£19.99

The C〜 uide
to Becoming an
English Teacher

D1352038

STEPHEN CLARKE is Senior Fellow in the School of Education, University of Leeds. For the last twenty years he has enjoyed writing and researching with others, on topics ranging from argument to language.

PAUL DICKINSON is Principal Lecturer and Head of the English Centre, Sheffield Hallam University. He is also the Subject Leader for the secondary PGCE English programme.

JO WESTBROOK is a Lecturer in the School of Education, the Sussex Institute, University of Sussex. She was previously Joint Programme Director of the modular (flexible) PGCE programmes at Canterbury Christ Church University College, and an Advisor with the Teacher Training Agency on flexible postgraduate programmes

The Complete Guide to Becoming an English Teacher

STEPHEN CLARKE, PAUL DICKINSON AND JO WESTBROOK

THE LEARNING CEN
TOWER HAMLETS C
ARBOUR SQUARE
LONDON E1 0P

P·C·P

Paul Chapman
Publishing

372.6521 CLA
111075

© Stephen Clarke, Paul Dickinson and Jo Westbrook, 2004

First published 2004
Reprinted 2006

Apart from any fair dealing for the purposes of research or private study, or criticism or review, as permitted under the Copyright, Designs and Patents Act, 1988, this publication may be reproduced, stored or transmitted in any form, or by any means, only with the prior permission in writing of the publishers, or in the case of reprographic reproduction, in accordance with the terms of licences issued by the Copyright Licensing Agency. Inquiries concerning reproduction outside those terms should be sent to the publishers.

Paul Chapman Publishing
A SAGE Publications Ltd
1 Oliver's Yard
55 City Road
London EC1Y 1SP

SAGE Publications Inc
2455 Teller Road
Thousand Oaks, California 91320

SAGE Publications India Pvt Ltd
B-42 Panchsheel Enclave
PO Box 4109
New Delhi 110 017

Library of Congress Control Number: 2002115858

A catalogue record for this book is available from the British Library

ISBN 0 7619 4241 6
ISBN 0 7619 4242 4 (pbk)

Typeset by M Rules
Printed in Great Britain by Cromwell Press Trowbridge Wiltshire

CONTENTS

Class: 373.6 CLA
Accession No: 11075
Type: L

LIST OF ABBREVIATIONS

APEL	Accreditation of Prior Experiential Learning
APL	Accreditation of Prior Learning
AQA	Assessment and Qualifications Alliance
AS	Advanced Subsidiary
CPD	Continuing Professional Development
DARTS	Directed Activities Related to Texts
DES	Department of Education and Science
DfE	Department for Education
DfEE	Department for Education and Employment
DfES	Department for Education and Skills
FE	Further Education
GCE	General Certificate of Education
GCSE	General Certificate of Secondary Education
GTP	Graduate Teacher Programme
HMSO	Her Majesty's Stationery Office
ICT	Information and Communications Technology
IEP	Individual Education Plan
ITT	Initial Teacher Training
KAL	Knowledge About Language
KS2	Key Stage Two (ages 7–11)
KS3	Key Stage Three (ages 11–14)
LINC	Language In the National Curriculum (Project)
MFL	Modern Foreign Languages
NATD	National Association of Teachers of Drama
NATE	National Association for the Teachers of English
NC	National Curriculum
NLS	National Literacy Strategy
NOF	National Opportunities Fund
QCA	Qualifications and Curriculum Authority
QTS	Qualified Teacher Status
SAT	Standardised Attainment Test
SENCO	Special Educational Needs Co-ordinator
SpLD	Specific Learning Difficulty
TESOL	Teaching English to Speakers of Other Languages
TTA	Teacher Training Agency

ACKNOWLEDGEMENTS

The three editors wish to acknowledge the great input that our fourth colleague, Dr Val Fraser, has made to the development of the original template of the materials, her intelligent and humorous discussions at our subsequent writing consortium meetings, and for her chapters as seen in the contents page.

We would also like to thank the three mentors who evaluated and commented on the materials as they developed:

Donna Bryant – Head of English at Camborne School and Community College, Cornwall
Alan Jones – Senior Teacher, Simon Langton Boys' School, Canterbury
John Perry – Pool School and Community College, Pool, Cornwall
The three editors are grateful for the large numbers of colleagues and student teachers who have provided some of the material for this book over the past four years:

Chapter 1
C. Gibson, PCGE English student teacher, Sheffield Hallam University
A. Grange, PCGE English student teacher, Sheffield Hallam University
J. Verney, PCGE English student teacher, Sheffield Hallam University

Chapter 2
Folens for the publication of lesson plans from English File 2 (2002)
L. Smith, PGCE English student, Sheffield Hallam University

Chapter 2
John Moss, Canterbury Christ Church University College, for permission to use his original materials for lesson observations, the management of whole class and small group work, outline of objectives, example of a lesson plan and pupil resources and points to consider in planning a scheme of work and its assessment
Sally Jellet and Larisa Curran, PGCE English student teachers on the PGCE Modular programme, Canterbury Christ Church University College for permission to use their contributions to the Blackboard VLE Discussion Board
Liz Hoult from Canterbury Christ Church University College for the lesson evaluation proforma

Chapter 4
Examples of work from pupils from Tupton Hall School, Derbyshire
School Curriculum and Assessment Authority (1995) *Exemplification of Standards in Key Stage 3, Levels 4–8: Reading and Writing*. London: SCAA

Chapter 5
Mary Chesshyre and Šally Jellett. PGCE English student teachers on the PGCE Modular programme, Canterbury Christ Church University College for permission to use their contributions to the blackboard VLE Discussion Board
Valerie Bloom for permission to quote the first stanza of her poem 'Wha Fi Call I' (from *Touch Mi, Tell Mi*, Bogle L'ouverture Press, 1983)
Donna Bryant, Head of English at Camborne School and Community College for permission to use her comments from an evaluation of this chapter

Louise Aitken, English teacher at Sandwich Technology School for her bibliography of texts from different cultures and traditions

Chapter 6
Kat Simpson, Leeds University English PGCE student, 2002–3. Thanks for permission to have her practice with a class described

Chapter 7
The quotation at the start of Section Two originated, as far as I know, from Michael Stubbs, lecturer at the Institute of Education, University of London from an MA (ed) session in 1988
John Moss from Canterbury Christ Church University College for use of his materials on classroom observations and management of whole class and group work talk
Stephen Clarke from Leeds University for his commentary on spoken Standard English

Chapter 9
M. Morgan (1995) for the poem 'Question Time' in the *Monster poems* collection by John Foster, Oxford University Press
D. Myhill for recommending websites and offering access to her grammar website
T. Hughes (1986) for the opening to *The Iron Man*, Faber and Faber
Folens for the publication of lesson plans from English File 2 (2002)

Chapter 10
Emily, Joseph and Simon Dickinson for providing examples of their work

Chapter 11
Chris Raeside, Senior School Improvement Officer, Excellence in Cities, London Borough of Haringey for permission to use her materials supporting pupils with EAL, for Activities 3, 8 and 9
Lucy Smith, student teacher on the PGCE modular programme at Canterbury Christ Church University College for her discussions on provision for pupils learning EAL at North Westminster Community School

Chapter 12
Thanks to Martin Coles, Assistant Director, Research, of the National College of School Leadership, Nottingham University, for permission to use his 'Strategies to encourage pupils to engage with texts' materials for Activity 7. Also the *Burton Mail* and especially Adam Leigh for permission to use newspaper articles

Chapter 14
J. Geeson from Anthony Gell School, Derbyshire for book recommendations
D. Wilcox from Deincourt School, Derbyshire for an example of a lesson using ICT

Chapter 15
A.C. Clarke for 'Hide and Seek' from *Of Time and Stars*, Puffin, Middlesex, 1972
Y. Coppard for *As if* Channel 4 Books, London, 2002
E. White for 'The House of the Nightmare', from *Ghostly and Ghastly* Hamlyn, London, 1997
S. Wrigley for ideas on collaborative writing NATE workshop, Manchester, 2003 (Activity 7)

Chapter 18
Thanks to John Moss of Canterbury Christ Church University College for the original input on Activities 11 to 14

Chapter 19
Thanks to Paul Dulley, student teacher on the PGCE Modular website at Canterbury Christ Church University College for permission to use his Blackboard VLE Discussion Board contribution

June Hopt, University of Leeds, for guidance and advice.

Chapter 20
Thanks to Paul Dulley, student teacher on the PGCE Modular website at Canterbury Christ Church University College for permission to use his Blackboard VLE Discussion Board contribution

Chapter 21
Thanks to David Gooch for the examples of coursework and teaching ideas

Chapter 24
Living Language. London. Hodder and Stougton. Copyright © 2000 George Keith and John Shuttleworth pp. v and vi. Reproduced by permission of Hodder Arnold.

Gill Winnett of Hipperholme and Lightcliffe School, for material reproduced on pp. 447 and 448.

Chapter 26
Thanks to David Gooch for his ideas and experience

THE BOOK AND HOW TO USE IT: INTRODUCTION

WORKING CONTEXT

English teaching in secondary schools in the United Kingdom is both a demanding challenge and a fascinating topic. Language and its development are at the heart of our culture and identity. In terms of recent official initiatives, becoming properly literate in English is seen as central to any educational programme. Teachers who extend language powers and language knowledge, even in the mother tongue, for most pupils, are involved in an activity that is historically deep, has great richness of ideas behind it and a consequent mass of diverse writing to energise it.

What is presented here starts from acceptance and willing acknowledgement of much of that previous analytical and creative thought. However, in extending that work the book intends to be a response to the needs of the times – to the changed curriculum contexts in which English teaching is carried out in the UK and to the new regulations through which teaching English is learned about and rehearsed in training centres and schools. In short, we have tried to acknowledge the wealth of ideas about our subject, whilst proposing ways of translating new demands into coherent practice for all those training under new standards, some of whom will be on traditional full-time courses and others on courses that are distinct departures from traditional Initial Teacher Training (ITT) one-year postgraduate routes into qualifying.

This text is aimed at a specific audience. Like others before it, it derives from teaching on courses designed to prepare postgraduates to become English teachers. We have designed it both to explain the mainstream ideas that have shaped secondary school English and to help readers rehearse teaching which is based on those ideas. Many of the activities and exercises set for readers are drawn from lectures and tutorials on courses where students meet in lecture halls and classrooms, have ideas explained to them, discuss those ideas, pool their thinking, try out activities, meet again and refine previous thinking, and so on. For generations collaboration has been essential to learning to teach, but this text grew originally from the need to create suitable teaching material for students who were unable to meet one another very often while undergoing teacher training.

Four authors, Stephen Clarke, Paul Dickinson, Val Fraser and Jo Westbrook, began to share ideas in the first place because the universities for whom they worked had each begun an innovative 'flexible' Postgraduate Certificate of Education (PGCE) programme in English. The authors, enabled to meet by funds helpfully provided by the Teacher Training Agency (TTA), shared the need to create material specially designed to cater for a new category of postgraduate student. Those on 'flexible' PGCE routes towards gaining Qualified Teacher Status (QTS) were pursuing, in part at least, an existing career or were caring for children while training to teach on a part-time basis. Many of them followed the new path bringing valuable prior experience with them; some had worked in secondary schools, as learning assistants or special needs support staff and/or unqualified teachers; some had taught English abroad, and some in Further Education (FE). Seen in this new pattern of recruitment and training is the changing trend in careers – downsizing, alternative lifestyles and 'portfolio' careers, and flexibility in the labour market. Our new students were, and their likes may well in future also remain, unable to join all the classes and activities available for the full-timers on the traditional PGCE course.

Previous editions, in effect, of this book have already enjoyed existence on university websites, accessed mainly by students working from home. To some extent electronic exchanges, between students and tutors and amongst students themselves, have helped to compensate for the lack of classroom meetings. Also acting to compensate for the lack of classroom meetings is the finding that students on the heavily individualised flexible routes are likely to be better read and to reflect more deeply. Why that is so should perhaps one day be the subject of a research project.

The arrangements for producing this book underwent some change as work continued on it. Certain chapters were specially commissioned from colleagues with particular expertise, and three of the original four authors took on responsibility for editing the book as a whole. The result is that very little of the following text is able to carry throughout a chapter's length a single identifiable author. Many chapters, however, although edited and revised do in fact retain their original authorial tone and direction of argument. For that reason the word 'I' still occurs in some places.

The audience now specified is the entire community of those who are learning to become secondary English teachers. We have taken regard of the needs of readers in professional contexts; we have made our text 'practical'. It maintains a steady focus on things that are required in the classroom, such as lesson plans, skill at applying open and exploratory approaches to literary texts, clarity of view about how pupils may be organised into becoming confident speakers, and so on. A large portion of each chapter takes the form of instructions on what and how to prepare. We hope that readers discover, as they carry out some of the tasks, not only that they help to create good lessons, but that they grant a deepening insight into the complexity of choices that every English teacher daily confronts.

THE SUBJECT ENGLISH AND ITS PERMEABILITY

In its history English has undergone quite radical changes, but lately it has been subject to continuous modification by central government, through such initiatives as these; the latest version of the National Curriculum (NC); the further spread of information technology; new examinations at A level; the Key Stage 3 National Strategy concerned with raising reading, writing and speaking and listening standards by all teachers, including English teachers; the requirement that impinges on English that all school pupils and students shall be educated in citizenship. These are not the only items in the list of imposed changes and new perspectives, but these and others do currently influence the English curriculum. They specify those things that are relatively specifiable, but threaten to displace other activities considered by some (e.g. Pike, 2003) to be less easily labelled but equally if not more vital to the intellectual development of the pupil.

English teachers need to see how on the one hand their subject is concerned with certain core values – with the idea, for example, of the sentient individual, the child growing up in a particular language, even if that is not his or her mother tongue. Certain values central to English teachers' common ideological stock have looked on tempests and have not been shaken. This despite the previous list of innovations. One such value is the key role of individuality. English teachers aim to generate differences in responses about such things as the interpretation of a poem, or skill at a method of narrating. The tradition in the UK is one of unease at placing too much stress on the orthodoxy of the single generic model for a way of writing, or the reduction of a poem to a series of questions susceptible to easily assessed convergent answers. None of us can seriously believe that male and female readers encounter, even under a wise teacher's guidance, Andrew Marvell's 'To His Coy Mistress' in identical ways.

On the other hand, English is mutable in a way that mathematics and science are not. In three briefly glimpsed ways we can see how. English is open, for example, to massive influence by apparently commonsense notions about literacy standards and the language-skill needs of the population of a democratic advanced state. It has also been permeated of late by notions of 'heritage', by having to obey the will of government ministers about which literary texts shall be studied by whom, and when. Thirdly, what 'reading' means in the 21st century could be different from what it meant in, say, the earlier part of the previous century. Citizens in an electronic and supposedly information-rich age must be taught about the media in their education, runs the argument. Schools now demand the teaching of citizenship, so, extending the line of argument, English teachers, already adept at explaining signs and images, should engage their pupils in critical discernment about the media products they read and produce, since the media play such a powerful role in shaping our views and values, and within democratic norms and expectations.

To learn to become an English teacher, therefore, means both understanding and being critically responsive to the core values, and keeping in clear view what the latest set of demands are upon what and how one teaches. Student teachers are freer to form critical perspectives than when they are employed, and thus committed to particular choices, or values, in a context often persuasive about the right values. However, ever since central government controlled the schools' curriculum directly the number of initiatives has stood, potentially, to increase, and thus to move towards a standardisation of approaches, regardless of individual positions and contextual variation. At the time of writing the latest regulations about initial teacher training (the Standards for QTS of 2002) make it every teacher's responsibility to know about not only literacy and how to help in its development at Key Stage 3, but inclusiveness, and how to involve and keep interested a wide spectrum of kinds of learners. Neither of these is utterly new; there has been much discourse about 'language across the curriculum' for 30 years, but only very recently has a certain version of that discourse made its way into becoming a compulsory item for all who qualify. Giving a set of pedagogical approaches statutory force may be a form of educational progress, but despite that new teachers still need critical insights into the ideas that enjoy official patronage.

TURNING UNDERSTANDING INTO PRACTICAL CRAFT

In any period of innovation the learner will need the guidance and help of those already initiated and skilled. The schools in which readers will be apprenticed, whether within a customary PGCE, or under a 'flexible' PGCE, Graduate Teacher Programme (GTP) scheme or similar route, will have much to teach and show that will be of use and permanent value. What is to be gained from schools is not just rehearsal in the practical aspects of the teaching job (though that ought to feature fairly largely), but also insight into how English teachers shape their thinking and respond to external demands upon their professional practice. This text should help to develop understanding about some essential rationales behind each of the major aspects of English teaching, and should enable insight into why English teachers adopt certain procedures as the basis of the construction of their work.

Teaching is a complex activity, but it is nothing if not intentional. A glance at the Standards mentioned above will show that teaching involves knowing, planning, preparing materials, being coherent with a class, explaining well both tasks and concepts, leading by example, assessing work intelligently and encouragingly and sustaining high expectations about progress. Teaching English involves skill in all of these things, but not one of them is necessarily as simple as the brief listing might suggest.

Take knowledge, for example. Anyone who sets out to teach reading in English will have to know the canon of texts that are required usage, whichever way they are selected from the National Curriculum (NC). Through shared encounters with their peers of plays, poems and novels, student teachers will have seen and understood how reading is often enhanced and deepened by being collaborative; how individual experiences, skills and predispositions may shape someone's ideas about what meaning even an apparently simple poem may have. Teachers also need to remember their own biographical progress as readers so that they have a clear grasp of how young readers, thrown into an encounter with a new text, possibly a new kind of text altogether, may well seek answers and right opinions from an instructive teacher. The pupils and students would be odd if they did not ask how firm ground could be defined on which they could stand. Yet the teacher knows that, ultimately, the pupils as readers will need to learn to interpret with one another, and by themselves, if they are to develop any worthwhile extensions of their powers and skills. The knowledge required for teaching reading is arguably multi-faceted in kind, combining familiarity with texts with an understanding of the complex processes of critical engagement and their biographical part in the formation of the kind of interpretative confidence that can enable the reader to feel that they know *Hamlet*.

Our aim, therefore, is to present an account of English teaching that can be constructed within the minds of readers as they start to practise it. We shall take the statutory framework statements, whether from documents relating to English teaching or from those relating to ITT and translate them, as it were, into terms that explain the context and indicate possible steps towards productive and worthwhile classroom encounters. The book is meant to be used literally as a handbook or guide, with the readers using the materials in a very focused, specific way according to their needs. This means, among other things, that some readers may find certain ideas and approaches being repeated. This repetition is inevitable, coming about as the means of preventing students who read only a few specifically chosen chapters (chosen after their needs analysis) overlooking some key ideas. There is no assumption of prior knowledge; each chapter, written with the beginner student teacher in mind, guides the reader progressively through to more complex readings, activities and solutions to problems. This allows for the selection and combination of particular chapters and activities by the learners, with some tutorial guidance. In this way a tailor-made programme should fulfil the needs of each individual.

Needs analysis

The specifications from the TTA for the new flexible programmes required:

an initial assessment of a candidate's training needs in relation to the QTS Standards . . . .
This should take full account of trainees' prior learning and achievement and might take the
form of a short, assessed school-based module. (TTA, February 2000)

The identification of individual needs was brought into the Revised Standards for QTS (TTA, February 2002) and now applies to all student teachers whether on full-time, part-time or flexible programmes. All student teachers therefore need some form of initial assessment of their prior experience and learning, and their needs then to be met through an individualised programme of study. For flexible programmes and, increasingly, full-time programmes, this can mean that the Accreditation of Prior Learning (APL) can exempt individuals from having to undertake sections of a programme on the basis of their qualifications. Accreditation of Prior Experiential Learning (APEL) could result in a student teacher who has been a Learning Support Assistant for four years claiming exemption from an inclusion session or chapter.

Any needs analysis should focus on subject knowledge in relation to the NC and to the *Framework for Teaching English: Years 7, 8 and 9* (DfEE, 2001): with drama, media and ICT now very much part of school English, no one student teacher will have a degree which covers everything. A simple audit using the NC headings and subheadings followed by a tutorial can easily pinpoint where the gaps in subject knowledge might be, and an action plan can be drawn up to fill those gaps in. For example, someone needing more drama input might be advised to complete some or all of the activities in the three drama chapters here, attend face to face sessions offered by their institution, focus on the observation of good practice in drama teaching on school experience and aim to plan and teach three to four drama lessons solo by the end of their school experience. Unfamiliarity with pre-1914 texts may mean that a suggested reading list is drawn up between tutor and student to be read over the duration of their programme, and the A level Literature chapter completed in full. In addition student teachers can share their own expertise through lunchtime or twilight sessions through 30-minute seminars arranged throughout the year.

The needs analysis process gauges how far readers have already fulfilled the learning outcomes of a particular programme – that is, knowledge about schools, teaching experience and pedagogy. Student teachers can claim exemption against the learning outcomes of each session, module or aspect of the programme or indeed, in a simplistic manner, even against the Standards for QTS. A portfolio of evidence with schemes of work, lesson plans, pupils' records and work, Continuing Professional Development (CPD) courses attended, pastoral roles and references will support the claims. Finally the early observation of student teachers in schools – two or more lessons – and discussions with mentors and Heads of Department will give a more accurate and realistic picture of their skills, knowledge and understanding.

All this information can be evidence in an individual training plan or programme for learning. Furthermore, as the student teacher moves through their programme both they and their tutor come to recognise their strengths and weaknesses far more accurately, and ongoing claims for exemption can be made and granted throughout, with the action plan adjusted accordingly.

To illustrate the above, here are three case studies taken from real English student teachers:

Student teacher A: Begins the teacher training course with seven years' experience of teaching in Further Education. She has a II.(i) Honours degree in English Literature. She has been teaching

AS levels in English Language and English Literature and has experience of teaching a range of vocational courses. As a result of her needs analysis and agreeing an individual training programme with her tutor she was given a 15-week placement in an 11–16 school with a focus upon KS3 and KS4. She was exempted from the post-16 modules. She had to work through units relating to Key Stages 3 and 4.

Student teacher B: Begins the teacher training course as an unqualified teacher with one year's teaching experience. However, his teaching is only at KS3. He has also been a National Opportunities Fund (NOF) trainer with a high level of Information and Communications Technology (ICT) skills. As a result of his needs analysis it was agreed that he should have some experience of teaching in another school and that teaching should include KS4 and post-16. It was agreed that he did not need to undertake the chapters on children's literature or planning at KS3 as the school had provided excellent training and models for him to follow and this was evidenced by a portfolio. It was also agreed that he did not need to cover all of the ICT chapter and was actually providing some training for the English Department

Student teacher C: Begins the teacher training course with a degree in Media Studies and two years' experience of TESOL (Teaching English to Speakers of Other Languages). As a result of her needs analysis her individual training plan included an emphasis upon the teaching of literature and she was exempted from some of the grammar chapters. She was advised to complete all the on-line poetry readings and activities as this was perceived as an area for development. She was exempted from the chapter on the media as this was a particular strength. Teaching practice was to cover a total of 20 weeks, with the first 10 weeks undertaken as three days a week, as she wanted some time with her young family, and the remainder was undertaken as a continuous block.

USING THE MATERIALS

The materials are designed to be interactive in the sense that they require as a minimum a one to one communication between student teacher and tutor, and ideally a larger community of peers, real or virtual. In addition the materials could be used as part of the required reading before or after a tutorial, or can be used by tutors to plan a session. For example, the English and ICT chapter lends itself to simply being worked through over two or three sessions in a computer suite with the help and support of an experienced English tutor. Each chapter can also be used to support student teachers who are unable to attend particular face to face sessions, or who need to improve their subject knowledge in particular areas independently in order to meet the standards.

SECTIONS

The book's sections are introduced by an overview statement about each area, and they group the chapters under one larger theme or standpoint. English teachers are commonly to be found, rightly in our view, arguing that the elements and purposes of the subject relate to one another in ways as complex as do the social, emotional and intellectual elements of learning to talk in infancy. It is never easy, therefore, to derive utterly logical divisions of the subject, as our first section, on history, ideology and values, illustrates. Central to the second section, on language use and its varieties, is the nature of language and learning. In the third section we show how teachers and learners are, ideally, cultural agents meeting one another in texts, as readers, writers and interpreters. After that we consider how drama and Shakespeare, vital to English and now related to one another more productively than they once were, may be taught. Finally, echoing the age-divisions of schools and colleges, we consider post-16 work in a section on its own, aware nevertheless that future thinking could well put far more stress on the later part of secondary education being framed in the expectation that most students will go on to higher or further study. At present, however, we have still the big divisions, or rather, dividing points, that history has given us.

THE TEMPLATE

Each chapter is sectioned in a broadly consistent way. The introductory paragraphs indicate what the chapter is about and what will be learned and better understood by the time it has been studied, and the suggested activities have been done. The language may well be reminiscent of the style that is used to introduce lessons to classes, and this simple act of modelling might usefully be followed.

Next comes a **Rationale**. Typically the purpose of this section of each chapter is to set the topic in hand against the background of ideas which helped construct it. Most of the significant elements within English teaching have a history of their own in the larger pattern of development of the subject as a whole. For example, crucial background to the teaching of Shakespeare is the work of Rex Gibson (1998). This was key in extending many English teachers' craft knowledge of how to make engagements with a Shakespeare play as active as possible. A beginner ignorant of Gibson's work might well not understand fully why the observed English teacher who is his or her mentor goes to such lengths to have portions of the play acted and presented. In the chapter given to A level English Language the similar intellectual leaders to Gibson are described.

Links to the National Curriculum and Key Stage 3 National Strategy:

In every chapter about an aspect of teaching below the sixth form, a section will be devoted to the requirements of statute. This section's main aim is to inform, but also to provide critical and historical perspectives on the NC.

Introducing readers to the requirements of the programme that has been, in the last two or three years, developed alongside the NC in English is slightly harder. The Key Stage 3 National Strategy (hereafter the 'KS3 Strategy') is to be understood as a complex of concerns within a single initiative. It is, in part, the follow-on to the National Literacy Strategy (NLS) and the Numeracy Strategy in the primary schools. Like the NLS the KS3 work in English – most readily understood by a reading of the KS3 Strategy *Framework for Teaching English: Years 7, 8 and 9* (DfEE, 2001) – relies on the idea that literacy may be fostered through attention to language at word, sentence and whole text level. Nothing in the *Framework* or in the many practical publications that support it is meant to be anything other than consistent with the requirements of the NC in English. As far as we can we clarify what the *Framework* means and how it can help the teaching of poetry, Shakespeare, grammar, children's literature or anything else that will aid literacy development. Beyond the concerns of English, however, the KS3 Strategy demands that literacy become a whole school matter, and that all departments seek to improve pupils' literacy.

In addition to the *Framework* itself are training materials, in printed form and video, and additional texts for pupils, such as the spelling banks and sentence banks. For readers and writers who are struggling to operate at Level 4 of the NC (which, ideally, most 11-year-olds should reach), Literacy Progress Units have been written for use by teachers with groups of six or so pupils in, roughly, 20-minute sessions, looking at how to improve such skills as: word identification when reading aloud, via phonics; spelling; reading between the lines; sentence construction or paragraphing. When material of this degree of planned support for literacy is available, any new teacher would be unwise to ignore it.

Most chapters have between six and twelve **Activities**. These are written to reflect progression and are linked, we hope, coherently, moving the student teacher on in terms of the level required, skills acquired and experience gained in the classroom. Several activities require a more reflective response, via such forms as a dialogue with a peer, tutor or school subject mentor, or to include in an English Portfolio. Some activities require school experience, whether observing a class, actually teaching a part or the whole of a lesson planned jointly, or holding discussions with regular teachers. Theory is therefore intimately linked with, precedes and depends upon observed English teaching. The overriding aim is to foster enough relevant and useful knowledge and confidence so that the student teacher can develop their own pedagogy, and use this to critique their own practice, and evaluate the effectiveness of the policies and strategies of others. Under 'Activities', where appropriate, links are made explicit between what is being done and the demands of particular Standards (see below under 'Continuous Threads').

The end of chapter **Scenarios**, or case studies, focus on particular classroom or department situations that are described as requiring either resolution in terms of action, or increased awareness of the issues raised by the example. These scenarios act as discussion points, drawing together the whole chapter, and are useful final exercises in INSET courses or face to face discussions.

Continuous Threads The chapters between them, but not all to an exactly equal measure, ask the reader to consider six threads which run throughout all aspects of teaching, and are directly related to the Standards for the award of QTS. As the chapters focus primarily on Section 2 of the Standards, 'Knowledge and Understanding', the continuous threads pull in the other standards to form a holistic and integral approach to the teaching of the particular aspect of English under discussion. The threads, in the order in which they will appear in most chapters, are:

1   Professional values and practice
3.1   Planning, expectations and targets (progression)
3.2   Monitoring and assessment
3.3   Class management
3.3.4 Differentiation
2.5   Information and communications technology (ICT)

Each chapter discusses most of these threads, not because every single lesson planned must show them all as having been equally considered, but because across a scheme of work or long sequence of teaching, attention should have been paid to each, even if it is only careful critical attention that ends in an argument about why a decision has been made, for example, that ICT has simply no role to play in a given sequence of lessons.

Expansion of particular areas discussed in each chapter is covered in the sections **Further Ideas** and **Further Reading**, and texts and resources are recommended to develop the topic. This is useful for the more academic requirements of ITT courses, but teachers are well accustomed to the idea that for every topic discovered there will always be more reading to be done than time to do it. Some references are made to Davidson and Dawson (1998), *Learning to Teach English in the Secondary School*, London, Routledge. As our book is going to print, this book has been updated and is available as a 2003 publication.

A NOTE ON TERMINOLOGY

A list of abbreviations has been included in the preliminary pages. Other terms we use are as follows: those in training to become English teachers we call 'student teachers', or sometimes just 'students' because no university we know of awards its certificates to 'trainees'; 'pupils' refers to learners in schools who are below, in age, the sixth form; 'students' does, in context, refer to sixth-formers; 'school practice' denotes time in school either as observer or practitioner spent by student teachers in learning to teach, and other terms, such as 'KS3' derive from official formulations entailed by the National Curriculum (NC) for the UK.

REFERENCES

DfEE (1999) *The National Curriculum for England. English: key stages 1–4.* London: DfEE and QCA

DfEE (2001) *Key Stage 3 National Strategy. Framework for Teaching English: Years 7, 8 and 9.* London DfEE

Gibson, R. (1998) *Teaching Shakespeare.* Cambridge: Cambridge University Press

Pike, M.A. (2003) 'On being in English teaching: a time for Heidegger?' *Changing English*, 10(1): 91–99

Teacher Training Agency (TTA) (2002) *Qualifying to Teach: Professional Standards for the Award of QTS.* London DfEE

HISTORY, IDEOLOGIES
AND VALUES OF ENGLISH

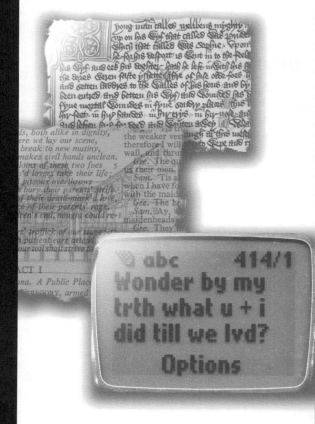

INTRODUCTION

> *During the past decade in particular, 'literacy' has indeed assumed higher prominence in national education, training, and social–civic agendas and become a keyword in educational discourse. This development has, however, been accompanied throughout by tendencies that keep the 'progress' of literacy tightly constrained within the parameters of larger purposes and agendas. These larger purposes and agendas, despite what may be said about them at 'official levels', inevitably require a literacy economy in which 'higher order, innovative and (otherwise) critical' qualities remain in strictly scarce supply. (Lankshear et al., 1977: 7)*

By studying this section and undertaking the chapter activities you should :

- Appreciate the development of English as a subject
- Understand and review the KS3 Strategy
- Develop an awareness of various models of English
- Appreciate planning in the short, medium and long term
- Understand the role of assessment in English
- Appreciate the recent emphasis on inclusion.

English as a subject has a relatively short but dramatic history and its evolution has been marked by strong political involvement, particularly since the 1970s. This section helps you understand the complexities of the subject and its place in the curriculum. It also encourages you to view the curriculum from a critical standpoint, guiding you through the benefits of the current curriculum with its emphasis on literacy skills as well as raising questions about some of the central issues concerning what kind of curriculum we should be providing for our pupils, including the place of creativity. Whether you are a student on a teacher training programme or a practising teacher you will have already formed a view of what English is about. This will have been influenced by many factors such as your degree (literature based, media emphasis, combined subjects and linguistics), your own experiences of being taught English, and discussions with other students and teachers. This diversity was recognised by Brian Cox's committee when they were appointed to set up the first National Curriculum for English. Brian Cox, reflecting upon the Cox Report, stated: '. . . people set in opposition individual and social aims, or utilitarian and imaginative aims, or language and literature, or reading for meaning and decoding or craft and creativity in writing, and so on' (Cox, 1991: 18).

He sums up by indicating that 'best practice reflects a consensus' (ibid.). Those aspiring to reach the professional standards of the regular English teachers whom they observe as student teachers will have witnessed the richness of different approaches adopted by these teachers to achieve similar outcomes or, equally validly, depending upon occasion, diverse outcomes. Agreed aims for a whole series of lessons do not necessarily entail identical methods of approach to achieving those aims. Whoever can invoke approaches that most readily engage the class in concentration and motivate large groups of pupils is at a professional advantage over one who arranges classroom experiences in much the same way on all occasions regardless of ability of group, text in hand, or desired outcome in terms of, say, writing in a particular mode or style.

Beginners may well be pleasurably surprised at, for example, the way in which one teacher uses role play to help pupils appreciate character and the way in which another successfully encourages pupils to share, honestly but with mutual respect, their reflections about a poem.

Variations in approach are one thing and variations in intentions and final ends are another, but the point about the debates entered by Cox, quoted above, is that those debates were about final outcomes and intended ends. The National Curriculum has not caused massive resistance among English teachers, most of whom recognised, if they were teaching when it began, its derivation from many enlightened existing intentions on behalf of the learners. Cox and his committee gave the nation a version of English that, encompassing diversity, was bound to be wide in the number of different kinds of verbal achievement that each pupil should show evidence of. Since the introduction of the National Curriculum teachers have enjoyed as much diversity in methods of approach as they ever did before it, but it is arguable, at any rate, that they may spend less energy deciding about content.

However, at the beginning of this millennium teachers in secondary schools are implementing a National Curriculum for English for pupils of compulsory school age, coupled with a national strategy for teaching English for Key Stage 3 (11–14-year-olds). English teachers are affected in their work and approaches by this strategy and their work is influenced heavily too by other changes in context, as will be explained below. Each of these changes imposes its own influence, each requiring the curriculum to cover very specific learning objectives.

At post-16 a variety of routes is now currently on offer, including AS levels and A levels. All A levels are now modular and divided into two stages (AS and A2 qualifications). AS levels are studied in the first year and A2s in the second year of any two-year course. There are also Level 2 courses (intermediate) as well as Advanced Certificates of Education. The latter two routes tend to be the vocational courses. The whole 14–19 curriculum is under scrutiny as the status of vocational courses is being raised. The point about these changes is that they have subtle, perhaps, but certainly powerful influences upon what the teacher feels he or she is doing when teaching English at that level.

INFLUENCE OF NATIONAL POLICY

There is a strong government drive to increase the participation rate in higher education with a future target of 50% of the population enrolling on a degree or equivalent course. The serious pursuit of this entails schools coming under pressure to produce well qualified students in large numbers able to begin degree level study. From this perspective you could argue that English teachers with their sixth forms now face the pressure of enabling averagely bright students, many of them, to fulfil themselves as readers and writers in ways that were, merely two generations ago, seen as within the scope of only a small intellectual elite. Moreover, schools are increasingly being encouraged to seek specialist status with the consequent financial benefits. Thus there are schools with sports or language college status; there are beacon schools and training schools. This political intervention to create diversity of kind (amongst supposedly equal status comprehensives) is coupled with an increasing level of monitoring and accountability that schools and teachers have to face.

We are clearly in a period in which target setting for pupils, schools and local education authorities (LEAs) is part of regular policy, with results displayed in national papers in the form of league tables, much like those of football teams! Data on pupils are being used to highlight the underachievers, to target the 'gifted and talented' and make comparisons between schools and in some cases even between teachers in the same school. The government has set itself high targets in a range of areas from literacy achievements to truancy rates. At subject level it is a period in which the very nature of English is being questioned. What is meant by reading? Does this recognise the skills of navigating websites? Pupils are increasingly immersed in virtual worlds, reading multi-modal texts, writing to real audiences on-line and researching topics at the click of a button. Yet schools tend to operate in an essentially print-based culture, one emphasised by the terms of the current KS3 Strategy in English. Whilst much of this strategy is worthy (the emphasis on modelling writing for example), schools need to recognise pupils' prior skills and knowledge in the widest sense, from popular fiction to the narrative of computer games (see Goodwyn, 2000). We need to acknowledge that pupils are interacting more and more with texts that are constructed using the affordances offered by ICT. With the increasing access to ICT it is likely that this increase will continue in the near future and that pupils will be creating texts on their computers at home and in school that draw upon this potential. As Cope and Kalantzis (2000: 234) note:

> mulitimodality itself is becoming more significant in today's communications environment where, from multimedia desktops to shopping malls, written text is represented in dynamic relation to sound, visuals, spaces and gestures.

This section not only offers an overview of the curriculum, but also provides you with a variety of models for planning to teach and operate successfully within the framework for teaching English, the National Curriculum and examination specifications. It recognises the need for effective planning to be based on short, medium and long term plans and for assessment to inform this planning. Different types of assessment are discussed, from formative to summative, and the value of diagnostic marking is given a central place. The chapters have been grouped in this section to provide you with an awareness of what English has become at the start of the 21st century and to help you to appreciate the close links between planning, monitoring and assessment. These links form the basis of all effective teaching.

English is meeting new challenges, with teachers needing to update their subject knowledge, to consider inclusion as well as teaching for examinations, life skills and creativity. It is an exciting time to be an English teacher from the point of view of devising ways of teaching that realigns the subject to fit external demands. The new teacher of English is likely to have numerous resources available to him or her in the form of publications, teacher-produced materials and web-based ideas for lessons. What should not be lost is the teacher's autonomy in selecting what is appropriate, adding to it and shaping the materials for the particular classes' needs and circumstances. This section demonstrates how to plan effectively so as to enable your pupils to meet the required external measurable targets. It also illustrates a range of methods to develop pupils' language potential and personal growth, and to raise their awareness of broader culture. It should take you on a journey through the development of English into the classroom, contributing to your

> knowledge and practical skills, the ability to make informed judgements, and to balance pressures and challenges, practice and creativity, interest and effort, as well as an understanding of how children learn and develop. (TTA, 2002: 2)

REFERENCES

Cope, B. and Kalantzis, M. (2000) *Multiliteracies*. South Yarra, Australia: Macmillan

Cox, B. (1991) *Cox on Cox: An English Curriculum for the 90s*. London: Hodder and Stoughton

DES (1989) *English for Ages 5–16*. London: DES

Goodwyn, A. (2000) *English in the Digital Age*. London: Cassell

Lankshear, C. et al. (1997) *Changing Literacies*. Buckingham: Open University Press.

Teacher Training Agency (2002) *Qualifying to Teach*. London: TTA

chapter 1

THE NATIONAL CURRICULUM FOR ENGLISH

By the end of this unit you will have gained an appreciation of the historical and political developments that have led to the current National Curriculum: 2000. (Copies of the National Curriculum are available at **www.nc.uk.net**. You will need to refer to this document during this chapter.) You will be introduced to the factors that contributed to the establishment of a National Curriculum and to the main implications for the teacher of English who is planning to base his or her teaching upon this curriculum. You will be encouraged to reflect upon your own views of what constitutes English teaching and upon the role of the English teacher in the secondary classroom.

RATIONALE

It was as recently as 1990 that England and Wales witnessed the first National Curriculum for the teaching of English. It was a curriculum revised five years later under Sir Ron Dearing in 1995 and again under David Blunkett in September 2000. The implications for English teachers have been immense. Each new curriculum was aimed at raising standards, and organised around programmes of study that 'set out what pupils should be taught in English in Key Stages 1, 2, 3 and 4 and provide the basis for planning schemes of work' (DfEE,1999). Each successive National Curriculum in English has retained, as if unarguable and unalterable, the division of the subject into Reading, Writing and Speaking and Listening.

Each new National Curriculum included attainment targets that set out 'the knowledge, skills and understanding that pupils of different abilities and maturities are expected to have by the end of each key stage' (DfEE, 1999). The current challenges facing teachers include 'delivering' the curriculum in a coherent, meaningful way, maintaining and developing pupils' enthusiasm for the subject, ensuring progression and enabling all pupils to attain their potential. (The concept of 'delivering' a curriculum, as if it were a material commodity rather than an organised series of transactions between minds, is one that might deserve a separate section, but suffice it here to note that it is one of those words which, having been originally imposed from above at the time of the inception of the National Curriculum, has been taken up spontaneously in the professional discussions that teachers hold amongst themselves.) The current curriculum retains much of the original 1990 curriculum. Examples include the centrality of Shakespeare, an emphasis on Standard English and writing for different purposes and audiences with a hardly notable shift to compulsory pre-1914 literature from pre-1900 literature. This at least makes the decision about which Hardy texts are placed under which category somewhat easier. However, there are changes at each revision that have affected the nature of English being taught in classrooms. These will become evident as you progress through the activities.

During the revisions to the National Curriculum for English there has been a gradual recognition of the growing importance of the media (with reference to the moving image), the significance of ICT and works from a range of cultures. Yet there is still much debate about the weighting of the National Curriculum towards a cultural heritage model (which places emphasis upon the works of significant literary writers from the past) at the expense of cultural analysis (with an emphasis upon a critical perspective on the texts that contribute to our view of English culture). Traditionalists may claim that the current curriculum promotes texts that are not 'classic' enough and that this encourages methodologies of teaching that are decidedly modern. Conversely, progressive teachers may well claim that there is too much emphasis on knowledge held externally rather than acquired inwardly and that Standard English has been over-emphasised along with the unnecessary prescription of pre-1914 writers. Certainly there does appear to be a large disparity between what pupils read at KS3 outside the classroom and the list of prescribed authors that includes Trollope and Dickens. Responses by two student teachers to a discussion board activity based on interviewing Year 7 pupils in 2002 about their reading preferences came up with these findings in two different comprehensive schools. These were not untypical of responses by pupils being interviewed in other schools. It might be argued that more should be done to build on this interest, or conversely that these pupils need some more of the literary canon as part of their Year 7 diet.

INTERVIEW BY J.VERNEY, PGCE ENGLISH STUDENT AT SHEFFIELD HALLAM UNIVERSITY

Name	Your favourite author? Why?	What do you read?	Do you read the same things at home and in class?	Why do you read?
Sally	J.K. Rowling – because *Harry Potter* books are a bit scary and weird – different from normal books.	Books, comics/magazines – *Mizz* and *Beano*	Home – Enid Blyton, J.K. Rowling, looking at dancing books. School – *Vampyre Diaries*	Calms her down when she gets in from dancing. Fun, you find out new things. Likes reading when she is tired – under covers
Nick	Michael Coleman – writes funny sports books on football, ice-hockey, cricket	Mostly comics/magazines – *Beano* and *Match* magazine	Doesn't really read at home, apart from comics. School – reads story books and sports books	'Don't know – just something to do while eating breakfast'
Alex	J.K.Rowling – likes *Harry Potter* books because adventurous and magic	Books	No, at home read *Harry Potter* books and *The Hobbit*	'If your friends are out or grounded it's the only thing to do'
Reece	J.K.Rowling – likes *Harry Potter* books because exciting. Favourite character is Fluffy, the three-headed dog	Books	At home, likes reading make-believe.	'My mum begs me'
Becky	Jacqueline Wilson – interesting books, funny	Books, magazines – *Smash Hits*	Sometimes	To learn, to enjoy it. Reads a lot on her own
Jessica	R.L.Stine – scary books – keeps you in suspense	Books, magazines – *Shout, Mizz,* every week	Not really – more horror books at home	It kills time. She likes reading because it gives her ideas for stories she writes

INTERVIEW BY CHRISTINA GIBSON PGCE ENGLISH STUDENT AT SHEFFIELD HALLAM UNIVERSITY

Name and age of pupil	Favourite Authors	What do you read e.g. books, comics, magazines?	Books read at home	Books read at school	Reasons for reading?
Emma age 12	R.L Stine, J.K Rowling and Jacqueline Wilson	Books e.g. *Dare Game*, *Double Act* by Jacqueline Wilson. I also read magazines for teenagers	TV guide and fiction books. I read magazines such as *Smash Hits* and *Mizz*	School textbooks during lessons. During the library lesson (once a week) I quite often look at the sports books – I really like David Beckham. I can't get into reading much fiction at school, there's not enough time	I just enjoy it. I like horror books; it's the suspense of not knowing who the killer is and things like that
Viki age 11	J.K Rowling, Enid Blyton, Jacqueline Wilson and Lena Kennedy	Books, newspapers, magazines and fact files, e.g. *The Human Body*	Newspapers: the *Sun* and the *News of the World*, books like *Amelia Jane* by Enid Blyton and *Harry Potter* by J.K. Rowling	Maths and Science textbooks. We sometimes use textbooks in Geography – oh, and atlases. I read stuff on the Internet and we read plays and books in English	It's educational and it's a hobby I enjoy the way my favourite authors express their character
Rachel age 11	Enid Blyton, Roald Dahl and Jacqueline Wilson	Mainly books but I do read some magazines – *Shout*	*The Twits* and *Fantastic Mr Fox* by Roald Dahl. I've read *Bad Girls* by Jeremy Strong, too	We've read some Judy Blume stuff in English and a Shakespeare play – *Macbeth*. That was good 'cos we had to make up our own spells. Otherwise it's all textbooks – boring!	The books I read are exciting and adventurous. I enjoy reading about animals
Thomas age 12	Roald Dahl, J.K. Rowling	I read books and magazines. The magazines I read are all about football	The *Harry Potter* books; my favourite is *The Goblet of Fire*	I read factual books in the library about football. Mainly the books I read at school are the ones we're given in lessons, like Maths books. We read plays in English	I just like reading, especially if it's something I've chosen and there's adventure in it
Rodger age 12	Roald Dahl, J.K. Rowling	Newspapers and factual sports magazines or ones about music	I don't often read books but I did enjoy *The Twits* by Roald Dahl and the *Harry Potter* books	Plays and textbooks	A teacher in my old school read *The Twits* and *The Witches* to me and I enjoyed these books so I bought them
Sonny age 11	Roald Dahl, Jacqueline Wilson and Dick King-Smith.	Newspapers, books and magazines	*Double Act* by Jacqueline Wilson, *The Twits* and *Charlie and the Chocolate Factory*, by Roald Dahl	Textbooks, *Macbeth*, poetry books, stuff like that	I like to read books that are funny and imaginable. Ones that are interesting and have a good story to them

A broad curriculum

There is clearly something in the curriculum for everyone, from the 'making, performing and critical analysis of drama, demonstrating progression throughout' (DfEE, 1999) which should encourage active approaches to the teaching of English to the more adult needs model of being able to write for specified purposes in order to advise, explain and analyse. Perhaps, as has often been the case, teachers will be creative when working with the curriculum and will marry some of these apparent extremes. For example the numerous websites providing stimulating approaches to teaching Shakespeare (Globe website http://www.rdg.ac.uk/globe/newglobe enabling the visitor to explore a virtual Elizabethan England) and videos based on Shakespeare plays may well result in teachers using more media and ICT to help pupils explore and interact with the Shakespeare experience. It is through examples such as this last one that we can begin to see the pointlessness, ultimately, of seeing English as territory fought over by 'traditionalists' and 'progressives'. How you teach Shakespeare may have much to do with how active pupil participation becomes in the classroom construction of parts of plays, and the new-ish media and computer technologies may be seen as undesirable at times, not because they are modern and thus linked to progressive ideologies, but because they may make the classes too static, silent and immobile.

Whilst there may be something in the curriculum for all teachers the current curriculum is unlikely to satisfy the aspirations of every English teacher. It is worth noting Brian Cox's comments on the first National Curriculum in which he believed there were five views of English teaching that could be identified: the Cox Report (DES, 1989) identified the five different models or views of English teaching as:

a) A 'personal growth' view focuses on the child; it emphasises the relationship between language and learning in the individual child, and the role of literature in developing children's imaginative and aesthetic lives.

b) A 'cross-curricular' view focuses on the school: it emphasises that all teachers (of English and of other subjects) have a responsibility to help children with the language demands of different subjects on the school curriculum: otherwise areas of the curriculum may be closed to them.

c) an 'adult needs' view focuses on communication outside the school: it emphasises the responsibility of English teachers to prepare children for the language demands of adult life, including the workplace, in a fast-changing world. Children need to learn to deal with the day-to-day demands of spoken language and of print; they also need to be able to write clearly, appropriately and effectively.

d) A 'cultural heritage' view emphasises the responsibility of schools to lead children to an appreciation of those works of literature that have been widely regarded as amongst the finest in the language.

e) A 'cultural analysis' view emphasises the role of English in helping children towards a critical understanding of the world and cultural environment in which they live. Children should know about the processes by which meanings are conveyed, and about the ways in which print and other media carry values. (Cox, 1991: 21, 22)

These views are described as not 'mutually exclusive' and most teachers will have a view that incorporates more than one aspect of these five models. It perhaps suggests that the Cox Committee were keen to embrace the breadth of what English constitutes and not to alienate teachers.

These different views of English are still relevant today, and are useful in identifying trends in government initiatives. For example, the great emphasis on the literary canon which was very evident in the Dearing Revised National Curriculum from 1995 was clearly a cultural heritage model, whereas it could be argued that the new Curriculum 2000 contains a stronger sense of the cultural analysis model in terms of the breadth of texts to be read, including media and ICT texts, but the emphasis on formal and informal Standard English use (and the *Framework for Teaching English*) moves the curriculum towards the cultural heritage and adult needs model.

What is important to grasp is that although most English teachers may favour one model over another, in practice all models can be visible at some point during a term depending on the precise focus of individual lessons. For example, when teaching Shakespeare the cultural heritage model will happily complement a cultural analysis approach – especially if Zeffirelli's film of *Romeo and Juliet* is contrasted with Baz Luhrmann's more modern version, and then set against the actual text.

By exploring the developments that led up to the National Curriculum, including the role of the Kingman Committee Report (DES, 1988), and the Cox Report (DES, 1989), you will appreciate how the current curriculum evolved with its particular characteristics and emphasis. In a climate of target setting, raising the standards of literacy and boys' underachievement, English departments have worked hard to implement successfully the demands of the National Curriculum. The compulsory requirements of Shakespeare, pre-1914 literature, Standard English etc. have led to some extremely innovative teaching methods. Pupils are regularly involved in writing directors' scripts, exploring the history of their local dialects and taking part in mock-interviews.

You will need to be familiar with the current curriculum in order to plan your schemes of work in a way that integrates the attainment targets of speaking and listening/reading/writing. The division into these areas for curricula is not a natural one and good teaching integrates them successfully.

LINKS WITH THE KEY STAGE 3 STRATEGY

It should be noted that the National Curriculum is statutory and thus its coverage underpins English departments' planning and assessment. At KS4, examination syllabuses are based on these requirements and most departments use the syllabus that they have chosen as the basis for their long term plans. At KS3 there is now the KS3 strategy which has meant that many departments have modified schemes of work to ensure coverage of the objectives in the *Framework for Teaching English: Years 7, 8, 9*. Teachers are rethinking lesson structures, with many adopting a less flexible, but arguably more focused four-part lesson structure as demonstrated in the next chapter. What should be remembered is that this is a framework and thus should be used flexibly to ensure that the most appropriate pedagogy is being applied. The KS3 strategy is discussed in greater depth in the following chapter and is referred to throughout the book.

Activity 1

WHY WE TEACH ENGLISH

(suggested time: 45 minutes)

Before beginning this activity list 10 reasons for teaching English (e.g. drama is important as it enables pupils to build their confidence and to learn to speak effectively in a range of contexts). Place these in your portfolio. Then look closely at the National Curriculum for English Key Stages 3 and 4 (2000). Consider the following:

Standard addressed: 2.1c

- Are there parts of the curriculum that you had not expected to be present?
- What do you think is being emphasised?

Place your responses to the above questions in your English portfolio.

Activity 2

ADVANTAGES AND DISADVANTAGES OF THE NATIONAL CURRICULUM

(suggested time: 30 minutes)

What do you view as the benefits of having a National Curriculum? List five of these benefits.

What are your concerns about the current National Curriculum? List five.

This is what one student teacher (A.Grange, PGCE English student at Sheffield Hallam University) noted on a PGCE discussion board before embarking on her first school placement.

1   What do you view as the benefits of having a National Curriculum?

- It provides a useful framework, so teachers can ensure that they are delivering a balanced programme of study.
- The National Curriculum gives equal value to oral work (EN1 – Speaking and Listening) as well as reading and writing skills. The speaking and listening section encourages the use of drama, especially as an active learning technique.

- It aims to standardise the goals that pupils studying English in secondary schools are aiming for – in theory, a comprehensive school pupil should have just as good a standard of education as someone who attends a private school. In fact, state schools may teach to a better standard as they are governed by more regulations.
- It provides a checklist for teachers to make lesson objectives clear.
- It makes clear the range of texts to be studied: from pre-1914 'classics' to contemporary literature, to media and ICT based texts. It also stresses the importance of studying texts from other cultures, and female authors to lessen the 'dead white male' accusations on the English Literature canon.
- It stresses reading in context: emphasising the historical, social and cultural backgrounds to texts rather than studying texts in isolation.
- The National Curriculum gives clear targets for students' attainment, and outlines for what pupils at different stages of development are likely to achieve.
- It emphasises the importance of learning grammar and learning to read and speak Standard English as the language of public communication, but also stresses the teaching of the historical and current background to Standard English (rather than just stating 'This is the correct way to use English').
- The section at the back deals with inclusion, and places emphasis on responding to pupils' individual needs.

2   What are your concerns about the National Curriculum?

- Teachers could feel that the National Curriculum stifles creativity (for both teachers and pupils).
- The National Curriculum covers so many areas in detail that it can seem confusing and overwhelming.
- Despite changes and improvements from the 1995 version, it still places emphasis on a 'canon' of 'classic' English Literature.
- It increases the already heavy load of bureaucracy that burdens teachers, and some could feel that it distracts them from actually *teaching*.
- It seems to assume that teachers don't have good ideas of their own, and that they don't know what to teach – this could be insulting.
- The National Curriculum generalises the attainment of pupils – the inclusion section is stuck at the back and could appear to be an afterthought when it could be integrated.
- It is sometimes optimistic when describing what pupils are expected to attain. It doesn't give clear targets for pupils with special needs or lower ability.

Standard addressed: 2.1c

Activity 3   THE EMERGENCE OF ENGLISH AS A SUBJECT

(suggested time: 45 minutes)

English as a recognisable school subject emerged in the early part of the twentieth century. In 1904 the Board of Education Regulations required all elementary and secondary schools to offer courses in English Language and Literature. There then followed a response to the growth of the late Victorian technology with a realisation that there was a need for a workforce that could read simple instructions and could both give and receive information. Thus the emphasis was upon reading and writing to provide the necessary skills for a large proportion of British employees. The early 1900s were also marked by numerous circulars to shape what was taught. The thrust was upon high culture, with the importance of literature as a moralising force being emphasised. Texts recommended included *Robinson Crusoe* and *Hiawatha*. Dickens was conspicuous by his absence as his works were deemed to 'venture into the realms of social realism' (Davison and Dowson, 1998: 22).

Standard addressed: **2.1c**

If you had to select two poets, two playwrights and two novelists (pre-1914) as needing inclusion in the current curriculum which ones would you choose and why? Note these down in your portfolio.

Activity 4

ENGLISH AND THE INTER-WAR YEARS

(suggested time: 45 minutes)

The First World War was followed by the first main examination of English in the form of what became known as the Newbolt Report (1921). It noted that English was hardly studied in boys' schools and was generally perceived as a subject of little importance. The concerns are reflected in the report (Board of Education, 1921), which states 'every teacher is a teacher of English' and points out that too much time was devoted to the study of spelling, punctuation and grammar. There were some radical recommendations that included encouraging pupils to be each others' critics and for there to be some explicit teaching of the writing process. By the 1930s the massive development of the media and popular press offered a challenge to traditionalists. Concern grew about the exposure to what were perceived as ungrammatical examples of English. As Davison and Dowson (1998: 29) state: 'high culture and popular culture were seen as objects of opposition and popular culture was not worthy of study'.

In this climate grew the belief that English and what it represented needed protection. Consequently, the literary canon including Shakespeare, Chaucer and Keats became the subject of literary criticism which was more about engaging with the constructed actualities of a text. It was felt that such intelligent and determined engagement would help protect against the corrupting influence of popular culture.

Standard addressed: **2.1c**

What popular contemporary writers would you like to see studied in the current curriculum and why? List four.

Activity 5   THE LANGUAGE AND LITERATURE DEBATE
(suggested time: 45 minutes)

The 'London School' emerged in the 1950s and 1960s. This became inextricably linked with the development of comprehensive education. The London School included such members as Britton, Barnes and Rosen and they emphasised the importance of understanding the use of the English language. This period also witnessed the creation of LATE (London Association for the Teaching of English) and NATE (National Association for Teachers of English). These two organisations, still active today, worked hard to meet the needs of classroom teachers, providing INSET, projects, publications and a voice for teachers of English. Issues today that may be debated at NATE meetings might include whether the strategy for Key Stage 3 has improved the standards of teaching. These organisations supported the introduction of policies designed to enable the authentic voices of teachers to be heard and to be validated, and they challenged retention of policies which treated school English as something of a foreign tongue, whose key and correct forms were to be learned in classrooms without a deep appreciation of diversity in language with its rich range of social and cultural dialects.

This increasingly language-based movement was matched by a literature-based one which emphasised the learning of and critical response to canonical texts and to a large degree this informed the grammar school curriculum. At the latter end of this period, CSEs (Certificate of Secondary Education) were introduced as an alternative to the traditional O level. This innovative route to qualifications at the school leaving age enabled pupils to gain an O level equivalent pass if the top grade (1) was achieved, as well as providing very different courses in content, emphasis and assessment type. There was less focus on a literary canon and assessment could be undertaken as coursework. In this period child-centred learning was the vogue and media concern about falling standards with the introduction of comprehensive education emerged. Pressure for an inquiry into education in English was prevalent and this culminated in the Bullock Report (DES, 1975).

This report

> *summarized much of the consensus of the 1970s on the nature of English teaching, particularly reflecting attitudes associated with the work of James N. Britton. Although sceptical about claims that literacy rates had fallen substantially, the Committee called for a major investment in training and development to improve linguistic skills and linguistic awareness among both teachers and learners, and drew attention to the number of English teachers whose training was not specifically for teaching in this area. The report has been criticized for its optimism, but reflects clearly the views on language which underlay the moves to a mass, comprehensive system of schooling through the 1960s–70s. (McArthur, 1992)*

Standards addressed: 2.1, 3.2.1

What do you consider to be the advantages of assessment by coursework? How would you teach a novel differently if pupils' assessment was to be undertaken in coursework rather than by a terminal examination? You could discuss this with your mentor. Note your ideas in your portfolio.

Activity 6

THE INTRODUCTION OF THE NATIONAL CURRICULUM
(suggested time 45 minutes)

The 1980s marked the final stages leading up to the National Curriculum. In 1984 Keith Joseph outlined the government's determination to raise standards through agreeing criteria for school subjects and their assessment. The HMI publication *English from 5–16* effectively provided a blueprint for the curriculum. It included age-related targets for speaking, listening, reading, writing and about language. It made explicit the importance of pupils studying high quality literature as well as the critical study of media texts. Whilst the emphasis upon speaking and listening was welcomed the range covered was so broad that many felt dissatisfied. Of particular note was the ensuing debate over what constituted knowledge about language and what pupils should be taught about the English language. The debate about 'correct' grammar and language use provided the opportunity for Kenneth Baker, Secretary of State for Education to push for a model of English teaching that placed greater emphasis upon prescriptive grammar. As a result he announced the establishment of the Kingman Committee to recommend a model of the English Language to 'serve as the basis of how teachers are trained to understand how the English language works' (DES, 1988).

This report was

> presented in 1988 to the Secretary of State for Education by the Committee of Inquiry into Teaching of English Language under the chairmanship of Sir John Kingman. The Committee was asked to recommend a model to serve as a basis for training teachers in how the language works and to inform professional discussion, to consider how far the model should be made explicit to pupils, and to recommend what pupils should know about how English works. The model which it produced has four parts: the forms of the language; communication and comprehension; acquisition and development; historical and geographical variation. It has been criticized as a checklist of linguistic topics without an internal dynamic connecting the parts, or relating them to educational processes. Nonetheless, some of the Committee's arguments prepared the way for a greater emphasis on knowledge about language in the National Curriculum requirements for England and Wales (1989) than in previous curriculum discussion. (McArthur, 1992)

The model that was being presented raised questions about teachers' knowledge of language and thus the government set up the doomed LINC (Language in the

National Curriculum) project which was aimed at producing materials to support teacher training in language. However, the materials did not marry well with the model of grammar teaching that the government had intended. These materials, many of them excellent, were never published, although you may well find copies in the backs of cupboards in some schools and its recommendations are quoted widely. The year 1989 saw the final draft of the National Curriculum ready for publication.

March 1990 witnessed the publication of the statutory order: *English in the National Curriculum* (DES and Welsh Office, 1990) and this was to be phased into schools. The curriculum which was to be 'broad and balanced' (DES, 1990) had, as its foundation, programmes of study organised into attainment targets (Speaking and Listening; Reading, Writing and Spelling; Handwriting and Presentation). It was made explicit that these attainment targets should not be viewed as separate and that effective teaching would interrelate them (e.g. reading the opening of a story could be followed with a discussion of the techniques used by the writer to gain the interest of the reader and then pupils could use some of the techniques noted in their own openings to a story). Progression and continuity were emphasised. The curriculum relied heavily on a cultural heritage model, but did address a cultural analysis view, with both Shakespeare and advertising receiving a place.

English departments were more inclined to draw up detailed schemes of work to ensure coverage of the curriculum. Despite pleas from many quarters, including Brian Cox (the chair of the committee that drew up the curriculum), to allow time for the new curriculum to bed down before making major changes, the DES decided on proposals for its revision in 1993. Following a period of consultation the revised order (known as the Dearing Report), led by Ronald Dearing, was implemented in 1995. It was agreed that there would be no revisions to the curriculum until at least 2000 as there was a general agreement that there had already been too many changes, too quickly. This revised order recognised the argument for English to embrace, much more fully, media, drama and information technology. Level descriptors were also introduced as indicators of achievement.

This period had seen the implementation of SATs (standard assessment tasks) following an initial boycott by teachers angry at the attempts to impose testing that was seen as ill-conceived, under-resourced and poorly piloted. Legally, however, the boycott had to relate, not to the nature of the tests, but to the additional and unpaid work which they required. SATs were introduced in 1994 with few changes to the original format and this marked the adoption of significant testing of secondary pupils aged 14. These tests are still with us today and are central to the target setting culture of schools and monitoring of pupil performance. Furthermore, since 1989, the division between O levels and CSEs was removed, with the introduction of GCSEs that covered the range of ability tested by both previous examination systems. These GCSEs were initially quite flexibly presented by examination boards with a variety of choices available to teachers, such as 'open' book, prior annotating on texts and coursework. GCSEs are still the main mode of testing at the school leaving age of 16, but are a little less flexible in nature than when they were first introduced, as all examination boards have clearly defined specifications, and what was originally a single-level examination has since become divided by ability into a two-level examination, echoing somewhat the older separation of O level and CSE.

Standard addressed: 3.2.1

Find out what the national targets are for pupils' achievement at Key Stage 3 SATs. Find out what they are for your local school. Place these in your portfolio.

Activity 7 ENGLISH AT THE END OF THE 20TH CENTURY

(suggested time: 60 minutes)

Five years after the Dearing Report came Curriculum 2000. This statutory curriculum is the one that now underpins what needs to be taught during the secondary phase. It is organised under three attainment targets of Speaking & Listening, Reading and Writing. There are also three main strands that run through the curriculum:

1   Knowledge, skills and understanding
2   Breadth of study
3   Standard English, language structure and language variation

Thus a broad plan for addressing National Curriculum requirements with a novel for Year 7 might look something like this:

LESSON PLAN

Topic/Text: *MRS FRISBY AND THE RATS OF NIMH*, by R O'Brien

Class: 7B   Age Group: 11–12   Approx. Timescale: 7 weeks

Aims: To foster enjoyment and appreciation of a literary text. Raise moral issues. Explore a range of written forms. Talk in a range of contexts and to use drama.

Resources   30 copies of the novel. Video *The Secret of Nimh*.

3 tape recorders and tapes.

A4 plain paper and coloured pencils.

Access to library.

If possible, use of Drama Studio.

	EN 1 Speaking and listening	EN 2 Reading	EN 3 Writing
BREADTH OF STUDY	(1) Teacher stopping the reading and asking questions about character, plot, main events	(1) Reading the novel in class. The teacher reading most of it, but allowing pupils to read for short periods (one side at a time). Sometimes giving pupils characters so they read the spoken text, the teacher reading the narrative	(1) Short character descriptions turned into acrostic poems (in pairs)
	(2) Discussing acrostic poems in pairs	(2) Reading their character poems to the class	(2) A plan of Mrs Frisby's house and that of the rats. This should be followed by a description of the houses
	(3) Discussing and analysing appropriateness of language for early primary school pupils. (Perhaps shown examples of story books for this age group)	(3) Presenting their storybooks and radio scripts	(3) Storybook with pictures for early primary school.
	(4) Drama presentation of story. Each group of 4–5 given a scene to dramatise. Teacher acts as narrator, could be mime? One pupil as narrator for each scene	(4) Research into animals being used for experiments. Use of the Internet	(4) Favourite scene turned into a radio script – include music and sound effects. (Put on to tape)
	(5) Debate based on 'Cruelty to animals'	(5) Watch video Recommend reading of: *The Borrowers* by M. Norton, *Wind in the Willows* by K. Grahame	(5) The Secret File of the Rats of Nimh. A History of their escape, their developing intelligence, journey to Thorn Valley
	(6) Discuss similarities and differences between video and book		
KNOWLEDGE, SKILLS AND UNDER-STANDING	Opportunities to adapt speech to different listeners. (e.g. present stories to primary school pupils) Opportunities to consider and discuss choice of language	Introduced to fiction and non-fiction texts	Encouraged to draft their work and proof-read it Encouraged to produce neat legible work To develop the use of dialogue to convey character Take notes from written sources

	EN 1 Speaking and listening	EN 2 Reading	EN 3 Writing
STANDARD ENGLISH, LANGUAGE STRUCTURE AND LANGUAGE VARIATION	Opportunities given to building confidence as users of Standard English in debate and to vary tone of voice in storytelling	Opportunities to respond imaginatively to what has been read To appreciate the motivation of characters and development of the plot To consider how texts are changed for different media – e.g. to radio script	Opportunities given to discuss each others' writing Opportunities given to discuss openings and closings in fiction

The current curriculum recognises a wide breadth within English and there is less reliance on literature; non-fiction, argument, travel writing and biographies are now all represented. Yet new literacies are emerging within a rapidly expanding digital age. Teaching to the national curriculum offers only part of what English is all about. As Andrews (2001: 18) states:

> the National Curriculum can be used as checklist to make sure that the curriculum has been properly covered; or as a proto-planning document, a starting point for learning design. But it cannot serve as a template for a rich and varied programme for English, nor can it obviate the need for creative, imaginative thinking about language and its application.

The National Curriculum was still seen as failing to deliver in certain areas, especially over the issue of transition from Key Stage 2 to Key Stage 3. There was also a growing view that the explicit teaching of literacy skills needed a more prominent role and that whilst the National Curriculum shaped content and assessment it had not changed pedagogy.

Internationally, during the last decade there has been a growing focus upon literacy, rather than English, and in the UK the National Literacy Strategy has moved on from primary education to a *Framework for Teaching English at Key Stage 3: Years 7, 8 and 9*. The promoting of new lesson structures and objectives at word, sentence and text level are demanding a rethinking of pedagogy.

Thus a medium term plan based upon short-story writing with an emphasis upon the *Framework* objectives might look like this:

LESSON PLAN: Medium-term plan
Title of unit: Raising Language Awareness through Short-Story Writing

Year: 8   Term: 2   Duration: 4 weeks   Set: All-ability

Objectives
Word

- 6c using dictionaries and spell-checkers where appropriate
- 7c understand and explain exactly what words mean in particular contexts
- 12 Recognise how the degree of formality influences word choice

Sentence

- 2 explore the impact of a variety of sentence structures
- 4 explore the effects of changes in tense
- 6 explore and compare different methods of grouping sentences into paragraphs of continuous text that are clearly focused and well developed
- 7 develop different ways of linking paragraphs, using a range of strategies to improve cohesion and coherence (e.g. choice of connectives, reference back)
- 10 identify the key alterations made to a text when it is changed from an informal to a formal text (eg change from first person to third person)

Text level

Reading

- 4 review their developing skills as active, critical readers who search for meaning using a range of reading strategies
- 10 analyse the overall structure of a text to identify how key ideas are developed (e.g. through the organisation of the content)
- 14 recognise the conventions of some common literary forms and genres (e.g. Gothic horror)

Writing

- 2 re-read work to anticipate the effect on the reader and revise style and structure, as well as accuracy, with this in mind
- 7 experiment with different language choices to imply meaning and to establish the tone of the piece

Speaking and listening

- 2 tell a story, recount an experience or develop an idea, choosing and changing the mood, tone and pace of delivery for effect
- 11 recognise and build upon other people's contributions
- 12 take different roles in discussion (e.g. develop ideas, seek consensus)

Teaching sequence
Week 1

Coverage:	Exploring texts of different genres
Focus:	Active reading of different texts and telling stories
Outcome:	Students to identify key characteristics of various genres and to be aware of some of the features of written and spoken stories

Week 2

Coverage:	Exploring the conventions of different genres

Focus:	Shared reading of short-stories and text modelling
Outcome:	To appreciate examples of short-story structures and be able to replicate them
Week 3	
Coverage:	Exploring a range of narrative styles.
Focus:	Incorporating a variety of 'ingredients' that help students to write an original story
Outcome:	Collaborative short-story writing and challenging the stereotype
Week 4	
Coverage:	Revisiting types of short-story writing and the writing process
Focus:	Writing in a particular genre for a designated audience
Outcome:	Individual short-story writing for an anthology/ display

Here the objectives are explicit and teachers will need to build into their lessons strategies for monitoring pupils' progress against these objectives. Whilst the National Curriculum is statutory and the KS3 strategy non-statutory, most schools are implementing many aspects of the KS3 strategy.

Standard addressed: 2.1

What do you consider to be the fundamental differences between English and literacy? Write out your thoughts in no more than 400 words. Keep these in your portfolio and discuss with your mentor.

CONTINUOUS THREADS

1 Professional values and practice

Standards addressed: 1.1, 1.2

You should read the section at the back of the document The National Curriculum for England. English (DfEE 1999) entitled 'Inclusion: providing effective learning opportunities for all pupils.' This provides advice about how you can develop a more inclusive curriculum. This is based upon three fundamental principles:

- Setting suitable learning challenges
- Responding to pupils' diverse learning needs
- Overcoming potential barriers to learning and assessment for individuals and groups of pupils

A range of strategies is suggested and you will need to consider these in your planning.

See Chapter 6 on inclusion for further details.

3.1 Planning, expectations and targets

Standard addressed: 3.1.2

Look carefully at the level descriptors for the attainment targets at the back of *The National Curriculum for English*. These describe what pupils need to demonstrate in the attainment targets to achieve that particular level. You will need to consider how you can move pupils from one level to the next (e.g. note the difference between Level 4 where pupils' writing 'in a range of forms is lively and thoughtful', whereas at Level 5 'pupils' writing is varied and interesting, conveying meaning clearly in a range of forms for different readers, using a more formal style where appropriate'). This suggests that you need to focus on the appropriate use of language for particular audiences in your teaching of pupils at Level 4. How might you target this in a scheme of work?

3.4 Teaching and class management

Standard addressed: 3.3.4

The demands of the National Curriculum, testing at Key Stage 3 and GCSE syllabuses have resulted in some English departments organising their classes into ability groups and this seems to be becoming increasingly common. However, some schools still retain all-ability groupings throughout Key Stages 3 and 4. What do you think are the arguments for all-ability groups? What are the counter arguments? Consider how you would organise group work if you had a large range of ability in your class. Would grouping by ability be used? If so, what are the social implications?

2.5 ICT

The meeting of specific Information Communications Technology standards is now a prerequisite for the awarding of QTS and students will also need to pass a separate test in ICT during their training. ICT training within your course is aimed to equip you with the knowledge, skills and understanding to make sound decisions about when, when not, and how to use ICT effectively in teaching. It is essential that you are aware of how to use ICT in English. You will need to have a sound personal understanding of ICT as well as how it should be applied to aid teaching and pupils' learning. It would be useful to meet Heads of ICT at your placement schools to ascertain the resources available and how they can be used. Make sure that at least some of your schemes of work have ICT integrated into them. Some examples of the potential of ICT in English to aid pupils' learning are provided by the TTA in *Using Information and Communications Technology to Meet Teaching Objectives in English* (TTA, 1998: 4). A few examples from this publication are listed below.

- enhancing and developing pupils' reading and writing, for example by increasing challenge and pace in a timed session through the use of a real time computer simulation or participation in an on-line newspaper day, both of which require pupils to receive, act upon and respond in a specified time; or through more direct contact with real audiences beyond the classroom and the local community, by providing access, for example through use of fax or the Internet, to a wide range of up-to-date learning resources;
- supporting and enhancing the study of literary texts, for example by bringing together on a split screen, texts by different authors to explore stylistic similarities and differences; by running a grammar check through the first paragraph of *Bleak House* and using the ensuing comments to discuss Dickens' sentence construction; by comparing pre- and post-1900 texts (say, Austen and Woolf) for changes in textual features such as sentence length;

- allowing pupils to engage with texts in ways that would not always be possible through a paper-based activity. In writing, pupils can experiment with synonyms, re-work texts into a different genre, re-sequence arguments, and explore the effect of changing from the first to the third person narrator with their own or others' texts. In reading, ICT can develop pupils' higher order reading skills in analysis, evaluation, and synthesis by, for example, comparing literary and non-literary material in standard print-based format with the combinations of text, still and moving images and sound which may be accessed in different layers through hypertext or multimedia;
- emphasising the link between the writer and the audience by allowing text to be presented in a variety of ways, extending the range of options available to writers in ways which could not easily be attained using pen and paper. Pupils can adapt the presentation and organisation of their writing to meet the needs of different audiences e.g. presenting information about the school to the wider community through constructing a Web page using text, graphics and possibly sound, video or animation;
- allowing literacy skills to be extended beyond reading and writing of chronological and linear text to multi-layered, multi-authored, multi-sourced texts. For example, when reading a multi-layered text such as a family history readers can take a number of different routes through it, accessing graphics, sound and text. Teachers need to recognise the different reading demands made by such texts.

Scenarios

1 You have been asked to teach your Year 8 class (12–13-year-olds) to write using 'imaginative vocabulary and varied linguistic and literary techniques' (National Curriculum 2000). How would you plan to achieve this? What resources might you use? How would you check prior knowledge?
2 You have one pupil in the class who always speaks with a strong local dialect whatever the context. How would you approach teaching her/him to use the 'vocabulary, structures and grammar of spoken Standard English fluently and accurately in informal and formal situations' (National Curriculum 2000)? What are the issues for the pupil and for your subject knowledge?

Further ideas

Consider how you might integrate aspects of the National Curriculum. This might include using media approaches when teaching Shakespeare, or ICT to support the teaching of a text.

FURTHER READING

Davies, C. (1996) *What is English Teaching?* Buckingham: Open University Press
Protherough, R. and King, P. (1995) *The Challenge of English in the National Curriculum*, London: Routledge

REFERENCES

Andrews, R. (2001) *Teaching and Learning English*. London: Continuum

Board of Education (1921) *The Teaching of English in England*. London: HMSO

Cox, B. (1991) *Cox on Cox: An English Curriculum for the 90s*. London: Hodder and Stoughton

Davison, J. and Dowson, J. (1998) *Learning to Teach English in the Secondary School*. London: Routledge

DES (1975) *A Language for Life*. London: HMSO

DES (1988) *Report of the Committee of Enquiry into the Teaching of English Language*. London: HMSO

DES (1989) *English for Ages 5–16*. London: DES

DfEE (1999) *The National Curriculum for England*. English: Key stages 1–40. London: DfEE & QCA

DfES (1995) *English in the National Curriculum*. London: HMSO

McArthur, T. (1992) *Oxford Companion to the English Language*. Oxford: Oxford University Press

TTA (1998) *Using Information and Communications Technology to Meet Teaching Objectives in English*. London: TTA

WEBSITE

http://www.nc.uk.net

chapter 2

THE KEY STAGE 3 STRATEGY

> *The language and literacy skills our pupils need to become citizens of the twenty-first century and the language and literacy teaching needed to achieve those skills will continue to be debated. That the goal, of improving literacy standards for all is worth striving for is, however, incontestable. (Lewis and Wray, 2000: 164)*

By the end of this unit you will have gained an understanding of the Key Stage 3 strategy which includes the *Framework for Teaching English: Years 7, 8 and 9*. You will also have been made aware of the implications of the strategy's implementation. The chapter will provide you with an overview of the strategy's development, assist your understanding of word, sentence and text level work and help you to consider planning for the teaching of the literacy objectives. Furthermore, this unit will provide you with a critical insight into the strategy's positive role in raising standards and some of the educational issues that surround its adoption. The *Framework for Teaching English: Years 7, 8 and 9* and the objectives for Key Stage 3 can be found on the following website **www.standards.dfes.gov.uk/**. For this chapter you will need access to this framework.

RATIONALE

The Literacy element of the KS3 Strategy was introduced to all secondary schools for Key Stage 3 (11–14-year-old) in September 2001. This followed a brief period of piloting in secondary schools covering some 17 authorities with no extensive lead-in time for detailed evaluations. However, the initial findings were generally positive and built upon the National Literacy Strategy in primary schools, which was an initiative well supported by most primary headteachers. Its implementation in secondary schools is likely to make Key Stage 3 teaching more objective-driven, whilst placing significant emphasis upon transition and focused planning. Whether this will result in more teacher-directed teaching is still not yet evident. This does not imply that good teachers were not doing much of what was being recommended in the strategy anyway and certainly some of the recent literacy strategy training for KS3 has been seen as patronising (see Goodwyn, 2002). However, it has meant a radical rethink in terms of the emphasis that is being placed on certain methods of teaching and content. The place of non-fiction is highlighted and access to a range of strategies for teaching spelling is offered by means of examples. Interactive starters for lessons have also been given a strong emphasis, along with a recognition that these might not necessarily be linked to the main body of the lesson. The strategy materials provide examples of teaching methodologies and these are certainly being debated and critiqued by teachers and academics.

In the English Department Training 2001 (DfEE 2001a) the anonymous writers of the KS3 materials set out the context for the introduction of the KS3 strategy. They were listed as:

- Success of the National Literacy Strategy in primary schools
- Reading standards higher than writing
- Girls achieving more highly than boys
- Dip at transfer and little progress during Key Stage 3
- Building on cross-curricular initiatives
- Teaching and learning gains in the Key Stage 3 pilot
- Support from the Key Stage 3 National Strategy.

Against this backcloth it was stated (DfEE, 2001a) that the Key Stage 3 strategy will:

- Safeguard and build on the gains made at Key Stage 2 through the National Literacy Strategy
- Improve continuity of teaching and learning from Year 6 to Year 7
- Provide early, tailored intervention to secure Level 4 for pupils still at Level 3, and those below
- Establish systematic and co-ordinated support for literacy across the curriculum
- Improve motivation for both teachers and pupils in Key Stage 3
- Make pupils better prepared for Key Stage 4.

Certainly, it could be argued that the National Literacy Strategy had made a strong impact on the teaching of English in primary schools. Its introduction was pitched against data stating that the standards of literacy had changed little in 50 years and that there were wide performance differences between schools. As Roger Beard (2000) noted:

> *Inspection, survey and observational research evidence suggests that, in the years before NLS was implemented, early reading in Primary Schools was largely taught by individualised methods in which the structure of commercial materials was often very influential.*

Other evidence suggested that 'direct teaching of literacy skills was surprisingly rare' (HMI, 1991; Ofsted, 1997 quoted in Beard, 2000: 246). In 1997 it was claimed that only 63% of pupils were meeting expected government targets for English on leaving primary school.

The evolution of the National Literacy Strategy was evident in the Conservative Party's National Literacy Project established in 1996 by the DfEE. This project was then built upon by the Labour government in May 1996 when they established 'The Literacy Task Force' led by Michael Barber. The brief for this task force was to devise a strategy for raising the standards of literacy in England's primary schools over the next decade. The report which followed was entitled *The Implementation of the National Literacy Strategy* and was published in 1997. Perhaps the most significant and controversial aspect of the strategy was the recommendation that all primary schools in England would have a daily literacy hour. The structure of the hour was clearly outlined:

1   The first section (approx. 15 minutes) to introduce the objectives, to model reading or writing and for this to be whole class teaching
2   The second section (approx. 15 minutes) to be word or sentence level work, again to be whole class teaching
3   The third section (approx. 20 minutes) to be group or individual work such as reading or writing at word or sentence level whilst the teacher focuses on one or more ability groups on guided text work
4   The final section (approx. 10 minutes) to be a whole class plenary reviewing the learning that has been undertaken.

This model was not a statutory requirement but was strongly recommended, as schools would have to justify alternative models. A structured literacy hour was a challenge to the pedagogy of primary school teaching, since it had its strong emphasis upon whole class teaching. According to Fisher and Singleton (2000: 243):

The Literacy Hour was introduced in order to bring about a number of changes to the teaching of literacy.

1 A clearer focus on literacy instruction with teaching that is:
- *Discursive*
- *Interactive*
- *Well-paced*
- *Confident*
- *Ambitious.*

2 Improved classroom organisation and management based on a Vygotskian model with pupils moving from dependence on the adult /skilled peer (shared work), to inter-dependence (guided work) to independent working.

3 Effective management of literacy at school level with a common structure within and between schools and common classroom practices.

The KS3 strategy and its literacy strand have been introduced on three main fronts. The first of these is at English Department level. English departments are being expected to deliver the Key Stage 3 *Framework for Teaching English: Years 7, 8 and 9* and thus schemes of work/lesson plans will need to address the learning objectives for each year group. Consequently pre-September 2001 schemes will require revisions/additions in order to ensure full coverage of the objectives. The objectives cover word, sentence and text level. In particular there is likely to be an emphasis upon planning to incorporate word and sentence level objectives. The challenge will be to include these objectives in an integrated manner so that they are explored in a meaningful context.

The second front is cross-curricular where, following auditing, all departments will be expected to undertake a commitment to improving the literacy skills of their pupils and they too will be covering some of the objectives from the *Framework for Teaching English: Years 7, 8 and 9*. In 2001 the QCA (Qualifications and Curriculum Authority) has published a support booklet entitled *Language at Work in Lessons – Literacy across the Curriculum at Key Stage 3*. This provides examples of how a variety of subject areas could cover some of the objectives from the *Framework*.

On the third front, pupils who are working below level 4 for English on entry to secondary education will be provided with support materials called 'Progress Units'. These cover six main areas: writing organisation, information retrieval, spelling, reading between the lines, phonics and sentences. Each of these areas has 18 planned teaching sessions that are designed in most instances to last 20 minutes each. These could form part of English lessons or be taught outside the main lessons. Some schools may decide to use teaching assistants to cover them. The recommended literacy hour structure with the 20-minute group/individual session could be an appropriate time slot for the teaching of these units. All of these units are available from the DfES and will be in secondary schools. Some schools are integrating them into breakfast clubs and lunchtimes. Some schools are adapting the units to help pupils in Year 9. The teaching of the units is ideal for student teachers at the start of a school placement as a structure is already provided and it gives the opportunity to work with a small group of pupils in a focused way.

It is noticeable that many of the objectives for Key Stage 3 focus on writing, which may be a response to criticism that at primary level the strategy was addressing reading more effectively than writing. The reading sections at Key Stage 3 make very close links with writing. For example Year 9 Reading 3 is 'note taking at speed' whilst Reading 5 is 'evaluating own critical writing'.

LINKS WITH THE NATIONAL CURRICULUM

It could be argued that a real strength of the KS3 Framework for teaching is that it sets out objectives for each year at Key Stage 3 and thus is much more explicit about progression than the programmes of study in the National Curriculum. It also builds upon the objectives at Year 6 (Key Stage 2). The structure for Key Stage 3 follows the same format as at Key Stage 2 and is based upon word level objectives, sentence level objectives and text level objectives. There is much debate amongst English teachers as to whether this order is appropriate and whether perhaps we should be starting with text level objectives (beginning with the whole rather than a part).

> At WORD LEVEL the coverage is: spelling, spelling strategies and vocabulary.
> At SENTENCE LEVEL the coverage is: sentence construction and punctuation, paragraphing and cohesion, stylistic conventions of non-fiction and Standard English and language variation.
> At TEXT LEVEL close links have been made with the attainment targets of the National Curriculum. The coverage is as follows:
> **Reading** – research and study skills, reading for meaning, understanding the writer's craft and the study of literary texts.
> **Writing** – plan, draft and present/imagine, explore, entertain/inform, explain, describe/persuade, argue, advise/analyse, review, comment.
> **Speaking and listening** – speaking/listening/ group discussion and interaction/and drama.

Teachers will need to look carefully at their planning to see how the objectives can be met if they are to avoid a checklist approach at the expense of coherence and creativity. The National Curriculum programmes of study will still need to be covered, although it is likely that the KS3 Literacy objectives will drive the short term and medium term planning whilst the programmes of study for the National Curriculum will shape long term planning. The National Curriculum requirements mean that the following must be covered in Key Stages 3/4:

- Two Shakespeare plays
- Drama by major playwrights
- Two pre-1914 fiction texts
- Two post-1914 fiction texts
- Four pre-1914 poets
- Four post-1914 poets
- Recent and contemporary works
- Writers from different cultures and traditions
- Literary non-fiction
- Information and reference texts
- Media and moving image texts.

Please note that the pre-1914 literature texts come from a prescribed canon. You will need to check the canon to ensure appropriate coverage of the requirements of the National Curriculum.

You are likely to find in your departments schemes of work and sample lesson plans that address the *Framework* objectives, but it is important that you gain an awareness of what are the best approaches to teaching and learning with your particular classes. The strategy has certainly made many teachers cover a greater range of genres in their teaching and we are increasingly likely to see objectives being made explicit to pupils and the use of interactive starter activities. Much of this is good practice, but as a student teacher you will need to consider whether the genre theory is too inflexible, whether pupils always need to know the objectives at the start of a lesson and whether the starter activity too often becomes a one-off decontextualised activity. A critical approach to the strategy will be a benefit, noting what works and reflecting upon how you should 'deliver' it. Teachers are having to consider how class novels can be taught in such a tight curriculum and whether the place of critical literacy has been marginalised.

Sue Hackman, the new national director of the Key Stage 3 Strategy, in a recent article in the *Times Educational Supplement* stated that she believed

> the Government targets for 14-year-olds are reasonable. But progress towards achieving them is slow. This year 66% reached level five in maths and English and 67% in science. A similar slow rate of progress, about 1%, was made in the 205 pilot schools who have been using the new English and maths frameworks for two years. By 2004, 75% are expected to get level 5 in English and maths and 70% in science.

> Ms Hackman has recognised the wisdom of allowing teachers time to turn the plans into action: 'Rather than carry on pumping out new ideas, schools need time to embed the strategy.

> 'There will be a greater emphasis on encouraging schools to develop and a recognition that it is better for them to do a few things well,' she said. There will also be a change of emphasis from individual subject departments to whole-school involvement. For instance, literacy will be expected to be taught across the curriculum, not just in English. Schools will also be encouraged to take what was a top-down, imposed strategy and tailor it to their own local needs.

> Part of this new emphasis is a behaviour drive. Consultants will be appointed this year to go into schools and help teachers tackle unruly pupils. 'Behaviour is closely tied in with how you run your classroom. We want to look at which classes encourage best behaviour,' Ms Hackman says. (TES, 17 January 2002; **from http://www.literacytrust.org.uk/index.html**)

The English teacher at the start of the 21st century will have an abundance of training materials from the KS3 Strategy at his or her disposal. There are units of work on transition for pupils to start in Y6 and complete in Y7 (DfES, 2002c) aimed at promoting continuity and progression. They are also intended to help inform Y7 teachers of pupils' achievement. There is a useful bank of materials entitled *Grammar for Writing: Supporting Pupils Learning EAL* (DfES, 2002a) which is accompanied by *Access and Engagement in English* (DfES, 2002b). These provide examples of how to identify learning needs of pupils in reading and writing and how these might be addressed, for example subject–verb agreement, through rehearsing aloud choices of reference to singular/plural in modelling writing. These publications stress quite rightly what pupils learning EAL bring to the learning process (openness to new input/understanding that grammars differ) as well as noting common weaknesses (use of connectives/word order/lack of subordination).

There will be many more publications/videos available from the KS3 strategy by the time this book is published. It is beyond the scope of this chapter to comment on all the publications, but most of them can be accessed from the standards website, **www.standards.dfes.gov.uk/keystage3**

Activity 1

EARLY DAYS FOR THE KS3 STRATEGY
(suggested time: 20 minutes)

The progress of the implementation of the National Literacy at Key Stages 1 and 2 has been closely monitored and debated. Some concerns had been raised about the lack of time and opportunity for extended reading and writing in the literacy hour and that there is less opportunity for individual work and student-centred approaches. Debate focused on the development of writing which resulted in suggestions that included the need for more emphasis upon guided writing and more modelling of the writing process. A NATE survey released in May 2001 in the *Times Educational Supplement* noted that 60% of 200 Key Stage 3 pilot schools felt that the strategy did not help children's learning. Yet the word 'strategy' suggests a long term plan and it will be several years before research can indicate whether there have been substantial improvements. However there is initial evidence to suggest that the strategy has provided a sharper focus for lessons with clear objectives, pace and rigour.

Read the article, 'The National Literacy Strategy – recognition of success,' by Professor Michael Barber, head of the Standards and Effectiveness Unit and list the benefits that he identifies of The National Literacy Strategy. Keep this list in your English portfolio.

This article first appeared in the March 2001 issue of
***Literacy Today* (issue no. 26)**

The National Literacy Strategy – recognition of success
Michael Barber

. . . The Government introduced the National Literacy Strategy into primary schools because an unacceptable number of eleven year olds were failing to reach the standard of literacy expected for their age – just 57 per cent achieved Level 4 or above in 1996. We therefore set an ambitious national target that, by 2002, 80 per cent of all 11 year olds would reach Level 4 or above in English.

There is strong evidence of the early success of the strategy. The Key Stage 2 test results in 2000 showed a 10 per cent improvement from 1998 in the percentage of 11 year olds achieving the expected level, taking the total to 75 per cent. This means that an additional 70,000 pupils achieved Level 4 last year in comparison with just two years earlier. With five percentage points to go, we are on track to achieve the 2002 target. There is also clear evidence of a narrowing of the achievement gap between advantaged and disadvantaged local education authorities, and of the gap between boys' and girls' achievement.

Ofsted's report *The National Literacy Strategy: the second year*, published on 28 November 2000, confirmed that the strategy continued to have a major impact on the teaching of English in primary schools and on the content of initial teacher education courses. It reported that there had been a transformation in the teaching of reading, particularly in the amount of effective whole class work, which had improved the standards achieved by both boys and girls.

There is also evidence of high levels of support for the strategy from the teaching profession, which has worked, and is continuing to work, extremely hard to raise standards. In a survey of Year 4 and 5 teachers, 91 per cent said that they supported the principle of a National Literacy Strategy and 75 per cent said that they enjoyed teaching the literacy hour. An independent survey of headteachers also showed that 95 per cent support the literacy strategy, and that 89 per cent said that pupils were positive about the literacy hour. The keys to this success have been the high quality materials, excellent professional development and consistent investment year on year (we are spending £192 million on the literacy and numeracy strategies this year and will continue to spend at this level until 2004) . . .

Standard addressed: 2.1c

(http://www.literacytrust.org.uk/index.html)

Activity 2

THE LITERACY TRUST WEBSITE

(suggested time: 30 minutes)

There is an extremely informative website that is updated on a daily basis and provides a useful overview of literacy issues. It is comprehensive, including articles, summaries, discussion boards and links to other websites. To open it click on:

www.literacytrust.org.uk

One issue that has been much debated is 'Boys and Literacy', particularly at Key Stage 4 where there is little evidence of boys closing the achievement gap with girls. It will be interesting to see if the KS3 Literacy Strategy with its emphasis on more direct teaching will have an effect upon this 'gap'. Many schools have adopted strategies to raise boys' achievement, such as single sex classes and placing greater emphasis upon speaking and listening. Look at the literacy trust website.

Standard addressed: 3.3.6

Click on index, then click on Gender. Under initiatives and case studies look at some of the initiatives to improve boys' writing. Note down some of the strategies that are being employed and place your key findings in your English portfolio. Ask the Head of English during your school experience if they have devised particular strategies that are gender specific.

Activity 3

PLANNING TO USE THE *FRAMEWORK FOR TEACHING ENGLISH: YEARS 7, 8 AND 9*

(suggested time: 2 hours)

Read through the three lesson plans below which address the KS3 Literacy objectives for Y8 in the *Framework for Teaching English: Years 7, 8 and 9* and are based broadly upon a literacy hour model. They comprise the first three lessons of a unit based on short story writing. Using this structure choose another one or two teaching objectives from the *Framework* for Y8 found on **www.standards. dfes.gov.uk/** and plan a lesson for a Y8 class with an accompanying resource sheet. Consider how progression is addressed in your lesson. Place your completed plan in your English portfolio. Presented below is a recommended lesson plan format used by PGCE students at one of our universities. It was completed by one student teacher asked to teach a lesson on personification at interview for a set 2 Y7 group. Electronic version of the template available at **www.paulchapmanpublishing.co.uk/resources/completeguide.htm**.

LESSON PLAN: Lucy Smith, PGCE English, Sheffield Hallam University

Date: 28/02/03   Room: Time: 50 minutes   Year Group: 7a2

Topic/text: Personification	Prior knowledge and skills: Some knowledge of personification.

Please complete this section on programmes of study and objectives as appropriate.

Intended learning outcomes:

NC Programmes of study:

EN2 – 1a – to extract meaning beyond the literal, explaining how the choice of language and style affects implied and explicit meanings.

Pupils will be able to recognise and use personification in their work and justify choices for doing so.

EN3 – 1d – use a range of techniques and different ways of organising and structuring material to convey *ideas*, themes and characters.

NLS Objectives:

Word level

Sentence level

Text level

Wr8 – experiment with the visual . . . effects of language

R14 – recognise how writer's language choices can enhance meaning

---

Resources	OHP Felt tips for pupils to underline OHP pen Whiteboard pen Acetate containing information for the starter activity Acetate stating objective of lesson 30 copies of *Mister Wind* (and one on acetate)

30 copies of *Rainbow* (and one on acetate)
Paper for the pupils to work on

Special considerations	Some aspects of the plan may have to be altered at the last minute as I do not know the pupils and am not aware how they will react to tasks set.

Time allocated

ACTIVITIES AND DEVELOPMENT

Introduction/Starter activity (recap of what they may already know)

Aim – to use personification to describe objects or settings and to justify the choices made in doing so.

(Put an example of personification on the OHP).

10 minutes

Ask pupils about personification – do they know what it is?

Class discussion – break down the word – **person**/ification – to give an object the attributes of a person. To personify. Discuss the sentence displayed on the OHP – why is this personification?

The verb develops the noun to make it appear to have human characteristics.

Dictionary definition – to attribute human characteristics to (a thing or abstraction).

Students now, in pairs, are to create their own descriptions using personification. (I will have my own example of this up on OHP and will ask the pupils to suggest reasons why I may have chosen the verb and noun.) They should be prepared to explain their intention as authors in using the personification.

Guideline list of words that pupils may use – sea, rain, trees, mountain, water, or they may use their own ideas.

Encourage some of the pupils to feed their ideas back to the class.

Development

5 minutes

Read the poem *Mister Wind*. I will ask for a volunteer to read the poem to the class, then repeat it myself if necessary, depending on whether I choose a strong reader. (Pupils will have individual copies of the poem as well as it being displayed on the OHP.)

15 minutes

Does this poem use personification?

Discuss the language used that personifies the wind. What verbs are used? Why are these associated with people primarily?

Pupils take turns to come to the front of the class and underline the words that suggest personification (the verbs). I will add any that are missed.

Push	Toss	whistle
Thump	rip	blow (possibly – discuss that we do also refer
Strewn	ROAR	to the wind as blowing but people do blow Tweak
slam		too – are we using personification every day when we say the wind is blowing?
		Another example – the wind is getting up)

5 minutes

Do we get a good opinion of the wind from this poem? How has the poet chosen to portray the wind? Class discussion on why the poet has chosen to use these particular verbs e.g. *push, thump, slam* and *rip* are all aggressive and angry words – how does this affect our opinion of the wind in this poem?

Briefly compare with *Rainbow*. (Don't spend too long on this, as it is only to show the pupils that personification does not have to be angry.)

5 minutes	Has this poem got a different tone to *Mister Wind*? Happier, more carefree – why? Choice of words – skip and dancing instead of slam and thump.
	Conclusion/plenary
	Put the rewrite of the first stanza of *Mister Wind* up on OHP. Read it through with the pupils.
10 minutes	Pupils are to continue the re-write using their own words and adapting it to suit *fire* rather than wind.
	[There will be a list of suitable verbs on the back of the copy of *Mister Wind* to help the pupils if they are struggling with the task. I will only point this out if I feel that some of the pupils are struggling.]
	Feedback of what the pupils have written. How has this changed the poem from its original format?

Homework/ Follow up work	
Further Ideas	In a follow-up lesson, it would be beneficial to the pupils to write their own stanza, or even a full poem, that uses personification to describe its subject. This would provide opportunity for assessment and would secure knowledge of the subject.

LESSON PLAN: Short story writing Lesson 1

LEARNING OBJECTIVE

Word 12 Formality and word choice

Writing 5 Develop the use of commentary and description in narrative

Starting points

(Note: This is the first of three units that should run concurrently to deliver this learning objective).

Before introducing the class to the examples on the student sheet, ask them to review what they feel makes an effective opening to a story. This exercise can be undertaken in pairs initially, with the resulting ideas brainstormed and noted on an OHT. Discuss any important points which then arise, such as that the opening makes you want to read on; begins with a dramatic event; raises questions in the reader's mind; has an interesting setting, effective use of pronouns and so on.

Whole class work

Read the student sheet together and explore the four texts, encouraging the class to explain how they differ in basic form and content. Ask what techniques the writers use to engage interest – for example are they aware that *Kit's Wilderness* appears to begin with the chronological end of the narrative? Work through each example, asking:

- What do we learn (if anything) about the setting and characters?
- Who is telling the story and what effect does this have on the reader?
- What sort of narrator is it? Is it written in the first person/personal or is it omniscient?
- What type of story do we think it is going to be?
- What are the clues as to what might happen next?
- What is particularly interesting or unusual?
- When was the text written? (Is it a new text, but written about the past?) What are the clues?
- What tense – or tenses – does the writer use? Why?
- What impact do all of the above have on the reader?

Guided group/individual work

Using the ideas discussed in the whole class work, ask the students to write the opening paragraph to a short story or novel. Provide them with *two* ingredients, such as the setting and first person narrative, before encouraging them to include *one* further ingredient of their own, such as adding a different genre of text (perhaps that it is a newsflash). Now introduce the idea that they must address the reader directly, and change the text accordingly.

Plenary

Invite some students to read out their story openings. Challenge the rest of the class to identify the techniques used to create interest in the story besides the two ingredients supplied by the teacher. How effective is it to address the reader as 'you'?

Further work

Plan, draft and present

Students reread their work to consider the effect it has on the reader, and revise the style and structure as appropriate.

Text level: Writing – Imagine, explore, entertain

You might prompt students to write the opening of a story using only pronouns for the main characters. Then ask them to provide a brief commentary on the effectiveness of this technique. Alternatively, encourage students to begin a story at the end so that the rest of the story is a flashback.

Or give the students a short story (two sides only) that has been divided into sections and muddled up, and ask them to identify the opening paragraph.

Resources

Kit's Wilderness (by David Almond)

They thought we had disappeared, and they were wrong. They thought we were dead, and they were wrong. We stumbled together out of the ancient darkness into the shining valley. The sun glared down on us. The whole world glistened with ice and snow.

We held our arms against the light and stared in wonder at each other. We were scorched and blackened from the flames. There was dried blood on our lips, cuts and bruises on our skin.

The Bound Man (by Ilse Aichinger)

Sunlight on his face woke him, but made him shut his eyes again; it streamed unhindered down the slope, collected itself into rivulets, attracted swarms of flies, which flew low over his forehead, circled, sought to land and were overtaken by fresh swarms. When he tried to whisk them away he discovered that he was bound. A thin rope cut into his arms.

The Bryant Letters (by Chris Harris)

Dear Shahena,

By the time you read this letter I will have made contact with Mr Bryant. I know you said it would be dangerous but how else will I find Emma? It is now two days since she left to see him and he told us that talking to the police was saying hello to our maker . . .

Shahena stared at the letter in disbelief. Mr Bryant, Mr Bryant, Mr Bryant. The name itself made her feel uncomfortable. Mr Bryant was a secretive, dangerous man whom no one crossed. Not if you wanted to remain in one piece.

The Girl from the Sky (by Fiona Macdonald)

Here is a newsflash . . . we interrupt this programme to switch over to the incredible events which are unfolding in Bandloch, a little village in East Stirlingshire. A small girl, of as yet unknown identity and caught here by a local amateur video enthusiast, has come hurtling from the sky on a broomstick, crash-landing on a house before falling into the pond belonging to the owner, Mrs Knowtrubel. After shaking the water from her clothes, the girl was reported to vow that the village would soon witness the strangest of happenings beginning at the next full moon. With this she apparently flew off, slightly unsteadily on her twisted vehicle, glancing back only momentarily at the confused faces of the villagers.

'Well I never,' said David staring at the television. 'Isn't that Vanessa's youngest daughter?'

Source: English Programme File 2 written by Paul Dickinson, Jim McDonagh and Jeff Wilkinson

LESSON PLAN: Short story writing Lesson 2

LEARNING OBJECTIVE

Sentence 7 Cohesion and coherence

Reading 10 Analyse the overall structure of a text to identify how key ideas are developed

Speaking and listening 7 Listen for a specific purpose

Starting points

Review and revise the following basic format of stories: opening (setting), middle (complication and climax) and ending (resolution). Also remind the class of the characteristics of openings as explored in the first lesson on story writing before asking the students to suggest how one of those stories might be continued. Brainstorm their ideas and write them on an OHT or on the board. Choose one of the ideas and, on another OHT or on a blank section of board, model the writing of the next paragraph, explaining the complication that you are introducing.

Whole class work

Retell the traditional version of the fairy tale *Little Red Riding Hood* by the brothers Grimm, and ask the class to identify the story structure. It consists of the opening (Little Red Riding Hood takes food and drink to her grandmother), the complication (she meets the wolf), the climax (the wolf dresses up as her grandmother ready to eat Little Red Riding Hood), and resolution (the hunter saves the day). Ask the students if they know of other versions where the climax is different. Now read the extract from Mary Shelley's *Frankenstein*. Explain how the complication comes to a head when the scientist steps beyond natural science and tries to play God by bringing his creation to life. If the students are unfamiliar with the story, ask them to suggest what the climax might be. Finally, show them the second story structure on the resources sheet. Which is based upon *Dracula*, and explain once again the model used for the story.

Guided group/individual work

Organise the students into groups of four or five, and number each individual 1–5. Tell them that person number 1 is going to describe the opening to a story, number 2 then follows by adding a complication, number 3 offers a climax and number 4 suggests a resolution. However, throughout the telling, one key idea has to be kept in the story (e.g. good vs evil). When this is completed, the next person then begins another story and the pattern is repeated. (If the students are in groups of four, suggest that a different person starts the next story, so that they all have the chance to try each story section.)

Plenary

Highlight the different stages of development in the story by asking one or two groups to tell their stories to the class. Ask if the key idea occurred throughout.

Further work

Drama: In groups, use a series of 'freeze frames' to illustrate the different stages of a story, such as a tale they have discussed earlier. For example, the freeze frames for *Macbeth* could be:

- opening – Macbeth winning battle;
- complication – he embarks on murderous path by killing Duncan;
- climax – the battle at Dunsinane;
- resolution – Malcolm is crowned king.

Text level: Reading – Understanding the author's craft

Group students three to a computer and provide a story opening for each group, preferably from different genres such as science fiction or horror. Give each group five minutes to write a follow-on complication. After five minutes, the groups move to the next computer to add the climax. Their writing can be either full prose versions or short notes about the basic elements and events.

Alternatively, provide the students with the beginning and end of a story and ask them to write the middle. Students give their introductory paragraphs from the previous unit to another student who adds the complication and climax.

Resources

Frankenstein (by Mary Shelley)

It was on a dreary night of November that I beheld the accomplishment of my toils. With an anxiety that almost amounted to agony, I collected the instruments of life around me, that I might infuse a spark of being into the lifeless thing that lay at my feet. It was already one in the morning; the rain pattered dismally against the panes, and my candle was nearly burned out, when, by the glimmer of the half-extinguished light, I saw the dull yellow eye of the creature open; it breathed hard, and a convulsive motion agitated its limbs.

Dracula (by Bram Stoker)

The basic four-stage structure –

Opening

Large castle, late at night in Transylvania. Man is lost and knocks at castle gate and is invited in for the night to avoid the terrible storm.

Complication

It is Dracula's castle and the man realises that his host is a vampire.

Climax

So he drives a stake through Dracula's heart.

Resolution

Dracula condemned to eternal Hell and will never wake again.

Source: English Programme File 2 written by Paul Dickinson, Jim McDonagh and Jeff Wilkinson

---

LESSON PLAN: Short story writing lesson 3

LEARNING OBJECTIVE

Writing 8 Develop an imaginative or unusual treatment of familiar material or established conventions

Starting points

Emphasise to the class that endings of narratives often provide the most challenging task for the writer – and writers have even changed the endings of their stories or novels to suit the wishes of their readership. One such example is Charles Dickens's *Great Expectations*. His original ending was viewed as too pessimistic and so, consequently, he created a more positive ending. Sometimes, of course, writers will deliberately provide a shock ending, as Roald Dahl did in his *Tales of the Unexpected*.

Whole class work

Look at the three different endings to *Little Red Riding Hood* on the student sheet and discuss the similarities and differences between them. Talk about the fact that they all share a form of resolution and are satisfying in different ways, and that they all conform to a closed ending model in the same way as a typical detective story. (In detective stories, a murder investigation often ends with the capture of the murderer, or with someone or something being found – the resolution.) Sometimes, however, story endings are unpredictable. Although good triumphs over evil in many stories, modern writers often deny readers this certainty. Point out also that good writers avoid 'let down' endings such as 'I woke up and it was a dream'. Ask the students which of the endings on the sheet is 'happy', which contains a twist, and which is resolved but not 'happy'. Also, draw attention to the text that uses the present tense to end, and *why* this is.

Whichever method writers choose, endings need to be 'realistic' or at least consistent with the character and the order of events. In this way, writers generally provide clues as to what will happen next – sometimes in very apparent ways, at other times less so. Two famous examples include the witches' strange prophecies in *Macbeth*, and Sherlock Holmes's ability to find clues. Read aloud three-quarters of a short story and ask the students to predict the ending, encouraging them to be explicit about any clues or inferences that have suggested it. Then brainstorm these ideas, writing them down on the board or on an OHT in two columns (actual events and linguistic clues). Students should note these down.

Guided group/individual work

Students write alternative endings for well-known tales or stories, aiming to subvert the convention deliberately, for example by making Prince Charming choose an ugly sister.

Plenary

Reiterate the key points about ending stories, such as: creating a sense of justice at the end; resolving the main problem; ensuring there is a twist at the end. Remind the class of how writers prepare the reader for the ending and how they sometimes provide a shock finale when they want readers to look at familiar material in a new way.

Further work – Inform, explain, describe

Students describe story structure clearly, conveying a sense of character and/or setting by including appropriate detail.

Text level: Writing – Imagine, explore, entertain

Ask students to consider different possible endings of the stories that they worked on in Lesson 2, 'Short story writing' and to suggest and write down a happy ending. In pairs, the students then swap stories and write an alternative sad or ambivalent ending. These endings can then be compared.

Resources

Little Red Riding Hood

Little Red Riding Hood found her grandmother safe and sound in the closet. When the huntsman returned, Grandmother opened the basket of goodies and the three of them ate a delicious lunch. When Little Red Riding Hood returned home, she told her mother what happened and promised never, ever, to talk to strangers again. (Traditional tale)

When the little girl opened the door of her grandmother's house she saw that there was somebody in bed with a nightcap on. She had approached no nearer than twenty-five feet from the bed when she saw that it was not her grandmother but the wolf, for even in a nightcap a wolf does not look any more like your grandmother than the Metro-Goldwyn lion looks like Calvin Coolidge. So the little girl took an automatic out of her basket and shot the wolf dead.

Moral: It is not so easy to fool little girls nowadays as it used to be. (James Thurber, 1939)

'What big teeth you have, grandmother!'

'The better to eat you.'

And upon saying these words, the wicked wolf threw himself upon Little Red Riding Hood and ate her up. (Charles Perrault, 1697)

Source: English Programme File 2 written by Paul Dickinson, Jim McDonagh and Jeff Wilkinson

Standard
addressed:
3.1.1

Activity 4 — WORD AND SENTENCE LEVEL OBJECTIVES

(suggested time: 30 minutes)

Standard
addressed:
3.3.2c

Choose two word level and three sentence level objectives from Year 7 in the *Framework for Teaching English: Years 7, 8 and 9*. Then note down in your portfolio how these might be integrated into a lesson. For example Y7 WORD 20 connectives could be linked to improving writing through the drafting process.

Activity 5 — SPELLING

(suggested time: 45 minutes)

Look at the following list of 10 key subject-specific spellings taken from the list recommended in the *Framework for Teaching English at Key Stage 3*. Then choose five of them and decide how you would help pupils to learn them. Bear in mind that some pupils in your class will already know some of the spellings. You might want to refer to the chapter on spelling, which suggests a range of strategies. Complete your responses in your English portfolio. Consider patterns of spelling mistakes made by your pupils.

Alliteration
Comma
Dialogue
Genre
Imagery
Playwright
Simile
Standard   Vocabulary
addressed: Scene
3.3.2c   Rhyme

Activity 6 — EXPLORING A VARIETY OF TEXTS

(suggested time: 40 minutes)

There is an emphasis on writing in the National Literacy Strategy, particularly in developing pupils' abilities to write in different ways for different purposes in non-fiction texts. In the training materials for the K53 Strategy eight main categories of non-fiction texts are identified. These are: instructions, recount (retelling an event or series of events), explanation, information, persuasion, discursive writing, analysis and evaluation. Think of two examples of text types under each category, such as recipes and giving directions for 'instructions'. This will help you to consider the range of texts that you could use in the classroom. Keep a list in your portfolio. You should also consider the main characteristics of these text types (e.g tense/viewpoint).

Standard addressed: 3.3.2c

Activity 7

A TEACHING SEQUENCE
(suggested time: 45 minutes)

The KS3 Strategy promotes particular models of teaching and learning. A teaching sequence that is recommended for writing is as follows:

1   Establish clear aims – these are to be made explicit and are related to the *Framework* objectives
2   Provide example(s) – a model of the text
3   Explore the features of the text – this could be through a variety of activities or guided reading
4   Define the conventions – the teacher makes clear the writer's choices at word, sentence and text level
5   Demonstrate how it is written – teacher models the writing, sharing with the class his/her reasons for choices
6   Compose together – teacher writes, building on pupils' contributions
7   Scaffold first attempts – pupils write but appropriately supported by bullet points/writing frame as appropriate
8   Independent writing – pupils apply their learning to another piece of writing
9   Draw out key learning – feedback offered and advice for further improvement
10   Review – progress is reviewed at a later date.

This is not supposed to be a rigid model but provides examples of how teachers can support the writing process. Also you will need to appreciate that this sequence might be undertaken over a series of lessons. You should be aware that not all pupils will follow this linear process in producing their writing. Some may even prefer to begin with designing the page layout before writing. Consider how you might use some of these strategies when teaching writing. Imagine that your objective is for pupils to write an effective persuasive speech. Practise modelling the opening to a persuasive speech.

A useful template that is provided in the strategy for exploring the conventions of different text types can be found below. You might want to modify this and/or give some examples of how it can be applied to different text types. However it should be noted that many texts are of mixed genre and do not always fall neatly into one category. Consider the following template for 'recount'.

Analysing Text types. Example taken from Standards and effectiveness unit *Literacy across the Curriculum*

Text type: Key features

Purpose

- What is its purpose?
- Who is it for?
- How will it be used?
- What kind of writing is therefore appropriate?

Text level

- Layout
- Structure/organisation
- Sequence

Sentence level

- Viewpoint (first/third person, etc.)
- Prevailing tense
- Active/passive voice
- Typical sentence structure and length
- Typical cohesion devices

Word level

- Stock words and phrases
- Specialised or typical vocabulary
- Elaborate/plain vocabulary choices

Completed examples are available in the *Literacy across the Curriculum* training packs in schools (DfEE, 2001c).

Standard addressed: 2.1c

Activity 8

THE EXIT MODEL

(suggested time: 60 minutes)

The work by Maureen Lewis and David Wray (2000) in developing support strategies for pupils' research has had a strong influence on the shaping of aspects of the National Literacy Strategy. They produced a model, which became known as EXIT (Extending Interactions with Texts). The original aim of this model was to support primary school pupils in their dealings with non-fiction texts. The theoretical underpinnings of this model were essentially sociolinguistic and cognitive. The sociolinguistic theories came largely from the Australian Genre model where pupils were encouraged to understand text features relating to purpose and audience. The cognitive model was based on an explicit writing process with support where required (see Harrison, 2002c).

Look carefully at the model and consider the various process stages. Fill in ideas for teaching strategies to address the process stages (e.g. brainstorming for activating prior knowledge) and for the purpose (e.g. for activating prior knowledge 'to remind pupils of what they already know'). Two other examples have been completed for you. This should be used to help inform your planning and teaching. Keep your completed sheet in your English portfolio.

The EXIT model

	Process stages	Teaching strategies	Purpose
1	Activating prior knowledge		
2	Establishing purpose		
3	Locating information		
4	Adopting an appropriate strategy		
5	Interacting with the text		
6	Monitoring understanding	● Teacher modelling ● Strategy charts	To review findings and adjust the research in the light of them
7	Making a record		
8	Evaluating information		
9	Assisting memory	● Review ● Revisit ● Restructuring	To place new knowledge in context and map it in with other knowledge
10	Communicating information		

Standard addressed: **2.1c**   Maureen Lewis and David Wray explore this model in some depth in Chapter 4 of *Literacy in the Secondary School* and in their book *Extending Literacy*.

CONTINUOUS THREADS

1 Professional values and practice

Standards addressed **1.1, 1.2**   You will need to make yourself familiar with the support systems within your placement schools. Be aware of the IEP (Individual Education Plans) process for particular pupils and of what short term literacy objectives might be appropriate for pupils working significantly below their age-related expectations. Open up the section on Inclusion in the *Framework for Teaching English: Years 7, 8 and 9* on: **http://www.standards.dfes.gov.uk/keystage3/strands/english/englishframework/s4/**

There is a useful section with case studies of pupils with disabilities (Cleo, James and Jason) that you should consider and a further section on English as an Additional Language. Under the latter it would be advisable to consider the case study of Mohammed. You will need to adopt many of the principles outlined in this section in your planning and teaching.

3.2 Monitoring and assessment

Standard addressed: 3.2.1

You will need to create opportunities within your lessons to assess against your learning objectives, through appropriate questions, pupils' written responses and in the plenary. Good use should be made of pupils explaining what they have learned in lessons to other pupils. Summative assessment will be against level descriptors for Key Stage 3 and examination criteria at GCSE for Key Stage 4. See Chapter 4 on assessment.

2.5 ICT

The objectives in the framework for teaching English are designed so that ICT can form an integral part of English teaching. Some objectives are explicit about ICT (e.g. Year 9 Sentence Level 8 'conventions of ICT') some imply its study and/or use, whilst others will require the teacher to consider when/where it should be incorporated. For example Y7 Reading 13 'non-fiction style' could include the reading and analysis of Web page constructs, just as Y7 Writing 1 'drafting' could include the use of word processor applications. Think about your own use of ICT in the teaching of the *Framework* for English. See below an example of a lesson using ICT.

LESSON PLAN

Learning objective
Reading 2 Undertake independent research using a range of reading strategies, applying their knowledge of how texts and ICT databases are organised and acknowledging sources

Starting points
Note: This lesson will need to be held in a room that has access to computers linked to the Internet.

Explain to the students that we often use a range of reading strategies to locate and access information that we need. For example, we scan by looking over a text quickly, locating information by identifying key words (as when using a bus timetable). We skim-read to obtain an initial overview of the subject or the main ideas in a text (as when looking through a newspaper article to get a sense of how a football team did on Saturday). In this lesson, students will be searching the Internet for information about the 1960s.

Whole class work
Give each student a number from 1 to 5 and explain that each number will be researching a different aspect of Britain in the 1960s: students numbered 1 will explore key political events; those numbered 2 will look at key dramatic events; number 3s will focus on music; number 4s will study memorable sporting events; and number 5s will look at fashion. Explain that, once they have accessed the Internet, they should use a search engine (for example Yahoo) to locate the relevant information. This might be achieved by writing in the search box '1960+music', an entry that is

likely to provide them with a number of websites. They should then access some of the websites, to a maximum of five in the first instance. (Obviously, careful monitoring of the sites selected will be important.)

Guided group/individual work

Using the student sheet, students should work in pairs or as individuals depending on computer availability to make notes on what they find out, and to record the source of the information. You might need to remind them how to make brief notes, perhaps recording key words, recording facts only, using abbreviations, and so on. After the students have collected their information, put them in groups of five, with one person of each number from 1–5, to share their findings. Invite them to select one person from each group who, in the Plenary, will feed back the most significant information and explain the sources of information.

Plenary

Invite one spokesperson from each group to report to the whole class the results of his or her group's research. From your observations, comment upon the reading and note-making strategies employed by the students. Ask them how easy it was to discern whether a site was useful or not. Could they tell from the title?

Further work

Group discussion

The group discussion activity will enable a representative from each group to summarise and clarify before reporting back to the whole class.

Text level: Reading

Research and study skills

Use the research materials as the basis for a classroom display on the 1960s, having added conventional library research.

Follow up the research with a presentation of the topic to the whole class, incorporating information from the Web and using an OHP to aid the presentation. If possible, use *PowerPoint*, or some other presentation software, to achieve this.

Resource Sheet

The Swinging Sixties?

TOPIC AREA (e.g. Music) =

Information	Sources

Source: English Programme File 2 written by Paul Dickinson, Jim McDonagh and Jeff Wilkinson

Scenarios

1 You are planning a Year 7 English lesson for your mixed ability class that contains three pupils working at Level 3. How will you incorporate the Progress Units, as it is your school's policy to have them delivered in English lessons?

2 The *Framework* recommends 10-minute interactive starter activities for your lessons, often with a word or sentence level objective. Imagine that you are about to introduce poetry writing. Can you think of a starter that could be used to address an appropriate objective without it being decontextualised from the main element of the lesson?

A book entitled *101 Red Hot Starters* (Adorian et al., 2002) offers a list of ideas that you can use, adapt, etc.

Further ideas

1 Please ask your placement schools for information about the training that they have undergone for the strategy which began in 2001. There should be videos, training materials and schools' responses to the training.

2 Activity Resources and Suggested Lesson Plans for The National Literacy and Numeracy Strategies can also be downloaded from the DfEE Standards site:
http://www.standards.dfee.gov.uk

3 The National Literacy Strategy is the most significant of a number of recent initiatives. For more information on the following initiatives please access the relevant websites. ENTER **www.literacytrust.org.uk** then click on the site reference and under E you will be able to locate information about the Excellence in Cities project. Under S there is information about summer literacy schools.

For information on Beacon schools and Education Action Zones, ENTER **www.standards.dfes.gov.uk/**

REFERENCES

Adorian, S., Brooke, B. and Gaudreau, L. (2002) *101 Red Hot Starters*. London: Letts

Barber, M. (2001) *Literacy Today* 26

Beard, R. (2000) 'Long overdue? Another look at the National Literacy Strategy, *Journal of Research in Reading* (Blackwell), 23(3).

DfEE (2001a) *Key Stage 3 National Strategy: English Department Training 2001*. London: DfES

DfEE (2001b) *Key Stage 3 National Strategy: Framework for teaching English: years 7,8 and 9*. London: DfEE

DfEE (2001c) *Key Stage 3 National Strategy: Literacy across the curriculum*. London: DfEE

DfES (2002a) *Grammar for Writing: Supporting Pupils Learning EAL* (0581). London: DfES

DfES (2002b) *Access and Engagement in English* (0609). London: DfES

DfES (2002c) *Transition from Year 6 to Year 7 English* (0113). London: DfES

Dickinson, P. McDonagh, J. and Wilkinson, J. (2001) *English Programme File 2*. Dunstable: Folens

Fisher, R. and Singleton, C. (2000) 'Symposium: The National Literacy Strategy', *Journal of Research in Reading*, 23(3).

Goodwyn, A. (2002) *Improving Literacy at KS2 and KS3*. London: Paul Chapman Publishing

Harrison, C. (2002) *Key Stage 3 English, Roots and Research*. London: DfES

Lewis, M. and Wray, D. (2000) *Literacy in the Secondary School*. London: David Fulton

QCA (2001) *Language at Work in Lessons – Literacy across the Curriculum at Key Stage 3*. London: QCA

WEBSITE

www.literacytrust.org.uk/index.html

PLANNING AND PROGRESSION

By the end of this chapter you will have developed an understanding of both the ideological and practical issues involved in the planning of schemes of work and lesson plans, with reference to the National Curriculum and the *Framework for Teaching English: Years 7,8 and 9*. Models of English teaching are given to demonstrate the range of views on what constitutes 'English teaching' today, and feed into a reflective and philosophical approach to planning and teaching. The links between sound class management, learning and effective planning are highlighted. The chapter also looks closely at progression in terms of externally measured exams, tests and targets, and at progression in terms of children's emotional and cognitive development. Continuity across the major transitions of primary to secondary schooling, and from Key Stage 3 to 4, to post-16 is also examined.

To complete this chapter it is recommended that you have access to the following documents:

The National Curriculum for Secondary English, DfES, 1999
Key Stage 3 National Strategy *Framework for Teaching English: Years 7,8 and 9* (DfEE, 2001)
The Cox Report (DES, 1989)
Your school's GCSE English and English Literature syllabus
and AS/A2 English Language and English Literature syllabus

RATIONALE

What is teaching?

Teaching is in part about the chopping up of the processes, knowledge or skills that are to be learned into smaller, more accessible and interesting chunks taking into account the profile of the class. Many of your decisions will be informed (and constrained) by the National Curriculum, the objectives in the *Framework*, and the schemes of work produced by your English Department and all underpinned by sound pedagogy. However, this is a teacher-led viewpoint; pupils are also active participants in the lesson, and the excitement of teaching English lies in the very non-linear development of content and skills, making room for tangential thinking. We can, if we choose, view our classroom as a place where new forms of culture are created and knowledge is produced, rather than simply reproducing society and culture (see Hardcastle, 1985). Teachers therefore need to strive for a creative balance in their planning and teaching between meeting objectives, and allowing space for their pupils to breathe. A planned 10-minute discussion on whether Skellig a character in a Key Stage 3 novel really existed or not may well take longer: the depth of discussion, and thought, and returning to the text in a search for details may go beyond the initial teacher objectives and planning.

Recursive nature of English

It is not possible to chop up the English curriculum into absolute sets of skills to be learned in each year– although the *Framework* does this for the sake of presenting teachers with a manageable framework and sets of objectives. In essence there is 'more of the same' or 'the same with greater understanding of the concept and appropriate use of terminology'. This recursive or spiral concept of the English curriculum means that in any one lesson certain skills or concepts may be revisited; the same activity of writing a story may occur in a Year 5 class, a Year 8 class and a Year 13 class, but the response is at a deeper and more abstract level.

Initial focus and classroom management

All lessons need an appropriate initial focus. Effective classroom management is inextricably linked to thorough prior planning. Pupil 'misbehaviour' – working off-task, talking out of turn, irrelevantly, distracting others, walking around the classroom – is most often a sign of a mismatch by the teacher of learning objectives or tasks to pupils' abilities and interests – 'Miss, I don't understand this, what's the point of doing it?', 'Sir, I can't do this' – or of disorganised grouping – 'Miss, he keeps taking my pen and not doing what we're supposed to do' – which prevents pupils from accessing the lesson content. It is hard to praise pupils when they do not achieve your planned learning outcomes, and harder then to get into a routine or rhythm of a sense of progression over a number of lessons where pupils do learn, and get an increasing sense of pride and satisfaction – and where you can then offer genuine praise back. The very relationships you build up with your pupils depend upon your effective lesson planning and classroom management. Of course, your own teaching style, delivery, mannerisms, even dress, can have a great effect on what and how your pupils learn but, without that initial secure, purposeful start, the safe boundaries needed for learning cannot happen.

Planning for progression

Progression is a fundamental premise of effective learning, and has been identified as such by research into teacher effectiveness (Hay McBer, 2000):

1.2.4

Teaching skills described   *Our lesson observations revealed that in classes run by effective teachers, pupils are clear about what they are doing and why they are doing it. They can see the links with their earlier learning and have some ideas about how it could be developed further. The pupils want to know more. They understand what is good about their work and how it can be improved.*

There is much anecdotal and empirical evidence of a 'learning loss' or a dip in achievement in the Key Stage 2/3 transition, which has led to a formalisation of 'progression' at Key Stage 3 through the *Framework for Teaching English: Years 7, 8 and 9* in an attempt to prevent this. Think of the whole picture of raising standards in English (stemming from the early 1990s), linking pupil progression from pre-school with the Early Learning Goals and Foundation Stage, through to the National Literacy Strategy at Key Stages 1 and 2, to the implementation of the *Framework* at Key Stage 3, and progression to GCSE and post-16.

For pupils to progress further in each lesson, therefore, the teacher needs to:

1   recognise pupils' starting points for the lesson through activation of prior knowledge and recap;
2   develop pupils' knowledge, skills, and concepts to move them on through direct input, modelling, questioning and the setting and correct sequencing of appropriate tasks;
3   monitor and assess pupils' interim progress;
4   recognise, record, report, and celebrate pupil progression.

This also entails building up an understanding of how to move pupils on in each attainment target, of having a whole picture of, for example, 'Reading Development' from beginner readers, decoding of words, and the importance of being read to, to the advanced skills of critical analysis. This is the theory which informs your practice and which 'lets you see where you are heading', as one of my student teachers put it. It also assumes a ready knowledge of your pupils' levels of attainment when they arrive in your class, and a knowledge of how they can best learn, whether they need to be directed to read more non-fiction texts or more challenging poems, or to work with other pupils apart from their friends, or that they work best alone. Pupils do not progress at the same pace but all need to be challenged in some way. Vygotsky's statement that 'the only good learning is that which is in advance of development' (Vygotsky, 1978: 89) crystallises the need for individual knowledge of each pupil.

Teachers therefore need both a 'bottom up' pedagogical approach and a 'top down' centralised governmental initiatives approach to progression. The two are not mutually exclusive.

The raising of national standards and target setting

Progression is also firmly linked to the raising of standards as manifested in the published school league tables. From January 2003 'value-added' data were also included to show how effective each school is at raising standards, looking at the actual progression of the pupils including their 'starting point' rather than simply the summative result of each pupil's achievements. Each school has an individual PANDA (Performance AND Assessment) Report compiled by the LEA, containing all the available data on the school. It encourages schools to compare themselves with others of the same kind (i.e. Specialist Status, or with the same number of pupils on free school meals), and to help in the development of the school plans to raise standards. It also supports the target-setting process for school improvement. Individual pupils and groups of pupils will have their potential achievement predicted at each stage in terms of some measurable gain in what they know, understand and can do. For example, a secondary school may be set a target by the Local Education Authority for 80% of their Key Stage 3 pupils to achieve Level 5 or above in the end of year Key Stage 3 tests.

This can mean that teachers may feel pressure to overtly push their pupils to obtain Level 5 or above or to attain the magic A*–C grade at GCSE. This gives a slightly different angle on progression perhaps, since it is the raw grades that pupils attain that demonstrate progression to the outside world. This can result in a narrowing of the curriculum to prepare pupils for the test; some schools drop the National Curriculum in January of Year 9 to do so. Progression that cannot be so easily measured – deeper enjoyment of reading, commitment and vitality in writing, sitting still in a chair, or a contribution to a school assembly – has to be recognised and celebrated in other ways. At the time of writing, teacher assessment is being given the same status as the KS1 NC tests for a more rounded assessment of each pupil: this may have implications for secondary pupils in the future.

LINKS WITH THE NATIONAL CURRICULUM AND THE KEY STAGE 3 STRATEGY:

Educational initiatives which impact on planning and progression

The National Curriculum

On page 6 of the NC it states:

'The programmes of study set out what pupils should be taught in English at Key Stages 1, 2, 3 and 4 and provide the basis for planning schemes of work.' The National Curriculum is the basic framework from which you choose the particular overall objectives as appropriate for long term planning over a year or a term. At GCSE the particular GCSE syllabus specification will have objectives covering the KS4 requirements of the National Curriculum. At Key Stage 3 the main document for medium (half-termly) and short term (weekly and daily) planning is the

Framework for Teaching English: Years 7, 8 and 9, which gives finer objectives than the National Curriculum. Refer to chapter 2 in this section on the National Literacy Strategy for more detail.

Cross-curricular planning

There are other cross-curricular aspects to include in your planning, for example the promotion of pupils' spiritual, moral, social and cultural development through English, the promotion of key skills, and citizenship and thinking skills. English is probably a fairly easy subject through which to embrace these other objectives. Inclusion (details on pp. 42-49 of the National Curriculum) and ICT in English are integrated into each of these chapters in a way that we hope will support your own constant consideration of them in your daily planning and teaching. Don't forget numeracy: plot graphs, bar charts of the class's favourite TV programmes, and diagrams to show relationships between characters are all part of numeracy. You will need to be aware of such cross-curricular initiatives and strategies.

The Key Stage 3 Strategy in secondary schools

The dip in attainment in the KS2/3 transition is due to a number of factors:

1   Change to a large school, with different teachers for different – and new – subjects, all requiring different ways of learning ('In Geography we have to underline the heading, in English we don't') for pupils, moving around the school, fears of getting lost
2   Being the youngest after having been the eldest in the school
3   Moving away from friends, old support networks
4   New ways of working even in familiar subjects like Maths and English
5   An increase in peer pressure to interact socially in and out of school
6   The fact that adolescent development begins in earnest at secondary school
7   Less frequent contact with parents.

There are other factors involved too; on your primary school experience you may well find out from the pupils themselves how they feel about moving. Conversely, underachieving pupils may do better at secondary school because of greater registration of pupils with additional educational needs (AEN) (see Westbrook et al., 1998). All schools received training for teaching the *Framework* at KS3 from Easter 2001 ready for full implementation in September 2001. Schools can opt for their pupils to take National Curriculum tests at Years 7 and 8. Those pupils who attained Level 3 in Year 6 resit their tests at KS2 in the May of their Year 7. Literacy Progress Units are provided for these pupils involving an extra hour of literacy sessions every week in addition to normal English. Continuity of pedagogy is therefore theoretically ensured by teachers of English in secondary school using a similar framework to the primary 'Literacy Hour'. Inevitably there is greater flexibility because of the idiosyncrasies of timetabling, with few English lessons being of one hour's length exactly.

The NLS came in the wake of great concern about a perceived drop in levels of attainment in English – now to be known as 'literacy' – with the emphasis on an 'adult needs' model of functional literacy. There was also great concern that pupils coming into secondary school were unable to cope with the demands of the secondary curriculum. Concurrently, there was a growth in understanding of the different definitions of what it means to be literate, with the new technologies of computers and the mass media demanding a new visual literacy, one that many pupils are highly competent in from early childhood. The notion of 'critical' literacy also came into the debate; pupils must learn how different texts were authored, for what purpose, for which audience. Understanding the multiplicity of texts bombarding us every day means being in control of how they are read, knowing how and why to read them – and being able to reproduce them in some form, too.

Along with the 1975 Bullock Report, *A Language for Life* came the 1990s version of language across the curriculum – 'literacy across the curriculum' – with the sharp difference that with each school being given targets specifically on literacy, it became a whole school initiative, rather than one solely directed by the English Department.

Activity 1

LANGUAGE AND LEARNING
(suggested time: 30 minutes)

This activity introduces you to the most important writers and theorists on language acquisition and development. These are Lev Vygotsky, Jerome Bruner and James Britton. You will also come across Harold Rosen, Martin Halliday, Gordon Wells and Douglas Barnes in your reading.

Chapter 26 of Brindley's *Teaching English*, 'Vygotsky's contribution to pedagogical theory' by James Britton, gives a very clear explanation of Vygotksy's theories on the importance of speech to our social development and cognitive development. Language, according to Vygotsky, is made up of a system of signs (think of Saussure and semiotics here); the young child's mediation with the world is transformed by their mediation with signs – language – and most dynamically through play. The child internalises the resources of the culture through using, and being immersed in, language.

> *Human learning presupposes a specific social nature and a process by which*
> *children grow into the intellectual life of those around them. (Vygotsky, 1978: 88)*

Children need to talk and to use language constructively in a variety of different social settings, interacting co-operatively with a variety of people, in order to 'grow into the intellectual life of those around them'.

> *Learning in most settings is a communal activity, a sharing of the culture. It is*
> *not just that the child must make his knowledge his own, but that he must make*
> *it his own in a community of those who share his sense of belonging to a culture.*
> *It is this that leads me to emphasise not only discovery and invention but the*
> *importance of negotiating and sharing – in a word, of joint culture creating as*
> *an object of schooling and as an appropriate step en route to becoming a*
> *member of the adult society in which one lives out one's life. (Bruner, 1986: 127,*
> *quoted in Brindley, 1994: 262)*

TASK

This begs large philosophical questions which are important to get to grips with at an early stage. Consider the following:

1   What are the implications for schools and the way in which classrooms are organised according to Vygotsky's theories?
2   Importantly, Britton highlights the role of the teacher in the context of the 'zone of proximal development' as being

> the distance between the actual development level as determined by independent problem solving and the level of potential development as determined through problem solving under adult guidance or in collaboration with more capable peers. (Vygotsky, 1978: 86)

What do you see as the role of the teacher in school – 'to make as rich an interactive learning community as we can, or continue to treat it as a captive audience for whatever instruction we choose to offer'? (Britton, writing in Brindley 1994: 263)

3   How do your answers above relate to real classrooms that you have observed?

Standard addressed: 2.4 Write a paragraph for each question, and place them in your English portfolio.

Activity 2   EXPLORING OUR LANGUAGE HISTORIES
(suggested time: 30 minutes)

The richness of language and the complexities of language are inherent in:

1   learning a language (learning your mother tongue through early parent/carer– child concrete interactions at home/childcare);
2   learning through a language (learning mathematics through English, or through English as your second language);
3   learning about a language ('metalinguistic awareness' through wordplay, rhymes, rhythms, analysing parts of speech, punning, enjoying crosswords, Scrabble).

These three aspects are the very stuff of being an English teacher.

TASK

Write a reflective piece of around 700 words on your own language history, recounting some important starting points for you in learning to speak, read and write. Previous student teachers who have been asked to write such a piece have found it most useful in really putting themselves into the shoes of learners; odd family ways of saying words, and the crucial role of parents, grandparents and teachers are always colourfully described.

Standard addressed: 2.4 NB: A similar task is also set for Chapter 7, 'Speaking and Listening' (see p. 164).

Activity 3

MODELS OF ENGLISH TEACHING AS A BACKDROP TO PLANNING
(suggested time: 20 minutes)

Look back to the five models of English teacher outlined on p. 30 from the 1989 Cox Report (DES, 1989). Which model best describes your own view of English teaching – and your own practice?

Standards addressed:
1.7, 3.3.2c

Refer to the kind of English teacher you assess yourself as in your future reflections, coursework, and lesson plans; do you recognise that you lean towards one or another model depending on the precise focus of the lesson?

Activity 4

PROGRESSION FROM KEY STAGE 2 TO KEY STAGE 3: PUPIL INFORMATION
(suggested time: 2 hours)

The introduction of the National Curriculum in 1988 aimed to set in place continuity and progression for all pupils across all key stages. Pupils moving to a new or different school should, theoretically, be able to pick up from where they left off, without a dip in attainment due to interruption or to having to learn new things. Good transition arrangements are necessary to:

- prevent duplication in learning; promote development in learning;
- maintain motivation;
- enable the National Curriculum to be covered effectively;
- help provide a clearer sense of shared goals.

The requirement for one key stage to build upon another has implications for our own familiarity with what pupils know at Key Stage 2.

TASK

1 Find out what information your placement school is sent from their feeder primary schools: Key Stage 2 National Curriculum test results, folders of work, details of pupils with AEN.
2 What does the secondary school do with the information? Who handles it, distributes it? How do classroom teachers/form tutors process and use the information?
3 How far do your investigations show that the four objectives given above can be met?

Standard addressed:
3.1.1

Write your answers to 1 and 2 as a chart if this helps, or in approximately 500 words of prose.

Activity 5   CONTINUITY FROM KEY STAGE TO KEY STAGE 3:
OBSERVING A LITERACY CLASS
IN A PRIMARY SCHOOL

(suggested time: at least a day in a primary school)

TASK:

1   Ask if you can see the *Framework for Teaching Key Stage 1 and 2* folder giving objectives for each year and each term. Write down the general topics that your class are learning about this term. How does the class teacher translate this into actual texts, activities and written work in the classroom? You will need to discuss this with the class teacher.

2   Observe a literacy hour in a primary school – and if possible one from Key Stage 1 to compare with Key Stage 2. Fill out the grid below for that lesson.

Year	Pupil activity and learning objective	Teacher activity
15 minutes' whole class text level work		
15 minutes' whole class sentence/word level work		
20 minutes' independent group work		
10 minutes' plenary		

Standard addressed:
3.1.1

What did you observe in terms of pupils' progression in literacy and the complexity of the concepts learned or tasks set from the two classes?

ACTIVITY 6   PROGRESSION AS DESCRIBED
BY THE ATTAINMENT TARGETS

(suggested time: 40 minutes)

The National Curriculum stresses that the four language skills should be integrated within each lesson, although one aspect will predominate. The attainment targets give some idea of the desired progression in each language skill at the end of key stages. These attainment targets have not been altered despite the revised National Curriculum for 2000.

The National Curriculum states that 'The level descriptions in English indicate progression in the attainment targets for speaking and listening, reading and writing.' The next sentence continues: 'The level descriptions provide the basis for making judgements about pupils' performance at the end of key stages 1, 2 and 3' (DfES, 1999: 7).

Up until 2003 teachers were expected to move pupils on according to the 'best fit' pattern, at a rate of a level every two years. Close reading was required to interpret the 'gap' between each level, the difference between 'Pupils talk and listen confidently in a wide range of contexts, including some that are of a formal nature' (Level 5 Speaking and Listening) to 'Pupils adapt their talk to the demands of different contexts with increasing confidence' (Level 6 Speaking and Listening). A more diagnostic form of measurement is being introduced into schools through the Key Stage 3 strategy which seeks to pinpoint pupils' progress more accurately, with sub-levels to indicate progression within a level. The new tests introduced in May 2003 seek to break down pupils' linguistic skills into segments so that schools can use the results in a more formative way than previously.

TASK

Read through the level descriptions for one of the attainment targets.

How far would you agree with this statement from *Learning to Teach English in the Secondary School:* 'Some of the Level Descriptions are so general that they are almost meaningless and the progression between them only nominal' (Davison and Dowson, 1998: 49)?

- What is your view of the progression as described here?

'Sub-levelling' is increasingly being favoured, especially by Ofsted, in order to motivate children who move slowly from one level to another. For example, in Reading, Level 4c is 'In responding to a range of texts pupils usually show understanding of some significant ideas, themes, events and characters. They sometimes refer to the text when exploring their views. They sometimes locate and use ideas and information.'

Level 4b is 'In responding to a range of texts pupils show understanding of significant ideas, themes, events and characters; beginning to use inference and deduction. They usually refer to the text when explaining their views. They usually locate and use ideas and information.'

Standard addressed: 3.2.3

- How useful do you find these descriptions of pupil development – for yourself, and for your pupils?

Activity 7

PLANNING: THE WHOLE PICTURE

(suggested time: 40 minutes)

Now that you have a preliminary grasp of the notion of progression, we need to look at how the larger picture of development can be brought into effect in the planning of key stages, schemes of work, and even individual lessons. You need to bear several concepts in mind at the same time:

- the general philosophy underpinning progression
- the National Curriculum descriptions of progression and level descriptions
- development over key stages and between them
- whole class development
- the specific developmental needs of your individual pupils

What does the big picture look like?

Long term planning for progression and continuity therefore assumes knowledge of prior learning, a wide vision of where pupils are heading and a sharper focus on particular individual aims and objectives for lessons and pupils. Issues arising out of pupil assessments inform and feed back into the planning of objectives for future lessons.

TASK

Arrange a meeting with your mentor to discuss the departmental structures within which your lesson planning will take place.

In particular, you need to know:

- How are the National Curriculum and the *Framework for Teaching English* used in planning in the department?
- What form do the school's schemes of work take for long term, medium term and short term planning?
- How will you be expected to make use of them when planning your lessons? How much freedom will you have to alter them according to your interests and the class?
- How does your particular department plan for continuity and progression?
- How do issues from individual pupil assessment inform short term and long term planning?

Standards addressed: **3.1.2, 3.3.2d** Discuss these issues with your mentor and make bullet points on them for your English portfolio.

Activity 8

CLASSROOM OBSERVATIONS OF ENGLISH TEACHING

(suggested time: 9 hours)

Before planning any English lessons yourself, you need to observe as many as possible, delivered by different teachers, to different classes, at different key stages, and at different times of the week.

TASK

To observe at least six different English lessons, focusing on the following three aspects of the lesson:

Responsibility for Content Planning and Delivery

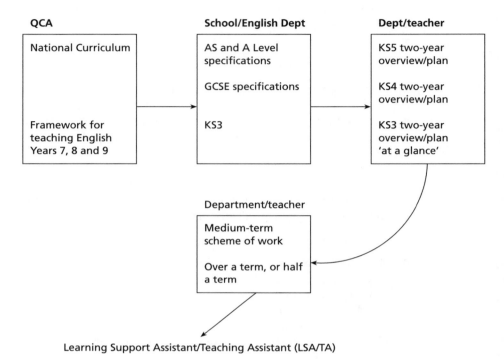

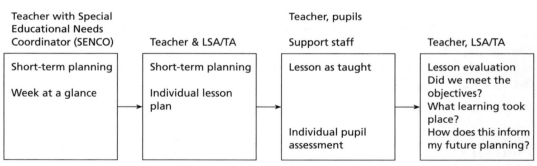

A   Teaching styles, lessons sequence and structure
B   The language used by teachers and pupils in English lessons
C   The management skills of English teachers

Methodology for classroom observation

You will need to conduct structured observations of at least **six** English lessons.

Before the lesson: you should prepare by choosing an observation focus and drawing up an appropriate observation sheet for making notes. Whenever possible, you should discuss with the teacher what kind of observation opportunities a particular lesson is most likely to yield.

During the lesson: make notes on your observation focus during the lesson. Whenever possible, discuss your observations with the teacher after the lesson, remembering that your role here is to seek explanation and clarification, rather than to offer judgements!

After the lesson: consider, in a brief commentary on the lesson, the matters suggested in the 'Prompt Questions' below. In some cases, the prompt questions will guide you towards discussions you may be able to have with the teacher.

TASK

A   To Observe a variety of English lessons, and consider teaching styles, lesson sequence and structure

Complete at least two lesson observations using these headings:

Time line   **Activity**   **Observations**

Prompt Questions:

1   What was the relationship between the time line and the teacher's lesson plan?
2   Comment on the way in which the processes of English – speaking and listening, reading and writing – were used in the sequence and structure of the lesson.
3   Which of the five Cox Report (DES, 1989) models of English teaching did this lesson demonstrate?

TASK

B   To observe the language used by teachers and pupils in English lessons

Complete at least two lesson observations using these headings:

Category of oral language   **Observations**

Prompt Questions:

- How was oral work linked to other activities in this lesson?
- What learning was taking place while talk was going on?
- What did the teacher do to make effective oral work possible?
- How much control of the talk that took place did the pupils have?

The five categories of oral language given here are taken from Douglas Barnes, in *Language, the Learner and the School* (Barnes et al., 1969). You are asked to use them, as he did, to consider the learning implications of various kinds of oral activity.

Categories of Classroom Oral Language Activity Guidance Sheet

1   The teacher asks questions

(a)   Closed questions checking recall, knowledge (What is this?)
(b)   Closed questions checking understanding of a process (Why/How do we . . .?)
(c)   Open questions asking for reasoning, use of observation (Why do you think . . .?)

NB: look out for 'pseudo-questions' which only <u>appear</u> to be open, because teacher and pupil know the teacher is fishing for a particular kind of answer.

(d)   Open questions asking for student use of own experience (Can you tell me about a time when you . . .?)
(e)   Social questions (for control/appeal) (Please will you . . .?)
(f)   Other

2   Specialist language

(a)   The teacher uses language specific to the subject to explain something.
(b)   The teacher mediates subject specific language with her/his idea of student language.
(c)   The student talks about the subject using subject specific language.
(d)   The student talks about the subject using his/her own language.

3   Student speech

(a)   'On task' speech is initiated by the student.
(b)   'On task' speech is sought by the teacher and provided by the student.
(c)   Student answers closed questions.
(d)   Student answers open questions.
(e)   Student asks questions about the subject/task.
(f)   Student thinks aloud.
(g)   Student describes own experience.

4   Social speech

(a)   Teacher uses language to exercise control.
(b)   Teacher uses language to offer praise, encouragement.
(c)   Teacher/student use language to negotiate course of work.
(d)   Teacher/student use language socially 'off task'.
(e)   Student uses language to interrupt/divert attention from teacher's purposes.

5   Organisation of speech

(a)   Teacher speaks to whole class.
(b)   Member of whole class speaks to teacher.

(c)   Member of whole class speaks to another student/other students.
(d)   Students speak in small groups/pairs.
(e)   Teacher speaks to member(s) of small group.
(f)   Teacher speaks to individual pupil in isolation.

TASK

C   To observe the management skills of English teachers

Complete at least two lesson observations using these headings:

Classroom Management Feature   **Observations**

Prompt Questions:

- Ask the teacher to comment on her/his approach to the aspects of classroom management you choose to focus on.
- Comment on any aspects of the teacher's classroom management which made very positive contributions to learning in the lesson.

Select a few categories to observe.

Aspects of classroom management   Guidance question sheets

How does the teacher communicate/negotiate the purpose of the lesson?

Aspects of classroom management   Guidance question sheets

- How are connections made to past/future lessons?
- How are learning objectives defined and explained, and how is their purpose made clear?

How does the teacher engage the pupils in working?

- How does the teacher create a positive working atmosphere?
- How is the work made interesting, challenging and fun?
- How is the work made relevant to the pupils?
- How is work made appropriate to each pupil in the classroom?
- How does the teacher demonstrate a concern for each pupil and his/her work?
- How are tasks organised so that they consist of an appropriate mixture of structure and freedom?
- How are pupils involved in supporting each others' work during the lesson?
- What use is made of pupils' knowledge and experience in the lesson?

How does the teacher use a blackboard/whiteboard/interactive whiteboard/OHT?

- What is the quality and nature of information prepared before the lesson?
- What techniques are important when using board(s) etc. during the lesson?
- What is the purpose of material recorded on the board(s) during the lesson?

How is the classroom organised for the lesson, and why?

- Where are the furniture, pupils and equipment positioned?
- What are the reasons for the positioning of furniture, pupils and equipment?
- What resources are available, and how are they distributed?

What is the position of the teacher in the room, and why –

- As the pupils arrive and settle?
- During parts of the lesson in which the teacher engages the whole class?
- When pupils are working, alone or in groups?
- When speaking to individual pupils or groups of pupils?
- When ending the lesson, and dismissing the class?
- And when does the teacher move around the classroom, and why?

How does the teacher use his/her voice:

- to gain attention?
- to present information and instructions in an interesting way?
- when reading to the class?
- when approaching pupils whose behaviour challenges the lesson's progress?
- to offer encouragement and praise?
- when asking questions?
- to suggest confidence and a relaxed state of mind?
- to convey enthusiasm for the work?
- and what use is made of variety of pace, volume, pitch, and silence?

How does the teacher organise an activity?

- In what sequence are working groups organised/resources distributed/instructions given/pupils asked to get out equipment, and why?
- What does the teacher do before the lesson to ensure that resources and equipment are available, appropriate and working?
- What techniques does the teacher employ to ensure that effective learning takes place when TV/videos/computers/tape recorders, etc. are used?
- How are resources designed to be interesting, appropriate and accessible?
- How are instructions made clear and comprehensible (e.g. written on board and reinforced by verbal explanations)?

How does the teacher manage the start and end of the lesson?

- How is the arrival and setting of the class managed?
- What are the expectations concerning bags, coats and lesson equipment?
- How does the teacher gain attention at the start of the lesson?
- How is the content and purpose of the lesson defined and explained, and to what extent is its sequence of activities explained at the start?
- What are pupils expected to do before leaving the classroom?
- How does the teacher manage the departure of the pupils?

How does the teacher manage pupil behaviour in the classroom?

- Where are pupils positioned, and how is their behaviour monitored?
- How are classroom behaviour expectations defined and reinforced?
- What are the signs of potential misbehaviour, and what action does the teacher take on noticing them?
- How does the teacher handle interruptions (e.g. late arrivals, shouting out)?

How does the teacher manage the work of pupils in the classroom?

- How does the teacher make working expectations demanding, appropriate and clear?
- How does the teacher monitor work rate?
- How does the teacher intervene to increase work rate?
- How does the teacher offer encouragement and praise?
- How does the teacher manage noise levels when students are working?
- When does the teacher insist on silence, and for what purposes?

How does the teacher give the lesson pace, momentum and variety?

- What makes a sequence of activities appropriate and effective?
- How are the transitions between activities in the lesson managed?
- How are time deadlines used when pupils are working?

What is the teacher's manner in the classroom?

- How does the teacher dress, present himself/herself to the class?
- How does the teacher convey enthusiasm and energy?
- How and when does the teacher use humour?

NOTE: Record your observations of lessons in a professional manner. Remain objective about what you write down, and remember that teachers may behave in ways you find puzzling because they have a range of kinds of knowledge, particularly about the pupils in the class, which is unavailable to you. It is very
Standard acceptable for you to ask questions about what you have seen, but not for you to *addressed:* **1.7** make judgements based on limited information.

Activity 9

BUILDING UP TO A LESSON – AIMS AND OBJECTIVES

(suggested time: 30 minutes)

As a student teacher you will need to show evidence in your lesson plans of an overarching aim – which can indicate the 'unknown' aspect of learning that may take place in your lesson, or the richer aim you wish to have. You do however need to clearly indicate the focus of your lesson through identifying specific objectives. These should be directly related to the National Curriculum (even quoting the relevant page number and section), the objectives in the *Framework*, or the appropriate examination syllabus. Two, maybe three, objectives are sufficient. Objectives, of course, are easily measurable, quantifiable; richer aims are not. Bear this in mind for both formal lesson observations by your mentor and tutor (and even external examiner), for lesson appraisals, and Ofsted in the future. Fulfilling your aims may well satisfy you, but if it means that observers see an unfocused, vague lesson with the objectives not reached, then you have either set the wrong objectives, or not provided a strong enough focus.

For example:

> *Pupils will use talk to analyse (NC p. 33 Speaking and Listening Group*
> *discussion and interaction, 10a) different genres and their characteristics (NC*
> *p. 35 Reading Printed and ICT-based information texts 4d) by comparing the*
> *newspaper report and poem on the same subject. All pupils should 'identify key*
> *features' and 'select information to support their views' (Level 5, AT2) and the*
> *more able should demonstrate Level 6 and 7 reading skills.*

TASK

Look back to one of the lessons you have observed (or even taught/
collaboratively taught)

- Write down the objectives of that lesson, and the aims at the beginning.
- How were the objectives realised? Were they covered?
- How well did the aims match the eventual outcome?

Standard
addressed:
3.1.1

- How would you rewrite both aims and objectives at the end, if you were able to magically rewind the time to before the lesson?
- What does this illustrate to you about both aims and objectives?

Activity 10

STRUCTURING THE LESSON

(suggested time: 60 minutes)

Having decided on your overall aims and objectives you now need to structure your lesson so that the tasks, or input and output, work towards the aims and objectives. Deciding upon the activities themselves, and the sequence they can go in, can be highly creative and enjoyable – and should be underpinned by a coherent rationale throughout by means of which you can explain *why* you have put those four girls into one group, or why you decided to start with a short written task.

TASK

Look at the lesson plan below for a Year 10 group:

1 Can you give a rationale as to why the tasks are sequenced as they are? For example, why should the teacher read the poem aloud twice? Why have the note taking before the improvisation? Why begin with this poem and not the Keats poem?

2 Can you critique this lesson plan? Would you structure this lesson differently? For example, do you think there are too many tasks to cover in one lesson? Think of a Year 10 class you have taught or observed – what parts would they enjoy, cope with?

LESSON PLAN

Group: Year 10   Date: 24 September   45 minutes

'First ice' by Andrey Voznesensky and 'La belle dame sans merci' by John Keats

Aims

To develop appreciation, enjoyment and understanding of poetry, including pre-20th century examples.

To develop pupils' ability to write about poetry, paying careful attention to detail.

Objectives

Pupil learning objectives (or outcomes)

Speaking and Listening

To adopt roles and communicate with audiences using a range of techniques (preparation for the oral coursework mark for 'Drama focussed activities'). NC En1 Speaking and Listening: Drama 4a.

Reading

Read with insight and engagement, making appropriate references to texts and developing and sustaining interpretations of them. NC En2 Reading: Understanding texts 1b.

Lesson content

Pupils hear two poems read, and take part in note making, pair work, improvisation and class discussion.

Brief historical input on Keats poem.

Method of delivery

- Issue 'First Ice' poem sheets and guidance question sheets.
- Set lesson in context of poetry scheme of work. Explain first task: teacher to read poem, followed by 5 minutes' noting of first responses.   3 mins
- Teacher reads poem twice: individual reading and note making.   8 mins
- Introduce improvisation task: get partners chosen first; then give a third of class each task.   2 mins
- Improvisation preparation time.   10 mins
- Hear/see some improvisations, link to poem; discuss possible titles.   10 mins
- Introduce Keats poem and read, identify two voices.   5 mins
- Pupils to read poem aloud, followed by class discussion of first impressions of 'knight' and 'questioner'.   5 mins
- Set homework – to complete guidance question sheet   3 mins

Resources

'First Ice' and 'La belle dame sans merci' worksheets.

Guidance question worksheet.

Pupil handouts and poems

Writing grid for pupil support

| What are your first thoughts about this poem? | 'First ice' | 'La belle dame sans merci' |

What is the story of the poem?

What is happening now (include your ideas about what absent characters are doing)

What has happened in the last 24 hours?

(include what you think has happened that the poem hints at)

What will happen in the next 24 hours?

(include what you think will happen that the poem hints at)

Where does the story of the poem take place?
How is this place important in the story?

Pupil copy of Andrey Voznesensky's poem' First Ice' with title removed.

1   Write down your first reactions to this poem. If you like, use the question sheet to get you thinking, but write your first thoughts here.

2   With your partner, prepare an improvisation of **one** of the following conversations, as directed by your teacher:

(a)   a conversation between the girl and her boyfriend 24 hours *before* the phone call in the poem.

(b)   the conversation over the phone which we are told about in the poem.

(c)   a conversation between the girl and a friend of hers 24 hours *after* the phone call in the poem.

Pupil copy of poem, 'La belle dame sans merci'

Standards addressed: *1.7, 3.3.3*

Assessment

Speaking and Listening

Pupils will make an entry in their oral record sheets, referring to the pair work undertaken during the lesson.

Pupils perform improvisations for the class. Teachers record assessment of these on their class oral record sheets.

Reading and Writing

Pupils are accumulating a collection of notes on a selection of poems. These notes will be used as the basis for one of a number of assignments on poetry which will be assessed using GCSE assessment criteria.

Differentiation

Worksheets provide focusing questions, structure and memory aids for all pupils.

The less able pupils will have support for essay writing and planning.

Some more able pupils *may* tackle the harder questions.

More able pupils will be given opportunity to make notes independently on further poems and begin to compare the two poems.

Student teacher's targets

3.1.2 They use . . . teaching and learning objectives to plan lessons, and sequences of lessons, showing how they will assess pupils' learning . . .

Activity 11　　　TOWARDS A REFLECTIVE AND PHILOSOPHICAL
APPROACH TO PLANNING

(suggested time: 40 minutes)

The last chapter in *Learning to Teach English in the Secondary School* (Davison and Dowson, 1998), entitled 'Teaching English: critical practice', reiterates the need for student teachers to reflect actively upon their learning in the classroom and in so doing to develop a philosophy to underpin that reflection. Together with an understanding of the historical contexts of English teaching, your own educational background, the particular stance of the English departments you observe and work with, and the Cox models of English, this should provide you with a sound basis for developing such a philosophical standpoint and therefore rationale for what you do every day in the English classroom.

TASK

The first philosophical stance quoted in Davison and Dowson (1998) is given below as a starting point. Some examples of two student teachers' discussions posted on the 'Discussion Board' of a virtual learning environment are given below to support you.

1. *An active involvement with literature enables pupils to share the experiences of others. They will encounter and come to understand a wide range of feelings and relationships by entering vicariously the worlds of others, and in consequence, they are likely to understand more of themselves. (DES and Welsh Office, 1989)*

Sally Jellett:

'Having discovered in a previous activity that I am an "adult needs" model teacher, it may come as no surprise that the first philosophical theory I responded to was the statement from the DES in 1984. As English teachers, the skills and knowledge we teach and share are not just relevant in the classroom. The notion of English teaching as "an education of the intellect and sensibility" is a wonderful description. I like to think as a teacher I will equip pupils with life skills and knowledge, but also that they will become confident in expressing their opinions and sharing their own views and ideas with others.

'[To me] the idea of a curriculum which "values the whole person" is vital. Everything a pupil can offer in English lessons should be taken on board and valued – their skills, creativity, reflection, knowledge, judgement and experience. In order to gain access to any of this though, and to ultimately develop it further, the situations and contexts we provide must be relevant, meaningful and accessible.'

Larisa Curran:

'I found that I am predominantly a "cultural analysis" view teacher and feel strongly that young adults should leave school with an ability to recognise the ways in which their thoughts, ideas and opinions can be and, in fact, are manipulated. They should be in a position to challenge both their own and others' opinions continuously. They should not leave school carrying the opinions of their teachers, or their parents, or their mates, but have been empowered to form their own informed opinions. Their personal attitudes and responses are vital to this philosophy. In addition, they should be able to communicate their ideas and opinions effectively by being able to create meaning in a variety of different media, which far from excluding creativity, embraces it. It is not of importance to me what drives the creative process – it could be money, idealism, a need for understanding, frustration, acceptance – but rather that it takes place on some level. The creation of a text of whatever kind, a novel, a film, a leaflet is creative but all creativity requires technical knowledge and skill for success.

Standard addressed: 1.7

'I don't disagree with the first statement quoted above by the DES and Welsh Office, 1989 but feel that the restriction to "an active involvement with literature" is a bit dated. An active involvement with media of many kinds, including film and tv encourages pupils' understanding of themselves and others. The problem is that the production of both literature and audiovisual media has historically been the domain of the privileged.'

Activity 12

LESSON EVALUATIONS: THE CYCLE OF PLANNING, ACTION AND REFLECTION

(suggested time: 15 minutes)

It is important to review what happens in each lesson, to evaluate what went well, and what didn't, and to try to work out why. Dialogue with mentors and other observers will be crucial here in helping you to focus your reflection, and giving you insights that you may have missed while you were so involved in the teaching. For example, you may have missed one pupil's attempts to gain your attention early on in the lesson, and this built up into the pupil working off-task and 'misbehaving'. Thinking constructively about what happens in a lesson must then go forward into the cycle of planning–action–review, so it has a direct impact on the planning, delivery and monitoring of the next lesson. Your ongoing, formative assessment of pupils in the classroom as they work and interact, and their more summative results – output – of the last lesson (if there was one) in the form of a written piece, or oral output, will also feed directly into the next lesson.

Lesson evaluations should be written after each lesson, to build up the evidence base of your development in the classroom when it is fresh in your mind. Some evaluations may be in the form of precise bullet points; with others you may wish to write longer prose versions where you really get to grips with what worked, or what didn't:

> *The lesson went far better than the one the previous week where I rushed through the material far too quickly and the pupils did not have the chance to explore the different figures of speech that we looked at. Today I took my time and went*

far more slowly. Also, in the last lesson I had sat at my desk for much of the time and this was not an effective way of establishing control over the group. Therefore, this time, I stood 'centre stage' at the front of the room at the very beginning of the lesson and thereafter. This worked much better. The group responded well to my formal greeting to the whole class and an effective 'mental set' (from Kyriacou) was established quickly. As the groups discussed the questions I talked individually to one of the groups and joined in with their discussion. My mentor said this was a good idea and that I should have done this with more of the groups.

One thing that could have been improved was when I was given an answer I was not expecting, and I just responded with 'mmmm' when I should have said 'Yes, good, 1 hadn't thought of that.' This would have been a far more encouraging and positive response.

I did feel much more relaxed today, and 1 was able to make some positive and enthusiastic comments after the group readings. I will work on the endings of my lessons, and on allowing real time for absorption of the poems/stories – whatever I am introducing.

The template below offers a more structured format and is available at
www.paulchapmanpublishing.co.uk/resources/completeguide.htm

LESSON EVALUATION
NB Must be completed within 12 hours of lesson

Comment on the effectiveness of the class management.
How successful were the learning activities in achieving learning objectives?
How effective were the teaching strategies used in the lesson?
What issues need to be considered for future lessons?

Standard addressed: 1.7

TASK

Teach and evaluate a lesson using either format. Place this in your English portfolio.

Activity 13

SCHEMES OF WORK
(suggested time: 30 minutes)

A scheme of work is your overview of what you plan to do over a half-term, or number of weeks with one class. It is your map, if you like, even if you veer off on minor roads in individual lessons. These are enjoyable to create, and give you a sense of the routes of progression for the learners from one lesson to the next.

Fleming and Stevens in *English Teaching in the Secondary School* provide an interesting analysis of the advantages and disadvantages of different approaches to planning, and give a useful starting point in the form of a spider diagram for planning schemes of work. Importantly, their structure suggests that starting from where the pupils themselves are 'will move pupils from the subjective and personal to the objective, giving form and expression to personal thoughts, feelings and ideas through reading other examples' (1998: 22). Pupils will then be able to track their own progress from a recognisable starting point and will be involved in reflecting upon their own progression.

Since the implementation of both the NC and the NLS English departments have devised their own schemes of work to ensure coverage of the objectives; student teachers will at least initially be teaching from an existing scheme, more often than not, and therefore need to be able to understand how it works, and to critique it, as well as tweak it for their particular class.

TASK

Use the following questions to evaluate the scheme of work on pp. 81–83, replying in bullet points, and referring to your own department schemes of work where possible.

- Does the scheme have a title which gives an indication of its scope and focus?
- Are some broad educational aims identified?
- Do the aims relate to programmes of study in the National Curriculum, *Framework* or examination syllabus requirements and are they compatible with the department ethos?
- Is it clear which group the scheme is intended for?
- Is it clear how the sequence relates to previous work and learning of the pupils for whom it is intended?
- Are the learning objectives clear? Do they promote a balanced, relevant and coherent approach to the topic?
- Does the scheme make explicit the opportunities for progression in learning and provide a structure and sequence of activities which will support this progression?
- Are the learning objectives compatible with the aims?
- Is there a suitable variety of learning tasks and teaching strategies in the sequence?
- Are the learning tasks compatible with the aims and objectives?
- Is there any evidence of differentiation to cater for pupils' differing needs?
- Do the lessons proposed follow a logical sequence? Is there progression and continuity in the learning tasks?
- Are the resources to be used appropriate and varied? Have any opportunities for the use of ICT been recognised and built into the scheme?
- Does the scheme appropriately address equal opportunities issues through its proposed strategies and content?
- Have the assessment objectives been identified and are the criteria clear?
- Is there sufficient variety in the range of assessment tasks?
- Do the assessment objectives relate to National Curriculum attainment targets?

- How will the assessment evidence be retained and recorded?
- Have the classroom implications of the activities been considered?
- What criteria will be used to judge whether the sequence is successful?
- What evaluation evidence does the student teacher propose to collect?

SCHEME OF WORK

PGCE Secondary English

SCHEME OF WORK

Class:	Year 9B	Dates (from/to):
		20 November–15 December

Number of lessons/lesson length
12 lessons x 1 hour each

Aims
To gain an understanding of the richness of fairy tales, and the concepts of satire and parody, and the idea of political correctness.

To look closely at the language used in fairy tales.

To revise Standard English and language terminology, including idiom and cliché.

Pupil learning objectives

En1 Speaking and Listening

1b: use illustrations, evidence and anecdote to enrich and explain their ideas

1e: vary word choices, including technical vocabulary, and sentence structure for different audiences

1f: use spoken Standard English fluently in different contexts

En2 Reading

1a: to extract meaning beyond the literal, explaining how the choice of language and style affects implied and explicit meanings

1c: how ideas, values and emotions are explored and portrayed

1g: how language is used in imaginative, original and diverse ways

1j: how techniques, structure, forms and styles vary

1k: to compare texts, looking at style, theme and language, and identifying connections and contrasts.

3d: how familiar themes are explored in different cultural contexts

En3 Writing

1c: exploit choice of language and structure to achieve particular effects and appeal to the reader

2a: plan, draft, redraft and proofread their work on paper and on screen

5c: make full use of different presentational devices where appropriate

6: . . . variations in written Standard English . . .

7e: the use of appropriate grammatical terminology to reflect on the meaning and clarity of individual sentences

Content (including breadth and balance)

Brainstorming traditional fairy tales, reading, viewing and writing own; research and reading on historical content, including 'gruesome' tales; close reading analysis of *The Practical Princess*; receptive reading of *Revolting Rhymes* and writing parodies; oral discussion of political correctness, and the power of language to persuade, with further writing; use of ICT to write final fairy story with a twist.

Method of delivery

Whole class discussion, viewing as a class, oral work in groups, researching in the library in pairs, reading stories as whole class, individual writing, whole class reading of *The Practical Princess*, and pair work on worksheets, teacher reading of *Revolting Rhymes*, an individual writing or collaborative writing, whole class discussion of PC language, and individual written work to end with.

Sequence of lessons (cross-reference to lesson plans)

1 Brainstorm usual aspects of fairy stories, e.g. giant or witch as baddie/set in a castle or forest/hero saves beautiful young princess or girl/good always wins through/happy ending. Discussion of cliché.

2 Watch cartoon versions of *Three Little Pigs* or *Red Riding Hood* – or read stories.

3 Oral work – in groups – presentation of a tradition fairy story (could include drama).

4 History of fairy stories – connection with Gothic literature, folk tales, myths and legends. Library visit to research topic.

5 Look at Angela Carter's work with twisting fairy stories – *Virago Book of Fairy Stories* – pupils could write their own 'gruesome' tale.

6 *The Practical Princess* – story and worksheets. Discussion of cliché and idiom.

7 Roald Dahl – *Revolting Rhymes* – read stories, then pupils parody rhyming story style.

8 *Politically Correct Fairy Stories* – discussion about PC and how it is either present or absent in literature. Discussion of power of language to persuade and influence. Discussion of racism and sexism.

9 Pupils to write own PC story.

10 Final task – write a fairy story with a twist. Plan story, brainstorm ideas, review material covered during scheme, use ICT to write, draft and revise, and to illustrate stories.

Resources

The Practical Princess – story and worksheets from *Changing Stories* from the English and Media Centre (1984)

Politically Correct Fairy Stories by J.F. Gardiner

Revolting Rhymes by Roald Dahl

Video of fairy stories in cartoon form

Virago Book of Fairy Stories, edited by Angela Carter

Assessment (including Examination Syllabus Requirements)

A PC fairy story or a fairy story with a twist

Oral presentation of a traditional fairy story

An analysis of words which are sexist and racist

IT – presentation of work

Reading and writing in a variety of styles

Differentiation

Oral work – mixed ability groups, and mixed gender. Groups worked out in advance.

Support from teacher-librarians and LSAs for the five least able readers in the library for research, and specific worksheet to focus their searches.

Whole class reading of stories and discussions will allow less able readers to access the content.

Support sheet to help with final writing with ideas for getting started. Individual support for writers. IT technician on hand to help with technological glitches.

Progression

Scheme starts with what the pupils already know, draws out their knowledge and makes it explicit. Audiovisual resource to further stimulate them. History of fairy tales will develop their own knowledge and individual research will allow pupils to progress as fast as their interests, and move from teacher-led reading to pupil-led reading.

Close reading of one story will introduce theme of equal opportunities and technical terminology, as will parodies. Specific linguistic structures will be identified too for use in writing, and the conventions of the genre so that writing will be purposeful and the format known.

Major discussion on persuasive language attempts to move pupils on to a more abstract understanding of a literary tradition, and subversive movements within that, making links between texts.

Equal opportunities Issues

Groups will have a good workable mix of genders, and consideration of the layout of the class and movement around it will be made to minimise off-task disruption.

Clichés of fairy tales will bring out issues of equal opportunities, especially the discussion of persuasive language in fairy tales. Tales from other European cultures will be looked at and compared.

Opportunities exist for both sexes to choose their preferred style of tale. The ICT suite allows for half the class to work at one time – the others will be drafting and revising. Good management will ensure that boys and girls have equal access and time to write and present their tales.

Student teacher targets

3.3.3:   teach clearly structured lessons or sequences of work which interest and motivate pupils . . .

3.3.4:   differentiate their teaching to met the needs of pupils, including the more able and those with special educational needs . . .

3.3.7:   organise and manage teaching and learning time effectively.

3.3.10: use ICT effectively in their teaching.

Standards addressed: 1.7, 2.1d, 3.3.11

Activity 14

HOW DOES ASSESSMENT IN A SCHEME OF WORK REFLECT PROGRESSION?

(suggested time: 40 minutes)

Planning programmes of work requires a focus on evidence and data relating to pupils and their attainments. Data can be quantitative: for example, about prior attainment (end of key stage tests) and inspection findings; or qualitative, such as views and opinions. Below is a quote from the Hay McBer Report on teacher effectiveness, relating to planning for progression:

> *Thoroughness in preparation, based on an accurate assessment of the stage pupils have reached – for the lesson, the term and the year – creates a framework for teaching and learning. Objectives and learning outcomes need to be clearly set out. Learning should be split into easily digested parts that make sense and have a logical flow. Milestones need to be specified so that pupils have a sense of progress and can measure their achievements against learning objectives. (Hay McBer, 2000: 44)*

How does your understanding of a pupil's general development have an impact on your teaching at different stages? Is there a connection between cognitive and emotional development? Pupils do not develop at the same rate, but are expected to take the same age-normed test regardless of their emotional and cognitive development. Pupils who attain a Level 4 at KS3 statistically find it very hard to attain a Grade C or above at GCSE; the motivational factor may also come into play. There is evidence to suggest that low attaining pupils understand both the criteria of the test requirements and what they can do in terms of study skills at home and school to enable them to reach those requirements at a later stage than higher attaining pupils, perhaps by the middle of their Year 10.

The following is a boy in Year 10 reflecting back on his experience of English at Key Stage 3:

> 'I like English this year. Last year, Years 7 and 8 we had a different teacher every lesson and they taught us different things. I got muddled up. We didn't do the homework, no one did, no one checked up on it. No one would teach us because we were naughty. Unless you are checked you aren't going to progress or learn. Year 9 I had the Head of English, he knows what you've learned, how you're coming along, your faults. He knows the things I'm going to do, tells me before class to take me face off, if I have the hump. He knows whether I need to do my work, by his marking of my writing, puts little things beside my work, I read what he puts, I read it, when to put quotes in, he teaches me.'

Boy from London comprehensive, who gained a Level 4 in his Year 9 SATS. From Westbrook et al. 1998: 49)

This illustrates the need to constantly check pupils' progression in lessons through spending time and energy getting to know the pupil, providing constant encouragement and explicitly showing pupils how to do certain skills, and being explicit over the test requirements.

TASK

How can you find out where your pupils have got to, and how do you get hold of this data?

Ask your mentor how the department ensures progression and continuity as pupils progress from one teacher to another.

- Do teachers pass on their individual pupil records, or discuss classes face to face with the next teacher?
- Are data on pupils kept centrally and released to all teachers at the beginning of every year (Cognitive Ability Tests (CATs) scores, results of NC tests, internal exams for example)?
- What use is made of the NC tests results at Key Stage 3 in any decision making about which tier pupils are entered for at GCSE, or about their predicted grade at GCSE?
- How are GCSE results used in Years 12 and 13?

Standard addressed: **3.2**

Activity 15

TRANSITION FROM KEY STAGE 3 TO 4

(suggested time: 30 minutes)

Although KS3 National Curriculum tests are now published, the GCSE is still the main benchmark for schools, and for parents. The GCSE is often seen by parents as a more solid measure of success, and therefore progression, being an older form of testing, with an element (albeit much reduced) of coursework, known external criteria, and administered by independent bodies. The GCSE is for some pupils the end point of their school career; for others their GCSE results allow entry to the next level of national qualifications. With the Key Stage 3 tests coming in early May, many departments are now introducing a 'pre-GCSE' unit, perhaps contrasting a pre-1914 poem with a post-1914 poem, or a more in-depth media unit as preparation for the substantial media unit at GCSE English. Indeed much of what is delivered at Key Stage 3 is now almost at GCSE level, and could be seen as important preparation for GCSE; a five-year plan devised to reflect overall continuity. The *National Qualifications Framework for 14–19* will further support progression for pupils.

TASK

- What do you consider to be the main points of difference between the curriculum at Key Stage 3 and that at Key Stage 4 as observed in your school?
- What similarities can you observe that can be used to focus on progression between the two?
- What strategies does your department employ to bridge the gap from Key Stage 3 to 4?

Standard addressed: **2.1c**

Make notes on this for your English portfolio.

Activity 16

PLANNING AT KEY STAGE 4

(suggested time: 45 minutes)

You will need to prepare a two-year 'at a glance' plan for your Years 10 and 11 – an excellent way of getting to grips with that syllabus!

You need to be sure what needs to be read as coursework, and what texts need to be read for examination purposes, and, if there is pre-release material in the form of an anthology, when to introduce that most effectively. Here are some prompts to consider:

- Ideally most pupils will be entered for both English and Literature GCSE.
- Speaking and listening should be fully integrated and recorded as appropriate.
- There needs to be lots of reading, both personal, independent reading, and close reading carried out with the help of the teacher.
- Much progression will happen in Year 10: good coursework is often produced here.
- Early diagnosis of individual weaknesses and strengths is required for early success.
- Most mature work comes in Year 11, so some coursework should be entered from Year 11.

You need to work out some kind of table. The one below gives one model of an English and English Literature syllabus.

AQA (NEAB) GCSE SPECIFICATIONS

Coursework		Examinations	
English 40%	**Literature 30%**	**English 60%**	**Literature 70%**
1 Reading: Shakespeare (5%)	1 Drama (pre-1914) (Shakespeare – crossover with English) (10%)	Paper 1 (30%) Section A: Unseen non-fiction and media texts	Written paper Section A: post-1914 prose (30%)
		Section B: Writing testing 'to argue, persuade, advise'	Section B: pre- and post-1914 poetry from anthology (40%)
2 Reading: Prose study (5%)	2 Prose (pre-1914) cross-over with English (10%)	Written Paper 2 (30%) Section A: Testing reading on poetry from different cultures and traditions	
		Section B: Testing writing 'to inform, explain, describe'	
3 Writing: Media – analyse, review, comment (5%)	3 Drama (post-1914) (10%)		

Coursework		Examinations	
English 40%	**Literature 30%**	**English 60%**	**Literature 70%**

4 Writing: Original writing – explore, imagine, entertain (5%)

Speaking and Listening

A variety of activities Assessment should focus on:

- extended individual contributions

- group discussion and interaction

Drama-focused activities (20%)

You now need to work out what, in practice, this means in terms of planning opportunities for speaking and listening, reading and writing over the two years.

You need a grid like this (available at www.paulchapmanpublishing.co.uk/resources/completeguide.htm):

GCSE COURSE PLANNER – THE TWO YEARS AT A GLANCE

Year 10	Year 11
Term 1 Autumn	Term 1 Autumn
Introduction to GCSE course and methods of working	
7 weeks	
7 weeks	
Term 2 Spring	Term 2 Spring
7 weeks	

Year 10	Year 11
7 weeks	Preparation of coursework folder and oral coursework assessments
	Exam revision and preparation
Term 3 Summer 7 weeks	Term 3 Summer Examinations
7 weeks	
Internal examinations – 3 weeks	

Standards addressed: 2.1d, 3.1.2, 3.3.2d

TASK

Work out your own two-year plan, referring closely to the syllabus, and to existing plans if need be. Put in specific texts too for each half-term. Ensure you cover all the requirements of the syllabuses.

Activity 17   PROGRESSION TO POST-16

(suggested time: 30 minutes)

The Dearing review of qualifications for 16–19-year-olds and the consultation process 'Qualifying for Success' resulted in the new Advanced Subsidiary and Advanced Level specifications, with implementation from September 2000. The one-year AS is both a final qualification 'allowing candidates to broaden their studies and to defer decisions about specialism' and counts 'as the first half (50%) of an Advanced Level qualification' (from the AQA syllabus on AQA website).

The implications for planning are that the two years must be fully planned and the differing needs of candidates taken into account. Some pupils may want to go the full distance with the two-year programme of the 'gold standard' as Advanced Level is still seen; others may want the opportunities of a broader education, going down the GNVQ and NVQ route, mixing and matching as appropriate to their skills and interests. The new White Paper on the 14–19 National Qualifications Framework *Opportunities and Excellence* sets out 'hybrid' GCSEs as well as the existing vocational

GCSEs to allow both an academic and a vocational choice of qualifications throughout the three levels of Foundation (GCSE Grades G to D), Intermediate (GCSE Grades A–C) and Advanced (AS, GNVQs, NVQs). What is certain is that the first year of post-16 study will be broad for all, with up to five AS being taken at any one point.

You will need to make a two-year plan in a similar way to GCSE, considering strategies to support pupils emerging from GCSE to make the transition to A Level. Your class may well be the most mixed ability class you will ever have taught, with GCSE results from the C/D borderline to A*, who go on to achieve A Level grades from A to E. Study skills, note taking, coursework/essay writing all have to be learned, and therefore taught explicitly as part of Key Skills (see post-16, Chapter 23). Many of the good teaching strategies used at GCSE can be used, extended and improved at A Level – imaginative responses to narratives, hot-seating, small group discussion work, DARTs (Directed Activities Related to Texts) activities.

Progression can be relatively seamless if the teaching and learning build creatively upon the high point reached at GCSE. The Wider Reading elements, the requirement to place texts in a social, historical and cultural context, the unseen poetry – all these have direct links to study in the sixth form. On a deeper level, the philosophy at A Level is that reading is seen as an active process, with the reader an active creator and not a passive recipient of second-hand opinion, with the meaning as dependent on what is brought to the text by a reader as by what is contained within it (refer to Chapter 12, below, on Criticial Theory). In all the syllabuses there is a well defined route through the two years, with the level of difficulty and complexity building up over the programme.

TASK

Get hold of an AS/A Level specification for English Language and English Literature GCSE syllabus. Trace the route of progression from Key Stage 4 to A Level using assessment objectives for GCSE and AS/A2. What seem to be the main differences and similarities between GCSE English Literature and AS and A2 English Literature? Put this in a table if it helps:

	GCSE Literature	AS	A2
Reading			
Writing			

Standard addressed: 2.1d

Activity 18   HOW CAN YOU ENCOURAGE PUPILS TO REVIEW THEIR OWN PROGRESSION?

(suggested time: 30 minutes)

Pupils need to be fully involved in their learning, and to take responsibility for it. As a student teacher you are constantly asked to be reflective, and to set yourself targets. How can pupils be similarly involved? By –

- Making the aims and objectives explicit at the beginning and over a series of lessons, and certainly concluding lessons with a plenary which revisits the objectives: 'Now, what have we learned today?' whether in a direct way, or through a quiz, or feedback from groups. This allows pupils to track their own progress within one lesson.
- Asking pupils to write commentaries on completed pieces of work analysing their progression over a unit of time. Pupils can also respond to the teacher's assessment comments.
- Keeping pupils' work in folders and on tape, and reviewing this at the end of every half-term or term with pupils. This is an excellent way of truly showing concrete progression, and pupils thoroughly enjoy this.
- Asking pupils to keep learning diaries or journals and giving sufficient time (and therefore status) in class for them to be filled in.
- Termly reviews or conferences face to face with pupils to go over their achievements, and review their individual targets.
- Allowing pupils into the 'mysteries' of marking and coursework moderation by giving them a moderation exercise to do at each stage, so they have to read, discuss and assess pupils' work according to the National Curriculum level descriptors criteria, GCSE marking schemes and A Level marking grids.

The key is to be explicit in what you are asking pupils to do and why.

Standards addressed: 3.2.1, 3.2.6

Which of the above suggestions could you implement immediately in your school? Are there other strategies for involving pupils in recognising, measuring and therefore working towards their own progression?

Activity 19   INNOVATION AND CREATIVITY, AND SYNTHESIS

(suggested time: 1–2 hours)

As a teacher you are working within several forms of constraint:

- the demands of your mentor and his/her immediate plans for a class
- the expectations of the department
- the National Curriculum, and the *Framework for English* at Key Stage 3
- the GCSE syllabus
- the targets set for that department by the school

- externally set national benchmarks
- the expectations of your tutor
- standards for QTS
- your own expectations of yourself
- the make-up of the pupils in your class
- your pupils' expectations of themselves, and of you.

It might seem a tall order then to finish this chapter on progression by encouraging you to be, in the end, an innovative and creative teacher in your use of materials, resources, teaching or assessment methods. Although there are many frameworks and specific ways of measuring your success, English teaching offers an infinite range of texts to be read, viewed, listened to, shared, argued over, and an infinite number of responses. This is a time to take some risks in your planning, and to revel in the vast number of choices of ways of putting together a lesson, a scheme of work.

Standard addressed: 1.7 That is your final task.

CONTINUOUS THREADS

1 Professional values and practice

Standards addressed: 1.1, 1.2

Does your choice of texts reflect both the demands of the National Curriculum, and the ethnic, social and cultural background of pupils in your classroom and in the UK as a whole? Have you planned a range of teaching and learning strategies which will appeal to all pupils? Have you considered the make-up of your groups before the lesson to avoid conflict and promote social cohesion in the classroom?

3.1 Planning, expectations and targets

Standards addressed: 3.1.1, 3.1.2, 3.1.3, 3.1.4

Here is one possible pro forma for a lesson plan: each institution will have its own preferred format. You should use this one to support your lesson planning to begin with. A template of this lesson plan is available as **www.pauchapmanpublishing.co.uk/resources/completeguide.htm**

LESSON PLAN PGCE Secondary English

Group   Date

Aims

Pupil Learning Objectives cross-referenced to Scheme of Work (linked to National Curriculum, *Framework,* or examination syllabus)

Content

Method of Delivery

Activity   Time

Starter

Teacher introduction

Development

Plenary

Resources

Mode of Assessment: diagnostic/formative/summative/recorded?

Speaking and Listening

Reading

Writing

Differentiation, including role of teacher assistant

All pupils (i.e. what all pupils will be able to do as a starting point)

Most pupils (i.e. further strategies to challenge the majority of pupils)

Some pupils (i.e. extension work and strategies for the more able)

Equal opportunities (with regard to gender, race, culture and class)

Cross-curricular considerations (ICT/literacy/numeracy/citzenship)

Student teacher's targets (referenced to the Standards for Qualified Teacher Status)

3.2 Monitoring and assessment

***Standards
addressed:
3.2.1, 3.2.2***

Assessment occurs in all lessons, all the time, even if it is the most informal kind of formative assessment where you as the teacher are assessing pupils' responses to your whole class delivery, or you are monitoring pupils' draft writing as you walk round each group. Below are some prompts to support you now:

- How will you assess the learning that takes place in this lesson?
- Does the assessment method match the learning objectives? (e.g. if these focus on speaking and listening are you using writing?)
- Does the assessment method have a diagnostic or formative function or is it summative?
- Does the assessment method give equal opportunities to all pupils, and cater for the range of ability in the group?
- Is the method used teacher assessment, peer assessment or self-assessment, and why?
- Is the assessment method related to National Curriculum attainment targets, the *Framework*, examination grade criteria, the school's marking scheme and policy?
- Will the assessment method assess all pupils or a selection?
- Does the assessment method allow what has been learned to be applied to a new situation, or to be used in communicating with an identified audience?

3.3 Teaching and class management

Standards addressed: 3.3.2c, 3.3.3

Student teachers usually admit that their greatest fear relates to managing their classes rather than to subject knowledge, assessment or any other area.

As stated in the rationale, good planning will prevent poor behaviour. A lesson that starts off with a swing, catching the attention of the pupils by a short sharp activity, involves them intellectually and culturally, gives pupils something purposeful, meaningful and challenging to do, and that ends with them understanding what it is that they have learned – all this will keep pupils on-task. A lesson which takes 10 minutes to warm up, where the teacher is rushing back to the stock cupboard for more books, or to shout at a pupil, where the pupils don't know the lesson objectives, or why they should open the book at page 60, where they are bored or patronised – all this gives opportunities for pupils to be off-task.

What are the main points of good classroom management in the English classroom? (These go hand in hand with good planning.)

- Orderly entrance into the classroom, with the teacher welcoming the pupils into the room, perhaps with an odd encouraging or humorous word.
- Clear instructions for pupils to sit down, take out specific books, exercise books, and for the first task to begin.
- Insisting on silence when the teacher – and other pupils – talk.
- Sharing objectives with pupils.
- Getting the first task under way quickly, perhaps with the task up on the board, or books and worksheets already laid out on the desks.
- Enthusiastic manner of delivery, with the teacher being unafraid to show their enthusiasm for the subject – in the way a poem is read out to the class or a play is acted out.
- Clear instructions for transitions from one activity to another.
- Resources to hand – pens, paper, worksheets, whiteboards and pens neatly sorted out, with pupils handing round the resources.
- Giving time limits to activities so pupils know what to talk/write/read about when and why: 'Five more minutes to rehearse your poems, class!'
- Being prepared to quietly split up pupils who are having a negative effect on one another, or a quiet word in private to someone working off-task; i.e. avoiding open confrontation
- Giving praise when due, quietly if necessary if open praise will embarrass. Celebrating work through reading aloud pupils' stories, display, or by writing letters or ringing home. Rapid marking and return of work so that pupils know you care about their work and can communicate this through your comments.
- Making effective use of LSAs in your planning and lesson, finding time to discuss the lesson beforehand.
- Knowing the whole school discipline policy to back up your classroom effectiveness.

- Orderly packing up and leaving of the classroom inside the lesson time (i.e. not after the bell has gone).

3.3.4 Differentiation

Standards addressed: 3.3.4, 3.3.13

You must say more than differentiation 'by outcome' or 'by task'. It is not appropriate to say 'not needed': all classes are mixed ability classes (especially many A Level groups). Be specific.

Planning with a teacher assistant (TA)

- Do you know who will be with you in your class for each lesson?
- Is the TA allocated to a specific pupil, or can they work with a group of pupils?
- Do you have the Individual Education Plans for pupils with AEN?
- Have you had the opportunity to plan in consultation with the TA so that you both know what your roles are in the classroom?
- How can the TA support you in integrating pupils with EAL/AEN?
- Is there time for a debrief of the lesson with the TA so that you can build this feedback into the next lesson?

Scenarios

1 The school you are placed with has full schemes of work already in place for teachers for each half-term. You want to have the freedom to plan your own schemes for your own good practice, and to suit the particular classes you are taking over. How might you go about discussing this with your mentor?

2 There are no schemes of work or lesson plans, and only some resources: 'it's all up here' they say, pointing to their heads. How do you find out what you need to plan for your classes during your placement, and where else can you go for models of schemes of work and lesson plans?

FURTHER READING

For a fuller discussion on literacy across the curriculum see Chapter 3, '(RE) Defining literacy: how can schools define literacy on their own terms, and create a school culture that reflects that definition?' in J. Davison and J. Moss, (2000) *Issues in English Teaching*. London: Routledge.

Chapter 8 in *English Teaching in the Secondary School* – 'English at Key Stage 4' – gives a sound background to the replacement of the 100% coursework GCSEs by the 60/40 and 70/30 exam/coursework weighting of the current GCSE English and GCSE English Literature syllabuses, and addresses the notion of adolescent development as a significant factor in pupils' ability to progress.

There is an excellent article mapping out progression in media in the *Secondary English Magazine* (available from the National Association for the Teaching of English), on 'Quality and progress at KS3', *Secondary English Magazine* 3(5) June 2000.

Chapter 11 in *English Teaching in the Secondary School* on 'English in the sixth form' gives a wide-ranging discussion of the various choices available post-16 and on page 123 gives the government's vision of the possibility of a 'seamless continuity' in 14–19+ education.

REFERENCES

Barnes, D., Britton, J. and Rosen, H. (1969) *Language, the Learner and the School*. London: Penguin

Brindley, S. (ed.) (1994) *Teaching English*. London: Routledge

Davison, J. and Dowson, J. (1998) *Learning to Teach English in the Secondary School*, London: Routledge

DES (1975) *A Language for Life*. London: DES

DES (1975) *English for Ages 5–16*. London: DES

DfES (1989) *English for Ages 11–16*. The Cox Report, paragraph 7.3. London: DES

DfEE (2001) *Framework for Teaching English: Years 7, 8 and 9*. London DfEE

DfES (1999) *The National Curriculum for Secondary English*. London: DfES

Fleming, M. and Stevens, D. (1998) *English Teaching in the Secondary School: A Handbook for Students and Teachers*. London: David Fulton

Hardcastle, J. (1985) 'Classrooms as Sites for Cultural Making', *English in Education*, 3(18).

Hay McBer (2000) *Report on Research into Teacher Effectiveness*. DfEE (June)

Vygotsky, L. (1978) *Mind in Society: The Development of Higher Psychological Process*. Cambridge, MA: Harvard University Press

Westbrook, J. et al. (1998) *Factors relating to Pupils who Attain below the Expectation in English at Key Stage 3*. London: QCA

WEBSITES

www.aqa.org.uk/ – 14–19 Opportunities and Excellence on DfES website, www.dfes.gov.uk/14–19/

www.dfee.gov.uk/performance/schools – DfEE standards site for performance league tables

www.qca.org.uk – Examples of schemes of work at Key Stage 3

www.qca.org.uk/nq/framework/ – National Qualifications Framework

chapter 4

ASSESSMENT

By the end of this chapter you will have gained an understanding of the relevance of a whole school assessment policy to English teaching. You will also have learned how to analyse and use assessment data to monitor pupils' progress. This will include appreciating the central role of assessment in informing and improving teaching and learning and how to apply English assessment levels at Key Stage Three and Key Stages 3 and 4. You will be made aware of the importance of positive marking strategies, particularly in relation to motivating pupils, and of the need for individual target setting to ensure progression.

> *It was during the 1990s that literacy became an education policy priority in several countries including Britain, Canada, the United States and Australia, with Governments demonstrating keen interest in standardised testing designed to generate quantitative data. (Wyatt-Smith and Murphy, 2002: 5)*

This has meant that often what has been emphasised is the most quantifiable that can be assessed, with teachers striving to find regular opportunities to test their pupils. Whilst appropriate assessment that generates action plans for pupils is welcomed we must avoid the routine of 'decontextualised assessment' (McClay, quoted ibid.).

Since the 1980s there has been an increased emphasis on accountability in the British education system. Consequently the process of assessment has been applied at every level. Local authorities and schools now have their results reported in 'league tables'.

Such information allows judgements to be made about the quality of education being offered. Educational assessment becomes as concerned with the quality of the institution as with that of the individual. Within schools each curriculum area has its exam performance scrutinised. Teachers are subject to individual appraisal and a 'Performance Management' system has been introduced. As a teacher of English you will be part of these formal assessment procedures. You will also be involved in the assessment of individual students from the moment they enter your classroom.

RATIONALE

The 1988 Education Act introduced the National Curriculum, a statutory curriculum for all state schools. It included a national assessment system for each prescribed subject. This involved a combination of centrally provided national tests and classroom-based teacher assessment. As a 'core subject' English became part of the programme of formal national testing from 1991. The original National Curriculum has been revised but it still provides a compulsory framework for teaching, learning and assessment. All English teachers must therefore become familiar with the English attainment targets and assessment level descriptors. At post-16, there has been a fundamental change in assessment procedures with the introduction of modular A Level courses, divided into the first AS and the second A2 year and the introduction of Key Skills. GNVQ courses also have their own assessment criteria and procedures. (For more information see Section 5 on Post-16.) It is then hardly surprising that C.V. Gipps (1994) notes the massive increases in assessment over the last decade.

To ensure consistency both within and across schools, English teachers are required to take part in standardisation procedures. This involves marking exemplar material, attending moderation meetings and providing samples of assessed work for external moderators. Clearly a wide range of assessment procedures are used in schools ranging from the most formal external examinations to the more informal process of making intuitive judgements such as when a teacher uses oral questioning in the classroom to assess the students' understanding. There is a variety of types of assessment. The main ones are listed below.

Forms of assessment

- **Summative** assessment gives a measure of a specific level of achievement at a given time, e.g. the formal assessment operating in external examinations.
- **Formative** assessment is used to inform teaching. Results are used to provide a basis for decisions about pupils' further learning needs.
- In **criterion-referenced** assessment the results give direct information about pupils' achievement in relation to objectives.
- **Normative** assessment gives a measure of how an individual has performed in relation to other pupils in the class. (e.g. giving a mark out of 20).

As a secondary English teacher, you will use all of these assessment strategies to monitor pupils. It is important to see assessment as a positive process. At best it should be an integral part of pupils' learning to raise achievement and ensure progression. C.V. Gipps argues that the challenge is 'to design accountability assessment which will provide good quality information about pupils' performance without distorting good teaching (and therefore learning) practice' (1994: 4).

Effective formative assessment is at the heart of successful teaching and for student teachers the skills required for its implementation take time to acquire. In an interview by B. Marshall, Dylan Wiliam (Professor of Assessment in the Department of Education at King's College, London) describes formative assessment as ' all those things that teachers and students do together that help the teachers know where the learners are when they are learning and what they need to do to improve and how to go about it' (Marshall, 2002: 47). This would mean the use of well selected questions, offering feedback, providing targets and recommending actions that will improve learning. In this interview Wiliam argues that formative assessment should involve pupils as learners having a 'construct of quality' and for teachers to help them understand how that quality is created. To unpick how this is achieved and to articulate it clearly to pupils is a challenge; the temptation might be just to correct the work.

Black and William produced a report (1998) in which they outlined recommendations for successful assessment:

- Feedback to pupils should concentrate on the qualities of the individual's work rather than fostering comparison with others.
- Pupils should be trained in self-assessment.
- Opportunities for pupils to express their understanding should be designed into the teaching.
- Dialogue between pupils and teacher should be thoughtful, reflective and focused.
- Texts and homework exercises must be clear and relevant to learning aims. (Quoted in Fleming and Stevens, 1998: 51–2)

It is worth considering all these in your short term and medium term planning.

LINKS WITH THE NATIONAL CURRICULUM AND KEY STAGE 3 STRATEGY

The foreword to the National Curriculum for English begins with this statement:

The National Curriculum lies at the heart of our policies to raise standards. It sets out a clear, full and statutory entitlement to learning for all pupils. It determines the content of what will be taught, and sets attainment targets for learning. It also determines how performance will be assessed and reported. (DfEE, 1999)

There are three attainment targets in English:

Attainment target 1: Speaking and listening
Attainment target 2: Reading
Attainment target 3: Writing

The level descriptions for these can be found in *The National Curriculum for England. English* booklet DfEE, 1999: (54–60). They provide the basis for making judgements about pupils' performance at the end of Key Stages 1, 2 and 3.

Pupils will arrive in Year 7 from a number of different primary schools. You will be informed of their KS2 test level in English and their 'Teacher Assessment' level. It is still a good idea to make your own baseline assessment of individuals in relation to the English attainment targets. Some English departments have a standard assessment piece across the whole year group. Many schools are now using CATS tests in the first term of Year 7. These are Cognitive Abilities Tests administered in schools but marked externally. The results can be used as an indicator for future performance at Key Stage 3 and GCSE. You will also need to explain the English department marking procedures to your pupils. Some departments use wall charts or printed sheets to stick in exercise books to explain what the National Curriculum levels and school effort grades mean. At the moment there is no compulsory national external assessment at the end of Year 7 or Year 8 but there are optional tests in these years. You will be involved in teacher assessment throughout KS3 and preparing the pupils for the SATs assessment towards the end of Year 9. You will need to use the level descriptions in the National Curriculum document to assess work.

At Key Stage 3 the main form of summative assessment is the SATs taken by 14-year-old pupils in Year 9 during the summer term. As from 2003 these consist of three tests: a reading test, a writing test and a test on a Shakespeare play. The outcome of the tests will provide separate levels for reading and writing, as well as an overall English level.

1   *The Reading paper.* This targets attainment levels 4–7. This is a one-hour exam based upon three linked texts with an additional 15 minutes' reading time. The emphasis is upon reading for meaning and successful pupils will have to be able to demonstrate knowledge of different text types. They will be expected to deduce, infer or interpret information, events or ideas from the texts. In particular pupils will be expected to comment on writers' uses of language, including grammatical and literary features at word and sentence level. Awareness of purpose of the texts and tone will also be expected. Pupils should be able to evaluate and respond critically to the texts, offering reasons and evidence. The most able pupils should be able to see how the social or literary context of a text influences its meaning.

2   *The Writing Paper.* This targets Levels 4–7. This is a 45-minute examination: 15 minutes is planning time and 30 minutes is allocated to writing. Only one writing task is set. Explicit planning is expected and the examination board provides a planning sheet. The task is supported by information about audience, purpose and form, as well as the level of formality. The expectation is that pupils should write imaginative, interesting and thoughtful texts. Pupils should produce technically accurate texts that are appropriate to task, reader and purpose. They will need to demonstrate skill in structuring their information. It will be marked under the following strands: sentence structure, punctuation; text structure and organisation; and composition and effect.

3   *The Shakespeare Paper*. This targets Levels 4–7. The paper is a one hour and 15-minute examination. The Shakespeare reading task will last approximately 45 minutes and will be based upon the detailed study of two sections set from one of three Shakespeare plays. There will be the choice of one task per play (and thus effectively no choice) as schools are likely to teach only one Shakespeare play. The task will focus upon two extracts from the play being studied. Pupils will be expected to write detailed responses that draw upon both extracts. The Shakespeare writing task lasts 30 minutes. Pupils are expected to write up to three paragraphs on a topic related to themes or ideas arising from their study of Shakespeare. Pupils will be asked to write precisely and concisely. The paper will be marked under the following strands: sentence structure, punctuation and text organisation; and composition and effect.

It is important to be familiar with how marks are awarded so that these can be explained to pupils. For example a writing task at KS3 taken from the QCA sample materials where pupils are expected to write a speech to a Parents' Association about the advantages and disadvantages of teenagers having part-time jobs is marked under three strands as listed above. For strand C, composition and effect (marks available 14), six bands of marks with criteria are offered. To illustrate the expectations of achievement in the bands, two bands are described: C2 Speech (marks 1–3) has an opening and closing and is presented in sections. Different perspectives on the subject are recognised. Chosen style of address to the audience is sustained, whether formal or informal. C5 Speech (marks 10, 11, 12) is adapted to achieve its purpose. It is a dispassionate account, which acknowledges complexity in the content and alternative views. The speaker's viewpoint is clear. A range of stylistic features is used, including devices which engage and convince the audience, such as repetition, humour and the use of deliberate contrast (QCA, 2002).

The higher level of understanding about the power of language, features of persuasive language and how to target your audience are evident in band C5. These band descriptions should help you when designing your lessons to move pupils forward in their reading and writing. However, it is important to recognise that not all pupils develop at the same speed.

A full set of sample papers and mark schemes is available on the QCA website at **www.qca.org.uk/ca/tests/2003sample**

Please note that whilst the assessment objectives are likely to remain similar for the SATs, the structure of the papers may well change for examination in 2004. Please check the QCA website.

At Key Stage 4 the main form of summative assessment is by national qualifications. The assessment objectives and grade descriptions can be found in GCSE and Certificate of Achievement syllabus documents. To give you a flavour of a 2004 GCSE syllabus (known as specifications) a broad outline of one is given below.

The AQA English syllabus is divided into two tiered papers for different ability ranges (A*–C and D–G). Each tiered paper is divided into two papers worth 60% of the marks in total and a coursework component worth 40%. This particular syllabus (specification A) covers reading response to non-fiction and media texts worth 15% in paper 1, as well as writing for a particular purpose (to argue, persuade or advise) worth 15%.

Paper 2 focuses on reading response to poetry from different cultures and traditions worth 15%, as well as writing for a particular purpose (inform, explain or describe) worth 15%.

The coursework element assesses speaking and listening worth 20%, and then two responses to reading and two responses to writing. The reading covers Shakespeare (5%) and prose (5%) and the writing component covers media (analyse, review, comment) worth 5% and original writing (imagine, explore, entertain) also worth 5%. Some of the reading in coursework can be used for assessment at GCSE Literature by meeting requirements for both English and English Literature.

You will benefit from speaking to the Head of English at your school experience about how the coursework is assessed, what feedback is provided for pupils and how assessment for terminal examination shapes the teaching.

(*Note*: This chapter will focus on the assessment of reading and writing. The assessment of speaking and listening will be addressed in Section Two.)

The marking of pupils' work in English should be:

- positive not negative
- varied but consistent
- regular not sporadic
- formative as well as summative
- respectful not dismissive.

As long as a pupil appears to have tried to the best of his or her ability, the work should be respected and valued, and any remarks written on it should bear this in mind. Constructive marking includes a teacher marking with the student, students marking each others' work, and individual drafting. The place of peer assessment is sometimes underplayed. Pupils will often provide suggestions to each other that the teacher would not and pupils will often accept harsh criticisms from one another that they would not accept from the teacher. These processes are all part of teaching.

When marking individual pupils' work you will need to consider a number of issues. What am I marking for?

Have the criteria been shared with the pupil?

Do I mark just the opening paragraph in detail?

Do I focus on patterns of spelling errors rather than all of them?

How many targets should I set, and have I made it clear how they can be reached?

How will I identify strengths?

Am I aware of previous targets?

Do my comments make it clear how the work can be improved?

Preliminary thinking

Look again at the four kinds of assessment – summative, formative, criterion references and normative. Reflect on your own education and make a list of specific times when you experienced these forms of assessment. In your personal 'case study' did one of these methods of assessment dominate? How does your experience compare with that of a pupil today?

Activity 1

CONSTRUCTIVE ASSESSMENT
(suggested time: 45 minutes)

The chapter entitled Assessment in *English Teaching in the Secondary School* by Fleming and Stevens (1998: 45) considers the problems of external, formal assessment, setting them against the advantages of the important role of assessment in informing teaching and learning. It questions the usefulness of 'vague and indeterminate' National Curriculum level descriptors when 'language development does not take place in a simple, linear fashion'.

- Make a list of the advantages and disadvantages of assessment that have emerged as a result of the National Curriculum.
- What strategies could you adopt to use assessment constructively in your classroom?

Standard addressed:
3.2.1

Record ideas in your portfolio and discuss with your academic tutor or mentor.

Activity 2

TYPES OF ASSESSMENT
(suggested time: 30 minutes)

After considering the definitions of formative and summative assessment (see p. 97), try and divide these examples of assessment into formative or summative assessment.

Complete a chart like the one on p. 103.

1 Teacher's 'in the head' monitoring of an individual pupil's close reading strategies as he/she scans for information and then reads a passage closely
2 Teacher Assessment for KS2 pupils
3 GCSE oral coursework grades
4 Teacher's written comments at the end of written work
5 Teacher's notes taken from listening to pupils read aloud from class reader
6 First drafts of GCSE coursework
7 Individual reading records of pupils' independent reading
8 Internal end of year exams for Year 10
9 Optional national tests for Year 8
10 The grades or marks in a teacher's mark book

11   Teacher's moderated grades for completed GCSE coursework
12   Speaking and Listening records recorded in prose
13   Group oral presentations at KS3
14   Collaborative writing completed in pairs at KS3
15   Self-assessment of written work
16   Teacher's notes taken from listening to 'response partners' working together
17   Pupil evaluations of one anothers' drama work
18   Individual Education Plans (IEPs)
19   AS Level module exams
20   CATs (Cognitive Assessment Tests) at the beginning of Y7
21   Pupils' peer assessment or oral work completed in pairs
22   Poems written as part of GCSE work
23   English Department annual report to Headteacher and Governors
24   Talk diaries completed after major oral work
25   Termly target setting for each pupil
26   Spelling tests
27   Reports written for parents
28   Pupils' peer assessment of written work
29   KS2 NC tests
30   KS3 NC tests

Formative assessment   **Summative assessment**

Standard addressed:
3.2.1   Are there any examples which you found hard to place? If so, which ones, and why?

Activity 3   ASSESSING CREATIVITY
                                          (suggested time: 30 minutes)

Standard addressed: Consider some of the issues when assessing a pupil's story that is creative,
3.2.1   imaginative and original but is weakened by many spelling errors. Note these issues
                         in your portfolio.

Activity 4

ENGLISH FACULTY ASSESSMENT POLICY

(suggested time: 30 minutes)

Read the English Faculty assessment policy provided and then respond to the following questions:

- What do you consider to be its strengths and weaknesses?
- Compare this with the assessment policy of your placement school.
- What are the most significant similarities and differences?

Standard addressed: **3.2.7**

Write your own marking policy. Place your responses in your portfolio and discuss with your mentor.

SCHOOL ENGLISH FACULTY ASSESSMENT POLICY

General principles

Marking

- The nature of work to be marked is completed written responses to English Profile Components: Speaking and Listening; Reading; and Writing.
- Written work in progress is monitored in pupils' drafting books; completed work will be written on file paper and kept in pupils' folders.

Recording of student achievement

At least every term pupils are assessed –

- at Key Stage 3 against the National Curriculum statements of attainment and assigned a level (1–8) and an effort score.
- at Key Stage 4 against GCSE criteria and assigned a grade (A–U) and an effort score.
- at Key Stage 5 against A Level, GCSE or GNVQ criteria and assigned a grade or level as appropriate.

This information is kept centrally in the English Faculty.

Student self-review

Each unit of work has a faculty cover sheet attached to it which includes teacher comment and suggested targets as well as a section for students to review their attainment and effort.

Teacher guidelines

Written work at Key Stages 3 and 4 is planned and drafted in exercise books, which may also be used for language exercises/skills work. This work will be checked with the students as part of the drafting process, but will not necessarily be physically marked. Each piece of written work will have a finished product which will be presented on A4 lined paper (usually), have a Key Stage cover sheet attached to it, will be assessed both by the teacher and the student and then put in the student folder.

Each piece of completed work will have the following:

- teacher comments noting achievement and development points
- pupil comment in response to the above
- an effort grade (A–E)
- at KS4 a GCSE grade relating to the AQA criteria.

At KS3 a National Curriculum level for each piece of work will be recorded in the teacher mark/record book.

At KS4 a GCSE grade for each piece of work will be recorded in the teacher mark/record book.

Activity 5

AWARDING NC LEVELS AT KS3

(suggested time: 30 minutes)

Look at the three examples of KS3 writing provided, which are taken from *Exemplification of Standards in English Key Stage 3, Levels 4–8: Reading and Writing* (SCAA, 1995).

Standard addressed: 3.2.3

Using the National Curriculum writing level descriptions, put a level on each piece. Next mark the work and write an appropriate comment at the end. What targets would you set for each student to raise achievement? Discuss the marked pieces with your academic tutor or mentor. The commentaries on these three pieces of work can be found at the end of this chapter as an appendix.

Example 1

FIRST Day at School

I can remember when it was the first day at school. I walked in the classroom with my mum. The teacher said "hello" and my mum said "Hello back". Then my mum took my coat off me then the teacher said "your coat goes in the cloakroom" "OK" I said then my mum went to hang my coat on my hanger. then came back and said "I am going now" and she gave me a kiss then she said "I will see you later on." I said "OK." Then the teacher said all come and sit down. She took the register. we did some painting, drawing, reading, playing in a big room and it was a play house. It had a sink, cooker, ironing board and a iron, tea and teddy bears Then after dinner we sat down and read a big, book Could Keppers birthday. and nobody wanted to go to his bithday party because thay what all too busy. So he decided to get his teddy bears down and have a party. So he made his own food and fed his teddy. bears to put them in the washing machine. His mum come in and said look at that mess Kipper, and that was the end of story and that was the end of School the bell want and my mum was waiting out side for me. Then we put our coats on then I went home and told my family what my first day at school was like and what I did

This is me hanging my coat and scarf up then my hat.

Example 2

Juliet's suicide letter

Dear Nurse,

I am sorry to upset if you if I have but I wish you had not also said for me to marry that Paris man as you knew I loved Romeo and him being banished was not going to make us split up. Frier Lawrence made a plan that I took a drug that made me apear dead but I was not. Then when I got put in the family tomb Romeo would have received a letter to come and collect me so we could run away. But Romeo failed to get the letter so he came to the tomb and took some poison after seeing my body. When I awoke Frier Lawrence was there. He tried to make me not see Romeo but I did. Then somebody was coming so he went off. I tried to get some poison off his lips but I couldn't. As the bottle was empty I took his knife and stabbed myself. As you proberbly know I could not live without my husband witch you may find silly killing myself over a man but I loved him more than any thing else in the world. Please go to my parents and tell them tha plan then the two families may make peace as a reaction to our deaths. Please thank Frier Lawrence and thank you for all our arrangements and marriage.

Example 3

Images of War

Nowadays, it is considered important by television and newspaper companies that we should all know the truth about what is going on. When the war in Yugoslavia first broke out, it seemed important that we had at least five or six reports crammed into every day. Because this was the first major war that had happened whilst I was alive, I was quite excited. However, after the first few days, this excitement soon turned to horror and anger. We would see images of people's blown up houses, of dead bodies – both human and animal. I was very moved by this and wondered how people could stand to kill other humans. I think, at first, everybody had the same reaction as me. We were horrified, we wanted to stop the animosity between the two sides.

In these first few months people were very concerned, they wanted to stop just looking and watching and being on the sidelines. They wanted to be there, or to start organising help funds. I too was like this. I got involved in fund raising. This was easy for about two months, but then interest started petering out. There were no more daily news bulletins about the Bosnians, or the Croats. We would hear a little news about once a week. The television companies who had been so interested in the war had decided that there were better stories to cover. The general public forgot, and when they did see these images of people dying they would seem wholly undisturbed. This frightened and angered me. Why should civilised people treat men killing men and animals as normal? There must be something wrong with a society that doesn't bat an eyelid when they see destruction.

But when I step back and think, I find myself wondering whether I will eventually become like that. I must admit that although I do sometimes find myself reduced to tears, it doesn't happen as often as it did when I first saw these images. Perhaps because people are used to seeing these pictures, they try to block their feelings out. Possibly the only cure for seeming lack of feeling would be to try and force some sort of world peace deal. But it is human nature to be greedy and always want more. Why should it change now?

It is quite obvious now that people have become immune to war. After the first few weeks many have the attitude that it is someone else's war – they can fight it themselves. I hope that these people will realise that something must be done to help others – before it is too late.

Activity 6

MARKING SATS PAPERS

(suggested time: 1 hour and 30 minutes)

Standard addressed: 3.2.3

When you are in school, ask for a SATs pack including previous SATs papers and mark schemes. Ask your school mentor if it is possible to be involved in marking 'mock' SATs papers.

Activity 7

MARKING AT GCSE

(suggested time: 30 minutes)

In teaching GCSE at KS4 you will need to work with coursework and examination assessment objectives. These are mapped on an assessment grid at the beginning of each syllabus. Individual coursework assignments are marked according to specific criteria and some pieces are 'double' marked for reading/writing or reading/literature. It is good practice to share assessment criteria with the pupils even if it is necessary to explain them in more 'pupil friendly' language.

Although examination boards employ external markers, all English teachers are involved in marking 'mock' examinations. It is really helpful to work with exam board mark schemes. They can be purchased for a small fee and provide a valuable insight for teachers into how the assessment criteria are applied. It is important to analyse 'mock' papers carefully with students to ensure they improve.

Most schools enter a small number of pupils for COA (Certificate of Achievement). This is aimed at students operating at Grade G or below and the formal assessment of each unit takes place in the classroom. More details are available on the AQA website.

Standards addressed: 2.5 and 3.2.3

Download the AQA GCSE language coursework grade descriptions for reading (En2) and writing (En3) from syllabus documents on the AQA website (http://www.aqa.org.uk/).

Activity 8

MARKING ASSIGNMENTS

(suggested time: 60 minutes)

Use the general grade criteria and the specific criteria for 'Media' to mark the two *Titanic* assignments provided. You should award a mark for writing (En3). Note that the AQA requires teachers to mark in the body of the text as well as making a final comment to indicate why a particular grade has been awarded.

Look at the assignments again and decide what advice you would give to these two students to improve their work. What specific targets would you set them? Put the marked essays in your portfolio and discuss them with your academic tutor or mentor.

GCSE Media Essay: 1

How is the disaster of the **Titanic** *presented in the media texts you have studied?*

Why have the texts been constructed as they appear for their intended audiences?

The media texts I have studied are: 'Titanic', directed by James Cameron in 1997 and produced by Paramount Pictures and Twentieth Century Fox starring Leonardo Di Caprio and Kate Winslet; 'A Night to Remember', directed by Roy Barker in 1958 and presented by Rank Organisation Film Productions, starring Kenneth More and Honour Blackman and the front page of a British tabloid newspaper, 'The Daily Sketch', printed on Tuesday, 16th April 1912. All of these texts were aimed at a very wide audience.

The R.M.S. Titanic sank on her maiden voyage from Southampton to New York. Out of 2228 people on board, 1523 perished. It had been declared unsinkable because of its sixteen water-tight compartments. It was sunk by an iceberg, south of Newfoundland, at eleven forty in the evening on the 14th April 1912. There was only enough room in the lifeboats for half the passengers and crew.

'The Daily Sketch' newspaper article is from 16th April 1912. The report is not set out as it would be in today's tabloid newspapers with colour pictures integrated into written text. It has three large black and white pictures dominating the front page, with very little text. Then it has four pages of writing with no pictures. The next two pages have more pictures of the ship, rich passengers and the luxurious interior. In 1912 printing techniques were not as sophisticated as they are today.

The written text in the newspaper is also different from today. Since there is an eighty-seven year gap, the language is bound to have changed. The language is very formal and has some complicated words and sentences. 'Details are yet fragmentary, but according to messages received ... Capt. E.J. Smith acted with commendable promptitude immediately after the disaster.' Today the language is much simpler. The headlines and sub-headings are quite different to those used today. They are small compared to a modern tabloid paper and now more use is made of alliteration, rhymes and puns. The headline in 'The Daily Sketch' was 'Terrible Disaster to Titanic' whereas today it would have probably been something like 'Titanic Super Ship Sinks'. I think the headline would have been shocking to the people who read the paper in 1912 because the Titanic had featured in the paper every day before the sinking to explain how technologically advanced she was.

'The Daily Sketch' puts a summary first and then the facts as they unfolded from Tuesday onwards. The summary is for brevity and gives the main details but it proves contradictory to the rest of the report. The facts are accumulated from the White Star Line offices and Marconi radio stations. However, the facts are mostly false because the paper reports that Titanic is being towed and that there were no casualties. The information was very slow coming through and today we have much more advanced communication systems, such as satellite. The newspaper is biased in the way it portrays the crew in a good light, 'The behaviour of the crew was exemplary.' The paper was also optimistic because it uses phrases like 'messages of encouragement' and 'not to worry'. The put '655 known to have been saved' in large print and how many may be dead in small print. This softened the impact of the bad news. The newspaper did use sensational words like 'perished', 'collided', 'alarming' and 'crushed'. It used the simile, 'broke them like an eggshell' to make the report more dramatic. The article concentrates on how much money was on board, 'Thirty millionaires . . .' and the third paragraph is devoted to listing all the wealthy people on the liner. Today's tabloid newspapers still report on the lives of rich celebrities because readers are interested in them.

When the Titanic sank, society was very different. People were treated according to perceived wealth and lifeboat space was allocated according to class with rich passengers taking priority. Also men were in charge and women were considered the weaker sex dependant on men. This coupled with an old fashioned sense of chivalry was why women and children were put into the lifeboats first. These values and relationships between men and women were portrayed in both films I have studied.

The 1958 black and white film, 'A Night to Remember' was the first to be made about the sinking of the Titanic. Forty-six years after the disaster, it was possible to look back and assess what had happened. The film was very 'tame' compared to Cameron's 1997 film, 'Titanic'. It had no sex and violence in it due to censorship laws and there was less emphasis on the class divide. This was because the class system still existed and to show that many steerage passengers died because of exclusion from the lifeboats would be an attack on their society. The film was made using models of the ship because the technology was not available to create a realistic ship and make it look like it was really sinking. The film did not focus on individual characters much because it was more of a documentary. 'A Night to Remember' gives a historic view of the sinking that was dramatic enough to hold the audience's interest rather than relying on fictional story lines.

The opening shows long shots of the ship to get across the sheer magnitude of the vessel. Also there is the triumphant music that gives the sense that we have been able to conquer the seas and produce a grand, impressive ship. There is a sense of great elation coming from the crowd. When the ship is sinking, the viewer feels that this can not be happening because all the way through the film we have been reminded the ship is unsinkable. As the ship sinks, there are medium shots of the vessel, showing its individual sections sliding under the water; it was like slow death. We also get close ups of the passengers to show the fear on their faces. There is constant tension building music and in the background, the screams of the passengers.

The whole idea of the 1997 'Titanic' film is based on the fact that the wreck of the Titanic has been found. A fictional salvage team explore it for a fictional diamond. James Cameron chose to put a lot of emphasis on class and the steerage passengers being locked below decks. As a result of this the majority of steerage passengers died. The film explores the extreme differences between the first class and steerage passengers and this is shown in their language. When the ship is being loaded, Rose and Cal, two rich passengers have a conversation. Cal says in an upper class accent, 'You can be blasé about some things Rose but not Titanic.' Then he gives one of the porters some money to take his baggage and says, 'I put my faith in you good sir.

Now kindly see my man.' The steerage passengers speak much less formally. When Jack is looking at Rose, one of his Irish friends says 'Oh forget it boyo – you'd as like have angels fly out of your arse as get next to the likes of her.' James Cameron said he wanted to entertain his audience and make his film as accurate as possible. 'There are responsibilities associated with bringing a historical object to the screen, even though my primary goal as a film maker is to entertain.' He is also critical of what happened on the Titanic and of the society at the time.

Cameron's film has four main story strands. The maiden voyage of the Titanic in 1912 is interwoven with a fictional romance between Rose and Jack, that happened during the journey. The third stand is a fictional salvage operation searching for a diamond in the 1990's and the forth is a fictional survivor, Rose, the owner of the diamond, telling her story of the last few days on board the Titanic in flashback. Rose is being forced to marry a wealthy man, Cal but falls in love with Jack, a steerage passenger. As the ship sinks, Rose leaves her first class family to try and get off the ship as a steerage passenger. She has obviously survived but the audience wants to know what happened to Jack.

The modern also film begins in black and white to take the audience back in time. It cuts to colour with the switch to the present and the under water shots of the salvage submarine. When the Titanic is being loaded, the audience is introduced to Rose and Cal but there are long shots of the crowd and close ups of their faces to show the excitement. There is a big build up of music to reflect the size of the vessel.

In the scene where Rose threatens to commit suicide, a lot of aerial shots are used to create tension and emphasise the sheer magnitude of the ship. There is a change in perspective looking from the deck down to the water to show how far it is. Close up shots of Jack and Rose's hands are shown. When Rose is hanging off the back of the ship, tension building music is used to create suspense to make the audience feel scared and concerned. Then when she is safe the theme tune cuts in to tell us that now Jack is here, everything will be all right.

All three texts have significant links with each other. 'The Daily Sketch' report and the film 'A Night to Remember' are both similar in the way they tell their story. The both rely on the facts that were available to them at the time. Unlike the film 'Titanic', 'A Night to Remember ' was not concerned with fictional story strands and it was a documentary style film. Both films did draw on the same facts; for example both films told us there were not enough lifeboats, that the ship Carpathia was too far away to help, that steerage passengers were held below deck and that the band was playing whilst the ship was sinking. Both films had the 'Molly Brown' character and used exactly the same quotation from John Jacob Astor when he is asked to put his life belt on, 'No – we have dressed in our best and we are prepared to go down as gentlemen.' The photographs in the newspaper can be compared with the images in the films as both directors had created sets to be as authentic as possible. However the newspaper photographs are of the real ship and real people and when you look at them you can't help thinking – if only they knew.

The modern film 'Titanic' is the most factually accurate of the three texts even though it is combined with fictional stories. The newspaper report was not very accurate at all. It said, 'Titanic is proceeding to Halifax, partly under her own steam, partly on tow by the Virginian.' We now know this was not true. The main purpose of the newspaper was to inform but it also wanted to give the people living at the time some hope. Survivors were interviewed before the 1958 film was made but some of the facts were still inaccurate. A member of the crew said the ship sank in one piece and because of his seniority, his story was trusted even though some of the passengers said that the ship broke apart. In the 1958 film the ship slid gracefully into the water in one piece but now the wreck has been found, we know that the ship did split in two as the rear of the ship is over half a mile away from the forward section. 'A Night to Remember' was also made to inform, reassess the disaster and it had another purpose to entertain. It was aimed mainly at an adult audience but the 1997 film was aimed at a wider audience. The younger generation are attracted to this film because it has actors in it like Leonardo Di Caprio. It is the most entertaining of the three texts and has the advantages of a huge budget, modern technology and special effects. James Cameron being interviewed on 'Sky Movies' said, 'I didn't want it to be just another Titanic movie.'

I believe the texts we have studied all achieved what they have set out to do and they were all excellent for the time they were written. I like 'The Daily Sketch' article because it was written just one day after the ship sank. I found 'A Night to Remember' slightly tedious because we did not really get to know any of the characters well. It was not a big budget film and the modern audience is rather spoilt with special effect films so it now seems rather dated. The film 'Titanic' was my favourite text because it really made you feel you were on the ship as it went down. The audience got to know the characters really well so it had a powerful emotional impact. It is also a step in the right direction to show the world how wrong it is to judge people on how much they own. They had a right to live whether they had ten pounds or ten million. I particularly liked this angle in the film.

GCSE Media Essay: 2

*How is the disaster of the **Titanic** presented in the media texts you have studied?*

Why have the texts been constructed as they appear for their intended audiences?

I am studying the film 'Titanic', and the Newspaper article from the DAILY SKETCH Which was published on Tuesday the 16 April 1912. The film produced in 1997 and produced by Paramount Pictures and Twentieth Century Fox starring Leonardo D Caprio and Kate Winslet. Leonardo plays Jack Dawson and Kate plays Rose, the rich person. The ship Titanic is 46,000 gross ton. 1513 people died and 700 were saved. The women and children had to go first into the lifeboats and that is why more women and children were saved.

The Titanic was meant to be unsinkable because of its 16 watertight compartments. The lifeboats had only been provided for half of the passengers but the Iceberg punctured five of them. On April 16 the newspaper mistakenly reported that all the passengers were safe. The Titanic hit the iceberg at 11.40 pm on the 14 April, approximately four hundred miles from newfoundland, At 2.20am the ship sank.

On the first of September 1985 the wreckage Was found in 13,000ft water. The iceberg They hit was 90ft from the water, the survivors Saw the result of sunlight. One man now dead Wrote the world woke on April 15 1912, the Titanic woke with a start. The daily sketch Newspaper article on Tuesday 16 April The daily sketch reported the facts of The disaster, the headline was, 'Disaster to Titanic on her maiden voyage'. On the first page of the daily sketch there is a Picture of the captian and the Titanic And a map of the route they taken to America and where the ship sank. The secound page tells you about the terrible Disaster to the Titanic and the quote feared loss of 1,700 lives in mid atlantic 655 known to have been saved, the quote rush of ocean linners is the beginning of the story. The third section is called 'calls for help' This page tells you when the Titanic gets into stress and the Titanic has struck an iceberg. The final section is two full pages of drawings 13 pictures of rich peoples 4 pictures of the rooms inside the Titanic they look exactly the same as the ones on the Titanic the language of the daily sketch bits of the language is not true and therte is a lot of exaggeration like 'many great linners' raced to the rescue there is a lot of heroic sentances like 'like an eggshell' there are a lot of famous sensations new york exited by perilof wealth passengers' the newspaper is like the times we have today and it is not like the tabliod which uses slang.

The film is about a ship called Titanic And a girl called Rose Dawson she leads you Through the things that happened on board The ship and all about her love life she even remembers falling in love with a steerage boy Jack she was a first class passenger, she Was a very prity lady. she tells the ship man she is looking for the heart of the ocean And the man starts to show her some pictures Of herself that Jack Dawson drew her seceret Lover drew of her. Jack won his ticket on the Titanic in a game of polka.

101 year old rose calvert and her grandaughter lizzy Rose is telling you the story from the beginning and it takes you to the beginning of the Titanic and thetre is a disaster the Titanic hit an iceberg, and two hours later it sank the maiden voyage of the Titanic most of the people that was on the Titanic have died so they have made a reconstruction they have even made the people look like the ones like the people on the ship at the time James cameron tried to make the film as accurate as possible and he used computer technology and wanted it to be a love story. The opening shot for the Titanic helps us to get used to the story. The theme tune My Heart will go on Celine Dion is black and white at the start of the film it is in slow motion the music starts to fade out the colour of the sea water and sky start to change colour In the next scens there is silence then there is tracking bleeps that the submarine is going under to the wreckage there are tacking over e starts to talk about the Titanic and then Rose has a flash back and she starts to remember all about Titanic and her Journey on Titanic as a young girl.

I think one of the scenes I remember the most is where Jack and Rose first meet they meet when Rose is hanging over the edge of the ship she says she will jump over the side if he comes any closer then Jack says if she jumps he will and he started to take off his Jacket and he grabbed her hand and then she slippped and was dangling over the water and he pulled her in then cal came and Jack was handcuffrd then Rose said

Standard addressed: 3.2.2

that Jack saved her and cal invited cal to come to dinner. Another dramatic scene is the sinking of the ship. the ship hits the iceberg at 11:40pm it starts with a high shot with these man playing the violin then there is a close up shot of people crying and screaming. There is a man leading a prayer and a close up of Jack and Rose and a slow motion shot of the passengers then there is a medium shot of the plated crashing down. Then the points of view on Rose then a long shot of Jack and rose as the ship sinks and Jack and rose hold there breaths and let go and kick there legs and try to get to the top of the water. They made it to the top and Rose couldn't find Jack she found him and they found a door and rose got on and she started to sing to Jack and Jack said don't ever let go of this promise Rose and then he died and sank to the bottom of the sea then a boat came and Rose got a whistle and started to blow it and then the ship came back and picked her up and everyone in the cinema was crying because it was so sad. My opinion is that the film was very good and I really enjoyed it and it was a box office success and it was really expensive to make.

Activity 9   DEPARTMENT MODERATION OF PUPILS' WORK

(suggested time: 30 minutes)

Standard addressed: 3.2.3

When you are in school ask to see the GCSE Written Coursework Standardisation materials. If possible, take part in the English Faculty moderation and discussion of these materials. Otherwise, mark the material independently and ask your mentor what marks the school awarded.

Activity 10   REPORTING TO PARENTS

(suggested time: 40 minutes)

The Qualifications and Curriculum Authority outline some recommendations for report writing to parents. They state that parents would like to know:

- how their child is performing in relation to their potential and past achievements, to the rest of the class and to national standards;
- their child's strengths and any particular achievement;
- areas for development and improvement;
- how they can help;
- whether their child is happy, settled and behaving well.

From **http://www.qca.org.uk/ca/tests/ks3/ks3_ara_2003_reporting.pdf**

Standard addressed: 3.2.7

Taking this into account, and looking at the examples on the QCA website, write three reports for different pupils in one of your classes. Discuss these with your mentor and place in your portfolio.

CONTINUOUS THREADS

3.1 Professional values and practice

Standards addressed: 1.1 and 1.2

In the National Curriculum document there is a section on 'Inclusion: providing effective learning opportunities for all pupils' (pp. 42-50). One of its three guiding principles is 'overcoming potential barriers to learning and assessment for individuals and groups of pupils'. Make yourself familiar with this as there is a detailed explanation of the special arrangements available during end of key stage assessments. The relative performance of boys and girls at Key Stage 3 and Key Stage 4 continues to be an area for concern, as boys are still seen to be underachieving.

3.2 Monitoring and assessment

Standard addressed: 3.2.2

This chapter highlights how formative assessment that is an integral part of classroom teaching can ensure progression. It is important to enter into a dialogue with pupils about their performance with regard to specific criteria, setting them SMART targets (specific, measurable, achievable, realistic and timed) so that they can improve. To check whether teaching and learning have been successful, it is necessary to reassess the pupils, celebrating achievement. Consequently this becomes a cyclical process of positive assessment.

It is equally essential for teachers to evaluate their own performance. In today's education system, others certainly will be assessing you.

3.3 Teaching and class management

Standard addressed: 3.3.7

External English assessment procedures are controlled by a strict code of practice. Detailed information is available from the QCA website (**http://www.qca.org.uk/**).

Individual schools will also have an internal assessment policy. For example, some secondary schools have an internal end of year examination system for year groups not taking external examinations. Some schools collect effort and achievement levels for each student in each subject (once a term/year) to help monitor individual progress. To be effective, a whole school assessment policy should be streamlined and consistent. It should report information to parents in a meaningful way.

English departments will have a subject-specific assessment and marking policy that will operate in the context of the whole school policy. It is likely to include effort and achievement levels and an approach to target setting. Since the National Curriculum levels are so broad, and pupils progress through them relatively slowly, many departments devise their own grading systems at Key Stage 3 to motivate students who may become disenchanted with their performance if they perceive themselves to be stuck on a particular level. At Key Stage 4 English departments may or may not put GCSE grades on pupils' work. It can be a negative beginning to the new course if Year 10 pupils have an accurate GCSE grade written on an assignment in the first term, as this grade is likely to be lower than the grades that they will be achieving towards the end of the course. Moreover, they may well see Grade F and translate it to mean F for fail.

Teachers of English need to work within the whole school and department assessment policies. However, it is the individual teacher's responsibility to make assessment a regular, effective and integral part of classroom teaching and learning. Good practice involves using a variety of assessment procedures, both formal and informal. Pupils should be given clear, explicit objectives for their learning. They should have opportunities to review their own work and be involved in self-assessment. It is desirable to devise class management strategies that create time for individual assessment and target setting.

3.3.4 Differentiation

Standard addressed: 3.3.4

With regard to formative assessment, it is possible to use differentiation by resource, task, support and outcome. All of these strategies involve the creation of teacher time for negotiating, tutoring, supporting, monitoring, recording and celebrating achievement. In more formal assessment situations, teachers still have a responsibility to help pupils of different ability to achieve their achievement potential. At Key Stage 3 there are three different assessment procedures available. Pupils working at Level 3 or below are able to do a series of 'tasks' to assess their level. Most pupils sit the SATs paper catering for Levels 4–7. At Key Stage 4, the examinations are organised into 'tiers', with the higher papers including more challenging material and questions. Students who are unlikely to achieve a GCSE grade can be entered for the Certificate of Achievement.

2.5 ICT

Computers are extremely useful for recording assessment data. Many schools now have their own recording systems in place. These can be used to monitor individual progress, track a pupil's effort and achievement levels across subjects and project anticipated levels based on earlier performance using CATs to KS3/GCSE indicator tables. Such data can be a helpful way to identify individuals who are underachieving.

Up to date information on national examinations at all key stages can be found on the Internet, for example on the QCA website (**http://www.qca.org.uk/**) and the BBC Bitesize website (**http://www.bbc.co.uk/revision**)

The latter also provides revision guidance and materials for Key Stage 3/GCSE external examinations – useful for teachers and students.

ICT has its own level descriptors for assessment. In some schools English teachers are required to deliver the communication strand of ICT within the English curriculum.

Scenarios

Look at the following school assessment data provided for a Year 7 class.

Year 7 class school assessment data (TA stands for teacher assessment)

Name	KS2 SATs	Year 7 CATs	KS3 SATs
Abigail Abbotts	5 (TA5)	122	
Ben Arrowsmith	2 (TA3)	73	
David Davies	4 (TA4)	94	
Zoe Fisher	4 (TA3)	91	
Simon Franklin	4 (TA5)	105	
Mary Jacob	4 (TA4)	120	
Isobelle Monk	3 (TA4)	77	
Sarah Pinker	4 (TA5)	119	
Joshua Reece	5 (TA5)	126	
Sonia Stevens	3 (TA4)	98	
William White	3 (TA3)	89	

Statistics never tell the whole story, but using the CATS table below what can you tell from this information?

CAT to KS3 to GCSE Indicator Table

Mean CAT Standard assessment score (SAS)	Indicated KS3 English	GCSE from verbal SAS
70–	4	F
70	4	F
71	4	F
72	4	E/F
73	4	E/F
74	4	E/F
75	4	E/F
76	4	E/F
77	4	E
78	4	E
79	4	E
80	4	E
81	4/5	E
82	4/5	D/E
83	4/5	D/E
84	4/5	D/E

Mean CAT Standard assessment score (SAS)	Indicated KS3 English	GCSE from verbal SAS
85	4/5	D/E
86	4/5	D/E
87	4/5	D
88	4/5	D
89	4/5	D
90	4/5	D
91	5	D
92	5	D
93	5	C/D
94	5	C/D
95	5	C/D
96	5	C/D
97	5	C/D
98	5	C
99	5	C
100	5	C
101	5/6	C
102	5/6	C
103	5/6	C
104	5/6	B/C
105	5/6	B/C
106	5/6	B/C
107	5/6	B/C
108	5/6	B/C
109	5/6	B/C
110	5/6	B/C
111	6	B
112	6	B
113	6	B
114	6	B
115	6	B
116	6	B
117	6	B
118	6	A/B
119	6	A/B
120	6/7	A/B
121	6/7	A/B
122	6/7	A/B

123	6/7	A/B
124	6/7	A/B
125	6/7	A/B
126	6/7	A
127	6/7	A
128	6/7	A
129	6/7	A
130+	7	A*

- Can you identify any students that are doing well or underachieving?
- Using the CAT to KS3 indicator table, fill in the projected level each student might be expected to achieve at GCSE.
- How could you make use of this data to inform your teaching of this class?

Your school operates a setting system at GCSE. Those set in 1 are expected to achieve high grades (A and B). The lowest set will not be entered for GCSE but will follow the Certificate of Achievement course. You have been given a Year 10 middle set who will be taking GCSEs in English. Some of the group will eventually achieve C grades but many of them will be operating on the all important C/D borderline. You are just beginning the GCSE course with them. They have achieved Level 4 or 5 in their English Key Stage 3 SATs.

- What assessment strategies would you adopt with this set in the first term to raise achievement?
- Remember you will be assessing them for speaking and listening, reading and writing. Which attainment target would be a good place to begin to build confidence? These students may not have performed well in an exam situation. How could you encourage them to show you their best possible work? Given that the class are all operating at level 4/5, what will you need to focus on to improve their writing skills?

Further ideas

- Exam boards sell external examination mark schemes for past papers (GCSE/ A level) for a small fee. Ask if your placement school has purchased any of these mark schemes. Marking 'mock' papers using such schemes provides a valuable insight into what examiners are looking for.
- When you make your primary school visits that focus upon transition, ask about assessment procedures at Key Stage 2. How are the pupils prepared for formal, external assessments and how is their English work marked in the classroom?
- Keep up to date with developments in assessment by consulting such websites as (**http://www.qca.org.uk/**), for the latest information on pilot testing at Key Stage 3.

APPENDIX: EXEMPLIFICATION OF STANDARDS – KEY STAGE THREE

From SCAA, 1995

Commentary: Example 1 Tammie – 'First Day at School'

Tammie develops her ideas well. She occasionally uses more imaginative vocabulary but tends to stick to known words. Ideas are logically organised and some sentences are demarcated by capital letters and full stops. In the piece on 'First Day at School', the support assistant showed Tammie where to put some of the correct speech marks and the commas in lists of words. However, Tammie was unable to do this independently. She shows greater control over letter size but still makes little attempt to join her writing.

Tammie's writing communicates meaning and shows adaptations for its intended audience. She uses a range of familiar vocabulary which is typical of Level 2 performance but the words she has chosen do not reflect the variety which is characteristic of Level 3. Tammie uses full stops and capital letters to demarcate sentences but not yet consistently. Her spelling of simple words is secure. More complex words are often incorrectly spelt, although they are usually phonetically plausible. Tammie's handwriting is a mixture of printed and joined writing and her letters are neatly and legibly formed. For these reasons, the overall range of her writing and its accuracy are best described by Level 2.

Commentary: Example 2 Aisha – 'Juliet's Suicide Letter'

In this example, Aisha makes a clear attempt at a different style. In places the letter conveys a sense of Juliet's desperation but the style is uneven as Aisha tries to include elements of plot retelling. There is plenty of evidence that she understands events in the play, but little that she understands the characters beyond their actions. The attempt to write in a lively way seems to have led to more shaky sentence construction. The piece might have benefited from proof-reading and rewriting to reduce the inaccuracies in the writing.

Levels 4 and 5 were considered. Aisha writes in a range of forms and shows awareness of how style varies according to the purpose and the reader. She does not yet have secure control of a more formal style but this is clearly developing. Sentences are usually demarcated accurately, though in some places they are not always grammatically elegant. In the narrative, there is evidence of using words for specific effects, although the vocabulary is largely straightforward. Spelling is not always consistent and some regular patterns have yet to be securely grasped. The handwriting is legible and Aisha is developing a personal style. She adjusts her writing in the different sections of the storybook, but there is no evidence of a fluent, joined style. This range of evidence suggests that Aisha's work matches the Level 4 description for writing. Her attempts at varying her style and her use of more sophisticated punctuation suggest there are elements of Level 5 in this collection but more consistent level of achievement would be needed before a Level 5 could be seen as best fit.

Commentary: Example 3 Isabella – 'Images of War'

The class read together the Tennyson poem 'The Charge of the Light Brigade' and compared it with a contemporary newspaper account of this event.

In this piece, Isabella reflects on her experiences and feelings. She conveys her involvement in the issues but also demonstrates that she can distance herself sufficiently to write an effective piece. The informal style works well, and there are examples of literary devices such as rhetorical questions and short sentences used for effect. Rather than write a detached discursive piece, Isabella gives her perspective on the issues in such a way as to engage the interest of the reader. The grammatical constructions are appropriate for this informal style and the writing shows effective use of punctuation and paragraphing.

Levels 7 and 8 were considered and Level 8 was judged to provide the best match. Isabella's writing is clearly confident and competent in a range of styles. The qualities of her work suggest it is at least Level 7. The degree of control of specific features, used for particular effects, evident in the narratives and the poem, are more characteristic of Level 8. The slow unfolding of the story in 'The Hidden Secret' and revealing of plot and character are markers of a mature writer. Her non-fiction writing is coherent and gives clear points of view. Her use of vocabulary and grammar is varied and interesting and her grasp of the more technical aspects of writing, spelling, punctuation and paragraphing is confident. In the light of this range of achievement, Isabella's work is best seen as fitting Level 8.

FURTHER READING

Butterfield, S. (1995) *Educational Objectives and National Assessment*. Oxford: OUP
Shorrocks-Taylor, D. (1999) *National Testing: Past, Present and Future*, . London: BPS Books

REFERENCES

Black and Williams, quoted in Fleming, M. and Stevens, D. (1998) *English Teaching in the Secondary School*. London: David Fulton.
Davison, J. and Dowson, J. (1998) *Learning to Teach English in the Secondary School*. London: Routledge
DfEE (1999) *The National Curriculum for England. Engish: Key Stages 1–4*. London: DfEE & QCA
Fleming, M. and Stevens, D. (1998) *English Teaching in the Secondary School*. London: David Fulton
Gipps, C.V. (1994) *Beyond Testing: Towards a Theory of Educational Assessment*. London: Falmer Press
Marshall, B. (2002) .Thinking through assessment: an interview with Dylan Wiliam, *English in Education*, 36(3): 47.Sheffield: NATE
QCA (2002) *Changes to Assessment 2003: Sample Materials for Key Stage 3 English*. London: QCA
SCAA (1995) *Exemplification of Standards in English Key Stage 3, Levels 4–8: Reading and Writing*. London: SCAA
Wyatt-Smith, C. and Murphy, J. (2002) 'An Australian proposal for doing critical literacy assessment: the case of writing', *English in Education*, 36(3): 5. Sheffield: NATE
For syllabus information, see past papers, mark schemes and exam reports.

WEBSITES

http://www.aqa.org.uk/ – AQA website
http://www.qca.org.uk/ – QCA website
http://www.qca.org.uk/ca/tests/ks3/ks3_ara_2003_reporting.pdf
http://www.bbc.co.uk/revision – BBC Bitesize website

chapter 5

EQUAL OPPORTUNITIES

By the end of this chapter you will have developed an understanding of the way in which issues surrounding class, race, culture, gender and sexuality can affect the way pupils learn in English. The chapter examines how English teachers can create a classroom culture which fully embraces, acknowledges and celebrates diversity and harnesses it to the very stuff of English teaching – language and literature.

RATIONALE

'Inclusion: providing effective learning opportunities for all pupils' has become the mainstay of the Labour government's stance on education, within the whole climate of raising standards for all. All schools have to monitor their results by gender and race, and must implement an Equal Opportunities policy in full: this includes a policy on anti-bullying.

Historical background

These principles emerged in the aftermath of the Stephen Lawrence inquiry of 1996, and the recent focus on the underachievement of boys in schools, specifically in English. The longer history of inclusion reaches back to the 1980s' focus on the underachievement of girls (see Brindley, 1994: Chapter 26, 'Girls and literature: promise and reality'), the Sex Discrimination Act 1975, the Race Relations Act of 1976, the multicultural and then anti-racism movements, also of the 1980s, and the funding of bilingual pupils from 'Section 11' government funding. This has now moved to the Ethnic Minority

Achievement Grant (EMAG) which includes funds to support the achievement of such groups as Afro-Caribbean boys – still the largest individual group to underachieve nationally, and the group making up the largest proportion of excluded children. The purpose of the grant is to provide equality of opportunity for all minority ethnic groups. In particular:

- to meet the needs of pupils for whom English is an additional language (EAL) and
- to raise standards of achievement for those minority ethnic groups who are particularly at risk of underachieving.

Schools are expected to monitor the attainment and performance of all minority ethnic groups, ensure that EMAG-funded staff receive appropriate training and that mainstream teachers have access to in-service training in relation to linguistic diversity and strategies to raise minority ethnic pupils' attainment.

Current focus

The current focus is new in that it is absolutely central to the National Curriculum, and statutory rather than relying on the 'goodwill' or conscience of individual schools or teachers or being marginalised. Section 1 'Professional Values and Practice' of the new Standards for Qualified Teacher Status exemplifies this, with the requirement for student teachers to recognise the diversity of their pupils' abilities, and backgrounds:

> 1.1   *They have high expectations of all pupils: respect their social, cultural, linguistic, religious and ethnic backgrounds; and are committed to raising their educational achievement.*

Previous strategies to teach bilingual pupils or to teach novels written by Black writers which were seen as radical only five years ago are now mainstream, and English departments who six years ago avoided GCSE anthologies with 'multicultural' poems, often because of unfamiliarity with their content and style, are now fully versed in such texts.

We have moved then some way from the 1980s' equal opportunities concept of ensuring that positive representations of girls are included in textbooks, and that pupils should read books which include children who are non-white and non-middle-class. Pupils are far more aware of the dangers of stereotyping, and are immersed in a multicultural world which is their norm – for many at least – due to the saturation of the media and popular culture (although many of the computer games feature violent macho characters, and the sexualised images of girls today are arguably providing a straitjacket of types for young girls to emulate). Today's youth are often used to growing up in mixed race schools, and are the first to point to any inequalities concerning race and gender. However, it should be noted that this is not always the case.

Current issues

So where are we in terms of equal opportunities? There is no room for complacency. Articles (e.g. *Times Educational Supplement*, 9 Nov. 2001) point to early concerns that the focus on improving the achievements of boys may over the next three years result in underachievement of girls, who are taking on the 'bad behaviour' of boys in terms of smoking, drinking and truanting. The gender gap at GCSE 'has remained constant over the past few years, with 10 per cent more girls gaining five good passes. More than 6 per cent of boys leave school with no GCSEs' (*TES* 17 Jan. 2003). Research by Ofsted, quoted in the *TES* (24 Jan. 2003) reports that 'Black pupils are four times more likely to be excluded than other pupils nationally . . . And while 59 per cent of white pupils get five Cs or better at GCSE, only 22 per cent of African-Caribbean pupils do.' Middle-class parents from all racial groups often actively ensure their children get the opportunity to go to 'good schools', leaving schools in socio-economically deprived areas to become 'sink' schools – a case of middle-class flight, rather than 'white flight'. Schools in older, more established mixed communities are able to embrace the full optimistic flavour of full integration while celebrating diversity but it is in mostly white schools that the real challenge exists to fulfil these statutory directives.

And finally, sexuality does not sit so comfortably with New Labour policies: Clause 28 introduced by the Conservative government in the early 1990s to prevent the 'promotion' of homosexuality in schools has not been rescinded. Much work needs to be done here to combat homophobia in the classroom, the playground and the staffroom.

LINKS TO THE NATIONAL CURRICULUM

The *National Curriculum* sets out three principles 'that are essential to developing a more inclusive curriculum':

A   Setting suitable learning challenges
B   Responding to pupils' diverse learning needs
C   Overcoming potential barriers to learning and assessment for individuals and
    groups of pupils (DfEE, 1999: 42).

It is B, 'Responding to pupils' diverse learning needs' that this chapter looks at in depth:

> *When planning, teachers should set high expectations and provide opportunities
> for all pupils to achieve, including boys and girls, pupils with special educational
> needs, pupils with disabilities, pupils from all social and cultural backgrounds,
> pupils of different ethnic groups including travellers, refugees and asylum
> seekers, and those from diverse linguistic backgrounds. (DfEE, 1999: 42)*

There then follows a sound list of strategies to create effective learning environments, to secure motivation and concentration, and to provide for equality of opportunity. This is the useful starting point it is meant to be.

CONTENT OF THE ENGLISH NATIONAL CURRICULUM

Standard English

Under AT1 Speaking and Listening the headings 'Speaking', 'Listening', 'Group discussion and interaction' and 'Drama' all point towards an adult needs view of oracy. There is an assumption here that all pupils speak English fluently as their first language, and any other differences are ignored; the one emphasis is on class with the imperative that all pupils should speak Standard English, with a comprehensive list of the most common uses of non-Standard English such as 'They was' and 'I done'. The clear message is that the working class form of English is not really tolerated, despite a line in Language Variation that pupils should be taught about attitudes to language use, and the differences between speech and writing. However, it is in this section that teachers can really be creative and grab the opportunity – the possibility – of openly discussing the variations of English that abound. And this is the aspect that pupils are interested in. Slang, the slippery, changing nature of English, words of abuse that change ('wicked, safe') should be debated and argued over in the safety of the well-run English classroom.

Reading

Under AT2 Reading there is a 'Literary criticism' approach, seen overtly in the list of 'technical terminology' objectives under 'Reading for meaning and understanding the author's craft', which are precise and helpful, assuming that all kinds of texts are indeed read. 'Texts from different cultures and traditions' spells out the need for teachers to make such texts a central part of the reading going on, without making them tokenistic or read as political texts. The examples of writers across the centuries and genres gives an exciting and rich picture of literature to share with our pupils which reflects the achievements of women and ethnic minorities, and even some 'classic' working-class texts such as those written by Alan Sillitoe and Bill Naughton.

However, David Blunkett, then Secretary of State for Education, made a last minute lurch towards an English Literary Heritage model NC when he made the exemplar list of pre-1914 major writers compulsory (i.e. teachers have to choose authors solely from that list), thereby maintaining the status of the canon. This means that pupils could read just one 'text from a different culture and tradition' over five years through Key Stages 3–4. The onus still lies on the department and teacher to bring alive and into their classroom the great diversity of texts that are available. Ironically, as a student teacher, Mary Chesshyre, has pointed out:

> 'When approaching texts by Asian, Irish, Scottish, Welsh, North and South American, black American, European, African, white South African, black South African, Australian, first nation or 'working class' writers, to name but a few 'different' cultures and traditions, we should remember that in many ways, the body of texts that make up the English literary canon may seem more remote to pupils today than texts from the National Curriculum's 'different' cultures – it too is from a different culture, even though we may have academic knowledge about the continuity that "our" culture recognises as being there. We can use

some of the practices, the discoveries and the reflection that are involved in teaching "different" texts to enrich and invigorate all our teaching.'

Writing

Under 'Writing' 'Breadth of study' pupils are to write imaginatively, drawing on this wide range of texts, both fiction and non-fiction. The genre approach to writing is clearly evident – but again there has to be a question: is there a dominant culture whose genres pupils are taking on board? Even with these last two queries, the National Curriculum is an odd mix of prescription, richness and innovation, demanding much subject knowledge from the beginner student teacher of English which may be new, and challenging.

The *Framework for Teaching English at Key Stage 3* emphasises the importance of pupils reading a range of texts (p. 14) as a contribution to progression in reading. The focus on word and sentence level work will help some pupils learning EAL, but there is also a danger that whole texts will be reduced to extracts in order to facilitate the teaching of this objective. Teachers will need to plan well in order to give all pupils the opportunities of reading a diversity of texts as a class, and as individuals in order to meet the demands of the National Curriculum and the *Framework*.

Know your pupils

The key point to keep in mind is that as a teacher you must take the time and trouble to get to know your pupils. This means talking individually, sometimes in private, to pupils, finding out what language they speak at home, or what their religion is (and if you don't know much about Sikhism, or Jehovah's Witnesses, then it is incumbent upon you to find out). In the same way you will find out what pupils read and write at home and at school – 'start from where the learner is'. Without this knowledge you will be teaching to a group of completely unknown pupils and run the risk of making assumptions particular to your own culture, class, race, gender and sexuality, and will not then be in a strong position to counter stereotypical judgements in your classroom, school and community. The school should provide you with data on the performance of its pupils from different ethnic backgrounds and other relevant information. You will need to show sensitivity here in your requests, and use of the data.

RACE

Activity 1

'OTHER' TO 'DIFFERENT' CULTURES AND TRADITIONS

(suggested time: 30 minutes)

The 'Dearing' NC of 1995 had one line dictating the need for pupils to read texts from '*Other* cultures and traditions'. The current *National Curriculum* has the semantic shift 'pupils should read texts from *different* cultures and traditions' (my italics).

TASK

Read the *National Curriculum* carefully with the Rationale above.

- What is the significance do you think, of this semantic shift?
- What texts are being referred to here – Black texts, Canadian or Australian novels, post-colonial texts, white working-class texts, Scottish texts, non-canonical texts such as very contemporary texts like Melvyn Burgess's *Junk*?
- Why should pupils read such texts?
- What issues could come up in teaching such texts in all-white schools or in a school with a mix of cultures?

Mary Chesshyre, the student teacher quoted above, responded in the following way:

'What texts are being referred to here?

'It might initially be assumed that it is black, Asian and post-colonial texts that should be studied by pupils here (how does American literature fit in? is it part of the English tradition for these purposes, or do only some authors "qualify", and if so, which ones?); there is a risk of this kind of study being treated as a token, a bit of political correctness, rather than an enormous opportunity to study a wide range of texts, including visual and moving image texts, that in some way represent a "different" culture, a different perspective, a different world. These texts do not have to be exotic; and always it is important to remember that many writers from cultures and traditions that are not in one sense "English" do in fact implicitly or explicitly subscribe to at least some of the principles and cultural values and habits inherent in the "English" tradition, by writing in English, by using the genres – novels, plays – of that tradition.

'Without stereotyping pupils and their possible reactions and sensibilities even before you start teaching them, you should consider how you are going to approach teaching texts from "different cultures and traditions", in the context of the planning for that teaching. Teaching in an all girls school that would be characterised as "white middle class", I found myself feeling uncomfortable in a general discussion about racism and slavery relating to a poem we were studying because there was one black girl in a class that I was teaching for the first time. Because I had not known this in advance I had not had the opportunity to consider whether my approach to this subject should be different, given this knowledge. Would it have been, or should it have been? As one of only a few black pupils in a predominantly white school, how did she "identify", or "position" herself culturally? I had assumed that the predominant values of all pupils would be middle-class-liberal, that you could take certain attitudes for granted, and that therefore a discussion of the kind we were having would not be problematic. Pupils did not have a genuine opportunity to express a view that dissented from the assumption that racism was an evil and that "we knew better"; after all, this discussion was only to provide a context for reading a poem, and was not a main aim in my planning for the lesson.

'In a school with a greater "cultural mix" different cultures must be explicitly valued, but what is the principle behind this? To promote tolerance and mutual understanding between cultural groups while allowing each to preserve and celebrate its distinctive characteristics? There is an inherent tension between "equality with diversity" as a liberal-left-wing priority and the valuing of tradition, hierarchy and conformity that may be identified with what might be regarded as more right-wing views. This tension may be experienced both within cultures themselves, and as a potential conflict between cultures, especially between that of the school (promoting a culture and equality ethos) and that of individual groups involved in the school (keen to preserve their identities). It will often be assumed, perhaps, that a school is the ideal place to promote the valuing of diversity and difference while at the same time "educating for citizenship", and in the English classroom this can and should be done, but it cannot be assumed that the relationship that the different ethnic groups present in the classroom have with their respective cultures and traditions is straightforward. The reality of the complexities of the relationships between pupils' individual cultural identities, those of their homes, their communities, their peers, their school and the "outside world", much of it experienced through the media, must be acknowledged by their teachers – and, gradually, by pupils themselves.'

Standard addressed:
3.3.14

Write a reflection of 500 words answering these questions. If you find it helpful, respond to Mary's comments above. Place these in your English portfolio.

Activity 2

TEACHING BLACK LITERATURE – GETTING AN OVERVIEW

(suggested time: 60 minutes)

To introduce Black literary texts into the classroom without being aware of some of the contradictions of a culture and its production, and some of the complex feelings students have in relation to it, creates problems. The potential the school may have to devalue the texts and their reading merely reinforces students' feelings about its otherness and may confirm their sense of the superiority of the dominant culture. Black literature as an oppositional cultural form cannot be taught alongside traditional literature in a way which leaves the cultural assumptions uncontested. It has to be used to question those assumptions and in order to do this effectively Black literature must be taught in the context of a completely revised approach to English teaching. (Scafe, 1989: 25)

Scafe, writing some 15 years ago, points out that Black literature is read in schools as a social commentary, as being 'problematic', rather than as a good piece of fiction or non-fiction, and suggests that it is read in 'multicultural schools', i.e. ghettoised, rather than in all schools. She points out the importance of placing all texts in their social, historical background to *inform* the reading (not to replace it) and with the language and human condition as the primary focus. The language, she says, is used 'to speak of the content' (Scafe, 1989: 136).

- This book was written in 1989; with inclusion now the main force of the statutory NC, are Scafe's arguments still valid for the school in which you teach?
- Are pupils being exposed to a wider range of Black texts over key stages which give them 'a tradition of Black literature'?

Sally Jellett, a student teacher teaching in a mostly white rural school, made this response to the above questions:

> 'I personally do not think of "black literature" as an isolated collection of texts. It is important to include black literature on the curriculum, and to place it in its context, but not more so than any other book, play or poem we read. I am not convinced that pupils are being exposed to a wide range of black literature, to give them "a tradition of black literature", but then the National Curriculum is very prescriptive in its demands of what we teach – and the lists of "major writers" we are expected to cover is not really an "inclusive" list in itself.'

Standard addressed: 3.3.6

How far do you agree with the points raised here?

You will need to discuss the issue with your mentor, and to study the resources in the English Department, and schemes of work. Place this in your English portfolio.

Activity 3

TEACHING TEXTS FROM DIFFERENT CULTURES – CHOOSING TEXTS AND SUBJECT KNOWLEDGE

(suggested time: 45 minutes)

Scafe goes on to suggest that teachers have to have some knowledge themselves of the Black literature – and the social, cultural and political context in which it was produced – in order to teach it as a cultural whole, to see such literature as part of a global literature, not as 'other', and therefore feel confident enough to challenge a reductive view of such literature. Rachel Redford (2001) warns of the dangers of seeking to avoid any suspicion of ethnic, gender, political and religious bias by the packaging 'of a few Grace Nichols poems and a Benjamin Zephaniah rap' into the English curriculum which has resulted, Redford argues, in a 'sanitised and Disneyfied' reflection of 'other cultures'.

TASK

1   Search through your departmental resources, and look at some GCSE and AS Level examination papers (your school should have copies of these). How far do you agree with Redford's argument as it relates both to your department and the examination questions?

Standard
addressed:
3.3.6

2   How would you audit your own knowledge and understanding of texts from different cultures and traditions in terms of being able to teach them at GCSE and A Level?

Activity 4

INTRODUCING A TEXT
(suggested time: 60 minutes)

The NEAB/AQA anthology often pairs poems up to compare and contrast, so that for example a pre-1914 poem 'The Despairing Lover' by William Walsh is compared to Grace Nichols's poem 'Even Tho'. They are paired by themes, thereby focusing on the universal theme, but also bringing up the different literary traditions, the different forms, and the very specific use of language.

TASK

Find a poem from a different culture or tradition which is challenging in terms of language, style and content, for example, 'Wha Fi Call I' by Valerie Bloom, the first stanza of which is reprinted below:

> *Miss Ivy, tell mi supmn,*
> *An mi wan' yuh ansa good,*
> *When yuh eat roun 12 o'clock,*
> *Wassit yuh call yhu food?*

Standard
addressed:
3.3.6

How would you introduce such a text to your class? How would you want it to be read? Plan the introductory lesson with a real class that you know in mind.

Activity 5

LANGUAGE AND DIALECT: DAVID'S STORY
(suggested time: 30 minutes)

Language lies at the heart of the identification of ourselves – inwardly as a way of forming our thoughts, and outwardly as a manifestation of our background, particularly in the UK where accent and dialect still pinpoint both social class and ethnic origin. Chapter 7 below on 'Speaking and Listening' looks at the differences between spoken and written language, and further on in this chapter we look at language and social class. But what are our responses to written pieces of work which contain – as the poem above does so skilfully – dialect and Creole? All children and adults 'code-switch' in their use of language to fit the linguistic context. Some pupils will have a wider repertoire of languages and dialects to draw upon. The unpublished Language in the National Curriculum training materials for teachers (1989–92) looks closely at these rich variations of English in the section 'Accent, Dialect and Standard English.'

> *Black British people have a strong sense of language choices to be made. So –*
> *depending on individual experience, on attitudes learned at home or with peers,*
> *and on age – black children and young people may have access to:*
>
> - *Standard English;*
> - *A local indigenous accent and dialect;*
> - *The accent and dialect of a Caribbean Creole learned from older people in*
>   *their family;*
> - *And a language which is a conscious expression of the identity of black*
>   *youth.*
>
> *(LINC 1989–92: 284)*

Additionally pupils in multilingual schools may form their own hybrid language taking on board elements of the dominant school and street culture, mixing Punjabi and Hindi slang with Black British and American slang, adding another linguistic layer, and moving away from Standard English (the dialect of the school). However, the National Curriculum and the attainment targets demand the use of Standard English (SE) for informal and formal situations, and certainly in written form. The need for clarity is important in the writing of a good story. But how do we identify elements of written English which are not Standard English – and how do we 'correct' such use for those pupils in a constructive and sensitive manner?

The LINC materials go on to point out:

> *Most children who can speak a local dialect of English or a Caribbean Creole*
> *learn to use Standard English in their writing without conscious instruction.*
> *They do this mainly as a result of their reading of texts written in Standard*
> *English. Sometimes this learning is a transitional process, with children making*
> *occasional unconscious use of local dialect or Creole forms for a time. Some*
> *children may, however, benefit from having attention drawn to differences in the*
> *dialects they use . . . The important general point to make is that unconscious*
> *use of local dialect forms in otherwise Standard English writing need not*
> *constitute a large problem requiring a major programme of intervention by the*
> *teacher. (1989–92: 291)*

A pupil–teacher discussion matching up dialectal features with their 'Standard equivalents' (LINC: 1989–92: 291) might be enough. The NLS focuses far more explicitly than previous government initiatives on the teaching of SE from Year 1, so that such a discussion may prove to be simply a reminder, or the start of a fruitful whole investigation of different dialects spoken in class.

TASK

Read through 'David's Story', written by a Year 9 African-Caribbean pupil under test conditions. He had been asked to write a story on the theme of 'conflict'.

- Where are the examples of the Creole he uses (i.e. unmarked forms of verbs)?
- Which verb forms *are* used correctly? Why might this be?

- What other influences on both his language use and the content of his story can you note?
- What would you write at the end of this story to encourage the writer, and support his use of (appropriate) Standard English?

David's Story

It was a nice hot summer day Saturday to tell you the true. I was sitting in my bedroom reading a book when 'my mum' ask me to go to the shop.

Do I have to? Yes you do, so I put on my shoes my mum told me what she wanted gave me the money and I was off. Put on my shad's out side my door and looked around feeling very good happy ' But it hadden yes the girl next door came out f*** I said to myself what does she want (I did not like her) Hello she said hi can't stop have to go shop. So di I we can go tighter yeah I said.

Walking down the street not saying a word then all of a sudden a black B.M.W pull up two men got out a took her Vicky being her name I tried to help

But it was no use I just got pushed aside like a real fool and drove off

O no what the f*** am I going to do I know I will go for help yeah go for help. No I can't they mite hurt her even do I don't care.

I've got it I will find her my self so I set off asking people were then one old woman said yeah man I saw them

Where did they go? Let me see now. Over there looked to my right and I saw the car thank a lot

I went in this like were house place and I saw her sitting down in a chair.

Standard addressed: 3.2.5

She saw me and I said like a fool, 'I've you come to help me' and then one man came and tried to hold me but I kicked him in the nuts got the girl like a hero and ran like mad all the way home.

Activity 6

POWERFUL TEXTS
(suggested time: 15 minutes)

One of your first questions in Activity 1 was to consider why 'texts from different cultures and traditions' should be taught. Now reconsider this in the light of powerful texts such as *The Other Side of Truth* by Beverley Naidoo (Puffin, 2000) which was a Carnegie Medal winner. This novel tells the story of two refugee children Sade and Femi from Nigeria, and tackles head-on the refugee experience both from a political perspective, and in relation to the politics of the school, class and playground.

TASK

- Can such texts alter the outlook of pupils in class?
- Is there a tension between Scafe's point of view about teaching texts which are good literature, while also wanting to teach a text because of the powerful themes and messages it conveys?
- How might a critical literacy approach help here with non-fiction texts – i.e. extracts from newspaper editorials about refugees and asylum seekers; interviews with refugees; television documentaries?

Write a paragraph putting forward your thoughts here, and place them in your English portfolio.

GENDER

Activity 7

PERFORMANCE DATA ON GENDER
(suggested time: 15 minutes plus time in school)

TASK

Open up the website below and look particularly at the case studies from both the secondary schools and the student point of view. You should also consider the presentation of performance data to look at the differences between boys' and girls' achievements, and then look at the strategies used to improve boys' under-achievement.

http://www.standards.dfes.gov.uk/genderandachievement/

Standard addressed: 3.3.6

- Can you find out what similar data are kept at your school in terms of monitoring gender performance?
- How do your school's data correlate with the national data?

Activity 8

RULER-WANGING
(suggested time: 15 minutes)

Read the following account by Margaret Sander, who in 1982 spent five weeks observing four classes in a South London comprehensive school which was in the process of going mixed. Please note that the year group references are pre-NC, so the 'first year class' is Year 7.

'I thought I had set myself, initially, a very simple task. I listed all the activities I saw pupils engaged in during one lesson . . .'

Ruler wanging

'"Ruler wanging" and "bag on table" may not sound very scientific but they do seem to have made sense to teachers with whom I have shared my observations . . . Certain activities in the classes I observed could clearly be identified with one sex or the other. Here are some of them.

GIRLS	BOYS
hand up	pencil tapping
chewing	calling out
reading	chair rocking
make up	bag on table
brushing hair	shove ha'penny
showing work to teacher	misusing materials

'Boys sat separately from girls at the centre of the room. This was the only space left to them since the girls, having arrived first, sat around the outside of the room. I observed girls moving chairs to achieve this position and interpret it as serving their best interests in keeping them away from the kicking feet and pinching hands of the boys.

'In a survey I conducted with the first year class on reasons for sitting separately the girls identified the boys as obsessed with fighting and football, selfish, inconsiderate, dirty minded and irrationally superior. The boys were more brief about the girls: they "nag and annoy" and are "do-gooders". However, all but two had attended primary schools where they sat in mixed groups and even changed for PE together.

'It was clear that the transfer to secondary school breaks friendship patterns and vulnerable "new" pupils turned to their own sex for security. Another reason for rarely sitting together was that such pairing was interpreted as sexual. "People say they are in love" said one girl. A boy reported "Friends make fun of boys who have to sit next to girls . . ."

'The [girls'] adjustment and attention to personal appearance had little impact on the conduct of the lesson. If either of the teachers observed it they pulled a face indicating disapproval and the girl would desist, sometimes only temporarily. I hypothesise that teachers tolerate such self-adornment behaviours because they are evidence of a culturally acceptable obsession with self and appearance allocated to women.

'. . . Girls controlled their environment by controlling themselves. Boys controlled the environment by controlling others: teachers, girls and other boys. This latter point is very important. Only a relatively small proportion of boys cause the disruption.' (Sandra, 1989: 19–21)

TASK

Note down your observations of differences in gender in classrooms taught and observed today.

- Are there similar differences in the ways in which boys and girls behave in English lessons?
- What strategies does the teacher use to minimise differences in gender (i.e. seating boys and girls together, ensuring space between tables, socially engineering relationships)?

Standard addressed: 3.3.6

- Would you so easily differentiate (and categorise) between ethnic groups in the way that you have differentiated between the genders? Can you elaborate on your answer here?

Activity 9

GENDER DIFFERENCE IN ACHIEVEMENT
(suggested time: 60 minutes)

In Caroline Daly's chapter 'Gender difference in achievement in English: a sign of the times?' in *Issues in English Teaching* (Davison and Dowson, 2000) Daly contends that boys and girls have different literary behaviours and that 'pupils' orientations towards reading and writing are inextricably bound up with their experience of power relations in the gendered and classed world outside of school.' (2000: 227) Daly quotes Elaine Millard who points out that it is boys who are continuing 'to control entry to the most influential ways of making meaning through the interrelated media of film, computer and CD-ROM' (Millard, 1997: 181). Girls do better at coursework, particularly in reading fiction and the empathetic response, and exams; boys do better, apparently in those areas which are not granted such a high status in the English curriculum – drama, media and argumentative essay-writing. 'English, historically, has been charged with delivering a basic, functional literacy to the mass working populace of a developed economy, while at the same time exercising a nurturing or a civilising influence, uneasily entrusted to the hands of women' (Millard,1997: 232). The question is, do we alter the content and the methodology to improve boys' exam results – more non-fiction, less pre-1914 texts, more genre-based writing, less imaginative and personal responses – or do we encourage boys to be more like the girls? The current focus on the underachievement of boys has meant a dramatic change in pedagogy for English teachers to try to keep boys on-task through the fast-paced tightly structured literacy lesson now in all our classrooms.

> *Boys' and girls' learning is inextricably bound up with their experience of class, race and sexuality, both in society at large and within schools in particular. For both working-class and middle-class boys, this is what characterizes their discriminating approach to what is worth learning, despite how differently they regard school and each other. (Millard, 1997: 233)*

TASK

1   How far do you agree with Daly's contention that the 'feminisation of English teaching has influenced boys' attitudes towards English'?

2   How does this match what you have noted down for Activity 2 above and
with your own experience of being taught – and teaching – English?
3   How could you as the English teacher build on the positive aspects of the
behaviours observed (e.g. praising girls for their empathetic responses, while

*Standard
addressed:
3.3.6*

encouraging the girls to speak out and not 'service' the boys ; encouraging
boys to channel their energy into their reading and writing by raising the
status of non-fiction and media texts in the classroom)?

Activity 10

WAYS FORWARD
(suggested time: 30 minutes)

Daly suggests some challenging strategies for teaching the four language skills in a
classroom environment which empowers both boys and girls – 'English teachers need
to avoid a polarized literacy focus for girls and boys, and rather plan for the curriculum
to be made accessible and enriching to all' (in Davison and Dowson, 2000:.234).
Chapters 7, 13 and 15 in the present book on Speaking and Listening, Teaching Reading
and Writing all elaborate on what is good practice for boys and girls. In his article 'Boys,
poetry and the individual talent' (2000) Mark Pike gives a detailed account of his own
practice in getting a more imaginative and empathetic response to poetry from boys. He
highlights the importance of allowing an initial personal response, with the real
possibility of a multiplicity of meanings. This, Pike suggests, appeals to boys' aptitude
for problem solving, and encourages ownership of the poem, taking away the (mostly
female) teachers' authority over them, and the text. Here is a summary of the article:

Causes of boys' antipathy to poetry

- Image of poetry and peer pressure make poetry uncool
- Teacher domination and pupil passivity abound
- An active reading stance is not adopted by readers
- Process and stance required for successful reading of the genre are not
  explicitly taught
- Relevance of poems to readers' lives not perceived by teachers or pupils
- Narrow range of poems
- Challenge lacking in the poetry read
- Poetry read infrequently
- Oral work and pair work under-represented
- Pace and structure either lacking or overly prescriptive
- Teachers' expertise and enthusiasm not sufficiently utilised.

Responsive teaching – the practice

1   Poem read twice or more by teacher
2   Individual pupils annotate poem as they wish and draw upon their own
memories or experience to make some intimate transaction, plus note
elements of style of language

3   Journal entries made

4   Paired talk to share their experiences of the poem

5   Whole class discuss – 'Well, who's going to start?' or 'What have you got?' = forum

6   Reader-centred activities – Directed Activities Related to Texts (DARTS), with a good pace and variety, where thinking and not regurgitation is predominant.

= Focus on the individual, the unique past that each reader could bring to the poem

= individuality in reading.

Teachers avoid prescribing what readers should find in the text and boys continue to be challenged.

> *The reader's attitude and stance have been shown to be of crucial significance: a hallmark of the readers reported here was their positive response to ambiguity – multiple meanings came to be seen as a source of pleasure. (Pike, 2000:52)*

TASK

Refer to Pike's suggested pedagogy and practise with a poem you are unfamiliar with. Discuss how bilingual learners as well as boys – and girls – could benefit from this approach, and from the issues raised. If you disagree with this methodology, then provide a critique of it.

SEXUALITY

Activity 11

HOMOPHOBIC BULLYING
(suggested time: 60 minutes)

Few Equal Opportunities policies, or strategy 'lists', focus specifically on homophobic bullying. Some schools are strong on the need to counter 'macho' or 'laddish' cultures, but seem to focus on outward appearance rather than on more intimate ways of behaving – or speaking. The term 'gay' is commonly used today by pupils as a derogatory form of verbal abuse; would you allow the term 'Paki' to be used in such a way without taking a stand against it?

TASK

Standard addressed: 3.3.14

Ask your mentor for the school's Equal Opportunities policy and discuss with him/her how the school, and the English Department, deal with homophobic bullying and name-calling, both in the playground and in the classroom. Does it deal with both gay boys and lesbian girls?

Activity 12

QUEER THEORY

(suggested time: 60 minutes)

In his chapter entitled 'What has sexuality got to do with English teaching?' (Davison and Moss, 2000) Viv Ellis gives a powerful account of how homosexuality is now 'allowed' or 'tolerated' in the classroom, but in so doing such liberalism still views – and forms the views of pupils in that classroom – heterosexuality as the norm, and homosexuality as 'other', with other forms of sexuality not discussed. Just as with the teaching of Black literature in the English classroom, the complexities around sexuality must be acknowledged, and then critiqued. There is an onus on us as teachers to produce new cultures, and not just unthinkingly reproduce the existing ones, the ones we are familiar and at home with. Most illuminating in this chapter is the extract from Poppy Z. Brite's novel *Lost Souls* where a boy dares to challenge the accepted interpretation of the relationship between Ralph and Jack in *Lord of the Flies*, where the love they have for one another is the root cause of their antipathy. This raises the question of 'permitted readings' of texts – and how teachers can disrupt such normalised readings, and focus on 'on how we read and write sexuality'. Chapter 12 on Critical Theory sets out the importance of disrupting such readings. Daly in her chapter points to the importance of recognising that 'Literacy is a social practice and the learning of it in school relates to the formation of sexualized identities within the worlds of family and work beyond' (Davison and Moss, 2000: 229).

TASK

- What is your reaction to the above paragraph as it relates to your own teaching, in your own school?
- What would be the issues for you in bringing out 'queer' readings of literature in your classroom?

One Head of English, Donna Bryant has commented on this issue:

'You may want to consider your colleagues' stance here. Colleagues and mentors may be reticent to explore this issue. You need to understand the school's policy and practice, and know the pupils well, and think through how you might structure a discussion in the classroom so as to engender an open debate rather than close down the arguments. This is to advise caution, not abandonment, of the issues.'

Mary Chesshyre, a student teacher, responded in this way:

'I agree with Viv Ellis's proposal that approaching texts in a way that allows or encourages the challenging of "traditional" interpretations of the sexual identities and behaviours represented in those texts is part of developing pupils' critical literacy, and, as such, is an appropriate and powerful teaching strategy. It is also an approach that genuinely encourages pupils to develop a personal response to texts, and to relate their own experiences to their reading and writing and vice versa.

'As always, as an English teacher you need to ask yourself what your aims are in adopting or encouraging any particular approach to reading, and as always as an

English teacher you can't imagine that the aims relating to the teaching of your subject have little relevance outside the English classroom. But your teaching may be viewed as highly threatening, inappropriate and politically motivated by some, including parents – and the pupils themselves. "Why are we doing this in an English lesson?" "She's obsessed with sex." "Perhaps she's gay herself." As a teacher, you may find that being prepared to discuss and "allow" "other" interpretations of texts earns you a reputation, labels you, among pupils and teachers, and you have to decide how you will deal with this. You would have to be clear about, and be able to confidently explain, what you were doing.'

Write a 400-word reflection on this and place in your English portfolio.

SOCIAL CLASS

Activity 13

IS SOCIAL CLASS IRRELEVANT?
(suggested time: 60 minutes)

Class is arguably the biggest single factor in underachievement. Boys from middle-class families usually understand that there is an investment in aspects of the curriculum and this will support achievement whatever a boy's race or sexuality.

White working-class boys and working-class African-Caribbean boys are statistically doing the worst amongst all groups, being found more often in lower set groups, and 'sink' schools. They are often separated from other groups and 'disproportionately judged as lacking the necessary "ability" or the right "attitude" to succeed' CTES, 1999: 13). Yet we are not that willing as teachers to discuss class differences as easily as race and gender. The current debates about 'top-up fees' for universities focuses on the need to means-test students from 'working families' – terms are batted around to avoid the word 'class'. What is at issue are the differences in expectations and culture that pupils from working-class backgrounds encounter in school. School culture is a middle-class culture which assumes both a particular way of speaking and behaving, and the expectation that learning will lead somewhere – to a better job, university, global experiences. This is not automatic for any pupil, but for the pupil coming from a home where parents are themselves educated, who are in broad agreement with the aims of the school, and who can provide computers, homework help and bedrooms because economically they can afford it, the home/school cultures dovetail positively. The 'right attitude' will support learning; such pupils know the 'right ways' of behaving and learning in school.

Additionally, as Jon Davison points out in his chapter 'Literacy and social class' (Davison and Moss, 2000: 247), the dominant culture is also reflected in schools through the *National Curriculum*, an ideological document reflecting what is still a mainstream, mostly white middle class literature and concept of literacy, propelled into schools via the National Literacy Strategy.

> Policy-makers espoused a moral, and almost evangelical approach to the teaching of 'Great Literature'. It was believed that nothing was more valuable, or indeed more civilizing, than pupils connecting with the great minds of the past. (2000: 247)

This statement refers to the Board of Education's 'Circular 753' of 1910, with its concomitant belittling of popular culture, including the cinema. The 1995 Dearing English curriculum demanded that pupils be introduced to both fiction and media texts 'of high quality'; Blunkett gave in at the last minute to his more traditional advisers and made the examples of pre-1914 texts compulsory.

TASK

Examine the current English curriculum and answer the following questions on it:

- Is it the role of schools to include popular culture in the curriculum?
- What other forms of popular culture would you want to bring into the English classroom? And what are the arguments against studying such texts?
- As Jon Davison asks (Davison and Moss, 2000: 259), 'are all types of culture equally valid?'

Standard addressed: 2.4

Activity 14

LANGUAGE AND SOCIAL CLASS

(suggested time: 20 minutes)

The use of non-Standard English is clearly unacceptable according to the National Curriculum for much of the oral work happening – and assessed – in English classes.

Look back at the 'Note on Standard English' in the *National Curriculum* regarding the examples of non-Standard English (p. 32). These give 'the most common non-standard usages in England'. Indeed these are so common that most of your pupils will use them at some point, and maybe there are non-standard forms which you yourself use, unconsciously. These are working-class dialects of English, many of which are fast becoming mainstream, and even middle-class forms of English. Remember that the upper classes of 100 years ago used the negative 'ain't' to differentiate themselves from the working class. The National Curriculum prescribes the following:

> 5 Pupils should be taught to use the vocabulary, structures and grammar of spoken Standard English fluently and accurately in informal and formal situations. (p.32)
> However, under 'Language variation', the curriculum widens to point out that
>
> pupils should be taught about how language varies, including . . .
>
> C. attitudes to language use
> E. the vocabulary and grammar of Standard English and dialectal variations.
> (ibid.)

TASK

Standard addressed: 2.4

You have many children who use specific forms of spoken non-Standard English such as 'I done it' and 'they was'. Bearing in mind the above points, how do you tackle this when you are assessing their spoken English in a formal situation you have set up such as a job interview or debate?

Scenarios

1 You are teaching *Of Mice and Men*. Your class is made up of mostly white pupils. How will you deal with the racist language used in the textbook? (Use a different text if this one is unknown to you.)

2 You have two refugee boys from Kosovo – they have been in England for three months. What strategies can you employ to bring them more strongly into the shared discourse of the lesson?

3 You have a group of boys in your Year 11 English classroom who label anything – and anyone – to do with emotions and the arts 'gay'. You want them to read a group of poems on the theme of Hearts and Minds which includes several Shakespearean sonnets and modern poetry written by gay writers. How might you go about this task?

4 You have a quiet reading session every week in the library with your Year 9. Two girls bring in popular romance novels to read and three boys refuse to read anything apart from non-fiction or football magazines. They read quietly all lesson, however. How would you deal with this situation?

FURTHER READING

RACE

The list below attempts to show that there is a 'history of black literature' in the UK, and a literature of 'different cultures and traditions'.

Achebe, C. *Things Fall Apart* – Novel about the fall of a Nigerian tribesman on the arrival of white missionaries

Amadi, E. *The Concubine* – Novel about a Nigerian village woman. Would read well in parallel with Achebe's *Things Fall Apart*

Ashley, B. *The Trouble with Donovan Croft* – Black boy goes to live with foster family

Bindha, M. *Stories from Asia* – Voices and themes from Asian culture

Darke, M. *The first of Midnight* – Black slave meets deprived woman in 18th century Bristol

Desai, A. *The Village by the Sea* – Children in poor rural Indian community take responsibility for family

Dhondy, F. *Poona Company* – Boys experience small town Indian society

Edgell, Z. *The Festival of San Joaquin* – Set in Belize. Women's rights, environmentalism and the class system

Gilroy, B. *Boy Sandwich* – Three generations of a West Indian family in Britain

Gordimer, N. *July's People* – White family shelters in black servant's village

Greene, B. *Summer of My German Soldier* – Jewish girl helps German PoW on the run in Arkansas

Harries, A. *The Sound of the Gora* – Cape Town trouble linked to South African's distant past

Holm, A. *I am David* – Boy on the run in WW2 Europe

Jones, R. *Delroy is Here* – Black London boy with Jamaican background makes moral choices

Jones, T. *Go Well, Stay Well* – Friendship between black and white girls in South Africa

Kaye, G. *Comfort Herself* – 11-year-old girl from Ghana experiences different cultures

Lester, J. *Basketball Game* – Black teenage boy plays basketball with white girl in Nashville

Naidoo, B. *No Turning Back* – Three young people and the forces that challenge them in South Africa

Naidoo, B. *The Other Side of Truth* – Two Nigerian refugees in London

Needle, J. (1978) *My Mate Shofiq* – Friendship between a white English boy and a Pakistani boy

Rhue, M. *The Wave* – A frightening experiment (learning about Nazism in History) which gets out of hand

Riffat, A. *A. Distant View of a Minaret* – Short stories describing everyday life in Egypt

Smucker, B. *Underground to Canada* – Cotton plantation slave girl plans her escape

Taylor, M. *Let the Circle be Unbroken* – Sequel to *Roll of Thunder, Hear My Cry*

Taylor, M. *Roll of Thunder, Hear my Cry* – Black girl grows up in 1930s USA

Walmsley, A. (ed.) *The Sun's Eye* – Collection of stories and poetry from the Caribbean

Zephaniah, B. *Face* – Facial injuries to a teenager cause a rethink

Zephaniah, B. *Refugee Boy* – Ethiopian/Eritrean boy taken to London to escape war

GOOD WORLD LITERATURE FOR GCSE AND AS/A2

Australia

Collected Stories by Peter Carey – A great selection of very accessible and sometimes gruesome short stories

Remembering Babylon by David Malouf – Novel about a white boy who is brought up by Aborigines and the problems that he has returning to white society

Lilian's Story by Kate Grenville – Australian girl who has trouble fitting in with her peers

Indian literature

The Man-eater of Malgudi by R.K. Narayan – A lovely Indian tale by one of India's most famous writers

Midnight's Children by Salman Rushdie – Epic tale about India's independence, lots of great imagery. Also *Haroun and the Sea of Stories* – a children's story about a fabulous journey and the battle between good and evil

Fire on the Mountain by Anita Desai – A young girl is sent to live with her strict grandmother in a remote village

Such a Long Journey by Rohinton Mistry – Tale of a man and the drudgery of his life in a poor Indian city

The Mystic Masseuer by V.S. Naipaul – Humorous story about a man who becomes a mystic healer, without really having any powers, and his rise to fame

African literature

Things Fall Apart by Chinua Achebe – A tale about Okonkwo, a member of the Igbo culture

A Grain of Wheat by Ngugi wa Thiong'o – About freedom fighters on the verge of Kenya's independence

The Slave Girl by Buchi Emecheta – A girl is sold into slavery by her own brother

No Sweetness Here by Ama Ata Aidoo –A collection of short stories by one of Africa's leading women writers

The Beautiful Ones Are Not Yet Born by Ayi Kwei Armah – A novel set in the last months of Nkrumah's rule of Ghana; deals with the disillusion that the population felt

Nervous Conditions by Tsitsi Dangarembga –About a young girl and her fight to be educated to the same level as her brothers

Selected Short Stories by Nadine Gordimer – A range of contemporary short stories about racism from a white, female, South African writer

SUPPORTING LITERATURE

Callender, C. (1997) *Education for Empowerment: the Practice and Philosophies of Black Teachers.* Stoke-on-Trent: Trentham Books

The teaching style and stance of Black teachers is examined in relation to the perceived norm of white teachers, and the conflict that can arise in schools.

Gaine, C. (1995) *Still No Problem Here*. Stoke-on-Trent: Trentham Books.

This text looks at the issues surrounding teaching in all-white schools and is particularly good on the history of multiculturalism and anti-racism, and the impact on teacher education.

Gilborn, D. and Gipps, C. (1996) *Recent Research on the Achievements of Ethnic Minority Pupils.* London: Ofsted/HMSO

An influential text on the current National Curriculum.

Jones, R. (1999) *Teaching Racism – or Tackling It? Multicultural Stories from White Beginning Teachers.* Stoke-on-Trent: Trentham Books

This text looks at beginning teachers in primary schools, and the issues raised for them in tackling, and accepting, diversity in their schools.

Richardson, R. and Wood, A. (1999) *Inclusive Schools, Inclusive Society: Race and Identity on the Agenda.* Stoke-on-Trent: Trentham Books

CLASS AND RACE

Brice Heath, S. (1983) *Ways With Words: Language, Life, and Work in Communities and Classrooms.* Cambridge: Cambridge University Press

An American ethnographer's account of working with three different communities in Carolina – white working class, 'mainstream' and black working class – focusing on the links between home and school literacy. Reads like a novel and raises questions about how and why young children succeed or fail in the early years of schooling.

REFERENCES

Bloom, V. (1983) *Touch Mi, Tell Mi*. London: Bogle L'ouverture Press

Brindley, S. (1994) *Teaching English*. London: Routledge

Davison, J. and Moss, J. (eds) (2000) *Issues in English Teaching*. London: Routledge

DfEE (1999) *The National Curriculum for England. English Key Stages 1–4.* London: DfEE and QCA

DfEE (2001) *Key stage 3 National Strategy. Framework for Teaching English: Years 7, 8, and 9.* London: DfEE

LINC *Language in the National Curriculum*, 1989–92 (unpublished materials)

Millard, E. (1997) *Differently Literate*. London: Routledge Falmer

Pike, M. (2000) 'Boys, poetry and the individual talent', *English in Education*, 34(3), Autumn: 41–55

Redford, R. (2001) 'Essential otherness', *Times Educational Supplement,* 9 February

Sandra, M. (1989) *From Gender, English and Media Centre*

Scafe, S. (1989) *Teaching Black Literature*. London: Virago Press

TES (1999) 'Weakest not at the table', *TES*, 26 November: 13

WEBSITES

www.blink.org.uk – links to many other organisations

www.childline.org.uk/racism

www.britkind.org.uk

www.cre.gov.uk

www.cre.gov.uk

http://www.standards.dfes.gov.uk/genderandachievement – Look at the performance data, case studies and strategies

chapter 6

INCLUSION

By the end of this chapter you should have a clearer idea of what is intended by the idea of inclusion and what is contained in that idea for the teacher of English. You should be able to see how English is at once inclusive by nature and, like any other school subject, open to particular methodologies and approaches which teachers need to employ in order to teach appropriately those who would otherwise lose out or go unchallenged and intellectually unsatisfied. Key terms in considering inclusion are; 'provision', 'differentiation' and 'assessment and diagnosis'.

The concept 'inclusion' has significance at a political and historical level, and that will be explained. For the beginner teacher the main questions, for action, that are prompted by the concept are those relating to:

- knowing about potential barriers to learning that have particular relevance for English;
- planning for a wide spread of abilities, learning-histories and aptitudes;
- planning to work with assistants and helpers in the classroom.

Simultaneously with understanding diversity and special treatment, inclusion means understanding how the subject itself seeks to build on the commonality of the language. By this we mean the applicability to everyone of forms of feeling, thought and expression that education in English enables pupils to meet, learn, and turn to their own use. English teachers need to structure their approaches in such a way that everyone is included in the central dimensions of what is being transacted. This has been clear since the days of David Holbrook's *English for the Rejected* (1964). However much we need to differentiate questions and tasks, or give particular support or stimulus where it is most warranted, or adapt texts, our aim has to be a common entitlement for all. This implies that somewhere, central to a lesson or a scheme of work, will be a common experience, or series of common experiences, not a string of individualised tasks tailored to a measurable level.

Ours is nothing if not a humane subject. When they first performed *Hamlet* at the Globe, a building predicated upon the idea of inclusion, Shakespeare's players may have utilised the idea of differentiated seating or standing by price, but the unique experience was available to all, simultaneously, in common. The script and the auditorium point to the intention to offer the full richness of the play to all kinds of people. Those who stayed, listened and reacted would have known what was happening, and been moved to greater or lesser degrees, but probably not in correlation with their literacy abilities. At the heart of our subject lie experiences through which we discover what we have in common as we watch and listen, not only as we read and write.

THE NATIONAL CURRICULUM, THE STANDARDS FOR QTS AND THE KS3 STRATEGY

The National Curriculum clearly states that 'An entitlement to learning must be an entitlement for all pupils' (DfEE, 1999: 3). The subject documents all contain a detailed section on inclusion which outlines the principles schools must follow in their teaching. The Standards for QTS are equally unambiguous about the need to include all students in the scope of one's teaching. The Standards do not actually employ the word 'inclusion' but statements relating to the need for all who qualify to understand their responsibilities towards all learners, regardless of ability and needs, are to be found under 'Professional Values and Practice' (arguably nearly all statements but 1.6 in particular), 'Knowledge and Understanding' (2.6 and the need to know about the *SEN Code of Practice*), 'Teaching' (3.1.2, 3.1.3, 3.1.4, 3.2.4, 3.2.5, and, 3.3.1 and 3.3.2c). The Standards iterate at different points that beginners – student teachers and those who have just gained QTS – may well need the guidance of experienced colleagues in an area where it is hard to gain quickly that subtlety of understanding about pupils which years of experience with the full range of them allows.

Schools have mainly to work on the assumption that all staff must, using their own resources, cope with the idea that pupils will exhibit variety in aptitudes, motivation, levels of achievement etc., but that the problems faced by some learners are such that they take them over the edge of being able to join in normally with what is done in class. These individuals, who may be diagnosed as, for example, severely dyslexic, or physically vulnerable, or autistic are granted an adult in a teaching role whose purpose is to help them, on a one to one basis, to learn the curriculum to which they are entitled in common with their peers. Although all secondary school staffs contain a figure known as a special educational needs co-ordinator, or SENCO, and although the SENCO leads a team of specialists who are qualified teachers in both a traditional subject and the requirements of teaching those 'whose attainments fall significantly below the expected levels', as the NC puts it, there are also to be found learning assistants, often not qualified teachers, working with individuals. These helpers need, for the sake of doing their work as well as possible, to liaise with the regular teachers of their selected pupil. Beginner teachers, therefore, have to learn how to plan lessons that will involve the assistant, how to clarify their intentions for the lesson to that person and draw upon her or his gifts and talent for the best benefit of the pupils.

Working with a range of ability

Each year a fair proportion of students on ITT courses have already been employed as assistant instructors to children with special and identified needs, and so will have a good understanding of the kinds of problems with learning that beset some children. The KS3 Strategy's Progress Units concentrate on short episodes of skills-based teaching, not for those with identified and named special needs, but for poor spellers or sentence-constructors, or those who find teasing out the implications of what they are set to read harder than most in their age group. This is not the right place to give a set of instructions about using these units, but anyone rehearsing to teach English would be well advised to try their hand at teaching two or three of them. They are to be employed with groups of about six in the recommended brief but busy sessions. Such willingness to work with lower achievers would be most welcome to a host school, and good practice at understanding the kinds of difficulties with aspects of English which some children show. This particular focus on areas of technical weakness is not intended to deny the entitlement of such pupils to the full set of literary, linguistic and cultural experiences given by statute in the NC. We can see that no one would be fully included in English if their 'special needs' or particular weaknesses, treated analogously to a diagnosed disease, resulted in a sole diet of spelling exercises and correct grammar drills. Yet we need also to understand the range of factors that might tend to exclude some pupils from taking a 'normal' part in the group; unless helped back into the community of learning by specific devices, strategies and acts of liaison with support specialists, some pupils will miss out on vital elements of learning English. It is these devices, strategies and acts of liaison that statutory documents foreground as the means of ensuring curriculum entitlement and inclusion.

RATIONALE

It is hard to argue against the case that a comprehensive school must seek to teach everyone, more or less by definition. Historically, comprehensive secondary schools came into existence as selection was phased out at age 11. They were there to include everyone: those who had been distinguished as 'special' by virtue of being in the 15% to 20% that had once gone to a grammar school, and the whole set of the erstwhile undistinguished majority remainder. Looking at comprehensive schools from the other end of the IQ range, it is clear that the direction of thinking about the 'less gifted' or 'slower learning' pupils in the last three decades has been that they should not, as far as is at all possible, be separated out from the rest of the student population, either in different schools, or in separate classes in the main school which, however much intended otherwise, often came to look like learning ghettos. Inclusion is a human rights issue, you could argue (and here see, for example, Frederickson and Cline, 2002: 73).

We may, of course, all have an equal right to learn, whatever our background or ability, and to do so in a school which includes everyone equally well. Those rights, however, entail nothing about how English teaching should arrange itself. Schools almost always stratify children by age, and often by ability too. Arguably neither of these fundamental aspects of the average secondary school is particularly inclusive, but then inclusion cannot so dominate the agenda that it dissolves all other considerations, such as the need to promote the best quality of learning in the limited time. English may be properly inclusive even though based on fairly traditional forms of distinction between groups of learners. Our subject may not be quite like others, insofar as no one learns maths or science with the same instinctual and universal skill by which they learn a mother tongue (or two), but it is like others in having grounds for putting together pupils whose skill levels are approximately alike. At this point the statutory insistence on the concept of entitlement takes on considerable significance. It serves as the guarantee that, regardless of where the school stratification system places an individual, he or she will be accorded the same rights to intellectually and culturally valued elements of the subject as anyone else.

Take writing poetry, for example. That whole issue is considered elsewhere in this text, but under the 'inclusion' heading it is worth noting the power of simple poetic forms. The haiku has achieved a certain affectionate knocking at the hands of such as Roger McGough, and no doubt it deserves it, but the evidence has been available for decades that children in low ability groups, or at the bottom end of the mixed ability group, can find in the power of the haiku's form both a comforting limit to the amount they have to say in order to have achieved a full utterance, and a focusing device, something which helps bring into strong form a singleness of vision. It is arguable that teaching writing through verse, through a series of provided structures, is at the very heart of English teaching and highly inclusive because such writing is like, to borrow from D. H. Lawrence, an absorbing game. The bright can enjoy testing their own creativity's degree of fit within the framework given. By comparison, something in the act of concentration, it seems, allows those not accustomed to writing well, or enjoying the demand very often, to achieve a breakthrough into naming an aspect of their nature or introspective world which demands to be given voice. This would be nonsense to assert, and dangerously reminiscent of the very worst excesses of the 1960s were it not for the steady flow of evidence to the effect that determined teaching in this area can lead to pupils writing original and memorable lines, and across the whole range of abilities and aptitudes. No doubt Sandy Brownjohn's volumes are applicable to this part of the argument (and see Chapter 16 below, on teaching poetry), but a recent publication by Barry Hymer (2002) starts with the importance of noting that an otherwise poor learner with social and literacy problems may nevertheless, under inspired teaching, manifest a gift. Hymer cites the magical line from a 10-year-old: 'Even the winter leaves have their own secret colours.' This is literally true in nature and it was, says Hymer, a metaphor as well for the writer.

To switch from writing verse to reading and performing it – all may consider how wrong Macbeth is to allow himself to be tempted into murdering his king. Depending upon age or ability, this issue may be apprehended and discussed in one set of terms or another. Few write better than Nicola Grove (1998) about how those with sensory impairments or unusually high barriers to ordinary means of learning may still, nevertheless, engage with issues that are at the imaginative heart of stories plays and poems, even if this means that little conventional reading or writing is achieved. Everyone in the cultures that find significance in Shakespeare's play (and some evidence, e.g. films, suggests that those cultures are not solely European ones) may grasp, even if not each nuance of meaning of every word of the soliloquies in Act I, the fact that Macbeth is fully conscious of his intentions and of their dreadful consequences. They can feel how his mind is at war with itself, how compulsions are fighting against moral knowledge, desire is pitched against conscience and temptation against reason. If inclusion is to mean more than techniques whereby special attention is given to a distinct minority, then the experiences gained from studying *Macbeth* together are to do with recognising some common experience which we all register as we engage with the elements of the play.

Including the 'less able' in aspects of the central significance of *Macbeth* is something that English teachers do in almost any comprehensive school, but it does not come about without careful thought about approaches to the play and about the dispositions of those 13- and 14-year-olds who are to encounter it. That they wish for the dignity of being included in serious literary study was seen recently on the faces of some urban youngsters as they were attending to their student teacher talking about Macbeth and his self-doubt. The attentiveness of the low-stream class had less to do with a prior relationship of trust (though that existed) than with the fact that the carefully chosen register of the explanations about Shakespeare's verse led the pupils to realise that their teacher took them fully seriously. They trusted his integrity and him when he was talking about what they themselves probably knew a bit about – self-doubt. You could argue that this was an example of setting suitable learning challenges, maintaining high standards and making professional judgements about what were realistic and achievable targets for the whole group.

Activity 1

AWARENESS OF INCLUSION

(suggested time: 90 minutes)

Standard addressed: 3.1.1

Familiarise yourself with the section on Inclusion in your *National Curriculum* document (DfEE, 1999: 42–50). As you read, make notes on some three to five pupils, of very different aptitudes, skills and dispositions, that you are reminded of or brought to imagine by the NC's discussion of 'Overcoming potential barriers to learning'.

Activity 2

GIFTED AND TALENTED PUPILS

(suggested time: 30 minutes)

Standard addressed: 3.2.3

We have to attend to the idea of giftedness and talent in our pupils. What signs from his or her work and achievements would lead you to believe that a given pupil had a particular gift or talent for English?

Activity 3

POTENTIAL BARRIERS TO LEARNING: PHYSICAL DIFFICULTIES

(suggested time: 60 minutes on school experience)

A glance at almost any standard textbook on special needs will show that pupils may be put at a disadvantage in learning terms by a diverse set of factors. Some of those factors may be physical, though the NC reminds us that physical handicap does not necessarily entail any learning disability. The teacher confronted by a pupil who has significant sight problems, however, needs to ensure that, for example, scripts for that person come out in a large font size, or that the words on the OHT are projected to sufficient size or that an audio tape (and tape player with headphones) of the poem or story being studied is given to that pupil in addition to the script, or that a helper, in the form of an amanuensis, guides them to write what they say in response to questions. In these obvious instances the emphasis is on more than just a softening of potential difficulties. It is on the idea of variety of provision.

That idea of variety of form is a key one to those who are convinced that learners come with different aptitudes. The audio tape may well help some others in the class, by providing them more than once with an intelligent and expressive reading of the poem or story. The task of providing that reading may well have been allocated to another member of the class, one particular pupil who is gifted at reading aloud, with understanding and warmth. In the case of some pupils, then, the overcoming of a potential barrier is not a daunting task for the teacher, and it even allows the possibility of a pupil contributing to special provision.

Activity 4

PHYSICAL BARRIERS TO LEARNING

(suggested time: 60 minutes)

Standard addressed: 3.2.4

When next in your placement or attachment school, find out about the pupils who have a potential barrier to learning in terms of their physical differences from the majority. Are any of them significantly hearing-impaired, for example, and if so, what do teachers habitually do in order to overcome the problems of deafness, however partial?

POTENTIAL BARRIERS TO LEARNING: SPECIFIC LEARNING DIFFICULTIES

Dyslexia

In the case of other pupils, the special provision may need to relate not to a physical difficulty, but to a specific learning difficulty, or SpLD. One of the most commonly diagnosed SpLDs is dyslexia, a Greek-derived term for what, roughly, was once called 'word-blindness'. Dyslexia is not an altogether easy term, however, since, as Riddick, Wolfe and Lumsden (2002: 2–3) note 'different definitions of dyslexia are constructed by varying social groups for different purposes'. They also, in a well-accessible text on the subject, note that dyslexia has been seen as a useful concept by those who need to explain why it is that some otherwise normal and bright children have unusual difficulties in coping with aspects of literacy or even speech. It seems safe to say that there are no royal roads to the 'cure' for dyslexia in treatment or methodology terms. Some things, however, are obvious, such as that an English teacher who made much of the dyslexic pupil's inability to spell consistently when the words, as lexical items, made good sense, would be using an assessment opportunity counter-productively. The English teacher who saw where the patterns of error, if patterns there were, lay, and who positively went out of his or her way to explicate some common aspects of our spelling system (especially as they related to an individual's spelling habits) in a quiet classroom one lunchtime might be using the result of assessment to good effect. Regular teachers might not always have much time for this kind of individuation; a student teacher ought to make time for it.

Returning to the question of good methods of teaching the dyslexic pupil, note that Riddick et al. list what to do on page 103. That list, which is all about being constructive, encouraging and knowing how to utilise a wide range of teaching methods, is a list that could apply to many other pupils in one's class as well as the dyslexics, such as those who choose, or seem to, as much invisibility as possible. Note at this point how, in the section 'Planning a lesson' on two poems, 'First ice' and 'La belle dame sans merci', from Chapter 3, 'Planning and Progression', there is, by deliberate intent, a variety of modes of engagement with the texts and issues by the learners. Pupils will listen, read the 'First ice' poem, make notes in a grid, improvise conversations in pairs, watch one another perform improvised conversations, discuss possible titles and rehearse reading the Keats poem aloud, possibly paired since it is a poem for two voices. That lesson plan instances well what is intended here by, if not a wide range of teaching methods, then a wide range of kinds of approach to text and task by the learners.

Activity 5

NOTING WHAT'S INVOLVED
(suggested time: 45 minutes)

Note how, in the kinds of approaches to the poems given above, a whole range of abilities, skills and aptitudes is brought into play and developed through being rehearsed and approved. To start off, note how much in this planned lesson has to

Standard
addressed: **2.4** do with speech and performance, and with pupils working with one another. How many of the texts and tasks could be adapted for pupils with distinct physical learning needs? How many for those with a degree of difficulty in reading and writing?

Autism

Like dyslexia, this psychological condition is not a matter that the new teacher is at all likely to be left alone to diagnose or treat, but it is mentioned here as another example of a named condition that affects a predictable proportion of the population. Individuals who are autistic may well encounter perceptual and cognitive difficulties in English. Those suffering Asperger's Syndrome, a variety of autistic experience more likely to be found in boys than girls, may lack imagination and flexibility in their thought, in their ability to communicate with ease and in their social awareness. Their thought-processes are logical, ritualistic and repetitive, and so they may use language in a way that looks oddly pedantic, or which lacks creative flair or metaphorical characteristics. However, as anyone may observe in Stephen Poliakoff's TV play *The Lost Prince*, those displaying a tendency towards autistic behaviour may have the ability to repeat word-perfectly what they've heard someone say, and not immediately either, so it appears that some elements of language are highly significant for such people. Those with Asperger's Syndrome may have good use of grammar, a large and sophisticated vocabulary and good use of language used concretely.

It is relatively easy to list those aspects of a particular syndrome that have been observed, but, of course, not all those displaying some of these characteristics in school English could be said to qualify for the syndrome, and what matters to the average English teacher is how best to overcome the difficulties that beset those with Asperger's Syndrome. The fullest possible use of ICT may help, since this may be structured in its use in such a way that pairs may co-operate at a single keyboard, or the 'threat' of having to communicate might seem to be offset by some immediate use of a machine. Such pupils may well be able to comprehend and respond to objective descriptive writing, or writing which involves lists (cull some of the great lists from fiction, from Dickens to John Updike via Auden). They may be helped in their writing by visual stimuli, or by being led to understand how particular kinds of writing are modelled by highlighting aspects of structure (e.g. key sentences) in an existing text, preferably together.

Activity 6

HELPING AN INDIVIDUAL
(suggested time: 45 minutes)

Standard
addressed: **2.4** Consider how you would support a pupil with Asperger's Syndrome who found it hard to use language creatively, but could memorise patterns of words to great effect.

POTENTIAL BARRIERS TO LEARNING: INVISIBILITY

Invisibility stands as a barrier to learning, as well as to self-esteem and future educational opportunities. These are some of the findings of James Pye's (1988) published research on a topic that may well need yet more research. There are a number of devices that a teacher may employ to prevent pupils sitting, lesson after lesson, on the fringes of the group, outside the main sightlines of the teacher, and outside the space that most pupils speak across when participating in a whole class discussion. If the teacher notes whom he or she has not heard from in a week, and deliberately goes out of his or her way to address some questions, by name, to those pupils at the start of the next week, then those pupils are able to show the rest that they exist and can talk as much sense as anyone else. We have seen student teachers in their host English departments put this approach into practice very effectively, prompted by a mentor. You do not have to be long-experienced in order to start achieving this significant form of inclusion.

If the teacher selects and reads aloud in a commendatory way certain scripts (even if anonymised) that pupils have written then both dyslexics and potential invisibles gain the reassurance of knowing that they can do well, and write in a way that their teacher can turn to good account in front of the whole group. This way the pupils feel secure within their learning environment and sufficiently motivated to draw on their own experiences and interests. Had pupils from both sub-groups been, by contrast, asked to read their own scripts aloud, they could well have ended up seemingly timid, or lost, and/or highly embarrassed. At other times pupils could be encouraged to read aloud, either from play scripts, novels or poems, or from their own work, if they are given the chance to work in a small and secure group, preferably made up of friends, actually rehearsing along with all the others in the class. In that way, within the general rehearsal sound in the room, they escape the dread of unrehearsed (and therefore probably unskilled) solo performance.

Note how the topic itself may have a positive effect: not just validating all pupils as much as each other, but validating varieties of cultural experience too. Using a range of resources can reflect the multicultural society in which we live and enable pupils to engage sensitively with key issues. For example in an English classroom pupils might be involved in: guided reading activities on refugee stories; a class discussion on the issue of arranged marriages in soap operas; an analysis of how disabled people are portrayed in certain (quoted-on-video) Hollywood films.

Activity 7

DIFFERENTIATING, INDIVIDUALISING, PREPARING TO ADAPT

(suggested time: 90 minutes)

Make sure that you are fully informed of the individual needs and experiences of pupils: this will include keeping up to date with Individual Education Plans (IEPs), previous targets, assessment documents and school bulletin information on pupils as well as liaising with parents, carers and outside agencies. In order to include everyone fairly, those who are least advantaged, apparently, need the English teacher to adapt material for them in ways already suggested. So too do others who are not under any specific 'disadvantage' label, but who just happen to be at either end of the normal ability range within the class. In order to adapt material most suitably so that the greatest support is offered where needed and the right kind of spur or challenge too, then do the following;

1   Prepare a list of questions for some that are subtly different from those provided for others, even if they tackle broadly similar issues on an identical text.
2   Adapt the text itself.
3   Require quite different kinds of response from different groups (e.g. straight written narratives from some, a series of narrative cartoon frames from others).
4   Extend the range of poems to be compared over and above the pair of poems that are the common starting point.

Standard addressed: 3.1.3

Those looking for an example, as a way of gaining initial reassurance, might do worse than consult the useful publication by the TTA, about the subject English, called *Supporting Assessment for the Award of QTS*. This booklet supports the use of a video recording of trainee English teacher, Juliet, at work. Its value under the 'inclusion' heading relates to Juliet's preparations for *Romeo and Juliet* with a Year 10 group. On page 45, under 'Differentiation', is noted the number of pupils with Special Educational Needs (SEN), the number that has English as an Additional Language (EAL) and the strategies which the teacher, Juliet, will employ to cope with those special needs. These will be

● Differentiated colour-coded versions of sequencing/quotations task for pupils with EAL: produced in collaboration with support teachers.
● The EAL support teacher to work with targeted pupils in groups; I will intervene in groups during other activities.

The point about the first bulleted stratagem is that all the pupils are intended to do the same thing – put quotes from the play in a temporal plot sequence – but that in order for all to be equally challenged, some have linguistically simpler quotations to work with than others. Juliet, having planned this, had then to prepare the different sets of quotes *in collaboration with the support teachers*. She had also to ensure that the copies were made on different colours of paper. To be effectively inclusive you may well have to prepare in fine detail like this as well as planning with knowledge of pupils in mind. To work well with the support teacher or teaching assistants available, you have to involve them, as Juliet does, at the planning stage as well as within the class itself. Presumably the support teacher advised expertly on which potential quotes her EAL pupils could work best upon.

Activity 8

COMPARING APPROACHES

(suggested time: 45 minutes)

Take Juliet's ideas about differentiation expressed above and the following, below, from the lesson plan from Planning and Progression (see p. 91), and compare the different ways in which each set of ideas intends an inclusive approach.

Standard addressed (however indirectly): 3.1.3

Worksheets provide focusing questions, structure and memory aids for less able pupils – only the more able pupils may tackle the harder questions.

More able pupils will be given opportunity to make notes independently on further poems while less able have lesson reinforcing essay writing expectations and planning.

Scenarios

1 A Year 9 pupil is returning to school late in the spring term after a period of extended absence due to a serious illness. You know that she has listened to a taped version of the Shakespeare play which your class has been preparing for SATs but she has been unable to complete any written work about it. How would you support her preparation for SATs in the remaining months?

2 The parent of a Year 7 pupil wants to meet with you to discuss his son's progress. He is concerned that the boy, who attained Level 6 in all his core subjects at primary school, is not being stretched sufficiently in his English lessons and is becoming 'switched off'. How would you prepare for this meeting?

3 A learning support assistant informs you that she is going to be working with your Year 8 mixed ability class in two of your four English lessons each week. She has been primarily assigned to work with a visually impaired pupil who has recently arrived at the school. How would you want to work with the LSA to ensure the pupil is fully included in all aspects of the lessons?

4 What strategies would you use to ensure that all members of your group of 30 GCSE students (19 boys and 11 girls) have equal access to school ICT facilities when completing their media coursework? You have managed to book the computer suite for three 55-minute lessons. Students can also book themselves in for 30 minutes during three lunchtimes and three afternoon sessions a week.

5 One of your new Year 7 pupils contributes extremely well to class discussion and small group work but she struggles to concentrate when writing her ideas down, often writing very little and making many spelling errors. How would you approach this issue? What kind of targets might you want to negotiate?

Inclusion and assessment

In the scope of thinking about inclusion in English it becomes clear that some interesting questions are raised in our minds by considering assessment, and, under that heading, what being 'good at English' means. Most of us would consider someone 'good at English' who consistently gave sharp answers to questions about the novel in hand even if those answers and affirmations came out in a tonally flat way caused by the speaker's deafness. This impression of skill in the subject would, naturally, be strengthened if that pupil were also a good writer about the novel. In respect of the deafness the teacher had written the questions on the board where he or she might otherwise have just spoken them aloud, but the pupil replies viva voce.

Would we consider someone equally good at English whose spoken words were just the same, though sounding very emphatic, funny even, and generally convincing, but who was also practically unable, for reasons elusive to one and all, to write down in any decent degree of coherence the same insights into the story that were given as spoken answers to questions?

When it comes to being 'good at English', is the second pupil in this little scenario less meriting than the first? With which of the two should the teacher, in the interests of fairness, spend the greater individual time?

Suppose a third point of comparison were with a pupil whose answers about the novel were full of insight, apparently, but often phrased in idiomatically very odd ways, and with some grammatical mistakes too, because English was a recently acquired second language. Where is this third pupil to go in the order of merit?

Issue for discussion

In very broad and general terms, how do English teachers, looking to provide a fully inclusive curriculum in their subject, use the processes of, and information gleaned from, assessment? How many of us would make, as the public examinations do, the ability to write the main means of judging skill gradations in English? If so, then what does that imply, in the interests of providing the greatest possible skill entitlement, about where the emphasis should fall in terms of work with those who need the greatest compensatory attention?

FURTHER READING

Bines, H. (2000) 'Inclusive standards? Developments in policy for special educational needs in England and Wales', *Oxford Review of Education*, 26(1): 21–33

Benton, P. and O'Brien T. (eds) (2000) *Special Needs and the Beginning Teacher*. London: Continuum

Daw, P. (1995) 'Differentiation and its meanings', *English and Media Magazine*, 32 (Summer): 11–15

DfES (2001) *Special Educational Needs Code of Practice*. London: Department for Education and Skills

Fleming, M. and Stevens, D. (1998) 'Teaching across the ability range', in *English Teaching in the Secondary School*. London: David Fulton

Frater, G. (1998) *Improving Boys' Literacy*. London: Basic Skills Agency – QCA guidance on planning work for pupils with learning difficulties and on meeting the requirements of gifted and talented pupils

REFERENCES

DfEE (1999) *The National Curriculum for England. English Key Stages 1–4.* London: DfEE and QCA

Frederickson, N. and Cline, T. (2002) *Special Educational Needs, Inclusion and Diversity: a Textbook.*Buckingham: Open University Press

Grove, N. (1998) *Literature for All.* London: David Fulton

Holbrook, D. (1964) *English for the Rejected.* Cambridge: Cambridge University Press

Hymer, B. with Michael, D. (2002) *Gifted and Talented Learners: Creating a Policy for Inclusion.* London: NACE/ David Fulton

Pye, J. (1988) *Invisible Children.* Oxford: Oxford University Press

Riddick, B., Wolfe, J. and Lumsden, D. (2002) *Dyslexia: A Practical Guide for Teachers and Parents.* London: David Fulton

TTA (2000) *Supporting Assessment for the Award* of QTS. London: TTA

WEBSITES

This is not an exhaustive list. Most of the pages listed below have links to other sites. There are a great number of American sites on this subject and you should be aware that legislation issues connected with inclusion may differ from those found in the UK.

http://inclusion.ngfl.gov.uk – Probably the most useful site for you to access as it includes an excellent resource search as well as access to documentation, discussion groups, helpline, etc. and is updated regularly.

http://inclusion.uwe.ac.uk – Some useful links to other sites

www.standards.dfes.gov.uk – Includes search facility for documents and statistics on inclusion

http://www.dfes.gov.uk/sen/documents/SEN Code of Practice.pdf

INTRODUCTION

Cats have clawses at the ends of their pawses,
and sentences have pauses at the end of their clauses.

Language lies at the heart of our identities, our cultures, and now more than ever is a focus in English lessons. Within our increasingly heterogenous, multilingual society what used to pass as 'Standard' and even acceptable as language use is being challenged from the streets and through the media. Newsreaders read with a variety of accents and no one comments in the papers; dialects and slang used by different groups are scooped up and celebrated nationwide – 'loadsamoney', 'innit?' 'that's pukka food'. Language is slippery. Any attempt to describe it will inevitably fossilise that particular language use – and yet some standard description, or yardstick of 'best use' or even 'most interesting, imaginative and varied use' in its widest term can illuminate how language works, and encourage a wider, exploratory study.

The current model of language seen in the National Literacy Strategy organises the study of language into the three levels of word, sentence and text. Such close examination of word and sentence structure prior to 2001 was relatively new to English teachers who were better versed in the text level approach such as teaching the class novel, or a poet's work. As such the NLS has challenged practising English teachers and those in training to revise and update their linguistic knowledge and terminology to be in a position to explain the function and use of, for example, main and subordinate clauses to pupils. Much of this is already implicitly known; but teachers have had to make this knowledge explicit firstly to themselves and then to their pupils. The chapters in this section make such knowledge explicit, and place the NLS in its historical context in order to enable comparisons with earlier models or descriptions of the English language.

The National Curriculum requires that pupils are taught about the importance of 'Standard English', and to use it in their informal and formal speech. The characteristics of non-Standard English in the National Curriculum are those which are 'widely stigmatised' and which amount to, according to Katherine Perera: 'a rather small set of frequently occurring features which are recognizably non-standard and serve as social shibboleths' (Brindley, 1994: 86).

Those whose home dialect contains such 'social shibboleths' may nevertheless be skilled code-switchers, speaking and writing in grammatically accurate English as the context requires. It is the job of the English teacher to make these contexts explicit. The context in which a text or word is read, viewed or listened to defines the choice, meaning and even pronunciation of a word. Words can be abstracted from their context but, like a fish out of water, they need to be put back into their right context for pupils to understand their use in any real sense.

REFERENCE

Brindley, S. (ed.) (1994) *Teaching English in the Secondary School*. London: Routledge

$$chapter\ 7$$

SPEAKING AND LISTENING

By the end of this chapter you will have gained an understanding of the importance of speaking and listening in the English classroom, and the ways in which constructive, purposeful talk can be planned for, encouraged, and monitored. It is the social, collaborative nature of talk, however, that is the primary focus in this chapter, facilitating learning through talk, and learning about the nature of talk and language – a distinct aspect of the English curriculum.

RATIONALE

Talk in the classroom is now firmly established across the curriculum as the means by which children learn to think, to get to grips with the topic in question, and to use group discussion to iron out problems and make the topic their own. There is no learning without speaking and listening.

Cognitive development occurs as small children internalise their speech and use their words as tools for thinking. This is why a running commentary of talk often accompanies their actions. The Russian psycholinguist Vygotsky theorised that:

> *inner speech [i.e. thought] develops through a slow accumulation*
> *of functional and structural changes . . . it branches off from the*
> *child's external speech [i.e. social speech] simultaneously with*
> *the differentiation of the social and the egocentric functions of*
> *speech, and finally that the speech structures mastered by the*
> *child become the basic structures of his thinking.*

> *. . . Thought development is determined by language, i.e., by the linguistic tools of thought and by the socio-cultural experience of the child. Essentially, the development of logic in the child, as Piaget's studies have shown, is a direct function of his socialized speech. The child's intellectual growth is contingent on his mastering the social means of thought, that is language. (Vygotsk, 1986: 94–5)*

Thus the social aspect of learning in schools has enormous implications for children's cognitive development, for the sharing of the culture; dialogue in the classroom becomes 'a device that permits the taking for granted what is known and shared between speaker and listener and going beyond it to what is a comment on what is shared and known' (Brunner, 1988: pp. 94–5).

The transition from home to school can extend language use by giving children access to a broader range of social contexts and other children (and adults), and to the guidance of professionals who know how and when to intervene in their learning. Any text is produced from a particular social context for the purposes of communication.

Texts, whether written, verbal, visual, graphical or computer-generated, can be shared orally as a 'social literacy event' (Brice Heath, 1983) before being acted upon by the individual through a written response. Talk allows pupils to incorporate new concepts by relating already learned concepts and their own experience to the new concept just learned – through the medium of talk. What is important for you as a student teacher is the notion of the teacher (or a more capable peer) 'scaffolding' the learning to enable children to develop their oral language themselves. This includes all the languages that form the linguistic repertoire of the pupil, not just English. The multilingual classroom will recognise the diversity of languages spoken within the class and the benefits of drawing on the differences and similarities between several linguistic systems – literally 'the shared culture' of the classroom.

LINKS WITH THE NATIONAL CURRICULUM AND THE KS3 NATIONAL STRATEGY

The present National Curriculum (DfEE/QCA, 1999) makes greater demands on the oral skills of pupils, seeing talk as both necessary for personal growth, and as a way of communicating in more adult fashion with the world around them –'for public and formal purposes'. Pupils are also expected to be able to listen critically, to analyse language use, and to evaluate their own and others' contributions. There are several sub-sections giving firmer direction to teachers on what and how to teach speaking and listening: 'Speaking', 'Listening', 'Group discussion and interaction', 'Drama', 'Standard English' and 'Language variation'. The predominant mode is however the move towards an adult way of using language for more formal, social occasions, almost a vocational, work-related fashion:

> *En1 Speaking and Listening knowledge, skills and understanding (DfEE/QCA, 1999, p. 31)*
>
> *Speaking*
> *1   . . . pupils should be taught to:*

> a) structure their talk clearly, using markers so that their listeners can follow the line of thought
>
> c) use gesture, tone, pace and rhetorical devices for emphasis
>
> f) use spoken Standard English fluently in different contexts
>
> Listening
>
> 2 To listen, understand and respond critically to others, pupils should be taught to:
>
> d) distinguish tone, undertone, implications and other signs of a speaker's intentions
>
> e) recognise when a speaker is being ambiguous, or deliberately vague . . .

Put these two together and you come up with the skills a politician needs in order to make, and to listen to, speeches in the House of Commons! Under the new section, 'Group discussion and interaction', the emphasis is on teaching and encouraging pupils to work together constructively as a group, reflecting the new government emphasis on citizenship for all pupils. Under 'Breadth of study' (p. 33) a more exploratory use of language is encouraged under this format, with a creative use of language encouraged under 'Drama'. However, the requirement to use Standard English in both informal and formal situations can be seen as limiting pupils' creativity with language (p. 32, 'Standard English'). Under 'Language variation' 'the importance of Standard English as the language of public communication nationally and often internationally' tops a list otherwise describing the richness and eclecticism of the development of the English language. Despite these implied criticisms there is enough breadth here for English teachers to exploit speaking and listening in the English classroom to the full.

The KS3 Strategy 'Framework' places 'Speaking and listening' alongside 'Text level – reading and writing' in the four sub-sections of the NC. Within these the specific objectives across the three years fall into three main areas of using talk as 'a tool for clarifying ideas', pinpointing in speech and when listening what makes a talk effective, and working constructively in a group. The progression across the years is towards an increased use of Standard English, and reflection and evaluation in talk. The strategy's emphasis on active approaches to learning, especially the use of directed activities related to texts (DARTS) ensures that pupils use talk in an exploratory way in pairs or groups to problem-solve. This is exciting learning, raising the status of speaking and listening considerably. We should perhaps be thankful that En1 is assessed only by teacher assessment and not by a NC test, thus allowing full curriculum time to achieve the objectives in a contextualised manner.

Activity 1

WHAT IS 'GOOD ORAL ENGLISH TEACHING?'

(suggested time: 1 hour)

Fleming and Stevens (1998:) quote Harrison's (1994:135) summary of 'the nature of good oral English teaching' as a possible model to consider:

Learners need confidence and expertise in talk . . . so that they can

- listen to, convey and share ideas and feelings;
- listen to, convey and share information;
- understand, convey and share the 'story' (their own and others');
- listen to, present, defend and interrogate points of view;
- consider questions, raise questions, work towards answers;
- understand accounts of process, be able to describe and evaluate processes;
- be sensitive (as listener and as speaker) to appropriate tone and rhythms of voice – for example, sometimes reflective and exploratory, at other times assertive and persuasive;
- be aware (as listener and as speaker) of the need for clear expression;
- know when to be tolerant, when to support, and when to challenge in talk with others;
- be confident in providing a personal presence in talking, without letting self-consciousness intrude on what you want to say – and accept the personal presence of others, while respecting what they have to say (rather than how they say it).

TASK

Re-read the Programme of Study for Speaking and Listening for English KS3 and 4 (En1) pp. 31–3.

Standards addressed: 2.1c & d

1 In what way does this dovetail with the National Curriculum Programmes of Study, and in what way does this depart from them?
2 At this early stage, can you state your own developing view of what should constitute 'good oral English teaching'?

Activity 2

YOUR OWN USE OF FORMAL AND INFORMAL LANGUAGE

(suggested time: 30 minutes)

You can encourage pupils to attain metalinguistic awareness by making their language use opaque and worthy of study.

Write a short description of your own oral language history.

1 When do you use informal language?
2 When are you most self-conscious, or most confident in more formal situations?
3 Can you analyse the conditions that help you perform the best in formal situations (interviews, discussions, presentations, speeches)?
4 How might this insight help you to support and assess your pupils in such conditions?

Informal language context	Type of language used	Formal language context	Type of language used
Home with parents	Informal, polite, warm, jokey	Job interview	Standard English, formal, deferential, complete sentences
With friends	Informal, use of slang and dialect, less authoritarian, even vaguer (use of tag questions and 'kind of . . .' sort of phrases)		

Standard addressed: 2.1

Activity 3   CLASSROOM OBSERVATIONS OF ORAL WORK

(suggested time: 3 hours)

What different contexts, types of language used and group activities can you observe in an English classroom? You need to conduct structured observations of at least three English lessons on speaking and listening taking place in the lesson.

TASK

Before the lesson – you should prepare by choosing an observation focus and drawing up an appropriate observation sheet for making notes on the use of language, drawing on the prompts here:

- Open and closed questions from the teacher (and pupils)
- Use of specialist language
- Use of social talk by pupils and off-task talk
- Use of talk by teacher to control/encourage/keep pupils focused
- Pattern of who talks to whom throughout lesson.

Try to discuss with the teacher what kind of observation opportunities a particular lesson is most likely to yield – e.g. a poetry lesson analysing different poems in groups and then performing it to the class will give an opportunity to observe close reading and discussion skills and exploratory, hypothetical talk for a specific purpose (trying to work out what the poem means), organisational talk to work out how to present the poem, and performance skills.

After the lesson – consider, in a brief commentary on the lesson, the matters suggested in the prompt questions below:

(a) How was the oral work linked to other activities in this lesson?
(b) What learning was taking place while talk was going on?
(c) What did the teacher do to make effective oral work possible?
(d) How much control of the talk that took place did the pupils have?
(e) For what percentage of the time did the teacher talk in comparison to the pupils?

Standards addressed: 3.3.1, 3.3.3

Activity 4   STRUCTURING TALK IN THE CLASS

(suggested time: 30 minutes)

Using your observation notes from Activity 3, and possibly your own language history notes, fill out the table below to distil further the factors contributing to effective oral work. The following two examples, from Davison and Dowson (1998: 78), are given to start you off.

Factors contributing to effective, purposeful talk	Factors inhibiting effective, purposeful talk
Clear instructions from teacher so that talk is purposeful and prioritized	Uncertainty and confusion as to the point of using talk so any talk revolves around what is supposed to be done
Planned grouping of pupils so that all feel happy and confident	Dominant member of a group represses quieter members

Standard addressed:
3.3.7

Activity 5   CLASS MANAGEMENT OF WHOLE CLASS DISCUSSION

(suggested time: 1 hour)

If we want our pupils to use talk for a purpose, often in whole class discussion, and at times in pairs or groups, what then is the role of the teacher? Here are some factors to consider in terms of whole class discussion:

- Ground rules – a way of making explicit the conditions which will facilitate effective talk, e.g. method for turn-taking (does it have to be 'hands up'?); listening expectations/sanctions for disruption
- Encouragement and support
- Clear notion of chairperson's role
- Agenda/time limits/target for conclusion/method of concluding
- Classroom organisation – different seating arrangements affect the focus of the talk: e.g. open circle, double horseshoe, 'open' groups, boardroom layout
- Building up to whole class discussion, e.g. use pair and group-work methods shaping whole class discussion, e.g. use agreed agenda
- Use personal experience, examples at the start
- Progress by seeking out explanation/generalisation
- Conclude by reaching overview/consensus/principles.

The teacher's role in whole class discussion

- Preparation: developing materials, build-up activities/ice-breaking
- Introduction: providing a context
- Stage management: working out groupings, sequence of activities, seating plan
- Orchestration: facilitating contributions
- Valuation of responses: e.g. through brief supportive comments
- Development of security: e.g. through 'diplomatic deafness' to blunders
- Extension: timing of introduction of key questions
- Toleration of silence: allowing opportunities for thought
- Clarification: especially, enabling pupils to do this by asking questions
- Encouragement of personal response: using questions which trigger memories/ examples
- Encouragement of reflection: providing 'time outs' for note making/consolidation
- Introduction of controversy: adding further materials/alternative viewpoints
- Management of change: timing move to generalisation/conceptualisation
- Management of contributions: e.g. keeping hold of interrupted contributions
- Summation/generalisation: e.g. consider appointing pupil 'observers'
- Participation: encouraging certain kinds of contribution by offering them/ democratising the discussion by entering at same level as pupils.

Managing whole class discussion is possibly one of the hardest skills a teacher has to acquire. What are some of the inevitable problems, and solutions?

- Teacher domination: detailed preparation by pupils/pupil chairperson/give pupils 'authority roles', e.g. leader of the council
- Pupil domination: detailed preparation and appointment of spokespersons/ confident pupils as observers
- Pupils not speaking: plan prepared contributions/all contributions take a form which involves developing ideas/support the most tentative offerings
- Conflict: be prepared to intervene when issues are personalised/define sanctions in advance/make the problem explicit to the class/allow discussion of issues to become enlivened while this is productive, then change direction
- Splintering discussion: allow 'time out'
- Loss of direction: inject new material/offer interim summing up/time for individual writing reflection/define new agenda on board or OHP
- Pupils not valuing discussion: create self-assessment/reflection programme/provide follow-up activity for issues to be pursued – see that the results of the talk can be seen to have helped them learn something
- Superficiality: usually due to inadequate preparation time/opportunity/ unclear task
- Lack of opportunity: clear mechanism for offering turns (e.g. 1, 2, 3, 4, 5/use of a 'your turn to talk' symbol such as a 'conch')

TASK

Drawing on the prompts above, plan in detail how you would organise a known class (where possible) to get ready for a whole class discussion on a subject of your choice. Write out in full the instructions you will give the class, including use of the board for bullet points or to confirm your instructions. Include any pre-planned questions to support your teaching and class management.

Activity 6   CLASS MANAGEMENT OF GROUP WORK

(suggested time: 1 hour)

Similarly, group work has to be carefully planned in advance, and constantly managed and monitored throughout the lessons. Before the lessons it is useful to consider the:

- purpose within the overall course/scheme/programme
- intended outcome.
- number in class = number of groups (five is the most effective).
- marshalling of resources – organise space (if possible); enough chairs? (six discrete areas in six groups).

Managing the lesson: making the groups

Who sits with whom? Do you decide the make-up of each group? According to friendship, ability, gender, mixed ability, interest groups (those interested in writing a football article on one table, those interested in writing a feature article on the environment on another), pupils learning EAL mixed with supportive native speakers, or with some pupils speaking the same mother tongue? Will best friends always make good reflective speakers? How do you insist that friends are parted and not-so-good friends work collaboratively together? What about the pupil no one wants to work with?

Teacher input

Think about where you stand in the class: you need to be seen as well as heard, and you also need to be able to maintain eye contact with all for control and engagement.

You may want to read out from material, or speak out to all (good for achieving a quiet focus). When distributing handouts, you may want to give one per group with a spokesperson or reader to read it out, or one to each pupil. Which method will increase the learning, and the shared talking? How can you be sure that each pupil has understood what the joint task is? By asking a pupil to repeat your instructions back to the whole class?

Set task

The timing of any speaking and listening lesson is vital: give definite times for small group work – 'OK, you have 10 minutes to unjumble these poems and put them in the right sequence.' 'Right, you have two minutes left.' Getting feedback from all tables at every lesson may not be necessary – pupils can be trained to give back short sharp purposeful feedback if that is appropriate. You can stop the class when appropriate to clarify or explain a point – or to give an example from a table. Choose your moment, or you will stop the flow of talk. Let the groups get into the swing of the task, and the talk.

Jenny des Fountain reminds us (in Brindley, 1994: 59) that:

> Whenever adults work together in small groups, they are aware of the need to take time out from the talk, which may involve a sidetrack into social talk or into silence. Often this actually enhances our ability to return to the task after some time to think – or to find another way into thinking about the problem at hand.

Discerning between disruptive off-task talk, and the kind of 'time out' talk described above may be crucial in creating a positive, relaxed atmosphere where pupils in your class feel able to speak freely, and without censure.

TASK

Standards addressed:
3.3.3, 3.3.7

The above discussion points are for you as the teacher. Now devise a list of helpful Dos and Don'ts for your pupils to read and discuss prior to embarking on group work. What rationale would you give them for doing 'talk in the class' at the outset?

Activity 7   STRATEGIES FOR SUSTAINING TALK

(suggested time: 40 minutes)

Fleming and Stevens (1998: 8–87) list some excellent strategies and ideas for using talk in the classroom in an energetic and enjoyable fashion. These include jigsaw techniques, the fruit bowl method, pair combinations, rainbow groups, envoy technique, goldfish-bowl method, buzz-session, Chinese whispers, snowballing, eavesdropping, storytelling, Just a Minute. Many of these strategies have become well known through the NLS.

TASK

Standard addressed:
3.3.3

Imagine you want to introduce four simple poems on a theme at Key Stage 3. Plan a short (15 minute) activity for a lesson using one of these speaking and listening class management techniques above, or discussed in earlier activities.

1 What do you want the pupils to learn?
2 What are the underlying pedagogical reasons for this strategy?

Activity 8   LEARNING THROUGH TALK, AND ABOUT TALK

(suggested time: 30 minutes)

Teachers can encourage pupils to reflect metalinguistically about their talk, and the roles of language. Pupils need to feel in control of what they say, and to have some understanding of what is being assessed in Speaking and Listening, if and when it is. Speaking and listening can suddenly become an overtly self-conscious activity if pupils are assessed continually. However, the use of such strategies as talk-diaries, pupil–teacher conferences on speech performances and peer evaluation of talk can create opportunities for pupils to reflect on their talk, thus making it opaque in the same way as we ask pupils to re-read their writing in order to improve it, and to become conscious of an active range of reading strategies (for example in guided reading) to improve their inference and deduction skills.

Standard addressed: **3.2.2**

1 What other strategies can we use (or have you seen) which encourage pupils to reflect upon their use of speaking and listening?
2 What, however, do you see as the possible dangers or restrictions of deploying these strategies in an oral English lesson?

Activity 9

SPOKEN AND WRITTEN ENGLISH

(suggested time: 1 hour)

Investigating the differences between spoken and written English is one of the first steps in getting pupils to look at spoken language opaquely. It also brings up opportunities to discuss the use of Standard and non-Standard English in an unthreatening, distanced way. The unpublished 'Language in the National Curriculum' laid out the differences between speech and writing succinctly: 'The speech situation is almost always a shared one, and the writing situation is usually an isolated one' (LINC, 1992: 254).

As a starting point, this is useful to share with pupils, but you can also discuss how this is increasingly not true with reference to the multi-authored texts on the Internet, and the use of email and texting – a form of writing more akin to speech, and which brings with it new forms of 'Standard English', i.e rules of dialogue and exchange. Language therefore reflects changes in society, and society's use of technology. The LINC (1992: 254–5) materials suggest that teachers list the differences between the situation of speakers and writers under these headings and using the following examples:

WHAT CAN SPEAKERS AND LISTENERS DO?

Speaker/listener	Writer/reader
Can make eye contact directly with addressee	Reader may be distant or unknown to writers
Can point to or refer to objects in the environment	Writers cannot assume a shared environment with reader
Can use all the resources of gesture, intonations, 'body language' and laughter to convey attitude and emotion	Writers have none of these resources at their disposal and therefore work much harder with the words on the page to convey these effects

WHAT CAN WRITERS AND READERS DO?

Writer/reader	Speaker/listener
Readers can choose their own pace, reading slowly or skimming quickly	Listeners are dependent upon the pace of the speaker
Readers can skip forwards or go back and re-read something	Listeners can ask a speaker to repeat something but cannot 'hold on to' the flow of words and later re-examine them, unless the conversation is tape-recorded
Writers can disguise all false starts and errors of composition in a final 'fair copy'	Speakers will make false starts, hesitations and 'slips of the tongue' in the course of speech, since they are making it up as they go along

TASK

1   Add another two or three examples of the differences between speaking/listening and writing/reading to consolidate your understanding.

Standard addressed: 2.1

2   Devise a task for pupils to undertake which would illuminate their own understanding, and which they could use in their own speech and writing acts.

Activity 10

SPOKEN STANDARD ENGLISH, ACCENT AND DIALECT

(suggested time: 1 hour)

Standard spoken English

For speaking and listening, En1, the 'Standard English' heading, has one statement; 'Pupils should be taught to use the vocabulary, structures and grammar of spoken standard English fluently and accurately in informal and formal situations.' The onus is upon the teacher to discover ways of having pupils employ standard forms of speech willingly enough – whether informal or formal. For example the usage 'we was' would have to be replaced by 'we were', but the teacher who corrected the pupil every time he or she said 'we was' might well stand in danger of sounding like one who was imposing some other group's social preferences.

It might be an easy pit to fall into to extend instruction in grammar to matters of accent. Good teaching of standard forms should be careful to avoid confusing accent with vocabulary and grammar, which are dialect matters. It is one thing to tell a pupil that 'he were' should be, in the dialect Standard English, 'he was' but quite another to suggest that spoken Standard English requires received pronunciation (RP) and thus a full, unambiguous aspiration of the 'h' of 'he'.

The NC in English is careful to avoid prescription about the pronunciation of words. Sensitive teaching of standard forms necessitates not suggesting to a class that the preferred speech forms of, say, their parents, are in some way lacking in linguistic adequacy. It should not be the speaker who is corrected but the speech powers that are extended. The teacher needs, by some means, to explain to the class that standard forms have no intrinsic linguistic merits. Equally, non-standard forms are nearly always perfectly adequate to convey meaning; no-one suffers any doubts about the meaning of 'he were'.

Despite that, however, English teachers need to agree, in the interests of putting the NC into effect, that intellectual, social and career opportunities may be missed if pupils are not able to adopt the dialect Standard English. This has widespread use as an accepted currency, and so in the interests of equality of opportunity we should try to ensure that all pupils can use it if they want to. Teaching the sophisticated linkages between accent, dialect, form and context is no easy task. It will take time and careful thought about approach and method in order to bring about in pupils informed and critical awareness of variation in language.

Bain in Davison and Dowson (1998) has a series of wise methods to use for instilling knowledge of the standard form. He advocates asking the pupils 'to find as many differences as they can between their local dialect and Standard English' (p. 157) as well as focusing on writing, in which mode standard forms are most likely to be found. The activities advocated by Bain usually allow the teacher to see that the class does in fact have full awareness of standard forms, even if large numbers do not use them. If the cumulative outcome of such teaching is the development of an enhanced power to describe differences between forms and genres of use (the class simply note what the differences are between standard and non-standard forms and where they lie), then the teacher will be seen to be promoting choice based on knowledge rather than merely advocating preferred usages.

Standard English is not the straightforward concept that it might at first appear. The NC has much else to say about speech and language under the next heading, 'Language variation', but it begins with a stress on the importance of Standard English and ends with the indisputable idea of language change over time. That in itself might suggest that Standard English is not fixed and is subject to the forces that drive change in any language.

Accent

Everyone speaks with an accent, and some accents, depending on social context, carry prestige, but that does not necessarily make them any clearer or more audible than other accents which some label 'lazy'. It is perfectly normal for someone to speak in the dialect of Standard English with a local accent, especially informal standard, but less likely that someone would speak a local dialect in received pronunciation. Most pupils can make fine gradations of how emphatic they should be in their use of the local accent. Accents may differ greatly in the same individual between the playground and the piano lesson.

All kinds of approaches to teaching about accent have validity in terms of:

- informing the class about the nature of some of the more prominent urban or rural accents of the UK;

- having them understand that there is no one right pronunciation of a word even though there is one right spelling of it; and
- sharpening their awareness of which sounds in particular characterise an accent, and how they can invoke the concept of vowels and consonants in describing accent features.

TASK

1   Read the 'Note on Standard English' on p. 32 of the NC (DfEE, 1999). Consider this in the light of Sections 5 and 6 of En1 in the NC and in light of the discussion above. What tensions do you note?
2   What is your own rationale for teaching spoken Standard English in the English classroom?
3   Is it possible to teach spoken Standard English in the classroom without making judgements about pupils' own speech patterns and origins?

Standard addressed: 2.1   Write a a 400-word reflection on the three points above and place it in your English portfolio.

Activity 11

PLANNING A WHOLE LESSON
(suggested time: 2 hours)

Standard addressed: 3.3.3

Plan one lesson of an hour for a KS3 mixed ability class where there is a combination of whole class discussion and small group work, drawing on any of the strategies discussed in the activities in this chapter. Use the lesson plan format on the Paul Chapman Publishing website **www.paulchapmanpublishing.co.uk/resources/completeguide.htm.** You may want to continue the lesson plan started in Activity 7. Provide a commentary outlining the underlying pedagogy for the choice and sequence of tasks.

CONTINUOUS THREADS

1 Professional values and practice

Look out for differences in the ways girls and boys approach collaborative tasks, talk in single and mixed sex groups, talk in whole class discussions, support and contribute to each others' talk. How will you assess what can be girls' more supportive listening, or willingness to sustain and develop each others' ideas? Do you give too much credit for boys' louder, leadership roles? How do you encourage girls and boys to adopt one anothers' tactics?

Bilingual pupils

How can you ensure that bilingual and multilingual students are fully integrated in your classroom, and that their knowledge of languages is recognised, valued and made use of? Are home languages openly discussed and seen in a positive light in the classroom by all students?

3.1 Planning, expectations and targets

You need to plan specifically for progression in speaking and listening. This involves the cycle of planning, action, monitoring, assessing, recording, evaluating and summarising, which then feeds back into the planning. This needs to be done at class level (macro level), and for each individual pupil (at micro level). The NLS key objectives for each year are useful in setting out a line of progression for speaking and listening.

3.2 Monitoring and assessment

'Assessment should be a continuous process which reinforces teaching and learning.' (*English for Ages 5–16*, DES, 1989: paragraph 14.12). Pupils are assessed in En1 formally at the end of Year 9 as Teacher Assessment, and at GCSE with three focused oral activities:

- extended individual contribution
- group work and interaction
- drama-focused activity.

You will need to devise some kind of focused assessment and recording which is not too burdensome, and which allows you to make regular assessments of individual pupils to build up a whole picture of a pupil over time. Remember that much of your assessment and monitoring is happening all the time 'in your head' as you go around listening to pupils. This is the most important form of assessment – but for reporting purposes, and to track progression, you need to write something down.

Possibilities include:

1   Keeping a notebook with you as you go round the class, jotting points down, and transferring these into a ringbinder with a page or half a page per pupil:

Date	Social and learning context	Comment
September	Reading class reader aloud to whole group	Natalie reads fluently, with some ease, but little variation or expression. Needs to be encouraged to develop her voice and gain confidence
November	Group improvised drama – understanding the interplay between characters in *Romeo and Juliet*	Improvised well, with great confidence and verve, using gesture and Lady Capulet's style of language beautifully
February	Paired work – telling a story to a partner	A lively, articulate speaker, giving a well-organised account of an incident and showing an awareness of the difference in the type of language used according to purpose

Example 1

Name: **Linda Cross**	Class: **9U**	**Speaking and Listening**		
Speaking describing, narrating, explaining, arguing, persuading, entertaining, evaluation of own speech	Listening Recall main features, recognise tone, ambiguity, ask questions and give comments	Group discussion and interaction, make different types of contributions, modify own views, summarise, helping group to reach conclusions	Drama improvisation, role play, devising, scripting performances, dramatic techniques, convey action, characters, atmosphere, appreciate dramatic effect, evaluate performances	Language variation, variety of word choice, sentence structure, use of Standard English
3/1 described Xmas holiday in Canada to class,used photos effectively	*4/2 listened carefully to outside speaker, took notes, asked pertinent questions*	*19/4 took role of chair in group discussion on uniforms, encouraged others to speak, drew group together*		

Example 2

2   Taking in pupils' talk-diaries every so often, and responding to them in writing.

3   Asking to look at your department's record keeping to see examples of record keeping in practice.

4   At some point you will be asked to make summative judgements on pupils' oral skills according to the National Curriculum level descriptions. You need to review all your records for each pupil and match them with a 'best fit' exercise against the levels. There is a useful video entitled *Exemplification of Standards, English, Speaking and Listening* produced by QCA on an annual basis; this has an accompanying booklet with details of the oral assignments given to the pupils shown on the video, and with the final grading, and its justification. You should view this with your department or with other students to discuss the pupils' performances. Just focus on three students – six are actually profiled.

3.3.4 Differentiation

Speaking and listening is a real leveller, allowing those who may be less able in writing to shine and gain confidence and self-esteem among their peers. Your skill as a teacher lies in cannily giving important roles to such pupils – chair rather than scribe – and praising and encouraging them. Pupils with learning and/or literacy difficulties need to be given plenty of opportunities to show through talk what they know, understand and can do. Many activities will use some written resource: you will have to plan ahead to ensure that if you want mixed ability groups then you allocate a good reader to read it out to your group so that the less able reader has access to it and so can participate fully in the subsequent discussion. You will have to ensure that all pupils get a chance to show and to stretch their oral skills, so that someone who is talented at comic role play also has to present a formal speech to an unknown audience.

2.5 ICT

Much talk can take place around the planning for work on the computer, and around the monitor itself. Pairs are best actually operating at the screen, creating new types of social literacy practices where talk around the on-screen text feeds into the creation or transformation of texts. The new technologies of email and use of the Web blur the distinction between speech and writing, and are worthy of study by pupils. Video conferencing can offer opportunities for different communities of pupils to interact and discuss topics.

Scenarios

1 You have a mixed ability class of Year 9 who are energetic and can be noisy at times. You want to channel their noise into meaningful talk, with a quiet hum rather than a deafening noise. How do you go about getting first silence, and then that quiet hum?
2 There is one quiet boy in your class who never makes a contribution to class discussion and rarely says anything even in a small group. How can you encourage him to speak out?
3 One girl has a strong northern accent in your southern school. The rest of the class laugh every time she speaks out. She is getting infuriated and beginning to withdraw. What can you do before this happens to present her accent as simply another form of English?

FURTHER READING AND REFERENCES

Bain, E. and R.(1996) *The Grammar Book: Finding Patterns – Making Sense: Teachers' Guide.* Sheffield: NATE

Barnes, D., Britton, J. and Rosen, H. (1969) *Language, the Learner and the School. London*: Penguin

Brent Language Service (1999) *Enriching Literacy – Text, Talk and Tales in Today's Classroom, a Practical Handbook for Multilingual Schools.* Stoke-on-Trent: Trentham Books

Brice Heath, S. (1983) *Ways with Words: Language, Life and Work in Communities and Classrooms.* Cambridge: Cambridge University Press

Brindley, S. (ed.) (1994) *Teaching English in the Secondary School.* London Routledge

Bruner, J. (1988) 'Vygotsky: A historical and conceptual perspective', in N. Mercer (ed.) *Language and Literacy from an Educational Perspective: Volume 1 Language Studies.* Buckingham: Open University Press.

DfEE (1999) *The National Curriculum for England. English: Key Stages 1–4.* London: DfEE and QCA.

Fleming, N. and Stevens, D. (1998) *English Teaching in the Secondary School.* London: David Fulton

Davison, J. and Dowson, J. (1998) *Learning to Teach English in the Secondary School.* London: Routledge

DES (1989) *English for Ages 5–16* London: DES

Harrison, B. (1994) *The Literate Imagination.* London: David Fulton.

LINC (1992) *Language in the National Curriculum: Materials for Professional Development.* LINC, unpublished materials.

McWilliam, N. (1998) *What's in a Word? Vocabulary Development in Multilingual Classrooms*. Stoke-on-Trent: Trentham Books

NATE (1991) *Teaching, Talking and Learning in Key Stage 3*. Sheffield: NATE

NATE (1993) *Teaching, Talking and Learning in Key Stage 4*. Sheffield: NATE

These two booklets draw on the work of the National Oracy Project.

Vygotsky, Lev (1986)*Thought and Language,* trans. A. Kozulin, Cambridge, MA: MIT Press

Wells, G. (1987) *The Meaning Makers: Children Learning Language and Using Language to Learn* London: Hodder & Stoughton

Wilkinson, J. (1995) *Introducing Standard English*. Oxford: Oxford University Press

chapter 8

TEACHING LANGUAGE

I have never met a person who is not interested in language.
Steven Pinker

By the end of this chapter you will have gained an overview of the place of English language studies in the context of the secondary English curriculum and will have considered a variety of strategies for teaching knowledge about what kind of thing the English language is, including language variety and change, and, somewhat isolatedly perhaps, the punctuation of writing.

RATIONALE

Language is one of the most fascinating of native human abilities, and is the one thing at which we all become expert simply by growing up inside it, surrounded by other users of it. The work of Stephen Pinker (1994) clarifies how well infant learners of language adapt what they hear in such a way as to suggest that we are all, literally, born to understand and use grammar for our own ends. Katherine Perera (1987) argues that language is so intrinsically interesting that it ought to be studied by those who use it. The KS3 Strategy is based on the concept that unless you have some idea how to describe and explain the workings of sentences – and sentences are rule-bound activities – then you are unlikely to develop and improve your language use very well. Alternatively, one could also argue that language studies should concentrate on works of literature as their virtually sole content. These texts, on this view, are composed in the most original, inspired and memorable uses of language. To study language at all should involve studying it at its best.

Children grow up showing spontaneous delight in such things as puns and verbal jokes built around self-conscious ambiguities and semantic tricks. They use apparent descriptions of the kinds of language ('slang', 'posh') used by others or by social groups not their own, and acquire some terms descriptive of language which are technically entirely proper, such as the word 'word'. Given our utter reliance on language, our apparent proneness to reflect on it, in any variety, becomes something which English teachers might well extend, refine and inform.

Being able to analyse what is going on as we speak, read, listen or write is a key way of understanding one of the most fundamental shared items in the culture. It is hard to believe that such understanding will not have its effects upon choice of words and creation of meanings, spoken or written. Building up this kind of understanding in school pupils and students does not imply our teaching the sterile application of labels such as 'gerundive' or the enforcement of rules whose purpose, as for the 18th-century grammarians, is the distinction of a polite group from the barbarous horde. An example of this would be the prohibition, without discussion or exploration of its actual use, on the split infinitive. We can dare to boldly go where we wish. Using grammatical terminology can be a tool which crystallises or 'caps' the concept lying behind the word or phrase. Studying the very tools of thought – words – can only support cognitive development.

LINKS WITH THE NATIONAL CURRICULUM AND KS3 STRATEGY

The Kingman Report (DES, 1988) had been commissioned by the Education Minister Kenneth Baker as the means whereby some systematic teaching about the English language across the age span would begin. Kingman chaired a committee whose report concluded that pupils should be taught that language has a system, is rule-governed and can be the subject of explanation and description. Missing from the report was what Baker's Prime Minister, Mrs Thatcher, wanted to see – the return to some straightforward grammar teaching. The state, by 1989, had politicised what had been previously a debate between sections of the English-teaching community on the place and point of teaching about 'grammar'.

Post-Kingman, a national project was funded to instil in primary and secondary teachers the right kind of knowledge about language. This was the Language in the National Curriculum, or LINC Project. When its final report was presented in 1991 to the then Education Secretary, Tim Eggar, he refused to accept it or publish it because, nominally, it might have been used as teaching material and not as guidance for teachers. In fact, its lack of a prescriptive and simple approach to teaching about language led to the prevention of its publication. Its fault was to suggest that language should be explored in common by teachers and pupils, under the teacher's guidance.

There was no resolution to this failure of minds to meet, but by 1990 the first National Curriculum in English, the so-called Cox Report, had given us the concept of 'Knowledge about Language', which was introduced by Professor Cox guided by advice which he'd sought from his professorial colleague Katherine Perera. This became known as 'KAL', and English teachers developed this idea, partly informed by unofficially reprinted copies of the LINC report. Consequent NC revisions to the Cox version of the English curriculum tended to take a more directive line on language teaching than the KAL philosophy would have welcomed. The 2000 curriculum (DfEE, 1999) for secondary English directly names subjects that must be taught, Standard English and grammar among them.

The first of these is more likely to be spontaneously acquired if you come, as a pupil, from a certain class background than if you do not. The second, grammar, may need equal amounts of explanation regardless of the social class location of the learners if only because 'standard' speakers may view their own grammar as essentially the right one. Grammar, however, is much more than a means to validate the rightness of the habits of speakers of Standard English.

Reading

For En2, 'Reading', the only statement under the same heading as for En1, 'Language structure and variation', is this: 'Pupils should be taught to draw on their knowledge of grammar and language variation to develop their understanding of texts and how language works.' This could well prompt some analysis of the way in which skilful writers shape their sentences. Bringing to pupils' notice how writing is shaped has now become, under the literacy element within the KS3 Strategy, an essential means of improving writing standards. The Strategy material works from the position that what the pupil as reader may observe as skill with words can be imitated as a skill by the same pupil when writing. The KS3 Strategy merges, as English teachers always have, the NC's distinctions between reading and writing. What improves one may improve the other.

See the 'Sentence bank' (DfEE, 2001) material for use with classes in Years 7, 8 and 9 and the progress units too. Not all sentences have to begin with article, noun or pronoun and then proceed to the main verb (pre- or post-modified). When the KS3 Strategy material gives models of text such as this:

> Mad for in-line skate action? Read on friends, read on. Top fellas Bauer have organised four wicked week-ends around this country this summer. In Brighton, Blackpool and London there'll be a vert ramp and specially designed street course . . . (DfEE, 2001: 111)

then any English teacher might care to point out how clever this kind of writing is at achieving variety in sentence structure types. The verb in the first sentence is implied. The first sentence is a question, the second a command and the third a statement. Such texts could also give access to the joys of slang, so that someone, doubtless male, could explain what a 'vert ramp' is, exactly. Anyone teaching English in KS3 who felt that his or her pupils needed help in seeing the semantic difference between, for example, active and passive uses of the verb could be helped by the sentences 'The tentacles of a man-eating plant barred their way' and 'Their way was barred by the tentacles of a man-eating plant' (DfEE, 2001:159). The class could then explore the meanings of such differences.

Writing

In what the NC has to say about En3, 'Writing,' the statements relating to pupils' use of language are more pervasive and are there under more than one heading. Also, for the teachers, the writing section is the one where the knowledge content about language is at its most specific. 'Pupils should be taught the principles of sentence grammar and whole text cohesion and use this knowledge in their writing' (DfEE, 1999: item 7 of En3). There follow five subheadings about word classes, phrases and clauses, paragraph structures, whole text structures such as openings and conclusions, and 'the use of appropriate grammatical terminology to reflect on the meaning and clarity of sentences' (for example, nouns, verbs, adjectives, prepositions, conjunctions, articles). You must teach some grammatical terminology, the NC insists, but it does not have to be the kind listed as examples.

These statements appear to have been inserted into the National Curriculum before the KS3 literacy material was fully ready, but nevertheless in anticipation of its arrival. The *Framework for Teaching English: Years 7, 8 and 9* (hereafter *Framework*, DfEE, 2001) within the Strategy promotes the explicit teaching of the parts of speech, and it justifies their functional value, but with a vocabulary slightly adjusted from the entirely traditional one. What most used to call 'conjunctions' are now 'connectives', for example, and a wide set of them is demonstrated in the service of sentence and paragraph cohesion.

A careful reading of the *Framework* would tell the English teacher where knowledge about language could come into play, and where it tails off into a larger set of concerns such as those denoted by 'writing'. In order to write you need to know about grammar (in action, at any rate), spelling, punctuation, word meanings and stylistic conventions, but none of those may be the principal knowledge required. That could be characterised as intentional – knowing what you want to say, and to whom, and how to explain, persuade, advise. These things require language knowledge in order to be fulfilled, but the point of, for example, 'persuasion' is not the demonstration of linguistic skill.

NLS, the primary–secondary transition and phonological awareness

Any discussion of this curriculum area is bound to look for the effect of the National Literacy Strategy (NLS) on children entering secondary school. Children may well enter secondary education now having a clear idea about what a phoneme is, and might be a little surprised if their English teacher were unaware of the fact that 'services' and 'lessons' have an audible difference in their final consonantal sounds even though represented by the same letter in each case. English has a tendency to pull plurals towards the voiced form – partly, no doubt, so that the plural can be distinguished from the singular possessive with ease. 'Life' becomes 'lives' in the plural, doubling the chances of the voicing being heard, since it is present in the final two consonants of the plural, not just the final one. The sound 'Life's' can thus be saved for unambiguous denotation of the idea 'singular possessive'. Such knowledge – phonology – can be made fascinating, especially in linking a general growth in consciousness about language between the English and the modern foreign languages (MFL) departments in a school. Visits to a host school could uncover which areas of phonology MFL and English are commonly keen to develop. Listening properly to words also helps the pupils learn to spell, insists the progress unit on spelling.

Activity 1

MODELS OF THE ENGLISH LANGUAGE
(suggested time: 2 hours)

As a teacher of language you will find it useful to develop your own model or diagram of the English language. The Kingman Report quoted above (and in Chapter 1 above 'The National Curriculum') gives one such model, and the NLS another. The National Association for the Teaching of English critiqued the Kingman Report for not including language acquisition: the LINC Project was not prescriptive enough.

Standard addressed: 2.1

Devise your own model of the English language, drawing on the content of the NC as a starting point and using visual images (circles, arrows, interlocking squares) to show how the various elements might be linked up. Exchange your diagram with another student for comparison. You may want to return to your model to alter or modify it as you work through this chapter and your ITT programme.

Activity 2

GATHERING EXAMPLES OF LANGUAGE IN USE
(suggested time: 90 minutes)

Put together a folder containing examples of forms, styles, grammatical patterns, public uses which are virtuous, inappropriate or erroneous, uses which are simply typical of genres (e.g. headlines in the present tense) or anything at all which serves to illustrate what you want a class to think about. This can vary from a photographic collection of punctuation errors (a sandwich shop near the writer had the title 'Taste Bud's ' until a new sign corrected it), to a collection of sentence examples which a class can be given as the basis of exploration of variations in form.

Standards addressed: 2.1, 2.7, 3.1.3

Here an example would be: 'Is it possible that you could tell me when they will arrive?' Where in that question could you insert the word 'please' and have it register as a grammatically correct sentence? At what insertion points would it render the sentence totally ungrammatical? Quite apart from correctness and incorrectness, what differences of meaning arise between, 'Is it possible, please, that you could tell me when they will arrive?' and 'Is it possible that you could tell me when they will arrive, please?' Such an exercise of choice in placing a word is often instinctual or subconscious, but the point of examining possible changes to the word order and structure of simple sentences is to show that the rules do exist, even though we are not consciously aware of linguistic moves so much as prior intentions that issue in language.

Activity 3

COINING NEW WORD MEANINGS

(suggested time: 30 minutes)

Sift through a computer manual or magazine extracting all the words and phrases from the page that look to be either new words in recent times (e.g. modem) or recent new usages of old words (e.g. ports). Design a grid headed: (1) new words, (2) existing words given new meanings, (3) the dictionary definition.

Fill the grid's squares with selected words from an article or advertisement.

Standards addressed:
2.1, 3.1.3

This exercise is designed to show you how a class might take a text-based look at the question of neologisms and recently arrived new meanings, and is directly applicable to the NC demand for a study of language change.

Activity 4

HELPING THE LEARNER VIA KAL

(suggested time: 30 minutes)

TASK

Take the table below, reprinted from the *Framework* (p. 11). Annotate it with ideas of how knowledge about language could help the learner. For example, the informed teacher of writing would teach his or her class to tolerate spelling uncertainty during the first stage of composition sooner than lose the flow by stopping to consult a dictionary. That is for the revision and editorial stage.

Key Stage 3

English

Word level	Sentence level	Text level		
		Reading	Writing	Speaking and Listening
• Spelling	• Speaking			
• Spelling strategies	• Listening	• Research and study skills	• Plan, draft and present	• Sentence construction and punctuation
• Vocabulary	• Group discussion and interaction	• Reading for meaning	• Imagine, explore, entertain	• Paragraphing and cohesion
	• Drama	• Understanding the author's craft	• Inform, explain, describe	• Stylistic conventions
		• Study of literary texts	• Persuade, argue, advise	• Standard English and language variation
			• Analyse, review, comment	

Standards addressed:
2.1, 3.1.1

Activity 5

LANGUAGE STARTER ACTIVITIES
(suggested time: 30 minutes)

Starter activities, championed by the KS3 Strategy, are meant to last only 10 minutes or so, and lend themselves to language activities. A typical language exercise would, for example, set pairs to work out which of two passages, and why, was the transcript of some actual conversation, and which the written dialogue from a TV soap opera which aimed to sound conversationally 'natural'. Alternatively, pairs might be set to design together a good opening paragraph for the making of an argument after the class had looked at examples of good argumentative writing and at how sentences led on, one from another, in the development of that argument.

Standard addressed: 3.3.2

Using one of your initial notes from Activity 4, devise one starter which looks at language structure and variation, commenting briefly on the learning objectives and underlying pedagogy.

Activity 6

TRANSCRIBING LANGUAGE
(suggested time: 60 minutes – because of transcription)

TASK

Standards addressed: 2.1, 3.1.3

Make a tape recording of news broadcasts which capture differences of style in lexis (word choice), pronunciation, and speed and tone of delivery between different radio and television stations and channels. Transcribe some comparable items, so that the class has two kinds of evidence available for later analysis of the differences. Differences are more keenly observed if the content of the news story is the same.

Punctuation

That punctuation is graphical is not lost on those writers in school who enjoy fancy question marks and outlined commas. Punctuation is one of the graphical means whereby writing renders language comprehensible. In writing we leave spaces between words, but we do not necessarily leave silences between words in speech. Written sentences are not like spoken utterances in many other ways. Punctuation in writing helps the sentence retain its cohesion and helps the reader to spot quickly what is going on, who is saying what and to whom, etc. Thus is disambiguation achieved. Asking pupils to read their work out aloud is the most effective way of encouraging them to see where a comma or a full stop should be placed.

Let an older or brighter class see selected (very carefully selected) extracts of Molly Bloom's unpunctuated stream-of-consciousness in the final section of James Joyce's *Ulysses* and puzzle out where the thoughts – or rather the topics – begin and end. Behind all this is the purpose of showing how a set of marks helps readers to be clear about what is being said and how. Molly Bloom is not so much unclear as the vehicle through whom Joyce explores how, if speech differs from writing, thought differs from speech.

Use the idea of graphics to help the class understand the handwritten (or word-processed) conventions of punctuating dialogue. With younger writers, have them put speech in speech-bubbles, as in comics, then the same speech in 'exploded' bubbles which have become "   ", mere shreds. On a word-processor, different colours can be used for different speakers' speeches.

Activity 7

PUNCTUATION IN USE
(suggested time: 20 minutes – school based)

Standards addressed: ***2.1, 3.1.1, 3.1.3***

Take a page containing dialogue from any book currently enjoyed by the class – anything from *Harry Potter* to a Point Horror – and simply count how many different kinds of marks are in use on that page. Next count how many rules are in use and select three which you would like an eighth- or ninth-year class to grasp securely and by deducing those rules from the same script.

CONTINUOUS THREADS

1 Professional values and practice

What matters for the beginner English teacher is overcoming fear of 'grammar' or knowledge about language. Look at Chapter 24 below, on teaching English Language at A Level, to discover how to acquire some of the necessary knowledge should any reader feel they lack it. Respect for the communicative strength of some varieties of English, such as might be encountered in ordinary school classrooms, is an essential professional matter, as is understanding the position of EAL speakers in the context of mother-tongue teaching. Having high expectations of pupils means, in regard to language, insisting that pupils can learn to reflect properly on the language that they use and hear, and can do so by willingness to think about the categories supplied for analysis.

3.1 Planning, expectations and targets

Good examples of lesson plans are to be found in such sources as *The Languages Book* (English and Media Centre, 1991) and the Bains' *Grammar Book* (1996). Ideas for approaches and content suitable by level can be gained from reading the KS3 Strategy's publications for Year 7 pupils – *The Sentence level bank*, *Spelling bank* and *Speaking and listening bank*, for example.

3.2 Monitoring and assessment

Good English teachers are conscientious in the way in which they read the written assignments they set their pupils, seeing where the problems lie for writers and then giving clear instruction on the solution to those problems. Some writers may fail in some sentences to achieve verb–noun correspondence, 'the boys was playing football when . . .' being a crude example of the failure to use plural verb form with plural noun. If something like this were encountered, then the teacher would be better to leave the sentence as it stands, put a red line through nothing, and note instead the whole offending clause or phrase and write it, entirely anonymously, on the board, telling the class that it can be improved, but can anyone see how? The chances are that class discussion would reveal the two possibilities for correcting the original error. If the teacher wishes to talk about noun–verb correspondences, so much the better.

With some scripts, however, the problems are much deeper, much more rooted in failure to achieve the textual cohesion which the NC is concerned about. For example, in the middle of a breathless car-chase narrative 'he' might switch to 'I' at a moment's notice, the narrative excitement having overtaken the writer to the extent of his (probably) quitting the third person narrator's role and descending into the tale by becoming the hero of it. Such writers tend to be the very people who are least able to understand 'first person' and 'third person' explanations. The writers who have deeper problems of correctness in basic sentence formation and textual cohesion can best be helped by, for example, telling their tales into tapes and then transcribing them with the help of a teaching assistant if one is available. Better still to set such pupils to work at word processors from time to time so that rewriting the 'I's to 'he's' can be done thoughtfully but without the sweat of rewriting all the other originally correct words too.

In the end, though, we must note that the NC's insistence on bringing knowledge of some grammar into play when it comes to correcting sentences and whole texts, although useful in practical terms, subscribes to the view that grammar is linked to deficiency or error. Ultimately, as Ron Carter (1990) reminds us, grammar is interesting as a way of enabling us to see how clever we can all be in creating different kinds of sentences with various correct combinations of clauses, main and subordinate, all of which convey subtly different kinds of meaning. That is what is worth exploring with writers as their written work is returned, not just their mistakes.

3.3.4 Differentiation

Language study works to bring the class together in its differences. It is a good place, the language class, to explore differences about any number of things, from idiolectal features to what the word 'tea' denotes in different families. Some will undoubtedly be quicker than others to grasp, say, the classical notion of the parts of speech, but there is no rule to say that the most talented academically are necessarily possessed of the strongest instincts for telling stories, for example. Someone with recourse to more than one dialect (e.g. Standard English, local speech styles, family patois) could be successfully challenged to show the rest how they switch codes. What matters is bringing together the full richness of what is available from the cultural and linguistic resources of the group.

2.5 ICT

Now that the word-processor is often used for writing, some of the previous conventionally employed devices of handwritten punctuation, such as the use of single inverted commas, are being replaced by other devices, such as the italic. Once it required, as writers in school, 'Hamlet' to help us to be in no doubt that it's *Hamlet* the play to which we refer rather than Hamlet the Dane. Now, if students word-process, it is *Hamlet*. The Saturday *Guardian's* arts pages to name but one, we might note, have ceased to indicate titles by any graphical means whatsoever on the assumption that the rest of the sentence's meaning, coupled with our likely knowledge, will suffice.

Word processors are brilliant in simple ways in helping, for example, to spot frequency of word use, or in providing spell-checkers which need to be the subjects of instruction about how they cannot work if presented with 'fare' for 'fair'. Other language-based offerings have much more dubious value, such as grammar checkers, but all these things might well be the subjects of an interactive whiteboard presentation with a group of students who have already made good progress with word-processors and are way past the basics.

Scenarios

1 'I ain't half tired, Miss' says a boy in your English class, as you are teaching a lesson on Standard English. How do you respond to his statement of fact in this lesson?
2 Teaching language is about encouraging pupils to zoom in close to see the small parts of language – word level work – and then drawing back to see the bigger picture of the jigsaw in sentence level work, and then further back still to see the complete picture of the text. How might you explain this to pupils? Could you draw a diagram to represent this?

REFERENCES

Bain, E. and R. (1996) *The Grammar Book: Finding Patterns – Making Sense: Teachers' Guide.* Sheffield: NATE

Carter, R. (ed.) (1990) *Knowledge about Language and the Curriculum: the LINC reader.* London: Hodder & Stoughton

Davison, J. and Dowson, J. (1998) *Learning to Teach English in the Secondary School: a Companion to School Experience.* London: Routledge

DES (1988) *Report of the Committee of Inquiry into the Teaching of English Language* (Kingman Report). London: HMSO

DfEE (1999) *The National Curriculum for England. English: Key stages 1–4.* London: DfEE and QCA

DfEE (2001) *Key Stage 3 National Strategy Framework for Teaching English: Years 7, 8 and 9.* London: DfEE

English and Media Centre (1991) *The Languages Book.* London: EMC

Perera, K. (1987) *Understanding Language.* Sheffield: National Association of Advisers in English

Pinker, S. (1994) *The Language Instinct.* London: Penguin Books

chapter 9

GRAMMAR

Two seven-year-old boys were working collaboratively on their story, which described a pig's escape from a farmyard. They had used a word-processor to create their first draft, and were now re-reading and revising the text. They came to the following two sentences: 'The pig ran across the farmyard. Suddenly she heard the noise.' The first boy said that 'the noise' didn't sound right. The second boy asked why? The first boy replied: 'It should be "a noise". If it was "the noise", the pig would have been expecting it!'

This is a good illustration of two fairly 'average' ability pupils reflecting very effectively on the 'meaning' produced by different grammatical effects. Whether terminology, such as 'definite/indefinite article', would have clarified the meaning of the text for the second boy is a debate central to grammar teaching in this chapter.

By the end of this chapter you will have gained an understanding of what constitutes grammar. You will also have been provided with a number of strategies for teaching grammar in the classroom context. There will be opportunities to explore the differences between spoken and written English. A priority will be to aid you in seeing the links between teaching grammar and improving pupils' literacy development.

Our focus on 'grammar' will raise the following points:

● Grammar, as an area of study, is linked, most frequently, to the teaching of writing.

- Differences in grammar can be too simplistically equated with differences in vocabulary. It is more than just choice of particular words.
- There is a need for students to reflect on their own, and others' use of grammar.
- A knowledge of some 'terminology' may well facilitate discussion of language use.
- Definitions of grammar may well inform, and elucidate, what is meant by Standard and non-Standard English.
- The role of grammatical investigations should provide a focus for challenging some of the myths about language use.
- Teaching grammar can be fun and interesting.

RATIONALE

Many current student teachers and experienced teachers will state that they were not taught grammar at school and feel somewhat disadvantaged when they are expected to teach grammar. In a recent self-audit (2003) undertaken by PGCE English trainees at Sheffield Hallam University grammar was the area of subject knowledge that most identified as requiring more attention. This raises the question of what is grammar and what knowledge is required to teach it effectively. Yet we all know about grammar from a very young age. Even at the age of two, babies are putting words in an established order to communicate. We construct our sentences using our knowledge of grammar. So what is grammar?

Grammar is usually seen as a way of conveying meaning and is not viewed exclusively in a narrow sentence-bound way, but is also seen as operating across clauses and sentences. Its study therefore focuses upon the process of creating meaning through the construction of sentences and parts of sentences. It should be noted that the situation, audience and purpose in which a text operates determine the specific grammatical choices that are made to create distinctive meanings. It would be wrong to assume that there is one approach to defining grammar. For example traditional approaches (prescriptive) tend to concentrate on the grammatical features of sentences and clauses, often focusing upon short sections of texts. These texts are usually deliberately chosen to illustrate particular features. This form of grammar teaching grew out of the importance of Standard English in the late 18th and early 19th centuries when there was a demand for books that explained the rules of Standard English. These types of school grammar were much relied upon with the advent of universal education in the 19th century. Exercises and drills in parsing and the identification of parts of speech marked traditional grammar teaching. Little emphasis was placed upon variety of sentence structure. Traditional formal grammar teaching persisted almost unchanged in at least some types of schools until the 1960s. Some research findings from this period claimed that grammar teaching of this form might actually be hindering pupil progress and thus a change of emphasis followed. By 1975 and the Bullock Report most English teaching integrated the teaching of language with emphasis upon writing for real purposes and audiences.

Academics like Henry Sweet developed descriptive grammars to account for forms and structures rather than relying on Latin-based grammar teaching in the teaching of English grammar. These (descriptive) grammars take account of the key differences between Latin and English. Descriptive grammars set out 'the rules that appear to govern how a language is used' (QCA, 1998). During the last 40 years linguistics has grown as an academic subject. Consequently grammar is viewed in broad terms with some linguists focusing on syntax, some focusing on sociolinguistics, others on pragmatics, etc. Progressive (descriptive) approaches tend to look at the grammatical features of the text as a whole.

Developing pupils' skills in grammar should also be about creativity and enabling writers to produce effective texts. The following statement game should help you to explore what is meant by grammar.

Statement Game: what is grammar?

Instructions: Consider the following six statements and record your immediate reactions to them. You can agree with the statement; you can disagree with the statement; or you can simply state that you do not know.

WHAT IS GRAMMAR?

	✓	✗	?
1 Grammar is a set of rules describing the correct way to write	❑	❑	❑
2 If we do not teach grammar pupils cannot be expected to write well.	❑	❑	❑
3 When correct grammar is not used the language has no meaning.	❑	❑	❑
4 *I be, we was* and *hisself* are examples of bad grammar.	❑	❑	❑
5 Grammar describes the rules for Standard English.	❑	❑	❑
6 Grammar inhibits the expression of imagination and experience in creative writing.	❑	❑	❑

Commentary: It should be recognised that there are strongly held beliefs about grammar. You might disagree with the forthcoming commentary on what grammar is but reconsider these beliefs after working through the chapter.

It is likely that the statements will have raised the following issues:

- Grammar can be used to discuss both talk and writing.
- Teaching grammar (e.g. identifying the noun, underlining the verb) does not, in itself, lead to improved language use.
- Grammar can often too easily, and simplistically, be associated with concepts of 'correctness' and 'incorrectness'.
- 'Bad grammar' can often be used to describe a method of organising words that is simply an alternative grammatical system, such as in a non-standard dialect.
- Grammar is sometimes confused with Standard English.
- Teaching grammar can also be mistakenly associated with notions of 'inhibiting free expression'.

LINKS WITH THE NATIONAL CURRICULUM AND KEY STAGE 3 STRATEGY

The National Curriculum for English places the teaching of grammar into the following three broad contexts:

1   That students should be given the opportunity to discuss and identify grammatical differences in texts (both spoken and written); for example the National Curriculum states 'pupils should be taught about the variations in written Standard English and how they differ from spoken language, and to distinguish varying degrees of formality, selecting appropriately for a task' (DfEE and QCA, 1999: 38).
2   That students should focus on the grammatical features of English only when directly investigating the 'meaning' of spoken and written texts; e.g. the National Curriculum states that 'pupils should be taught the principles of sentence grammar and whole text cohesion and use this knowledge in their writing' (DfEE and QCA, 1999: 38).
3   That any approach to describing grammar should be concerned with 'the ways in which words are combined into meaningful units'. For example the National Curriculum states that 'pupils should be taught to exploit choice of language and structure to achieve particular effects' (DfEE and QCA, 1999: 37).

With the introduction of the National Literacy Strategy at Key Stage 3, which groups English objectives into word, sentence and text level, there is a greater emphasis on the teaching of grammar at word and sentence level. For example the objectives at sentence level for Year 7 include:

> Pupils being taught: to extend their use and control of complex sentences/to expand noun and noun phrases/ to keep tense usage consistent/and use the active or passive voice to suit purpose. (DfEE, 2001b)

You will need to familiarise yourself with these objectives and reflect upon what knowledge of grammar you require in order to teach them.

In the DfEE publication, *English Department Training 2001* (DfEE 2001a) a whole section is devoted to grammar. The writers state some main principles for teaching grammar and these are outlined below:

- Pupils' implicit knowledge about grammar should be acknowledged and used as a positive base from which to develop more explicit awareness and control of language.
- Explicit grammar teaching should be integrated into the English curriculum.
- Grammar teaching should have a well-defined focus.
- Systematic planning should ensure progression and development over time.
- Grammatical features should be related to function, effect and meaning. (DfEE, 2001a: 130)

The last point is of particular significance if pupils are to create the most effective texts. The same publication recommends a teaching and learning sequence that follows these stages:

- Explore the objective
- Define the convention
- Demonstrate how it is written
- Share the composition
- Scaffold the first attempts.

And there is a supporting publication 'Year 7 sentence level bank' (in DfEE, 2001) that follows this model with examples of different objectives and how they might be taught, such as expanding nouns and noun phrases/using active and passive voice. When planning to teach aspects of grammar, consider using this model but note that the aim is to remove the scaffolding as soon as the pupil has gained confidence and can work more independently.

Activity 1

GRAMMAR WEBSITE
(suggested time: 40 minutes)

In order to support and develop teachers' and trainees' knowledge of grammar Debra Myhill from Exeter University has set up an excellent website. The site is designed to meet everyone's needs – from those with 'little' knowledge of grammar through to those with quite extensive knowledge. It is organised into three sections: word classes, sentences and discourses. There is also a 'test yourself ' facility. Access the website

Standard addressed: 2.1 http://www.ex.ac.uk/~damyhill/grammar and make a note in your portfolio of four things that you have learned and four things that you want to learn more about.

ACTIVITY 2

A FUN GRAMMAR WEBSITE
(suggested time: 45 minutes)

There is a fun website called Grammar Gorillas. On this web site you are provided with definitions for key terms such as noun, verb and adjective. You are then given sentences and asked to click on the appropriate word. Based on your response you are given a score and the gorilla collects a banana. Play the game yourself and consider how you would use this website in an English lesson. The web address is **http://www.funbrain.com/grammar/**

Standard addressed: 2.5
Acknowledgement to D.Myhill for noting this one for us at a conference.

Place your ideas in your portfolio.

Activity 3

STANDARD ENGLISH AND GRAMMAR

(suggested time: 60 minutes)

In Chapter 8 of *Learning to Teach English in the Secondary School* by Davison and Dowson (1998) there is an excellent overview of Standard English. It also highlights some of Cox's explanations as to what Standard English is not (e.g. the same as 'good', 'correct', 'formal', 'logical', 'Received Pronunciation'). The writers suggest some approaches for teaching Standard English. These are three of them:

- a focus on writing: as most writing is in Standard English, a focus on writing is almost inevitably a focus on Standard English;
- contrasting speech and writing: looking at the differences between spoken forms and written forms will highlight many features of Standard English;
- contrasting regional dialects: contrasting local dialects with Standard English will highlight the Standard English forms and make pupils more aware of the subtle choices which they make subconsciously when they switch dialects. (Davison and Dowson, 1998: 157)

TASK

Think of one activity that you might use as the basis of a lesson for Year 7 to teach standard written English. Below is an example of a Year 8 lesson.

LESSON PLAN

LEARNING OBJECTIVE

Understand the main differences between Standard English and dialectical variations

Starting points

The point of these activities is to review and revise the differences between accent and dialect, so it is worth starting by reminding students that accent (pronunciation) and dialect (grammar and vocabulary) are not to be confused. Stress that Standard English is also a dialect of English, albeit the dominant and most widely used one.

Whole class work

Invite the students to suggest local dialect terms and list these on the board or OHT. This might be an exercise they have done before, but is worth revisiting in order to emphasise the points mentioned above. Discuss alternative Standard English forms for their suggestions. If students have focused on vocabulary in their responses, explain that dialect also includes grammatical features such as multiple negation (for example, *I never done nothing to nobody*). This often leads to quite heated arguments about 'correctness', although 'appropriateness' would be a better term.

On an OHT or board write up a number of dialect forms that are extensively used throughout the country, and ask students to provide written Standard English alternatives. For instance:

I ain't going to school. He done it wrong.

She's took my pencil. You wasn't in when I called.

I don't know nothing. He's the man what wrote that book.

Point out that many dialects have regular forms for terms that are irregular in Standard English (for example, the present tense of *to be*), and that they mix the past tense and past participle of certain verbs (such as *done, come, seen* and *took*). You might then, of course, refer to Scottish English in which there are many dialect features, some of which are influenced by Gaelic.

Read aloud to the class the extract at the top of the student sheet before handing it out. Ask the students if they understand any of the dialect words or if they can guess the meaning in the context. Write up some of their suggestions on the board. Point out that this is a text that has brought together many dialect forms, and that it would not necessarily appear in speech in this way. It is instead likely that individual words or phrases would creep into more standard forms (e.g. *wee* is still used quite regularly).

Guided group/individual work

In pairs, pupils read the student sheet and translate the passage forms into Standard English. As they do so they should keep a record of any other changes they have had to make, apart from translating vocabulary (i.e. syntax).

Plenary

Compare the students' responses to their earlier suggestions recorded on the board.

Ask students to read out their descriptions to the class, encouraging other class members to work out the meaning as the passage is being read.

Resource sheet

Standard English and dialect

> It was a braw forenoon and the orraman, who was
> ganging frae the clachan to the bothy where he lived,
> crossed the brig over the burn and passed the wee but
> and ben that belonged to the souter. It was not busy
> and when he looked back at the glen he had come
> across, all he could see were a tattie bogle in the
> loaning, twa weans playing peevers and a wee bairn
> greeting. The orraman looked a wee bit like a tattie
> bogle himself. He was wabbit after walking and his
> bauchles were covered in glaur. He bided awee by a
> byre before reaching the yett of his bothy. There was
> somebody in because he could see the lum was reeking.

Some examples of dialect terms:

English *Scottish*

alert/lively *gleg*	beautiful/fine *braw*	big *muckle*
bridge *brig*	brook *bur*	building *biggin*
careful *canny*	child *bairn/wean*	chimney *lum*
church *kirk*	cosy *couthy*	cottage *bothy*
cowshed *byre*	cry *greet*	daft *gyte*
dirty *clarty*	thirsty *drouthy*	dust *stoor*
each *ilka*	ear *lug*	English *Sassenach*
exhausted *wabbit*	a few *a wheen*	field *loaning*
freckles *fernitickles*	from *frae*	gate *yett*
go *gang*	good *guid*	foolish *glaikit*
greasy *creeshie*	hard/serious *dour*	hill *brae*
hit *ding*	hopscotch *peevers*	house *but and ben*
horse or donkey *cuddy*	know *ken*	labourer *orraman*
long-legged *lang-shankit*	look *keek*	make a mess *slaister*
morning *forenoon*	mountain *ben*	mud *glaur*
neat *dink*	nose *neb*	odd *orra*
one *ane*	pale/washed out *peely wally*	pocket *pouch*

mashed *champit*	pretty *bonny*	remember *mind*
potatoes *tatties*	scarecrow *bogle*	shoe *bauchle*
shoemaker *souter*	shy *blate*	cunning/smooth *sleekit*
small *wee*	smoke *reek*	sore *sair*

(Dickinson et al., 2001)

Standard
a ddressed:
2.1c

Activity 4

WHY WE TEACH GRAMMAR

(suggested time: 40 minutes)

E. and R. Bain (2003: 3) state that there are seven common purposes for teaching grammar:

1 To correct grammatical errors, e.g. subject–verb agreement
2 To develop awareness of regional dialect 'intrusions' into Standard English writing or speech, e.g. we was, he done it
3 To improve the clarity and effectiveness of students' speech and writing
4 To develop students' critical awareness
5 To extend students' control of style
6 To develop concepts and terminology for use in foreign language learning
7 To develop language awareness.

TASK

Standard
addressed:
3.3.2c

Consider the above and then choose two and note down how you would address them in a meaningful way. So for example you might share a text with pupils and discuss what changes would need to be made if it was aimed at a younger audience.

Activity 5

THE CRAFT OF WRITING

(suggested time: 40 minutes)

Read the article entitled 'The craft of writing' at the following website address:

http://members.aol.com/MacedonPg/writing.htm

The article outlines various technical aspects of writing narrative. The writer argues that the most important skill of an author is to say what you want to say well. He identifies several writing basics that underpin effective narratives, but challenges conventional opinions, such as it is always good to find alternatives to the word 'said'.

***Standard
addressed: 1.8*** Write the opening to a story incorporating some of the author's principles. List which ones you have tried to incorporate. Place this in your portfolio.

Activity 6

ARE ALL VERBS DOING WORDS?
(suggested time: 10 minutes)

We need to be careful about providing 'simple' descriptions for parts of speech such as 'a verb is a doing word'. Some verbs are dynamic (e.g. racing, running, attacking, shouting), but some are stative, such as forms of the verb to be (e.g. is/will be/am/was/are). Stative verbs are useful for describing things and providing information. For example: 'He was a ten-foot beast. He was also very strong.' The use of such forms might be more common in a non-fiction text. Conversely, 'The ten-foot creature rushed out of the forest, eyes searching the landscape for prey' might be more akin to a horror story. There are also verbs which identify emotions often found in the romance genre such as love, hate and desire.

TASK

***Standard
addressed: 2.1*** Rewrite the following three sentences adding dynamic verbs. Consider how this affects your text.

The man was in a black car. He was on the M1. He was incredibly sad.

Activity 7

PUNCTUATION AND GRAMMAR
(suggested time: 30 minutes)

Consider the importance of the relationship between punctuation and meaning. For example: *The man shouted out aloud, ' help me she gasped'.*

The man shouted out aloud.

'Help me,' she gasped.

***Standard
addressed: 2.1*** You might like to consider some activities with children where punctuation changes the meaning in different ways. You might want to select some anonymous examples from your pupils' work to share with the class.

CONTINUOUS THREADS

1 Professional values and practice

Perhaps a good starting point would be to begin with each pupil's language experience. This could take the form of pupils creating a brief language biography and then sharing the influences upon their language development. Also differences between pupils' spoken language (use of contractions/fillers/tags/repetition/pauses/incomplete sentences/intonation) could be compared with writing. It might be interesting to explore the gender-based features of pupils' writing. Thus, you could select a range of stories written by a particular year group and encourage pupils to consider which ones might have been written by girls and which ones by boys. Evidence should focus on the grammatical features used. You might also want to explore genre preferences. Opportunities should be built in to explore the grammatical features of different languages. This is particularly important for pupils learning EAL. Their experience and knowledge of different languages should be recognised and used to benefit their development in English.

3.2 Monitoring and assessment

Pupils are expected to be familiar with the grammatical terms and concepts relating to word, sentence and whole text structure that are outlined in the English programmes of study. They should be able to name parts of speech and grammatical structures, analyse their functions and evaluate their effects. They should be able to make use of this knowledge when reading, or when writing their own texts. (QCA,1998: 41)

What is important is that the assessment of grammar must recognise the interplay of word, sentence and text level. You will need to be aware of pupils' implicit and explicit knowledge of grammar. This can be achieved in a number of ways:

- Informal observations in a number of classroom contexts
- Focused tasks to check that knowledge has been learned (e.g. Grammar Gorillas scorecard on the website for Activity 2)
- A focus on a particular aspect of grammar when marking work (e.g. subject–verb agreement or use of adverbs in descriptive writing)
- Encouraging pupils to identify and explain grammatical features in their own or others' texts. This could take the form of a commentary such as explaining the use of persuasive techniques in a political speech.

Over a period of time, it will be important to provide a range of oral and written contexts which place different linguistic demands upon pupils. These could relate to where different levels of formality are required, exploring language change over time and discussing the effects of active and passive sentences (e.g. in newspaper reports)

Below is an example of one pupil's writing, with a commentary (LINC, 1992).

The Dead Pigeon (by Lesley)

To day at afternoon play just when we was comeing back in to school Mrs B found a pidgin on the floor next to the Haygreen Lane side. Some children had gone in but I was ther when Gary Destains said hay up thers a pidgin on floor. WE all rusht up but Mrs B showted 'stop come back and let me look whats appened to it poor thing.' I just thout it was resting a bit but Dobbie said its ded. It was when Mrs B picket it up its kneck just flopped over poor thing I said to Dobbie. She lifted it up with its wings and they were like lovely grey fans. I didn't know wings were so lovely and big with so meny fethers espeshily. When we had gon in we was just sittind in are class and telling Mrs Sandison and the others about it when Mrs B came and held it up with its lovly grey wings. I was sorry for it poor thing and Mrs Sandison was sad and we all was.

Commentary focusing on achievement

Lesley asked her class teacher if she could write a personal narrative in response to the incident with the dead pigeon. She wrote her piece quickly and without revisions: key features included personal narrative, chronological, specific incident and past tense.

At text level Lesley uses the actual occurrence of events to provide the ordering of the sentences in the text. However, it is not quite as simple as that. The order of events reported in the first few sentences is in actuality:

> Some children go into school after play.
> Others including Lesley follow behind.
> Gary finds a pigeon on the floor.
> The group of children rush to see it.
> Mrs B calls for them to stop.

Lesley, in fact, manipulates this sequence in a sophisticated way. She puts the focus of the first main clause on Mrs B finding the pigeon *Mrs B found a pidgin*. In the second sentence *Some children had gone in but I was ther* she builds up a comparison which provides a focus for her own participation *I was ther* using the past perfect *had gone* to contrast with *was*. The event that might appear most significant, the finding of the pigeon, is then recounted in the subordinated adverbial time clause *when Gary Destains said . . .* This again throws prominence on to her own participation, consistent with the personal nature of the account.

In the third sentence Mrs B, as it were, takes control of the situation. This provides the answer to the apparent contradiction between the phrase in the first sentence *Mrs B found a pidgin* and the second, which provides the information that Gary was the first to notice the pigeon. Lesley, in fact, is concerned primarily with her own involvement in the incident and secondarily with her reactions to it. She also sees Mrs B as the central figure in the finding of the pigeon because she was presumably the teacher on duty.

It is generally to be expected that a chronological or time-related sequence of events will contain time expressions. Apart from the circumstance elements just noted in the first sentence, Lesley uses several adverbial time clauses in her text which emphasises its time-related nature:

Just when we was comeing back in to school
When Gary Destains said
When Mrs B picket it up
When we had gon in
When Mrs B came

Sentences and punctuation

It is also noteworthy that the grammatical structure of clauses and sentences is well handled, though the absence of punctuation does, at times, hinder comprehension. For instance, the fifth sentence as punctuated in the text might be read as *It was when Mrs B . . .* since this is a construction that might be anticipated in the light of the number of adverbial clauses and the comparative absence of simple sentences. Lesley, however, shows a fitting dramatic control in her writing, as can be seen in this edited version of the passage – *I thought it was just resting a bit but Debbie (?) said, it's dead. It was. When Mrs B picked it up, its neck just flopped over. Poor thing, I said to Debbie.*

Choice of vocabulary

Lesley's account is highly personal and anecdotal. The particularity of place and persons that is so central to her text shows in the speech and more so in the regional dialect forms in the speech which are, of course, perfectly legitimate in speech situations. Lesley, however, does on a few occasions use dialect forms that are not appropriate in the main narrative. There are three instances of *we was* where the Standard English form appropriate to writing is *we were*. (NB: You might want to argue that these non-standard forms are influenced by the informal nature of the writing situation.)

Circumstances

It is also interesting to note the emphasis given to elements that describe the circumstances. Narratives typically involve participants doing things (event or action processes). As well as participants and processes sentences contain slots for circumstances, as follows: (S) participant; (V) process; (O) participant; © further information about participant(s); (A) circumstances. Lesley gives great prominence to circumstances. Apart from the main clause *Mrs B found a pidgin* all the other elements in the first sentence describe circumstances. This gives great particularity to the account and this is also evidenced in the number of personal pronouns and specific names in the text.

Summary

This analysis provides a way of identifying the nature and extent of Lesley's achievement. It shows her confident control over the handling of time and tense; her conscious manipulation of sentence and clause structures to throw into prominence her own involvement in the incident; and the use of attitudinal expressions to record her reactions (LINC, 1992).

Progression

Whilst the National Curriculum states what aspects of grammar pupils need to know and use, it does not make explicit when they should be taught. Teachers need to plan explicitly for teaching grammar even if it is integrated into existing schemes so that continuity and progression is ensured. Consideration will be needed of the level of detail required, what grammatical terms will be necessary and how to ensure that these terms are understood. The *Framework for Teaching English: Years 7, 8 and 9* now makes explicit which objectives should be covered for each year. This can be used as the basis for planning progression for grammar teaching. However, it does not mean that learning about grammar takes a linear form.

Examples from the *Framework*:

Word level Y7 focus upon word meaning in context
Word level Y8 focus upon word formation
Word level Y9 focus upon layers of meaning
Sentence level Y7 focus on subordinate clauses
Sentence level Y8 focus variety of sentence structure
Sentence level Y9 focus on degrees of formality
Text level (Reading) Y7 infer and deduce
Text level (Reading) Y8 bias and objectivity
Text level (Reading) Y9 authors' viewpoint

You will need to be familiar with the framework objectives and look at the assessment criteria for the KS4 GCSE syllabuses.

3.3 Teaching and class management

Grammar teaching is likely to take an integral approach to English teaching rather than being treated as a selection of discrete exercises. Thus classroom organisation would reflect the diversity of English teaching.

Below are some examples of how you might organise the teaching of grammar within your classroom.

Example 1: Paired work

Pupils are asked to discuss the possible verbs in a cloze exercise based on the opening to Ted Hughes's short book, *The Iron Man*. Verbs are selected as these are crucial to understanding the Iron Man's origins and power. It is interesting to note that the verbs Hughes chooses are high frequency verbs. The extract follows:

The Iron Man   (1) to the top of the cliff. How far had he   (2) Nobody   (3) Where had he   (4) from? Nobody   (5) How was he   (6)? Nobody   (7).

Taller than a house, the Iron Man   (8) at the top of the cliff, on the very brink, in the darkness.

1   came
2   walked
3   knows
4   come
5   knows
6   made
7   knows
8   stood.

This could then be followed up with writing a description of the Iron Man accompanied by an illustration.

Example 2: Small group work

The aim of this exercise is to help pupils to develop their sentences in greater depth and to give them access to connectives to enable them to do this. Organise your class into groups of four and then give each person a list of four connectives or cards with a connective written on each of them. Explain that they will then be telling a story around the group, but each contribution must include a connective from their list. They should not repeat the connective, but include a different card or one from their list each time.

Connectives might include:

because
finally
otherwise
above all
however
although
thus
next
then
alternatively
for example
apart from
consequently
meanwhile
indeed
especially
such as.

This could be developed into categorising when these connectives might be used (to illustrate/to sequence/to compare). A glossary of terms could be provided to pupils and they could then be encouraged to use them for writing different types of texts.

Example 3: Whole class exercise on shared reading

The class reads an example of instructional writing and is asked to identify the grammatical features specific to this text.

GROW YOUR OWN PLANTS

You'll need . . .

- *approximately a dozen seeds (e.g. wheat seeds; cress seeds; bean seeds; sunflower seeds)*
- *glass jar*
- *one small plastic ice-cream carton*
- *hammer and nail*
- *potting mixture or seed-raising mixture*
- *cardboard label, sticky tape and scissors*
- *large bowl*
- *large plastic bag and a rubber band*
  1. *Place your seeds in the glass jar and soak them overnight.*
  2. *With the hammer and nail, punch about five holes into the bottom of the ice-cream carton for drainage.*
  3. *Fill the carton about two-thirds full with potting mixture.*
  4. *Place your seeds on top of the potting mixture and then cover them carefully with about half a centimetre of mixture.*
  5. *Stick a cardboard label on the carton with sticky tape to identify your plants.*
  6. *Fill the bowl with water and stand the carton in it until the water soaks through to the top.*
  7. *Let the carton drain. Cover the carton with a plastic bag, using a rubber band to keep it in place.*
  8. *Put the carton in a warm place until the seeds germinate.*

Key features that pupils might identify include the following:

- chronological sentences
- adverbial phrases (e.g. *through to the top*)
- imperatives (*stick/fill*)
- classifying adjectives (e.g. *rubber band*).

Pupils are then asked to write their own set of instructions, e.g. recipe, board game, making a toy, and then to write a brief accompanying commentary outlining the main language features.

3.3.4 Differentiation

This can take a number of forms:

- By resource

Following diagnostic marking of pupils' writing the teacher designs individual pupil checklists based on individual grammatical features. So, for a period of time each pupil has his or her own checklist. A pupil might be asked to check subject–verb agreement whilst another might focus upon consistency of tenses. Opportunities for peer review might aid with differentiation.

- By support

Collaborative writing with pupils, for example based on setting the scene for a short story, focusing on the grammatical features that help to establish atmosphere (adjectives, adverbs, pronouns).

- By response

This could be an investigation into the regional features of a non-standard dialect.

- By task

A cloze exercise in which some pupils are given a word bank, some are given gaps for specific grammatical features, and the more able are given further gaps to complete in the text.

2.5 ICT

ICT lends itself to grammar work and ICT in itself is changing language. Pupils could draft their work in Word and then use the tool bar for the spelling and grammar check facility. The sections underlined in green show where the program has identified the writing as grammatically incorrect. Pupils could work individually or in pairs, changing their drafts so that the lines disappear. This could be followed up with group discussion about why the sections were highlighted. Examples of sections from classic literature could be tested against the grammar check and discussion follow where published writing appears with the green lines. Try the opening to Dickens's *Bleak House* available at **www.paulchapmanpublishing.co.uk/resources/completeguide.htm**

Another interesting area is where ICT has affected language change. Of particular note are the exchanges in chat rooms and text messaging. Both these forms often rely on quick exchanges and this need has produced abbreviated forms and written forms that approximate speech. Pupils could be given examples from Internet chat rooms carefully selected by their class teacher and compare these with Standard English. Examples could be shared with pupils, e.g. THX for Thanks and 2nite for tonight. The use of emoticons might also be examined e.g. ☺ or ☹. Pupils could be asked to devise messages using code words from a given glossary and asked to add some of their own. This fun way of exploring language is an effective way into challenging what is meant by grammar.

Scenarios

1   You have been asked to recap with a Year 7 class specific grammatical terminology (e.g. noun, verb, adjective, adverb and preposition). An interactive way of doing this is to link it to creating a poem. For example organise the class into pairs or threes. Give each group an A3 sheet of paper and ask them to fold the paper in half (landscape). On the left-hand

side ask the pupils to create a drawing of a monster and then give it a generic name, e.g. an Ichyipod . Keep the name short. Then on the right-hand side use each numbered box to generate lists of suitable words, e.g. for box 1 friendly and four legged. Look at the illustration below as an example. All five boxes should be completed. Box 6 is optional.

Pupils could read their lists out aloud. Then read aloud to the pupils the original poem and ask the pupils to create a similar monster poem.

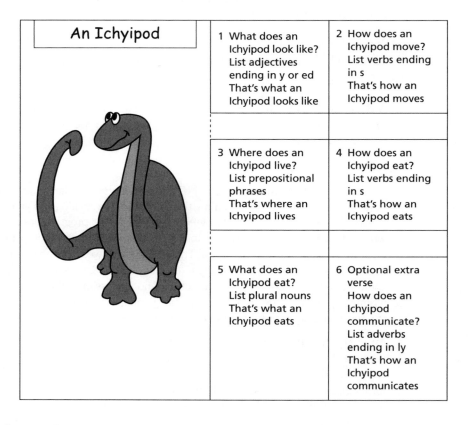

Question Time

What does a monster look like?

Well . . . hairy

and scary

and furry

and burly and pimply and dimply and warty and

naughty and wrinkled and crinkled

> *That's what a monster looks like*

How does a monster move?

It oozes

it shambles

it crawls and it ambles, it slouches and shuffles

and trudges, it lumbers and toddles, it creeps

and it waddles

> *That's how a monster moves*

Where does a monster live?

In garden sheds

under beds

in wardrobes, in plug holes and ditches

beneath city streets, just under your feet

> *That's where a monster lives*

How does a monster eat?

It slurps and it burps and gobbles and gulps

and sips and swallows and scoffs, it nibbles

and munches, it chews and it crunches

> *That's how a monster eats*

What does a monster eat?

Slugs and bats and bugs and rats

and stones and mud and bones and blood

and squelchy squids . . . and nosy kids

YUM!

> *That's what a monster eats*

> Question Time *by Michaela Morgan*

Another poem structured in a similar way is Wes Magee's 'The Blob', which starts:

And . . . and what is it like?

Oh, it's scary and fatbumped

And spike-eared and groany.

It's hairy and face-slumped

and bolshie and bony.

(*extract from* A Third Poetry Book *compiled by John Foster, Oxford University Press, 1982*)

Now think about another activity that could be used to recap the same grammatical features.

2 Pupils are writing about religious beliefs in one of your lessons. One pupil learning EAL writes the following:

> People believe in God and they believes that there in the world not only bad but good things as well. They believes that God is helping good people so then they will know that the God is really exsist in the world.
> God can see that not all bad people are evil, some of them can find their own way to change their mind. And sometimes when people seen miracles, they starting belive . . .

Consider what aspects of grammar this pupil needs to know to improve the effectiveness of his/her writing. How would you help the pupil to improve?

A useful template for analysing written work by pupils learning EAL is provided in *Access and Engagement in English* (DfES, 2002: 20–1).This template identifies the learning need, such as subject–verb agreement, and recommends a lesson that would address this need. See Chapter 11 below on EAL for more detailed information.

FURTHER READING

Barton, G. (1997) *Grammar Essentials*. London: Longman
Carter, R. (1990) 'The new grammar teaching', in R. Carter, *Knowledge about Language in the Curriculum*. London: Hodder & Stoughton. pp. 104–41.

REFERENCES

Bain, E. and Bain, R. (2003) *The Grammar Book Supplement*. Sheffield: NATE
Davison, J. and Dowson, J. (1998) *Learning to Teach English in the Secondary School*. London: Routledge
DES (1975) *A Language for Life* (The Bullock Report). London: HMSO
DfEE (2001a) *English Department Training 2001 0234/2001*. London; DfEE
DfEE (2001b) *Framework for Teaching English:Years 7, 8 and 9*. London: DfEE
DfEE and QCA (1999) *The National Curriculum for England. English: Key Stages 1–4*. London: DfEE and QCA
DfES (2002) *Access and Engagement in English 0609/2002*. London: DfES
Dickinson, P., McDonagh, J. and Wilkinson, J. (2001) *English Programme File 2*. Dunstable: Folens
Foster, J.L. (ed.) (1995) *Monster Poems*. Oxford: OUP
Hughes, T. (1971) *Iron Man*. London: Faber
LINC (1992) *Language in the National Curriculum: Materials for Professional Development*. LINC. Unpublished materials
QCA (1998) *The Grammar Papers*. London: QCA.

chapter 10

SPELLING

By the end of this chapter you should know how to enable those you teach to become confident in spelling the words they wish to write. English teachers have a public duty, one recognised most often by teachers of all other subjects in the secondary school, to see to it that words are correctly spelt in any assignment, and so the best approach for you to adopt is a positive one. Better by far to see yourselves as teachers of spelling rather than as proof-readers of endless if unintended mistakes by school students. Spelling is interesting; students can be made aware of how well they have learned to spell as well as how much more they have to learn. They can be made aware too of the relationship of individual words to meaning rather than to a simpler or 'purer' phonetic alternative. They need also very often to be taught how to use dictionaries skilfully, but the skilful teacher arranges for dictionary-based games to be a productive way of sustaining concentration in lessons, perhaps at the end of the day or end of the week. Spelling – learning to spell – needs to be seen in context, both of the work in hand and of the individual's abilities and difficulties.

RATIONALE

The first *National Curriculum for English* (1990), usually referred to as 'Cox', after the name of the chairman of the report, emphasised spelling as part of the 'secretarial' aspect of learning to write. Sadly this sane view of where spelling fits into the process of learning in English has not been sustained by later versions of the NC. All the same, spelling still needs to be seen as part of a larger complex of intentions on the young writer's part when sitting down with pen and paper, or at a word-processor. Fear of error may be a great detractor from the creative and thoughtful intention to employ the right word in the sentence. As English teachers we need to keep creative thoughtfulness at the forefront of young writers' minds. So, in place of fear we need to instil the view that the right word is to be used and that it may need to be spelt provisionally and then corrected when a dictionary or spell-checker is to hand. Ultimately, for many but not all habitually practised writers, spellings seem to be formed by the hand, without the need of conscious and slow thought. Conscious thought and compositional skill are best saved for the more demanding and significant aspects of the writing process.

In between teaching individuals how to cope with their own needs at particular points we could do worse than analyse the spelling strengths and spelling needs of each class we teach. As a result of these analyses we then conduct whole group lessons based on patterns and general principles. An example is the unvoiced labial-dental, often supplied by 'f'. This may be represented in English by 'ph' or 'gh', but the latter is never used at the start of a word, and often the 'gh' digraph occurs after a vowel digraph such as 'ou' as in 'cough', 'tough' and 'enough'. A sound general principle to bear in mind when teaching spelling is that like examples need to be taught together. Only when the class is secure with 'rough' and 'laugh' in addition to the examples above do you explore, preferably in a different week, all the examples of 'gh' having no obvious consonantal work to do, such as in 'dough', 'bough', 'ought', 'lighting' and 'fight'.

Many young writers not in top sets perpetuate errors because they have been encouraged to do so by their well-meaning but misguided teachers. For example some teachers point out too often how 'they're' differs from 'their' and 'there'. Better to teach 'there' along with 'here' and 'where' and other place words. 'Their' belongs with 'our' and 'your', being words of possession that share two vowels followed by a final 'r'. 'They're' can be saved up for occasions when you are talking about other commonly elided words where apostrophes of omission are used, such as 'aren't' and 'who'll'.

In seeking to enable the class to be equal to the demands of correct spelling there is every virtue in pointing out that spelling is complicated in part. We have in English some 44 sounds, but only 26 letters to call upon, so that some single letters have to be prepared to represent quite different sounds, such as 'a' in 'bath' (received southern pronunciation), 'rate' and 'cat'. For all the complications, however, there is no choice about outcome. The correct spellings just have to be learned, and if they cannot then writers should aim at limiting to a relatively small number those words which they know they just cannot remember but about which they are prepared to consult when in doubt. School students are not alone in their struggles; some famous writers have had great difficulties with spelling. Furthermore, the standardisation of spelling came about through editors, dictionary-compilers and the like. Some of these would-be perfecters and self-appointed authorities are responsible for some strange forms with which we are now all stuck. The word 'scissors' was once spelt, according to the *Collins*

English Dictionary, 'sisoures' and would never have been given that 'c', but that the people who successfully ordained that particular spelling thought that the Latinate origin of the word should be recognised.

Possibly out of print now, but nevertheless worth looking for in a library, is an excellent brief pamphlet by Mike Torbe about the teaching of spelling, but the classic text in this area for years has been Margaret Peters's *Spelling: Caught or Taught?* with its invitation to consider how many plausible ways there might be in English to spell 'saucer'. This unsurpassed little guide is perhaps of more direct use to the primary rather than secondary teacher, but its emphasis on variety of approach by individuals is still the crucial point. Pupils learn to spell words in chunks, in clusters or units of letters, perhaps of syllable length or maybe just digraphs. Certain combinations that recur frequently, such as the 'th' or 'ch' of English, need to be rehearsed as movements or feelings of the hand forming the right shapes. For secondary pupils the 'ch' or 'sh' equivalents might be common vowel digraphs like 'ei' in words such as 'neighbour'. For some, then, spelling might be a kinaesthetic matter, but for others a visual one. All pupils need to be presented with the chance to rehearse different ways of memorising the words with which they have difficulty. This point is made neatly in Chapter 3 of Davison and Dowson (1998). Furthermore, Sue Hackman and Liz Trickett's *Spelling 9--13* provides a range of interesting approaches to the teaching of spelling from exploring patterns within words to linking spelling to ancient word roots.

Questions

What are your own spelling needs? Are they merely particular and unrelated words with which you have trouble, such as – to take an example from the TTA's literacy test for would-be teachers – 'accommodation', or 'liaise', the latter being a word which even a few teachers, who claim to know it, sometimes misspell as 'liase', or are there general patterns which puzzle you? To take another recent TTA example, does 'queuing' look right to you? What general rule can you instance to a class to explain to them why 'queueing', a possible alternative spelling, would be wrong?

If you give a class a spelling test (never a bad way to make everyone attentive at the start of a lesson), then what principles might guide your selection of items?

Which other words are there besides 'judgement/judgment' and 'lovable/loveable' which, according to certain dictionaries, are the subjects of legitimate alternative spellings? Why not interest the class in the fact of differences between US and UK English spellings, as in 'anaesthetic/anesthetic', 'instil/instill', 'centre/center'.

LINKS WITH THE NATIONAL CURRICULUM AND KEY STAGE 3 STRATEGY

The NC for English addresses spelling in the writing attainment target. At Key Stages 3 and 4 it states that pupils should be taught to:

a) increase their knowledge of regular patterns of spelling, word families, roots of words and derivations, including stem, prefix, suffix, inflection
b) apply their knowledge of word formation

c) spelling increasingly complex polysyllabic words that do not conform to regular patterns

d) check their spellings for errors and use a dictionary when necessary

e) use different kinds of dictionary, thesaurus and spellchecker (DfES, 1999, p. 38).

Fostering an interest in words and providing strategies for pupils to help them check their work for spellings is crucial to making them accurate spellers. Regular access to dictionaries, time allocated to proof-reading and finding ways that help individual pupils, such as visual mnemonics (there is an ear in hear) should form part of common practice. For proof-reading encourage pupils to read each line carefully and underline any words they think might be spelt incorrectly and ask them to write the correct spelling above or check with a dictionary.

Central to the raising of standards in literacy is the improvement of pupils' ability to spell correctly. Two major strands run through the KS3 strategy at word level, entitled 'Spelling' and 'Spelling strategies'. Under these headings are clearly defined objectives. For example under Y7 **spelling** pupils should revise, consolidate and secure: vowel choices, pluralisation, word endings, prefixes, high frequency words, apostrophes and key words. Under **strategies** pupils should continue learning, constructing and checking spellings in their personal spelling, sound out phonemes and syllables, draw upon analogies, employ a range of strategies for learning challenging spellings, use dictionaries and spell-checkers. The above examples are taken from the *Framework for Teaching English: Years 7, 8 and 9*.

In *English Department Training* 2001 (DfEE, 2001b: 48) the following key points are highlighted:

- There are no perfect spelling rules but there are conventions that can help pupils to make informed choices.
- Many spellings are dictated by grammar (e.g. -ed for the past tense).
- Many spellings are dictated by morphology (units of meaning), etymology (word derivations) or word changing (i.e. adding prefixes and suffixes).
- Even some advanced spelling conventions are dictated by phonics (e.g. doubling consonants after a short vowel sound).
- The importance of revisiting critical weaknesses left over from previous years.

The KS3 strategy team recommend how the teaching of spelling should take place. They include the following:

- **A starter activity at the beginning of each lesson**

This has the benefit of potentially being interactive, but could result in spelling becoming a decontextualised activity. Examples of starters might include a focus on s and -es plurals with the following approach. Pupils are given on OHT two lists of words: one that has just s plurals and another list of those ending in es. Patterns are identified, for example singular words ending in a hissing, shushing or buzzing sound have es added. Then the teacher reads out some words and pupils using mini whiteboards in pairs agree the ending, write it on their boards and hold them up.

After a series of starters on pluralisation a fun activity is Millionaire plurals. This could be undertaken with two teams or just the class. A different volunteer is used for each word. The pupil on the spot is given a singular noun and must write the plural form on the board. The team or class has three lifelines: ask the audience; phone a friend (choose one other pupil for the spelling); and 50/50 (offer the pupil two choices). The words at the beginning are easier (for £100 *car*) and get progressively more difficult (£4,000 *loaf* and £64,000 *forum*). (Idea from Adorian. S et al, 2002.)

- **Followed up through work with texts**

This is important so that spelling is seen in context and revisited. For example if you are beginning a unit on poetry, introduce pupils to a small list of poetic terms.

- **A focus for shared and guided writing**

So for example look at rhymes in poetry.

- **Personal targets and lists**

Pupils are encouraged to respond to set targets and have a list of spellings for reference.

- **The keeping of a spelling journal**

This is useful for teachers to refer to when setting individual targets and for monitoring patterns of spelling difficulties.

- **Homework learning**
- **Subject-specific spellings across the curriculum**
- **In marking**
- **Literacy progress units**

Activity 1 — CHECKING THE SPELL-CHECKER

(suggested time: 20 minutes)

The essential question for the English teacher is about the psychology of learning to spell. A whole number of methods are available which help school pupils to learn to improve their spellings, including setting them to spell-check the following poem on the word-processor which has already been found error-free by that spell-checker, so that they learn the limitation of reliance on the machine:

> I'm a confidant young computer buff
> I have a fine spell chequer
> It always terns wrong spellings write
> You could not sea a better.
>
> You ask me what I do to rite
> The errors which I meat,
> Well actually I leave awl that
> For Bill Gate to con pleat.

Any teacher's good wit would enable them improve on this doggerel, but whatever you provide your classes with, design it so that you make the point that when we spell words we spell meanings, and the electronic machines – the spell-check circuits – have not one clue about meanings and the intentions which precede them. Your pupils need to perceive how spell-checkers can only help, not provide whole sets of answers.

Standard addressed: 2.1

Try creating a short text in which words are spelt incorrectly because of the context but would not appear as incorrect on a spell-check. This could be developed into an activity with pupils.

Activity 2

EXPLORING YOUR OWN STRATEGIES FOR LEARNING SPELLINGS
(suggested time: 15 minutes)

The best approach to teaching spelling is to become interested in the topic, and to take all that implicit knowledge and explicate it. Here is one brief example. Most of us know that we write 'fuming' not 'fumeing', just as we know from our instinctive knowledge of the pronunciation–spelling relationship that people who make and sell hats are hatters not haters. Do we work out, however, that there are systematic rules which we nearly all apply all the time about doubling the central consonants after short vowels in the first or preceding syllable, e.g. sit/sitting, input/inputting and leaving single central consonants for long-vowelled first or preceding syllables, e.g. hating, riding, imputing? The 'e' disappears from 'hate', 'ride', and 'impute' as the infinitive verb form is changed to a noun or present participle. There may be no need to confuse 11-year-olds with prematurely encountered technical words, but the basic rules can nevertheless be systematised, shown, rehearsed and understood. Non-existing but plausible words can be invoked here; if lads went out together maybe they'd be 'ladding'. They certainly wouldn't be 'lading', most of the class would feel instinctively.

Standard addressed: 3.2.2

Consider three ways in which you have learned to remember difficult spellings and place these in your portfolio. One of the writers of this chapter remembers learning Wednesday by sounding it out as wed-nes-day, and that library has a bra in it.

Activity 3

DEVELOPING A VISUAL MEMORY
(suggested time: 15 minutes)

Another greatly sensible method to use for applying one possible – namely visual – approach to spelling is to engage in the following sequence. This has the virtue that it has nothing to do with computers, and may be done to and with a whole class, and with no more aid than a black- or whiteboard

- Look at the word whose spelling is a problem,

- say the letters of it aloud or sub-vocally,
- look again,
- cover the word,
- write the spelling from memory,
- uncover the word,
- check and confirm or start again.

Standard addressed: 3.3.2

Try it yourself on an item such as 'desiccated', 'anaesthesia' or 'unnecessary.' This approach should form a regular method for pupils learning their individual spelling lists.

Activity 4

MODELLING THE PROCESS
(suggested time: 20 minutes)

The wise teacher is careful to relate the spellings to be taught to the words which the class spell badly or which individuals in the class repeatedly have trouble with. The advice here is to make a collection of a week's worth of spelling errors from a given class, and rather than spending time that week correcting every error on the page, spending it instead prioritising the most common errors, and making them the subjects of explanation to all. Put the five most common errors on the board, tell the class to study them in order, and rub each out while the class write it themselves, restoring it for checking purposes. Then you will have modelled a process which thereafter individuals can enact for themselves, becoming, not anxious writers as they compose, but increasingly confident spellers who know that editing provides opportunities and that composing provides satisfactions.

Standard addressed: 3.3.2

Whilst on teaching placement, model the above process and then encourage pupils to use this method with their own individual spellings.

Activity 5

USING DICTIONARIES
(suggested time: 20 minutes)

Central to good dictionary use is lots of rehearsal, with the class divided into groups, when you feel confident enough about handling pairs and triads. Actually bother to explain how the alphabet works for the word-order process. Explain how some words may not begin with the letter which it sounds as if they begin with, for example 'pneumatic', 'elicit', 'psychology', etc. When the basics appear to be grasped by most, then move on to group games which have all the class consulting the dictionaries for one purpose or another. An example would be a 'Call My Bluff' approach, named after the TV game show, in which groups discover a word which they think the other groups do not know, and then write out both the correct definition and two false but plausible definitions. Answering groups must keep their dictionaries closed until the definitions have been given and the resulting choices made. If your class has access to the *Oxford English Dictionary* on CD-ROM, then games can be played with deciding the year in which the selected item first appeared, such as 'aqualung' in 1951.

Groups can be guided to see that many common words have two or more distinct meanings, or may exist in both noun and verb forms. 'Form' as noun for example means: a type; a bureaucratic printed paper for puzzled civilians to fill in; for sports people something which it is better to be on than off, and which might be summed up as 'condition'; a class in a school; the bench to sit on, and so on. As a verb it is how people construct queues, relationships, attachments and opinions. In short it means 'make', but not 'create solo'. No great spelling-learning advantage, perhaps, in looking up such simply spelt items, but for more obscure items, which each group is trying to puzzle the rest with, there could well be spelling advantages. Apparently, however, the spelling is only an incidental part of the game. We are back with the great methodological key to English teaching, that by indirections do we find directions out.

***Standard addressed:* 3.3.2**

Using dictionaries make a list of 10 words that can be used as a noun or a verb. Use this list as the basis for asking pupils to write sentences in which the chosen word is being used first as a noun and then as a verb.

Activity 6

WORDS WITHIN WORDS
(suggested time: 30 minutes)

***Standard addressed:* 3.3.2**

A method that is often applied to help pupils remember some spellings is for them to be aware that there is another word within this word. Common examples are: there is 'a rat' in *separate*, a 'table' in *vegetable*, 'rain' in *brain* and *train*. Identify some that you use and then ask pupils to do the same. You might want your pupils to learn some key ones such as 'end' in *friend* or 'ru' in *February*.

Activity 7

PREFIXES
(suggested time: 20 minutes)

***Standard addressed:* 3.3.2**

Think of a list of prefixes (approximately 10, such as *pre*, *tele*, *re*) and ask pupils to add root words to make new words (telescope, invent). This can be undertaken in a variety of ways, such as by matching given root words with prefixes or by seeing how many words you can make beginning with one prefix. It could be developed into adding suffixes, or working out what the prefix might mean by looking at the impact it has on the meaning of a number of roots to which it has been added.

Activity 8

PUPILS AS INVESTIGATORS

(suggested time: 20 minutes)

Encourage pupils to identify patterns in groups of words that you present. An example from *English Department Training 2001* (DfEE, 2001b: 52) is summarised below.

> Pupils are provided with lists of words that contain long *a* sounds e.g.
> Play, say, tray, day, pay, may, fame, crane, space, fake, fail, aim, sail, rail.
> They are then asked to identify patterns and then exceptions. So for example words with long 'a' sounds from this list usually end with *ay*. This technique can be applied to a range of spelling 'clusters' such as words ending in *ible* or *able*. The ending *able* is usually added to words that make sense on their own (accept/ notice) Words ending in *ible* are usually those that do not make sense on their own before the *ible* is added. (vis/horr).

Standard addressed:
3.3.2

Activity 9

MARKING PUPILS' WORK

(suggested time: ongoing during teaching experience)

Avoid over-marking pupils' work by correcting too many spellings as this can be demoralising and your pupils will not know what to focus upon. Underline a selection of mistakes. You may decide to put the correct spellings in the margin to be copied into the individual pupil's spelling book. Focus on patterns and on rules recently taught and make sure that your pupils are aware of how they are to learn the correct spelling. This should then be followed up later, possibly as peer group testing.

Standard addressed:
3.3.2

CONTINUOUS THREADS

1 Professional values and practice

Standard addressed: 1.2

Spelling errors often strike the reader of children's work quite dramatically and in the past the teaching of spelling has often had negative associations – tests, red ink, corrections, marks out of ten and the writing out many times of the correct version. Accurate spelling in the English language is not easy, for many pupils to achieve as English is not written as it is spoken. In fact less than half of the most common words in the English language have a regular sound–symbol correspondence. The importing of words from other languages, such as *ghost* with its Dutch 'h' and *ski* from Norway, has made learning to spell even more difficult. At the time when English was copied by monks from transcripts alterations were made to some words in the interests of presentation rather than accuracy: an example is *women* (see Stubbs, 1980). It is these various influences which mean that simple strategies and conventions do not always help. Achievement in spelling should be recognised, ways of improving pupils' spelling should be introduced, rather than just identifying the mistake and expecting the pupil not to do it again. The use of spelling games, finding words within words, putting keywords up on display around the room, encouraging pupils to take risks in their spelling and to reflect upon their reasons for spelling words in certain ways are all positive approaches. Spelling is only one aspect of a much larger picture and whilst spelling matters it is important to encourage pupils to be confident investigators of language.

3.1 Planning, expectations and targets

It is important to be aware of the stages of development in children's spelling so that a diagnostic approach can be taken to help the pupil to move forward to the next level.

J.R. Gentry (1987: 19–26) identified five main stages of development in spelling, but it should be remembered that pupils will move through these stages at different speeds, depending upon a range of factors including teaching strategies employed and experience of reading. These were the stages that he identified:

- *Stage 1 Pre-communicative*
  The writer knows that symbols create meaning/might invent some of their own.

- *Stage 2 Semi-phonetic*
  The writer begins to understand that letters have sounds/may abbreviate words and combine them with pictures.

- *Stage 3 Phonetic*
  The writer uses sound-symbol correspondence/may not appreciate the accepted letter strings in English.

- *Stage 4 Transitional*
  The writer applies the simple conventions of the English writing system/he or she realises the visual aspect of spelling in letter strings which involves more than simple sound–symbol correspondence.

- *Stage 5 'Correct'*
  The writer understands basic spelling patterns/knows something about word structure/uses visual strategies/has a large bank of correctly spelt words/can identify homonyms/has some control over 'borrowed' words.

Once you have identified at which stage the pupil is in his/her development the right strategies can be used to move him/her on to the next stage. So for example pupils at stage 1 should be encouraged to talk about letter shapes and to notice letters in familiar words. At stage 2 letters and their sounds might be taught and pupils helped to discover words within words. At stage 3 the focus might be upon letter strings and letter–sound correspondence. At stage 4, use look–say–cover–write–check and encourage the writer to use joined-up writing and to collect words for display. At stage 5 the writer should be encouraged to explore word meanings/derivations and the use of dictionaries/thesauruses.

Look at the three examples of writing below and consider what each pupil knows about spelling and how their spelling might be moved on to the next stage.

My party by Emily, aged just 4

My favourite film by Simon, aged 6

Once upon time ther
was a robot called
Sporfy He did a lot
of sprot His foravree sprct
Was foot ball He
Nromly tiked Tennis but
He chaged His min to
football but one day
ther was going
to be a foot ball
mach Eagans
English robots agerist
amarcan robots Sporty
Play for Amarca
becaase He lived in
America And His
team won becase
they Hird Sporty the
next day Sporty
got up at 1 o clock
becase he went to
foot ball trainlng

the End
by simon

All about Joseph by Joseph, aged 7

all about Joseph

My name is Joseph my favarite
colur is green because it reminesd
me og the green grass. my addey
is planes. I licke planes because
I want to be a plane triwer
when I gnaw up I have a
braiter and sister called siman
and Emily. and I have a
dady called paul and a mummy
called Marie. Mast og the
time I play with my planes
my Savarite fish isa sharck
age 7

Tannayldo

by Joseph

Each of the above children wrote their unrehearsed and unaided texts in about ten minutes.

We need to ask ourselves: what do they know about spelling?

Emily is aware that letters are made up of different shapes. Some of the letters are recognisable such as the 'e', 'm' and 'y'. Some of the symbols are invented. There is a clear attempt to keep the letters to approximately the same size and they are written as if in lines. The most recognisable letters come from her name as she is in the process of learning how to spell it. She recognises the letters from her name in books and will often say 'That's in my name'. To her the text makes sense and she will explain what it means, even though it makes no sense to the reader.

Emily could best be described as at the pre-communicative stage.

One strategy to improve Emily's spelling might be to teach her to locate other letters in the books that are read to her so that she points for example to 'l' for lizard.

Simon spells a high percentage of words correctly with a mixture of lower and upper case, although these are not always selected appropriately. Initial word sounds are almost always correct and there is evidence of a bank of words that are visually recognised such as 'day', 'was', 'they'. Where words are unfamiliar there is use made of phonic knowledge, such as 'agenist' for against. There is also an awareness of -ed ending for the past tense. Simon has a good sight vocabulary and in general is using his knowledge of letter sounds to attempt unfamiliar words.

Simon could best be described as at the phonetic stage and moving towards the transitional stage.

One strategy to improve Simon's spelling might be to teach the spelling of 'there' with other place words such as 'here' and 'where'.

Joseph shapes his letters clearly and this may help with spelling later. In general he has a good bank of words drawn from visual recognition such as 'green', 'grass', 'name'. He makes effective use of his phonic knowledge such as 'reminesd', and 'sharck' and 'Tornaydo'. More work is required on his visual memory 'licke' for like and 'broter' for brother. However there is evidence that he is using a range of strategies with much success. When asked how he learned to spell 'because', a difficult word to learn visually or phonetically, he said *Ben elephant can add up sums easily*. The use of the mnemonic here has been a valuable strategy.

Joseph could best be described as at the transitional stage.

One strategy to improve Joseph's spelling would be work on word families, e.g. like, bike, hike and shark, bark, dark.

It is important not to just correct pupils' spelling mistakes but to identify the patterns of their mistakes and offer strategies to help rectify them. An effective way of undertaking this is recommended in the KS3 training materials, *English Department Training 2001* (2001b: 57) under the heading 'self review'. The suggestion is that you:

Ask pupils to log their last 25 spelling errors for analysis. Some of these spellings they may find for themselves, and some may be ones marked by the teacher. From this list, teachers can, at a glance, identify patterns, set personal targets and suggest useful strategies. DfEE (2001)

Thus a list of words that included 'lonly', 'lovly', hobbys and 'ladys' from one pupil would highlight the need for reminding the pupil that the original word does not change when 'ly' is added. Secondly that words ending in *y* when made plural become *ies* if the letter before the *y* is a consonant.

3.2 Monitoring and assessment

All pupils will make spelling mistakes and whilst it is the teacher's role to monitor and assess pupils' spelling it is essential that pupils do not have their confidence as spellers damaged by numerous red pen underlinings, or unstructured spelling tests. In fact success is likely to come from pupils being encouraged to self-monitor their progress. This can be achieved in a variety of ways. Pupils should be encouraged to proof-read their written work and then keep in a spelling journal a list of words that they find difficult to spell. Peer reading of each other's work where pupils offer advice to one another can be very effective, and they can also test their partners on their personal spelling lists. Pupils could be asked to underline in their draft work words they think they might have spelt wrong even if they are unsure how to spell them. They can then use a dictionary to check the spellings. If pupils keep lists of words they have difficulty spelling then in a separate column they could be encouraged to list a strategy to help them learn the particular words or you as the teacher could write it down for them. So for example the following might be applied, as demonstrated in Hackman and Trickett (1996: 6):

Syllabification yes–ter–day

Roots bi (two) + cycle (circle) = bicycle

Prefixes and suffixes dis+satisfied (hence two ss)

Pupils should be aware of the importance of spelling correctly and be made aware of requirements in examinations. In such a crowded curriculum there is precious little time for sustained individual attention to spellings, thus the emphasis must be on self-help strategies. When marking a pupil's piece of work for spelling think carefully which spellings you want to correct and why.

3.3 Teaching and class management

As a classroom teacher you will need your pupils to understand the importance of spelling, including how it affects meaning, the view of the reader and in relation to marks in written examinations, (look at examination assessment criteria). However, do not stigmatise pupils as a result of their spelling. You are likely to have in any one class a wide range of spelling ability. Thus you will need to differentiate spellings; hence the value of using spelling journals and open-ended questions. Try to avoid just giving the answer when pupils say, 'Miss how do you spell . . .?' Provide clues, or say, 'How do you think you spell that word?' As a teacher you should also be introducing pupils to new words with unusual or irregular spellings.

2.5 ICT

There is the obvious use of spell-checkers, but there is also an increasing number of spelling games available for pupils to use in guided group work or as support for individuals. Many schools have programs like Successmaker where individual progress is identified.

> Nicolson, Pickering and Fawcett (1991) carried out a study using a multimedia environment for dyslexic children which encouraged them to construct their own rules for the spellings of their problem words. Synthesised speech was used to augment the written text and different levels of help are available at all times. The interesting feature of the software was that the user was encouraged to identify and then fix his/her own 'spelling bugs' by creating a specific 'bug card' for each mistake. (in Mumtaz, 2000: 33)

An evaluation of the above software indicated 'substantial and lasting improvements in the spelling and motivation of a group of dyslexic children of average age 13 years' (ibid.).

On your school experience ask the SEN department and English Department what software is available to support the teaching of spelling. It would also be useful to do the same on any primary school experience. The use of ICT to make flash cards, to explore the structure of words such as prefixes and suffixes visually should not be underestimated.

Scenarios

1 You have some pupils in your Year 7 class who achieved Level 3 in writing at KS2 SATs so it is likely that they will need to follow some of the literacy progress units. How do you know whether they should follow the spelling units?

A useful audit is recommended at the start of the Spelling Literacy Progress Unit, reference 0475/2001 (DfEE, 2001c: xv). The audit is outlined below:

- *Stage 1*: Can the pupil spell all but one of these words: enemy, favourite, families, journeys, hospital, knives, photograph? If the answer is YES this LPU is not needed. You will note that to be successful the pupil will have needed good visual recognition, phonic awareness and a range of other strategies such as knowing when the final y remains in plurals. If the answer is NO then move on to the next stage.
- *Stage 2*: Can this pupil spell all but one of these words: thought, writing, clock, hopeful, stopped, because, heart? If the answer is YES this unit could be of benefit, but it may be more effective to diagnose and deal with the specific aspects of spelling which are causing difficulties. If the answer is NO move on to the next stage.

- *Stage 3*: Can the pupil spell all but one of these words: sleep, day, moon, new, fight, make, hoping, crawl? If the answer is NO the unit may be of benefit, but it may be better after the **phonics** unit rather than before it. If the answer is YES move on to the next stage.
- *Stage 4*: The unit should be of benefit to the pupil.

2   You have a pupil who has an excellent vocabulary in speaking and listening work, but because he has difficulties with spellings tends to play 'safe', avoiding the use of words he may spell incorrectly. As a result the richness of his vocabulary is not fully exploited in his writing. How do you encourage him to take risks in his writing and always choose the best word at his disposal?

FURTHER READING

An excellent resource for strategies to help pupils in their development of spelling, which includes detailed explanations of the use of spelling journals, is:
Department of Western Australia (1999) *Spelling Resource Book*. Sydney: Rigby Heinemann.

REFERENCES

Adorian, S., Brooke, B., Cardreau, L. (2002) *101 Red Hot Starters*. London: Letts
Davison, J. and Dowson, J. (1998) *Learning to Teach English in the Secondary School*. London: Routledge
DfEE (1999) *The National Curriculum for England. English: Key Stages 1–4*. London: DfEE and QCA
DfEE (2001a) *Key Stage 3 National Strategy: Framework for Teaching English: Years 7, 8 and 9*. London: DfEE
DfEE (2001b) *English Department Training 2001*. London: DfEE
DfEE (2001c) *Year 7 Spelling Bank* (Reference 0475/2001). London: DfEE
DES (1990) *English in the National Curriculum*. London: DES
Gentry, J.R (1987) *Spel . . . is a Four Letter Word*, Ontario, Canada: Scholastic
Hackman, S. and Trickett, L. (1996) *Spelling 9–13*. London. Hodder & Stoughton
Mumtaz, S. (2000) *Using ICT in Schools: a Review of the Literature on Learning, Teaching and Software Evaluation*. Warwick: The Centre for New Technologies Research in Education
Peters, M. (1985) *Spelling: Caught or Taught? A New Look*. London: Routledge and Kegan Paul
Stubbs, M. (1980) *Language and Literacy: the sociolinguistics of Reading and Writing*. London: Routledge and Kegan Paul

chapter 11

TEACHING PUPILS WITH ENGLISH AS AN ADDITIONAL LANGUAGE

By the end of this chapter you will have gained an understanding of how pupils learn EAL (English as an additional language), and the implications of this for schools, and the English classroom. There is an emphasis on the need to diagnose the language levels of pupils learning EAL, and for you as their English teacher, to provide appropriate support, drawing upon teaching assistants where necessary, and challenging such pupils cognitively and at times emotionally.

RATIONALE

The principle of inclusion which embraces the National Curriculum is also a very prominent standard for QTS, seen in all of Section 1 of the Revised Standards for QTS, 'Professional Values and Practice', specifically:

> 3.2.5: With the help of an experienced teacher, they [student teachers] can identify the levels of attainment of pupils learning English as an additional language. They [student teachers] begin to analyse the language demands and learning activities in order to provide cognitive challenge as well as language support.

And

> 3.3.5 They [student teachers] are able to support those who are learning English as an additional language, with the help of an experienced teacher where appropriate.

All the activities below address both standards.

Thus there is a requirement to know how to diagnose the language competencies of pupils learning EAL at the outset, and then show that you can support the learner in their development. This is a requirement for all student teachers – and is therefore an issue to be considered in homogeneous white schools, as well as in urban schools which may well have a larger number of pupils learning EAL. The UK has a long and rich history of providing a safe haven for refugees, together with a diverse population originating in the UK as an imperialist country. With increasing movement of people looking for work within the EU over the last few years there are now relatively few schools with no pupils learning EAL. Many pupils are truly bilingual, moving competently in and out of their first and second tongues, and equally literate in both. Other pupils use a mother tongue at home, but may only be literate in English. Multilingual schools are the norm: most people in the world speak two or more languages from birth – and there is growing appreciation of the benefits of such multilingualism in our schools for all pupils, and teachers.

Support for pupils learning EAL

Pupils learning EAL may need five years to attain the same level of English as those pupils who speak English as their mother tongue. It will be important for you to recognise that pupils learning EAL may well be at very different stages in their acquisition of English. Some may have been living in England for a short time and have few reading and writing skills; others may be becoming familiar with English, appearing confident in social talk but still not confident in the more academic registers. Others could be good readers when reading aloud, but their comprehension skills may be less developed and in their writing there may be evidence that they draw upon the syntax of their first language: e.g. 'Paul has made today a plane big' (Spanish syntax). Continued support all the way through the pupils' school career is therefore necessary – not just in the first year. As discussed in Chapter 5 on Equal Opportunities, The Ethnic Minority Achievement Grant (EMAG) administered by the DfES within the Standards Fund supports schools in providing specialist EAL support staff.

The link between possible underachievement of minority ethnic groups and their language skills must be strongly made; the whole linguistic, cultural, social and religious background of pupils is bound up in their success at school.

LINKS TO NATIONAL CURRICULUM AND KEY STAGE 3 STRATEGY

Curriculum English discusses language constantly, so there should be plenty of opportunities to integrate and include pupils learning EAL, more than in, for example, Science or Maths. The NC does not look specifically at the needs of pupils learning EAL, but the increased emphasis in each attainment target on Standard English and language variation should mean that as English teachers we are investigating and discussing language in close detail in most lessons – all of which will support the pupil learning EAL. Drawing on pupils with access to two or more linguistic systems will enrich such lesson objectives as 'Looking at the development of English . . . borrowings from other languages, origins of words' and 'Attitudes to language use'. The requirement for drama within the English classroom will certainly support such pupils, as will the requirement to read texts from different cultures and traditions. Texts which reflect pupils' backgrounds or experiences will raise the status of such pupils, and act as a powerful shared discourse for the class in understanding the differences and similarities between pupils and groups of pupils. However, all pupils have to get to grips with complex pre-1914 English literary heritage texts that use language unfamiliar to all groups. Writing will be the hardest attainment target for pupils learning EAL, as it is for most pupils. Careful scaffolding, and lots of modelling, with close attention to content, cohesion and paragraphing for organising ideas, are the best support. Planning and drafting will be important for pupils learning EAL: response partners who are at a more sophisticated level of English will also be able to help.

The NLS with the four-part lesson planning, explicit delivery and focus on sentence and word level work helps the teacher translate the NC objectives into smaller parts which will support the pupil learning EAL.

In *Access and Engagement in English* (DfES, 2002a) there is a useful section that provides a range of approaches for addressing certain learning needs under text level, sentence level and word level. These strategies are aimed for use with pupils learning EAL who have reached Levels 3/4. They are also aimed at pupils likely to have been learning English for at least two years. It is worth noting that these suggestions can be used flexibly and that writing approaches need to be supported by purposeful talk to encourage pupils to rehearse in their heads the models of English sentences being presented.

An example from each section under 'Writing' is listed below:

TEXT LEVEL

Learning need	Starter activity	Introduction	Development	Plenary
Paragraphing; grouping, developing and expanding ideas appropriately	Text sort: grouping and ordering sentences, under topic sentence for a paragraph. Support could work with pair or small group	Shared writing: demonstrate how to develop ideas from a topic sentence	Pair work: pupils write the next sentences, developing ideas on whiteboards. Support could work with targeted pupils	Pupils contribute their ideas to whole class discussion before independent homework on next paragraph. Support could provide writing frame to support organisation and cohesion of ideas

SENTENCE LEVEL

Learning need	Starter activity	Introduction	Development	Plenary
Subject–verb agreement	Quick matching activity: halves of sentences with subject split from verb (of limited use unless reference is made at point of pupils' own writing)	When modelling writing, rehearse aloud the choices, mark on text the points of reference to singular or plural	Guided writing: orally rehearse and practise agreement in particular contexts before writing. Does this sound right? Why? Why not?	May not be applicable to whole class objectives

WORD LEVEL

Learning need	Starter activity	Introduction	Development	Plenary
Uncountable nouns	Sort activities: plurals. Could use specific vocabulary related to text or lesson writing focus	Plan to discuss countable and non-countable nouns explicitly during the writing process (where it is relevant)	List examples as prompt for pupils in back of books or diaries	Not appropriate for plenary

Source: (DfES, 2002a: 20–21)

The attention to the genre and grammar of texts, vocabulary, paragraphing and spelling points at times to a Teaching English as a Foreign Language (TEFL) approach: student teachers with such teaching background will find their skills and knowledge useful for pupils learning EAL.

Activity 1

GETTING THE RIGHT INFORMATION ABOUT THE PRIOR LEARNING AND EXPERIENCES OF THE PUPIL LEARNING EAL

(suggested time: 3 hours)

As a starting point for working with a pupil you need to ask a member of the Ethnic Minority Achievement Grant (EMAG) team for the appropriate information on the language levels of a newly arrived pupil, or for those in the class you are taking over. Many schools, especially in urban areas, have intensive induction training for pupils arriving with very little English. This will be outside the curriculum. It will be your task to successfully integrate these pupils into your classroom when their level of English is judged to be at an appropriate level to deal with 'curriculum English'.

You will need to find out:

- their point of entry to the UK, and family circumstances (as far as this is helpful for your diagnosis);
- their mother tongue and other languages spoken outside the school (which language do they speak with their mother/father/siblings/friends?);
- their literacy levels in other languages (what is their level of literacy in their mother tongue? Do they attend Hebrew or Arabic classes at the weekend?);
- their previous school history;
- their English comprehension and literacy levels.

You need to make time for a language conference with the pupil(s) so that you can begin to understand for yourself their language needs. This is possibly the best strategy you can implement, demonstrating an interest and respect for the culture and language which the pupil brings with them to the class. Their confidence in you as their teacher may well be the most important element in their development. You may simply wish to discuss the previous questions with the pupil, and ask them to bring you something to read aloud in their mother tongue and in English. You may wish to carry out a miscue analysis to fully diagnose their reading levels. Photocopy the text they wish to read aloud, and mark the text according to their omissions of words, substituting one word with another, noting difficulties with decoding, and importantly, the pupil's level of comprehension through effective questioning at the end.

- What is your immediate understanding of the level of this pupil?
- What specific kinds of activities might you set in place to support their development in English? (You may want to come back to this question at the end of the chapter.)

Standards addressed: 3.2.5 and 3.3.5

TASK

Carry out this activity, and place the notes, and your diagnosis, in your English portfolio.

Activity 2 COGNITIVE DEVELOPMENT IN BILINGUAL LEARNERS

(suggested time: 30 minutes)

Bilingual pupils have a greater cognitive and academic proficiency than may be seen or heard in their surface production of speech and writing.

Much of what is produced at the 'surface' by pupils learning EAL will appear proficient in terms of comprehension at a conversational level. The deeper ability to analyse and evaluate may not be immediately visible because the pupils have not yet acquired the language to communicate this. If you can speak two or more languages, then you may appreciate the frustration of not quite having enough of one language to enter into debate and philosophical argument, and yet you may be perfectly fluent to all intents and purposes when buying potatoes in a shop. Importantly, pupils who are bilingual or have English as an additional language should be treated the same as monolingual pupils, and *not* as if they are pupils with learning difficulties or SEN.

Standards addressed: 3.2.5 and 3.3.5

TASK

Refer to this diagram with reference to your diagnosis of your pupil with EAL in Activity 1 above. How does this clarify or confirm your initial understanding of their level of competence?

Activity 3

BENEFITS OF BILINGUALISM: TALK IN THE CLASSROOM

(suggested time: 1 hour)

Bilingual pupils can:

- express the same thought in different languages, often in speech and in writing
- understand that L1 (mother tongue) is one particular system among many = 'metalinguistic awareness'
- have a greater facility in concept formation
- be good at divergent thinking
- have a greater social sensitivity.

But the inequalities of race, ethnicity, social class and gender in the classroom can sometimes counteract these potential benefits. How can we use these benefits of bilingualism in the English classroom?

Diana Cinamon's chapter 'Bilingualism and oracy ' (Chapter 8) in Brindley (1994) gives many excellent strategies to encourage bilingual learners to talk, and also encourages the use of home languages.

> *If talk is accompanied by practical activities and concrete experiences it helps children to understand concepts, develop skills and learn English while doing so. But what if the talk that is valued and encouraged is English only? What about the crucial relationship between language and learning? (Brindley, 1994: 72)*

This is shown to support both the mother tongue and the language being acquired: suppressing the use of mother tongue in the classroom may also suppress pupils' cognitive development.

The writer of this chapter once taught English to secondary school pupils in Uganda. All their schooling was through the English medium (with few if any models of English in their daily lives), with the result that any discussion was slow and teacher-led. When I asked them once to discuss the character of Juliet (they had to do *Romeo and Juliet* at O Level) in their own mother tongue, they immediately broke into the quickest, liveliest discussions I had ever heard. They successfully brought back to the whole class the points they came up with in English in a far more confident, and informed way than previously.

If you are a monolingual speaker of English, think back to situations – on holiday, travelling, learning a language for pleasure – when you were forced to make yourself understood in another language, or did not comprehend what was said to you. Now imagine trying to take Maths or Science GCSE in, say, French, or Gujarati. You would need to use your English to sort out concepts, moving in and out of the two languages. Keep that in mind when you teach pupils learning EAL.

Some schools have to work at providing models of English which are not there either in the home or in the playground, because of the large numbers of pupils learning EAL. Your bilingual pupils will need to be given many opportunities to speak in a variety of situations, with an increasing focus on formal situations – and the breadth of study for En1 in the NC insists on this. Well-structured group work with specific roles given to pupils such as scribe and chair will support pupils learning EAL. Giving very clear instructions on the purpose of the discussion, and prompt sheets for all pupils – differentiated or not – will offer further support.

Newly arrived pupils learning EAL may not contribute for some months. They should still be encouraged to work in groups; their silence is to be taken as a sign not that they are not understanding the issues, but that their level of English production is not at a sufficiently high enough level to contribute (as well as their confidence).

Placing pupils with the same language in a pair or group to discuss a character's feelings will further support both their cognitive understanding of the text, and their confidence in expressing their viewpoints. Diana Cinamon gives some valuable advice here:

> If children are talking together in groups we have to trust them to get on with the task, and also to trust them as they express opinions, argue points, disagree with what we think. It's not such a big step to encourage some of this to take place in a language we do not understand. We need to think about the control we exercise and how to hand over some of this within a clear structure, with objectives the children understand. Bilingual children will not exclude teachers who do not share their language and will usually switch in groups according to the needs of the task as well as the composition of the group. (Brindley, 1994: 77)

Further support at GCSE can be given in the form of a 'Talking Frame' to encourage a pupil learning EAL to enter into the discussion (and all pupils). This might be a series of questions, or even a few phrases appropriate for the discussion such as:

'I think that Juliet is . . .'
'I disagree with the last speaker . . .'
'To pick up on a point you just made . . .'
'Finally I think that . . .'

TASK

Standards addressed: 3.2.5 and 3.3.5

Think of a lesson you have taught which included much oral work. Did you have bilingual learners in your classroom? If you did, at which point did you encourage them to use their own languages? If not, can you include that lesson plan, and enlarge on the tasks where bilingual learners could more usefully use their own language?

Activity 4

MOVE TOWARDS 'CURRICULUM ENGLISH'

(suggested time: 20 minutes)

Bilingual learners need a range of contextual support and cognitive challenge in talk in the classroom. There are four types of language use, which, according to Brent Language Service (1999: 19) need to be considered in the development of pupils with EAL:

Register of English	Level of cognitive challenge	Level of cognitive challenge
	Low	High
Every day	*Type 1*: for example, chat about everyday events and plans, and about TV programmes, pop stars, sports, etc	*Type 3*: for example, talk within the context of structured exercises and activities which require genuine communication
Curriculum	*Type 2*: for example, giving rote-learned answers, copying from books, doing 'comprehension' exercises	*Type 4*: for example, writing answers in SATs and GCSE and written work in preparation for all such tests

TASK

Standards addressed: 3.2.5 and 3.3.5

Where would you place your pupil's abilities with regard to the four types of language demands at school? Have you observed him/her in the playground? In informal discussion with other pupils? Would it be helpful to observe the pupil in other lessons, or to see a sample of their work in lessons for Type 2 above?

Activity 5

WORKING WITH SUPPORT STAFF – AND PUPILS

(suggested time: 2 hours)

Time for joint planning and collaborative teaching are crucial in the effective use of support staff. Their expertise is to be sought, and their specific roles in the class need to be worked out. For example, Lucy Smith, a teacher working in a London school with a very high percentage of pupils with EAL, has described her work with the specialist teachers supporting pupils in class:

> 'I read through a poem, and then the EMAG teacher explains the meanings of the words which are unfamiliar to the pupils, listing uncommon words on the board. With complex GCSE readers we use lots of drama, she gives brief summaries [in the mother tongue], translates particular words, and gets the pupils to discuss the characters' feeling and emotions.'

TASK

Find out how the EMAG team works in your school, and the time and resources given both to preparing for lessons, and for INSET for class teachers on teaching pupils learning EAL. Write bullet points to record your investigations here and place them in your English portfolio.

Standards addressed: 3.2.5 and 3.3.5

It is also wise to draw upon the strengths and experiences of the pupils in your class to support the pupil learning EAL. Those with the same mother tongue but different levels of English may be able to translate for one another, so allowing all access to the discourse of the lesson. This will also enhance the more able speaker's English by forcing them to crystallise their understanding of what is happening in the lesson for another pupil.

Activity 6

SUPPORTING PUPILS IN REACHING 'CURRICULUM ENGLISH': READING TEXTS
(suggested time: 2 hours)

The question is, how can we support pupils with EAL in reaching Type 4 for academic success?

Routes for bilingual learners (from Brent Language Service, 1999: 24)

From

The language of everyday interaction

through:

Key visuals ← Collaborative group work → Writing frames

with

High cognitive challenge ← Respect for pupils' personal, cultural and linguistic identities → Lively interest in words + language

and:

Texts which inspire and empower

within the framework of whole school policies
towards the language of the National Curriculum

Strategies for using texts with classes that include pupils learning EAL

- Provide a good hook for reading the novel through discussion at the outset.
- Use illustrations to help with an understanding of the text.
- Provide summaries throughout a reading.
- If other pupils read aloud from the shared text, ensure that they are audible for all pupils.
- Prepare an audio tape with bits of the text being read so pupils can replay and refer to a spoken as well as a written text at a later point or at home.
- Use a film or video version, particularly at the beginning of the shared text to get the pupils into the discourse, the plot, understanding the characters.
- Build in a lot of oral work, drama and role play.
- Clearly explain uncommon words, idioms or phrases.
- Use the board to consolidate such meanings, giving translations of words if possible.
- Using pictures to represent the storyline, ask pupils to sequence the pictures according to plot, theme, etc.
- Remember that work on a text does not have to always include written work.
- Provide support (see Activity 9 below) for written work, and give a variety of tasks.

Source: Adapted from Bilingual Learners: support materials. (The English Centre, 1989, p. 9).

TASK

Standards addressed: 3.2.5 and 3.3.5

Sketch out the first rough plans of the first two lessons teaching a whole novel of your choice at Year 10. Indicate what other activities you would include to allow your six pupils learning EAL full access to the text. Draw overtly on your previous reading and the guidance given above. Provide a brief commentary of 400 words to explain the thinking behind your planning.

Activity 7

WORKING WITH WORDS

(suggested time: 2 hours)

Pupils learning EAL need lots of rich input at word level, which is a key focus of the NLS. You will need to provide a 'Talking Wall' with examples of peculiarly English idioms and phrases for all to enjoy, such as the ambiguity behind 'draw the curtains' or even prepositional phrases such as 'down the hall' or 'along the road' – words which children learn almost as one word because they are so common, but which to a pupil learning EAL may sound strange and need explanation. You will also need to continuously enrich your pupils' vocabulary – that of all pupils, not just your pupils with EAL. Providing opportunities for finding synonyms for words using a dictionary (or finding opposites, or oxymorons) will support all your pupils.

TASK

Standards addressed: 3.2.5 and 3.3.5

What other idioms and phrases can you find which such pupils might find difficult to grasp? Start a collection of these to place in your English portfolio, which could be part of a display to get your pupils started on adding their own in your classroom. See Further Reading for helpful resources.

Activity 8

PROGRESSION IN WRITING

(suggested time: 30 minutes)

Read the following extracts from writing by a girl who arrived from the Indian sub-continent at the age of 14. Use a different coloured pen to underline or to highlight the following:

1 Features of L1 (mother tongue, or first language) interference
2 Transition to formal written Standard English, with some errors made from attempting to write in such a formal way
3 Successful progression to 'writerly' or NC English
4 How you would describe her progression over the year in terms of her writing?

1 November, Year 10

Lady Macbeth hade some ambitious to be a queen one day but she didn't know how, so now the time was between her hands and shee new if the witches seid which her husband is going to be a Kind soon so she could be a queen is well, she was weiting for a good time to tell her husband about that.

Lady Macbeth telles he husband about that thing which the witches seid he is going to be a kind soon and then she told him which he has to kill the kind (Duncan) of Scotland then he will become a King.

2 March, Year 10

Marriage is a Decision which a girl has to take for her self which some times is well thought and some times can be misleading.

Every country has got their own way of choosing the correct partner for instance in India, Indian girls get marriad when they are young like 17 or 18 years old. When you're that age you don't know enough about life and relationships to be able to make such an important choices about marriage for yourself so the parents often help them with that important decision.

There are of course ekceptions. Some parent don't let the girls make this decision and they force the girl to marry a man which she doesn't know, or a man she doesn't love.

3 January, Year 11

In this play Miller uses a good language to express loman's 'American Dream' which will never become true.

Miller expresses Willy as a person that puts lots of effort in what he wants to do, but everytime he wants to start Something and to get on with his life, it just wouldn't work out; He was in his Sixties and still hasn't got a definite job for himself.

In that part Willy mentions a sentence to biff, that was 'never leave a job 'till you're finished', my point of view is that, this part could go with the 'American Dream' because when Willy mentioned this, he meant not to leave a jobe like polishing a car, or something like that, What he ment was, in their future, if they find a job, not to give it up so easily, if they decided to find another job, because it would be too hard to find another.

Willy always wanted Biff and Happy to be something and not to go through what life put him through. Willy loved Biff very much even more than Happy. He stood up for Biff lots of times, even when biff used to take things with out asking for it.

Standards addressed: 3.2.5 and 3.3.5

5   What does this pupil know about how language works, and grammar and syntax in particular?

Activity 9 MOVING TO TYPE 4 LANGUAGE USE – GCSE ESSAYS

(suggested time: 30 minutes)

Look at the writing frames devised to support pupils learning EAL to write a GCSE essay on *The Crucible*.

The Crucible by Arthur Miller

Abigail Williams

Look carefully at the following quotations and statements about Abigail Williams. Where you have been given a statement, find a quotation to go with it. Where you have been given a quotation, think of a suitable statement about Abigail which you think sums up what that quotation says about her.

Quotation	Statement
Abigail is described as '. . . an orphan, with an endless capacity for dissembling.' (p. 6)	
	Abigail is a bully
Abigail says, 'I know how you clutched my back behind your house and sweated like a stallion whenever I come near!' (p. 18)	
	Abigail is capable of pretending to be sweet and innocent

The Crucible by Arthur Miller

How far is Abigail Williams to blame for the events in Salem?

Use the following writing frame to help you draft this essay. In each box there are words and sentences to help you begin each paragraph about Abigail and to help you structure your work so that it makes sense.

You can use the frame in three ways:

- To give you ideas and to help you put together planning notes. Then use your own words to structure the essay.
- To guide you through your first draft, using the words of the frame but adding your own as you progress. Then develop all this in a second draft, which uses entirely your own words.
- To guide you through the essay from start to finish, using the words of the frame and just adding your own sentences. Then, next time you do an essay like this you will be able to do all the planning on your own.

When I first read *The Crucible* by Arthur Miller, my reaction to the character Abigail Williams was . . .

My reasons for taking this view were . . .

After thinking about and studying tthe play in more depth, I discovered that Abigail was a more complex character than I had realised. It is very easy to blame her for the events in Salem. However, if I wanted to defend her I would say . . .

I would also say . . .

The evidence I would give to support these arguments is . . .

When Arthur Miller created Abigail, I think he wanted to create a character who . . .

His reasons for creating this kind of character might have been . . .

My own attitude to Abigail, after considering all the different aspects of her character is . . .

I feel about her because . . .

I do/do not think she is to blame for what happens in Salem because. . .

> I would sum up the character Abigail Williams and her role in the events of the play in the following way:

Standards addressed: 3.2.5 and 3.3.5

1 What is the pedagogy behind the planning of these frames as it relates to pupils learning EAL (and perhaps monolingual speakers of English?)?

2 What is the pedagogy behind the three possible ways of using the frames? Draw on your knowledge of Vygotsky and other language theorists.

3 Would you want to add to (or take anything away from) these frames to further support your pupils learning EAL?

CONTINUOUS THREADS

1 Professional values and practice 1.7, 1.2

The Ofsted report, *Managing Support for the Attainment of Pupils from Ethnic Groups* (October 2001, in DfES, 2002: 2) identified the following factors that enable bilingual learners to develop English successfully:

- Joint planning between mainstream and specialist ethnic minority achievement (EMA) staff
- A focus on the content of the lesson, ensuring appropriate cognitive challenge
- A parallel focus on the language necessary to complete the task
- Activities that enable pupils to rehearse and explore the language they need
- Opportunities to use and build on their first-language skills, where appropriate
- Continuing support with writing through, for example, the use of matrices for organising information and writing frames for more extended contributions.

It is important to note that social language is usually acquired much more quickly than the language of school classrooms with its academic element. When planning your schemes of work consider the points raised above and ask yourself if you are putting in place the factors required to facilitate successful learning.

Adopting a positive approach is a prerequisite to successful teaching and to appreciating what pupils learning EAL bring to the classroom. This is foregrounded in *Grammar for Writing: Supporting Pupils Learning EAL*, as listed in the bullet points below.

- Knowledge of fluent talk in their first language(s)
- Commitment and purpose
- Openness to all kinds of new input
- Understanding that languages and grammars differ
- Sometimes written knowledge of other languages

In addition, pupils learning EAL are likely to develop a greater knowledge and understanding of grammars and how they work than their monolingual peers (DfES, 2002b).

3.2 Planning, expectations and targets

You will need to consider the particular grammatical errors made by pupils learning EAL and then put in place the appropriate strategies as part of your planning. So for example a pupil needing to develop text cohesion through greater use of connectives could be provided with a list of connectives for different purposes. The example provided below is taken from *Grammar for Writing: Supporting Pupils Learning EAL* (DfES, 2002: 36).

For sequencing

> Next
> Then
> First, second, third
> Finally
> Meanwhile
> After

Key areas in which you might expect pupils learning EAL to have difficulties fall broadly into these categories, as indicated in *Grammar for Writing* (DfES, 2002b: 9), depending upon their stage of learning and first language.

Text cohesion

- Verb tense forms
- Pronoun ambiguity
- Use of connectives

Sentence construction (subordination)

- Subject–verb agreement
- Word order
- Lack of subordination

Word choice

- Modification
- Use of prepositions
- Use of determiners

Native English speakers (Key Stage 3 upwards) usually have an excellent grasp of English grammar and errors might appear only in relation to dialect and confusion between speech and writing. However, pupils learning EAL may still need to appreciate how the English grammar system works in order to be effective communicators in it. Consequently, there may well be the necessity to explicitly teach English grammar with reference to the areas mentioned above. So for example at text level explicit teaching of cohesive devices may be necessary.

3.3. Monitoring and assessment

Monitoring of individuals' work for specific grammatical features will need to be undertaken. An example is provided from *Grammar for Writing* for you to consider.

Think about what this writer knows about grammar and what she needs to be taught.

> *Razia (YEAR 7) has been learning English for two years and is a Sylheti speaker, who does not read or write Bengali. Here she writes about her sister.*
>
> *As she is now at 18 years she look more nice. She has a brown shiny small eye. She got long lack hair like a snack tidy up at the back. My sister when she talk so softly you can understand anythink she says. She is not that tall not that small She lives at home with my family . My sister the way she walks is so fast that the first minute she is there the second minute she just venisht.*

Razia knows

- That a simple sentence usually has the pattern of subject, verb, object and adverbial e.g. She lives at home with my family.
- That she needs to vary her sentences, in order to make her writing interesting.

Razia needs to be taught

- How to combine ideas in her writing by using subordination
- How to use connectives effectively. (DfES, 2002b: 58)

It could also be argued that subject–verb agreement should be taught. This close analysis of pupils' writing is essential to inform your planning, teaching and target setting for pupils.

3.4 Teaching and class management

Whilst there will be times when you will need to differentiate your work carefully, there will be some activities when teaching native speakers of English aspects of grammar can be undertaken simultaneously with pupils learning EAL. The teaching of the differences between spoken language and written forms can be of value to all. In speech, shifts in tense and in meaning can be conveyed through tone of voice and para-linguistic communicators whilst in writing these shifts need to be highlighted more explicitly, such as in the ordering of clauses. Teaching these aspects of language can have learning benefits as much to pupils learning EAL as to those who have English as their first language. Similarly, when exploring dialect grammars the knowledge of other languages by pupils learning EAL can be exploited.

2.5 ICT

Think about the grammar-check facility for pupils with EAL not simply as a check, but also as a discussion point. Designing cloze exercises with connectives or other parts of speech which need strengthening in particular pupils can be highly supportive. Some pupils learning EAL may be highly ICT literate; others may not have had the opportunity to use a computer, and will need to be taught the basics while also developing their English. You might find it useful to refer to the 'Grammar Gorillas' website in Chapter 9 on Grammar in this section for further ideas on using grammar and ICT for pupils learning EAL.

Scenarios

1 You have two Year 9 refugee boys from Kosovo – they have been here three months. They sit at the back in a pair and are quiet but disengaged in the reading of *Macbeth*. What strategies can you employ to bring them more strongly into the shared discourse of the lesson?

2 In your class you have a girl from Ethiopia who is a refugee. She is keen to do well, but is inhibited by the antipathy towards her from other members of the class, both black and white. Group work seems impossible. Who will you turn to amongst the staff (and outside agencies) to support you here, and what might you do immediately to support her, and make the class a friendlier place for all?

FURTHER READING

McWilliam, N. (1998) *What's in a Word? Vocabulary Development in Multilingual Classrooms*. Stoke-on-Trent: Trentham Books

This is an excellent resource book, highly knowledgeable on how pupils learning EAL learn in the classroom, and providing a wealth of examples of idiomatic phrases and strategies to support the vocabulary development of such pupils. There is a great emphasis on drawing from the pupils' daily environment and on the visual impact of words.

Ofsted (March 2003) *Writing in EAL at Key Stage 4 and Post-16* and *More Advanced Learners of EAL in Secondary Schools and Colleges*. London: Ofsted Publications

These two highly detailed reports focus on the more fluent pupil learning EAL and their continued need for specific support for their writing skills.

OTHER RESOURCES

Video clip from *Literacy across the Curriculum* (DfES, 2001) Module 13 All Inclusive – this gives an excellent example of teaching pupils learning EAL.

Refugee Council
3 Bondway House
London SW8 ISJ
020 7582 6922

REFERENCES

Brent Language Service (1999) *Enriching Literacy – Text, Talk and Tales in Today's Classroom: a Practical Handbook for Multilingual Schools*. Stoke-on-Trent: Trentham Books

Brindley, S. (ed.) (1994) *Teaching English in the Secondary School*. London: Routledge

DfES (2002a) *Access and Engagement in English*. London: DfES

DfES (2002b) *Grammar for Writing: Supporting Pupils Learning EAL*. London: DfES

The English Centre (1989) *Bilingual Pupils: support material*. Compiled by J. Jugner. London: The English Centre

WEBSITES

www.blss.portsmouth.sch.uk
Look especially at their case studies, and types of bilingualism
http://www.standards.dfes.gov.uk/ethnicminorities/
http://www.standards.dfes.gov.uk/keystage3/strands/english/englishframework/s4/eal
Gives an overview of strategies with a good focus on the support of teaching assistants

SECTION THREE

READERS, WRITERS AND TEXTS

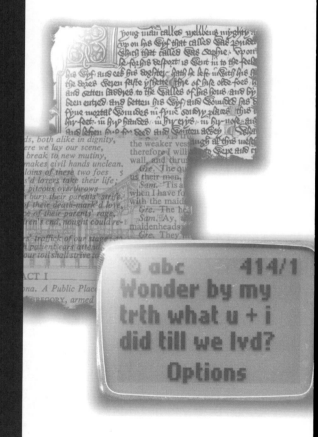

INTRODUCTION

Children come to school from an oral skills base. By the time they leave compulsory schooling at 16 they are required to have critical reading skills, and to independently generate a range of written forms. The shift in this century away from the written form towards the visual through the development of new technologies has resulted in multiple literacies; children are increasingly adept in their use of multi-modal means in their production of texts, using mixed symbols of text, images, graphics or media. This cultural revolution is slowly being recognised in revised editions of the National Curriculum, but the pedagogy of teaching media – a technology less than 100 years old and constantly changing – is still catching up with that of traditional print-based texts:

> What is certain is the audio-visual image is absolutely central to the child's organisation of knowledge, and that this centrality is still not much appreciated by schools and forms of teaching. (McCabe, 1998, p. 36)

This section on 'Readers, Writers and Texts' not only therefore includes media and ICT alongside teaching reading, narrative texts, writing, and poetry, but starts with a crucial chapter on critical literacy which is designed partly to influence and to impinge on the issues within the subsequent chapters. Those larger questions about form, purpose and audience which we need to ask – for less able as well as more able pupils – are the starting points for the study of all texts. This also allows for comparison between texts, illuminating the 'reading/viewing' processes of each:

Genre	How do we watch/read it?	Where do we watch/read it?	Who has the control? Authorship?
Book	Sequential, fixed order – BUT flashbacks, references backwards and forwards embedded in text, a negotiated construction of meaning in which both the reader and writer actively participate in representation of life through rapid decoding of words on page, drawing on context, syntax and grapho-phonic skills, specific and practised eye movements	Anywhere – very portable Usually a private activity, done alone Can be a shared, social activity – class, adult reading group, performance reading	The individual reader in turning the pages The author The teacher The parent The performer
TV	Engaged and silent, or shared viewing with commentary; disrupted reading (adverts, making tea), reading of people, and juxtaposition of text and image; aural and visual representations; increasing choice of programmes, interactive viewing rather than passive; eyes move according to action, camera angle, framing, focus, lighting, text	At home, the pub, alone or with others, selective reading or TV on as wallpaper	The individual viewer using the remote/on/off button The parent The one holding the remote control TV producers and directors Ratings BBC Governors Advertisers

Such an approach complements the more specific professional skills that a teacher of English needs to know – how children learn to read, the different stages of spelling development – and also contextualises debates such as the 'Real Books vs Phonics', or the 'Genre vs Process' models of writing.

Vygotsky wrote that 'Children grow into the intellectual life of those around them' (1978: 88), which can be paraphrased as 'Children grow into the textual practices of those around them.' We need to put all kinds of texts into our classrooms, encourage pupils to question them, and forge creative and intellectual links between them, in a spiral curriculum – one which includes pupils' home and social 'textual practices'.

REFERENCES

McCabe, C. (1998) 'Television and literacy', in B. Cox (ed.) *Literacy Is Not Enough*. Manchester: Manchester University Press

Vygotsky, L.S. (1978) *Mind in Society: the Development of Higher Psychological Processes*. Cambridge, MA: Harvard University Press

chapter 12

CRITICAL LITERACY AND LITERARY THEORY

In this chapter you will explore the role of critical literacy and literary theory in English teaching. You will be challenged to think about the value of disrupting absorbed reading processes; to consider and explore models of critical literacy developed in England and Australia; and to focus in turn on the roles of the reader, of social, cultural and historical contexts, and finally, of the text itself in the construction of meaning. Throughout the chapter your thinking will be challenged by questions which educators working in these fields have asked, you will be directed to examples of practice, and invited to develop and evaluate your own.

To complete the work in this chapter, you will need to make reference to: the Programme of Study for English Key Stages 3 and 4, En2 Reading, in DfEE and QCA (1999) pp. 34–6 or at **www.nc.uk.net**); and the criteria for GCSE, A and AS Level Specifications for English Language and English Literature published by QCA at **www.qca.org.uk/nq/framework/gcse_criteria.asp** and **www.qca. org.uk/nq/framework/main.asp**. You will also need to make reference to the specifications for GCSE, A and AS Level used at your placement school, which you can find on the examination board websites: Assessment and Qualifications Alliance (AQA) (**www.aqa.org.uk**); EdExcel (**www.edexcel.org.uk**); Oxford, Cambridge and RSA (OCR); (**www.aqa.org.uk**) and Welsh Joint Education Committee (WJEC) (**www.wjec.co.uk**).

RATIONALE

The National Curriculum for English (1999) does not offer a rationale for the curriculum it defines. However, there is obviously some correlation between what teachers think English is, what they think it is for, and the way in which they teach. This chapter is intended to help you determine what *you* think English is and what it is for, by challenging you to explore the rationales for particular teaching approaches which can be derived from some of the most significant thinking about these issues in the 20th century.

Critical literacy is an educational concept with origins in the work of Paulo Freire, which has challenged all teachers of literacy to consider the relationships between language and power. In the second half of the 20th century in particular, a proliferation of varied literary theories challenged all previously held assumptions about the character of texts and the processes of their production and reception. This chapter will invite you to consider how far the influences of critical literacy and radical literary theories have penetrated English teaching in schools.

The first National Curriculum for English, *English in the National Curriculum* (DES, 1990) was explicitly built on a compromise defined in *English for Ages 5–16* [The Cox Report] (DES, 1989). Cox reported that five views of the purposes of English were common among teachers. Among these, the 'cultural analysis' view emphasised 'the role of English in helping children towards a critical understanding of the world and cultural environment in which they live'. This view argued that: 'Children should know about the processes by which meanings are conveyed, and about the way in which print and other media carry values' (para. 2.25).

'Cultural analysis' as defined here has much in common with both critical literacy and the radical critical theories which had penetrated many university English courses by the 1980s, and it has clearly had some influence on the school English curriculum. For example, the National Curriculum for English states that 'Pupils should be taught . . . to understand the values and assumptions in the texts' they study 'from different cultures and traditions (En2 Reading)' (DfEE, 1999: 49). The national criteria for GCSE English Literature, which all specifications must meet, include a requirement for pupils to 'develop awareness of social, historical and cultural contexts and influences in the study of literature' (**www.qca.org.uk/ nq/framework/english_literature.pdf**).

Moreover, the introduction of Citizenship into the National Curriculum has given greater scope to teachers who wish to promote this kind of critical reading: the Citizenship National Curriculum states that: 'Pupils should be taught to . . . think about topical political, spiritual, moral, social and cultural issues, problems and events by analysing information and its sources, including ICT-based sources' (DFEE, 1999: 184): analysis of information and its sources should involve accessing the values informing it.

However, what the Cox Report called the 'cultural heritage' view, which emphasised 'the responsibility of schools to lead children to an appreciation of those works of literature that have been widely regarded as amongst the finest in the language' (DES, 1990: para. 2.24), remains equally influential in the English curriculum: 'Pupils should be taught . . . the characteristics of texts that are considered to be of high quality' and 'the importance of these texts over time (En2 Reading)' (DFEE, 1999: 49). The 'cultural heritage' view casts the reader in the role of an appreciator or admirer of excellence, rather than as an interrogator of values and assumptions, and this is reflected in another of the GCSE English Literature national criteria: pupils should learn to 'appreciate the ways in which authors achieve their effects'.

Despite the Cox Report's attempt at a compromise definition of English, some readings of texts are distinctively and rigorously interrogative, while others are fundamentally appreciative, and teaching can be geared to induce one response rather than the other. Some teaching approaches, such as reading aloud to a class at length, are more likely to promote absorbed appreciation; others, by engaging pupils in a wide range of interrogative activities such as underlining key words and ideas, predicting how texts will develop, and unpacking the sequences in which they are meant to be read, are more likely to result in critical questioning. (Active reading strategies of this kind are known as directed activities related to texts, or DARTs, in recognition of the development work of Lunzer and Gardner, 1979.) If teachers are to make effective connections between teaching strategies and learning outcomes in their planning, they must cut through the Cox compromise and determine what kinds of readers and reading they are working to promote.

This chapter invites you to investigate, and indeed to question critically, reading approaches founded on critical questioning, which are ultimately incompatible with the depoliticised appreciation of the texts in a preconceived literary canon.

LINKS TO THE NATIONAL CURRICULUM AND THE KS3 NATIONAL STRATEGY

Activity 2 will prompt you to investigate how far the National Curriculum and public examination specifications suggest it is appropriate for you to incorporate approaches based on critical literacy and radical critical theories into your English teaching.

Activity 1   CHANGING STORIES

(suggested time:
Task 1: 3 hours: planning, teaching and evaluation;
Task 2: 1 hour to write contributions to a WebBoard discussion or seminar)

If critical literacy and most forms of literary theory have much in common, it is a shared concern with disrupting acquiescent, absorbed forms of reading.

Changing Stories by Bronwyn Mellor with Judith Hemming and Jane Leggett (1984) is a set of resources which can be used to teach the disruption of acquiescent, absorbed readings of folk and fairy stories. The materials can be used in different ways with pupils from Year 7 to Year 13.

In the first unit of work, 'The Princess', the following activities are suggested:

(a) Pupils are told some key facts about a fairy story and asked to predict other elements of content (based on their expectations of the genre):
e.g. Bedelia is given three gifts by fairies when she is born. What are they?
(b) A story, 'The Practical Princess', is read, in which some, but not all, conventions of the genre are challenged or reversed.
(c) Pupils identify the challenged or reversed conventions.

TASK 1

Either using the materials from *Changing Stories* or constructing some of your own, teach a lesson in which you ask pupils to identify conventions of a genre which are undermined in a text they then share. Ask them to identify the challenged conventions. A further activity may be to invite pupils to write a piece in which they exercise choice over whether or not to subvert the conventions of the genre. Find out, using a strategy appropriate to the group you are teaching, what the pupils have learned by carrying out this work.

Note: Among other things, *Changing Stories* includes five versions of 'Little Red Riding Hood' to compare, showing how the story can be manipulated for different conscious and unconscious purposes. It also contains stories which promote different behavioural expectations of boys and girls, men and women.

TASK 2

Question (for discussion with other teachers and student teachers via WebBoard or seminar)

Martin and Leather use a metaphor from drug culture to describe the escapism and involvement they see as essential to reading development: 'Before long you are hooked and cannot do without a regular fix' (Martin and Leather, 1994: 7).

What are the possible advantages of deliberately disrupting acquiescent and absorbed reading when teaching reading?

Note: One student teacher, Kathy Rees, responded to this question as follows. You may like to use this response to stimulate your own.

'Possible advantages of disrupting absorbed reading when teaching reading might include:

'1. The stimulation of questions at a time when the pupil is personally involved in the story. Once a book is finished, the questions do not have the same impact, because the story is resolved and the reader has become more detached.

'2. In the case of a class reader, pupils might be surprised to learn that the same book can be experienced/perceived in a different way, according to one's individual cultural and ideological repertoire. When the pupil resumes the book, his/her reading may be enriched by the observations of others.

'3. By disrupting a text and asking the pupil to predict the likely ending, he/she may – quite unconsciously – draw on previous experience of that genre so that the suggested resolution feels 'appropriate'. A pupil thereby acknowledges an understanding of the conventions of the genres.

'4. Half-way through a book, the teacher may alert pupils to intertextuality – concepts, references, imagery to be found in other texts, or across the media – thereby heightening and enriching the pupil's continued experience of the book.

'5. Disrupting the narrative to examine the intention of the author may alert the pupil to the way the author manipulates reader responses. Questions like: Why did the author decide to write about this particular subject? What ideological/cultural repertoire influenced the author to write in this particular way? Disruption may temporarily frustrate the reader, but at the same time make him more aware of the author's craft (production) and the nature of the reader's developing responses (reception) and hopefully better able to articulate those changes (linking in with Speaking and Listening, Writing work).

Standards addressed: 1.1, 2.1c and d
'6. A discussion part-way through a book about any sexist, classist, racist or ageist ideas within it may alert the pupil to evaluate how such ideas are developed. This may help the pupil to develop a critical position. Where does the author position the reader? Does this positioning differ as the book develops? What effect does the book's structure (and authorial devices) have on the reader?'

Activity 2   CRITICAL LITERACY AND LITERARY THEORY IN THE NATIONAL CURRICULUM

(suggested time: reading of sources: up to 3 hours;
analysis of curriculum documents and response: up to 2 hours)

Read the following quotations, and, if possible, the texts from which they are taken.

The main effect of theory is the disputing of 'common sense': common-sense views about meaning, writing, literature, experience. For example theory questions

- the conception that the meaning of an utterance or text is what the speaker 'had in mind',
- or the idea that writing is an expression whose truth lies elsewhere, in an experience or state of affairs which it expresses,
- or the notion that reality is what is 'present' at a given moment.

> . . . *As a critique of common sense and exploration of alternative conceptions, theory involves a questioning of the most basic premises or assumptions of literary study, the unsettling of anything that might have been taken for granted: What is meaning? What is an author? What is it to read? What is the 'I' or subject who writes, reads, or acts? How do texts relate to the circumstances in which they are produced?*

(*from Culler, 1997: Chapter 1*)

A set of questions which might be asked by a practitioner of critical literacy:

- What version of reality am I given here?
- What perspective on the world is this?
- What other knowledge and perspectives are there that I'm not given, and if I know them, how might this alter my reading of this version?
- What viewing angle or position am I being given by this text, and what kind of reader am I assumed and encouraged to be? What response am I being coached to make?
- If I have access to other discussions, will this enable me to take up a different reading position and redefine the kind of person I am and how I can respond?
- How does this text set up the authority of its information and so encourage me to trust it?
- If I have other information, will I reassess the authority as sufficient?
- Does this authorised view confirm the position of those who stand to benefit from it?
- If I have other information, might I see more clearly who does not benefit and why? (Morgan et al., 1996: Chapter 1)

TASK

In the light of these passages, which reach towards definitions of literary theory and critical literacy by defining the questions they are concerned with, consider how far you are expected to inform your English teaching with literary theory and to develop critical literacy in your pupils.

You should refer to the following documents:

1   Programme of Study for English Key Stages 3 and 4, En2 Reading, in *The National Curriculum for England. English: Key Stages 1–4* (DfEE and QCA, 1999) pp. 34–6 or at **www.nc.uk.net**)
2   The criteria for GCSE, A and AS level Specifications for English Language and English Literature published by QCA at **www.qca.org.uk/nq/ framework/main.asp**.
3   The detail of at least one of each of the following:
    a scheme of work used for Key Stage 3 at a school you visit;
    GCSE and A Level specifications used at a school you visit.

Standards addressed: 2.1c and d, 3.3.2c and d

You should make a distinction between national criteria, examination board specifications, and local interpretations of them. When discussing schemes of work, you should consider how far expectations of pupils defined in aims and objectives are realised by the planned learning objectives and assessment outcomes.

Activity 3   CRITICAL SOCIAL LITERACY FOR THE CLASSROOM

(suggested time: reading Lankshear chapter and reflection
on citizenship education issues: 2 hours; planning,
teaching and evaluating lesson(s): 3 hours minimum)

In Chapter 2 of *Changing Literacies* (1997) Colin Lankshear identifies a pedagogy for teaching critical social literacy in the classroom. Writing with reference to the corpus of research on critical literacy, Lankshear argues that its essential characteristics are 'the element of evaluation or *judgement,*' or analysis of, an '*object* of evaluation or judgement' (p. 43). In different versions of critical literacy, the object of evaluation may be literacy itself, particular texts, or the '*social practices, arrangements, relations, allocations, procedures* etc., which are mediated by, made possible, and partially sustained through reading, writing, viewing, transmitting, etc., texts' (p. 44).

In this broad context, Lankshear describes an experiment in the development of 'an interdisciplinary practice of critical literacy' (p. 52):

He quotes a text headed 'The Face of Starving Africa' from *The Australian*. He invites analysis of the passage using the following questions which he attributes to Luke and Fairclough:

1   *What version of events/reality is foregrounded here?*
2   *Whose version is this? From whose perspective is it constructed?*
3   *What other (possible) versions are excluded?*
4   *Whose/what interests are served by this representation?*
5   *By what means – lexical, syntactic, etc. – does this text construct (its) reality?*
6   *How does the text position the reader? What assumptions about readers are reflected in the text? What beliefs, assumptions, expectations (ideological baggage) do readers have to entertain in order to make meaning from the text?'*

Lankshear then, more radically, suggests that reading the text can be enhanced by the following activities:

1   *Locate for [a range of curriculum subjects e.g. history, geography, science] a range of texts relevant to situations like that in Somalia (viz. disasters).*
2   *Ensure that among them the texts reflect different perspectives.*
3   *Identify and describe key differences in the perspectives, in terms of their underlying theories, the questions or issues with which they are most concerned, their key assumptions, whose standpoint they most reflect, where you would locate them on a continuum.*

TASK

Read the whole of Lankshear's chapter carefully. Using material which is relevant to the pupils you teach, plan a lesson or series of lessons in which pupils investigate a text or texts using questions based on those listed by Lankshear above and/or Morgan et al. under Activity 2 above.

If possible, extend the work by experimenting with the approach suggested above by Lankshear for enhancing this reading. You are only likely to be able to do this in collaboration with specialist teachers from other subject areas.

QUESTION

Lankshear identifies the following goals for the critical social literacy project: power awareness, critical literacy, desocialisation and self-organisation/self-education. He refers readers to Ira Shor's definitions of these terms, which need careful consideration. However, they collectively constitute a form of citizenship education.

What objectives of the National Curriculum for Citizenship Education could be addressed by systematic teaching of critical social literacy?

(See Citizenship, *The National Curriculum* (DfEE and QCA, 1999 or **www.nc.uk.net**)

Activity 4

CRITICAL LITERACY FOR THE CLASSROOM AND COMMUNITY

(suggested time: Planning, teaching and evaluating lesson:
up to 3 hours; reflection on discussion question: 1 hour)

In *None But Our Words* (1998) Chris Searle describes the principles of critical literacy as:

> *creation . . . the mobilization of words and the imagination in response to a certain situation . . . consideration . . . acts of individual and collective thinking . . . consciousness . . . thoughts freshly forged, newly expressed . . . confidence . . . both in the creative self and others who have worked in collaboration . . . consolidation [leading to] the determination . . . for cultural action . . . [which may involve] crossover of culture.*

Importantly, Searle acknowledges the debt of critical literacy to Paulo Freire, in works such as *The Pedagogy of the Oppressed* (1972) and *Education: the Practice of Freedom* (1975). *None But Our Words* goes on to describe Searle's work in promoting critical literacy in a range of school and community contexts. He records the extent to which his work has been controversial, describing how, for example, the publication of *Stepney Words,* an anthology of pupils' work about the community they lived in, against the wishes of the school governors, led to his dismissal and a strike by pupils.

The Crick Report, *Education for Citizenship and the Teaching of Democracy in Schools* (QCA, 1998) contains a section on the teaching of controversial issues (56–61). Having described the 'neutral chairman', 'balanced' and 'stated commitment' approaches, and indicated that all have shortcomings if used in isolation or too rigidly, the report recommends the following:

The guiding principle should surely be that teachers are encouraged to use whatever means they find most effective in bringing home to those they teach that, by their very nature, controversial issues do not admit of easy answers. Nevertheless, whatever approach a teacher chooses to adopt, good practice will always seek to provide assurance that the risk of bias is avoided by making sure that every aspect of an issue is examined fairly and thoroughly by means of a checklist of questions such as the following:

- *What are the main features and probable causes of this issue?*
- *How, where and by whom are these matters normally resolved?*
- *Are there other ways in which this issue might be resolved?*
- *What are the main groups involved in this issue and what do they say needs to be done and why?*
- *What are their interests and values? What are the likely consequences of their policies?*
- *How can people be persuaded to act or change their minds?*
- *How can the accuracy of the information be checked and where can additional evidence and alternative opinions be obtained?*
- *How does this issue affect us and in what ways can we express our point of view and influence the outcome?'*

TASK

In the texts referred to above, Searle (through education for 'cultural action') and Crick (through education for 'influence') suggest that critical literacy and citizenship education need to go beyond the analysis of issues and provide opportunities for pupils to influence matters they feel strongly about.

In close negotiation with a placement school, plan and, if possible, teach a lesson or series of lessons which aims to give pupils an opportunity to give real expression to their views.

QUESTION (for discussion with other teachers and student teachers)

Standard addressed: 2.2 'Empowerment' has become a buzz word in education: teachers often write it into their policy aims. From your reading of the texts above, and your experience undertaking the task, what conclusions have you reached about whether pupil empowerment is a realistic goal of education?

Activity 5

MEANING LOCATED IN READERS
(suggested time: Planning, teaching and evaluating lesson(s): 3 hours minimum; reflection on discussion questions: 1 hour)

Read the first part of 'How should critical theory inform English teaching?' Chapter 13 of Davison and Moss (eds) *Issues in English Teaching* (2000), especially the section headed 'Theories locating authority for meaning in the reader', pp. 199–203. This section of the chapter argues that, in the light of reader-response theories, which explore the role of the reader in determining, or even generating, meanings of texts, teachers need to recognise that the teaching methods they use have an effect on the extent to which pupils are enabled to determine or generate meanings. It follows that good teaching will also help pupils to *understand* that the relative power of the reader and writer in determining or generating meanings varies, depending on both the characteristics of a text and the kind of reading of it which takes place.

Reading Stories (1987) by Bronwyn Mellor, Marnie O'Neill and Annette Patterson is a collection of teaching resources for investigating the reader's role in the construction of meaning from texts. For example, the first section of the materials invites exploration of the following questions:

- What expectations do readers have of stories?
- Where do readers' expectations come from?
- Can a story ask to be read in a particular way?
- Do readers read a story in the same way the second, third or fourth time?
- Can stories have 'messages'?

The activities in this section are as follows:

1   Pupils are asked to predict the content of the story 'The Good Corn' by H.E. Bates, having been told the title, gender and ages of the characters and the setting. After reading the story, they discuss and note down the usefulness of each of these pieces of information in making predictions, the kind of ideas each piece of information suggested, and the origin of their ideas.
2   A second story, 'Turned' by Charlotte Perkins Gilman, is gradually revealed in sections. Pupils are prompted to make new predictions by answering questions before each section is revealed.
3   A series of role play and discussion activities drawing attention to similarities and differences in the stories invites pupils to consider matters such as textual gaps and how re-reading each story will be affected by having read the other.

TASK

Using either materials from *Reading Stories* or some of your own, plan and teach a lesson or series of lessons in which you explicitly challenge pupils to explore what they bring as readers to the meaning of a text.

Standards addressed: 2.1d, 3.3.2d

QUESTIONS (for discussion with other teachers and student teachers)

1   What are the implications for practice of recognising the contribution that readers make to the meaning of texts they encounter?
2   (See *Issues in English Teaching*, p. 210) To what extent, in practice, is 'authority for meaning' constructed by pupils as located in teachers, and by teachers as located in nationally imposed requirements of readers?

Activity 6   MEANING LOCATED IN CONTEXTS

(suggested time: planning, teaching and evaluating lesson(s):
3 hours minimum; reflection on discussion questions: 1 hour)

Read the second part of 'How should critical theory inform English teaching?'
Chapter 13 of Davison and Moss (eds) *Issues in English Teaching* (2000), headed
'Theories locating authority for meaning in the social, historical and cultural
contexts in which texts are produced and received', pp. 203–6.

This section of the chapter argues that an investigation of critical theories which locate
primary authority for meaning in the social, historical and cultural contexts of texts,
suggests that 'teachers can develop the range and complexity of meanings which are
generated by texts and readers in classrooms, by exposing and exploring the
ideological and cultural elements of text and extending those of the reader' (p. 206).

Examples of teaching resources for 'exploring the ideological and cultural elements
of text' include the following.

Studying Literature (1987) by Brian Moon is a set of materials for teaching literature
to advanced students. It includes a section headed: 'Reading in terms of gender',
which aims to help pupils answer the following questions:

● What is gender and how is it constructed?
● What part does literature play in the power structure of society?
● Do all representations of gender reinforce cultural prejudices and stereotypes?
● How can readers challenge representations of gender in literary texts?

The section introduces pupils to the idea that gender is a cultural term by exploring
the vocabulary of gender with reference to a range of texts including 'Never would
birds' song be the same again' and 'The aim was song' by Robert Frost.

Pupils are then led towards the following questions which they are asked about texts
including Donne's 'A Valediction: forbidding mourning' and the story of Rapunzel:
which character is mobile? static? emotional? rational? strong? weak? active? passive?

Further activities include the deconstruction of texts including 'The essence of a
man' by Alan Sullivan and *The Company of Wolves* by Angela Carter.

Wuthering Heights by Emily Brontë: A post-16 Study Guide (1998) by Christine Hall
and Mary Bailey includes a section on 'Contexts and connections'. The guide is one
of a series entitled *Critical Reading* for use in A Level teaching.

This section includes contemporary reviews, a contemporary preface by Charlotte
Brontë, a critical history of the book which includes extracts from psychoanalytic,
Marxist and deconstructive readings, and summaries of five other Brontë novels.

TASK

Construct a set of materials and lesson plans, either for teaching a critical approach
to reading which addresses issues of economics, power, gender, race, class or

marginalisation (taking ideas from Moon's treatment of gender issues), or for teaching a range of critical approaches to a single text (taking ideas from Hall and Bailey's treatment of *Wuthering Heights*).

QUESTION (for discussion with other teachers and student teachers)

Standards addressed:
2.1d, 3.3.2d

(See *Issues in English Teaching*, Davison and Moss, 2000: 210). At what stage in pupils' reading development, and how, should 'context-centred' critical theory(theories) begin to influence pedagogy?

Activity 7

MEANING LOCATED IN TEXTS

(suggested time: Planning, teaching and evaluating lesson(s): 3 hours minimum; reflection on discussion questions: 1 hour)

Read the third part of 'How should critical theory inform English teaching?,' Chapter 13 of Davison and Moss (eds) *Issues in English Teaching* (2000), especially the section headed 'Theories locating primary authority for meaning in the text', pp. 206–9.

This section of the chapter challenges teachers to take account of the facts that:

1   the terminology traditionally used in the analysis of texts in schools (such as 'character') has been reinterpreted by critical theory in ways which classroom practice could acknowledge more;
2   there is a wide range of text-centred literary terminology available to teachers from a range of literary theories of which much more use could be made in classrooms.

Both *Literary Terms: A Practical Glossary* (1992) by Brian Moon and *The Concise Oxford Dictionary of Literary Terms* (1990) by Chris Baldick provide clear definitions of a range of useful terms.

Moon for example (pp. 3–6), defines binary oppositions as 'structural features encoded in texts and reading practices. They are patterns of opposing concepts or values which work to reproduce a set of beliefs or values, and they serve particular interests.' This definition is illustrated by the identification of binary oppositions in the opening paragraph of *A Tale of Two Cities* and a summary of *High Noon*. Moon then invites consideration of which elements in each set of oppositions are privileged.

TASK

Standards addressed:
2.1d, 3.3.2d

Identify some terminology from the list in *Issues in English Teaching* or from Baldick or Moon which is new to you, but which sheds light on a text you plan to teach. Devise a lesson plan which makes use of the concept(s) in a manner which is appropriate for the pupils concerned. Evaluate the lesson.

Activity 8

SUMMARY QUESTION

(suggested time: 1 hour)

Standard addressed: 1.7

How can you plan to continue to extend your own 'semiotic, generic, cultural and ideological repertoire' (see *Issues in English Teaching,* p. 210) so that this repertoire can inform your developing practice as an English teacher? Identify some specific targets which include the development and application of new subject knowledge, and which you can realistically achieve during your initial training.

CONTINUOUS THREADS

1 Professional values and practice

The Standards for the Award of Qualified Teacher Status require new teachers to learn how to teach in ways which respect the social and cultural values of pupils, address the needs of all individuals and groups while taking account of these values, and enable all pupils to progress. The policy of inclusion which informs the Standards is founded on a sensitive response to diversity which must inform all aspects of practice.

Thus, it is a fundamental professional value to 'respect [pupils'] social, cultural, linguistic, religious and ethnic backgrounds' (1.1). Planning must be 'relevant to all pupils' (3.1.1) and take account of 'pupils' interests and their language and cultural backgrounds' (3.1.3) and assessment must also support pupils of all abilities and backgrounds (3.2.4, 3.2.5). Teaching must 'establish a purposeful learning environment where diversity is valued and where pupils feel secure and confident' (3.3.1) and be differentiated to meet the needs of all pupils (3.3.4–3.3.6).

Critical literacy and many radical critical theories are concerned with identifying the social and cultural values which inform texts, including the ways in which texts can privilege individuals and groups, and exclude or marginalise others. They are also concerned with voices which may otherwise be unheard: for example, reader-response theory gives a voice to the reader in the generation of meaning; Marxist, post-colonial and feminist theories, among others, expose the ways in which texts reinforce or challenge existing power relations, and give voice, or fail to give voice, to particular groups in society.

It can consequently be argued that English teaching which draws on critical literacy and those critical theories which are concerned with power and representation has a very specific and principled contribution to make to the inclusive education promoted in the Standards. Pupils who learn to critically question the texts they encounter are learning to question privilege and exclusivity. Pupils who learn that all texts are informed by particular social and cultural values are also learning to recognise that they and their peers all bring sets of social and cultural values to the classroom which underpin their individual identities.

Scenarios

How would you respond to the following situations, and how far would you change your practice for the future in the light of them?

1 You plan a unit of work on genre for your Year 7 class using, among other things, some of the materials from *Changing Stories*. The Head of English asks you to explain what the unit has got to do with National Curriculum and Key Stage 3 Strategy objectives and priorities.

2 You have encouraged your Year 9 pupils to explore what they bring as readers to the texts they study. You read the first stanza of Blake's 'Tyger' to the class and ask for the pupils' responses to it. A pupil puts up his hand and tells you enthusiastically that Blake clearly didn't like maths because he talks about '*fearful* symmetry'.

3 You invite your Year 10 pupils to read a text of their choice using the critical questions Lankshear attributes to Luke and Fairclough in Activity 3 in this chapter. A group of four articulate pupils produces a well argued critical reading of the school's code of conduct, pointing out how it reinforces the power and privileges of the staff. They inform you that in the light of the learning that has taken place in the course of producing this analysis they no longer intend to follow the code of conduct.

4 You develop an A level induction course which introduces your pupils to Marxist criticism, post-colonialist and feminist theory using Shakespeare's *The Tempest* as a text to investigate. A Year 12 pupil comes to see you at the end of the first fortnight to tell you that she is going to give up English because you are destroying the magic of literature for her.

FURTHER READING

In the references section below, Paulo Freire's books will give you an inspiring introduction to critical literacy, while the work of Lankshear, Morgan et al. and Searle explore its application in a range of English and Australian educational contexts. Baldick and Culler, and Moon (1992) provide accessible introductions to literary theory, concepts and terms, which, because of their differences in approach, complement each other well. Hall and Bailey and Mellor et al.'s materials will give you further practical insight into the classroom possibilities, while Davison and Moss contains chapters on a range of related issues which will prompt you to develop your thinking.

REFERENCES

Baldick, C. (1990) *The Concise Oxford Dictionary of Literary Terms.* Oxford: Oxford University Press

Culler, J. (1997) *Literary Theory.* Oxford: Oxford University Press

Davison, J. and Moss, J. (eds) (2000) *Issues in English Teaching.* London: Routledge

DES (1989) *English for Ages 5–16.* London: DES.

DES (1990) *English in the National Curriculum.* London: DES.

DfEE (1999) *The National Curriculum for England. English: Key Stages 1–4.* London: DfEE and QCA

DfEE (1999) Citizenship, *The National Curriculum.* London: DfEE and QCA

Education for Citizenship and the Teaching of Democracy in Schools (The Crick Report) (1998). London: QCA

Freire, P. (1972) *The Pedagogy of the Oppressed.* London: Penguin

Freire, P. (1975) *Education: the Practice of Freedom.* London: Writers and Readers Cooperative

Hall, C. and Bailey, M. (1998) *Wuthering Heights by Emily Brontë: A post-16 Study Guide*. Sheffield: NATE

Lankshear, C. (1997) *Changing Literacies*. Buckingham: Open University Press

Lunzer, E. and Gardner, K. (eds) (1979) *The Effective Use of Reading*. London: Heinemann Educational Books for Schools Council.

Martin, T. and Leather, B. (1994) *Readers and Texts in the Primary Years*. Buckingham: Open University Press

Mellor, B., Hemming, J. and Leggett, J. (1984) *Changing Stories*. London: English and Media Centre

Mellor, B., O'Neill, M. and Patterson, A. (1987) *Reading Stories*. Scarborough, Australia: Chalkface Press

Moon, B. (1992) *Literary Terms: A Practical Glossary*. London: English and Media Centre

Moon, B. (1987) *Studying Literature*. Scarborough, Australia: Chalkface Press

Morgan, W. with Gilbert, P., Lankshear, C., Werba, S., Williams, L. (1996) *Critical Literacy Readings and Resources*. Norwood: Australian Association for the Teaching of English

Searle, C. (1998) *None But Our Words*. Buckingham: Open University Press

chapter 13

TEACHING READING

By the end of this chapter you will have been introduced to the theories of learning to read and reading development; considered the place of reading within the National Curriculum and the National Literacy Strategy; understood the qualities of being a reader and evaluated a range of teaching strategies to promote reading within your classroom.

To complete this chapter it is recommended that you have access to the following documents:

> *The National Curriculum for England. English: Key Stages 1–4* (DfEE and QCA, 1999)
> *Guided Reading in English at Key Stage 3* (DfES, 2002)
> Accompanying video, *Guided Reading at Key Stage 3* (DfES, 2002)
> *Framework for Teaching English: Years 7, 8 and 9* (DfEE, 2001)

RATIONALE

To read means more than to simply decode print. It means to make sense of the print that we engage with. In order to do this a reader has to bring their prior knowledge and understanding to bear on the texts that they encounter. There are many different levels of comprehension that a teacher can encourage a pupil to develop:

- Literal comprehension means to read the lines of print to determine what is said in the text.
- Inferential comprehension means to read between the lines of print inferring what the writer might mean.
- Applied comprehension means to read beyond the lines of

print, linking what is read to other knowledge, situations and issues.

The ability to read fluently and with meaning is the basis for most school learning and one of the prerequisites for academic success. Every teacher, whatever their subject, is a teacher of reading, and our role as reading teachers is to ensure that our questioning encourages pupils to search for meaning not only on the lines of print but between and beyond them too.

The reading process: making it visible

The job of the English teacher is to make the reading process visible to those learning – not just beginner readers but all the way through school. In learning to read, even very young children draw on three sources of knowledge in order to make meaning:

Context   Knowledge of the world – drawing on what they know about how the world works, from their own experience, and that gained from talking with peers and adults, and what is re-presented to them through the media. This knowledge has then to be mapped on to what is represented in the text. If a child has no experience of, for example, seeing a tractor plough a field, then words such as 'furrow' and 'clods' may be unknown semantically and experientially.

Textual ('Text level' in the *Framework for Teaching English: Years 7, 8 and 9*) Knowledge of how texts work, and are organised – recognising that this text is a story, this a poem, this an advert, gained from reading and being exposed to a multiplicity of texts. Text level also means understanding how the different elements of the text relate to one another.

Language ('Word and sentence level' in the *Framework for Teaching English: Years 7, 8 and 9*)

Semantic knowledge – understanding the meaning of words;

Syntactic knowledge – understanding how words link to each other in a sentence to create sense and coherence;

Grapho-phonic knowledge – decoding at word level, i.e. relating phonemes to graphemes (the sounds we make with our mouth and voice to make spoken language which relate to the written form of these on the page in their smallest form), understanding letter blends (*cr, sh, st*), and initial (onset) and last sounds of words (rime) for example, 'street', 'str' = onset, 'eet' = rime.

Children draw on all three forms of 'decoding' of written language when reading texts, and unfamiliar texts in particular, using one form of knowledge more overtly, depending on the need. For example, with unknown words in a sentence we all may slow our reading down to look more closely at the individual letters and morphemes (smallest units of meaning) to help us to decode it.

The psychology of reading

Reading out loud, reading silently, being able to carry in the mind intimate libraries of remembered words, are astounding abilities that we acquire by uncertain methods. And yet, before these abilities can be acquired, a reader needs to learn the basic craft of recognising the common signs by which a society has chosen to communicate: in other words, a reader must learn to read. (Manguel, 1996: 67)

What follows is an examination of the research in relation to how children begin to learn to read print, what is sometimes called the 'psychology of reading' (Stanovich and West, 1981).

Reading is a complex system of skills, knowledge and processes that are continuously developing in us all. Perceptual, comprehension and social skills are all needed to enable a reader to gain meanings from texts and to interact with others to give purpose to these meanings. It is in this sense that competence in reading can be considered text dependent and there is never a final moment when we can consider our literacy learning complete. 'We begin learning to read the first time we make sense of print, and we learn something about reading every time we read' (Smith, 1978: 128).

Theorists in early reading   Earlier writers claimed that the processes of learning to read were the same as those involved in learning to talk. The Goodmans (1988) and Frank Smith (1978) asserted that literacy is learned in much the same way and, to some extent, at the same time, as oral language: 'Many of the skills employed by a child in learning about speech are relevant to the task of learning to read' (Smith, 1978: 2). Kenneth Goodman's model of reading (1976), as a psychological guessing game, relied upon the notions that good readers depend on context for word recognition and that they make less use of letter information than poor readers as they read. Frank Smith argued that being read to is a basic means by which children come to understand the functions and structures of written language (Smith, 1978).

To deal with Goodman first, current views of the reading process attack Goodman's conclusions on fluent readers. Stanovich (1984) and Adams (1990) are authoritative critics of Goodman's theories. Goodman argued that fluent readers are not only more efficient users of the visual cues in print, they need to use very few of them. However, advances in eye movement technology (Harrison, 1996) show that not only do fluent readers fixate all main function words very rapidly, they also appear to process individual letters in words. They sample the text more quickly and use fewer resources to do so. However, the poorer reader who cannot recognise a word straight away has *more* need of context, uses valuable resources in the process, and so reduces the capacity for comprehension.

The importance of developing word level reading skills, underpinned by language comprehension   Keith Stanovich's work was influential in discrediting Goodman's model of reading. He adapted the Posner-Snyder theory of expectancy (1975) that provides a framework for studies of contextual effects on word recognition. Stanovich's 'Interactive-Compensatory Model' of the reading process

(1984) is now more widely accepted than Goodman's model. He points out that reading involves a number of interactions with a text. One of the many resources that a reader brings to the reading experience is a 'processing capacity'. If fewer resources are needed for word recognition then more can be allocated for comprehension and vice versa.

Marilyn Jaeger Adams also poses strong arguments for developing word and letter recognition skills early in young children, 'well before first grade' (1990: 374). However, she also laments that the debate on reading has become a polarised discussion of understanding versus the skills to recognise print. Visual perceptual abilities are *underpinned* by language comprehension and understanding print is more than simply making sense of the words on the lines. Reading should be defined more broadly and focus on the discovery of meanings in texts. This is not simply the case of meanings being inherently present in the text to be understood by the reader, like a code to break. 'The ultimate power of text is not from its understanding but from its broad interpretation, its critique, its extension through the reader's own knowledge and thought to the reader's own needs and interests' (Adams, 1990: 405). Meanings are only meaningful when they are interpreted and processed.

It is in this way that reading is a means to an end and only very rarely an end in itself. The process of reading involves supplementing incoming information from the text with a reader's prior experience of language and of the world. Engaging with text is the proper pursuit of reading and this is when there is 'the active encounter of one mind and one imagination with another' (Meek, 1982: 10). The lessons that young children need to be taught in learning to read are not decoding skills but are about 'attitudes, strategies and experiences' (Dombey, 1992: 9). 'They find in books the depth and breadth of human experience' (Meek, 1982: 17) and the relevance of these findings is applied to their own experiences.

Reading readiness: behaving like a reader   If children are to learn to read, right from the start they need to be invited to behave like a reader with the emphasis on sharing texts, extracting and creating meanings from those texts and integrating these experiences into their lives. This can be taught by their first literacy teachers, which, for most children, will mean that their early 'lessons' are from their parents. Yetta Goodman explains that children can and do learn much about reading from listening to and watching skilled adults who show them how it is done (Goodman, 1990). Margaret Meek talks of the four assumptions which many parents operate from: (1) reading is important; (2) reading is learned by reading; (3) what the beginning reader reads makes all the difference to their view of reading; (4) reading must be genuinely shared (Meek, 1982). These assumptions encompass what it means to read and practising them assists the beginning reader.

As discussed earlier, pre-school children are acquiring reading and writing behaviours when they engage in literacy-related experiences and the most fundamental behaviour needed for learning to read is 'learning to behave like a reader' (Meek, 1982: 24). This is why a toddler turning the pages of a book and telling himself a version of the story can be described as in the beginning stages of reading.

LINKS WITH THE NATIONAL CURRICULUM AND KEY STAGE 3 STRATEGY

The National Curriculum at Key Stages 3 and 4 assumes a high level of reading skills for pupils, with a focus on inferential and deductive reading, for example,

EN2 Reading: Knowledge, skills and understanding – Understanding texts

Reading for meaning

A to extract meaning beyond the literal, explaining how the choice of language and style affects implied and explicit meanings

B to analyse and discuss alternative interpretations, ambiguity and allusion. (NC, p.34)

This is in essence a traditional literary criticism approach, with a focus on the effects of the writer's language on the reader. There are moves towards a critical literacy response, as in:

Printed and ICT-based information texts

4 To develop their reading of print and ICT-based information texts, pupils should be taught to:

. . .

- sift the relevant from the irrelevant, and distinguish between fact and opinion, bias and objectivity for Media and moving image texts;
- how the nature and purpose of media products influence content and meaning. (Ibid., p. 35)

The *Framework for Teaching English: Years 7, 8 and 9* has a close focus on word and sentence level work to balance what was seen as the predominance of the text level work which secondary English teachers have often started from, using the class reader or poetry as the stimulus for work. The three levels should work in harmony, with pupils progressing to more complex reading objectives. For example, Year 7 Word Level: Vocabulary looks very closely at the semantic level of words:

16 work out the meaning of unknown words using context, etymology, morphology, compound patterns and other qualities such as onomatopoeia. (p. 23)

Text level – Reading focuses on using a wide range of active strategies for reading:

2. use appropriate reading strategies to extract particular information, e.g. highlighting, scanning (p. 24)

At Year 9 this has progressed, for Vocabulary, to:

7 recognise layers of meaning in the writer's choice of words, e.g. connotations, implied meaning, different types or multiple meanings

and Text level – Reading:

2 synthesise information from a range of sources, shaping material to meet the reader's needs.

The ability to actively select a particular reading strategy is one of the most interesting aspects of reading highlighted the National Literacy Strategy.

Guided reading

'Guided Reading' is an initiative of the National Strategy, whereby the teacher focuses closely on the active reading skills of a small group of pupils for about 20 minutes during the 'Development' part of the lesson (and while the other pupils are similarly working in groups on reading but more independently). The teacher plans in advance which groups of pupils are to work on which text, using a particular set of reading strategies. These will have been taught as part of whole class reading techniques – scanning, skimming, inferring, predicting, decoding, breaking words down into morphemes, highlighting words, annotation, visualising, empathising, relating to own experience, identifying implied meanings, note taking, re-reading, asking questions, speculating, reinterpreting, making an informed personal opinion. The teacher will have also planned out searching questions to support pupils in their reading, so making the reading process visible, and explicit. The actual teaching sequence is as follows:

- introduction to text (providing a hook into the reading – 'Michael goes into the garage in this chapter, and finds something extraordinary!')
- strategy check ('can you remember how we predicted something in the text, Joanne?')
- independent reading and related task (pupils read in silence on their own, perhaps with the teacher listening to two or three read aloud to them, and then moving on to a task)
- return to the text: developing response (the teacher probes deeper into their reading, and re-reading by careful questioning)
- review (reading target and next texts)
- evaluation by the teacher and assessments noted down.

The point of guided reading is to provide a scaffold for pupils to empower them to become independent readers of the kind able to fulfil the reading objectives of the NC. The teacher is probing the pupils' reading strategies, to analyse texts at a deeper level. Examples of such prompts can be seen in the training file on *Guided Reading at Key Stage 3* (DfES, 2002) in Appendix 8.1:

Text level questions to ask:

- What is my purpose in reading this?
- What can I immediately begin to understand?
- What do I know and what do I expect?
- Can I predict what is likely to take place in the short/medium/long term from what I have already read?

Sentence level questions to ask:

- What is the average sentence length? Do the sentence lengths vary, or are they consistent? What do these facts help me to understand? What effects do they create?

- Are there any special effects in the language the author uses for particular purposes?

The teacher needs to take notes, if possible, on this small group of pupils, even making a simple checklist of which strategy was the focus, and noting which pupils were able to activate this successfully. A simple tick list can be useful: this can be used to get an overall picture of which strategy each pupil is using. A miscue analysis on less able readers as a diagnostic tool before the guided reading will also inform the teacher on which strategies a pupil may be over-dependent on.

The literacy progress units have particular units focusing on reading which can be used with small groups, or adapted for use with the whole class:, e.g. *Reading between the Lines* (DfEE, 2001) looks at first impressions, inference and deduction, picking up clues, visualisation, looking forward and backwards, predicting possible ends, amongst many other skills distilled into 20-minute sessions.

Activity 1

READING AN UNFAMILIAR TEXT YOURSELF
(suggested time: 30 minutes)

It can be helpful to remind yourself – as an expert reader – what the reading process can be with an unknown text.

TASK

Ask a fellow student or tutor to give you an unknown text, without a title or author. Annotate the text at the points at which you began to understand what the text was about. Re-read the text, and annotate further to indicate which source of knowledge you overtly drew on (refer back to Rationale) in order to make meaning from the text as in:

'C' = context
'T' = knowledge of how texts work
'L' = Semantic'/syntactic/graphophonic

- What does this exercise teach you about the way in which you read unknown texts?
- How can you apply this knowledge to your pupils' developing reading skills?

Place your responses on a discussion board to share with another student teacher.

Standard addressed: 2.1   Margaret Meek analyses a group of her student teachers engaged in a similar activity in Teaching English (Brindley, 1994: 156–9). You may find this very useful to support you in this exercise.

Activity 2

PRINCIPLES FOR A BEGINNER READER
AT SECONDARY SCHOOL
(Suggested time: 20 minutes)

Standards addressed:
2.1, 2.3

For almost all secondary school pupils the process of becoming a fluent reader is well under way. However, every English teacher encounters pupils for whom decoding print is a challenge. From your understanding of the reading process, as outlined above, list some of the principles that you would apply to assist a pupil who is still at the beginning stages of learning to read.

Activity 3

WAYS OF READING IN THE CLASSROOM
(suggested time: 1 hour)

The National Literacy Strategy suggests four different ways of reading:

Shared reading	Group reading	Guided reading	Independent reading
The whole class and the teacher read the same text; teacher/pupils read aloud and talk about the text	Pupils work in a small group independently on a set reading task, or read the next chapter of a novel together with prompts from the teacher	Small groups work closely with a teacher or TA on a focused reading activity	Pupils read independently in a library session, in the class or at home having selected their own text
Whole class work stemming from this text can include drama, visualisation, drawing, debates, class writing	Individual groups select group texts from book boxes in the library once a week and read together	Teacher assessing the reading skills of one group after modelling a particular reading strategy	Personal research on the Internet
Activity observed:	*Activity observed:*	*Activity observed:*	*Activity observed:*
Objective:	*Objective:*	*Objective:*	*Objective:*

Source: Handout 1.3, in *Guided Reading in English at Key Stage 3* (DFES, 2002)

TASK

You will have observed many English lessons during your placement, with many different such reading strategies going on.

- Can you add to the descriptions in the table above under each heading, detailing what the activity was, and its specific reading objective? You may need to discuss this with the mentor or class teacher.
- Which kind of reading have you taught so far?
- By the end of your training programme you should have planned out and taught all four models of reading at school, including guided reading. You may need support for this model from the class teacher or the teaching assistant, and a well-managed classroom.

Standard addressed:
2.1c

Activity 4

SUPPORTING THE BEGINNER READER IN PRACTICAL TERMS
(suggested time: 30 minutes)

Understanding how children learn to read is the first step. Creating a supporting reading environment is the next step. How would you ensure that your classroom is a supportive reading environment?

As a class teacher I used library sessions to give short readings of the first two or three paragraphs of different books to tempt reluctant readers; would interview pupils about their reading habits (one boy said he always read the tabloid paper aloud to his parents at the kitchen table after school); create a class library that pupils could browse through at the beginning and end of lessons and once stole two old worn library chairs stored in a cupboard to create a comfortable reading zone.

TASK

List in bullet point form the priorities for you in terms of approaches and resources that you would use within your teaching. You can be as detailed as you like. For example you can specify the range of materials in book boxes/class libraries and the time you would allow for private reading as well as how you would group pupils and the strategies you would emphasise. You may even want to describe the physical layout of the classroom.

Use the following prompts to support you:

- Do you know what kinds of texts your beginning reader reads outside school? In what context? On the bus? At home? With an adult? On their own?
- What kinds of texts are available in school to support and interest beginner readers in their teenage years? You may need to discuss this with the Learning Support Department.

Standards addressed: 2.1, 2.4, 3.1.1

- What kind of pairings of pupils might work in a structured library lesson to support one another's reading?
- How are you including such pupils in the shared class reader?

Activity 5

LISTENING TO PUPILS READ: MISCUE ANALYSIS
(suggested time: 2 hours)

You will need to diagnose your beginner readers' reading skills, and this begins with listening to pupils read, but also to liaise with the Learning Support Department here to find out how reading levels are diagnosed on entry to the school. A simple miscue analysis sheet which records and diagnoses pupils' errors and strategies in reading (substitutions, errors in syntax, over-reliance in 'sounding out' unknown words, omissions of words, ability to re-read and self-correct, not reading for meaning) can help you pinpoint specific areas for development.

TASK

Find out the following from the Learning Support Department:

Standard addressed: 3.3.4

- Which reading tests are given to pupils on entry, and at the end of each year?
- What is done with this information? Do class teachers have access to the reading ages of their pupils?
- Is there a miscue analysis sheet used in the Learning Support Department which you can use yourself in listening to pupils read?
- If so, ask for support in listening to pupils read on a one to one basis.

Activity 6   EFFECTIVE QUESTIONING: EFFECTIVE READING.

(suggested time: 1 hour)

Shared and guided reading lessons depend on the teacher's effective probing and questioning of the pupils' understanding of the meaning in texts, and on the teacher's acting as a model for pupils to begin to ask their own questions of texts. Skilful questioning requires planning in advance. Hints for question setting:

- To assess literal comprehension skills you could set questions such as, 'Why did character X . . .? 'What reason did Y give for . . .?
- To assess inferential comprehension skills you could ask questions such as, 'What clues are there to suggest that . . .?, 'Why do you think . . .?, 'Now that you have read the complete text/extract and looking again at the title of this chapter/story/section can you explain why it is a suitable title?'
- To assess applied comprehension skills you need to consider questions such as, 'Imagine that X and Y meet again several years later. What would their conversation consist of?', 'Have you ever experienced a similar situation to X? Tell your story'.

TASK

Standard addressed: 3.3.3

Choose an extract from a reader that you would use with a Year 9 mixed ability class. Remind yourself of the levels of comprehension (see above) that as a teacher you are to encourage in your pupils. Now devise six questions you might ask your pupils to answer to demonstrate their understanding of the extract. Make sure that you are asking them to access meanings that exist on the lines of print but also between and beyond them too.

Activity 7

STRATEGIES TO ENCOURAGE PUPILS
TO ENGAGE WITH TEXTS

(suggested time: 1 hour per strategy)

Secondary English teachers need to *teach* reading. Even pupils who are fluent readers need explicit instruction on how to engage more fully with texts. Many of the directed activities relating to texts (DARTs) described in Chapter 14 below, on teaching narrative texts, are useful strategies for developing pupils' reading abilities. The essential element in all of these strategies is to encourage young readers to make meanings from a range of printed materials – and to talk about how they do this to their peers and teachers. Further, they all stress that reading is more than decoding and that readers, in order to make meanings, have to bring their prior knowledge and understandings to bear on the texts they encounter.

For all the activities below you will need to work in co-operation with others. A group of three is appropriate. Arrange to work with other students or friends.

A TEXT COMPLETION ACTIVITIES, INCLUDING CLOZE AND DISRUPTED TEXT

Cloze procedure was originally designed as a measure of readability, but it can be used in a variety of ways to encourage both individuals and groups to engage meaningfully with text. In a cloze activity, a text is provided in which some words have been deleted. If the intention is to encourage readers to explore a text in a general way, words can be deleted on a random basis – every 9th, or 7th or 5th word (structural deletion). It is also possible to delete words in a more specific way – for instance by deleting all the pronouns or all the words dealing with a particular subject, issue or idea (lexical deletion). The point here is that the teacher can decide on the significant features of a text to which pupils' attention is to be drawn.

Disrupted text activities are similar to cloze in that gaps are left in a text which the reader has to fill, but in this case, whole sentences are omitted. These sentences are provided for the reader, who has to work out which sentence fits into which textual gap. The teacher has flexibility to decide how much or how little information to provide about the deleted words. Pupils could be left with just the gaps, they could be provided with an initial (or final) letter as a clue or the omitted words could be printed below the text. Pupils are able to respond to and reconstruct texts using cloze procedure and disrupted texts because they have implicit knowledge about the way in which language works.

Cloze and disrupted text activities aim to provide a structure for discussion and response, through which pupils' implicit knowledge becomes open to scrutiny. Pupils need to use inference, deduction and previous reading experience in order to unlock the meaning from the text. In this way, the teacher is able to become aware of what pupils actually know about language and can therefore plan more effectively for future language activities. The National Curriculum particularly stresses these aspects of reading behaviour.

TASK

All readers make use of a number of strategies and skills that reflect our knowledge about language and the way print works. This activity will help you to realise what some of these strategies and skills are. It can also be transferred easily into the classroom situation.

Read through the whole task before beginning.

1   Select a prose passage of about 200 words from any text that is not too subject specific, e.g. a novel, a description of an event, an article from a magazine.
2   Choose a method of deletion, i.e. structural or lexical (see above).
3   Give the passage with deletions to a friend and ask them to try and suggest suitable words to fill the gaps. The object is not to get the 'right' word but a word that makes sense in context.
4   While they are doing this, observe and note any strategies that they use to select suitable words, or complete a cloze passage prepared by a fellow student and consider the strategies you use yourself.
5   When the task is completed, list the strategies used and the linguistic knowledge upon which you drew:

- reading of whole passage to get an overview;
- reading aloud for clarification;
- checking title, writer, date;
- showing awareness of style of writing, punctuation;
- showing knowledge of parts of speech, e.g. 'It has to be a noun' or: 'It has to be a verb';
- showing awareness of the tense of verbs, agreement between pronouns, gender, knowledge of prepositions and conjunctions;
- checking with a partner;
- discussing alternatives, familiar expressions. Note any words you found difficult to position. Which were the easiest/hardest words to do? Did the group disagree? What did you disagree about and why? What reasons did people give for their point of view?

Cloze procedures – developing your own materials

Devise an activity or series of classroom activities using the techniques of cloze and disrupted text which would help children to employ and develop the skills and processes identified above.

- The aims are to encourage groups to use their implicit grammatical understandings to identify how written texts are constructed.
- We suggest pairs as an appropriate grouping, although you could plan individual activities.
- The work could be presented either as a whole class lesson, or as one group activity amongst others.

- Plan to include a reporting sheet to enable children to record what they do.
- We see it as important that pupils are encouraged to share their findings with others.

Note: Cloze is an oral activity, not a handwriting exercise. It can also be carried out by means of the computer programs.

SEQUENCING ACTIVITIES

Sequencing activities undertaken in small groups can encourage young readers to make explicit through collaborative efforts their understandings about how language systems work to create meaning within texts. Sequencing activities build upon and develop pupils' understanding of how particular types of text are organised. Many early years classrooms utilise the techniques of sequencing, often of narrative texts. These are usually pictures, but sometimes pictures and captions. In such activities pupils draw on their knowledge of narrative structures, familiar contexts and their innate knowledge about language to reconstruct a text from its constituent parts. Such skills are vital in enabling readers to access meaning through the interrogation of texts. The talk which is generated as pairs or small groups of pupils discuss the reordering of the various sections provides evidence of the extent of their implicit knowledge about language and encourages them to articulate this knowledge. Pupils are provided with opportunities to hypothesise, reason, justify and argue a point of view.

TASK

1 Each person should select a text which has a limited number of sections. (Newspaper articles with no more than a dozen paragraphs are ideal: and short poems, cut into either stanzas or single lines can also be profitable.)
2 Photocopy the original text and cut the photocopy into sections. Give each section a random number or letter to identify it for purposes of discussion and reporting.
3 Each group member in turn should give the other members of the group the scrambled texts which they have prepared. The idea is for group members to sequence the tumbled paragraphs or sections of text in a meaningful way and to reflect briefly on this process. (You could use the reporting sheet provided or work out your own method of reflection.)

REPORTING SHEET This is the order we agreed

First section	☐	Seventh section	☐
Second section	☐	Eighth section	☐
Third section	☐	Ninth section	☐
Fourth section	☐	Tenth section	☐
Fifth section	☐	Eleventh section	☐
Sixth section	☐	Twelfth section	☐

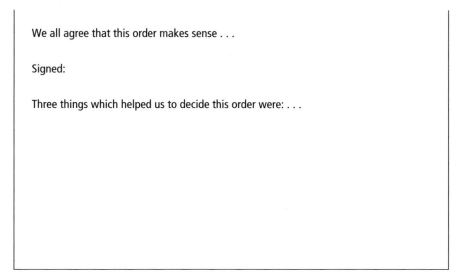

We all agree that this order makes sense . . .

Signed:

Three things which helped us to decide this order were: . . .

Sequencing – developing your own materials

Devise an activity or series or classroom activities involving sequencing.

Sequencing can be employed throughout the primary years and beyond, using, as well as newspaper articles and poems, other material relating to specific themes and topics being studied in the classroom. The technique can be used to reinforce knowledge and concepts as well as providing an interesting and stimulating way of introducing new work.

We see the talk generated as one of the most important aspects of the work. Also important is a small group's ability to reach consensus and there is a section on the reporting sheet for group members to sign, indicating that they agree with the completed report.

If a class is not familiar with the idea of collaborative group work, they may take a little time to develop appropriate skills. However, the sequencing activity is designed to support collaboration because the task itself is clear and straightforward – although the ideas in the texts may be challenging. Also, the task moves from the concrete and specific – ordering the text – to the more abstract analysis of how the task was accomplished.

PREDICTING

Very simply, prediction activities provide children with an incomplete segment of text and ask three basic questions:

- What will happen next?
- What makes you say this?
- Where's your evidence?

It is also possible, as an alternative, to feed the information to groups one paragraph at a time and ask them to predict one paragraph at a time.

Prediction activities build upon and develop pupils' understanding of how particular types of text are organised and can give them opportunities to use such knowledge in their own writing by, for instance, asking them to continue the text as they think appropriate. The aim in 'continuation' prediction activities is to encourage small groups to use their imagination and their world knowledge to develop interesting and entertaining writing. They are also encouraged to pick up on the contextual clues embedded in the texts provided and to use these as a foundation for their own work. It is not intended that they reproduce the original texts or even that they develop their own writing along lines comparable with the original.

TASK

We have provided four examples of headlines with the introductory sections of stories. As a group, outline the way in which you think the story might continue.

BATHING IN CUSTARD

Customers at Gateway Supermarket in Swadlincote were asked to dip into their pockets while a store employee took a bath in a vat of thick custard. Assistant grocery manager Mr Paul Sherratt . . .

FALLING PREY TO PERSECUTION

Conservationists have launched a plan to protect birds of prey from illegal persecution.
The move – linked with a £400,000 appeal – comes as new statistics reveal that . . .

RIDING INTO ADVENTURE

Intrepid adventurers, Ms Linda Bootherstone and Miss Mel Bradfield rev up ready to take off on a 2000-mile trip by motorcycle to Malta. Once there, the two Burton bikers will . . .

IT'S ALL IN THE GAME

Murder, mystery and mutants as gamers gather.

More than 150 people had fun and games locked in the shadowy depth of Burton Town Hall at the weekend.
Some were doing battle with mutant creatures from outer space; others were fighting the American Civil War; while the more constructive were . . .

Share your responses with another group, giving some reasons for the decisions you made about how to develop the stories.

Predicting: developing your own materials

Devise an activity or series of classroom activities which will involve pupils in predicting and recording what might happen next in a text. Try to include opportunities for them to produce their own texts as a response and to reflect on how and why they made particular decisions with regard to vocabulary or structure.

- If pupils are to produce their own texts it may be necessary to provide additional reference materials – dictionaries, information books of various kinds, etc. This will give an opportunity for pupils to practise information-retrieval skills in a meaningful context.
- If pupils have done work on textual cohesion they could be encouraged to identify the cohesive links in their own texts as a way of checking that the story makes sense and relates in some way to the original starting point.
- We see the talk generated as one of the most important aspects of the work.
- Newspapers are a readily available and inexpensive resource. Teachers – or the pupils themselves – can select their own headlines and opening paragraphs and develop the activity in the manner already outlined.

COHESION ACTIVITIES

A text is more than just an arbitrary collection of sentences. The way in which a written text is structured to convey meaning relies on links between one section and the next. Such chains of reference often look forward in the text – for example:

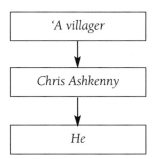

'A villager	*is threatening to call in the Ombudsman to settle a dispute over the siting of a children's play area.*
Chris Ashkenny	*and other Fradleigh residents were opposing . . . they say that the area is unsuitable . . .*
He	*says the land in question . . .*

Occasionally, references are made to knowledge beyond the text which is common to the reader and the writer. Such shared knowledge could relate to current events, or well known people within a family or community. In any text there will be a number of meaning strings relating to the subject of the text and also identifying the main participants in the events of the text.

Texts that work well are those which balance new information with that which already exists on the page and has been assimilated by the reader. By identifying the meaning strings within texts, pupils can make decisions about the effectiveness or otherwise of the writing they encounter. Further, if groups and individuals are encouraged to identify the meaning strings within their own writing, it is a helpful way for them to think about the structures of their own texts. If pupils see their own writing examined in the same way as the work of adults, then this can send an important message to them about themselves as writers.

TASK

1   • Read the newspaper story 'TODDLER IN FIRE DRAMA'.
    • Decide who is in the story.
    • Circle each person's name and all the other words which are used instead of their name in the story.
    • Use a different colour for each person.
    • Link together all the references for the people in the story.
    • Check that you haven't missed out any references.

2   Collect sets of words from the story which identify (a) actions; (b) feelings; (c) fire and its associations

3   Using the evidence generated by the 'sets and strings' activity, consider how successfully the story is structured. If necessary, suggest modifications which would make the story more appropriate for its intended purpose and audience.

THREE-YEAR-OLD ESCAPES BLAZE BY HIDING IN CUPBOARD

TODDLER IN FIRE DRAMA

A Burton toddler was today recovering in hospital after being trapped in his blazing bedroom.

Three-year-old Curtis Denley cheated death by hiding in a cupboard while flames and choking black smoke filled his Ash Street home shortly after 9 p.m. last night. He was rescued by firefighters but suffered minor burns and was treated for shock.

His mother, Miss Gill Denley, seven-year-old sister, Natalie, and 1-month-old brother, Michael, escaped the fire.

Today, Miss Denley told the Mail how she was beaten back by smoke as she tried to reach Curtis.

'I was standing outside the house when I saw smoke coming from the side window upstairs. I ran in and shouted at Natalie and Michael to get out. I never heard Curtis crying. I ran up the stairs and opened his door. Black smoke just hit me in the face and singed my hair – there was no way I could reach him,' she said.

'A neighbour called the fire service – I was terrified while we waited – I thought Curtis was dead.'

Two firefighters wearing breathing apparatus dashed into the house and brought Curtis out within seconds, said Miss Denley.

The cause was under investigation today, but was not said to be suspicious. Curtis was taken to Burton District Hospital where he will stay until the weekend.

Cohesion – developing your own materials

The aim is to encourage groups to use their implicit grammatical understandings to identity how written texts are constructed.

You (and your pupils) will readily find other stories, articles and passages which can be used successfully. Even less 'successful' texts are useful in demonstrating structural strengths and weaknesses.

- Pupils will need a copy of the text(s), and possibly a response sheet. They are asked to highlight and link sets of words in different colours. You could also add another dimension to this activity by providing a selection of possible headlines for the story and asking pupils to choose the most appropriate, giving their reasons.
- It is important to demonstrate the 'stringing' procedure to pupils new to the activity.
- We see it as important that pupils share their findings with others: get pupils to apply this process to their own writing, (use a photocopy).

READING FOR MEANING ACTIVITIES

Trackread

'Trackread' was originally devised and developed by Paul Francis in the mid-1970s. At that time, he was Head of English in a Derbyshire school and his intention was to encourage the use of authentic texts in schools. Very simply, the approach offers teachers the opportunity to devise activities using environmental print and 'real' non-book material to develop in pupils the higher order reading strategies of skimming, scanning and homing in on meaning. It is relatively simple to create your own 'Trackread' resource.

Begin by making a collection of 'real' materials – leaflets, catalogues, timetables, posters, maps, advertisements, etc. Now devise a series of questions for each text. Between 5 and 10 is about the right number, depending on the length and/or complexity of the material. The questions should cover the whole text, and be arranged in a random way. For example, you could begin with a question asking for the postcode of the firm which printed the text and then move on to ask which page contains a specific detail, the price of a particular product or other relevant information, depending on the precise nature of the resource used.

The questions can be simply factual, or can ask pupils to make decisions based on information provided in the text. The approach is suitable for children in both early and later years, although questions for early years 'Trackread' need to be carefully framed to take account of younger pupils' relatively limited literacy experience. For example, a question referring to very small type like this in the text might not be suitable, whereas it would be appropriate to ask about larger sections of text, or illustrations and visual images.

When you have devised the questions, put the text and questions into an envelope and note the answers on a separate card so that pupils can 'mark' their own responses. Make sure that text, question card and answer card can be clearly identified.

Figure 1. 'Trackread' envelope, text, question and answer card

Again, for early readers, 'Trackread' materials do not have to insist on written answers; oral approaches can be equally effective.

READING TO GAIN INFORMATION

To extract information effectively from text we need to draw upon a range of skills. This is as true for younger readers as for adults. You may like to consider your own reading behaviours with regard to this kind of reading. The following activity is designed to draw your attention to some of the many skills which we perhaps take for granted as adult readers.

Tick the appropriate box every time you do any of the following:

- ☐ Consult the index
- ☐ Consult the table of contents
- ☐ Consult a dictionary
- ☐ Consult an atlas
- ☐ Obtain information from illustrations or diagrams
- ☐ Look quickly over a page to locate information
- ☐ Select some parts or the book as relevant to your needs
- ☐ Reject the book as being unsuitable for your needs
- ☐ Select some parts or a page as relevant
- ☐ Reject some parts of a page as irrelevant
- ☐ Decide whether or not you agree with the book
- ☐ Summarise what the book said .
- ☐ Consult another book
- ☐ Supply information that you already know
- ☐ Decide whether you were reading information or opinion
- ☐ Reorganise the information you have obtained
- ☐ Make inferences based upon what the book tells you
- ☐ Read a paragraph very carefully
- ☐ Re-read
- ☐ Read rapidly to get a general idea of the passage
- ☐ Use the bibliography.

You may like to consider how you even began to do this task. For example, how did you find the book you consulted? Similarly, consider how, or if, you do the following things in locating, selecting and recording information:

- choose appropriate books (e.g. refer to subject categories, etc.);
- pay attention to title (eg. front cover), blurb (e.g. back cover);
- define the purposes for consulting the book e.g. did you have particular questions you wanted answering or were you researching an issue?
- use contents list, index (alphabetical order), chapter headings, section headings, footnotes, page numbers etc.;
- consider the writer's qualifications and experience;
- consider the book's publication date;
- skim and/or scan;
- identify key words e.g. capital letters for names, italic, underlining, heavy print, etc.;
- interpret charts, illustrations, maps, etc.;
- read for the main ideas, and/or general gist;
- check information against other sources – e.g. books, people, your own experience;
- summarise or reorganise information or translate it into another format;
- apply or act on information;
- decide when to discard information – or even to discard a book.

Reading for information – developing your own materials

If you are attempting to design materials suitable for classroom use, you may find the following points worth considering:

- Who defines the purposes for consulting books? Are they realistic and interesting?
- Who decides the questions to which answers are sought? Are the questions clearly understood, and are they appropriate to the books being used?
- Should the pupils work individually or in groups?
- Are the pupils skilled in choosing suitable books or do they need some screening done for them, to limit their choices?
- Are the books at a suitable reading level for the readers? Does this always matter?
- Do the pupils have the skills necessary to achieve their goals, or will they need help, guidance and/or direction (index, chapter, page, line or even word)?
- Is there an acceptable reason for recording information?
- Are the pupils practised in choosing and using a range of recording formats – e.g. charts, graphs, maps, flow/Venn diagrams, or will they need a model of each suitable format?
- How will any work produced be used, displayed and/or stored as a resource for others?

When you have chosen the theme or topic you want to explore with your pupils, you will need to design a task or series of tasks which involve them in using information books in a purposeful way. It can be very effective to ask pupils to plan and create their own information books within the subject area. This will enable you to teach explicitly about indexes, contents, chapter and section headings, page layouts and the appropriate language registers to use.

Standards addressed: 2.1, 3.3.4

CONTINUOUS THREADS

1 Professional values and practice

There is much concern about how little reading boys do at school and at home. You need to find out what reading both genders do in your class. If boys are viewing complex computer games, surfing the Net and reading papers this is only to be encouraged in the light of the new technologies and therefore literacies in our world. You may also be surprised at the fiction boys are reading. Providing challenging, rich and varied material that appeals to both genders, and reflects the diverse pupil population in our schools, will get pupils reading.

3.1 Planning, expectations and targets

What information will you want to have from the previous class teacher in terms of the reading levels and experiences of a class you are about to take over? How quickly can you ascertain how each pupil has developed in their reading, and where they need to go in the time you have with them?

How would you attempt to ensure that your A Level students continue to read for pleasure? What strategies would you employ to encourage independent reading at this level?

3.2 Monitoring and assessment

The National Curriculum levels emphasise the need for pupils to use inference and deduction. Read the attainment targets for Levels 4, 5 and 6 in Reading. What are the main 'leaps' that a pupil working at Level 4 needs to make to get to Level 6?

Reading Records: do you know what kinds of books your pupils are reading privately at home? How can you find out? Do you keep records of what they take out of the library? Are you in the position to offer individuals more challenging texts while keeping them interested? Are you assessing their reading only from their reading aloud from the class reader (in front of their classmates)? Are you assessing reading from pupils' written work, or from their spoken responses to texts, including drama activities?

3.3.3 Teaching and class management

Reading the class reader as part of shared reading is still a main activity for teachers of English – and so it should be. The teacher reading aloud the shared text draws together the class, and allows access to the text for all pupils at their own level. This needs practice: you need to bring the words alive as an actor does in performance, while continually scanning the class to check that all are following and are engaged in the text. Knowing when to ask others in the class – the Teaching Assistant, able and willing pupils – to read aloud is also a skill, to avoid fragmentation of the storyline. Asking less able readers to take particular characters' parts can be most effective in including all in the reading, with the teacher acting as the narrator, keeping the reading moving onwards. Planning when to stop and ask pertinent questions, or letting pupils ask questions, is also a skill: stopping constantly to ask for the meaning of unfamiliar words may be unnecessary and cause pupils to 'break' out of their engagement in the text. Conversely, as Chapter 12 on Critical Literacy and Literary Theory points out, this disruptive reading can be crucial in showing pupils how the text works on many levels.

Many English departments have strategies for supporting pupils' private reading. Sometimes this is an allocated time period each week or each lesson and sometimes the library is made use of. Lots of careful thought by each teacher is needed in order to make sure that this is a successful use of time. Contingency plans for forgotten books must be clear, and consideration should be given to how children will record their reading experiences and how a teacher will monitor them. Find out about paired and guided reading and reading buddies/partners/mentors schemes. Evaluate each for strengths and weaknesses.

3.3.4 Differentiation

This is a particularly important issue when using a class reader. Take one extract of a class reader you would use with a Year 8 class. Consider how you would conduct the reading of this extract to fully support all ability levels. Set a range of tasks (three or four) on this extract that would meet pupils' individual needs.

3.3.5 Pupils learning English as an additional language

Consider how you would support the pupil for whom English is an additional language. You will need to diagnose the level of English of these pupils, and find ways into a shared text through frequent summaries, diagrams of the main action, use of dual texts, and dual language teachers to translate where necessary particular words or paragraphs, or characters' motives, showing films, and pictures from the text, using drama to act out the story and to flesh out the characters' feelings. All of the activities suggested in this chapter are of direct relevance to pupils learning EAL.

2.5 ICT

A computer-based text requires different reading strategies from a traditional print-based text. How will you teach these skills? Refer to Chapter 18 on English and ICT in this section. Many of the strategies for encouraging pupils to engage with texts can be transferred to ICT and the speed and provisionality of computers exploited.

Scenarios

1 In your mixed ability Year 7 English group you have a girl with a reading age of 7.5 years. What strategies will you employ to assist her independent reading as well as the whole class and group reading activities she will be required to undertake?

2 You have a Year 10 boy who is a very reluctant and inexperienced reader. He claims to find English boring, especially the reading of books. He is very keen on sport and excels at football. How might you use his interest in sport to help him access a variety of texts?

3 You have a reasonably bright Year 9 girl who reads a lot but the material is exclusively from the teen romance genre. You feel she is missing out in her private reading. How would you hope to move her on and encourage wider reading?

FURTHER READING

Dean, G. (2000) *Teaching Reading in Secondary Schools*. London: David Fulton
This book gives an overview of all the reading requirements for the English Department pre-NLS; it is useful to remind ourselves of the underlying pedagogies feeding into the NLS. The section on 'Qualities and Characteristics of Readers' is particularly effective at spelling out what good readers can do, and how to devise a four-point scale to monitor pupils' progression in reading for each quality.

REFERENCES

Adams, M. J. (1990) *Beginning to Read*. Cambridge, MA: The MIT Press

Brindley, S. (ed.) (1994) *Teaching English*. Milton Keynes: OUP

Dombey, H. (1992) *Reading in the Early Years of School*. London: Longman

DfEE (1999) *The National Curriculum for England. English: Key Stages 1–4*. London: DfEE and QCA

DfEE (2001) *Reading Between the Lines*. London: DfEE

DfES (2002) *Guided Reading in English at Key Stage 3*. London: DfES

Goodman, K. S. (1976) 'Reading: a psychological guessing game', in *Theoretical Models and Processes of Reading*, (eds) H. Singer and R.B. Ruddell. Newark, Del: International Reading Association

Goodman, Y. (1990) *How Children Construct Literacy: Piagetian Perspectives*. Newark, Del: International Reading Association

Goodman, K. and Goodman, Y. (1988) 'Learning about psycholinguistic process by analysing oral reading', in *Language and Literacy From an Educational Perspective*, (ed.) N. Mercer. Buckingham: The Open University Press

Harrison, C. (1996) Interchange No. 39 *Methods of Teaching Reading: Key Issues in research and Implications for Practice*. Edinburgh: The Scottish Office Education and Industry Department

Manguel, A. (1996) *A History of Reading*. London: HarperCollins

Meek, M. (1982) *Learning to Read*. London: The Bodley Head

Posner, M.I. and Snyder, C.R.R. (1975) 'Facilitation and inhibition in the processing of signals', in *Attention and Performance*, P.M.A. Rabitt and S. Dornic (eds). New York: Academic Press

Smith, F. (1978) *Understanding Reading*. New York: Holt, Rinehart and Winston

Stanovich, K. E. (1984) 'The interactive-compensatory model of reading: a confluence of developmental, experimental and educational psychology,' *Remedial and Special Education*, 5: 11–19

Stanovich, K.E. and West, R.F. (1981) 'The effect of sentence context on ongoing word recognition: tests of a two-process theory', *Journal of Experimental Psychology*, 7(3): 658–72

CHILDREN'S LITERATURE AND
NARRATIVE TEXTS

By the end of this chapter you will have gained an understanding of the place of children's literature in the English curriculum and of the educational value of children's literature, and will have considered a variety of strategies for teaching children's literature. The focus will be upon high quality popular fiction at Key Stages 3 and 4. You will also be shown a range of ways of investigating story and be encouraged to consider how best as a teacher to select appropriate tasks for the specified learning objective(s). Furthermore, you will have practised devising a unit of work on teaching narrative texts.

However, before reading the rest of this chapter spend some time reflecting upon your own reasons for teaching literature.

RATIONALE

Why teach literature? The National Curriculum for English makes it very clear what pupils should be taught, e.g. 'How meaning is conveyed in texts' and 'to understand the values and assumptions in the texts' (DfEE, 1999), but does not always make explicit the reasons why. An English curriculum should provide pupils with the opportunities to explore, discuss and evaluate their views of the world. It should bring pleasure and enable pupils to share and develop their imaginative worlds. It should empower and inform. Ultimately it should enthuse and challenge the pupils that you teach.

It will be important for you as a teacher to provide an appropriate range of reading experiences for your pupils and to build upon their prior learning. Quiller-Couch (quoted in Knight, 1996: 115) stated

> *it matters little for the moment, or even for a considerable while that a pupil does not perfectly, or even nearly, understand all he reads, provided we can get the attraction to seize upon him. He and the author between them will do the rest. Our function is to communicate and trust.*

As teachers we need to prevent barriers to this 'attraction' and provide an environment where readers engage in the wonders of narrative writing. Young readers are usually aspiring to be adults in their response to texts. Reader-response theory suggests that whilst individuals strive to make sense of the texts that they face this sense becomes increasingly significant when shared by interaction with other young readers. The teacher's role is often to facilitate this interaction without imposing her/his own interpretations. It is important that pupils find their own interpretations. Ways of helping pupils to engage with literature and to reach their own views will be explored later in this chapter. There are some excellent writers of teenage fiction such as David Almond, Anne Fine and Jacqueline Wilson, not to mention the currently fashionable Harry Potter novels by J.K Rowling that can fire up young minds, take readers to new worlds and in some cases help pupils understand that they are not alone.

The role of any English teacher is to help pupils tell stories better, select good fiction, respond to stories more thoughtfully, analyse them with more insight, read them with more enjoyment and knowledge and to write a greater range of stories with a greater degree of accomplishment. Stories are important for several reasons: Stories develop us intellectually and emotionally. Any act of reflection involves us narratising our experiences as we attempt to make meaning from them. Stories help us to make sense of our identity. When we read and tell stories we have the opportunity to learn about ourselves.

Engaging in stories involves us in sophisticated intellectual endeavour. Any story is a complex system of communication as we evaluate the characters through their thoughts, feelings and knowledge and as we navigate the subtleties of the plot. Stories have social and cultural contexts. Our social lives are inextricably bound up with story as it creates, maintains and transforms our relationships within our families, communities and societies. Only by telling and listening to stories can we come to know or have a view about others and come to understand our experiences of living in social contact with each other. Reading and listening to stories are themselves social experiences: through the text a relationship is established with the writer/teller.

LINKS WITH THE NATIONAL CURRICULUM AND KEY STAGE 3 STRATEGY

The National Curriculum for English states that 'during key stages 3 and 4 pupils read a wide range of texts independently, both for pleasure and for study. They become enthusiastic, discriminating and responsive readers, understanding layers of meaning and appreciating what they read on a critical level' (DfEE,1999). Teachers will note that the National Curriculum provides examples of writers post-1914 but these are not compulsory and thus teachers will have some flexibility in selecting classroom readers and recommending extension/private-reading texts. However, there is a canon of writers pre-1914 that must be studied. Here teachers will have to consider which texts are most appropriate, how they should be introduced and how they should be explored in the light of the quote by Quiller-Couch. Teachers will also need to consider how they introduce an appropriate breadth of study for their pupils. *English Department Training* (DfE, 2001: 85) lists what effective teaching of reading in Key Stage 3 is built upon and these are shown below:

- Making close connections between reading and writing
- Modelling reading strategies
- Widening the reading repertoire
- Exploring and analysing texts and their features
- Justifying views with close textual reference
- Relating the author's purpose to the language, structure and organisation of the text, using appropriate terminology.

It is interesting to note that some publishers have linked children's literature to framework objectives. *Witch Child* by Celia Rees (a book for Y8/Y9) includes a section at the end of the book of activities that relate to literacy objectives (e.g. R18 'Discuss a substantial prose text, sharing perceptions, negotiating common readings and accounting for differences of view'). However, we must not forget that we read the same text differently if we are reading it at night in our bedroom for pleasure rather than as a class reader in the build-up to an academic assignment (a book that is read by the whole class).

Activity 1

READING BOOKS
(suggested time: 30 minutes)

Fleming and Stevens (1998: 54–5) explain the current debate about the nature of English in the light of historical comparisons and the recent 'drive to improve basic literacy'. In particular they highlight some of the central issues regarding the changing place of reading in the secondary school classroom during the last 50 years. They raise a number of pertinent questions. Here are just three:

> *'To make sense of what others write' sounds pretty uncontroversial, but one person's (pupil's?) sense may be another's (the teacher's?) nonsense: how far should we give free rein to subjectivity in interpretation?*

> *What place exactly do 'pleasure and inspiration' have in the reading curriculum in view of the pressure to meet basic literacy targets and achieve examination success at all levels of secondary education?*

> *What other forms of reading are there – and might there be – apart from the printed page?*

Standard
addressed: **2.1**   What do you think are the key issues to consider when teaching reading? Make a list of these issues and write them in your English portfolio.

Activity 2

READING LOG
(suggested time: 60 minutes, spread over a fortnight)

Keep a record of all the types of reading that you undertake in the next fortnight. Make a list of these and then write down the purpose of the reading and the skills required to decode each text. Put these into your English portfolio: e.g. bus timetable to locate information using skim reading (reading quickly in order to gain an initial overview of the subject matter or ideas in a text) and scanning strategies (using key words to locate information). This should help you to appreciate the range of reading that people experience over a short space of time, the variety of purposes of reading and the skills required to achieve these purposes. You might want to use the following pro forma. This should help you to appreciate the range of reading that pupils will also encounter over a short space of time.

READING LOG

Text type	Purpose of reading	Skills required
Radio Times magazine	To find out about film	Skim read

Standard
addressed: **2.1**

Activity 3

LITERARY AND NON-LITERARY TEXTS
(suggested time: 40 minutes)

Fleming and Stevens (1998: 58) articulate some of the teaching approaches used to help pupils access texts. They make reference to the Cambridge Literature questions, which are as follows:

> Who has written this text and why?
> What type of text is it?
> How was it produced?
> How does this text present its subject?
> Who reads this text, and how do they interpret it?

As is pointed out, these questions encourage debate, interpretation, analysis and reflection.

Choose a literature text (e.g. short story by R. Dahl) and a non-literary text (e.g. travel writing or reportage) and try to answer the above questions. Keep these in your English portfolio. Consider the similarities and differences. Why do you think that these exist?

Standard addressed: 2.1

Activity 4

READING ACTIVITIES
(suggested time: 60 minutes)

Choose one of the Key Stage 3 literature texts recommended at the end of this chapter. Then list two reading and writing activities that could be used in the teaching of this text. For example in teaching the book *Stone Cold* you might consider encouraging pupils to research the Internet for information about homelessness and writing/performing a drama script based on interviewing the serial killer. Plan out a lesson that incorporates one of the reading or one of the activities. See the section in this chapter on ICT (p. 361) for an example of a lesson. Downloadable lesson plan templates are available at **www.paulchapmanpublishing/resources/completeguide.htm**

Standards addressed: 2.1, 2.5, 3.3.10

Activity 5

THE CLASS NOVEL
(suggested time: 60 minutes)

In many English classrooms the use of a class reader is still seen as central to teaching a vast range of objectives across all the attainment targets of Speaking and Listening/Reading/Writing.

In no more than 300 words write a justification for using a class reader. Keep this in your English portfolio.

Standards addressed: 2.1, 3.1.3

Activity 6

WAYS INTO BOOKS I
(suggested time: 30 minutes)

Lunzer and Gardner (1984) pioneered an approach to reading in order to help pupils to develop their reading and comprehension skills. This was to become known as DARTs: the 'Directed Activities Related To Texts'. A brief rationale for DARTS and some examples can be found in Davies (1996: 116–17). Look at the examples below and add some of your own. Consider which approaches would be useful with particular narrative texts. You might want to consider the following points.

1   Pupils attend more closely to meanings if given an incomplete test rather than a complete one, if they are actively involved in constructing the text and if they are asked to draw upon their previous knowledge (of stories, of language, of life). This is because a reader has to get close to a text that is in fragments to gain meaning from it.

2   A reader has to attend more carefully if they are required to project forward.

3   To sequence a story a reader has to understand and draw upon the knowledge of how stories work.

Activity	Specific task /text	Objective
Cloze	Delete adjectives and ask pupils in pairs to complete the gaps	To encourage reading for meaning, to introduce/revisit the term 'adjective' and to develop vocabulary
Hot-seat	Take on the role of a character after an incident and be questioned by others	To appreciate characters, their motives, etc.
Diary/letter	Writing in role as one character to another	To help pupils to appreciate plot, perspective, etc.
Storytelling	Urban myths	Small groups promoting collaborative talk
Drawing	*Robinson Crusoe* extract	To facilitate close reading by producing a labelled drawing of the character
Role play		

Standards addressed:
2.1, 3.3.2

Activity 7

ANALYSING STORY
(suggested time: 30 minutes)

To help pupils to read more critically you could consider the use of the two approaches outlined below. The first is the employment of a *story analysis table* that pupils can be asked to complete (Year 7):

TITLE			SERIES (if part of one)		
AUTHOR					
Place where story is set			Time when story is set		
Main character		Sex	Nationality		Age
Occupation			Special features (if any)		
What sort of person?					
Main character		Sex	Nationality		Age
Occupation			Special features (if any)		
What sort of person?					
What problem do the main characters face?					
How is the problem solved?					
Unusual features of the story					
Who tells the story?					
What do you think is the author's message?					

The second is the use of questions for pupils to ask themselves about a book that they have read.

Background

Period and place(s) the story is set in: How do they affect the characters and their actions? Do they create a particular mood or atmosphere? Are they familiar to you?

What happens in the story?

What is the story about? What length of time does it cover? Is what happens unusual? ordinary? How does the author manage the start of the story? Do the events in the story follow on from one another? Is there some kind of mystery in the story or is everything made clear when you're reading? What is the climax of the story? How is the climax built up? What kind of ending is it? (any loose ends?)

Characters

Who are the main characters? What are they like? (strengths and weaknesses? behaviour?) Which do you find most interesting? most sympathetic? How do these main characters change through the story? What kinds of relationships and/or conflicts are there between the characters?

How it was written

How did the author show you what was going on? How was the description of people and places handled? How were feelings and attitudes presented? What use was made of dialogue? What did you think about the division into chapters?

What did you think about the length of the book (too brief? too long for itself?) Were the title, cover, etc. of the book right?

General

What reason do you think the author had for telling this particular story? What do you think the author was trying to get you to experience or understand?

How did you feel during and after reading it? (hopeful? annoyed? amused? uncertain?)

Do you think you learned anything from the book about people? ways of life? problems? Do you think it has changed your attitudes or ideas in any way? How would you compare it to other books you've read recently? What kind of people would it appeal to? What else do you think it's important to say about it?

Standards addressed:
3.3.2, 3.3.12

Try using one of these approaches with your pupils in one class based on their private reading. Put one example into your English portfolio.

Activity 8

WAYS INTO BOOKS II

(suggested time: 30 minutes)

The chapter by Traves on reading in *Teaching English* (1994) by Brindley explores the central aim of schools to produce confident, ambitious and critical readers. Traves notes that in reading narrative pupils need to be aware of a large number of conventions:

> *They need to be able to read within or against the rules of particular genres. These rules help the reader to decide what is acceptable, plausible rather than possible, within the world of the story. (Brindley, 1994: 93)*

Traves also argues that pupils need to be able to read from particular positions (girl, boy, insider, outsider).

Standard
addressed: 2.1

Consider how you would encourage pupils to become critical readers of the narrative texts that they encounter. Write out your responses to the above question and keep these in your English portfolio.

Activity 9

CHILDREN'S READING HABITS

(suggested time: 30 minutes)

Interview six pupils from a Y7 or Y8 class (choose three girls and three boys) to ascertain their reading habits, why they like particular books and what created their interest in these books. List your findings in your portfolio. Your questions should cover the following areas:

Standard
addressed:
3.3.6

(a) Favourite authors and why
(b) Range of reading, e.g. comics, novels
(c) Books read at home and books read at school
(d) The reasons for reading.

Activity 10

DEVELOPING YOUR OWN KNOWLEDGE OF KEY STAGE 3 CLASS READERS

(suggested time: 60 minutes)

Recommend one good Key Stage 3 novel to other student teachers or to your school based mentor. Keep a copy of your recommendation in your English portfolio (no more than 300 words). Explain the rationale for your choice (e.g. appeal to age range and gender/style/characterisation/themes/action).

Standard
addressed: 2.1

Activity 13, 'Creating Databases' in Chapter 18 of this book ('English and ICT') outlines how you can build up a database of Key Stage 3, and 4 readers and anthologies throughout your year of training, and beyond.

Activity 11

GENRE TRANSPOSITION

(suggested time: to be undertaken if appropriate on school placement)

Standard
addressed:
3.3.2

It is important to link the attainment targets. One effective approach would be to take the opening of a story and, using a film script or a radio script template, ask pupils to rewrite it in a different genre. This activitty can generate excellent discussion about film shots or sound effects and what is lost or gained in the change of genre.

Activity 12   GHOST STORIES AND SCIENCE FICTION

(suggested time: 4 hours)

You now need to consider the implications of teaching the genre approach to narrative texts.

GHOST STORIES

TASK 1 PLANNING TO TEACH THE GHOST STORY GENRE

Using some short stories from the ghost story genre such as Thomas Hardy's 'The Superstitious Man's Story', E. Nesbit's 'The Violet Car', Catherine Storr's 'Crossing Over' and Rosemary Timperley's 'Harry', plan a unit of work (medium term plan) for a mixed ability group at Key Stage 4. You can use the medium term template available at **www.paulchapmanpublishing.co.uk/resources/completeguide.htm**. Take the following into account:

- Clarify (by listing) the features of the ghost story genre exemplified in these stories.
- Assume three of the stories are to be taught. Plan activities to aid pupils' comprehension and critical enjoyment of each story.
- Work out a series of rough lesson plans. Consider here the timing, variety of activity and the coverage of the genre features that you listed earlier.
- Design a series of creative writing tasks, from which pupils can choose, which will allow (and encourage) them to make use of what they have learned in their own writing.
- Design one 'wide reading' GCSE assignment (consult a GCSE syllabus for criteria) in which one of the modern stories should be compared with a pre-1914 story such as one by Hardy. Assume that you are aiming to differentiate by task in this case and direct less academically able pupils towards one assignment and more academically able pupils towards the other. Set the questions and work through the teaching points that you would want to cover to ensure that all pupils were appropriately challenged.

TASK 2 EVALUATING SOME SCHEMES OF WORK

Evaluate the schemes of work for the ghost story genre and science fiction genre that are contained in this activity. Before describing the individual stories a context is provided for each genre. How might you get this information across to pupils? What are the implications of teaching genre? The stories need to be taught as well as read. Choose one story and plan the lesson(s) for teaching it. How would you support less able pupils who are working on the wider reading assignments? List the strategies you would use for teaching each of the genre assignments.

Outline of scheme

Ghost stories provide us with ways of thinking about death and dying. They help us explore our uncertainties about the supernatural and whether there is any form of life after death. They build upon the fact that, whatever we believe, no one can be definite about what happens to our spirit when our bodies die. All of us will experience a fear of dying and most of us will experience great grief when someone we love dies. Ghost stories use our fear of death and the unknown to create suspense in the reader. They draw on deep rooted superstitions and the belief that perhaps we all have an allotted time to die. They portray the meeting of two worlds – the worlds of the living and the dead – and they create tension about whether a character will step over the border from one world to the other.

They also draw on our experience of what happens to people who are grieving. When people we love die, grief can make us lose our grip on everyday reality. Life can seem pointless, and we so desperately want to see the person we are missing that it is common to imagine catching sight of the dead person. Ghost stories often keep the reader guessing about whether a character has actually seen a ghost, or is being driven by grief or fear to imagine that they have.

Most commonly, ghost stories deal with the premature or violent death of the ghost character. They build a story around the idea of an interrupted life, to which the ghost needs to return to tie up the loose ends. Places and times are highly significant in ghost stories. The exact time or spot that a person died can take on a symbolic significance. So can objects, music or perfumes associated with the dead person.

Because ghost stories are hard to believe, writers use devices that make the story seem more authentic. The stories are often told in the first person, to suggest that the writer actually had the experience. Many contain a lot of direct speech, with people apparently telling the story 'in their own words'. The central characters are often sensible, down-to-earth people who would not usually have wild imaginations.

The tension in ghost stories usually builds up as we wait to see whether the world of the dead or the living will win in the end. But because we know that we cannot go on living for ever, we are also aware that any victory for the living characters is only a temporary one. This leaves writers with lots of possibilities for dramatic twists at the ends of their stories.

EXAMPLES OF GHOST STORIES

The Superstitious Man's Story by **Thomas Hardy**

This is from a collection of Hardy's stories called *Life's Little Ironies* which was first published in 1894. 'The Superstitious Man's Story' is one of a series of linked tales which are grouped together under the heading 'A Few Crusted Characters'. Hardy has invented a set of neighbours who meet up with an interested traveller returning in the coach with them to his father's home in Wessex. The local people tell the traveller stories of the 'crusted characters' to bring him up to date with the local news. Each of the nine tales is told in direct speech by one of the Wessex people, and there are short linking conversations between the stories.

Thomas Hardy, who lived from 1840 to 1928, wrote about rural life in his novels, poems and short stories. He lived at a time of rapid change in the countryside, as work patterns and social life and attitudes were altering and he hoped that in his writing he could 'preserve for my own satisfaction a fairly true record of a vanishing life'. In this story, based on West Country folklore. Hardy records the superstitions connected with Midsummer's Eve. Time and place are highly significant. Strange and symbolic events occur, but set within a context of ordinary people living their everyday lives.

The Violet Car by Edith Nesbit

Edith Nesbit is best known for her children's books, particularly *The Railway Children* and *Five children and It*. In fact, she wrote a great many short stories and articles for adults as well as children since her family depended upon her making money from her writing. Edith Nesbit lived from 1858 to 1924; she was a devoted mother, a keen socialist and partygoer, and a friend of H.G. Wells.

In several ways 'The Violet Car' is typical of well told ghost stories. The narrator is a sensible, plain-speaking woman, a nurse who soon gives up the attempt to write in a fancy style. The central characters are consumed by grief; the whole story turns upon what is reality and what is grief-induced imagination. The location and setting of the story are very clearly drawn, and the ending raises as many questions as it settles.

Harry by Rosemary Timperley

'Harry' is a chilling story. Its setting is warm and loving, a world of small children and protective parents. Like the other ghost stories in this selection, it is simply told. Conversations are directly reported, and the first person narration gives the reader an insight into the mother's point of view and her increasing anxiety about her child. As in the other stories, places and times are very significant. Everyday items become highly symbolic. And the tension mounts, as we move from the everyday world of children playing, to the intensity of the supernatural world in which a teenager's life has been cut short by violence.

Rosemary Timperley, born in 1920, has been publishing ghost stories since 1952. She has written over 100 short stories, and is particularly respected for her ghost stories in which the ghosts are usually gentle rather than horrific, but none the less frightening!

Crossing Over by Catherine Storr

Catherine Storr's fiction often has an interesting psychological angle to it, which is not surprising since she is both a writer and a psychiatrist. The story included in this collection, ambiguously titled 'Crossing Over', gives us an insider's view of how the main character is thinking and feeling.

As with the other stories, the setting is very ordinary. The girl too seems quite ordinary – she is not even given a name. The incident being described is an everyday event – walking a dog. The story is told in a matter of fact, simple way which makes the readers think they understand what is happening. But the response of Mrs Matthews and her dog Togo at the end of the story makes us see events rather differently.

1 Comparing stories for wide reading

Compare and contrast Thomas Hardy's 'The Superstitious Man's Story' with **either**

> 'The Violet Car' by Enid Nesbit **or**
> 'Harry' by Rosemary Timperley **or**
> 'Crossing Over' by Catherine Storr.

Consider the main similarities and differences in the way the stories are written, and decide which of the stories you find most successful as a ghost story and why.

You might like to comment on:

- the way the stories are told – who the narrator is, the point of view expressed and the style of language used in the telling;
- the use of place in the story;
- the importance of time in the story;
- the relationship between the central characters, and the effect that has on the supernatural part of the story;
- the underlying emotions that the story is dealing with. Are these portrayed effectively?
- the way the 'ghost' appears and influences events;
- how the ending works. is it satisfying to readers? is it ambiguous?
- the use of symbolism in the stories.

2 Opportunities for original writing

When you have thought about what you have learned from this section on ghost stories, do one of the following:

- Write a story from the ghost's point of view. (You might like to keep the reader guessing about whether the narrator is dead or alive until the end.)
- Write a story based on the idea that a character's grief at the death of a loved one is so intense that the dead person seems to return as a ghost.
- Choose a ghostly place and time (such as the church porch on Midsummer's Eve in Hardy's story). Describe three separate spooky incidents that take place in the location you have chosen. Give the year of each of the incidents, but remember they could take place hundreds of years apart and the place will change over the years. Build up the atmosphere of the place and occasion in your description.
- Use diary entries and letters to tell a ghost story.
- Write a comic ghost story about a haunting that goes wrong.
- Write a story about a ghost who lived a thoughtless and selfish life. The ghost is given a last chance to put right some of the damage by being allowed to return to Earth for a limited amount of time. What happens?

SCIENCE FICTION

Science fiction has its roots in the story, *Frankenstein* published by Mary Shelley in 1818. In 1864, the French writer Jules Verne published *Journey to the Centre of the*

Earth, and followed it up a year later with a novel about travelling from the Earth to the Moon by space rocket. In the same year there were at least four other novels published in France about interplanetary travel. In 1895 H.G. Wells published *The Time Machine,* and later went on to write about an invasion by Martians in *The War of the Worlds* (1898), and about *The First Men in the Moon* (1901).

For a long time, writers have tried to predict the future. They have been interested in how new technology will change people's lives and how people will adapt when machinery and computers take over some of the jobs that people previously did. Writers have used their imagination to think about the potential of science and also the possible dangers, and they have worked through these ideas in their stories. The stories are usually written in the third person; they often include reports and technological descriptions, with new names for the people, places and objects that the writer has invented.

The best science fiction helps us think freshly about our own world and our own society. Sci-fi stories often take a current trend or new development and show what could happen if it is allowed to get out of hand. Some science fiction is concerned with aliens, spaceships, amazing technology and other worlds. Other science fiction focuses more on the organisation of society or home life in the future. Either type of science fiction will show the reader something about the concerns and values of the writer and the society he or she lives in.

The Time Machine by H.G. Wells

Herbert George Wells, who lived from 1866 to 1946, had a very important influence on the development of science fiction in Britain. *The Time Machine* was published as a short book in 1895, but in the year before that it had aroused a great deal of interest when it appeared in instalments as a serial. the text can be accessed at **www.bartleby.com**.

Wells called his novels 'social fables' and they certainly all carry strong social messages. Wells was a committed socialist and keen to comment on the political and social issues of his day. *The Time Machine* is written as a series of after-dinner conversations in a middle-class gentleman's home, and Wells takes every opportunity to debate ideas and engage in philosophical discussions. The dinner guests include an editor, a doctor and a psychologist, but they are there to represent points of view connected with their work rather than as individual characters. They are in conversation with the Time Traveller, who had built and travelled in his own time machine.

The Time Machine is an early example of science fiction, and not entirely typical of the genre as we know it today. However, certain important features of the genre are easily recognisable: the interest in science and the technology of the time machine; the portrayal of alien life forms and environment in the future. Also typical is the social question which underpins the story. Wells is interested in the future of the human race – read on to find out his vision of what we may become!

The Veldt by Ray Bradbury

'The Veldt' (which refers to areas of open grassland in South Africa) takes the reader into the future. Technology has advanced to the point where you can switch on a whole house to do the household chores and to provide entertainment. But how does this affect the families who live in those houses? Does the technology help children grow up as psychologically healthy individuals? What are the parents' responsibilities?

These are some of the questions that are explored in Ray Bradbury's story, which comes from his classic science fiction collection *The Illustrated Man,* published in 1952. In the Prologue and Epilogue to the book, Bradbury tells the story of a traveller who meets a man who has been tattooed all over his body. These are magical tattoos – 'illustrations' – which move and act out stories of the future on the man's body. 'The Veldt' is one of those stories, which the traveller finds himself almost compelled to watch. Seventeen other varied and powerful stories follow, before the sting in the tail which emerges in the Epilogue.

Harrison Bergeron by Kurt Vonnegut, Jr

Like Ray Bradbury's story, 'Harrison Bergeron' takes place in the future, and in a domestic setting. New technology is having an important impact on people's lives. The story is told clearly, and with a degree of detachment. Vonnegut explores a different social theme: the idea of what it might mean to make sure that all people were equal. Vonnegut treats the subject with irony and a darkly humorous touch, but the story suggests some serious social questions – about the place of the media in our lives and our freedom to act as individuals.

Kurt Vonnegut is an American writer, born in 1922, who often uses features of the science fiction genre in his novels and short stories. 'Harrison Bergeron' is from a collection of Vonnegut's short stories called *Welcome to the Monkey House,* which was published in 1968.

Science Fiction

1 Comparing stories for wide reading

Compare and contrast an extract from H.G. Wells's *Time Machine* with a 20th century science fiction short story.

You could choose **either** 'The Veldt' by Ray Bradbury or 'Harrison Bergeron' by Kurt Vonnegut, Jr.

You might like to comment on:

- the way the story is told;
- the kind of new technology which is described;
- the attitude the writer seems to have to this new technology;
- the settings in which the stories take place;
- the main characters – their jobs, their attitudes, how they are described;
- the vision of the future portrayed in the story;

- the broad social and philosophical questions that the stories explore;
- how these broad questions might relate to the time when the stories were written.

2 Opportunities for original writing

When you have thought about what you have learned from studying the stories in this section, write a science fiction story using one of the following ideas:

- Time travel – you could set your story in a future when time travel is as common as catching an aeroplane is today, so that people can take time travel holidays to the future or the past.
- A seemingly innocent piece of new technology, for example answerphones or voice mail, takes on a life of its own.
- A party of aliens contacts the Prime Minister and asks to make a peaceful diplomatic visit to Earth. What happens when they arrive?
- A story set in a future society where social problems have been 'solved' by electronic tagging of people, curfews and constant surveillance so that people are forced to stay in their homes.
- A story set in a school, house, prison or hospital of the future.

Standards addressed: 2.1, 3.1.2, 3.3.4

CONTINUOUS THREADS

3.1 Planning, expectations and targets

Standards addressed: 2.1, 3.1.2, 3.3.4

You will need to choose your class reader carefully so that it appeals wherever possible to the range of interests/abilities in your class. This might mean choosing a text with themes that relate closely to the adolescent experience, or a fantasy fiction. During Key Stages 3 and 4 you will need to provide a variety of types of reading: pre-1914, texts from a range of cultures, and texts with male and females as central characters. The issue of boys' underachievement in literacy is a significant one and you need to consider how to motivate boys. So for example you may want to encourage the reading of picture books in Year 7 such as *The Watertower* by Gary Crew. These types of picture book build upon the form of science fiction films and include a series of problems that need to be resolved. Such texts build upon the pupil's experience of the visual media and are thus likely to be considered as culturally significant by pupils. Millard notes that in a research project in the mid-1990s boys were more likely than girls to neglect fiction; this, she states, puts them at

> *a greater disadvantage in a subject where the reading and writing of narratives . . . is essential for success. Further the individual tastes of those boys who do read regularly for stories which emphasize action over personal relationships, excitement over the unfolding of character, and humour most of all, set them at odds with many books chosen for study at school. (Millard, 1997: 61)*

You should note P .Traves's charter for reading in schools in Brindley. Here he argues for a minimum entitlement for all pupils and concludes with the view that:

> The overarching aim of schools ought to be the production of confident, ambitious and critical readers who see reading, like other aspects of their language facility, as a key part of their engagement in and understanding of the world. (Brindley, 1994: 97)

You may also want to consider the readability of texts. Almost all readers will find it hard to interact successfully with a text if it is unfamiliar or too complex. Issues around readability are well explored in Harrison, *Readability in the Classroom* (1980).

2 Monitoring and assessment

Standard addressed: 3.2.1

You will need to be aware of the range of reading of your pupils and assessment should be used to ensure the development of their ability to read for meaning. Some strategies for developing critical readers are well outlined in Davison and Dowson (1998: 119–22) and include suggestions such as the use of reading journals and dramatisation of parts of the text. The assessment of reading may well come in speaking and listening activities or in the written tasks you set (e.g. the writing of an event in a novel from a different perspective). You will need to consider what objectives you have in mind when planning your scheme. Davison and Dowson note that to develop progression pupils should be taught to make individual meaning, to broaden their reading experience so that they can approach the unfamiliar. See also our chapter 4 on assessment.

In order to build successfully upon pupils' prior reading it is important to audit their reading habits, perhaps using a reading log or questionnaire. Appleyard presents an interesting model of pupils' development in reading. This is cited in Goodwyn (1998: 8). He indicates that teenagers in particular when confronted with printed or visual texts learn in a 'fairly predictable sequence'. He categorises this as follows:

1   THE READER AS HERO OR HEROINE – here the reader escapes into a world that provides an alternative to their own.
2   THE READER AS THINKER – here the reader is looking for a greater understanding of the meaning of life and of role models.
3   THE READER AS INTERPRETER – here the reader approaches the text as a body of knowledge, learning to analyse it and appreciate its history.
4   PRAGMATIC READER – here the reader is able to choose the use they make of the texts that they read.

This view of reading development, from 'unreflecting engagement' (Goodwyn, 1998) to selective purposeful reading, places particular challenges upon the teacher. To ensure the development of the higher reading order skills what approaches are required? Can they be gained from reading almost entirely popular culture? The opening chapter to Goodwyn's book explores this debate. You will need to consider how we move readers from one stage in their development to the next stage.

Certainly you will have to introduce texts that help pupils to experience a wide range of values and messages.

3.3 Teaching and class management

Standards addressed: 3.3.2, 3.3.3, 3.3.4

You will need to provide a variety of opportunities for different types of reading in your classroom. Consider when teaching the class reader whether you read most of it to your class, whether you allocate sections for your pupils to read aloud, whether some is read at home, etc. Thought needs to be given to what are the most appropriate speaking and listening activities and/or written activities to include in your lessons to help pupils discuss and explore such areas as the language of the text, characterisation, narrative structure and themes. You will also want to consider the opportunities for silent reading (e.g. USSR–uninterrupted sustained silent reading) and be aware of the benefits of reading your own book/s (as a model) when pupils are reading their books as part of private reading.

You might also want to recommend books to your pupils for silent reading sessions and even provide a book box of interesting reads. Many schools encourage silent reading, possibly at the start of two lessons a week for 10–15 minutes, as many pupils do not get the opportunity to read at home. Small group readings can be useful to enable differentiation by interest group/ability/gender. Thus consideration should be given to the purpose of the reading activity and to what type of group organisation would best suit it. Some ideas for encouraging independent reading are listed below:

- Recommend books to pupils.
- Encourage pupils to recommend books to one another.
- Provide regular opportunities for uninterrupted sustained silent reading.
- Act as a role model.
- Encourage pupils to keep reading logs.
- Create regular opportunities for your pupils to discuss books.
- Keep up to date with children's fiction, e.g. Carnegie shortlists.
- Integrate reading with speaking/listening activities and writing activities.
- Encourage pupils to visit children's literature websites.

2.5 ICT

We must not ignore the fact that we now live in a time when much communication takes place via electronic means. Pupils should be encouraged to read about books on such websites as **www.ucalgary.ca/~dkbrown/index.html**. The use of websites to aid the teaching of children's literature is well illustrated in the lesson plan below.

LESSON PLAN

Date: Room: Time: One Hour   Year Group: Year 9

Topic/Text	*Stone cold* by R. Swindell	**Objectives** What will the pupils have learned?
NC Programmes of study:	To develop reading of print and ICT-based information To identify the perspectives offered on individuals and society To reflect on the writer's presentation of ideas and issues.	To appreciate central themes To explore information on websites To role-play on-line To evaluate choices
AT1–Collaborative group work and formal evaluation AT2–Reading for information AT3–Writing to review		**Resources** 15 computers with Internet access **Last lesson** Read the opening to *Stone Cold* and discuss the writer's ability to create suspense. Brainstorm reasons for homelessness

Time allocated	Activities and development
5 to 10 mins	Introduction: Recap previous lesson's learning outcomes. Log on to the Internet **www.centrepoint.org.uk** Explain the task, the purpose of the website and the purpose of 'virtual homelessness' Let the pupils work through the game in pairs, with them noting down their responses
20 mins	They then print out the material
10 mins	Using the key questions as guides, the pairs prepare their evaluation of the site
10 mins	Presentations of the site
10 mins	**Conclusion** Plenary. Discussion about the value of the site and what was learned about homelessness
Homework/ Follow up work	Produce poster about the causes of homelessness for teenage audience. Access other sites: **www.shelter.org.uk**
Special Considerations	Sarah was absent last lesson
Evaluation	(Include successes and targets for future action)

In this lesson pupils access information about homelessness. This is a good starting point for reading R. Swindells's novel, *Stone Cold*.

Scenarios

1 In your class you have three very able pupils who are always keen to read out aloud, but you also have three pupils who refuse to read out aloud. How are you to address these issues?

Some thoughts that might help you with the latter:

- Explore why they don't want to read aloud.
- Provide opportunities for small group readings.

- Encourage pupils to read out their favourite sections of books.
- Let them choose when to stop reading.
- Read drama scripts and give the latter three only the smallest parts.
- Paired reading approaches.

Now consider the issues for the most able.

2 Imagine that you are about to begin teaching a class novel to a Y8 group of 30 mixed ability pupils. Consider the following:
- How do you choose the text?
- What do you need to know about your pupils' prior learning?
- What preparation do you need to do with your class?
- How long have you allocated to work on this text?
- Who will do most of the reading? Why?
- What related work will you set?
- In your class you have one pupil who has significant reading difficulties. How will you cater for his/her needs?

FURTHER READING

Gender issues have recently become a major concern in the drive to raise literacy levels. In reading, girls are generally outperforming boys. Teachers are being encouraged to use strategies to improve boys' attitudes to reading. A particularly informative book on this subject is E. Millard's *Differently Literate* (1997).

In relation to using texts from a range of cultures and traditions, consider works by Maya Angelou, or M. Taylor's *Roll of Thunder, Hear My Cry* (for Years 9–10). You could take a thematic approach, e.g. beliefs/animals/languages/costumes/weather, and explore these in a range of texts. A list of recommended writers from different cultures can be found in the National Curriculum document 2000.

Some key books for 11–14-year-olds

Year 7	Year 8
D. Almond	*Skellig*
B. Doherty	*Street Child*
M. Morpurgo	*Why the Wales Came*
R. Swindells	*Room 13*
B. Doherty	*The Snake Stone*
S. Cooper	*King of Shadows*
R. Swindler	*Stone Cold*
D. Almond	*Kit's Wilderness*
G. Cross	*Tightrope*
N. Hinton	*Buddy*
J. Wilson	*The Lotty Project*

Some popular Key Stage 3 texts are reviewed here by Jane Geeson (Head of English at Antony Gell School, Derbyshire).

These books are all strong enough to be 'class readers' but the most appropriate year group will depend on the school.

David Almond, *Skellig* (Year 7/8) Fantasy/adventure

After moving house, Michael explores the derelict garage and finds a strange creature, 'Skellig'. The magical adventure begins when Mina, a local girl who does not go to school, makes friends with Michael and they share their secrets. Tension grows in the story as Michael's baby sister fights for her life.

Comment: Well written with some excellent description and humorous dialogue.

Themes/issues: Being different, outsiders, friendship, education, imagination.

Tim Bowler, *River Boy* (Year 6/7) Fantasy/adventure

Jess goes for a holiday with her sick grandfather back to his roots. Whilst swimming, she meets the 'River Boy', who suggests Jess should help Grandpa with his painting. The 'River Boy' wants Jess to swim from the source of the river to the sea with him but Grandpa is dying. The Jess/Grandpa relationship is the centre of the novel.

Comment: The river becomes a metaphor for life and death. A well told story.

Themes/issues: Life, death, the past, love and family ties, talents, choices, identity.

Melvin Burgess, *An Angel for May* (Year 7/8) Time slip/adventure

Angry with his parents for separating, Tam escapes to 'Thowt it' farm and sees a young girl (May) in the ruins. He follows her and finds himself in another time (Second World War) where he makes new friends and has adventures. It is much more appealing than his home life where the horrible 'old bag lady' hangs around.

Comment: A touching story. A rich text for social issues and imaginative spin-off.

Themes/issues: War, prejudice, tolerance, outsiders, friendship, family conflicts.

Gillian Cross, *Tightrope* (Year 8/9) Teenage/adventure

Ashley seems to be the perfect daughter but her secret nightlife as a graffiti artist gets her involved with Eddie, a powerful character in the neighbourhood. He begins to control Ashley's life in a sinister way until she decides she must stand up to him and face the consequences.

Comment: A powerful multiple narrative with some disturbing ideas to discuss.

Themes/issues: Breaking rules, risk, violence and crime, freedom and responsibility.

Berlie Doherty, *The Snake Stone* (Year 7/8) Teenage/adventure

James travels through the Derbyshire countryside in search of his real mother and his own identity. The 'Snake Stone', which he finds in an old envelope, holds the clue to who he really is. His real mother's story is intertwined as they both make a journey over the hills at different moments in time.

Comment: A moving story tightly structured in a dual narrative.

Themes/issues: Identity, truth, trust, family conflicts, parental responsibility.

Robert O'Brien, *Mrs Frisby and the Rats of Nimh* (Year 6/7) Fantasy

When mouse Timothy is ill, Mrs. Frisby seeks advice from the super breed of Rats who live under the rose bush. In a story within a story, Mrs Frisby is told how the Rats came to be there following a laboratory experiment which made them so intelligent that they escaped and built their own society.

Comment: A story with excellent animal characterisation and sinister implications.

Themes/issues: Social, moral, political, power, cruelty, new beginnings, courage, trust.

Philip Pullman, *Northern Lights* (Year 6/7) Fantasy/adventure

Lyra and her daemon live in a parallel world where 'Dust' and 'severed children' are an intriguing puzzle. Lyra sets out to investigate, rescue her friend Roger and find her father Lord Asriel. She has an alethiometer to help her find the truth but first she must learn to read it. (The first book in 'His Dark Materials' trilogy.)

Comment: An intricate plot, well told with mystery and tension.

Themes/issues: Good/evil, truth, trust, courage, friendship, betrayal, other worlds.

Louis Sachar, *Holes* (Year 6/7) Mystery/adventure

An innocent Stanley Yelnats finds himself at Camp Green Lake, an unusual boys' detention centre in the desert. The warden insists that each boy must dig a five foot hole every day as a character-building exercise. Stanley struggles to fit in at the camp but hopes his luck will change when he discovers something in a hole.

Comment: Told with humour in a direct and simple style. It will appeal to boys.

Themes/issues: Hope, determination, injustice, outsiders, crime, deceit, friendship.

Robert Swindells, *Stone Cold* (Year 9) Teenage/crime

After his parents split up, Link finds himself homeless on the streets of London and without Ginger he'd never have survived. Then suddenly, Ginger disappears and Link teams up with Gail, a new girl on the street. Meanwhile Shelter, a retired sergeant -major, is offering 'help' to the destitute.

Comment: A sinister dual narrative, tightly structured and told with chilling suspense.

Themes/issues: Homelessness, outsiders, friendship, trust, abuse, evil, madness.

Benjamin Zephaniah, *Face* (Year 8/9) Teenage/adventure

Martin, the leader of 'The Gang of Three' is in a fatal car accident that changes his life. He has to come to terms with the fact that his face has been burned beyond recognition, and with his new face and all that means. His girlfriend Natalie is increasingly distant and he finds himself the victim of cruel name-calling.

Comment: A hard-hitting narrative, action packed from the start. It will appeal to boys.

Themes/issues: Peer pressure, gangs and victims, survival, prejudice, identity.

REFERENCES

Brindley, S. (1994) *Teaching English in the Secondary School*. London: Routledge

Davies, C. (1996) *What is English Teaching?*, Oxford: OUP

Davison, J. and Dowson, J. (1998) *Learning to Teach English in the Secondary School*. London: Routledge

DfEE (1999) *The National Curriculum for England. English: Key Stages 1–4*. London: DfEE and QCA

DfEE (2001) *English Department Training 2001*. London: DfEE

Fleming, M. and Stevens, D. (1998) *English Teaching in the Secondary School*. London: David Fulton

Goodwyn, A. (1998) *Literary and Media Texts in Secondary English*. London: Cassell

Harrison, C. (1980) *Readability in the Classroom*. Oxford: Oxford University Press

Knight, R. (1996) *Valuing English*. London: David Fulton

Lunzer, E. and Gardner, K. (1984) *Learning from the Written Word*. Edinburgh: Oliver and Boyd

Millard, E. (1997) *Differently Literate*. London: Falmer

WEBSITES

http://www.bbc.co.uk/schools (For GCSE and SATs revision materials)

http://ourworld.compuserve.com/homepages/Harry_Dodds (Provides a good link to the Virtual Teachers' Centre)

http://www.teachit.co.uk

http://www.englishonline.co.uk

http://www.inform.umd.edu/edres/readingroom (Excellent for obtaining electronic versions of all sorts of texts – including narrative ones)

chapter 15

WRITING

By the end of this chapter you will have gained an understanding of the writing process, the demands of different types of writing and be able to appreciate a variety of ways of developing pupils' written skills. Before reading the rest of this chapter it is worth reflecting upon your own writing. Start by listing the types of writing that you have undertaken during the last fortnight. You might want to use the following framework: What do I write (e.g. diary/letter)? Why do I write (e.g. reminder of appointment)? How do I write (e.g. is it planned, is it reflective)? Who do I write for (e.g. partner, bank manager)? Keep this record as ongoing whilst you work through the chapter. It will be useful when comparing your experiences with those that you expect from your pupils, particularly in relation to extended writing.

RATIONALE

The focus of this chapter will be upon the development of compositional skills and writing as central to creative development. Writing can take a variety of forms, and effective writers convey a clear sense of purpose and successfully target their audience. Consequently much of this chapter will explore the three areas of: form, purpose and audience. As J. Sargeant states, writing is often viewed as of paramount importance because:

> *prospective employers, examiners and the general public see the art of writing as the most fundamental test of a person's ability to communicate clearly and accurately. (Protherough and King, 1995: 65)*

Certainly this 'adult needs' approach to writing means that it is critical that teachers pay heed to the quality and fluency of the written expression. However, there can be a tension between emphasising the technical aspects of writing at the expense of the creative process. M. Rosen captures this succinctly:

> *writing has to live on fertile ground. It has to be wanted and loved for it to survive. It cannot survive in an atmosphere of indifference, cynicism, and harsh judgement. This means that amongst the best things that a teacher can do with students' writing is to discuss with them ways of sharing and distributing their work. (Brindley, 1994: 198)*

As teachers we must be sensitive to the created texts that pupils give to us. In our efforts to improve pupils' writing we should recognise their often tentative steps towards inviting the outside world to view their efforts.

In the quest to improve pupils' writing there have been a number of research projects in the last five years. One that is worth noting is the QCA *Technical Accuracy in Writing* research project. This came in response to the SCAA/Ofsted report, *Standards in Public Examinations 1975–1995* (referred to in QCA, 1994: 4), which expressed some concerns about the levels of literacy among 16-year-olds in English GCSE examinations. The QCA report presents the findings of an analysis of the 1998 GCSE scripts for English. It was based on the accuracy and usage of six aspects of written English: spelling, punctuation, sentences/clauses and different word classes, paragraphing, textual organisation, and non-Standard English.

The results outlined in the report suggested that there were certain linguistic characteristics associated with particular grades e.g. Grade A candidates used fewer finite verbs per sentence and fewer co-ordinated clauses than C or F candidates. Such findings might affect the approaches that teachers adopt when teaching writing, although a reductive approach relying heavily upon mirroring the key linguistic features of a particular grade might discourage creative exploration. Debra Myhill has written a thought-provoking article based upon this report in *English in Education* (1999). It raises some interesting debate about the importance of a shared understanding of how texts are constructed.

> *For teachers and learners, knowing what devices or linguistic techniques constitute the effective establishment of a reader–writer relationship or the maintenance of cohesion through paragraph links is a powerful tool, deconstructing and demystifying the process of writing. (Myhill,1999: 77)*

Myhill argues that such shared knowledge helps pupils to appreciate that writing is a 'craft which is at once intrinsically creative and eminently learnable' (ibid.). It is through such knowledge that pupils can gain confidence, become independent and challenge conventional structures, styles and genres.

LINKS WITH THE NATIONAL CURRICULUM AND KEY STAGE 3 STRATEGY

The *National Curriculum for English* states that:

during Key Stages 3 and 4 pupils develop confidence in writing for a range of purposes. They develop their own distinctive styles and recognise the importance of writing with commitment and vitality. They learn to write correctly, using different formats, layouts and ways of presenting their work. (DfEE, 1999)

The National Curriculum makes it clear that pupils must be taught how to write for a variety of purposes and lists 12 (e.g. persuade, entertain, and inform). It should be noted that many of these purposes overlap and that the primary purpose for the writing is what is significant. Thus a narrative approach could be used to inform.

Besides the compositional element to writing there is much emphasis on the secretarial elements of writing such as spelling, grammar and presentation. These elements are considered in other chapters. It is gratifying to discover towards the end of the section on writing that 'pupils should also be taught to use writing for thinking and learning' (DfEE, 1999). This emphasis on the way in which writing is a vital element in learning to extend and deepen thinking – by the process of allowing reflection on one's own first ideas – must be central to our teaching if we are to produce good creative writers.

In the *Framework for Teaching English: Years 7, 8 and 9* writing is given a separate place at text level and is broadly divided into two key categories. The first relates to the organisational and process aspects such as planning, drafting and presenting work and the second focuses upon the purposes for writing under 12 headings. These are then clustered into groups of three (e.g. inform, explain and describe). There are thus implications for you to help pupils to generate ideas for their writing (e.g. through reading, pictures, music) to teach them to draft work and revise it (e.g. through guided questions, response to peer comment). You will also need to help pupils write for these different purposes and in different forms (e.g. analysing conventions of certain genres to help pupils appreciate that form and language choice relate to audience and purpose).

Activity 1

PROCESS AND GENRE

(suggested time: 40 minutes)

The teaching of writing in the English curriculum has been dominated by two main approaches. The first one has been termed *process writing* and it has a number of distinct stages, from initial discussion of ideas through to drafting, conferencing, revising, editing and publishing. In this approach to writing it is important that the writer has a sense of ownership, although supported by the teacher. It emphasises a personal growth model with the writer seeking to find the appropriate voice with guidance from the teacher. Its advocates would argue that there is an emphasis on creativity and self-expression, whilst its critics may comment that the teacher's 'reluctance to intervene positively and constructively during conferencing and the consequent mystification of what has to be learned for children to reproduce effective written products' (Martin, 1985 in Myhill, 1999: 71) could be disadvantaging pupils who do not have a wide range of discourses to draw upon. The principles of the writing process are well outlined by Davies (1996: 121–2).

The second model is *the genre approach*, which emphasises the explicit teaching of different genres and their main linguistic features. Writers need to appreciate that genres are structured in different ways depending upon the purpose of the text and the intended audience. This approach requires that the writers have a sound awareness of their culture as texts are made within certain cultures and societies and thus even if texts have the same purposes they may be very different, depending on the culture and society in which they were shaped. Writers also need to understand the structure and language of explanation, report writing, procedures, narratives, etc. Approaches teachers might use here include sharing exemplars, perhaps modelling the writing and highlighting key language and organisational features. Myhill comments that proponents of the genre approach might claim that:

> *By learning explicitly about the differences between genres and through studying the features of genres, writers can imitate and reproduce these genres more effectively. (1999: 71)*

This approach is clearly prevalent in the National Literacy Strategy, where genres are clearly categorised and pupils are encouraged to analyse their main features.

These two approaches underpin most teaching of writing although the critical literacy movement does challenge the over-reliance on form that the genre approach can promote.

What do you consider to be the main advantages and disadvantages of each model?

Standard addressed: 2.1 Write down your thoughts in your English portfolio under the titles 'Process writing' and 'Genre approaches'.

Activity 2

GENRES AND NARRATIVE

(suggested time: 40 minutes)

Consider the following text and see if you can identify the different types of narrative text from which it is constructed. What are the clues? (Adapted from an approach in Carter, 1997.)

> 'Come on!' He looked into my eyes and I saw that he wasn't just after gossip; he really cared about me.

> There was a mildewed, chilly smell, but the bed looked freshly made up and clean, although it felt clammy.

> He moved cautiously forward towards the transmitter. To his surprise the signal faded.

> I was in darkness as absolute as if I were sealed in a jet vault, yet the shudder of the nightmare instantly subsided.

So I told her. On the Net.

I WANT YOU.

I NEED YOU.

I WANT TO DOWNLOAD MY LOVE FOR YOU.

Then, with a series of jerks that could not have been very enjoyable, the cruiser began to move down to the horizon.

Usually Sooz spits and snarls a bit, finds a cool way to settle the score and then moves on.

This time my terror was positive and not to be shaken off.

Once, when she would have led him out into the full sunlight, he let her fall below the horizon until he could only just pick up her signals.

Extracts from narrative texts acknowledged at the start of this book.

Standard addressed: 2.1

Consider how you were able to identify the three different types of narrative text. How would you teach pupils to write in these very different ways? Place your answers in your English portfolio. You might want to create a text with extracts from instructions, story and adverts and see if pupils can identify the genres of the texts.

Activity 3

FEATURES OF DIFFERENT GENRES

(suggested time: 40 minutes)

Choose two texts that represent different genres ,e.g. a report and an argument. Then write out the underlying structure of the text and list its main language features. Keep the texts with your commentaries of the structures and language features in your English portfolio. If you were doing this for a **discussion genre** you might discover the following structure:

- Presentation of the issue with central arguments outlined
- Arguments for, with evidence
- Arguments against, with evidence
- Overall viewpoint offered as a conclusion

Key language features:

- Simple present tense
- Logical conjunctions (therefore/ consequently).

For **short stories** the structure might be:

- Exposition – the story begins with an explanation that . . .
- Complication – the complication begins when . . .
- Climax – this is reached when . . .
- Resolution – some form of solution is reached when . . .

Key language features:

- Use of adjectives
- Formal/informal spoken English.

Standard addressed: 2.1   It is important to note that many writers will mix genre styles for particular effects using our understanding of the genre structures, for example using a story to persuade.

Activity 4

THE WRITING EXPERIENCE
(suggested time: 20 minutes)

List in two columns the positives and negatives of writing in the English classroom context. Here are a few to start you thinking. You might not agree with where they have been placed. Consider what implications this might have for you as a classroom teacher.

Positives	Negatives
Writing is a tool for developing thinking	Writing is the main medium through which pupils are assessed
Writing for real audiences can be highly motivating and liberating	Getting pupils to write is a great way of controlling them

Standards addressed: 1.6, 2.1

Activity 5

WRITER'S BLOCK
(suggested time: 40 minutes)

Often pupils find it hard to get started on their writing and teachers need to provide the appropriate stimulus and support. Consider how you can facilitate the writing process and then make a list of the ideas. So you might model examples of writing, provide pictures as stimulus and/or provide writing frames (for example, in the persuasion genre – I think that . . ., the reasons are . . ., the most important point is . . . before making up your mind, remember . . .). See Lewis and Wray (1995) for examples. Keep your ideas in your English portfolio.

Standard addressed: 3.3.4

Activity 6

READING AND WRITING
(suggested time: 50 minutes)

The significance of the relationship between reading and writing should not be underestimated. It is often useful to encourage pupils to consider the choices that writers make in their writing and then to do the same for their own writing. A useful framework for reflecting upon the creating of a written text was provided by the LINC Project and is quoted in Fleming and Stevens (1998: 39). This is outlined below:

A FRAMEWORK FOR LOOKING AT WRITING

What do you think is the writer's purpose or goal? How can you tell?

How is the text structured or organised? What specific features of language show this?

What is the text about?
    e.g. people or things? individuals or groups? concrete or abstract?

What kinds of actions or processes are there?
Are verbs concerned with:
    Physical actions?
    Ways of behaving?
    Thoughts and feelings?
    Processes of communication?
    Describing things – by what they are ? (definition)
                    – by what they have? (attribution)

What tenses are used?

Are verbs concerned with:
    Possibilities? (e.g. might, could, ought)
    Certainties? (e.g shall, will, must)

What is the relationship between reader and writer? How is this shown?

Does the text read as a coherent whole? What helps it hang together?
    e.g vocabulary; references forward and back; linking of clauses and sentences.
What kind of text is this? (Fleming and Stevens, 1998: 39)

Standard addressed: 2.1 Using this framework for looking at written texts apply it to a newspaper article and a letter. Put these two texts into your English portfolio with your responses to the questions. You might want to adapt the model above to use with pupils to help raise their awareness of the writing process.

Activity 7

COLLABORATIVE WRITING
(suggested time: 60 minutes with a class, if the opportunity arises)

As outlined in Chapter 2 on the Key Stage 3 strategy, the training materials (e.g. *English Department Training 2001*) recommend a 10-stage sequence for teaching writing which is focused heavily on the initial support given to the writing process by the teacher through modelling, scaffolding, etc. What should be remembered is that whilst we have a curriculum that is highly assessment-driven with the focus on individual achievement we must not neglect the power of collaborative learning between peers. A well-illustrated example of this was shown by Simon Wrigley at the NATE 2003 conference when he demonstrated the use of pictures and collaborative work to facilitate the writing of poetry. The example he used was based upon the stimulus material of a picture entitled *Miss La La* by Degas. This painting shows a trapeze artiste hanging by her teeth from a chain as she is suspended high up near the roof of the Big Top in Paris.

We were asked to discuss our initial ideas/thoughts as a whole group and these were placed on a flip chart. We were then organised into groups of four and asked to write down what we saw in the picture. Our ideas were placed in an envelope and passed on to the next group. We were then asked to list the sounds that we might hear and placed our note of these into the envelope that had been passed to us. This was then passed on to the next group. We were then asked to note down what the artiste might be thinking. Our ideas were then passed on to the next group. Finally we were asked to write down what the artist might be thinking. This too was passed on. Each envelope thus had four sections of ideas/notes in it:

- *What was seen*

- *What might be heard*

- *What the artiste is thinking*

- *What the artist is thinking.*

We then became the editors of the notes in the envelopes provided by different groups. We had to write a poem or another type of text using ideas/words from each section, adding some of our own plus one idea from the flip chart. No more than 50 words were to be used. We also had to choose a title or titles. This collaborative task provided detailed discussion about meaning, perspectives, lexical choice and audience. It was then followed up by the reading of the poem 'Look, no hands' which was the response by U.A. Fanthorpe to viewing this picture. This was a stimulating and supported activity. Choose a picture and try out this activity with one of your classes.

Standard addressed: 3.3.3

Other collaborative writing work includes: writing parts of stories and passing them on to another pupil to continue, planning drama scripts in small groups and co-writing PowerPoint presentations.

Activity 8

CHANGING THE FORM
(suggested time: 50 minutes with a class, if the opportunity arises)

It can be an excellent collaborative experience if small groups of pupils are asked to write in a certain form and then try to change the form. This can be undertaken with pairs writing in prose and passing their work on to another pair to reproduce as a screenplay. This can help discussion about audience, choice of description, speech and what needs to be made explicit. Try writing the opening to a thriller in prose (no more than 300 words) then try rewriting this opening as a radio play. Take into account the points below. This will be a useful preparation for trying it out in the classroom. Keep a record in your portfolio.

Radio script

- Always number each scene
- Identify where the scene is taking place
- Describe sound effects (FX)
- Identify each character alongside dialogue (number each utterance)
- Minimal use of direction e.g. (PAUSE) (CALLING)
- Identify music effects (GRAMS)

TIPS:

- Radio has no scenes like a play. Do not allow scenes to go beyond their natural length.
- Establish character through speech.
- Avoid stage directions. These should be in the dialogue.
- Use sound effects sparingly. Use them to set the scene.
- Hold the listener's attention by altering the lengths of sequences (e.g. number of people speaking, space of dialogue, volume of sound, background acoustics, location of action).
- The beginning is everything.

Standards addressed:
2.1, 3.3.3

Activity 9

PLANNING TO TEACH A GENRE
(suggested time: 90 minutes)

Create a series of three or four lessons using the lesson plan format provided on the Paul Chapman Publishing website at **www.paulchapmanpublishing.co.uk/ resources/completeguide.htm** taking heed of the points that you have considered during this chapter. The lessons should demonstrate how you would introduce pupils to writing one genre type (e.g. persuade, report, narrative, explanation) and have clear objectives.

If you were teaching persuasive writing your first lesson might focus upon studying the language of advertising or political speeches with a glossary of terms such as

Standards addressed: 2.1, 3.1.2

alliteration, use of statistics. The following lesson could focus on the drafting of an advertisement for a given audience. The third lesson could be the final write-up with a list of the techniques employed. Place the lesson plans in your English portfolio.

Activity 10

CONSIDERING PUPILS' WRITING

(suggested time: 40 minutes)

Marking: Look at the following two examples of pupils' work. One is a narrative, the other is non-narrative.

- Comment on what you feel each pupil has achieved in terms of their writing skills.
- Comment on how you would help these pupils to improve their writing.

In particular focus upon content and organisation. After you have considered the above turn to the end of this chapter for our suggestions.

The Lost Coin (by Lee) – Narrative

One day a man was out walking and there was a hole in his pocket but he didn't notice and a coin fell out. Suddenly the coin came to life and ran away when a dog came rushing towards it suddenly. But luckily the coin dodged it and fell down the drain. Unfortunately he couldent swim a piece of paper floated by and he jumped on it. When he met a rat. When a log stopped them but cleverly he picked up the log and hit the rat with it but while they were doing it a water snake come up behind them but they got away in time they sailed on a bit more when they saw a light in front of them they thought it was the sea but it wasn't they started going faster but it was a pirranha with his mouth open and he swallowed the coin, and carried them into the sea not knowing what was going to happen there just suddenly they rocked it was the suirs getting thinner when they stopped and was coughed out they finally they was at the sea and they swam home.

Game Rules (by Rosalind) – Non-Narrative

- You have a card each with a colour on it, whatever colour you have, you go to the square with the name on it – e.g. Europe.
- Each player shakes the die in turn and moves the number of squares shown on the dice.
- When you land on a coloured square the same colour as your card, you are allowed to go 5 spaces forward.
- If you come to a square with yellow lines you just stay there and do nothing until your next go.

Standard addressed: 3.2.1

- When you land on the yellow squares you go across the equator.
- When you land on a square with instructions you have to obey them.
- When you come to STOP You must stop and follow the instructions.

CONTINUOUS THREADS

3.1 Planning, expectations and targets

Standard addressed 3.1.1

In general when pupils arrive at secondary school they have a huge body of knowledge about language that teachers can build upon. Brian Cox states (in Brindley, 1994:171) that 'this will differ according to the richness of the environment provided by the home and wider community, but all children live and grow up in a print-rich world full of writing and people who write'. It is important that you access the data available on your pupils' writing ability so that your expectations are realistic and appropriate targets can be set. Aim to create a writing environment that is rich and meaningful, involving collaborative work as well as individual writing. Sharing each other's writing, writing with your pupils, showing them how 'real' writers create texts should all form a central part of this environment.

3.2 Monitoring and assessment

Standards addressed: 3.2.2, 3.2.4

This should be both formative and summative and can include peer advice, discussions with the teacher, self-evaluations and grading against National Curriculum/GCSE criteria. Points to consider:

Peer advice – You may want to allow pupils to choose their own partner. You could suggest to pupils that they must say three things that they like about their partner's work and offer one or two comments of advice (e.g. I really liked your description of the seaside, but the ending was a bit unrealistic).

Discussions with the teacher – you will need to create a relationship where the pupils want to share their work with you and respect your advice. This might be achieved by sharing your own writing, focusing on the positive elements of pupils' work and explaining why you recommend particular alterations.

Self-evaluations – One effective strategy would be to provide prompt questions for pupils to check against, e.g.:

- Have you read over your work carefully?
- Have you checked for full stops?
- Have you made sure that you have addressed the particular audience?
- Have you checked to make sure that your work is organised into paragraphs?

These questions could be based on whole class, group or individual targets.

Grading – You will need to check on the department policy, as it might be only comments on pupils' work in Key Stage 3, or effort grades only. However, it is important that you gain experience in grading against National Curriculum levels and thus you should keep a record of these in your mark book. Share some examples with an English teacher or your mentor. Always give pupils access to the grading criteria as this helps them to understand why particular grades have been awarded and what is required for the next grade. Although pupils will often just focus on the grade given, your feedback comments are vital in helping each pupil to improve.

You will need to meet the needs of all your pupils and you may well have some pupils working at level 3 in your Year 7 group. There is a Literacy progress unit entitled 'Writing Organisation' that targets pupils with good ideas, but who have difficulty expressing them effectively, perhaps because of poor planning skills, lack of knowledge about paragraph construction and a limited awareness of cohesive ties.

In order to identify which pupils would benefit from this unit the following audit is recommended in the unit.

Look at a recent piece of extended writing by the pupils you think may be at level 3, or low level 4 in your Year 7 group and tick each number if your pupils' writing contains these characteristics:

1 Paragraph breaks are used.

2 The order makes sense.

3 Paragraphs start where there is a shift in topic, time or perspective.

4 Paragraphs are coherent, i.e. contain information which hangs together.

5 There is a 'topping' and 'tailing' e.g. key sentences, a concluding paragraph.

6 There are links between paragraphs, e.g. 'Next . . .' Another reason . . .' The next day . . . '

Note: tick 3–6 if the pupil has organised the material even if they have neglected the break itself.

Result

5–6 ticks; You could probably address the outstanding problems by teaching the particular point to these pupils and getting them to go back and use proofreading marks on their old work to catch the error. Follow up in marking.

0–3 Enter the progress unit

4 ticks Borderline case. Be guided by the feel of the work.

(DfEE, 2001)

This unit provides a series of objectives, many relating to paragraph construction supplemented by 20-minute teaching units that follow the teaching sequence of:

Remember
Model
Try
Apply
Secure.

3.3 Teaching and class management

*Standards
addressed
3.3.1, 3.3.6*

As you will be encouraging pupils to write for different purposes and different audiences it is useful to create opportunities for pupils to write for real purposes and real audiences, so you might have pupils writing to pupils in other classes or feeder schools. This may take the form of emails. You might also have pupils writing to different people within the same class, e.g. boys writing for a teenage girls' audience and the boys' writing being evaluated by the girls. There should be opportunities for collaborative writing and thus organising the class into pairs: perhaps to produce the opening of a story would facilitate discussion about what constitutes an effective opening. A particularly good way of introducing the structure of short story writing is to take the four areas outlined in Activity 3 (exposition, complication, climax, resolution) and give pairs of pupils five minutes to write an exposition and then pass it to another pair to write the complication before it is then passed on to another pair to write the climax, etc. This encourages reading, discussion and developing awareness of genres.

There will also be times when you want pupils to be 'critical readers' of each other's work. Consider how you would choose 'critical readers' or whether you would let the author choose. What guidelines would you provide? There will also be times when a quiet or silent thinking/writing time is needed. For this you will have to make it clear why the silence is needed for individual work and how long you expect it to last.

There is much current debate about boys' underachievement in literacy and various theories have been presented, including a lack of positive role models and the type of literacy deemed appropriate to assess as English. The Ofsted report, *Boys and English* in 1993 found 'little evidence of boys discussing the affective aspects of experience or of their writing with conviction about personal feeling' (in Millard, 1997: 28). It is thus a complex issue to try to raise boys' achievement. Perhaps we need to widen our own definitions of literacy to include emailing and other aspects of computer literacy, to provide opportunities for boys to write on topics and in ways that interest them. Their work must be valued and teachers should appreciate that boys' reading habits are often very different to those of girls and this impacts upon their writing. Millard (1997: 45) states that her research of Y7 reading showed:

> *'Boys' understanding is focused on action and the factual information provided by the texts they read and the narratives the watch. Girls on the other hand develop more sophisticated understanding of psychological expansion of character and employ more literary devices such as antithesis, suspense . . .'*

Whilst there are no clear answers to helping boys to perform as well as girls, our awareness of some of the theories is important. Ultimately we aim to raise everyone's standard in writing and we must also avoid stereotyping: you may well find for example that boys enjoy creative writing as much as girls and that stereotyping only reinforces prejudices. Some ideas for encouraging writing in the classroom are listed below:

- Provide a variety of stimuli, e.g. music, food, pictures, examples of good quality writing.
- Write with your pupils.
- Use collaborative approaches.
- Encourage pupils to talk about their writing.
- Provide opportunities for pupils to read each other's work.
- Display pupils' writing in the classroom.
- Encourage drafting.
- Emphasise the positive as well as offering support for future development.
- Provide a range of audiences.

2.5 ICT

We are rapidly moving into an age when ICT is affecting every aspect of the curriculum and English teachers must decide how they can make best use of its potential. This may include using ICT for editing, drafting and presenting texts. Such an approach can be a confidence builder for many writers (boys are generally keen to use ICT). You could have pupils writing on-line to each other. This would make it 'live' and interactive. Simulation activities can be excellent motivators (e.g. pupils allocated a variety of roles – as reporter, editor, presenter – and then requested to produce a five-minute news report in a given time slot). Pupils could be encouraged to compare the changing nature of literacy, by looking at letters in Victorian times and comparing them with the language of emails and text messages.

The need to provide real audiences and purposes for writing can be largely addressed through the use of websites where pupils' work can be published. For reading and contributing book reviews try Cool Reads on **www.cool-reads.co.uk**. For young poets try **www.poetryzone.ndirect.co.uk**. This has a poetry gallery for 4- to 18-year-olds. Writing activities are available on the BBC Listen and Write site at **www.bbc.co.uk/education/listenandwrite**.

3.3.4 Differentiation

You will need to consider how you can meet the individual needs of each writer so that each pupil reaches her/his potential. Thus you will need to challenge the most able, perhaps through providing a range of complex models of writing for pupils to analyse and adopt (e.g. use of flashbacks/multiple narrations in short story writing). You will also need to support and challenge the weaker writers, possibly through the use of writing frames (see Lewis and Wray, 2000: 91–9) to help scaffold the writing process. If you have a classroom assistant, you need to discuss her/his role in aiding the learning of individual pupils. It is important to have assessed the abilities of your class so that you can build upon prior learning. Pupils need to feel that they can succeed and so such factors as how do I motivate them to write? what stimulus and resources do I need to provide? (e.g. a tape of Martin Luther King's famous 'I have a dream' speech when encouraging pupils to write a persuasive speech) must be given appropriate consideration. Consider the rationale for setting word lengths to written activities, as a long assignment might not be appropriate for certain tasks and certain pupils.

The opportunity for pupils to draft work with your intervention is at the heart of differentiation in writing. Pupils should be made to appreciate that even 'great' writers often had many attempts before going to print. A useful exercise is to share with pupils examples of recognised writers' rough work and to discuss why the writers might have made the changes that they did (see W. Owen's 'Anthem for Doomed Youth' and 'Anthem for Dead Youth'). Remember that differentiation can be by task and by outcome if the appropriate strategies are employed to enable all pupils to achieve their potential.

Scenarios

1 Imagine that your Y7 class has only limited experience of writing for different audiences. How would you encourage writing for a greater range of audiences?
You might want to consider these four areas:
- Audiences within the class
- Audiences within your school
- Audiences in other schools
- Audiences in the community.

For the first item it could be wall displays, report on a school trip, class anthology of poems, playscripts to be acted out, etc.

2 Imagine that you have taken over a class that has little experience of collaborative writing and you recognise the value of collaborative writing. How do you facilitate this approach? Think about the use of paired work, consequence exercises (pupil A begins the story with a setting, passes it to pupil B who has to introduce a character, etc.).

Commentary on Lee's writing
- Lee is influenced by his reading of Hans Christian Andersen's tale, 'The Constant Tin Soldier'. For example the soldier makes a boat out of paper, meets a rat and is swallowed by a fish.
- Stories contain one or more problem–solution sequences. Lee is influenced by narratives that contain many problem–solution sequences, such as action adventures or cartoons.
- His story changes direction in the second line, which indicates that he is thinking and writing simultaneously.
- Lee needs to be more aware of audience as he is not consistent in his choice of pronouns.

Ways to improve Lee's writing might include: model a story with one problem–solution structure and give more guidance in the composition stage.

Commentary on Rosalind's writing
- Rosalind has some awareness of the language of instructional writing, e.g. the use of direct address ('You').
- She has constructed a multi-modal text as an appropriate form for her audience.
- Evidence of appropriate lexical choices e.g. 'land on', 'shakes'.

Ways to improve Rosalind's writing might include: greater awareness of purpose as there is no clear end to the game; this could be achieved by reading a variety of board game instructions.

This text could be piloted with peers.

FURTHER READING

Western Australia Education Department (1998) *First Steps:Writing*. Melbourne, Australia: Rigby Heinemann

Lewis, M. and Wray, D. (1995) *Writing Frames*. Exeter: Exeter Extending Literacy Project

REFERENCES

Brindley, S. (1994) *Teaching English in the Secondary School*. London: Routledge

Carter, R. (1997) *Working with Texts*. London: Routledge

Davies, C. (1996) *What is English Teaching?*, Buckingham: Open University Press

DfEE (1999) *The National Curriculum of England. English: Key Stages 1–4*. London: DfEE and QCA

DfEE (2001) *Framework for Teaching English: Years 7, 8 and 9*. London: DfEE

DfEE (2001) *Literacy Progress Unit Writing Organisation 0473/2001*. London: DfEE

Fleming, M. and Stevens, D. (1998) *English Teaching in the Secondary School*. London: David Fulton

Lewis, M. and Wray, D. (1995) *Writing Frames*. Exeter: Exeter Extending Literacy Project

Lewis, M. and Wray, D. (2000) *Literacy in the Secondary School*. London, David Fulton

Millard, E. (1997) *Differently Literate*. London: Falmer Press

Myhill, D. (1999) 'Writing matters: Linguistic characteristics of writing in GCSE English examinations', *English in Education*, 33(3): 71–81 Sheffield, NATE

Protherough, R. and King, P. (1995) *The Challenge of English in the National Curriculum*. London: Routledge

QCA (1999) *Technical Accuracy in Writing in GCSE English Examinations: Research Findings*. London: QCA

WEBSITES

www.eastoftheweb.com/short-stories

This site provides numerous short stories from a range of genres. Many are by classic authors. The site also publishes short stories.

www.kelly.mcmail.com

This site provides scriptwriters' templates free to be downloaded.

www.stonesoup.com

This site publishes writing and art by children.

chapter 16

TEACHING POETRY

By the end of this chapter you will have considered the links between your own knowledge of poetry and your role as a teacher; made connections between pupils' general language use and poetry; located poetry within the oral tradition and considered teaching strategies for ensuring that the analysis of poetic form can continue to be an interactive process for pupils.

Most of the pupils that you will teach will already have formed attitudes about poetry by the time they get to secondary school. Your job as an English teacher is to acknowledge those attitudes, work with them and, at the same time, broaden and deepen their experiences of poetry. You will then be in a good position to widen and deepen pupils' appreciation of poetry and its role in their language development.

RATIONALE

As a teacher of English you will need to consider the place of poetry in pupils' development as readers and writers. One good place to start is to make some links between your own experiences of poetry as a reader, writer and literature student and your role as a teacher of English. If you read verse and enjoy it, know about poems and wish to convey some idea of why they matter to you, then you have a much better chance of success as an English teacher than if you think of yourself as a reader, but a reader who omits poetry. In any event, and whatever your reading inclinations, you may do well to identify the forms of support that you can access in your training year.

Consider these points:

- Children develop a sense of themselves as readers of poetry if they are
  hearing, reading, speaking and dramatising poems on a regular basis.
  There are many ways of making bridges between children's general language
  use and poetry:
  (a) The rhythms of poetry have their roots in the patterns of ordinary speech.
  (b) Children have a strong oral tradition upon which to draw – playground
      chants, jingles, nursery rhymes, etc.
  (c) Everyday language is full of metaphor, e.g. 'He stormed his way to the
      finish.' 'She cut him to the quick.'
- There is no one way of teaching poetry: appropriate, purposeful activities
  should be like keys that unlock poems.
- We do not read poems as we read continuous prose. We usually see a poem
  as a whole like a painting, photograph or sculpture.
- We also attend to the language of poetry differently to other speech – it is
  more like listening to music.
- As teachers, we need visual and aural emphases in our approaches.
- The emphasis should be on poems that work on readers as well as readers
  who work on poems.
- Children's appreciation of poetry will be enhanced if they are also writers of
  poetry.
- Poems are constructed objects and it is our role as teachers to show pupils
  how they work.

As a successful teacher of poetry you will need to become familiar with a wide range
of fruitful approaches to teaching/using poetry in schools. To gain this knowledge
you will need to evaluate several strategies that you might later use in your teaching.

LINKS WITH NATIONAL CURRICULUM AND THE KS3 NATIONAL STRATEGY

The National Curriculum in English is quite insistent that pupils in secondary
schools learn some poetry, and poetry drawn in part from the heritage. According
to statute, eight poets should have some of their verse studied. The teacher must
select four of these eight from a set list of some 28 major figures whose work was
published before 1914, and the other four from within or without an example list
of those whose work was published after 1914. Selecting from the lists is an
interesting activity: one would need to consider a number of somewhat different
factors in determining which poets and which poems were to be read with a class.
Think, for example, of the links between the statement above that children can draw
upon a strong oral tradition, and the work of William Blake.

For decades eighth- or ninth-year classes have read *The Rime of the Ancient Mariner*,
and done work on it afterwards concerning the narrative and the moral, but what
else is there from the poems of Coleridge that might attract a class? Almost all the
poets in the list of 28 have had, over the years of the existence of comprehensive
schools, their powerful advocates among the influential teachers of poetry. The

championing of the work of John Clare by Geoffrey Summerfield comes to mind as simply one example, and there are plentiful others.

Often the younger classes, learning to write poems, compose a verse or two in the shape of an object in the world which is the subject of the poem, like an apple with a worm in it, or the spring of a clock. Teachers could well, if the class had shown some creative skill in that art, introduce them to George Herbert's 'Easter Wings', where verbal meaning and visual form correspond to one another in a way that thoroughly vindicates the idea above that we usually see a poem as a whole like a painting or sculpture. The newly qualified English teacher can see the pre-1914 NC list as a challenge to their own creativity rather than as a daunting demand.

One of us recently heard an engaging and highly intelligent account from a PGCE English student – Kat Simpson – of how she introduced Blake's 'London' to a Y7 class in an inner-city comprehensive in an economically deprived area. The class had been reading 'Skellig', about an angel figure. That provided the stepping-stone, as it were, to illustrations of angels by William Blake (a London poet and engraver), which led to showing illustrations of London by William Hogarth ('Gin Lane' and 'Beer Street') and from attention to and talk about the details of the Hogarth depictions (which, of course, include a plagued harlot) to Blake's poem, 'London'. Yet more was woven in – a modern computer game called 'Vice City' – before the pupils produced their own imitations of 'London'.

As for the moderns, the same generality about seeing the list as an opportunity applies. Most of the poets listed have their work already well represented at some point or other in the English curriculum: for example Ted Hughes. Some others are well represented although their names do not appear in the 'Examples of major poets after 1914' list, such as D.H. Lawrence, Simon Armitage, Carol Ann Duffy or Grace Nichols, but there is nothing to prevent their inclusion and everything to warrant it.

Once the poets and poems have been selected, then the next major matter concerning meeting the requirements of the NC is ensuring that the poems are read in ways consistent with the ideas of reading for meaning, for understanding the author's craft and explaining the poems for what they are – significant items in the culture which pupils are entitled to know about.

Note that some, for example Nicola Grove (1998), will see in poems an importance that transcends anyone's ability to read them or write about them. Poems should be known by being heard, repeated aloud or 'seen', but not necessarily read, if by that is meant pupils comprehending the print on the page. This is an argument to the effect that the NC is to be used as a way of insisting, on behalf of those whose reading and writing are unlikely ever to develop very much, on their rights of access to poems. Poems are forms of language which take them (and all of us) to the heart of states of knowing and feeling that are unavailable in any other form. Homer's audience, most of it, could not read even as he (or she or the collective) sang the *Iliad* and the *Odyssey*. Those poems remain the subject of continued fascination and enquiry. The story of Telemachus' father, Odysseus, coming home and chasing off, assisted only by his son and a faithful old servant, the foul pack of men trying to make it into his wife's bed remains something which all adolescents might like to hear about, regardless of their literacy abilities.

Whether the best ways of reading poems (and writing them) are instanced in the KS3 Strategy's *Framework for Teaching English: Years 7, 8 and 9* might be in question, but certainly that document is concerned to ensure that literary texts receive their fair share of reading time and emphasis. Take, for example, what is said under 'Reading' for Year 8. That would encourage the English teacher to take, say, objective 14: 'pupils should be taught to recognise the conventions of some common literary forms, e.g. sonnet, and genres, e.g. Gothic horror, and explore how a particular text adheres to or deviates from established conventions'. Imagine what an invitation this could be to take some narrative poems, and look at how they are alike and unalike. You could start with revisiting a poem read in Year 7, NC poet Robert Browning's 'The Pied Piper of Hamelin':

> Rats!
>
> They fought the dogs, and killed the cats,
> And bit the babies in the cradles,
> And eat the cheeses out of the vats,
> And licked the soup from the cooks' own ladles,
> Split open the kegs of salted sprats,
> Made nests inside men's Sunday hats,
> And even spoiled the women's chats
> By drowning their speaking
> With shrieking and squeaking
> In fifty different sharps and flats.

It is not hard to explore, from verses such as this, how the poet tells the story. The rhyme scheme is part of the technique of narration, insofar as it helps to push the story along, with a certain degree of anticipation included. The rhythm of a poem so obviously for children is also something which a class could be brought to understand. (Telling the Year 8s that they've quite outgrown the childish pleasures of sitting back and enjoying the tale of this poem, as they did in Year 7, might just help to get them looking at the poem as critics. A simple iambic four-beat paradigm example of ti-tum, ti-tum, ti-tum, ti-tum, for some lines is under continuous interruption, as it were, from two-beaters with six syllables, such as the penultimate two lines.)

Compare Robert Browning's way of using the convention of rhymed and regularly stressed lines with Coleridge's, in the *Ancient Mariner* or, to choose another Robert from the pre-1914 list, Burns. Take, as a contrasting example to the above:

> The wind blew as 'twad blaw its last;
> The rattling show'rs rose on the blast;
> The speedy gleams the darkness swallow'd;
> Loud, deep, and lang the thunder bellow'd:
> That night, a child might understand,
> The Deil had business on his hand.

This, from 'Tam O'Shanter', keeps to much the same eight-syllable per line pattern as the Browning poem relies upon, but within each line the rhythms are quite different. See Fenton (2002: 53–5) on the tetrameter's forward push. With Burns's couplets you get much less rhythmic slack. Whether the Browning poem or the Burns is better at conforming to the convention of telling a story could be the subject of discussion by the class. It depends who the story is for and whether Burns's language is seen as breaking rules.

There are, of course, quite other and valid ways (than attending to line stresses) of 'recognising the conventions of literary forms' if the form in question is the narrative poem. Think about how strange and unrealistic are the events in the three narrative poems mentioned, and how they may be compared in terms of presenting their extraordinary plots.

Below in Activity 2 we mention John Taylor and the idea of the 'auditory imagination'. What the pupils need, in reading Browning, Coleridge or Burns, is to hear the verse aloud in their heads every bit as much as understanding the gist of the story from looking rapidly at the print on the page. Building in pupils the ability to hear pre-1914 verse is not something that will be achieved quickly, but there is no reason why it should not be a long term aim. There is nothing gentle or polite in much of this; imagine 15-year-olds, rehearsing these lines aloud, from Donne's (another NC poet) 'The Canonization', facing one another in tactfully selected pairs:

> For Godsake hold your tongue, and let me love,
> Or chide my palsie, or my gout,
> My five gray haires, or ruin'd fortune flout,
> . . . So you will let me love.

Activity 1

MAKING CONNECTION

(suggested time: 1 hour)

Consider all the reasons for teaching poetry to secondary pupils from the philosophical to the practical. What are the challenges that exist?

What do children know about the conventions of poetry and where have they learned these from? How can a teacher resurrect that knowledge? Try and list all the playground rhymes and chants that you remember from your childhood. What do these reveal about a child's prior knowledge and what sort of classroom activities might build upon that knowledge? A useful reference for this work is *The Lore and Language of School Children* by Iona and Peter Opie.

Standard addressed: 2.1

Activity 2

POETRY TO BE HEARD

(suggested time: 1 hour)

In Chapter 24 of *Teaching Poetry in the Secondary School* (Brindley, 1994: 210–19) John Taylor talks about developing an 'auditory imagination'. Consider the associative power of language; make some descriptive lists that arise from considering colours or animals. How might you orchestrate a reading of a poem such as Auden's ballad 'Oh What Is That Sound?' or Edwin Morgan's 'Canedolia – an off-concrete Scotch Fantasia'? Think of as many different ways as you can to provide opportunities for pupils to perform poetry (their own and others') in a supportive environment.

Standards addressed:
2.1, 3.1.1

Activity 3

PATTERN AND FORM

(suggested time: 1 hour)

The pattern and form of poetry play a useful role in familiarising pupils with poetry before they undertake a close scrutiny of the poem. Sometimes the attention to form and pattern is sufficiently rigorous in itself to provide the intellectual challenge and stimulus you require for your pupils. Consider Edwin Morgan's 'Opening the Cage'. How would you use this with pupils?

Read carefully the work of Sandy Brownjohn (1989) as she describes haiku, tanka and cinquain. These forms illustrate the requirement to use the style of concentrated language that many people associate with poetry. Brownjohn ensures that they are also exciting for pupils to explore. Consider how to teach poetry so that the pleasurable aspects precede the more analytical activities. How might you organise your lessons to provide the necessary stimulation and challenge?

Standards addressed:
2.1, 3.1.1

Activity 4

CONNECTING WITH POEMS

(suggested time: 90 minutes)

Consider different ways of stimulating a pupil's imagination when teaching poetry. As well as the aural aspects of a poem (its sound as heard) you should consider the oral aspects (the pleasures of giving a poem voice) and the visual, and look for ways for pupils to make such connections with poems presented to or chosen by them. Read the two worksheets 'Things to do with a Poem' and 'Sixish Ways of Working on Poetry' on pp. 332–3. Now read some collections of poetry that have been put together for secondary pupils. (Two that are recommended are both by Michael and Peter Benton: *Examining Poetry* and *Painting with Words* but you may come across many others.)

Take an individual poem of your choice that is suitable for KS3 pupils.

- List reasons for your choice.
- Consider preparatory work or whether the poem will be introduced immediately.
- Decide choice of approach and the time required.
- Identify possible difficulties and then the strategies that will take pupils beyond these difficulties.
- Plan pupil activities.
- Prepare the first three minutes of a lesson.
- Outline how the lesson will continue.

Activity 5

BUILDING UPON EARLIER EXPERIENCES
(suggested time: 90 minutes)

Get hold of a GCSE English and English Literature specification from your school or from the exam board itself. Consider the content areas and the skills that pupils are expected to develop within the requirements for poetry in GCSE English and English Literature. You will need to match the teaching approaches to the specification demands and this will vary depending on whether the poetry being studied is for course work or the examination. The GCSE assessment objectives will also influence your choices. Read at least one GCSE specification.

You will need to emphasise the continuity between work that stresses enjoyment/ activity/experience/understanding that you will pursue at KS3 and producing confident readers of poetry at KS4. Active learning approaches are still vital in helping pupils to acquire a vocabulary for talking about poetic forms and technical features in poetry. A didactic style of teaching will reverse a lot of the investment you are making in pupils' attitudes to poetry at KS3 if you change your approach too radically. Pupils need to be gradually moved to a more analytic approach of examining poetry where stimulus and pleasure are still features of their learning.

Standards addressed:
2.1d, 2.3,
3.1.2, 3.1.3

Choose two poems from the AQA 2004 Anthology (GCSE specification) or any preferred pair of poems. Consider ways of linking these poems. List a range of approaches that might engage pupils' interests in the early stages. Now select one of these approaches. Plan the opening sequences of a lesson. Outline the rationale for the strategy you have taken. Why did you reject the others?

Activity 6

POETS AS WELL AS POEMS
(suggested time: 75 minutes)

You need to help pupils become explicitly aware of the poet's/poets' use of language, structure and form. Make a list of activities that might develop this awareness. Now choose poems from a GCSE specification and try to match them with the activities. What challenges still exist? All GCSE specifications require the study of *poets* as well as poems. Think about what this does and does not mean for classroom-based work. Look at some examples of questions asking exam candidates to write on two poems by the same poet. Try to frame a question accessible to a wide ability range which asks pupils to write about a pair of poems by the same poet. Consider the different demands of a coursework essay and one preparing pupils for writing in an examination.

Standards addressed:
2.1d, 2.3,
3.1.2, 3.1.3

CONTINUOUS THREADS

1 Professional values and practice

Perhaps the most appropriate note to make under this heading is the importance of an individual teacher's commitment, in becoming an English teacher, to teach poetry. To some this is natural, obvious and indeed second nature, but other student teachers and beginners are left feeling like ambassadors for an aspect of the culture that pupils appear to regard with something worse than reluctance. Professional development may well come to mean, in regard to teaching poetry, getting to know more about verse in English and getting to understand how successful teachers in this area succeed.

3.2 Planning, expectations and targets

Much could be written under this heading, but much of what would appear is contained or implied in the Activities. Plans, as stated below, will give prominence to active and performative approaches to poems from the moment the pupils arrive at school. It is good to hear about the standing ovations given to poets as they perform in front of crowds of Year 11s in town halls and lecture halls in the run-up to GCSE examinations in English. Better to build on this kind of expectation than to plan for defensive strategies that aim not so much to teach poetry as to minimise conflict over it.

3.3 Monitoring and assessment

Assessing how well a pupil has written a poem is an interesting and sophisticated task, and it can be quite difficult. There are no easy rules to formulate; sometimes it is even a challenge to comment meaningfully to the pupil about their poems. However, a reading of pages 250–1 and page 257 of Davison and Dowson (1998), and seeing how to use the headings of sense, sight, sound and structure introduces a framework for assessing and responding to pupils as writers of poetry.

There are strong arguments for placing pupils' poetic efforts in assessment-free zones, especially when remembering that composing poems is one of those areas of writing that pupils may well do, at a certain age, quite alone and off the premises, prompted, as it were, only by themselves. Such verse as is produced as part of the normal English curriculum (Haiku, Tanka, Cinquains etc.) might just as well have its virtues noted, in achievement recording terms, for use in reports, as be marked out of 10 in most cases. Some young writers of verse might welcome editorial guidance by a teacher – good advice about what to leave out, and where to insert and refine. This kind of writer–editor relationship may have to be constructed with care in the first place, but there are plenty examples of it working perfectly well.

Remember also that a well-mounted, frequently changed, easily legible display of poems by pupils is a good device for celebrating what they do, a positive result of monitoring and assessment. Known to the writers are English classrooms where one wall (and much of the ceiling) is covered in the professionally printed work of published poets (e.g. 'Poems on the Underground') and another wall is covered in the poems of school students, but in equally high quality typography, so as to avoid the elemental division between professionals and amateurs in the minds of the readers.

3.4 Teaching and class management

Good poetry lessons may be characterised in a dozen different ways, but what they are all likely to have in common is interest and enthusiasm about the matter in hand on all sides, much reading aloud by all at different moments, but also concern to select, edit, group, anthologise, pair, promote and display poems. The idea of having a class write a poem based on the index of first lines from an anthology may have, as a lesson, the appearance of a mass copying session, but in fact, if it works well, the pupils will be thoughtful and creative, as well as absorbing several lines they may not have known before.

There will be time for traditional straightforward exposition and explanation work by teacher to class about a particular poem, but the pupils, in a five-year span of learning about poems in secondary school, should not come to see the expository session as the essential paradigm form. There is every reason for giving over the last lesson of the week, on Friday afternoon, to the making of posters of poems. These should be large, bold visual statements that have been known to do much to help interpret a poem. The good class manager foresees the problems, and has the right poem for the particular individual to work upon.

Poetry needs to be read and discussed by pupils. Developing purposeful talk in the classroom is one of the most important roles of a successful English teacher. Poetry lends itself to collaborative pair and small group work. If you are considering teaching a thematic approach to poetry then do consider jigsaw grouping. This provides a robust structure and the potential for much interaction with other pupils in a purposeful manner.

Under the equal opportunities heading, the role of a teacher of poetry is to raise all pupils' achievements. Using a wide range of different poems that appeal to pupils' interests and abilities is essential in achieving this aim. Some boys, and quite possibly Charles Clarke, Secretary of State for Education for England and Wales at the time of going to press, may regard poetry as a 'soft' subject with little utilitarian value. There is an old argument that teachers need to rise to the challenge of 'softness' by finding robust, hard-hitting poetry that engages boys' emotions and intellects and raises issues about its role in education and the wider community. There already exist volumes of verse in school, with such titles as *Axed between the Ears*, which are aimed at persuading reluctant readers of poetry to give it a fair hearing. In short, the 'tough' tradition has obvious merit, but a sole diet of such verse would be misplaced if it blanked out, effectively, the lyrical voice, something not unknown in the songs that even mainly male bands perform, and in public too.

3.3.4 Differentiation

DARTs are a good way of providing additional support for less able pupils. Read pages 255–6 in the Davison and Dowson book for examples of how to scaffold pupils' learning experiences with poetry. Chapter 6 on 'Inclusion' in the present volume has a certain amount to say regarding how best to interest and reward, in terms of poetry teaching, those who often do least well in English, and this is consistent with the notion of scaffolding.

Differentiated activities might well require more able pupils to work at a higher intellectual level. They may finish class work more quickly than their peers but they do not simply need additional tasks to occupy their time. It may be that at KS3 you require these pupils to work in a more analytic manner but their need to enjoy poetry remains the same as their counterparts'. Sometimes asking them to write in the style of a poem they have studied is the challenge and stimulus they seek. Make sure before they are asked to do this that they have identified the essential features of the poem(s).

At KS4 and at sixth form level you may wish to lift the levels of the most able pupils' thinking still further. Considering the generic aspects of a selection of poems (perhaps by the same poet or on the same theme) may be the intellectual challenge that these learners need. It may be that they can move on to a consideration of the cultural conditions that influenced the poet(s).

2.5 ICT

ICT is good for transforming texts. Editing prose and transforming it into poetry will help make explicit the distilled essence of language used in poetic texts. Use computers to do some text mapping. Download, scan in or type out suitable poems. Instruct the pupils on the various functions that will enable them to, for example, italicise imagery or highlight poetic form. For an orchestrated reading they could also map the text to show crescendo (<<<) and diminuendo (>>>) etc. It is in this way that they can develop a personal response to poetry and make a poem their own.

Twenty years ago an innovative teacher, Brent Robinson, noticed that if you arranged for a computer to load a poem on to a screen, two lines at a time over a minute or more, then whoever was looking at the screen began, quite without instruction, to read the poem aloud. If you want to know how Chaucer sounds, read aloud in the original Middle English accent, then you can sit at a computer and listen, whilst being able at the same time to read the text scrolling in time with the voice, says Richard Lanham (1993). Both of these small devices promise much, in terms of voice–script relationship, that remains largely unexplored. New English teachers, with a keen interest in computers and what they can do, as well as in poetry, may find that there are exciting discoveries to be made. Who would read Yeats's 'Lapis Lazuli' in print when they could read it on screen alongside a brilliantly reproduced image of the stone to which the poem refers, all its carved details clear? *Beowulf* may be introduced via the interactive whiteboard, with images of the original text, and pictures of contextual objects, such as the famous Sutton Hoo burial treasure, all downloaded. And so the list may go on.

Scenarios

1 Imagine you have 'inherited' a Year 8 class who claim that they have never studied any poetry but also that they do not want to as it is unstimulating. How would you hope to change their views?
2 You have a Year 10 class who are a reasonably able group. However, when it comes to studying for their exam they want you to deliver their lessons in a lecture style format. How would you explain the rationale for your approach? What activities would you devise to demonstrate the rigour, intellectual challenge and stimulating style of your approach to poetry teaching?

FURTHER READING

Andrews, R. (1991) *The Problem with Poetry.* Buckingham: The Open University Press
Brownjohn, S. (1989) *The ability to name cats: teaching children to write poetry.* London: Hodder & Stoughton
Dymoke, S. (2003) *Drafting and Assessing Poetry: a Guide for Teachers.* London: Paul Chapman Publishing
Fenton, J. (2002) *An Introduction to English Poetry.* London: Penguin/Viking
Stibbs, A. (1991) 'Walking like an elephant: what's gained in (impossible) translation', in James L. Collins, *Vital Signs 2: Teaching and Learning Language Collaboratively.* Portsmouth, NH: Boynton Cook. pp. 109–22
Stibbs, A. (1995) 'The specialness of poetry', *English in Education,* 29 (3): 14–19
Stibbs, A (2000) 'Can you (almost) read a poem backwards and view a painting upside down? Restoring aesthetics to poetry teaching', *Journal of Aesthetic Education,* 34 (2): 37–48

POETRY HANDOUTS

Sixish ways of working on poetry

Here is a summary of the rationale for choosing a particular approach to a poem. All of these approaches focus on reading the poem carefully as a starting point before analysis or discussion.

(a) Modelling   This activity focuses on the structure and style of a poem. Pupils are asked to understand either the pattern of metaphor as in 'A Martian Sends a Postcard Home' by Craig Raine; or a pattern of structuring observation as in 'Thirteen Ways of Looking at a Blackbird', by Wallace Stevens. It may also look at the use of repetition as in 'A Boy's Head', by Miroslav Holub or lists as in, 'I sit out and look upon the sorrows of the world' by Walt Whitman and 'These I have loved' by Rupert Brook.

(b) Sequencing This technique is best for poems that are structured chronologically, as in a narrative poem such as: 'Green Beret' by Ho Thien; or time line as in 'Yesterday, Today Tomorrow' by Maureen Miles.

(c) Visualisation A visualisation can be used to identify either the key moments of a narrative poem as in Tennyson's 'The Lady of Shalott', using a storyboard; or its imagery – Macbeth's speeches make very good subjects for visualisations with their imagery of blood and desolation.

(d) Creative and re-creative writing This has the same focus as Modelling but the patterns are used to create pupils' own versions.

Shape poems encourage play with words and sounds as well as shapes – Try e e cummings, Edward Morgan (and for advanced classes George Herbert).

Group Poems help classes who have no confidence in poems to write together. Model on 'Love is . . .' or 'Men are . . .' Acrostics also provide an easy pattern for weaker pupils to follow. Be careful though, they are much over-used in primary school at KS2.

(e) Cloze Design your own cloze to focus on imaginative descriptive detail, as in 'Warning' by Jenny Joseph or a particular use of verbs, adjectives or adverbs. Also use cloze to examine an underlying extended metaphor as in 'The Mirror' by Sylvia Plath and 'The Sea' by James Reeve.

(f) Performance The emphasis here is on reading out loud with expression – good for dialect poems, rap poems, and poems from other cultures, and also a good starting point for drama. You can ask pupils to use highlighters to colour in words that seem particularly effective, pull them out from the poem and test their effect or write comments round the poem centred on these words; or ask them to prepare a set of questions to which they might want a response and try to supply the answers.

Things to do with a poem

First reactions

1 Jot down first reactions for five minutes. (This works even better if, as in Chapter 19 below, you have the poem typed out or photocopied so that there is plenty of space on the page for reactions, comments and questions.)
2 Listen to taped reading.
3 Read same poem every day without discussion.
4 Display poems on wall (change them, too).

Sharing and presenting

5 Groups prepare own readings.
6 Groups present poems in dramatic form.
7 Groups make poetry tape; exchange with other classes, schools.
8 Class prepare choral readings, using sound effects or music.
9 Groups prepare movement work to accompany poem.
10 Groups choose photographs or slides to accompany poem.
11 Groups make a poetry videotape.
12 Groups make a frieze to illustrate a ballad or narrative poem.

Becoming familiar

13 Compile a personal anthology.
14 Make poetry posters.
15 Learn poetry by heart!
16 Discuss different versions (manuscript drafts, translations).

Exploring

17 Ask groups to underline sections (bits they like; difficult bits).
18 Small group discussion; report back.
19 Type poem with plenty of space for comment; pass on after adding own comment/question/response to those of others.
20 Delete key words/phrases/rhymes/images; speculate on what these might have been, before seeing the intact version.
21 Give poem untitled; choose/discuss titles.
22 Ask groups to decide where they would split a poem into sections; discuss reasons for choice.
23 Present poem in segments; chunks/stanzas/lines/pairs of lines/ (even single words?); reconstruct poems, discuss choices, compare with original.
24 Attempt parody or imitation.
25 Make picture/collage/poster with (or even without) text.
26 Invent sequel/ 'prequel' ('Tadpoles Revisited', 'Paradise Mislaid', 'Resurrection of a Naturalist', 'A Shropshire Pensioner'?).
27 'Chinese whispers' on a poem.
28 Rework poem in a different genre (e.g. nursery rhyme as a sonnet; epic as a limerick).

Collections (best to support these with a poetry book box)

29 Class anthology of favourite poems.
30 'Found poems' (newspapers/graveyards/uncertain translations).
31 Anthology of TV advertisement jingles!
32 Build up a collection of recorded poems.
33 'Desert Island poems' – tape with readings/comments.
34 'Top of the Pomes' – your top 10 poems, ranked in order, maybe made into a poster.

A few even more eccentric things to do . . .

35 Write a class epic!
36 Make concrete poems – hand poems/shape poems/sound poems (e.g. washing machine, football match).
37 Get your class's poems into the local newspaper, on to radio.
38 Organise a school poetry competition (warning: this can easily generate 1,000 poems!).
39 Use computer programs which produce 'poetry'.
40 Invite a poet into school (this is easier than you might think).

REFERENCES

Benton, M and P. (1986) *Examining Poetry: A Practical Guide for 15–18 Year Olds*. Sevenoaks: Hodder and Stoughton

Benton, M. and P. (1994) *Painting With Words*. Sevenoaks: Hodder and Stoughton

Brindley, S. (ed.) (1994) *Teaching English in the Secondary School.* London: Routledge in association with the Open University

Brownjohn, S. (1989) *The Ability to Name Cats: Teaching Children to Write Poetry.* London: Hodder and Stoughton

Davison, J. and Dowson, J. (1998) *Learning to Teach English in the Secondary School: a Companion to School Experience.* London: Routledge

Fenton, J. (2002) *An Introduction to English Poetry.* London: Penguin/Viking

Fleming, M. and Stevens, D. (1998) *English Teaching in the Secondary School.* London: David Fulton

Grove, N. (1998) *Literature for All.* London: David Fulton

Lanham, R A. (1993) *The Electronic Word: Democracy, Technology and the Arts.* Chicago, IL: University of Chicago Press

Opie, I and B. (1976) *The Love and Language of Schoolchildren.* Oxford: Oxford: University Press

WEBSITES

Not all of these websites are specifically on poetry but they are listed here because they include good poetry sections that are easily accessible.

http://geocities.com/Athens/Acropolis/2012/poems/index.html

Contains some 5,753 works by 659 poets, mostly pre-1923

http://www.bbc.co.uk/schools

For GCSE and SATs revision materials

http://ourworld.compuserve.com/homepages/Harry_Dodds/

Provides a good link to the Virtual Teachers' Centre

http://www.teachit.co.uk/

http://englishonline.co.uk/

http://www.inform.umd.edu/edres/readingroom/

Excellent for obtaining electronic versions of all sorts of texts –including poetry

http://www.aqa.org.uk

Website address for AQA 2004 GCSE English Literature specifications.

chapter 17

MEDIA EDUCATION

By the end of this chapter you will have been introduced to the theory underpinning education in media studies; will have considered the position of media in the NC; evaluated that theory with reference to media languages, media audiences, media agencies and media representation by engaging with some media resources, and will have been offered a range of teaching and learning strategies for the media classroom.

This chapter makes no assumption about prior knowledge of media education. The textbooks listed under 'References' and 'Further Reading' will offer support and subject input beyond the remit of this chapter. Those who have studied media more formally will be able to draw upon their expertise at several significant stages in the plans. Those who are teaching media as part of English without any formal qualification in media will see quickly that they can apply to different kinds of text the analytic expertise they learned to construct around, presumably, verbal texts.

RATIONALE

Media education is taught within the English curriculum in most schools. In some schools these studies are timetabled as a separate subject although this is not usually the case before KS4. Pupils can sometimes take a separate qualification in Media Studies at GCSE and at A level.

The relationship between media education and English is often now seen as obvious. Many of those doing PGCE English have a degree in which media studies have figured very largely; English graduates from more purely language- and literature-based courses are already well equipped to explain about images, narratives, connotations and denotations, and they can explore the linguistics of different texts from an expert position. The media that pupils study will take the form of 'media texts'. This use of the word 'text' to describe a film, a song, a photograph or a fashion magazine is obviously drawing upon a broad definition of the term, but it is one that has the virtue of neutrality. It is helpful to consider that when pupils encounter media texts they will deploy various 'reading' strategies in their attempts to understand them.

Pupils are certainly very familiar with media texts and may well be more familiar than you are. However, much of their knowledge is implicit: they have seldom been required to articulate what they know about TV programmes, billboard posters or pop videos. The role of an English teacher who is teaching media is to make more explicit the knowledge that pupils have about the media and to provide opportunities for them to refine, develop and even at times discard this prior knowledge. In order to do this it is sometimes necessary to defamiliarise media texts. This means using a familiar text in a different way from the way a pupil normally would encounter it. Various strategies exist for achieving this: you can use the remote control and pause a TV text frequently; you can use only the opening sequences of a film; you can crop a photograph; you can turn the sound off when using a clip of the news; you can remove the written text from a magazine advert, etc.

The arguments above on behalf of bringing media knowledge to fuller consciousness, by explicating what is already mutely understood, are similar to those used by teachers of English language as a mother tongue study. Pupils need to be able to state what kind of thing language is, and how it works. Media are comparable to a language in that they are constructed through common understanding of the meanings available in certain forms, and like languages media develop extensive varieties of form and differences of purpose.

LINKS WITH NATIONAL CURRICULUM – WHAT THE NC SAYS ABOUT MEDIA

English teachers must introduce pupils to the analysis and composition of the media within the National Curriculum for English. 'Media' may be held to include newspapers, television and film, and gaining a developing understanding about them will happen for pupils through activities which:

(a) demonstrate some of the ways in which meaning is presented by the media and consider how form, layout and presentation contribute to impact and persuasion;

(b) teach about the institutions that produce media and require pupils to evaluate the messages and values communicated by the media;

(c) require pupils to consider the ways in which audiences and readers choose and respond to media.

It is interesting to see how the NC in English, with its essential three-part division into speech, reading and writing, places work on media. Media study comes under, almost entirely, En2, Reading. The (a)–(c) list above is based far more on interpreting and reading than on constructing different kinds of texts. The actual media content – the products as it were – suitable for the NC in English are mentioned under. 'Non-fiction and non-literary texts', where we are told that 'The range should include:

b) *print and ICT-based information and reference texts*

c) *media and moving image texts (for example, newspapers, magazines, advertisements, television, films, videos).'*

Also, under the heading, 'Promoting other aspects of the curriculum' (p. 9) we see:

English can play a part in promoting citizenship and thinking skills through, for example:

● *learning about the social, historical, political and cultural contexts which shape and influence the texts pupils read and view . . . evaluating critically what they hear, read, view, with attention to explicit and implied meanings, bias and objectivity, and fact and opinion.*

In effect these National Curriculum statements amount to a way of theorising media within English; media products and texts exist in certain forms and the English teacher should make their forms clear. Media texts are influential, and as such need to be subject to a critical view. They have the same discursive power as literary ones. The current NC's entire formulation acknowledges that there is not an infinity of time in English to deal with media topics and approaches, and far from dismissing media products as valueless compared to literary ones, it places them as significant within a broader social and political scheme.

ASPECTS OF THE MEDIA

Activity 1

STUDYING A SERIES OF PERSPECTIVES ON THE TOPIC

(suggested time: 1 hour)

Anyone seeking to understand the theory that accompanies teaching media education could well begin by reading Cary Bazalgette's 'Key aspects of media education' in Alvarado and Boyd-Barrett (eds.) *Media Education: An Introduction* (1992). In this article the six key aspects are described and illustrated. In delineating the key aspects it is not intended that your approach to them should become formulaic: they do not represent a list of contents to 'deliver' but more a way of organising a reader's thinking about the media and/or a particular media text.

The theory of the key aspects has been condensed into a form of Signpost Questions;

The following six questions are to be read as if contained within a traditional signpost form, pointing at the two-word upper-case answers.

WHO is communicating, and why?   MEDIA AGENCIES

WHAT TYPE of text is it?   MEDIA CATEGORIES

HOW is it produced?   MEDIA TECHNOLOGIES

HOW do we know what it means?   MEDIA LANGUAGES

WHO receives it, and what sense do
they make of it?   MEDIA AUDIENCES

How does it PRESENT its subject?   MEDIA REPRESENTATIONS

(Bowker, 1991)

Be clear that not all of these questions need to be asked of a media text nor are they the only questions to ask. However, they are questions that *can* be asked of any and every media text. In their being reduced to concise questions the key aspects come to represent a cluster of concepts without strict boundaries; indeed they are, in many usages, interdependent. Refer to the complementary scheme, reproduced here, that shows the relationship between the questions and the key aspects (Summary Areas of Knowledge). They are also not set out to suggest linearity of importance.

Summary of the Areas of Knowledge and Understanding in Media Education

MEDIA AGENCIES	Who produces a text; roles in production processes; media institutions; economics and ideology; intentions and results.
MEDIA CATEGORIES	Different media (television, radio, cinema, etc.); forms (documentary, advertising, etc.); genres (science fiction, soap opera, etc.); other ways of categorising texts: how categorisation relates to understanding.
MEDIA TECHNOLOGIES	What kinds of technologies are available to whom, how to use them; the differences they make to the production processes as well as the final product.
MEDIA LANGUAGES	How the media produce meanings; codes and conventions; narrative structures.
MEDIA AUDIENCES	How audiences are identified, constructed, addressed and reached; how audiences find, choose, consume and respond to texts.
MEDIA REPRESENTATIONS	The relation between media texts and actual places, people events, ideas; stereotyping and its consequences.

Standard addressed: 2.1

(Bowker, 1991)

Activity 2

SEEING THE SAME THING DIFFERENTLY
(suggested time: 30 minutes)

Prepare for use with a class a set of customary visual puzzles. This set might include the duck/rabbit drawing; the cubes that are seen either in a convex or concave perspective; the old woman/ young woman-with-feathered-hat drawing, or one in similar style that shows a young woman combing her hair or a man's puckered grin depending on how you look at it or for how long; the lines that appear to be different lengths by virtue of the arrows on the end of them, and verbal statements arranged like this one:

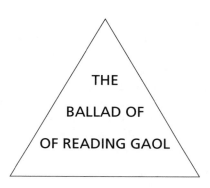

Most people unfamiliar with the device would fail to spot the repetition of 'of' the first time they were presented with such an image.

After taking a 'reading' of each one, answer the two questions that follow:

Standard addressed: 2.1

1 What can we say about how we see/read images?
2 What teaching points do you want to make from these resources?

It is clear that any image has a plurality of meanings depending on how a reader interprets its 'messages'. Let us try to demonstrate this further.

Activity 3

REHEARSING INTERPRETATIONS –
STILL IMAGE ANALYSIS
(suggested time: 2 hours for all of separate interpretive activities)

Start this exercise – about the understanding of a still image within a typical media text – by yourself, but with a view to turning it into an exercise for your students. Sift through as many newspapers as you need until you establish what for you is an interesting black and white photograph, and one that carries a caption. Cut the caption from the picture, and then study the picture. Next, write down from memory everything that you saw (denotation). Now write your interpretation of it (connotation). At that point this is an 'open image'. Next, place the caption to the side of or beneath the photograph, and re-read the 'text' (image and words) as a whole with an enhanced understanding of it – one which will anchor the reading of it for yourself and others who come to that photograph with the caption already in place. It has now become a 'closed image'.

Now consider the 'Signpost Questions' in relation to this image.

- How many can you answer?
- How much more information do you need to complete the exercise?

Be aware of the need to categorise a text before understanding can be secure. How would you attempt to get this point across to pupils?

In the topical news programme *Have I Got News for You*, the captioning contest always produces humour. Can you explain how that humour is generated so that pupils understand it from an image analysis perspective?

Standards addressed: 2.1, 3.1.1, 3.1.3

Another way of making explicit the reading of an image is to assign thought and speech bubbles to the characters portrayed in the image. Keep an eye out for any images that you come across that would be suitable for teaching purposes. Scan them in and send them to fellow English PGCE students, inviting responses.

Cropping images

Cropping images (strategically cutting photographs or pictures to get a particular point across) is another important way of getting pupils to attend more closely to the construction of them. These are best as black and white images, since they photocopy well. Exploit the richness of the visual media products of the everyday world to produce examples of photographs which can be used in class to explain about cropping. A class can explore what they think they are seeing as the cropped OHT of a photograph is uncovered in successive stages.

A fairly recently chosen example by one of us showed three elements in one frame. The most strikingly obvious consisted of coffins surrounded by flowers, as at any traditional funeral. The next element was a guard in uniform by the side of the coffins. This challenged the idea that the funeral was routine or customary. The onlooker might wonder how the guard related to the coffins other than through ensuring their remaining undisturbed. Above the coffins and their guard, however, at the top of an embankment and behind a balustrade, stood a group of onlookers. Perspective made them much smaller figures than the foregrounded guard, but the presence of that group suggested quite clearly that in order to understand what was being depicted you would have to know how they related to the guard and to the dead. The accompanying news story explained most of what the photograph showed, but the image without the story changed in meaning depending on which elements were included or excluded; a class could have explored what they thought they were seeing as a cropped OHT of this photograph was uncovered in successive stages.

Looking at printed images in this way might well gain a class's attention, and the point of the work would be twofold. As an initial point the class could grasp that newspaper editors might crop photographs like this at any time it was felt persuasively convenient to do so. Within the same session, however, they could almost certainly grasp a broader idea, namely that the selection of elements by the viewer is a continuation of the process begun by the photographer, who, of necessity, selects his or her image from a potentially infinite set. Working from this conceptual base, school pupils and students could be helped to see what kind of medium photography is. They could see how asking about choice and learning about the ordinary (analogue) camera is a question for media technologies or media languages (camera angle, lighting, use of colour, focus, framing, subjects, objects, effects) or media agencies (what kind of newspaper would carry this image?), but it could easily become an opportunity to discuss media representations. It may be, of course, that some cameras are available for use by the class, who could explore, through their pointing and clicking, after proper discussion about likely places to look in and around the school grounds, how the same image could take on quite different connotations.

Combining images

We mostly encounter a media image surrounded by other media images. We need to examine an image's altered meaning when it is placed alongside another image. One way to do this would be to juxtapose figures that have some point of similarity – such as that they are of the same age and sex, and one obvious point of dissimilarity – such as that one is from an advertisement for a cosmetic product and the other from a charity appeal, or an image from a documentary programme about shortage and suffering. It would be interesting in terms of media agencies questions to have the class spend no more than 10 minutes leafing through magazines seeing whether such juxtapositions ever occurred. Our experience is that editors are careful not to disturb the viewers of advertisements with much in the way of matter that might make them tense or anxious about what else might be over the page. Usually, in magazines, images of suffering or injustice are sectioned off by one graphic means or another from the flow of commercial versions of what the world looks like. This comes about because advertisers who pay, do not want their products to be linked with negative or disturbing images.

Sequencing images

When images are sequenced together the meanings can be multi-layered and can build upon each other. Detailed analysis of a number of opening sequences to programmes such as *The Bill* are crucial before any pupil production. Examining each frame (if you have the technology – otherwise just use the 'Pause' button) in terms of media language and representation is worth the time. One good way of getting pupils to discuss their knowledge of TV genre is to get them then to sequence some four or five still images as a plan for a pre-credits opening 'teaser' of an episode or a trailer for a programme. A class could create the opening sequences for a new police drama by photomontage, or drawing, or downloading images from some suitable sites. Any lesson plan or scheme of work designed to bring this activity to fruition should state clearly what knowledge pupils are drawing upon when they undertake it. The plan or scheme should also have worked out how the classroom is best organised for this kind of work. Both theoretical and practical issues will need to be considered, such as what materials are needed, how the groups will be organised and how the work will be displayed. The theoretical issues will need to be introduced at a certain point, and the learning outcomes of this activity should be made explicit at some point in the sequence of time or lessons.

A greatly helpful resource in developing this kind of teaching about the media is a CD ROM called Picture Power from the English and Media Centre. Ask to borrow it from your tutor or school-based mentor (if they have it). Pupils are able to choose the news by cutting and pasting images from a large selection and then choosing a sound track (a theme tune or voiceover) to accompany them as they appear in sequence on the screen. Consider what the use of ICT is adding to this activity. What is it taking away?

Activity 4 — INTERPRETING MOVING IMAGES
(suggested time: 45 minutes)

Watch the opening sequences of a film that is unfamiliar to you. Try to make a random choice and not pay attention to the title, write-up, cover of video box, etc. Watch the first two or three minutes of the film several times. Use the freeze frame facility of the remote. Turn the sound off. Adjust the brightness so the picture does not appear and you can attend to the soundtrack.

Use the following Guide Questions to help 'recognise' this text:

1 What can I see and hear?
2 What is the story?
3 What might happen next?
4 What can't I see or hear properly? What can't I understand yet?
5 What sort of text is this?
6 What are its origins?
7 Who is it intended for?
8 What's my opinion of it?
9 What is its ideological message?

Now examine the extract alongside the signpost questions. What further information do you need about this text? How will you get it?

Consider the relationship between the key aspects theory (see pp. 338–9) and our existing, almost unconscious attempts to analyse the media texts that we encounter. Remember that the use of theoretical categories helps organise our thought for specific curricular purposes but that as a reader of a media text we are actively engaged in understanding its meanings by posing our own questions, often at an implicit level. There is much overlap of the two kinds of analysis but how will you demonstrate this to pupils?

Standards addressed:
2.1, 3.3.3

Activity 5

ADVERTISING IMAGES
(suggested time: 90 minutes, possibly longer)

Standards addressed: 2.1, 3.1.1, 3.1.3, 3.3.8

Think about the match between text and image in advertisements. Collect as many images from magazines as you can. Try to ensure that your collection has appeal for pupils. Remove the written text and any reference to the brand name or corporate image. What knowledge is a pupil drawing upon in attempting to identify the product and brand name? How will you organise the classroom for this activity?

Activity 6

CLOSE TEXTUAL ANALYSIS
(suggested time: 45 minutes)

Watch a popular television commercial that is based on a narrative (e.g. new recruit to the car factory refuses to stick badges for what he thinks are and should look like cheap cars on those in the production line which are visibly high in quality. Production line has to be stopped and we are left to infer the remainder of the story – the explanation that, yes, these fine models do indeed bear the name Skoda). Examine the construction of this kind of, in effect, short film, analysing it through any one of four strands:

1 main musical statements of a theme
2 location
3 story versus advertisement (e.g. romantic involvement instead of pleasure in the instant coffee/the stubbornness of a new boy's prejudices instead of the high quality recent models)
4 narrative (how the story is cut into episodes, how we are invited to predict, etc.).

Further analytic questions that could usefully be considered are as follows:

- What would a feminist reading of the Skoda advert be?
- How might this resource be used in the classroom?
- Is this short film commercial effectively a silent movie, or is speech important?
- How might the whole advertisement be analysed with reference to audience, representation and language?

Standards addressed: 2.1, 3.3.8

Activity 7

TEACHING THE POSTMODERN
(suggested time: 1 hour)

What is your understanding of the postmodern? If you were to record some TV ads that consciously acknowledge their borrowings, alienation effects or fragmented structures (e.g. modern soap powder commercials recalling styles and speech from 1950s soap powder commercials), then you might use them in class in a double role. Through the questions considered before this, you could not only cast some light on them but cast some light too on the idea of postmodernism. This concept may be a little difficult for average Year 9s to become greatly excited about, but they could grasp the notion that a text may gain its meaning through quotation, or apparent quotation, from other examples of the genre. Even an engaging media text may be like a second-hand bike – fully working, but made up of bits from a variety of sources. Media work in English could echo what is commonly understood in the art room, and soften up potential sixth-formers for later encounters with T.S. Eliot's *The Waste Land*.

Standards addressed: 2.1, 3.3.8

Make notes on whether the same categories of audience, representation and language apply to deconstructing this kind of text as to others, and if so, how they apply.

How would you use this resource in the classroom?

Activity 8

BOOK COVERS

(suggested time: 1 hour)

You will want to consider getting pupils to deconstruct and reconstruct images and texts used to sell books. You will also want to teach them about the role of commerce in the choices that children make concerning their reading. First task is to photocopy the covers of a paperback book popular in the school at which you are placed, and analyse every part of it, from the font and colour used for the title to the significance of the picture that occupies the central space on the front, to the blurb, to the barcode above the price.

Next, make a skeletal plan of the lesson where you provide these learning opportunities to a given class. Consider using the recent publishing success of J.K. Rowling as a source of possible examples. Plan for the class to be working on a piece of blank A3 paper at the centre of which is glued a photocopy of the book's cover. Arrows and lines are to point from the explanatory notes, handwritten on the A3, to the particular features the notes explain on the photocopy in the centre.

Standards addressed: 2.1, 3.1.1

Activity 9

TEACHING THE NEWS

(suggested time: 1 hour)

What values are conveyed by news companies? Tape the national news and watch it without image and then without sound. Review the principles of defamiliarising a text discussed earlier in the chapter. Compare this clip with news from other stations.

- What are the common features?
- What distinguishes them?
- What is the relationship between the media institutions (news companies) and other institutions (the legal, health and civil services, the government, education, etc.)?
- How will you attempt to convey this information to pupils?
- Can it be applied to the newspaper industry?

Work on newspapers is a traditional part of English teaching. Pupils ought at least to know, through school, something about newspapers. They should leave school understanding what the main national daily papers are. From the start they should have a chance to sample the readerly pleasures of each (if they exist at all in some cases), from the puns of the *Sun* to the short sarcastic letters in the *Guardian*. They should see how the tabloids (a word and concept worth explaining) may take views as utterly opposed to one another on important issues as the broadsheets do. They should be helped to understand that the same event (e.g. London march in February 2003 in protest against the planned invasion of Iraq) may be photographed identically but written about in utterly different ways.

Textual conventions should be explained, from the letters page to sport's pre-eminence at the back, via demonstrating how an obituary is the first draft, perhaps, of a biography, and may often be full of matter that enables us to appreciate the talent and achievement of the best. Left to themselves, pupils may never discover that fact about obituaries and many other things too that are simply assumed by habituated readers of the heavier papers. The KS3 Strategy brings in the idea of understanding at textual level; let the conventions of the text 'newspaper' be made clear, not necessarily by the teacher's words alone, but by setting the class up to determine rules about sections from examples in front of them. On a more sociological level, let the young detectives of Y9 look for clues in the text of a series of extracts from quite different dailies as to the likely readership is, by gender, age, obsession or otherwise with pets, income, sport preference etc. More will be said below about productive *Standard* rather than receptive activities as a way of generating understanding about the forms *addressed: 2.1* of newspapers and the forces behind their composition.

Activity 10

PRACTICAL PRODUCTION
(suggested time: 45 minutes plus preparation time)

The process of pupils engaging in practical media production enables them to develop their media knowledge of all signposted aspects. However, as teachers we also need to provide pupils with the tools to critique some of the media processes, otherwise we may inadvertently teach pupils to empathise with profit motives and to sympathise with ethical compromises at the expense of citizenship issues. Always de-brief pupils so that they can see the relationship between production decisions (audience, budget, technical constraints) and the wider context.

Pupils often undervalue production experiences, seeing their own attempts as amateurish versus the more professional polished products. Stress the process not the product as the important issue. The situation can be compromised by a lack of real purpose and/or audience.

Storyboarding, therefore, is an important concept. Pupils not only need to be taught how to use one, they need to know that even professionals use storyboards. A useful first exercise is to ask pairs or threes to illustrate the theme of 'love' or 'time', 'fear' or 'anxiety', in just four carefully selected shots – from just within the classroom and possibly a corridor. Give them a blank storyboard as a frame. Prior learning of the detailed analysis of still images, and how images are sequenced together, including details of camera shots, should come into explicit play here. Get the group to run it through using fingers in a 'square' to simulate the camera view, focus, angle etc. Only then should the video camera be given to the group – and a sharp time limit given for its return. Celebration of the four-shot sequences together with evaluation from the whole class is a crucial step in learning, and progression on to longer storyboarded sequences, such as a 10-shot film with selected images representing good points about the school carried out by one group, with another selecting images to represent the school in a poor light.

How will you introduce this to pupils?

With practical production avoid 'busy work'. Cutting and sticking occupy pupils' time but it is important that we require them to make critical choices about the language, codes and conventions within a given genre. Make sure that you stress the accompanying written text as well as the pictures/graphics when asking them to compile brochures/adverts, etc.

Further possibilities for practical work

- TV presentation of a poem, South Bank Show style
- TV news of a narrative event
- Newspaper stories of main action events in Shakespeare play
- Invent, describe and market a pop group
- Devise poster campaigns for public services e.g. drugs education, drink driving

Activities relating to newspapers

Much work can be done in productive terms if time and space allow (a day, a newsroom set aside for education) with your local newspaper. Have a section of the class take editorial responsibility for some local news. If someone in your host English Department is doing this, go with them if possible. Help can be obtained from The Newspaper Society (http://www.newspapersoc.org.uk) that is directly practical and advisory.

If, as is more than likely, only a small section of the class can gain hands-on experience with the local newspaper, then why not give everyone a chance to rehearse, in a simulation, the role of being in an editorial team? Provide groups of four with, say (depending upon age and ability), five stories of which only one can be the headlined main front page top story. As they wrestle with what elements make for the likeliest best story for their paper and its readers (each group could have the same stories but they could be designated *Mirror*, *Mail*, *Sun*, *Telegraph*, etc.), and with rules about libel (one of the filters you have created, together with a blatantly libellous story as one of the contenders), you start to drop in to each activity table another late-breaking story only 10 minutes before the bell which, of course, is also the deadline time for going to press.

Standards addressed: 3.3.7, 3.3.8

CONTINUOUS THREADS

1 Professional values and practice

The materials of media – the products which you are to have a class understand – are likely, some of them, to be controversial. Bias and opinion are present both overtly and in less obvious ways, such as through selection and omission. The English teacher needs to know in advance how he or she is going to handle the political and social angles on key questions. The handling of controversial issues is too big a matter to be dealt with here, but in a classroom context of mixed ideologies, religions, ethnic allegiances and so on, the traditional value of neutrality commends itself. Such a teaching stance seeks quite openly to describe and clarify values and to compare like with like in terms of text type and function. Debate should be valued not for its finality, necessarily, but for its capacity to keep a conversation going which reveals the complexity of reporting the actual, and which uncovers the rhetorical history of persuasion towards any decision deeper than whether to buy shampoo x or shampoo y.

3.2 Planning, expectations and targets

What curricular opportunities would you like to see in place for Key Stage 3 pupils that lay the foundations for a more formal study of the media that will result in a qualification in later years? List the areas of study you would include in your teaching of the media in Years 7–9.

3.3 Monitoring and assessment

In media education some of the hardest assignments to assess are those pieces of work that represent a pupil's original and creative output. These may include brochures, posters; photo stories; even audio or video recorded items. And yet it is important that these endeavours are regarded as equally important as the more traditional written assignments. Criteria for assessment need to be set and explained to pupils

3.4 Teaching and class management

In general, and broadening out from newspapers to any form of practical or creative work in media, bear in mind that pupils need opportunities to become active media readers, audiences and writers. As such they are better able to evaluate for themselves any media text in terms of content, form and context if they have tried to make one or two. Therefore media classrooms need to be:

- democratic–individual views are encouraged – a variety of 'readings' are possible (with information given about a preferred reading as a dominant interpretation within a particular cultural context);
- participatory – reflective;
- active;
- collaborative – involving dialogues between learners and between learners and teachers.

Within this, a disciplined approach to practical production is crucial: an emphasis on teamwork, and possibly division of roles (director, cameraman, editor, actors, 'gofers') can share responsibility and prevent inappropriate arguments; it also serves to emulate media industries' need for a hierarchy of roles. Insisting on deadlines with penalties will allow all access to the (perhaps sole) camera/radio mike etc., and will result in better quality of work produced.

3.3.4 Differentiation

Media education lends itself very well to differentiating by outcome. The accessibility of the texts means that you use the same text and often set the same tasks/questions in mixed ability groups. Pupils' responses will vary in terms of sophistication and depth according to their ability. Issues relating to how to group pupils obviously need careful consideration. However, try to anticipate activities that will require both more support and more challenge built into the task to ensure that all pupils' individual needs are met.

Scenarios

1   You are showing the opening sequences of a recent popular film to your Year 10 English group as part of their GCSE work on genre studies. When you complete the showing of the extract the pupils start to put a lot of pressure on you to show the rest of the film. How do you respond to their requests and how do you explain your decision to them?

2   Your Year 8 group have been working in groups on producing their alternative school prospectus for incoming Year 7 pupils. After four lessons one girl approaches you to say that she cannot work in her group any longer because she has fallen out with the other members. How do you handle this situation?

FURTHER READING

Bell, A., Joyce, M. and Rivers, D. (1999) *Advanced Level Media*. London: Hodder & Stoughton

Buckingham, D. (1993) *Children Talking Television: The Making of Television Literacy*. London: Falmer Press

Dahlgren, P. and Sparks, C. (1992) *Journalism and Popular Culture*. London: Sage

Hart, A. (1991) *Understanding the Media*. London: Routledge and Kegan Paul

Nelmes, J. (1996) *An Introduction to Film Studies*, 2nd edn. London: Routledge.

REFERENCES

Alvarado, M. and Boyd-Barrett, O. (eds) (1992) *Media Education: an Introduction.* London: BFI Publishing in partnership with the Open University on behalf of the Media Education Course Team

Bowker, J. (ed.) (1991) *Secondary Media Education: a Curriculum Statement.* London: British Film Institute.

Branston, G. and Stafford, R. (1999) *The Media Student's Book.* London: Routledge

Davison, J. and Dowson, J. (1998) *Learning to Teach English in the Secondary School: a Companion to School Experience.* London: Routledge

O'Sullivan, T., Dutton, B. and Rayner, P. (1998) *Studying the Media.* London: Arnold

chapter 18

ENGLISH AND ICT

By the end of this chapter you will have gained an introductory understanding of the use of ICT to teach English-specific objectives: word-processing; the Internet; email; CD ROMS; databases and spreadsheets. You will have developed your own ICT skills, in a theoretical context, engaging with the pedagogy necessary for the successful practical application and learning through ICT in the classroom. There are three stages or aspects of this:

> the operational (knowing how to use the technologies), the 'cultural' (understanding the contexts of appropriate use) and the 'critical' (being able to make judgements about the skills, values, beliefs, practices and effects associated with this use). (Goodwyn, 2000: 53)

The chapter can also serve as an initial audit of a student teacher's ICT skills, and show where both strengths, and weaknesses may lie. These activities have been tried and tested by students at Canterbury Christ Church University College and have proved effective in producing ICT-literate English teachers.

RATIONALE

Circular 4/98 from the DfEE laid out a lengthy list of Standards of ICT for student teachers, and teachers in general, with commensurate funding for training in schools through the New Opportunities Fund (NOF). Those standards were replaced by the Revised Standards for QTS in 2002, with two standards specific to ICT which assume an understanding derived perhaps from the prior learning in 4/98 with their subject-specific annexes:

2.5 They [student teachers] know how to use ICT effectively, both to teach their subject and to support their wider professional role;
3.3.10 They use ICT effectively in their teaching.

To a degree these mirror Goodwyn's three stages above, but the 'critical' aspect is a longer term aim lying outside the Standards. Developing your own competence may involve you spending time in front of your computer screen learning how to effectively search the Web, produce exciting worksheets, build up databases, and create spreadsheets; these are simple skills which only need time rather than external expertise to develop. It is the use of ICT in the English classroom that is more complex, and time and experience are needed if ICT is to be used successfully. Although not now in force, *Information Technology in the National Curriculum* (DfEE, 1995) can still be seen to be influential in shaping the ICT strand in the KS3 Strategy which seeks to teach ICT skills and knowledge now through subjects. The demands therefore on teachers to deliver ICT are comprehensive; experienced, practising teachers have difficulty putting them all into practice, and many schools are still not equipped resource wise, time wise or trained staff wise to make them all a reality.

English successfully incorporated drama and media for use in the classroom for over two decades, and used them primarily for the personal growth models and cultural analysis views of English; these are now subjects in their own right. ICT can be viewed as another tool which can be used successfully in the English classroom to enhance and extend reading and writing skills by exploiting the speed, capacity, provisionality and interactivity of ICT. Multi-modal ways of reading, writing and talking about ICT texts also offer very different experiences of interacting with texts. The English teacher is in a unique position to exploit this by making these new 'readerly and writerly' ways of approaching ICT texts opaque to pupils; in a similar way, we look at language metalinguistically: hence the rationale for placing this chapter alongside chapters on reading, writing, and the media.

Many pupils already have sophisticated ICT skills from home – computer games, email and surfing the Net – but they may not have a conscious understanding of their skills, and what they read, view and write may not as yet (computer games, texting) be part of the school curriculum. Conversely, many pupils will have no home access to computers; it is the job of the English teacher to audit pupils' prior skills and to ensure equality of access and opportunity to ICT.

LINKS WITH THE NATIONAL CURRICULUM AND THE NATIONAL LITERACY STRATEGY

En2 Reading in the NC has a section 'Printed and ICT-based information texts' which requires pupils to be taught to: 'synthesise information, evaluate, distinguish between fact and opinion and identify the language features of different types of text'. This calls for proactive reading, as does the section on 'Media and moving image texts' which takes a critical approach to texts, and is stronger in tone than the more neutral (and traditional) literary criticism approach underpinning the 'Understanding texts' sections. The whole of En3 Writing can be applied directly to the use of ICT, as, in reality, can the whole of Reading, and much of EN1 Speaking and listening. The possibilities then for using ICT to meet the National Curriculum objectives for English are enormous, and exciting. Essentially pupils need to become autonomous users of ICT, understand its potential and limitations as well as some of the social and ethical issues involved in its use, and be taught to model, communicate and handle information at increasingly sophisticated, conscious levels.

The KS3 Strategy

The emphasis on different reading strategies demanded by ICT texts is included in The KS3 Strategy and highlighted in the examples given, with the assumption that a large proportion of English time will be carried out with access to a computer.

WORKING THROUGH THIS CHAPTER – LINKS WITH OTHER CHAPTERS

You may wish to cover this chapter in conjunction with others so that the ICT tasks are completed in a meaningful context. For example, while doing Chapter 16 on poetry, it would be useful to do Activity 8 below on using ICT to 'do things' with a poem, and in planning a lesson for Chapter 3, 'Planning and Progression,' you may want to refer to Activity 4 below on planning for the use of ICT in the English classroom. Some of the basic technological skills can be practised alone, but much of this chapter depends you learning how to apply such skills in the English classroom. Class management skills need to be sound for this, as does your own experience of your placement schools' ICT resources. For this reason many of you will find that completion of this chapter may not come until your last school placement.

Activity 1

FROM PAGE TO SCREEN
(suggested time: 30 minutes)

Chapter 13 in Brindley (1994) gives a good introduction to the new literacies. Here the authors show how our concept of literacy has altered through the challenge of invisible, unreliable authors and multi-authoring, non-linear text and hotlinks that the computer screen, and especially the Web, offer us. Even the way we think may have changed to thinking in whole chunks of movable text rather than discrete words or sentences. The public, collaborative nature of these new texts on the Web, and the centrality of the visual image, graph or icon, has also transformed the way we read, view and write texts. The speed of electronic communications has reshaped our social world, and redefined what is Standard English, and even the concept of speech, with text-messaging, chat rooms and email being closer in nature to speaking and listening than writing and reading.

TASK

How far do you agree with the viewpoints expressed here? In about 400 words describe your own experience of moving from 'the page to the screen' in terms of your reading and writing. Specify your use/habit of email, the Web, word processing, use of CD-

Standards addressed: 1.7, 2.1

ROMs and computer games, and compare this to your use/habit of reading paper-based books and using a pen and paper. For example, do you still write letters by hand, or do you word-process them, or just use email? Do you take handwritten notes when completing activities for this book, or can you only think by typing directly on the keyboard? Do you use two fingers, or do you use the QWERTY finger places?

Activity 2

ICT RESOURCES IN SCHOOLS
(suggested time: 30 minutes)

Schools vary enormously in their attitudes towards the use and resourcing of ICT despite statutory requirements for pupils to reach particular levels of competency. Some schools such as technology colleges or specialist schools have up to date ICT suites. Some schools have opted to put three or four computers in each teaching room, rather than have a specialist suite, to more fully integrate their use in daily teaching and learning. Some schools have what Goodwyn describes as an 'innovative' attitude and practice to ICT (Goodwyn, 2000: 11) where the potential of ICT to transform learning is seen as exciting: other schools have a 'preservative' attitude which is seen in the difficulty of booking ICT suites, or as a perceived threat and 'Luddite' claims from teachers in their own ICT competency.

TASK

- How would you describe the attitude and practice of your teaching practice school or any school you know well to the use of ICT with pupils, using Goodwyn's terms of 'innovative' or 'preservative'?
- What policies exist to ensure that development takes place in ICT knowledge and skills in your placement school, and are they effective?
- How is ICT resourced and what are the implications of this for teaching and learning?

Standard addressed: 2.5 Write a paragraph for each bullet point and place these in your English portfolio.

Activity 3

HEALTH AND SAFETY
(suggested time: 45 minutes)

Teachers need to be aware of current health and safety legislation as regards ICT. Lighting, providing a variety of activities away from the screen in lengthy sessions, encouraging good posture, and the supervision of pupils making hardware connections are initial health considerations. Data protection legislation ensures that 'individuals have a right to privacy, (the protection of) an individual's intellectual property and copyright, and protection of individuals from exposure to obscene and inflammatory material' (Canterbury Christ Church University College, 1998: 93).

TASK

Identify three examples of classroom ICT practice in which the following issues are significant from either your own practice, or that of teachers you observe:

- Health and safety issues (e.g. seating arrangements, lighting, time in front of a screen)
- Legal issues (e.g. data protection, copyright)
- Ethical issues (pupil access to inappropriate material, use of 'filters').

Standard addressed: 2.5 Discuss these three examples with your mentor or a specialist ICT teacher, and place your findings in your English portfolio.

Activity 4   PLANNING, EXPECTATIONS AND TARGETS
(suggested time: observation time plus 1 hour)

It is too easy to use ICT inappropriately as a carrot – 'If you behave well this lesson we can go into the computer room for the next lesson' – or to make nice final printed copies of handwritten drafts. Good planning is the key to appropriate and constructive use of ICT. The template below gives prompts for consideration when planning an ICT lesson. An electronic version of this template is available at **www.paulchapmanpublishing.co.uk/resources/completeguide.htm**

ICT PROMPT SHEET

(for use in conjunction with schemes of work and lesson plans)

ICT focus: (e.g. WP, email, multimedia)

Overall teaching aims

Pupil Learning Objectives (Refer to National Curriculum)
AT1 Speaking and Listening

AT2 Reading

AT3 Writing (and Knowledge about Language)

ICT focus and functions (NC for ICT)

How will ICT be used to meet teaching and learning objectives in English (as above?)

Benefits of using ICT/disadvantages/ inappropriateness of using ICT for above teaching and learning objectives

What is the prior knowledge or skills of the pupils in terms of the use of this ICT function? How can this be assessed before use?

Classroom organisation
Activities needed prior to ICT use (in English classroom) to support and dovetail into specific functions of ICT

Preparation needed by the teacher of ICT equipment to be used:
(including prior planning with ICT specialist support teacher or technician)

How will the room be set up? (layout, use of tables, and monitors, pairings of pupils)

Focused teaching

How will the particular teaching and learning objectives be introduced (at beginning of lesson, in another room, use of electronic whiteboard for whole class discussion, modelling of ICT function on data projector?)

Prompt questions to ask groups and individuals to assess their understanding of the task and objective during use of ICT?

Reporting back of attainments in use of ICT in the plenary?

Differentiation

What support can be offered to pupils learning EAL?

What support can be offered to pupils with AEN?

How can high attainers (in ICT) be extended?

Do boys and girls have equal access to the equipment?

Assessment and monitoring of pupils' progress

How will pupils' language skills be monitored during use of ICT?

How will individual and group attainment be recognised and recorded?

TASK

Standards addressed: 1.2, 2.5, 3.1.1, 3.1.2, 3.1.3, 3.2.2, 3.3.4, 3.3.5

1 Observe an English lesson where ICT is used to meet the English objectives drawn from the NC. Fill in the 'ICT prompt sheet' for that lesson by observing, interacting with the pupils and discussing the lesson before and after with the classroom teacher.

2 Are there any other classroom planning and management issues that came up that were not on the pro forma, or that you had not considered? How were they dealt with (or not)?

3 Refer to this prompt sheet when planning ICT lessons in completing the activities in this chapter as appropriate, and in your own practice.

Activity 5

CLASSROOM MANAGEMENT

(suggested time: 30 minutes)

Good planning will reduce off-task behaviour but classes can still find being in the ICT suite a novelty. The skills of class management are no different in this context and needed rather more overtly to ensure effective learning. Some pointers are:

- Pupils must be quiet and face the teacher when required, and away from the monitor, with 'hands off' the keyboard.
- Instructions to log-in and locate the work already in the intranet must be clear, and reinforced by written instructions on the board.
- The aims and objectives of the lesson must be made clear.
- Timings for activities need to be given.
- Off-task behaviour, i.e. surfing or emailing when working on a small piece of text, will not be tolerated.
- Some tasks are better suited to pupils coming together as a class or group (many ICT suites have tables in the middle to convene on) to discuss issues raised or responses to reading texts.
- Pupils can work well in groups or pairs if the seating allows for equal access to the mouse: as in speaking and listening activities, the teacher can allocate roles to members of the group –'scribe', mouse controller, muse.

● Pupils must save their work and log off properly in good time.

Standards addressed:
3.3.7, 3.3.8, 3.3.9

TASK

Drawing on your observations of English and ICT lessons above, add another four bullet points to the list above on what seems to you to be good class management, and good practice. Relate directly to your own school.

Activity 6

WRITING AND COMPOSING TEXTS

(suggested time: 30 minutes)

Writing and composing texts is the most straightforward use of the computer where the Editing functions of *cut, copy, paste, delete, search* and *replace* functions can be used for redrafting purposes, so creating a text for a particular purpose, context and audience.

TASK

You want your pupils to write a short story on a theme studied previously in class, using the computer to 'scribble' with, draft, redraft, and revise, rather than writing a rough draft in hand and transferring it to the screen..

1   What planning and preparation activities/lessons need to happen before pupils get to this stage?
2   How important to you is the process of writing compared to the end, polished product (the presentation, and the re-presentation)?
3   How will you as a teacher encourage pupils to retain their drafts?

Standard addressed:
3.3.10

4   Who will read the final draft? *How* will it be read (pairs swapping over, sending it out on email and exchanged with another class/school; printed into a class story book, burned on to a CD ROM)?

Activity 7

TRANSFORMING TEXTS

(suggested time: 20 minutes)

Manipulating form and changing text is the next obvious stage forward. The NC explicitly points out the requirement for pupils to 'consider how meanings are changed when texts are adapted to different media' and to look at 'how techniques, structure, forms and style vary' (1999: 34) There are many exciting and innovative uses of ICT here:

● Changing a narrative into a script, focusing on form, structure, syntax and punctuation
● Condensing texts or expanding them to investigate figures of speech
● Altering the gender of a narrative with search and replace to understand the tone of the piece

- Offering different endings to stories
- Playing with layout by changing, e.g. a paragraph from Dickens (the opening paragraph of *Bleak House* works well) into a poem.

Goodwyn suggests (2000: 18, 19) taking the irony out of a Jane Austen paragraph, and taking 'a paragraph of Henry James and "Hemingway" it into short sentences'. These exercises are particularly effective in getting under the skin of what 'style' means, at AS/A2 perhaps.

TASK

Standard addressed: 3.3.10

Do one of the transformations above yourself. Which NC objective was met through this activity? Write a brief analysis of your re-reading and (re)interpretation of the text(s) or discuss your findings with your tutor or other student teachers in a discussion forum.

Activity 8

READING TEXTS

(suggested time: 30 minutes)

The interactive and provisional nature of ICT can be exploited to support pupils' close reading of short texts for inference and deduction. The 'deep structure' of texts, their patterning, and the way meaning is built up can be deconstructed. The teacher's Annotation of texts through the functions of bold, italic, different fonts and colour to highlight figurative language or the rhyming scheme can demonstrate in a visual format how the poem is constructed and patterned. This can be placed on the school's intranet in advance, and pupils working in pairs use the 'demolished' poem as a reading prompt. They can then highlight a different poem – including graphics – to send to another pair to comment on.

Pupils can do this activity on paper with coloured pencils, too. Perhaps you should have a go at both methods.

TASK

1 What advantages are there in using ICT?
2 What advantages are there in using pencils and paper?
3 Find a poem you like for a Year 9 class. Produce a simple activity which could be used in teaching poetry: e.g. re-sequencing a jumbled poem, highlighting particular words, deletion of specific words. Pre-1914 poems can present the appropriate challenge: e.g. Wordsworth's 'Upon Westminster Bridge' with its regular rhyme and imagery.
4 Write a brief commentary on what you wanted your pupils to learn here, and how you plan to assess that learning in the ICT suite or classroom.

Standard addressed: 3.3.10

5 Send this as an attachment to another student for comment. Save both your original version and the emailed commentary in your ICT folder.

Activity 9

PRESENTING TEXTS FOR A PARTICULAR PURPOSE, STYLE AND AUDIENCE

(suggested time: 1 hour)

Any text is written for a specified audience, purpose and context, with a corresponding particular use of language. Many non-literary texts – leaflets, newspapers, newsletters, guides, pamphlets, advertisements, memos, reports, accounts and letters – communicate their meaning through a particular computer format, layout and use of graphics. Some desk top publishing packages give ready-made templates, and some programs, e.g. Microsoft Word, have simple templates to choose from in the 'New document' window.

TASK

Create your own simple leaflet or newsletter (or another format of your choice) using a template or DTP package. Specify the audience, purpose and context in a separate short commentary and incorporate graphics to enhance the text.

Some ideas for this:

- A newsletter for English student teachers on your programme
- A flyer advertising your favourite novel
- A leaflet on how to encourage children to read, to be placed in libraries.

Standard addressed: 2.5 Send this as an email attachment to a colleague/friend/tutor and ask for feedback.

Activity 10

MULTI-AUTHORING TEXTS FROM THE WEB

(suggested time: 1 hour)

The vast capacity and range of information available allow for real research opportunities. There are numerous excellent websites devoted to English teaching (See WEBSITES, at the end of this chapter), from interactive soap websites, to sites containing all the poems you could ever imagine. Indeed the challenge for both teacher and pupil is to know exactly what you are looking for, and to know how to use the search engines accurately and efficiently.

Jane O'Donoghue in her chapter 'To cope, to contribute, to control' in *English in the Digital Age* (Goodwyn, 2000) discusses new understanding of the way we read 'innovative, demanding, non-conformist texts, which require the reader to become involved in the process of decoding and therefore to take up a position of power within the author–text–reader process' (p. 74).

English teachers can take control of the potential of the Web for their own classes – using it ' to make things happen', and sanctioning the alteration of web-based texts and building up a list of useful websites as bookmarks.

TASK: *Creating learning material using Web resources*

You are going to use the Web to locate information on some aspect of literature to copy, paste and revise/reuse in another format, e.g. a newsletter on Dickens in Kent. This task develops your skills in using the Web for a specific reason – rather than randomly surfing through endless websites.

(a) Open up a word document or newsletter, memo, report template – whatever format you want. Keep Word open behind as you access the Internet.

(b) Plan and put together a search strategy on some aspect of literature – women and education, or the Industrial Revolution in Victorian England. The sharper the focus, the better – for you and your pupils.

(c) Search for the information on the World Wide Web.

(d) Use skimming and scanning techniques to locate the specific bits you want.

(e) Use the copy, paste, and save functions to carry those bits of information you want over to your Word document or template. Continue this until you get as much information as you want.

(f) Now use the editing functions to revise, delete, rearrange the information into the format you want. Remember to be creative in your use of fonts, letter size, bold, underline, and the use of graphics.

Keep this as an example of your own ability to use the Web for a specific purpose.

1 How would you use this exercise in a class and to meet what objectives for English? How would you raise the issues about who authors the final text?

2 Who will control what can be downloaded from the Web? (See Activity on health and safety)

Activity 11

RESOURCES REVIEW

(suggested time: 1 hour)

The range of resources available is, as already stated, enormous – from the Web, from CD-ROMs, from school intranets, from databases. You need to spend time exploring what is available at your placement school in terms of CD-ROMs, and flexible learning resources such as Integrated Learning Systems (ILS), for example SuccessMaker.

TASK: *Supporting reading and writing development*

Evaluate the use of a software resource intended to support reading or writing development (e.g. Dev Tray or SuccessMaker) by making a list of the advantages and disadvantages. The table below sets out some examples from *Talking About Information Communications Technology in Subject Teaching* (Canterbury Christ Church University College, 1999: 65)

Title of software:

Advantages	Disadvantages
Immediate feedback – no waiting for the teacher or work to be marked	The cost!
Failing in private – no one else will know that the answer is wrong	Investment in time for training, the timetable and support staff is necessary to enable the system to be successful

TASK: *CD-ROM reviews*

Discuss the educational value of a CD-ROM after making use of it in a classroom teaching situation at your school placement, or observing a lesson where it is used. (If this is not possible, evaluate it as a potential tool for the classroom.)

Some prompt questions:

- Does this resource promote good practice in English teaching?
- Is it accessible, in terms of the language it uses and the procedures which must be followed to use it?
- What English learning objectives for pupils did it help you to meet?
- How successful was it in practice for teaching one or more classes and developing their knowledge and skills in English?

Standard addressed: 2.5 A useful address for this that includes CD-ROM evaluations is at: **www.becta.org.uk**.

Activity 12

ASSESSMENT SPREADSHEET

(suggested time: 1 hour)

You need to know how to create simple spreadsheets to support your teaching, not specifically for your pupils to use in the classroom. You will need to record, evaluate and report on the progress of each of your classes – and using a spreadsheet can help you in this. You can look for patterns in particular pupils' progress in, for example, writing, or giving in of homework; you can analyse progress and achievement in terms of gender, or ethnicity; you can compare classes against one another or over two or more years. You can also include pupils' KS2 results, their CAT scores, optional tests, Year 9 NC tests, and predicted grades at GCSE. Schools provide this information so that all teachers can plan for learning and assess pupils' performances more effectively. You will need to be sensitive to the data protection policies; consult with your mentor if uncertain.

TASK

You are to produce a spreadsheet in which you record the assessments of one of the classes you teach. The spreadsheet should include:

- pupil names
- dates of assessments
- numerical marks/grades and/or comments for each assessment.

Use at least two spreadsheet functions to analyse the data, and print out the results. For example:

- use the sort functions to rank the pupils;
- use the average function to analyse marks;
- make a graph showing a particular pupil's performance in comparison with the average.

Standards addressed: 2.5, 3.1.1

Write a brief commentary considering the possible uses you would make of spreadsheets and assessment and reporting.

Activity 13

CREATING DATABASES
(suggested time: 1 hour)

It is useful to know how to use, and create, databases for your own professional development rather than get pupils to create their own databases from scratch. You may need to create databases of your classes for administrative purposes (be aware of the Data Protection Act), and also set up databases for your classes to access, and add to. Ideas for uses of databases range from entering data about a large collection of letters (junk mail, computer-generated, handwritten, printed) or a number of fairy tales, or a class database of all the books read by that class over one year, into a pre-prepared database.

TASK

You will undoubtedly read 20 novels, plays and poetry anthologies written specifically for young people over your course. Compile a bibliography of these texts in the form of a database, in which you create a record for each text consisting of the following fields:

Title, author, date, publisher, themes, age/ability suitability, key passages for classroom use, teaching ideas

From here you can learn how to do a simple search on your database, entering search criteria such as:

THEMES = adolescent love

You can also develop your skills in accessing information from other more complex databases, such as CD-ROMs and then the Internet.

To create a database suitable for the required task using Access:

- Double click on the Microsoft Access icon.
- Create new blank Access database.
- Filename: Reading.mdb – Create.
- Select Create Table in Design View.
- A table will appear for entering Field Names and Data Types.
- There will be a box with Field Size at the bottom of the screen.
- Enter the following data:

Field Name	Type	Field Size
Title	Text	100
Author	Text	30
Date	Text	10
Publisher	Text	20
Themes	Text	255
Age/Ability	Text	255
Key passages	Text	255
Teaching ideas	Text	255

- Field Size information is entered in a box which appears towards the bottom of the screen.
- Do not create a Primary Key when asked.
- In the View menu select Data Sheet.
- Use the Format menu to find Row height: change this to 80.
- Use the Format menu to find Column Width.
  Change this for the columns by clicking in each column first –
  Title: 15; Author: 15; Date: 6.5; Publisher: 15; Themes: 26; Age/Ability: 13;
  Key Passages: 26; Teaching Ideas: 26
- You are now ready to enter data in the columns.

Standard addressed: 2.5
- Before printing, use the File menu to find Print Set Up: change to landscape from portrait: your table will run across the page.

Activity 14

USING ICT TO TEACH ENGLISH OBJECTIVES IN A SCHEME OF WORK

(suggested time: 2 hours)

This task is a culmination of all the small activities that you have developed for your own ICT competence and the classroom-based activities which require you to consider the planning and organisational aspects of using ICT in the English classroom. This task also assesses your ability to monitor, evaluate and assess your teaching and pupils' learning in English when using ICT, and to evaluate the contribution that ICT can make to the teaching of English.

Standards addressed: **2.1, 2.5, 3.1.1, 3.1.2, 3.2.1**

You need to submit a scheme of work you have taught in which ICT is a prominent component. The scheme of work must be accompanied by a detailed evaluation using the prompt sheet fully. Include the scheme of work, any worksheets or instructions used and, if possible, evidence of pupils' work, both written and on screen, to show their learning and progression through your scheme of work.

Scenarios

1   Your school library has state of the art computer networks and is accessible to all pupils at lunch and after school. You notice that boys dominate the access to the monitors at lunchtimes, surfing the Net and playing computer games while girls seem to be content to read library books. How might you alter the balance here?

2   Despite having organised an ICT lesson to research 'First World War poetry' on the Web, you begin to despair when pupils go off-task quickly, send email to each other, search for other subjects outside of your specified one, and do not leave their keyboards alone when asked. What prior discussions with the pupils or other teachers might have helped here, and what strategies would you put in place for the next lesson to keep pupils solely on-task? What cross-curricular strategies could also help here?

CONTINUOUS THREADS

1 Professional values and practice

If you have a group of three pupils around a monitor, who has control over the mouse? Boys are still often more skilled at using computer equipment from home, and are perhaps more willing to take control of the mechanics, as a diversionary tactic away from the actual subject matter. You will need to ensure that there is equal access to the mouse, and that pupils work individually at monitors as well as in pairs or groups.

3.2 Monitoring and assessment

You will need to plan for the assessment of the four language skills when using ICT – what are your learning objectives? If the primary focus is on close reading of a poem through a transformation of it, then you will be assessing the talk that surrounds that activity. If the primary focus is on scanning and skimming on the Web, and rewriting copied prose, then the relevance of the text scanned and then copied, and the quality of the revision according to purpose, context and audience are the defining criteria. Assessment can be difficult and unreliable if the technical aspects hide the real work; pupils' lack of keyboard skills, jammed printers, uncertain or overly complex instructions.

You will need to monitor pupils' progression both in English, and in their ICT skills, matching their development in both to your objectives and tasks. It would be useful to find out what they are doing in their ICT specialist classes, and in other curriculum areas.

3.3.4 Differentiation

Some pupils will have greater technical skills than others because of access to computers at home; you will need to channel these skills constructively into the lesson rather than allowing those pupils to intimidate others. Conversely you will have to give one to one time to those pupils who are really stuck. Sensitive pairing of pupils either in same ability or mixed ability can help, as can having good extension work for those who work more quickly. For a reading lesson, the same considerations come into play – choose less complex texts to deconstruct or highlight for the less able reader.

FURTHER READING

Canterbury Christ Church University College (1998) *Talking about Information and Communication Technology in Subject Teaching.* Canterbury: Christ Church University College
This text gives an accessible account of basic functions of ICT as related to the classroom, including practical advice on word-processing, creating spreadsheets, and the use of images.
DfEE (1995) *Information Technology in the National Curriculum.* London: DfEE.
DfEE (1999) *The National Curriculum for England. English: Key Stages 1–4.* London: DfEE and QCA.
Goodwyn, A. (ed.) (2000) *English in the Digital Age: Information and Communication Technology and the Teaching of English.* London: Cassell
The whole book is worth reading – and enjoyably too, but read especially Chapters 1, 2, 5, 7 and 8.
NATE English and the New Technologies Committee (1993) *Developing English approaches with IT.* Sheffield: NATE
This book gives good examples of real work done with pupils, and has sections on planning and management, and assessment.
Tweddle, S. et al. (1997) *English for Tomorrow.* Buckingham: Open University Press
This book takes an in-depth look at the profound changes that ICT is bringing to the way we think, and teach about texts, and therefore the very subject of English. An important book to read. It has useful and entertaining 'vignettes' of pupils' possible, and real work with ICT.

REFERENCES

Brindley, S. (1994) *Teaching English.* London: Routledge
DfEE (1995) *Information Technology in the National Curriculum.* London: DfEE
DfEE (1998) *Teaching: High Status, High Standards.* (Circular 4198). London: DfEE
Davison, J. and Dowson, J. (1998) *Learning to Teach English in the Secondary School: a Companion to School Experience.* London: Routledge
DFES, (2002) *Qualifying to Teach.* London: DfES

WEBSITES

www.ngfl.gov.uk – National Grid for Learning
www.vtc.ngfl.gov.uk – Virtual teacher centre
www.becta.org.uk/cd-rom.html – BECTa CD-ROM reviews

Two sites on John Steinbeck's *Of Mice and Men:*
www.bbc.co.uk/history/programmes/centurions/steinbeck/steibiog.shtml
www.englishresources.co.uk/workunits/ks4/fiction/ofmicemen/wkunitvt/micementunit.html

Two sites on popular soaps:
www.homeandaway.seven.com.au/homeandaway entry.html
www.bbbc.co.uk/eastenders/home.shtml

Useful sites for English teachers:
www.teachit.co.uk
www.englishonline.co.uk
http://ourworld.compuserve.com/homepages/Harry_Dodds/
www.qca.gov.uk/schemes of work/

Two sites giving hundreds of poems in their entirety:
www.inform.umd.edu/edres/readingroom/
http://geocities.com/Athens/Acropolis/2012/poems/index.html

Chor. *Two households, both alike in dignity,*
   In fair Verona, where we lay our scene,
From ancient grudge break to new mutiny,
   Where civil blood makes civil hands unclean.
From forth the fatal loins of these two foes 5
   A pair of star-cross'd lovers take their life;
Whose misadventur'd piteous overthrows
   Do with their death bury their parents' strife.
The fearful passage of their death-mark'd love,
   And the continuance of their parents' rage.
Which, but their children's end, nought could re-
      move,
Is now the two hours' traffick of our stage
The which if you with patient ears attend,
What here shall miss, our toil shall strive to

ACT I

SCENE I.—*Verona. A Public Place*
Enter SAMPSON *and* GREGORY, *armed*

the weaker vess
therefore I will
wall, and thrus
Gre. The ou
us their men,
Sam. 'Tis a
when I have fo
with the maid
Gre. The he
Sam. Ay,
maidenheads
Gre. They

abc
Wonder
trth wha
did till w
Opti

INTRODUCTION

Drama is probably an older subject on the school curriculum than English. We can see that this is true if we trace the history of school productions of plays as a key element of education, from the very earliest days of there being schools in this country at all. In the last hundred years, and well within the history of universal compulsory education, drama has been able to claim significant ground for itself under certain conditions. Sometimes an exceptional teacher has made and held space for the subject to flourish (at primary and secondary level), or at other times an arts-inclined Chief Education Officer has seen to it that the subject gained support across a county. When in the 1960s newly created comprehensive schools were set up, they welcomed teachers of a subject that appeared, in the hands of persuasive and often charismatic figures, to offer a great deal across a wide ability range. Drama seemed at times, in that period, to embody all that was valued about freedom, self-expression and improvisation with its necessary, if instantaneous, creativity.

As more than one chapter in this section makes clear, drama is not English, however, and if it once flourished in the hands of a few, at the same time it could flounder in the hands of young English teaching enthusiasts (if contemporary journal articles are any guide to what happened) who lacked knowledge of the history, purposes and essential disciplines of the art. Drama teachers were and are specialists, who know from within the body of their own practical experiences, as performers, what kinds of concentration levels are required before anything worthwhile can be created by a group. Drama teachers know how the kind of trust and mutual respect demanded of a collaborative art form cannot happen instantly. This experience is inevitably reflected in their teaching.

On balance, though, English teachers have a fair recent history, many of them, of wishing to exploit to its best advantage, and through practical methods, the drama inherent in the literature they teach. Also important to many of them are the raised levels of concentration that deliberate or rehearsed movements can give rise to, and the development, if all goes according to plan, of good speech and listening. Drama can help greatly in allowing some pupils – the more reticent – to find a voice, and to discover, that in role they have things to say which, in other circumstances, under habitual social constraints, they would never be able to say. Participating fully in even the most disciplined drama can give rise to freedom of expression indeed, but a freedom grounded in the clear, right and confident occupation of your own space, confirmed by a complex of skills which include listening, speaking in turn, looking at and moving in tune with others.

Drama is a difficult subject to learn about from the page. As with philosophy, you do not know what it is to do drama until you have done some. It is hard to describe from an anterior or external view, but the history of English teaching is full of anecdotes of beginners daring a path with a class and exciting admiration for their success. If you want to re-enact, with your ninth-years, the murder of Julius Caesar in the Capitol, then you'll need to prepare with a good deal more than a general warning not to hurt the victim as you take the group down to the drama studio or specialist room. As is made clear in what follows, you cannot force a pupil to perform; that is simply impossible, but what the English teacher can do is use time and the routine orderliness of the English lesson to build confidence in all members of the class that they will, none of them, be made fools of if they do perform.

You may do well to begin in Year 7, with controlled and limited performances of well-selected extracts, such as poems with dialogue in them, like 'The Owl and the Pussycat'. There are parts for only four voices in this poem – the three characters and the narrator – but four is a good number for small group rehearsals, and although the Piggy has only two words to say, there could surely be much humour extracted from the way he or she says them, and from the way in which the words are introduced within the performance. Not all the narration, by the way, has to be left to a single voice. The Pig could share the storytelling. If Owl and Pussycat hit it off, dramatically, by the time they are 12, then they could surely be doing justice to Lysander and Hermia by the time they are 15.

In what follows, especially in Chapter 19, 'Teaching Practical Drama', we both outline the absolute need for caution in the early steps and at the same time describe plausible safe strategies that work towards the right kind of disciplined practice and concentration. The advice about watching a specialist at work and contributing to the teaching at first in limited ways will enable the growth of insight about the subject drama in an English teacher keen to see how it can enrich, deepen and extend what he or she wants to achieve in any case.

Drama improves the quality of learning in English, but part of the content of English – the plays that are central to the literature to be learned – stands greatly to enrich the quality of drama. This is most commonly apparent with Shakespeare. Good teachers of English know their Shakespeare well in any number of different ways, but not least they know, from seeing them variously performed, how differently the plays may be interpreted. What they can understand from those productions is that any slant or particular interpretation may work well providing that certain beliefs and practices are common to them. For example, actors, directors and everyone else will move or sway the audience or make them laugh if the raw material – the script – is treated as if it could all make sense and register significantly with them. That kind of conviction about the plays and their value is what the pupils need to experience. They may start by mass group work under teacher direction – chanting the Prologue to *Romeo and Juliet*, or swaying into (or being) the storm that wrecks the boat that starts *The Tempest* and they may progress from the large choric group to dialogues or improvisations in small groups, but the constant unchanging aim of the teacher will be to have the individuals discover from within how powerful the play is.

To say what has just been said is to do no more than paraphrase the ideas of Rex Gibson. Gibson's Gulbenkian 'Shakespeare and Schools Project' (Brindley, 1994: 140) at the Cambridge Institute of Education has had a long term effect on the practice of English teachers. The drama which Gibson put into or back into Shakespeare study in school was realised at a key historical moment – namely the beginning of the National Curriculum in English. At the point when the politicians were insisting on there being more Shakespeare, in effect, across the English curriculum, so Gibson insisted that that Shakespeare should be true, in its teaching, to its form. He did this having shown what his approaches could achieve, and having gained the confidence of Professor Brian Cox, chair of the first English NC Committee.

Such projects as Gibson's have now been followed up by others on how drama could improve English, or on how English could strengthen drama with, say, advice on written assignments at GCSE, examples of which are given in Chapter 21, 'Teaching drama for GCSE'. Looked at together, these two subjects have a natural dialogic relationship: learning may be begun, enthusiastically and with personal commitment, through action and movement; it may be refined and deepened by writing, by reflection and the opportunity that writing alone gives, as a form of language, for the exploration of alternative ideas and the placing and critical understanding of one set of experiences in the context of a considered wider set. We remain hopeful, not just that these chapters will help beginner English teachers to see how to take some productive first steps into drama teaching, but to see also that the two subjects could well, if related to one another properly, combine in helping school pupils and students achieve a better understanding of the word and better power with words, in school and out.

REFERENCES

Brindley, S. (ed.) (1994) *Teaching English in the Secondary School*. London: Routledge

chapter 19

TEACHING PRACTICAL DRAMA

By the end of this chapter you will have gained an understanding of the place of drama in both the English and Arts curriculum and considered ways of structuring drama lessons to incorporate a variety of techniques and conventions in your classroom.

RATIONALE

Classroom drama is a vast subject. It differs from theatre in that the class is communally involved in creating the drama together. They are participants in it rather than observers. There will, of course, be times when pupils will watch the work of others as an audience, but this will usually be in a far less formal setting and will be a sharing of 'performances' where the watchers will in turn be watched themselves. Classroom drama does however use and adapt many of the techniques used by actors as they explore and rehearse plays for performance, for example conventions such as hot-seating and improvisation.

It would, of course, be neither possible nor appropriate to attempt to cover the entire discipline within these few chapters. Drama is very specialist and many teachers have trained specifically to teach this alone, having first studied the subject for three years at university. However, the reality is that since the relatively recent inclusion of drama within the National Curriculum for English, a vast amount of drama teaching is now done by teachers who are English, rather than drama, specialists. It is therefore the responsibility of English teachers to ensure that they begin their careers with at least the basic tools necessary to explore the subject in a practical way with their pupils.

Since student teachers will initially be expected to concentrate on teaching drama within English the emphasis of the chapter will be on acquiring the strategies and conventions to enable you to develop your practice beyond the model of 'getting into groups to make up a play' and connecting practical drama work with reading and writing. The chapter makes the assumption that student teachers' previous knowledge of classroom drama is minimal, but will allow for those with more experience to develop their practice accordingly. Consideration will be given to making the drama classroom a safe place for both teachers and pupils to explore the art form and take risks, i.e. that the teacher is still able to manage the class effectively and that pupils feel able to express themselves without feeling exposed or threatened. The range of drama teaching that is taking place in schools, as a part of the National Curriculum for English and as a subject in its own right, will also be explored.

LINKS WITH THE NATIONAL CURRICULUM

There is no National Curriculum for Drama, as such, but the subject currently has a higher prominence within National Curriculum English than ever before. Whilst this is positive and to be welcomed there is a danger that the description given to drama activities in the National Curriculum could suggest that the subject can be taught without any specialist training and is simply a part of English. This is not the case if drama lessons are to provide meaningful learning experiences for pupils. There is a concern that there may be a return to groups making up plays and performing them, without any real understanding of the art form, thereby threatening the future of properly trained drama specialists. English teachers may not, other things being equal, become drama specialists overnight, but many have proved quick to understand something about the art form, especially since some have studied it, and about its positive contribution to the quality of engagement with texts in English lessons.

The National Curriculum document requires pupils 'to participate in a range of drama activities and to evaluate their own and others' contributions'. It states, 'they should be taught to use a variety of dramatic techniques to: explore ideas, issues, texts and meanings' and to 'evaluate critically performances of dramas that they have watched or in which they have taken part' (DfEE, 1999). Whilst this can include a formal presentation of a group play, the chapter will also consider ways of enabling teachers and pupils to evaluate their work from within the drama process. For example a teacher may assess the pupils' ability to question appropriately and stay in role during a hot-seating session or pupils may assess their own or a partner's role work in an improvisation that was not shown to the class.

The chapter will consider ways in which the drama process can deepen and expand pupils' experience of language, which in turn feeds into both reading and writing in English. Neelands states,

The language experience offered in the classroom is usually restricted to teacher–pupil and pupil–pupil talk related to the classroom situation, unless the teacher decides to provide alternative language experiences by transforming the classroom situation into a different one through the use of drama. (In Brindley, 1994: 203)

This change in language use will inevitably affect other areas of the English curriculum, in addition to the drama work, i.e. pupils may be better able to write a journal entry or a report as if they were a different person if they have had experience of thinking and talking in role first.

A list of suggested further reading, directly linked to the following activities, can be found at the end of the chapter.

Activity 1

YOUR OWN EXPERIENCES OF DRAMA
(suggested time: 15 minutes)

Begin by considering your own knowledge of classroom drama before you undertake the drama units in this chapter. Think about and write down some of your experiences in drama from school, university and/or participating in any productions. Write down what you think happens in a drama lesson (as part of English or otherwise). Keep a record of this in your English portfolio and compare it to your Subject Knowledge Audit on Drama (see Introduction, p. 5).

Activity 2

OBSERVING DRAMA LESSONS
(suggested time: 90 minutes in post-observation reflections and note-making)

Watch several drama lessons in your school, preferably taught by different teachers. At least one of these teachers needs to be a qualified, recognised drama specialist. If your school does not have such a teacher you may wish to consider finding another school that does, if this is possible, simply for the purpose of completing some of the activities in this chapter, and in some of the following ones. You will need to use these observations for Activities 3, 4 and 5, so read ahead before doing them.

Use some or all of the following pointers to structure your observations if you wish. You may also add anything else you think is relevant.

- How was the studio/classroom arranged? (Was this done in advance by the teacher or were the pupils organised to rearrange the space?)
- How did the lesson begin?
- Was there any kind of warm-up activity?

- Was anything used as a stimulus for the drama, i.e. a piece of text or a prop?
- Was any lighting or sound used in the lesson?
- What drama conventions and techniques were used?
- How were students grouped to work in the lesson?
- How did the pupils respond to the work and was there any undesirable behaviour?
- Were any other resources used in the lesson? If so, what and how?
- What kinds of questioning did the teacher use?
- How did the lesson end?

Standards addressed:
3.3.1, 3.3.3, 3.3.7, 3.3.9

How were the lessons you observed similar to or different from the ideas you wrote down in Activity 1? Record your thoughts and include them in your English Portfolio.

Activity 3

DIFFERENT DRAMA CURRICULA
(suggested time: 20 minutes plus interviewing time)

Fleming and Stevens (1998: 136) state:

> *The inclusion of drama in the National Curriculum for English is something of a mixed blessing. It does ensure that some participation in drama is now every pupil's entitlement; and in many schools it continues to flourish as a separate subject and is popular at GCSE and 'A' level. In other schools, however, drama has ceased to be taught as a specialism and is subsumed under English.*

Consequently drama teaching varies enormously from school to school.

Neelands (1998) outlines three different types of drama curriculum, all of which are possible in a climate where schools are fairly free to design their own. He defines these as 'Drama as personal and social education', 'Drama as English' and 'Drama as subject'. In the first of these, 'drama is valued for the contribution it makes to the personal, social and moral education of the students as well as for being an immediate and practical forum for creativity' (p. 6). Little is offered at exam level. In the second model, drama is linked closely to the guidelines for National Curriculum English for KS3, in terms of both structure and assessment and is taught within English lessons by English teachers. In the third model, 'drama is taught by specialist teachers and the curriculum at KS3 is seen as preparation for the GCSE course' (p. 7). Neelands believes that all of these models have weaknesses and that none is ideal. He goes on to propose a new model for a drama curriculum at KS3 which draws on the best of these traditions.

John Moss states (Davison and Dowson, 1998: 201), 'Before you begin to teach drama in a placement school, it is very important for you to establish what kind of rationale underpins its drama teaching, and *how this will have influenced pupil expectations and perceptions of drama work*' (my italics). This is important, even if you only ever teach drama within English, because it will have a bearing on how pupils are likely to respond to the work and how you will need to plan.

Refer back to your lesson observations from Activity 2. Use the following questions to help discuss the lessons with the teachers involved. Make some notes about your discussions in your English portfolio. Does your school resemble any of Neelands's curriculum models outlined above?

- Is drama taught as a separate subject or within the English curriculum?
- How much of the timetable is allocated to drama?
- What are the school's schemes of work for drama at KS3 and 4 and how does the lesson fit into these schemes?
- What drama is offered at exam level, if any?
- What resources are available for teaching drama and do all pupils get access to these?
- What drama activities happen in the school outside of lessons? Is there a school production, for example, and who gets involved in it?

Standards addressed:
2.1.c, 2.1.d,
2.2, 2.3

Activity 4

CREATING AN ENVIRONMENT FOR EFFECTIVE DRAMA TEACHING
(suggested time: 20 minutes)

Drama differs from other subjects in that it is very difficult, nigh on impossible, to force students to do drama, and particularly to perform. It is altogether more exposing than writing or completing a worksheet. Neelands (1998: 55) states:

> *There has to be an agreement to do drama. This agreement is easier to make if there is a visible and negotiable framework of ground rules, codes of conduct and behavioural objectives. The framework serves the same purpose as the rules of a game. The 'players' know that the rules of the 'game' provide a safe and fair means of becoming involved. Knowing what to expect from others and what is expected of you gives confidence, security and protection. Knowing what the rules are and what happens if you, or others, 'cheat' removes the fear of getting it wrong.*

Standards addressed:
3.3.1, 3.3.8,
3.3.9

Use your lesson observations from Activity 2 to consider how different teachers created an environment for effective drama teaching in which pupils felt safe to take risks. How did pupils enter the room and was there a common routine or structure to signal the start of lessons? Did you notice any negotiated rules posted up in the drama space? What sanctions did teachers use to deal with any undesirable behaviour? Record your comments in your English portfolio.

Activity 5

DRAMA CONVENTIONS AND TECHNIQUES
(suggested time: 20 minutes)

The following are examples of three popular drama conventions and techniques:

Hot-seating

Someone in the group, a pupil or teacher or classroom assistant, takes on the role of a character in the drama and is questioned by the rest of the group. The class may ask questions as themselves or may also be in role, for example they might be social workers questioning a child. Hot-seating is a popular rehearsal technique used by actors.

Teacher in role

The teacher may simply take on a role alongside the pupils in order to join in with creating the drama. They may also take on a role of their own which is different to the class and which the class may respond to either in role, or as themselves. This could be the case in the hot-seating convention outlined above. Sometimes it may be better for a teacher to take on a role, rather than a pupil, if the role is particularly emotional or controversial.

Thought tracking

A character's thoughts are spoken aloud by the person playing the role, or by others. This can be a useful convention for developing a still image or for freezing an improvised scene to find out more about the characters in it.

There are *many* others including **conscience alley**, **forum theatre**, **iceberg** and **mantle of the expert**.

What different conventions and techniques did you see employed in your lesson observations from Activity 2? Make a list of all those you saw, including a brief note on the context in which the convention was used and how the pupils responded to the work. Your list may or may not include the examples given above.

Add to this list any other drama conventions you may know about or have seen in the past. As your course continues include any others that you read about or see taught. This will serve as a useful resource for your drama teaching in the future.

Standard addressed: 2.1

If you are a complete beginner, or have very little previous knowledge of drama teaching, it may be advisable to research some drama conventions and techniques *before* beginning this activity. Some useful starting points are listed in the suggested reading section at the end of this chapter.

Activity 6

DRAMA AND KS3 ENGLISH
(suggested time: 30 minutes plus teaching time)

Look again at your list of drama conventions from Activity 5. Make a list of those drama activities you would feel happy to undertake with a KS3 English class on a class reader or poem. These may be short tasks where the usual classroom layout remains unchanged (e.g. working in groups to make iceberg diagrams on the central character in a novel) or longer activities in a proper drama space (e.g. preparing a sequence of still images to be performed while a poem is narrated by the teacher). 'Iceberg diagrams' may be defined in this way. Everything that we know about a character (could be an improvised role in a drama or a central role in a novel or play) is written in the top part of the iceberg outline, above the water line. Everything we think we know about the character ('guesses' from the way they are behaving or hints about them in the text) is written in the bottom part of the diagram, below the water line. It's a good way for students to understand text and subtext. Lower ability students could stick teacher-prepared statements about characters on to the diagram.

Think carefully about what you hope the pupils might learn about the art form of drama as well as their text. For example, in the sequence of still images suggested above, you might hope that the pupils will learn something about how characters might be positioned in order to demonstrate something about their relationship with each other. This understanding and use of the art form might then in turn illustrate something about the contents of the poem that stand to be revealed through this kind of interpretation. Form and content used together add another dimension to the meaning.

Try out one or more of these activities in a school, either as a whole or part of a lesson. Include your list in your English portfolio, together with an evaluation of the activity (or activities) you tried out.

One student teacher, Paul Dulley, observed the following lesson at his girls' comprehensive school:

> 'In each lesson, there was a mixture of small-group drama and whole group drama, the small-group work being sandwiched between a whole class activity and the final presentations. One year eight lesson, for example, began with a discussion upon the relation between body language and power. By selecting volunteer pairs to address one another with one standing up and the other crouching down, the teacher questioned the class about their perceived power relationship. In order to emphasise that this body language can override even physical size and age differences, she became the 'weak' partner in one of the demonstrations, asking the whole group "Who has the power now?" The point established, the teacher then arranged pupils into groups of four and asked them to construct a tableau in which one character was being bullied by another. This exercise was followed by one in which a freeze-frame was created showing the bully being reprimanded by one of the victim's friends. In both exercises, the teacher encouraged pupils to use a variation of Neelands' space between technique (Neelands, 1998) in order to demonstrate power relationships. As a final elaboration, the pupils not otherwise involved in each scene were asked to create a soundtrack involving sound effects and character thoughts.'

Standard addressed: 2.1c

Activity 7

FACILITATING THE WRITING PROCESS
(suggested time: 30 minutes plus teaching time)

Neelands states, 'Just as working in drama can help students to turn abstract ideas and written language into concrete and living representations, so it can also help students to translate lived experiences into a wide variety of written representations' (Neelands, 1988: 32). For example the use of the hot-seating convention to explore a central character in a novel would help pupils across the ability range. Those who find writing difficult will have the character fleshed out by asking questions and listening to responses, and will consequently have more to draw on in their written work. A more able or articulate pupil may be able to take on the role themselves and to develop and extend their understanding of the character through having to think of and provide answers to questions. This in turn will improve the quality of a written response later.

Write down some situations in which you might be able to use a dramatic context, no matter how simple, to facilitate writing with your pupils. For example the teacher (in role) narrates the introduction of a story about a group of Year 8 pupils who are to be confined in a school because of the leak of dangerous bacteria from a nearby hospital. The pupils, also in role, write letters home requesting supplies.

Standards addressed: 2.1.c, 3.3.2.c

Expand one of the situations that you have written down and break it up into specific activities. Teach one or more of the activities in school. Include a brief evaluation (a paragraph or two) of the work, together with your original list of situations, in your English portfolio.

Activity 8

IMPROVISATION
(suggested time: 30 minutes)

Write down what you understand by the term 'improvisation'. How have you seen improvisation used by other teachers in both English and drama lessons? What areas/types of improvisation would you feel confident about tackling at this point in your training?

In what contexts might you consider using improvisation in the classroom? (i.e. a pair's improvisation between a police officer and a shoplifter, not necessarily performed to the class, could lead to writing a police incident report in role.)

A student teacher, Paul Dulley, made the following observations in response to the above task:

'Spontaneous improvisation is drama work in which there is little previous preparation time for actors – perhaps only enough to establish a general idea of location, characters and the order of arrival. In contrast, prepared improvisation often extends over several lessons and utilises several techniques such as research, discussion and even spontaneous improvisation to allow pupils to gradually bring an idea of location, story and character into focus. Of course with such extended work, the teacher needs to tread a fine line between giving pupils the freedom to explore and dictating form so rigidly that the class gets bored. In my own teaching, I would be reluctant to use any form of improvisation with a *new* class as I feel that it is a technique that is much less 'safe' for individuals than, say, tableau. I would find it necessary to ascertain the character of a particular class before deciding whether improvisation is a suitable tool for them. If there are less confident individuals in the group then improvisation could make drama a source of embarrassment and dread for them, leading to their effective exclusion from the learning activities. Conversely, if a class is confident and/or experienced in drama, then improvisation is an ideal tool with which to allow pupils to create 'consensual drama', constructing scene, characters and plot as a true group.'

Standards addressed:
3.3.2.c, 3.3.3   Write your answers in your English portfolio.

Activity 9

ASSESSING DRAMA
(suggested time: 1 hour)

Find out how drama is assessed in your placement school. In a school where the KS3 curriculum is a watered-down, but more appropriate version of GCSE, this may include areas such as *'pupils' ability to use exploratory techniques'* i.e. hot-seating, *'use of the art form'* i.e. creating tension in improvisation, *'evaluation'* and *'social development'*.

Email your findings to other modular students and compare them with the assessment procedures for drama that are used in their schools. Are there any common areas?

How could you use these assessment models to help you with assessing the drama element within KS3 and 4 English? What other areas of the English curriculum could also be assessed alongside this to record what children are learning? (For example a journal entry, written in role, could be used to assess pupils' ability to use 'varied linguistic and literary techniques' (DfEE, 1999: 37) as well as their ability to understand the character of the drama.)

Standards addressed:
3.2.1, 3.2.2, 3.2.3

Activity 10

PLANNING AND TEACHING A WHOLE DRAMA LESSON
(suggested time: 1 hour plus teaching time)

Using what you have learned in Activities 1–9, now plan a whole drama lesson, as part of either the English or the drama curriculum. Plan according to your own

Standards addressed: 3.1.2, 3.3.3, 3.3.7

ability/confidence in using drama conventions, remembering the rationale for drama at the school and how your pupils will be likely to respond. If the lesson is part of a scheme of work, explain how it fits into the whole. Teach and evaluate your lesson and include this with your plan in your English portfolio.

Scenarios

I   Your Year 8 English class are nervous about doing drama. A few pupils tend to show off and make the others feel embarrassed. What strategies could you employ to overcome these problems and provide a safe environment, whilst using drama to develop pupils' reading and writing skills?

2   Imagine you will be teaching drama to a mixed ability Year 7 class who are new to the school. What sort of activities would you want to include in the first few lessons in order to introduce them to drama as a subject (i.e. *not* as part of the English timetable)?

CONTINUOUS THREADS

1 Professional values and practice

In the same way as a teacher needs to choose reading materials that do not represent limited aspects of society, so a drama teacher needs to ensure that topics or stimuli used in lessons are not restricted by the characters or issues involved. Since pupils will frequently respond to drama work with ideas of their own the teacher needs to be aware that they themselves may be restrictive in which aspects of society are represented. It is the teacher's job to fill in the gaps and introduce characters or situations that will truly extend pupils' thinking. For example, in a drama about racism, pupils in a GCSE class might prefer to represent roles which were anti-racist (in spite of the fact that some may privately harbour racist views). It would be the teacher's job to find a way to introduce an actual racist view into the drama (although this may seem controversial) that would enter into dialogue with the pupils' roles and so genuinely develop the understanding of the class because they would need to argue against it.

Standards addressed: 1.1, 1.2, 1.3, 1.5, 1.7

3.1 Planning, expectations and targets

Drama allows for a variety of conventions to be incorporated in both schemes of work and individual lessons. This means that it is possible to ensure that work is suitable and appropriate for all pupils.

Consider using any support staff you may have in your lesson to take on roles, particularly for activities such as hot-seating. You will obviously need to plan any such work carefully and communicate it to the staff concerned in advance of the lesson.

Standards addressed: 3.1.1, 3.1.4

Progression in drama works best using a spiral curriculum, i.e. the pupils look at one area of the subject, such as role work, and return to it as they move up the school. In this way their understanding and ability deepen as they also bring their experience of other areas of the curriculum to their work.

3.2 Monitoring and assessment

Assessment is covered in Activity 9 of this chapter.

You will need to consider, however, how to actually organise your class in order to assess pupils' drama work, particularly if you are looking at the process rather than the finished product. The fact is that you cannot assess everybody at the same time. It is a good idea to keep a notebook or register handy in all lessons so that you can make a note of any individual's work as you go along. You will usually only give one assessment mark per scheme of work or half term, for each pupil, and by making relevant notes on different pupils each week you should be able to cover everybody over a few weeks. If you are planning to mark everyone in one lesson you may need to consider using a video or tape recorder so that you can look back after the session. Drama assessment, like speaking and listening, is something that gets easier with experience of both teaching and the curriculum.

Standards addressed: 3.2.1, 3.2.2, 3.2.3, 3.2.4, 3.2.6

Don't forget that a self-assessment sheet for pupils to fill in after a unit of work is extremely useful in supporting your own marking. They will usually be harder on themselves than you will be on them.

3.3 Teaching and class management

It is particularly important in drama lessons to have a routine and structure to start the lesson and this ideally needs to be one that is a recognised start to any other one in the school, i.e. lining up outside the classroom until told to enter or sitting in a circle without talking while the register is taken. This will be a sign to the pupils that it is a proper lesson even if other classroom routines are altered.

There are other safety issues to consider in drama lessons in addition to those of any other lesson. Pupils will be moving about and using the classroom in a different way to other subjects. It is important that pupils have a designated place to put bags and coats in the drama studio, so that they will be out of the way, and that the teacher establishes rules and routines for moving chairs and other furniture, etc. It is a good idea to establish a signal which means 'stop talking and listen' since there is likely to be more noise generated in the drama classroom than in many other subjects. Some teachers stand still with one arm in the air, others have resorted to whistles! Either is better than shouting.

Standards addressed: 3.3.1, 3.3.3, 3.3.8

Of course, if drama is a low-key part of an English lesson in a classroom much of the above will not be relevant and teachers will find themselves using the part of organisation that might be employed for other group work or a speaking and listening activity.

3.3.4 Differentiation

Drama is an excellent leveller. Pupils who otherwise are low achievers in the school frequently excel at drama, and the opposite is also possible. It is not unusual to be handed a pile of Individual Education Plans (IEPs) for a group of pupils, only to be surprised that they have special needs at all. However, you do need to make it your business to find out which pupils have behavioural special needs. You may need to decide where to seat them or consider groupings if the class are to be involved in activities where safety might otherwise be an issue.

More often than not drama is taught in a genuinely mixed ability class. It will sometimes be necessary and possible to differentiate according to task. For example, specific roles could be allocated to particular pupils according to their ability, if this was appropriate.

An early lesson for Year 7 pupils is that, in representing a role, the most important thing is to play the attitude of that person and not try to be them completely. (This is something that might be achieved by a gifted A Level student!) Consequently it is quite acceptable for boys to play female roles and vice versa. From a gender perspective, the sooner this is accepted by pupils, without inhibition, the better.

Standards addressed: 3.3.4, 3.3.5, 3.3.6

Some schools with a high proportion of EAL speakers allow pupils to work on improvisation, in pairs or small groups, using their first language. This can have a positive effect in the classroom and allow some pupils to express themselves more confidently. Any presentations can be interpreted or followed up with an explanation, if necessary, but quite often pupils may just need to report back in English.

2.5 ICT

There are opportunities to use computers in a drama situation to present stimuli (perhaps pupils may be given different information on the screen that can be pieced together during the course of the drama) or for pupils to record their progress or outcomes.

Consider as well how you might be able to use audio and video resources in your lessons, either to introduce stimuli (i.e. the recorded log after a spaceship has crashed) or again for students to record their work.

Jonothan Neelands has published *Drama and IT* (available through NATE) which is a compilation of different projects using ICT and drama. This is definitely worth looking at.

Further ideas

Watch as much good drama teaching as you can as an ongoing project. If you see good practice, email your observations to other modular students.

Find out about other drama courses or conferences and attend workshops. Begin by referring to NATE, NATD (National Association for the Teaching of Drama) and National Dram.

Watch videos of Dorothy Heathcote teaching (see Johnson and O'Neill, 1991). Good for whole class improvisation and the theory behind conventions.

Team-teach drama lessons with an experienced teacher. This will allow you to try out conventions such as teacher in role more safely.

Look up Ken Taylor's website (**www.kentaylor.co.uk**) for excellent links to other sites on drama and education.

FURTHER READING

For models of classroom drama and drama curricula see:
Fleming and Stevens (1998: 134–7)
Neelands (1998: 6–21 and 71–92)

For ideas on protecting students into taking risks in drama see:
Davison and Dowson (1998: 202–5)
Neelands (1998: 55–8)

For drama conventions and techniques see:
Fleming and Stevens (1998: 137–45)
Neelands (1998: 93–8)
Johnson and O'Neill (1991: 160–9)
Jonothan Neelands (ed.) (2000) *Structuring Drama Work*. London: Cambridge University Press

For drama and writing see:
Brindley (1994: 202–9)
Neelands (1998: 32–4)

For improvisation see:
Davison and Dowson (1998: 209–12)

For assessment see:
Neelands (1998: 22–7)
Bolton (1992)
Byron (1986)
NATE (1993)
O'Neill (1977)

REFERENCES

Bolton, G. (1992) *New Perspectives on Classroom Drama*. New York: Simon and Schuster

Brindley, S. (ed.) (1994) *Teaching English in the Secondary School*. London: Routledge

Byron, K. (1986) *Drama in the English Classroom*. London: Methuen

Davison, J. and Dowson, J. (1998) *Learning to Teach English in the Secondary School: A Companion to School Experience*. London: Routledge

DfEE (1999) *The National Curriculum for England. English: Key stages 1–4*. London: DfEE and QCA

Fleming, M. and Stevens, D. (1998) *English Teaching in the Secondary School*. London: David Fulton

Johnson, L. and O'Neill, C. (1991) (eds) *Dorothy Heathcote: Collected Writings on Education and Drama*. Evanston, IL: Northwestern University Press

NATE (1993) *Move Back the Desks*. Sheffield: NATE

Neelands, J. (1998) *Beginning Drama. 11–14*. London: David Fulton

O'Neill, C. (1977) *Drama Guidelines*. London: Heinemann

chapter 20

TEACHING DRAMATIC TEXTS

By the end of this chapter you will have considered different ways of using and teaching dramatic texts within both the English and drama classroom. You will have gained a deeper understanding of the relationship between an active teaching approach and the production of written work on dramatic texts.

RATIONALE

Neelands (1998: 8) states that 'students' "making" is dependant on knowing how to make'. The study of dramatic texts, with their narrative structures, portrayal of characters and treatment of themes, is invaluable in developing students' skills in knowing how to make a play.

Unlike a novel, a dramatic text presents the reader with not much more than dialogue. There is little in the way of action since the playwright assumes this will be provided by the actors when the play is realised in performance. When pupils read a dramatic text it is difficult for them to imagine how the play might look in performance and the role of the teacher becomes something akin to that of a theatre director. Many of the drama conventions and techniques which are adapted from the theatre and which were explored in the previous chapter can be applied to the teaching of dramatic texts. This enables students to fill in missing scenes and to consider characters and their relationships with each other more fully in the same way as an actor might in rehearsal.

The focus of the chapter will be on how to use and teach texts to a range of age groups and abilities at Key Stages 3 and 4 and on the link between practical drama and written work. Particular consideration will also be given to Shakespeare for SATs and GCSE English and to dramatic texts appropriate for teenagers.

LINKS WITH THE NATIONAL CURRICULUM

The National Curriculum document states that 'pupils should be taught to: appreciate how the structure and organisation of scenes and plays contribute to dramatic effect' and that drama activities 'should include: devising, scripting and performing in plays' (DfEE, 1999: 32). It is essential that in order to understand something of the structure and organisation of a play, pupils will need to study existing texts, as well as participate in making their own. The National Curriculum lists in its range of recommended literature 'two plays by Shakespeare . . . drama by major playwrights, recent and contemporary drama written for young people and adults . . . and drama by major writers from different cultures and traditions' (DfEE, 1999: 35–6). The chapter will look at active approaches to teaching this range.

Activity 1   ACTIVE APPROACHES TO DRAMA TEACHING
(suggested time: 30 minutes, following any observations)

Observe a variety of lessons where a dramatic text is being taught, either in an English or a drama context. These may include some of the observations undertaken in Chapter 19, 'Teaching Practical Drama' if these are relevant.

Refer back to the activities on drama techniques and conventions in the previous chapter. What active approaches have you observed teachers using in these lessons? Record your observations in your English portfolio.

Activity 2   CONTEXTS FOR USING DRAMA TEXTS FOR KS3 DRAMA, ENGLISH AND KS4 ENGLISH
(suggested time: 30–40 minutes)

Drama texts can be used in a number of ways and for a variety of reasons in the classroom. Pupils may be required to study a play as part of their English GCSE or you may simply wish to use the storyline from a play as a stimulus for a KS3 lesson.

Make a list of the contexts in which you think you could use a dramatic text in your teaching. Use the headings KS3 drama, KS3 English and KS4 English to help you. A 'text' need not necessarily be the whole text; you may just use an excerpt or another aspect of a play. For example, Ben Jonson's cast lists for his plays offer names which could be used to explore stereotypes with a KS3 class who would find the actual text much too difficult. It is perfectly legitimate to narrate large amounts of a play and then ask pupils to improvise around the storyline of a key scene. You may then decide to read the original as a comparison.

As an example, a student teacher, Paul Dulley put forward the following:

'Ideas for using *Our Day Out* in the following contexts (for each type of lesson, I have included work that explores character, context and dramatic language):

KS3 English	KS3 drama	KS4 English
Referring to the play script, pupils write a prose account of the children's return to inner-city Liverpool on the coach.	Pupils act as a board of school governors, hot-seating the characters of Briggs and Mrs Kay about events on the trip before deciding who to dismiss.	Contrasting *Our Day Out* with video excerpts from *Scully* and *The 51st State*: how and why is the presentation of Liverpool similar in these pieces? How does it differ? (era, genre, writer's perspective, etc.)
Pupils write a letter to Briggs from Carol in which she explains her feelings about school and her teachers.	Pupils improvise scenes involving the characters from *Our Day Out* in their everyday lives, i.e. before or after the play's events.	Pupils write an extra scene for the play in which Mrs. Kay and Briggs discuss the trip the day after they return.
Pupils do project work on the areas of Liverpool and Conwy in Wales. This can include writing in role as local people from these places.	Using the playscript, groups of pupils must compile director's notes for the first scene in the play. These should give details of costume, sound effects, set design and props.	Pupils are given photocopies of certain scenes from the play with the task of adding a 'subtext' to the dialogue of each character.

Standards addressed:
3.3.2c, 3.3.2d

Activity 3

DRAMA TEXTS FOR TEENAGERS

(suggested time: 1 hour plus reading time)

Research some drama texts which are suitable for teenagers. Some examples of such texts appear at the end of this unit under 'Further ideas' and 'Further reading'. Choose one play that you particularly like and would like to work with. Write a summary of the play and email it to other modular students. Perhaps also include any other good recommendations.

Standard addressed: 2.1

Activity 4

USING DRAMA CONVENTIONS AND TECHNIQUES TO TEACH DRAMA TEXTS

(suggested time: 30 minutes)

Consider again the drama conventions and techniques studied in Chapter 19, 'Teaching Practical Drama'. Think of as many different ways as you can to use the drama text chosen in the previous activity. This may vary from formally rehearsing and performing a scene, to selecting a key moment in the play to make into a still photograph with headlines, to hot-seating characters. Record your ideas under the following headings: KS3 drama, KS3 English and KS4 English. Keep the lists in your English portfolio.

Paul Dulley chose *The Granny Project* for Activity 3 above, with the resulting ideas for using different conventions and techniques:

KS3 English	KS3 drama	KS4 English
Pupils research proverbs (perhaps also some Russian ones) using them as headings for different sections of the play.	Alter ego/hot-seating: one student plays the 'public' Granny, the other gives voice to her real feelings during a hot-seating session.	Students to create 'flashback' scenes illustrating Granny in her youth that are to be juxtaposed with those depicting her treatment in old age.
Pupils create iceberg diagrams of the primary characters in the play.	(Cross-curricular opportunity: history) What would it be like to come to Britain from a Communist country in the 1980s? Pupils to plan circular dramas in which Natasha has her first experiences of the country.	Students are presented with a scenario in which Granny leaves a large sum of money but no will. How should the money be spent? A family meeting could be improvised.
With reference to the text, pupils must create a list of three props to be allocated to each character in a production of *The Granny Project*. The props should enable an audience to infer important facts about each character.	The scene in which the children interrupt their parents' dinner party is performed twice; each time the narrator puts a different 'spin' on the events.	Students arrange characters so that the physical space between them is indicative of their emotional differences. They can explore how this distance evolves over time.

Standard addressed: 2.1

Activity 5

TRYING OUT ONE OF THE ACTIVITIES IN THE CLASSROOM

(suggested time: 20 minutes plus teaching time)

Which of the activities outlined above would you feel most confident about teaching at this stage in your training? Select one activity and try it out in school, either as

Standard
addressed:
3.3.3

part of, or as a whole, lesson. Link this to Activity 6 if you wish. You may have to consider issues such as availability of texts, if appropriate, when you make your choice. Evaluate for your portfolio.

Activity 6

LEAD INTO WRITTEN WORK
(suggested time: 20 minutes plus teaching time)

Look back over Activity 8 from 'Teaching Practical Drama' to remind yourself about using drama to generate writing activities. Now take your lists of ideas for using your chosen drama text (Activity 4). Which of these tasks could lead into written work? It might be a simple homework, writing in role after a drama lesson or a more formal piece of coursework for GCSE English. Written work could be undertaken by individual pupils: for example letter writing; or in pairs and groups, for example putting together a programme for a performance of a play. Also consider activities which might enable pupils to use ICT in response to the drama work.

Standards
addressed:
3.3.3, 3.3.10

Select an activity and teach it. Evaluate your work and include some examples of the written work produced by pupils in your portfolio.

Activity 7

SHAKESPEARE AT KS3
(suggested time: 20 minutes)

Jane Dowson states that Shakespeare's 'plays are examples of good theatre and suitable for developing critical analysis of drama as a genre' (Davison and Dowson, 1998: 226). The place of dramatic texts on the curriculum as a means of teaching children about how a play is put together has already been discussed, but this, added to the fact that Shakespeare is a compulsory part of the curriculum from Year 9 up, makes a good case for introducing it earlier in KS3.

As we saw earlier in the chapter it is not necessary to study a play in its entirety for pupils to have a meaningful learning experience. In fact part of the KS3 NC test asks pupils to focus on one or two short scenes from a play for the exam. As it is often the story that is the main level of interest for pupils in the first instance, it makes sense to begin there when introducing Shakespeare. For example, groups could be given still photographs to devise from different key moments in the story which would then be used to 'illustrate' a teacher's narration to the class. You might then focus on one scene to explore in more depth, making the decision on whether or not to introduce the original text according to the ability and age of the class.

Rex Gibson states: 'Shakespeare is remarkably resilient. It has a long history of surviving all assaults, adaptations, interpretations, and can obviously take care of itself. So don't worry about fracturing the Shakespeare script' (in Brindley, 1994: 146).

Standard
addressed:
2.1.c.

Look at Chapter 22 on Shakespeare teaching to remind yourself of the requirements and issues surrounding this area of the curriculum.

Activity 8

SHAKESPEARE AT YEAR 7 OR 8
(suggested time: 40 minutes)

Choose a Shakespeare play that you know well and rewrite the story as simply as you can. Try breaking it into episodes and giving each a title.

Take an episode or section of the story that might be of interest to a Year 7 or 8 class. How might you introduce this to the pupils? Some moments may not need a complex introduction, for example the discovery of Juliet's dead body.

Standard
addressed:
2.1.c

What practical drama activities could you do using your episode? Record your storyline and your ideas in your English portfolio.

Activity 9

KS3 NC TESTS: THE WRITING PAPER
(suggested time: 20 minutes)

The sample paper (2003) for Key Stage 3 English Assessment includes a task asking pupils to write the text for a publicity booklet on a video of *Macbeth* in modern dress, which is aimed at schools.

To prepare pupils to respond to such a question, the class could work in role for a number of lessons as if they were members of a film or video company, using the convention of **mantle of the expert**. This is perhaps best done with the pupils working in small 'company' groups or small sections of one larger company. Try working in role yourself as a sponsor for them to pitch their ideas at.

'Mantle of the expert' is a phrase used by a number of writers on Drama, including Bolton (1998: 240–1). A group of pupils take on the responsibility of finding out enough about a particular activity or phenomenon (such as a tiger hunt or mountain rescue or making a film of *Macbeth*) to rehearse in role expert and authoritative positions about that activity or phenomenon. Becoming worthy of the 'expert' status results from a number of research and presentation processes, such as consulting accounts from authoritative sources found in libraries or on the Web, sketching imagined scenes, comparing previous films of the same play, seeing how to read a map, edit a text, explain a decision or argue a case. This way of working has a number of justifications, among which is developing the process of integrating knowledge, information and role-based performance. However, as the 'mantle' idea reminds us, the expertise is in role: an English GCSE group might work as a film company making a film of *Macbeth*. The pupils might plan and design costumes or special effects and might storyboard some sequences but wouldn't go as far as actually making the film, not least because their ideas will exceed their ability to execute them.

What activities might you ask the pupils to do within this 'mantle of the expert' framework? For example you might consider the use of language and whether the text should be updated or abridged, using still images and storyboarding to record key dramatic actions from the play or designing locations for filming that would create the necessary atmosphere for particular scenes. The key to this work (and to the 'Mantle of the Expert' convention) is that the pupils will never actually make the video. Their ideas will far exceed their expertise in film making, but it enables them to move away from the written word and into the action of the play.

Standard addressed: 2.1c

Record your answer in your English portfolio.

Activity 10 — KS3 NC TESTS: THE SHAKESPEARE PAPER
(suggested time: 30 minutes)

The same Key Stage 3 Assessment paper referred to in the last activity also asks students to explain how the actor playing Macbeth should show his reactions 'in Act 1, scene 7, (line 28 to end) and Act 5, scene 3'.

Get hold of the *Macbeth* scenes in question and photocopy them. Use this to make a set of director's notes for yourself. Consider where and how the actor should stand, how he might position himself in relation to other characters, how he might use movement, gesture and facial expression and what might happen to his voice. It's actually quite hard and will help you to appreciate what the Year 9 students are being asked to do. (Questions of this type are usually to be found on an A Level Theatre Studies paper!)

Standard addressed: 2.1c

Make a list of any drama conventions and techniques which might help pupils when they come to answer a question of this type.

Activity 11 — PULLING IT ALL TOGETHER – TEACHING A LESSON
(suggested time: 40 minutes plus teaching time)

Using what you have learned so far in this and the previous chapter, plan a lesson (or lessons) on a Shakespeare text for GCSE English to teach in your school. You will need to find out what specification and text are currently being taught if you do not already know. Consider the ability of your class and their previous experience of Shakespeare and drama before you plan. Some of the work should include practical

Standards addressed:
3.1.1, 3.1.2,
3.3.2.d, 3.3.3

drama but not necessarily for all of the lesson. The drama may also be fairly low key, i.e. hot-seating characters. The lesson(s) should produce or be working towards the production of a piece of written coursework.

Evaluate your work and include this with your plan in your English portfolio.

Scenarios

1   Your Year 8 English class finds reading difficult. What practical drama strategies could you employ to lure them into the study of a dramatic text?
2   Your Year 10 English class is studying a contemporary play as part of their GCSE. You would like to use active drama teaching to help them with a piece of written coursework, but want to avoid groups performing extracts. What methods might you use?

CONTINUOUS THREADS

Standards addressed:
1.1, 1.2, 1.3,
1.5, 1.7

1 Professional values and practice

The comments outlined in this section of Chapter 19, 'Teaching Practical Drama' are equally relevant to this chapter. Please refer to the comments at this point in the previous chapter.

3.1 Planning, expectations and targets

In addition to the comments in this section of Chapter 19, you will need to consider how to organise your dramatic texts, in the same way that you would for any other reading lesson. For example, will you need to give the whole play to each pupil or a group? Will you need to prepare, edit or photocopy extracts? Are there some in the class whose reading needs are such that they would benefit from a well-prepared text that coped with their particular problem? (See Chapters 5, 6 and 11 and the remarks under 'Differentiation' below.) Over a period of time you will build up resources that save you time in the long run and cope with a breadth of types of learners.

Standards addressed:
3.1.3, 3.1.5

There is plenty of opportunity to organise visits to the theatre or to invite theatre companies into school to perform set texts or other plays to pupils. In practice the latter is often easier with large groups of younger pupils.

3.2 Monitoring and assessment

Standards addressed:
3.2.1, 3.2.2,
3.2.3, 3.2.6

The issues outlined for assessing practical drama work are equally relevant to assessing work based on dramatic texts. Teachers will also need to consider the assessment and recording of reading and writing as a response to drama work. Consult the current National Curriculum documentation for assessing KS3 and 4 and also the GCSE specification that you are teaching.

3.3.4 Differentiation

In terms of the practical drama work involved in teaching a dramatic text, the comments in Chapter 19, 'Teaching Practical Drama' are relevant in differentiating the work. You will need to consider the reading ability of pupils if you are intending to present them with text in the lesson, and whether any of your pupils are learning English as an Additional Language. If you are teaching drama within an English lesson you will already be used to working with other texts with your class and will simply need to adapt the work accordingly as you would in any other reading lesson. If you are using text in a drama lesson there is more likelihood that you will have a genuinely mixed ability group. In this case you may need to consider either grouping pupils yourself so that those with weaker literacy skills can be supported by others who are more competent, or grouping pupils according to ability and presenting each group with different pieces of text. This will depend on the work you are doing and knowing what will work with your pupils.

Standards addressed:
3.3.4, 3.3.5

Since it is legitimate to introduce very small amounts of a dramatic text into a drama lesson, particularly with younger and lower ability pupils, it is easy to see how pupils' ability to read and understand a text can be developed by introducing bigger and more demanding extracts as they move up the school towards KS4 and A Level.

Further ideas

- Use the metaphor of the play being a house. Ask pupils to design the rooms in which scenes take place (not necessarily one that would be used as a performance space). They will need to think of the size of the room, what furniture or pictures might be in it and what the light is like. For example, a scene in which characters are not truthful with each other might be a room with little natural light and dark corners. This helps pupils to think about mood and atmosphere, in addition to character.
- If you think the storyline or language of a play will switch pupils off, look for an analogy and start with that: for example, *Macbeth* could be a gangster story.
- Present pupils with only one half of a dialogue i.e. Lady Macbeth in Act 1, scene 7. Pupils can improvise Macbeth's response and then compare this to the original.

Some dramatic texts suitable for teenagers include:
(Obvious classics have been omitted in favour of some contemporary, lesser known plays.)
The following are available through Heinemann:

Alan Ayckbourn, *Ernie's Incredible Illucinations*
Richard Cameron, *Handle With Care*
Michele Celeste, *Mariza's Story*
Anne Fine and Linda Le Versha, *The Granny Project*
Adrian Flynn, *Burning Everest*
Helen Forrester, *Twopence to Cross the Mersey*
Nigel Gray, *Black Harvest*

Joanna Halpert Kraus and Cecily O'Neill, *Mean to be Free*
Rob John, *Living With Lady Macbeth*
Jan Mark and Stephen Cockett, *Captain Courage and the Rose Street Gang*
Jan Needle and Vivien Gardner, *A Game of Soldiers*
Jan Needle and Vivien Gardner, *The Rebels of Gas Street*
Cecily O'Neill and Simon Adorian, *The Ratz*
Willy Russell, *Our Day Out*
Sue Sanders and Cecily O'Neill, *In Holland Stands a House*
Mark Wheeler, *Too Much Punch for Judy*; *Legal Weapon*; *Hard to Swallow*; *Why Did the Chicken Cross the Road?*

The National Theatre's *New Connections* compilations (London: Faber and Faber, 1997) are also good but may contain strong language so may not be suitable for younger pupils or acceptable to the school.

See also:

Chapman, G. *Teaching Young Playwrights*
Good on the structure of plays and helps with deconstructing texts.
Kempe, A. *The GCSE Drama Handbook*. London: Nelson Thornes
Useful activities using dramatic texts which can be lifted or adapted for KS3 drama and GCSE English.

FURTHER READING

For conventions and techniques for teaching dramatic texts see:
Davison and Dowson (1998: 212–14)
Neelands (1998: 93–8)

For teaching Shakespeare see (in addition to Chapter 22):
Fleming and Stevens (1998: 144)
Brindley (1994: Chapter 16)

REFERENCES

Bolton, G. (1998) *Acting in Classroom Drama: A Critical Analysis*. Stoke on Trent: Trentham.
Brindley, S. (ed.) (1994) *Teaching English*. London: Routledge
Davison, J. and Dowson, J. (1998) *Learning to Teach English in the Secondary School*. London: Routledge
DfEE (1999) *The National Curriculum for England. English: Key Stages 1–4*. London: DfEE and QCA.
Fleming, M. and Stevens, D. (1998) *English Teaching in the Secondary School*. London: David Fulton
Neelands, J. (1998) *Beginning Drama. 11–14*. London: David Fulton
QCA (2003) Sample English Test, Writing Paper, Key Stage 3

chapter 21

TEACHING DRAMA FOR GCSE

By the end of this chapter you will be familiar with some of the different types of syllabuses or, as they are now called, specifications being taught for GCSE Drama and the ways in which this examination is assessed.

RATIONALE

This chapter makes the assumption that the majority of English student teachers will not go on to teach drama at exam level. You do not need quite the depth of theory to teach GCSE as you would A Level, but it is not advisable to teach the course unless you are reasonably experienced and knowledgeable about the subject. It is a very different issue to teach some KS3 drama or use some drama techniques and conventions within your KS3 and GCSE English lessons. This is not to say, of course, that you could not acquire the relevant knowledge for this level as your experience grows.

Having said all this, it is still useful to have an understanding of what is taught on a GCSE course since it is likely to affect the general ethos of, and attitudes to, drama in the school. If there is a separate drama department or specialist teacher, the likelihood is that the curriculum for KS3 (and you may be expected to teach this) will be a scaled-down version of what is offered higher up in the school. From this point of view there is also a great deal that even a pure English teacher can adapt or use to his/her own ends.

For those teachers who have some expertise and might go on to teach GCSE Drama it is worth noting that there are now a number of course books available that link directly to the specifications for particular examination boards. These are useful for pupils to read but could also be invaluable when you begin to teach for the first time. If you are serious about GCSE in the future it may even be worth getting hold of the book which relates to the specification taught in your school at this point. (You may find that the school already has a copy.) Andy Kempe's *The GCSE Drama Coursebook* has been recently updated. This is a more general approach but is very accessible and can easily be adapted to suit the specific requirements of different examination boards.

The chapter will focus primarily on the similarities and differences between some of the key GCSE specifications and suggest approaches to teaching them.

LINKS TO THE NATIONAL CURRICULUM

There is no National Curriculum for drama (the NC uses lower case 'd') at examination level. It is included within the requirements for KS4 English: these issues have been covered in the previous two chapters.

Activity 1

LOOKING AT DIFFERENT GCSE DRAMA SPECIFICATIONS

(suggested time: 40 minutes)

Some GCSE specifications are examinations based on coursework and a practical assessment, where others are almost all practical or involve a written examination. They are usually selected according to the needs of the pupils and the personal preference and skills of the teacher(s) involved.

Get hold of two or three different GCSE specifications via the appropriate websites. Some examination boards such as MEG incorporate three very different options in the one course. You could also try Edexcel and AQA (used to be SEG).

Standard addressed: 2.1d

Read the specifications. Most include a summary or overview, which should give you something of the flavour of the course. Make a note of the basic structure of each course. What are the main differences and similarities? What problems might they present to the teacher? Make a note of your answers in your English portfolio.

Activity 2

DRAWING ON YOUR STRENGTHS

(suggested time: 15 minutes)

Standard addressed: 2.1d

If you were going to teach or share the teaching of a GCSE course, which specification do you feel you could do best? Write down what strengths you could bring to the course and include a note of this in your portfolio.

Activity 3

TRANSLATING A SPECIFICATION TO THE CLASSROOM

(suggested time: 20 minutes)

Standard addressed: 2.1d

Find out what GCSE specification is taught in your school. If there is none, find a school where there is one. Read the specification thoroughly, if you have not already done so. Observe several lessons to familiarise yourself. What sort of specification is it? (i.e. is it mainly practical with some coursework or is it geared to preparing students for a written exam?)

Activity 4

PLANNING A PART OF A GCSE LESSON

(suggested time: 30 minutes plus teaching time)

Standards addressed: 2.1.d, 3.3.2d

In collaboration with the GCSE teacher, plan to teach part of a GCSE lesson. This might take the form of leading an activity, for example, or perhaps working in role to support the work of the usual class teacher. Evaluate the lesson. How does it fit into the specification overall? Include your plan and evaluation in your English portfolio.

Activity 5

DRAMA COURSEWORK

(suggested time: 45 minutes)

The following is a guide for students to help them with a piece of coursework which focuses on a how a range of different drama conventions were used to explore *The Odyssey* and stories about Second World War evacuees. It was designed following a specific piece of drama work for Unit 1 of the Edexcel GCSE examination.

> **Unit I GCSE Drama Coursework**
> a   Put your name and form at the top of the page.
> b   Put the title **Unit I GCSE Drama Coursework** on the next line down.
> c   Make sure you answer the following questions in **enough** detail. You may use clearly labelled diagrams or pictures to explain your answer.
> d   Remember to use the correct Drama language at all times.
> START A NEW PARAGRAPH
>   1   Briefly describe what you are going to talk about in no more than two sentences.

2   What was the overall learning area of the lessons about Jimmy and the evacuees? (What issue or subject were we trying to find out about?)

START A NEW PARAGRAPH

3   Compare how you used **still images** to explore the learning area and stimulus for Drama in the Dramas about Odysseus and the evacuees. How helpful was this technique? (Give solid reasons.)

START A NEW PARAGRAPH

4   Compare how you used **thought tracking** to explore the learning area about Odysseus and the evacuees. How helpful was this technique? (Give solid reasons)

START A NEW PARAGRAPH

5   Compare how you used **cross cutting** to explore the learning area and stimulus for the Dramas about Odysseus and the evacuees. How helpful was this technique? (Give solid reasons.)

START A NEW PARAGRAPH

6   What did you find out about Jimmy/Odysseus and the evacuee through playing the roles?

7   How did you use space and levels differently to play the **two** roles?

8   How did you use body language differently to play the **two** roles?

9   How did you use your voice/different language to play the **two** roles?

10 Which was the more difficult role to play, Jimmy or the evacuee? Why? Give reasons and examples.

START A NEW PARAGRAPH

11 Compare how you used dramatic contrasts in the Drama about Jimmy and the evacuees?
    Dramatic contrasts are sound/silence, stillness/movement and light/darkness.

START A NEW PARAGRAPH

12 Compare the most important symbolic actions or objects used in the two Dramas. What did they stand for? (Use pictures and diagrams if you wish.)

START A NEW PARAGRAPH

13 Compare the similar and different things you have found out and learned about human behaviour from the two different Dramas of Jimmy's Odyssey and the evacuation of children during World War Two.

Standard addressed: 2.1d

After reading the guide, choose another piece of coursework from a specification you are familiar with and design a new guide to support students who will have to write it. Even if you never teach GCSE Drama, this is a useful thing to do for pieces of English coursework, no matter how able the students. Email your guide to other modular students and compare it with theirs.

Activity 6

ASSESSING GCSE DRAMA COURSEWORK

(suggested time: 45 minutes)

The following are two pieces of GCSE coursework based on the Paper 1 practical exam of the Edexcel 2003 specification.

Piece one   *The Evaluative Phase GCSE Drama*

Coursework.

I am going to write about what I have learned about and understood from these two Dramas and discuss my contribution and the contribution of others to the drama

The most symbolic action in the drama of Jimmy was when I was hot seated and sitting in the middle of the room with the spot light on me. I think it sands out most because I did not have much time to get into the character, as I was just picked. But as the drama went on I started to act talk and fell more like Jimmy. I had to think like Jimmy and I feel I adopted the role well. This gave me a better view of what Jimmy's life is like and how he feels. The most symbolic action of the evacuees was when we had to get in a family portrait and the audience would ask questions. The group who had Natasha was very good, they were very organised they knew their status and acted decent quality. This is why it stands out the most.

I have learned a lot about adapting two very different roles. For example I found it hard to get accents in the time of World War 2, so I thought about the way Oliver twist spoke as we where in London. But with Jimmy I found it easy to adapt the voice as the drama is set in our time now, and a London accent is easy to adopted as I have family and friends from London. Also I sometimes did not know how to act in 1940s so Becky and I tried to get some information about the different every day life like Rations, and Becky found out posh and popular names like Victoria.

The work I was best pleased with was the voice college work with the Jimmy drama. I think the group I worked with we worked very well. I think what worked very well because Carly who sometimes does not give her views did and her views was very good and this made everyone in the group bring their ideas out, The drama worked very well and what I liked most was it was different from everyone else in the whole class. The piece I enjoyed most about the evacuee was when we had to do a Drama about in the bomb shelter. I liked the way Charlotte acted as she got her status sorted straight away and did not go out of role once. I would like to work with her more.

The drama in Jimmy would have liked to work on was the Jimmy and Odyssey's crosscutting. I was not sure what the Odyssey drama was about, so this put me off the drama. But I would have liked to work on it more. I did not understand the similarities between the two dramas. But pupils like Alex she knew what was happening and this shows how strong she is at drama. The Drama I would have liked to work on with the evacuee's would be when we had to do a portrait I think my group was unorganised and did not know our family status and what to expect when the audience was firing questions at us. I think I need to work on adopting role quickly and staying in role.

I think The piece of work Alex's group worked on showing still images of what Jimmy's life is like on the inside (prison) and what the girl friend of Jimmy is like on the outside. The still images were very strong they used no action or narration and still got the symbol across to the crowd. They work well together and give a lot of effort and work into their work I would like to work with strong characters like Alex, Rachel, and Adam. The work what impressed me most about the evacuee was Natasha she was a very strong character and made me laugh like when There group was in the bomb shelter and any other would be fearing for their lives but her character was more worried about what this cramped space is going to do for her mothers authorities. She stayed in role well and showed off her skill.

I would have liked to improve the drama what sir done showing us when Jimmy is at the door but the little boy (sir) would not let him in. I think that scene was not to true to life, because if I had not seen my dad all my life and then he is at the door, I would be the first one to open the door. I would have changed the approach what the young boy would do. The work I would of like to improve on the evacuees drama would be when Chelsea group was on the train, there was a lot of fighting and babyish comments, I think this was very unrealistic and also there voice was low and actions needed perfecting a lot.

I think my main aim was to stay focus and listen. I think I done this and I always give my ideas to what ever group I am working with and try my best at all times I have learned a lot of new skills and tips and have tried to use them and tech others like Becky. I made up most of story line on the drama we are doing present, I try to get to do a drama or show my drama.

I think Kirsty has worked very well, she has shown many of her different skills and worked with different members of the class and has impressed me a lot also Alex and Natasha. Kirsty always was asking sensible questions and trying to get involved as much as possible in the two dramas.

Piece two   *Unit 1 – Evaluative GCSE Drama Coursework*

I am going to write about what I have learned about and understood from these two Dramas and discuss my contribution and the contribution of others to the drama.

In the drama about Jimmy, the most symbolic actions were the still images showing the reactions from his wife when she received his letters, and how he was coping with life in the prison. These particular images stood out to me because they were so powerful.

In my group we used our bodies to show the walls in Jimmy's cell. This could also have been interpreted as the state of jimmy's mind (feelings of oppression). In the drama about the evacuees, the most symbolic action was in our final performance, where Lucy and Sophie are talking on the train and they express their concerns and hopes. Behind them are two still images, one showing two children playing happily, the other showing a child looking very upset. The still images are representative of what they two girls are feeling and thinking. The good image was shown in a green gel and the bad one was shown on a red gel.

In both of the Dramas I have learned about relationships within families. In both of the Dramas it is the mothers' who try to protect their children. In the drama about the evacuees, the children's mother sends them away from London to the countryside to save them from the blitz. In the drama about Jimmy's Odyssey, the mother attempts to keep Jimmy away from her son, because she fears that he will be a bad influence on him and that Jimmy is not to be trusted. I have also learned about the close bonds between family members, and how people have to change depending on their environment. In my groups play about the evacuees in WW2 the two children are very close and find it very hard to adapt to their new environment. It is also very hard for some members of their new family to accept them in to their home.

When devising our play for the evacuees' drama, we had to take in to consideration that as it would be set over 60 years in the past, there would be many social and cultural differences compared to the present day. So as a group we decided to research the 1940's and life for people from different areas in Britain. We also took in to consideration that as the people in the drama would be from different areas from England, we would need to have different accents to show this. We found out that many evacuees went to the West Country so Adam and I had to develop accents that would be fitting for people from the Dorset/Cornwall/Somerset area, we also put in phrases that we thought that the may have used. We also wanted to be suitably dressed, to show the class what they would have worn, this made the drama more authentic/ true to life. We also had to consider what went on historically.

In the drama Jimmy's Odyssey, we also had to consider accents. It was decided early on in one of the lessons (during a sound collage) that Jimmy would be from London. For most this accent was particularly easy to adopt because, being from, and living in Kent, the accents are pretty similar. And so it takes little effort to adapt. We also had to consider that jimmy is susceptible to giving in to temptation, and the area in which he lives is extremely tough. So when playing anyone from the area, we had to play them as people who have suffered great hardships.

I was particularly pleased with a piece we did in Jimmy's Odyssey, it was where he had just come out from prison and was walking past a shop, he sees some of his old friends stealing from a shop and goes to walk past them in the hope that they don't see him. But they do, and they stop him. In my groups drama I played Jimmy, and Louis and Owen were his old friends, Annika played the police officer. In the drama the two men noticed that Jimmy had a bag with him (we carried this on from a previous lesson), and the two men wanted to put their stolen goods in his bag and ended forcing themselves upon Jimmy to do so. A police Officer (Annika) pulls over, the two men scarper and Jimmy is caught and arrested, there was a real climax to this point. This was fuelled by the lack of sound at the beginning of the piece which lead up to a lot of noise when jimmy was arrested, there was also an increase in movement. I have not worked with Louis, Annika and Owen that often, and I found that we worked very well together, we got down to work very quickly, and I was pleased with the end result.

In the Drama about the evacuees I was very pleased with my group's final performance. Mainly because we had worked so hard on the script and we'd spent a lot of time organising props, costumes and our actual performances. We had little time to write the script and when it came to our first run-through we were displeased with it. So to make each scene better we'd run it a couple of times and those who were not involved in it would sit and watch it. We would then discuss what we thought would make it better, and sometimes other people would take on the roles to show the actors in the scene how they would do it. It was like forum theatre, except we did not alternate the ending of each scene.

I think that by discussing each part of the scenes we made definite improvements on our final piece. For example, in the scene I wrote, I had Mrs Jones standing waiting for Susan, and then Susan running over to Mrs Jones, then the dialog began, but we changed it so that Mrs Jones would be seated and would start speaking as Susan ran on. This helped to show that she had a higher status than Susan. This made the piece flow and made it more comic for the intended audience.

While working on the odyssey drama, I was only ever really displeased with one piece that I did. The task that we were set was to cross cut a day where Jimmy is tempted by an old friend to take drugs with a story from the Odyssey (where he goes to an island with plants that act as drugs). Our group was asked to show ours to the class. I was not confident with the piece because people in the group had not worked in the time we were given. And I felt that they had put all the responsibility of directing it on to my shoulders. And as a result we did not finish it and we did not add narration over the top. Had we had more time, I think that it would have been better, because we would have been able to add the narration and we would have been able to run through it a few more times to make sure that everyone knew what they were meant to be doing (which I found they did not when it came to the performance).

I was not very pleased with the first piece that I did in the evacuees' drama. We were to make a photo of the family and then step out in character and say a small piece about ourselves. The class then asked each of us questions. I think that it would have been better if we'd thought more about what questions we'd be asked. Because we were taken off guard a bit by some, for instance, I was asked 'What do you want to be when you are older?' and I wasn't sure what my character would want to be. Mainly because I'd not developed my character very far, as it was only the first piece that we'd done on the drama, and secondly, I was unsure of what jobs would have been open to women in the 1930s! 1940s. I think that we ought to have sat down together and tried to decipher what questions the class may ask.

I was very much impressed by Natasha, Alice, and Rachel C. in the Drama about the evacuees. They stayed in role remarkably well, even though they were quite funny. Natasha took on her role as the mother of a rich family extremely well and she had a great heir about her because she put on a great middle class English accent and was very poised. Alice played the father, it is hard to play a member of the opposite sex but she managed it with aplomb. And Rachel played the spoilt younger child Francis, she spoke as though she was constantly boasting, the family seemed rather vulgar and smug.

In the drama about Jimmy's Odyssey I enjoyed the performance by Rachel Fisher and Annika. They cross cut how Jimmy would have coped with someone stealing his bag (aggressively and using violence) and how he reacts in the same situation now that he's reformed (he talks through the problem with the thief). With the current situation they ran the piece, but every now and again they would pause back to a moment, showing the 'old' Jimmy. The sound from the current Jimmy's scene would be continued. I thought that this was very effective because it made the piece flow and you could continue to hear what was happening.

I would have liked to improve the performance of Laura and Jacks group during a sound collage (where Jimmy goes through all of his old haunts), they sat down and did not give any eye contact to one another through out, apart from when there was an awkward silence and they'd look at each other in annoyance and confusion. I don't think that they had gotten themselves very organised because compared to other groups their performance was very short and did not have much to it.

If I had to direct them I would have gotten them all to think of some of the places that Jimmy may have gone to and I would have gotten them to pick out noises that they would hear in these places, for example, in a betting shop the noises you would hear would be; people shouting at TV's, the noise of a commentator, groans, cheers, a bookie taking the bets/giving out the winnings. I would tell them never to have any silence, and if there ever was a silence then for one of them to cough, or make some noise that would provoke others in the group to start up the sound collage. I would have gotten them to stand up, because it is easier to project your voice when you are standing, I would have also told them to look at each other so that they'd know when to speak and when not to.

In the drama about the evacuees I would have wanted to improve Rachel F and Chelsea's piece on the photo of the evacuees' at the train station. I had not even realised that they'd begun there piece because Chelsea was so quiet, the performance was uninspiring because they all looked bored or they had their heads in their hands, they did not make much effort to be heard when they were speaking and it did not grab your attention. I would have told them to have faced toward the class, as some of them were hidden behind one of the blocks. I would have told them to look up and at the audience when they were telling us their piece, this would have drawn the audience's attention towards them and their minds would not have wandered of what was happening.

In every lesson I always put a lot of effort in to what the group is doing. In our individual groups I think I worked well, each time I tried to work with different people, and I think that the majority of the time this made the work I did really well, because I got to hear new ideas of doing things that I'd then share with other groups that I'd work with. I often have a large say in what happens in the groups work because I tend to voice my ideas and opinions a lot I think that by doing this I helped to shape the drama. For example in the sound collage, where Jimmy walks through some of his old haunts, I tended to give my ideas to the group and then encouraged others who are more quiet to give their ideas also. In the final performance that we gave in the evacuees' drama, it was my idea to use forum theatre to change how we played parts of the script. I think that by doing so we really improved our play. I think that I gave a good and positive contribution to each of the dramas and I also allowed for others to do so as well.

I think that the person who gave the best work and the best contribution to the project was Kirsty. I was extremely impressed by how quickly and efficiently she works. I found that she was easy to work with because she was very enthusiastic and she would give ideas as well as listening to others. I worked with her on more than one occasion and neither time did she fail to give a great performance and to work hard on the task set. Working on Jimmy's Odyssey with her was good fun and rewarding, I think that we learned different approaches to drama from one another. I think that she contributed well to the lessons and to the group as a whole because she is always willing to show her work and to add to class discussions (e.g. whilst hot seating Louis as Jimmy she asked many questions).

Using the 'Assessment Criteria' on the following page, which band would you put these two pieces of work into? Discuss and compare your answer with another modular student or your mentor.

EDEXCEL GCSE DRAMA

Assessment Criteria for Paper 1: Drama coursework

Students will:

Marks	1–3	4–7	8–12	13–16	17–20
A01 Responding	– make little or no connection between different texts (Unit 1) or – make some basic responses to the play (Unit 2).	– attempt to make a connection between different texts (Unit 1) or – show that they can interpret some aspects of the play with guidance (Unit 2).	– recognise a number of similarities and differences between the texts (Unit 1) or – demonstrate a viable interpretation of the play that is intuitive rather than considered.	– make clear connections between texts and make comparisons with some justification (Unit 1) or – interpret the play with knowledge and understanding, giving reasons for the chosen approach (Unit 2).	– recognise and articulate a range of connections between texts and compare them in a knowledgeable way (Unit1) or – present a thought-through interpretation of the play that is fully justified (Unit 2).

Marks	1–3	4–7	8–12	13–16	17–20
	– occasionally contribute a few ideas and suggestions. – present ideas in a basic way	– contribute ideas and suggestions that may be somewhat derivative. – present ideas with little sense of form and structure.	– focus their ideas and suggestions on form and structure for most of the time with occasional originality in the shaping. – present their ideas in an appropriate form so that there is some sense of shaping.	– focus their ideas and suggestions on aspects of form and structure and with some originality in the shaping. – present their ideas in away that shows they are being shaped with a sense of form and structure.	– clearly focus their ideas and suggestions on aspects of form and structure and they will be shaped with originality. – present their ideas in ways that clearly demonstrate an understanding of form and structure.
A02 Developing	– demonstrate a basic development of issues and ideas but without reflection or understanding of structure.	– demonstrate some development of issues and ideas but with limited means of expression.	– demonstrate their ability to explore issues and ideas, displaying some insight but with little depth or reflection.	– demonstrate their ability to explore issues and ideas with some thought, imagination and understanding.	– demonstrate their ability to explore issues and ideas in an expressive, analytical, reflective and personal way.
	– take part in the use of forms and materials during the development process with guidance.	– select and use some forms and materials as part of the development process.	– use a range of forms, approaches and materials with some invention as part of the development process.	– make imaginative use of forms, genres, approaches and materials as part of the development process.	– experiment creatively with forms, genres, materials and approaches as an integral part of the development process.
	Communicate some of their intentions in the portfolio but errors will be difficult to ignore.	– attempt to communicate the way they have shaped ideas despite lapses in spelling, punctuation and grammar.	– select a style of writing and/or presentation that communicates a sense of how the ideas have been shaped.	– select a method of presentation that captures and communicates the shaping of ideas with some success.	– use a suitable structure and style of writing that clearly communicates the ways in which the ideas have been shaped.
A04 Evaluating	– describe the work of others in a simple way without reference to the language of drama (Unit 1) or without making connections between a written and performed text (Unit 2).	– recognise some of the ways others are using the elements and medium of drama (Unit 1) or the ways in which written text is realised in performance (Unit 2).	– discuss the ways in which others use the elements and medium of drama, making some informed judgements (Unit 1) or recognise connections between written and performed texts (Unit 2).	– recognise and discuss the way others use the elements and medium of drama in their work (Unit 1) or the way others interpret a written text in performance (Unit 2) and make judgements that are informed and to some extent justified.	– show a clear and consistent understanding and appreciation of the ways in which others use the elements and medium of drama in their work (Unit 1) or in realising a written text in performance (Unit 2), making critical judgements that are informed and well justified.

Marks	1–3	4–7	8–12	13–16	17–20
	– occasionally evaluate the drama in a simple and descriptive manner with little or no recognition of the social, cultural and or/historical influences.	– attempt to evaluate the effectiveness of the drama with passing references to the social, cultural and/or historical influences but criticisms will not always be informed or appropriate.	– evaluate the effectiveness of the drama constructively and objectively making informed judgements about the ways in which the social, cultural and/or historical influences are communicated.	– evaluate the drama by being able to describe its effectiveness with occasional attempts to show how the social, cultural and/or historical influences are communicated.	– evaluate the effectiveness of the drama with some insights into the social, historical influences showing an intuitive sense of how and what is communicated.
	– communicate a simple meaning but errors in spelling, punctuation and grammar will impede clarity.	– communicate their views using a basic vocabulary that prevents the development of an argument. Technical errors will be apparent.	– evaluate their work using the vocabulary of drama with some facility and a reasonably accurate use of spelling, punctuation and grammar.	– evaluate the work in a satisfactory way with some attempt at using an appropriate means of expression with considerable technical accuracy.	– evaluate the work using an appropriate style of writing that communicates clearly and with almost faultless accuracy.

Standard addressed:
3.2.3

CONTINUOUS THREADS

1 Professional values and practice

Standards addressed: 1.1, 1.2

Look at specifications carefully to consider the best one for your students. Some pupils will be happier and achieve better with a more academic, exam-based, course while others will do better with something that includes more practical assessment. GCSE Drama courses which include a high percentage of practical work and coursework allow the teacher to be more selective in choosing material which is relevant to the whole class and so providing a curriculum that has more equal opportunities for the students, regardless of gender and race.

3.1 Planning, expectations and targets

Standards addressed: 3.1.1 3.1.3

Depending on the attitude and maturity of your students it may be possible to relax some of the routine start to lessons, i.e. GCSE students may enter the studio as they arrive, providing the previous class has left. It helps not to allow the lesson itself to feel too relaxed, however, as plenty of exam level students will switch off if they think it's not a proper lesson, particularly at GCSE. You will have to get to know the students first and alter the structure as you feel appropriate. As a beginner teacher, however, be wary. This is something to aim for when you have taught the same pupils since Year 7 or 8.

Tasks within lessons can be allocated to different pupils according to ability. For example, a short activity to produce a series of still images could be extended to include a dramatic action and a line for those pupils who need it. Many schools who have a drama specialist and offer examination drama will be employing a scaled-down version of their GCSE specification at KS3 and the majority of pupils who take the option at KS4 should have no problem in progressing on to their examination years.

3.3 Teaching and class management

Standards addressed: 3.3.1

It is worth reinforcing rules about respecting the work of others in the drama studio, particularly with a GCSE class that is new to you. Whilst it is entirely natural to laugh *with* others it is never acceptable to laugh *at* anyone's work. The drama studio must be a place where students can feel safe, take risks and extend their learning.

3.3.4 Differentiation

Standards addressed: 3.3.3, 3.3.4

At GCSE level a drama group is much more likely to be mixed ability than an English class which has probably been set according to the ability of the pupils. Consequently the drama group is likely to be about 20 in number and contain pupils who may get A* through to those who will struggle to reach even a D or E grade. Since there is likely to be more coursework than at KS3, you may need to consider using tiered guide sheets (like that prepared in Activity 6) that are aimed at different levels of ability. You will know which pupils have problems with literacy and may even gear something specifically towards them. In some instances preparing a worksheet to be filled in by the pupil, perhaps with help from the teacher, or tape-recording an interview that can then be transcribed is the best way to obtain a written record of practical work. More able students can be given more difficult or analytical questions to extend their work.

2.5 ICT

Standards addressed: 3.3.10, 3.3.12

In addition to using computers to produce coursework and essays at exam level, there are now computer packages available for designing stage sets and lighting, which are relevant to GCSE courses with a high performance element. Students could also be involved in preparing sound effects for performances that they might put on for others as part of their coursework.

It is worth developing your own web pages on the school's website and using this as a place to bookmark relevant websites for GCSE students to use as a resource. This will ensure that they get the most out of any lesson time allocated to the Internet. You could include listings of current theatre productions, information on set texts and practitioners and even the GCSE coursework guides discussed in Activity 6. Students could also add to the website and include information and photos relating to current work in progress and school productions. The better your Web page becomes, the more other staff and pupils will be aware of your lively drama department!!

FURTHER READING

Beneditti, J. (1982) *Stanislavski – An Introduction*. London: Methuen

A particularly concise and clear guide to Stanislavski. Useful for non specialist teachers of GCSE (and A Level Theatre Studies students).

Chapman, G. (1991) *Teaching Young Playwrights*. London: Heinemann

Good on the structure of plays and helps with deconstructing texts.

Cross, D. and Reynolds, C. (2002) *GCSE Drama for OCR*. London: Heinemann

Kempe, A. (2002) *The GCSE Drama Coursebook, Third Edition*. Cheltenham: Stanley Thornes

Useful activities using dramatic texts which can be lifted or adapted for KS3 Drama and GCSE English.

Price, R., Morton, J. and Thomson, R. (2001) *AQA GCSE Drama*. London: Heinemann

Taylor, K. and Leeder, J. (2001) *GCSE Drama for Edexcel*. London: Hodder

The National Theatre's *New Connections* compilations (London: Faber and Faber, 1997) are also good but may contain strong language so may not be suitable for younger pupils or acceptable to the school.

REFERENCES

Edexcel (2003) *GCSE Drama Assessment Criteria for Paper 1: Drama Coursework*. London: Edexcel

Kempe, A. (2002) *The GCSE Drama Coursebook*. 3rd edition. Cheltenham: Stanley Thornes

chapter 22

TEACHING SHAKESPEARE

By the end of this chapter you will have gained an understanding of what some aspects of Shakespeare teaching entail at some levels within the English curriculum. You will be informed about the demands of the NC in relation to Shakespeare, but the main purpose of this chapter is to outline available approaches to and a rationale for the teaching. The best methods are experiential; pupils and students are to play out the play, so it is important to think about Shakespeare teaching in terms of planning activities and experiences. This chapter should be read in conjunction with Chapter 19, 'Teaching Practical Drama', and Chapter 20, 'Teaching Dramatic Texts'. It draws upon the methods outlined in both of those.

For many of us any play is a great thing to be teaching – a rich and fascinating area for exploration, full of opportunity for lively encounters and the satisfactions of dramatic engagement interwoven for study purposes with varieties of spoken and written response. Yet at the same time the notion of overcoming the supposed reluctance of the class towards Shakespeare and of conveying the difficulties of any text must give us pause. Beware, however, the frequent mantra that it is the language that's difficult and stands as the main obstacle to having any play well understood and engaged with.

RATIONALE

The best reason for making Shakespeare studies active, practical and dramatic in nature lies both in the nature of the texts themselves and in the nature of how young minds engage with the plays. The texts, runs the now-familiar argument about the thing to be learned, are scripts, mere representations of a reality which can only be captured by acting.

The argument about how best to bring about learning has, since Plato's time, made much of the power of play. Adolescent children are helped in their grasp of some of the complexities of human relationships by creating enactments of them, or by re-creating scripts of scenes depicting relationships that turn from the relatively simple to the undoubtedly complex. The Athenian heroines of *A Midsummer Night's Dream,* Hermione and Helena, whose friendship disintegrates as they both chase the same man, criticise each other's looks. These characters may well be played with true tonal conviction by those who, even if they have never encountered a Shakespeare play before, know exactly what is going on as insults are hurled at a former friend out of jealousy.

Experiences may be absorbed most safely, perhaps, by playing with them. The value of play may be great at the psychological level, but it can also become the mainspring of the development of self-confidence and personal skill if it helps the subject – the student – to project an experience, to act it out within the confines of a dramatic form, the containing shape of a scene and the guiding path of a plot with both endings and resolutions. Shakespeare's plays can never reveal all about themselves within or from any one production, and so it does not matter if the young encounter them in something other than their full or most revered forms when the teacher first introduces them.

Scenes may enact the unfolding narrative of events, but they do so only by the direct verbal interaction of character with character. The teacher's skill may well lie in selecting the right moment for a particular group to rehearse and act out. See Rex Gibson (1998) on how a great deal of *Romeo and Juliet* may be understood from a first encounter if that first encounter is a group rehearsal of everyone, in a chorus but dividing up the lines, voicing the Prologue to the play:

> Two households, both alike in dignity
> In fair Verona where we lay our scene,
> From ancient grudge break to new mutiny,
> Where civil blood makes civil hands unclean.

Surely, in a group of four, ninth- or tenth-years could sound convinced as they threatened civil blood and hands unclean? What's more, amplifying Gibson's point, is that the whole story of the play, only without a named cast list of characters, is contained in that Prologue.

If, then, the point of an active methodology is that it engages constructive interest and turns the idea of script into a dramatic reality in the classroom, then note also that it has other virtues. Active methods of rehearsing and realising moments become the basis of reading, writing, interpreting and thinking along lines that run throughout the English curriculum.

LINKS WITH THE NATIONAL CURRICULUM AND THE KS3 STRATEGY

It is almost impossible to conceive a secondary school programme of teaching English, at any rate in England, that ignores the teaching of Shakespeare. To some, such as Dollimore and Sinfield (1985) his presence on the National Curriculum is politically problematic as well as predictable. English teachers know that they'll have to introduce classes to Shakespeare plays, and so if this introduction enables the class to make a live and productive relationship with the chosen play, then critical thinking with regard to political and social questions may be begun as part of that relationship, though not necessarily the first part. There is no compulsory interpretation as far as regulatory frameworks go, of what any one play 'means' in terms of its ideological slant, and so it is feasible and proper to explore with a class what the play offers by way of its forming a critical perspective on an issue of gender, class, political power, religion or any other area where contention arises.

You could argue that events in *A Midsummer Night's Dream* – the pattern of courtship, flight, confusion and return – not only happen within and marginally without a steeply hierarchical society, but ultimately serve to validate its order, complete with its half-literate mechanicals. From a slightly different angle you could argue that only by escape into nature, magic and the anarchic social arrangements of the Fairy Queen's court can the participants engage in the necessary self-discovery and sexual identity – work which, later, will enable civilised Athens and its familial, autocratic marriage arrangements to work at all. The anarchic goings-on in the woods stand not as a dark foil to show off the goodness of the Duke's civilised control of matters political and personal, but as its psychological critique. This point might be understood better once the class has seen how the same actor could play Duke and Oberon.

Ninth- or tenth-years can be brought into an engagement with the moral and social questions of the play even if in relatively plain terms. They would certainly have views about the rightness of fathers to tell their daughters whom to marry and they could probably see the point of asking whether any harm befalls Bottom because he has a brief holiday among those given to taking 'potions'. The NC demands quite explicitly that English lessons should be seen as possible places for the promotion of pupils' spiritual, moral, social and cultural development; arguing about values in a fiction could be a key method of achieving this.

The NC makes the encounter with a Shakespeare play begin by Y9 if not before. Certain plays are set for study and assessment. The current plays are *Twelfth Night, Macbeth* and *Henry V*. The quantity of cruelty, planned murder and general slaughter is well up on that contained in earlier selections for Y9. The NC list should have included the idea of children's political development along with the other four kinds of development given above; *Macbeth* and *Henry V* ask a good many awkward questions, whose presence many classes could begin to see, about the morality of state action. Note, for example, and in terms of contemporary relevance, with what care Henry presents the justice of his case for making war.

The chosen play is not there to be studied in every word, with each detailed nuance or point of verbal interest explained. What is sought instead is that some sections of the play are studied in detail sufficient for each member of the class to understand what is going on between whom, and how and why, and that the remaining sections are understood sufficiently well for the selected scenes to signify as parts of a whole. Questions of acting and dramatic production are to be considered, and in that regard the NC appears to accept the need to posit the text as script.

A list of teaching requirements from the TTA is given here that starts with the idea of script. The document from which it is taken no longer has statutory force, but it remains a helpful prompt for any would-be Shakespeare teacher. It comes from a now superseded National Curriculum for English teachers in training;

Trainees must be taught how to teach Shakespeare's plays, including how to

a   *explore Shakespeare's plays as script for performance,* e.g. by presenting scenes, improvising around the play's theme; directing particular passages attending to action, music and set; devising and performing modernised versions of the scenes;

b   *ensure that pupils gain access to texts and appreciate the force of ideas, language and dramatic qualities by using a variety of approaches;*

c   *enable pupils to gain an appreciation of Shakespeare's language including its poetic qualities, how character and action are conveyed through language, and how it differs from contemporary English;*

d   *set Shakespeare's plays in their social and historical context,* e.g. performance in the Globe Theatre; the nature of monarchy; conventions of love and courtship. *(DfEE Circular 4/98, Annex F, original emphasis)*

This is a neat summary of things which teachers are inclined to do in any case, though the harmonics are those of the latest approaches for examination work at advanced level, particularly setting the plays in 'social and historical context'. At the beginning of a programme of study (scheme of work) on the set play, it would seem appropriate to show the class, by every available means, how Shakespeare's plays were originally staged, and why, for example, we have the Prologue at the beginning of *Henry V* come and tell us to imagine the battlefield within the 'wooden O'. Towards the end of the teaching programme some questions about what view of the protagonist we are meant to take away from the play should be discussed. Is Henry a straight hero, or a clever political mover? If the class were given an appetite to see the Olivier film, it would be helpful to work with the history teacher who takes them and have him or her expound on how although the film was intended for a particular time, another set of men than Henry's troops were perhaps in a position in 1944, by their courage and dedication to a great cause, to merit King Hal's praise.

If the class could be helped to see how the play had propaganda value in the Tudor era and had been used much more recently but in a different kind of argument, then it would have grasped something fundamentally important. If the start and finish of the scheme of work has the class being told things, and shown things, then the middle part should be centred upon their encounters with particular moments and scenes.

So far so good, we could argue; we see that the present NC for pupils and a past one for trainee teachers run in alignment with practice conceived of as enlightened by the leaders that English teachers are keen to follow, particularly Gibson. Against that, however, we have to notice at KS3, as at other levels, that the pay-off for students is gained by writing well about what has been read and performed rather than by reading and performing. The English teacher, throughout the curriculum, has little choice but to believe that active and collaborative approaches in class will in fact have better pay-off on the examination day than closed, invariably individualised and competitive systems of learning in the run-up to it. (See also below under 'Assessment'.)

Standard addressed: 2.1

Activity 1

CHOOSING A PLAY

(suggested time: 45 minutes)

Standards addressed: 1.1, 2.2, 2.6, 2.7, 3.1.3, 3.3.3, 3.3.4

From the current set list on p. 413, select which play you would prefer to teach to a Year 9 group. What is there, in the nature of the chosen play, which you would particularly want the students to understand? Bear in mind Gibson's (1998) dictum that you should 'address the distinctive qualities of the play'. Record your thinking here in your English portfolio.

Activity 2

SHAKESPEARE AND THE ABILITY RANGE

(suggested time: 1 hour)

Work out, from some of Gibson's ideas, as found in *Teaching Shakespeare*, and some of Davison and Dowson's, in *Learning to Teach English in the Secondary School*, and by reference to some given in the DfEE Circular 4/98 above, how you could enable the active and gainful participation of a pupil who had reading difficulties in the learning of a Shakespeare play at KS3.

Activity 3

SHAKESPEARE'S GLOBE

(suggested time: 1 hour)

Standards addressed: 2.5, 3.1.1, 3.1.5

Explore what knowledge you already have of the Elizabethan theatre, including via a visit to the resurrected Globe, with or without a performance, or, failing that, the Globe's website. (**http://www.shakespeares-globe.org/**). In particular check that you view the virtual pictures of the theatre: here you can view the entire building as if you were, like Malvolio, revolving on stage, able to cast up and down at the same time. When, in the teaching of *Macbeth* to ninth-years, might you remind the class of the effects of that theatre on the way certain lines and movements are performed? (e.g. why are so many characters so often commenting upon night and darkness?)

Activity 4

SHAKESPEAREAN INSULTS
(suggested time: 30 minutes)

Go to a Shakespeare insults page on the Web (e.g. **www.insults.net/html/shakespeare/index.html**) and from that select or create from the word-kit several key insults which either derive from *Henry V*, *Macbeth* or *Twelfth Night*, or which might suit moments within them. How might these insults be used as a way of introducing moments from the play to the Year 9 class, given that you want a mix of activities of practical performance work on the one hand and reflection and further planning by pupils on the other?

Standards addressed:
2.7, 3.3.3

ASSESSMENT

Studying Shakespeare for examinations is one of the predictable experiences of secondary school. The arguments about the possibly dire effects of testing on study are at least 70 years old. Rex Gibson in Brindley (1994: 143–4) makes one essential point starkly: examination Shakespeare is typically solitary, silent, individual, competitive, literary. In contrast, 'active Shakespeare is co-operative, social, a matter for negotiation in groups of various sizes engaged in self-chosen tasks'.

The assessment section here concentrates on the Y9 Shakespeare testing arrangements in the hope of casting light on what they are, where more information about them may be found and what they mean in terms of influencing the teaching that leads up to testing. Those teaching Shakespeare at GCSE level should consult the list of suggestions from one examination authority (the AQA) about how teachers might structure the assessment of their Year 10s or Year 11s engaged in GCSE English or English Literature, in which Shakespeare is assessed within the coursework component of the examination. See the last item under 'Further Reading' on p. 422. This list suggests that the QCA in conjunction with the examination boards, such as AQA, have ensured that, by placing the Shakespeare play within the coursework component, and by encouraging teachers to seek the most suitable kinds of assessment from a broad and imaginative range, teaching is in the lead rather than assessment in this particular province of the curriculum. Someone starting out as an English teacher could do worse than give each one of the suggestions listed by the AQA a try, the better to develop their professional judgement about which kinds of task are best suited either to a teaching approach or even to individual pupil aptitudes.

The notes that follow are to be read in conjunction with Activity 9 – on the topic of the tests in Shakespeare for KS3 SATs in English – in Chapter 20, Teaching Dramatic Texts' (see p. 392). A visit to the website **qca.org.uk/ca/tests/ks3/2003sample/2003sample_ks3_en_shakespeare.asp** or whatever the contemporary equivalent is when it takes force will clarify what is happening in regard to assessment in Year 9. The 2003 arrangements for testing Shakespeare within the SATs, or incorporating prior study of a Shakespeare play within the English tests, could be summarised as follows. The Shakespeare test has two sections, A and B. The first draws upon knowledge of a play but does not reward that knowledge; and the second, which posits the idea of writing in the role of director, does reward knowledge of the play and aspects of its characterisation, language and performance. Under this arrangement the first question was, effectively, a writing test which looked for text, sentence and word level skills such as, it was and is hoped, are developed through the KS3 Strategy. Section B's task was assessed only for understanding of and response to the play – not for written expression.

Comment on the above methods of assessing Shakespeare study, or rather, of using the study of a play as the means of assessing writing skills, involves a return to Gibson's comment about how Shakespeare in school is assessed in ways not consonant with the best ways of understanding and interpreting the plays themselves. The QCA was quite clear that knowledge of *Macbeth,* for example, could be utilised but not credited at all in a task that asked the writers to create a publicity booklet about the launch of a '*Macbeth* video' for use in schools with young people. See especially the notes in Chapter 20 about how the *Macbeth* booklet opportunity may best be given fulfilment in terms of teaching the play at that level (Activity 9, p. 392).

A whole critical account could be made of the way in which Shakespeare study in Y9 and the literacy aspect of the KS3 Strategy were merged in 2003 at the point of the assessment of pupils. Three imperatives, it seemed, were forced into a relationship:

- Literacy skills must be tested and acknowledged.
- Shakespeare must, as previously, be studied and tested.
- Not too much time must be spent by pupils in being tested.

Prior to the 2003 tests it looked as if what would yield as these three imperatives were brought together was fairness in crediting what may have been learned about a play. There was no harm in having a class devise some publicity for a video, but if, surely, they drew upon their knowledge and their wit to create something convincing, then they should gain credit for more than varied sentence lengths or confident use of the passive verb form. The exemplar writing was hailed for these virtues, but a greater virtue was conscious irony in the wording of an advertisement, evident in its stating that Shakespeare has trouble conveying a troubled state of mind in words. That virtue escaped credit, or appeared to.

It would be inappropriate to dwell at length on the arrangements for a single year. Under any retention of the present arrangements the new teacher, keen to have his or her Y9 class do well in their SATs, will need to ensure that they can graft their understanding of the play on to a generic form of writing which is more than just a critical or explanatory narrative. Rehearsal in a variety of styles, with supportive examples provided, might well be needed. It is and will remain good to have the class develop their knowledge about language to the point where they can create passive verb forms and varied sentence lengths, but why not look also, when the play is becoming well known, at how Shakespeare does those things, both in prose and verse? Shakespeare study could inform literacy work at word, sentence and text level.

Section B of the Shakespeare paper, the reading task, assessed in writing, told the writer in 2003 to explain as if director, from provided extracts, to the actor playing Macbeth how he should show his reactions. Behind this, for all its difficulties and possible limitations, lies the notion of script as performance waiting to be given life. This particular piece of assessment might be adapted into a useful method of teaching. For more specific guidance on structuring practical work in preparation for Section B, see Chapter20, Activity 10 (p. 393).

Activity 5

WRITING ABOUT SHAKESPEARE
(suggested time: 1 hour)

Standards addressed: 3.2.1, 3.3.1

Consult some published examples of answers to the Shakespeare questions, both from the website already given and from the QCA's printed material, available to training institutions and schools. Consider what you'll need to do in order to have your pupils write as confidently and as well as the pupil writers of the best examples printed. In other words, from the best answers, what appear to have been the learning experiences that the writers have enjoyed?

Activity 6

USING DRAMA TECHNIQUES
(suggested time: 1 hour.

Standards addressed: 3.1.1 to 3.1.5 inclusive

Consult what is said in Chapter 19 about hot-seating, teacher in role and thought tracking. Sketch out, for placing in the Shakespeare section of your English portfolio, how you might employ these techniques in teaching any Shakespeare play.

Activity 7

REWRITING A SCENE
(suggested time: 45 minutes)

Standards addressed: 3.3.4, 3.3.5, 3.3.6

You may have to rewrite some scenes in order to have them understood by those struggling with aspects of Shakespeare's verse or prose. Rewrite the text of the scene quoted in the lesson plan below, so that it enables some to grasp what the scene is about before they encounter Shakespeare's actual words.

CONTINUOUS THREADS

1 Professional values and practice

Under this heading what matters regarding the teaching of Shakespeare is partly improving one's own teaching by continual study of the plays, the history of their performances and critical evaluations, and about how particular kinds of knowledge (for example about language) can improve what pupils may, through their teacher, come to understand. What matters also is the teacher's taking account of how some Shakespeare plays may have already enjoyed a history in cultures and religious backgrounds that are not English, British or Christian.

3.1 Planning, expectations and targets (progression)

A number of crucial issues arise here, from knowing how to plan properly and carry out safely a visit to a theatre (check carefully with mentoring staff about how they do this, and offer to accompany a visit by a class in order to see what background work has to be done) to knowing how to teach a play inclusively. Differentiating practical work (see below) is by no means impossible. Even if all are set to do the same task in terms of live performance, you can control who works on which sections, and with whom. Note also, please, comments in Chapter 6 'Inclusion' about the success of a student teacher working on *Macbeth* with bottom set Year 9s in an urban setting who had them taking seriously ideas about Macbeth's self-doubt. Serious work arose from high expectations rooted in good planning.

3.2 Monitoring and assessment

Note, in addition to what has been said already, that many practical drama techniques, such as hot-seating, allow for useful monitoring of how well individuals are coping with the matter in hand.

3.3 Class management

The skilled English teacher borrows from drama specialist colleagues very definitely practical devices for keeping proceedings orderly when all are out of their desks. In the lesson plan given below, the practical work is limited to pairs. This is one way of keeping things defined, limited and within bounds in the early stages. Good responses may be rewarded by giving the class more open tasks and directorial powers, with larger and larger portions of script.

3.3.4 Differentiation

Rewriting a portion of the play may be necessary for all for some of the time, or some for all of the time, or a mixture of both. No one, however, except perhaps the severely shy (e.g. elective mutes), should be altogether excluded from the chance to speak some lines.

2.5 ICT

In addition to the richness of support material to be found on line, and in such CD-ROMs as those produced by the BBC for the study of *Macbeth*, among others, please see Clarke (2000) for an idea about how the technology can support comparative views of the same play.

FROM IDEAS TO LESSONS

Probably the ideal way of teaching a Shakespeare play, of making the class aware of the entertaining experience of, say, *Twelfth Night*, is to be allowed to do nothing else in school for three whole days, working up from the girls imitating the boys in their most bragging and swaggering behaviour prior to cross-dressing to watching the comedy in full, preferably as a theatre trip at the end of the three days. This happens in schools, if at all, very rarely, and usually only when the timetable can be allowed to shift into an 'arts festival' week. In other words, teachers have to work with lesson times, fragmentation and disrupted continuity.

Time, as all good guides to teaching emphasise, is precious. Lessons need to be planned to be well related to one another in a coherent sequence or 'scheme of work' which has itself a clear end in view. In order to begin to write a coherent scheme of work you would need to start by listing, simply, what you might want your work with, say, Y9s on *Twelfth Night* to have accomplished by the time it was over. Most English teachers would probably aim for such a list as this:

(a) Each pupil will have acted some part of the play in a way that has brought about understanding and enjoyment.
(b) Each pupil will have learned and will be able to summarise, roughly, the main narrative of events.
(c) Each pupil will have gained an insight into some element of the character, as well as the language, setting, staging and performance of the play.
(d) Each pupil will have furthered their critical literacy skills through all the other exercises and engagements with the text.

Not every single lesson planned in a sequence such as this has to fulfil each of the intentions listed. That may well be impossible, but the series, the overall scheme of study, should take account of the necessity to do something to fulfil each one at some point.

Pupils' degrees of knowledge of the play will change as work on it progresses, so that initial exercises in familiarity with some of the main characters, situations and themes will probably yield, over the weeks, to different kinds of exercises concerned more with reflecting on the resolution of the plot and the themes within that resolution, such as the comic convention of an ending in marriage or debate about the justness of Malvolio's punishment.

Bearing in mind that *Twelfth Night* is not the easiest of the plays to begin as a straight reading-aloud exercise, some way in is needed which makes the class keen and also gives them some satisfaction from speaking the play enjoyably.

An early lesson plan might resemble the following:

LESSON PLAN

Class: middle band Y9, 15 boys, 15 girls   **Time**: one hour
Space: English classroom – cabined, cribbed, confined.

Resources: text of II.ii on single sides of A4, wide-spaced for marking up; clip of video of *Some Like It Hot*; video extract from BBC Shakespeare; video player.

Aim: to introduce the class to the mainspring of one comic idea and to the opening of *Twelfth Night* via some active approaches.

Differentiation: most differentiation in this lesson is by outcome, but the pairs rehearsing the Viola–Malvolio script will be chosen so that no pair will be of those likely to incite one another to do nothing.

Time	Teacher's Work	Pupils' work
10 minutes	Sit everyone attentively and show them a clip from *Some Like it Hot*. Jack Lemmon, disguised as female, is wooed by a man. Tell the class that the play about to be studied is also a comedy about, among other things, cross-dressing, and the unexpected perils of that.	Attend to what is said and shown.
5 minutes	Give the class an outline, prepared well in advance, of the plot of the opening of the play – Viola's arrival in Illyria and the lack of love-play among Illyrian high society. (This outline, in a well-equipped ICT environment, could be available to all as a word processed document, to be kept for possible adaptation later.)	Attend to what is said, or copy two minutes' writing from the board if the class looks to be inattentive, and needs to focus its attention.
10 minutes	Hand to everyone the text to be spoken in pairs; pairs to face each other, seated first while they rehearse aloud the Malvolio-Viola dialogue, below, and then standing, so that gesture and intonation can be better worked at.	Rehearse; ask questions of the teacher. If the class has on-line computers, they can consult the source and click on the words in blue.

Text here taken from: **http://www.cs.cmu.edu/Web/People/rgs/12night.html#II-II**

[Enter VIOLA, MALVOLIO following]

MALVOLIO: *Were not you even now with the Countess Olivia?*

VIOLA: *Even now, sir; on a moderate pace I have since arrived but hither.*

MALVOLIO: *She returns this ring to you, sir: you might have saved me my pains, to have taken it away yourself. She adds, moreover, that you should put your lord into a desperate assurance she will none of him: and one thing more, that you be never so hardy to come again in his affairs, unless it be to report your lord's taking of this. Receive it so.*

VIOLA: *She took the ring of me: I'll none of it.*

MALVOLIO: *Come, sir, you peevishly threw it to her; and her will is, it should be so returned: if it be worth stooping for, there it lies in your eye; if not, be it his that finds it. [Exit]*

Time	Teacher's Work	Pupils' work
10 minutes	Have some of the stronger pairs perform their dialogues aloud, looking for and pointing out Viola's ability to stand up (now she's pretending to be a man?) to pretentious and over-wordy Malvolio. Instruct listeners to note the good points in performances.	Perform as directed. The rest to listen and note the points they like.
5 minutes	Perform yourself, to the class, the soliloquy of Viola's that follows Malvolio's exit here, and ask, when you have finished, (a) what she is so worked up about; (b) what she will tell Duke Orsino.	Answer questions – speculate about what Viola will do to resolve her dilemma.
15 minutes	Show the whole of Act 1, scene v on the BBC Shakespeare video, so that they can understand what led up to the dialogue which they rehearsed.	Watch and listen.

Homework Pupils to write out three questions about the plot so far to which they would like answers. These questions to be read aloud, by random selection of individuals, at the start of the next lesson.

Evaluation (e.g.) Sarah, Gemma, Sam and William were v good, but others will need more rehearsal time and help in future. What threw some of the readers was the rhythm of the prose; more instruction in this will be required. In a play that contains much prose, practice is likely to be necessary. Class appeared to take readily enough to the performance part of the lesson, and perhaps the rest was too sedentary, but the plan is not to leave things too open at first.

FURTHER READING

Davies, A. and Wells, S. (eds) (1994) *Shakespeare and the Moving Image*. Cambridge: Cambridge University Press

This is an important guide for those who wish to bring into their Shakespeare teaching records of previous productions, and to work from watching others perform as well as having the class perform.

Hawkes, T. (ed.) (1996 *Alternative Shakespeares*, Vol.2. London: Routledge

http://www.flf.com/twelfth/

This is the URL of a film of *Twelfth Night,* listed as a reminder of the richness of some accompanying texts to Shakespeare plays which the Web contains. Students might well be convinced by material on the site that the play is indeed about things still current in the culture.

Garfield, L., illustrated by Michael Foreman (1988) *Shakespeare Stories*. London: Gollancz

See: http://www.aqa.org.uk/qual/pdf/AQA-3702-w-sp-04.pdf page 33 for useful notes about teaching and assessing Shakespeare for the GCSE in English.

REFERENCES

Brindley, S. (ed.) (1994) *Teaching English in the Secondary School*. London: Routledge

Clarke, S. (2000) 'Changing technology, changing Shakespeare, or Our Daughter is a Misprint', in *English in the Digital Age, ed.* A. Goodwyn, London: Cassell Education. Chapter 7

Davison, J. and Dowson, J. (1998) *Learning to Teach English in the Secondary School: A Companion to School Experience*. London: Routledge

Dollimore, J. and Sinfield, A. (1985) *Political Shakespeare*. Manchester: Manchester University Press

Gibson, R. (1998) *Teaching Shakespeare*. Cambridge: Cambridge University Press

Tillyard, E.M.W. (1990) *The Elizabethan World Picture*. London: Penguin in association with Chatto and Windus

SECTION FIVE

ENGLISH POST-16

INTRODUCTION

In this last section we outline the general picture of post-16 provision in English, and follow that with chapters on Language, Literature and Drama and Theatre Studies. Post-16 English has seen some marked developments in its curriculum during the last quarter-century, and Drama and Theatre Studies A level has enabled a subject to thrive at the top of the age range when it looked at times near likely to die of neglect lower down the secondary school and in the primary because of its absence from the NC.

Back in the early 1980s a fledgling A level English Language syllabus or two had been encouraged to make experimental flights, but the initial take-up was not widespread, and the idea seemed a distinct innovation. It was an important innovation, however. English Language was to broaden the appeal of the subject. Since 'English' at advanced level had come to mean, for nearly all schools, English Literature, then some students felt excluded. Adding English Language as one of the embodiments of the subject was part of an ongoing process of making greater choice available.

Numbers for English were, in some schools, sustained by the arrival of English Language. Through these new syllabuses English proved itself capable of innovating and adapting, as it had in the 1960s but with younger pupils. The subject responded to the needs of the population and of the context. English may have been permeable and open to influences, but it was also taught by people ready to create something new, workable and yet principled. The early English Language syllabuses demonstrated how language itself could be made a lively, discursive, investigative matter. Since that time English Language has fully vindicated its early claims, but is not, still, as widespread in its availability as Literature courses are at the same level.

It is easy, then, to point to certain areas, such as English Language and the way A level Literature became examined during the early 1980s, and to assert that these changes represent clear progress and rejoice. There is no doubt that English teachers have played their part in full in helping more and more students achieve good results beyond 16, and it is true also that we now have less of a problem than we did (looking negatively) with what Robert Protherough (1983: 10) called the 'broken-backed' curriculum. English and drama below 16 now look forward to English and drama post-16 better than they did. English post-16 now makes habitual recourse to an imaginative breadth of styles of learning which the students have been accustomed to all along. Post-16 drama definitely requires more knowledge of the theatre, its history and variety of styles, than the subject requires at GCSE level, but the concept of practical workshop approaches remains powerful either side of the age gap.

Literature remains characterised by some verbally fairly dense and historically 'distant' texts, but there is more concern than before the last set of curriculum reforms (see Chapter 23) with setting those poems, plays and novels in their historical and social context. This contextualising is not necessarily easy, but the move to achieve it is part of a general measure of introducing more explicitness into an area that once relied on an intuitive grasp of rules. There would have been nothing wrong with intuitive grasp had not those from an advantaged and already literate background been the far more confident possessors of it than others. Explication might also help to equalise social chances. Changing the structures of examination has also led to a more precise analysis of what kind of exercise the critical process is. Some elements of coursework remain in place, even after the reforms.

The new teacher may not be overly concerned with history, but he or she still needs to keep a critical eye on how structures and constraints affect their teaching. As successive governments and social forces encourage or push ever more students into post-16 studies, questions must arise about how far examinations once designed for a distinct minority are applicable, even after reform, to large numbers of students of very varied abilities, prior dispositions and depths of background. Writing about the poems of Sylvia Plath may not be at all easy for those boys who enter Year 12 with only average writing abilities and no predisposition to read. They are the kinds of students who will need very specific guidance on how to write an essay of a literary critical kind. Their fellow-students are also likely to want to attend the English Language classes, as shown in Chapter 24, 'Language' via an example of student writing.

English Language and Literature and Drama and Theatre Studies at this level involve gaining credit, even if not all of it, through the ability to write. Whoever studies any one of these, whether for one year or two, should become conscious of being stronger at writing. This has implications for how lessons are organised and time is spent. The critical essay is likely to remain the best vehicle for the statement of verifiable knowledge and for assessment, but other forms of engagement with dramatic, literary and linguistic texts may have much to offer as ways of learning to write. Students entering the sixth form should not cease to rehearse parody, for example.

In some high-status centres English is a very strong subject indeed, with extremely well read and skilful teachers who are also editors of texts, authors of critical accounts, contributors to journals, writers of textbooks and examiners. The beginner teacher has much to gain from seeing how others presented with the same challenges have proceeded. Commonly now teachers provide their students with passages of commentary, drawn from critical accounts of the text in hand, whether book-based or Internet-based, and these are to be read and reported on, later, in class in sessions that hand much of the responsibility to the students. A good class would be characterised not only by the students showing freedom to explore a text, topic or approach, with informed comments guiding their analyses, but by their looking at a range of examples of student writing, or acting performance, and commenting on the varying strengths of each.

Even, however, in the small sixth form in an inner urban comprehensive where the students would be unlikely to have the intellectual confidence of their counterparts from the suburbs or polite small towns, there is a great deal of intellectual development to be gained across the two years of sixth form study in English or drama, or even one year, for those who start at AS level but who do not proceed to A2. Anyone who began their sixth form teaching in such a centre could find it hard at first to grant the necessary confidence to their students to contribute very much, but one way forward would be to encourage the students to learn to put trust in their own spoken language. In centres such as these, the need to study together the forms and conventions of the well-shaped essay and for the teacher to explicate ways of constructing such a thing might give greater proportional pay-off, in terms of marks gained under assessment, than similar work in a context with a longer history of intellectual assurance.

All students should be involved in a programme in which they perform parts of the Shakespeare play, or any other play. They should rehearse poems, write pen-portraits of well-known figures within and without the school in the style of the Chaucer of the General Prologue, and describe their town as if it were Dickens's Coketown or Eliot's London. They should be made, unthreateningly perhaps, to report back explaining what sections of Crystal's *Encyclopedias* (which they have been lent) mean, or attend a local production where a popular TV actor makes *Hamlet* more exciting and memorable than they ever thought possible. Faith in the students has to be combined with the provision of a structure for them, and with making demands on them.

Things can go wrong in detail that mar the general impression of the teaching, as when, to take an actual example, a student studies, among others, a subject of this section at AS and A2 without having once been told to consult a book that would explain much that was demanded of coursework essays. No reading list was provided. No books were to hand to be borrowed in the main teaching room of that subject. No indication was given about whether they existed in the school library. This student was compensated through her parents finding out which books were needed and bringing them home. Imagine, now, the same figure, but from a background where the youth of the family were expected to cope, intellectually, on their own. Where this points is that the A level teacher has a great deal to do in terms of foreseeing the world – of what ought to be increasingly autonomous study – from the student's point of view. Intellectual frameworks are needed, variety in tasks and approaches, physical facilities, occasions and opportunities. Teaching sixth form English or drama could be joyous labour in the sense that it is imaginative and informative work directly concerned with aspects of the subject at the highest level they will reach in ordinary secondary school.

We hope that what follows is of positive value in enabling the student teacher or beginner to see how they can start relatively confidently in an area of teaching work that many regard as their natural home. Those who are freshly inspired by degree courses to want to inspire others to see where the rewards of engaged reading and serious study lie should indeed watch with care what the well-rehearsed teachers do, as is so often advocated in what follows, but they need to develop simultaneous clarity about where their own aims point.

REFERENCE

Protherough, R. (1983) *Developing Response to Fiction*. Buckingham: Open University Press

$chapter$ 23

ENGLISH POST-16

By the end of this section you will have an overview of English teaching within the context of non-compulsory education at 16+ in regard to A level English Literature, English Language and English Language and Literature. Most schools and colleges choose to use pairs of teachers to teach A level courses collaboratively, with each taking responsibility for half the lessons and certain areas of the course. In addition to course planning you will consider, within the scope of teaching the students and assessing their work, the specification requirements and methods of teaching which include learning and enrichment activities.

RATIONALE

In 2000 government legislation introduced a number of reforms to post-16 qualifications with the aim to 'address undue narrowness and lack of flexibility in the post-16 curriculum by encouraging broader programmes of study, underpinned by rigorous standards and key skills' (see QCA website).

As the curriculum becomes broader and more students are encouraged to mix and match vocational and academic qualifications on post-16 courses, many more students will be studying 'English' in some form. English teachers may find themselves teaching components of vocational A levels and key skills alongside English AS and A2 Levels. As a teacher of English or of Drama & Theatre Studies you will need to stimulate and develop all students' engagement with texts in ways that are meaningful and appropriate both for those intending to go on to specialise in English or Drama studies in Higher Education and also those taking any of the subjects to offer breadth to Science A levels or to complement a vocational course in say, Health and Social Care.

English courses at post-16

A levels are now divided into two qualifications: AS (Advanced Subsidiary) and A2 (Advanced Level). AS and A2 contain three units each, with A2 being the more demanding. The AS level can be awarded as a discrete qualification after the successful completion of three units, whereas the A2 cannot stand alone. Sixth form students will be able to take subsidiary vocational certificates and vocational A Levels alongside or instead of A levels in traditional academic subjects. QCA stresses that, 'The standards of the revised A levels will be the same as those of the current A level' (see QCA website).

The following chart demonstrates where A levels and key skills fit in the new national framework:

Level	General	Vocational/ Vocational-related	Occupational	Key skill level
Higher 5	(Postgraduate/professional)		NVQ5	5
Higher 4	(Degree/HND)		NVQ4	4
Advanced 3	AS/A	Advanced GNVQ	NVQ3	3
Intermediate 2	GCSE A*–C	Intermediate GNVQ	NVQ2	2
Foundation 1	GCSE D–G	Foundation GNVQ	NVQ1	1

There are six key skills included in the National Qualifications Framework: Communication, Application of Number, Information Technology, Working with Others, Improving Own Learning and Performance and Problem Solving. Initially students will be assessed on the first three of these key skills by a combination of portfolio evidence and external examination. Many of the requirements for the key skills qualification will be covered during the A level courses, and key skills count towards UCAS points.

One result of the rapid rate of change is that some textbooks on A level teaching are still out of date when they refer to specific aspects of the syllabuses and they often cite detail from what is now known as the 'legacy syllabus' for a subject that ended in 2001. Many of the ideas for teaching and learning that were in force before the reforms remain very relevant but you will need to find out details of the new specifications from the relevant examining bodies. The subject-specific criteria for GCE Advanced Subsidiary and Advanced Level are set down by QCA and each examination board has to present specifications that adhere to these. Clear assessment objectives are identified and given weightings for discrete parts of the AS and A2 specifications so there is a very clear focus on what is being assessed in each part of the course. It is very important for the teacher to identify the relevant assessment objectives for each component and structure the teaching and learning around these. For example at A2 in English Literature students must 'evaluate the significance of cultural, historical and other contextual influences on literary texts and study', and this must be demonstrably present in the examination answers.

Activity 1

FORMAL REQUIREMENTS

(suggested time: 2 hours for the whole set of readings)

The following are designed to provide you with background to post-16 provision:

Go to the QCA website at **http://www.qca.org.uk** and read through the aims, specification content, key skills, assessment objectives, scheme of assessment and grade descriptions outlined for the AS and A levels in English Language, English Literature, English Language & Literature or Drama & Theatre studies.

Go to the websites of the relevant examination boards you will be teaching and download the relevant specifications. Familiarise yourself with the content of these.

Read Chapter 11 in Fleming and Stevens (1998).

Read Chapter 13 in Davison and Dowson (1998).

The chapters in Fleming and Stevens and Davison and Dowson give an overview of the issues surrounding teaching at post-16 level and provide practical examples of related activities for teaching A level English. Appendix 1 provides a representative sample of the authors you may encounter when teaching English Literature. Conduct a personal audit of your familiarity with these authors, noting any gaps in your knowledge.

Standards addressed: 1.1, 2.1d

On page 124 Fleming and Stevens summarise the 'tensions, contradictions and concerns' which often arise from teaching the English A levels. Write out the list for your English portfolio, but in the order of what you consider to be the most important issues. Try and add some more of your own concerns.

Activity 2

SELECTING AND PLANNING

(suggested time: 90 minutes)

Using the AQA English Literature Specification B complete the following tasks and, if appropriate, email them to your academic tutor:

Standards addressed: 2.1, 3.1.1, 3.1.3 and 3.1.5 (possibly), 3.3.3, 3.3.4

1 Make a list of the texts you would select for study to fulfil the specification requirements and to provide a broad and stimulating course. Explain the reasons for your choice.

2 Look at the exemplar plan for the course outline (Appendix 2). Complete the plan to demonstrate how you and a partner teacher would teach the chosen texts, address the required assessment criteria and integrate the key skills. Place the completed plan in your portfolio.

Activity 3

ASSESSMENT
(suggested time: 1 hour)

Standard addressed: 3.2.3)

Turn to pages 277–9 in Davison and Dowson, where they outline some assessment issues at A level and provide an example A level essay on Keats. Using the broad outline of grade descriptors given on pages 49–50 of the English Literature, Specification B from the AQA/NEAB website, assess where you think this essay would fall within the grade band criteria (remember that not all the assessment criteria will be addressed in one aspect of the course, only those targeted).

Activity 4

DEVISING TITLES
(suggested time: 2 hours)

Below are two exemplar questions on Coleridge's *The Rime of the Ancient Mariner*:

1   There have been many different interpretations of *The Ancient Mariner*: pagan myth, Christian allegory, psychological examination of isolation and loss, for example.
    How do you stand in relation to these interpretations, and what aspect of Coleridge's use of forms, structure and language do you select in order to support your own view?
2   How important is the wedding guest to what you consider to be Coleridge's purposes in *The Ancient Mariner*?

Standards addressed: 2.1, 3.1.1

Using Assessment Objectives A01, A03, A04 and A05ii for A Level English Literature, draft out three alternative essay titles on pre-1900 poetry. Email your academic tutor with your grade for the essay and your three alternative titles.

Activity 5

COLLECTING RESOURCES
(suggested time: 2 hours, perhaps, over three weeks)

To teach English Language A level you must provide a wealth of material to stimulate discussion about language usage and to act as models for students' own writing. In addition to this the A level requires students to have knowledge of the theoretical concepts and of major research findings in areas such as language change, sociolinguistics and language acquisition. In the section 'Preparing to teach a particular aspect of English Language', Davison and Dowson (1998: 284) emphasise the importance of selective reading and the collection of resources. The following tasks will help you to focus on this preparation:

1   Over a period of three weeks collect as many varieties of written language as you can and categorise them in terms of audience and purpose. (This is a

very easy activity and you will soon be overwhelmed by the printed word. It is a good opportunity to recycle rubbish in the form of sweet wrappers, junk mail, flyers etc as all can be transformed into valuable teaching resources!)

Standards addressed: 2.1, 3.3.3

2   Scour the newspapers for and build up a collection of articles that deal with the issue of language usage. Plan a 15-minute discussion activity around one of these articles.

ORGANISING ACTIVITIES IN CLASS

Maintaining a classroom environment in which students feel confident to explore ideas and express personal opinions is of paramount importance in English lessons at post-16 level. Students need to be given time and opportunity to develop the skills of presenting an argument, defending a point of view and thus analysing texts in an open and enquiring manner. These things can be aided by class organisation: discussing and presenting as a pair is less daunting and ultimately more productive for some students than a solo presentation. Make sure you change around the individuals when doing pair or small group work so the same people do not always work together. Think about the layout of the classroom: often a horseshoe shape helps whole class discussion whereas clusters of tables work well for small group work.

Some students may come to A level lessons expecting to take notes and be given information in a direct manner, so when you are setting different tasks and activities make sure you make their purpose clear to the students in terms of outcomes and assessment criteria. It is important to be clear about the different preparation needed for the various outcomes at A level. Class work will support and scaffold both coursework and preparation for timed examination work. Consider the following points:

- *Methods to help classwork* might include: discussion; jigsaw groups (when students work on a particular aspect of a task and then come together to share ideas and create the whole picture); preparation of presentations; collage production on characters or themes using quotations and visual images; identification of and comment on key lines; tableaux and freeze frames where students physically put each other in positions to represent what is occurring in the text.
- *Methods to help coursework* might include time allocated for individual tutorials, negotiated titles with student choice, drafting, Internet research, trialling on intended audiences and peer response.
- *Methods to help examination work* might include: assessment criteria made clear from the outset; students writing their own exam questions; the demonstration of planning techniques such as spider diagrams; peer marking of anonymously presented essays (preferably from a previous year or another class's output) against the mark scheme; the structural analysis of essays looking at the first line of each paragraph; colour coding students' own essays to identify exactly when they are addressing the assessment criteria and where the writing is irrelevant to the question asked.

In *English Teaching in the Secondary School* (1998: 129), Fleming and Stevens state:

> It is important to emphasise the creative overlap between literature and language, and innovative English departments are developing exciting teaching opportunities in the light of this cross-fertilisation – cemented as it is by syllabus change incorporating the AS structure, key skills and modular framework possibilities.

There are many teaching and learning activities which are generic to and useful for all three A Level English courses and the strategies explored here which focus on the combined course can also be usefully employed on the discrete Literature and Language courses. Before starting the activities below which relate to the English Language and Literature courses, read pages 129–31 of Fleming and Stevens and reflect upon the areas of productive crossover between language and literature study.

Activity 6 PLANNING CRITICAL ENGAGEMENT WITH TEXTS

(suggested time: 1 hour)

Assessment Objective AO2i for the combined English Language and Literature course requires students to:

> distinguish, describe and interpret variation in meaning and form in responding to literary and non-literary texts

Standards addressed:
2.1, 3.1.1

Consult the following website: **http://www.aqa.org.uk/qual/pdf/AQA-5726-6726-w-sp-os.pdf** from page 757. When you are in your host school, obtain a copy of the 'small anthology' referred to on page 19 of the AQA Specification. Pick out three different types of text, for example a poem, an extract from a contemporary novel and the transcript of a spoken narrative, then plan out three short activities which will engage students with these texts and address the assessment criteria. Remember that many of the teaching and learning activities you would employ lower down the school will be just as appropriate for A level classes. Put these in your portfolio.

Activity 7 KEY SKILLS

(suggested time: 45 minutes)

Standards addressed:
3.2.1, 3.2.3

Key skills in communication can easily be integrated into A level English lessons. C3.1a requires students to 'Contribute to a group discussion about a complex subject' and this could be addressed in many A level English lessons. Remember that it is important to have evidence of competence in the key skills so you will have to be aware when you are assessing and recording key skills. Think of and list three opportunities that address communication skills in A level English Literature and English Language lessons. Post these to fellow students of the modular PGCE course.

Activity 8

GAINING STUDENTS' VIEWS
(suggested time: 45 minutes)

Standard addressed:
3.1.1

If you are on placement get at least ten students of A level English to complete the questionnaire on page 126 of Fleming and Stevens and use this information when planning your lessons.

Scenarios

1 Imagine that you are teaching a group of A level Literature students who you feel need to develop a broader knowledge of classic and contemporary literature. How would you encourage them to explore more texts?

   You might want to consider:
   - asking them to read and review books for short presentations to the class;
   - creating a wall display of published book reviews;
   - organising extra-curricular trips to the theatre and poetry readings.

2 Imagine that you have an A level English Language class who are struggling to find creative and inspiring ideas for their Original Writing assignments. How would you help them to develop a greater diversity of forms and audiences for their writing? (Consider the importance of building on their interests and experiences, the importance of 'real' audiences and also the need to provide models of different types of writing.)

CONTINUOUS THREADS

1 Professional values and practice

In terms of high expectations, remember that A level groups may contain a very wide spectrum of pupil motivation and ability. English has often been perceived as a 'girls' subject' and more girls than boys do study English at A level, although there are considerable variations in the gender ratios across the different specifications for Language, Literature, the joint course and Drama & Theatre Studies. It is necessary to consider the issue of gender, culture and race when selecting texts to create a broad and balanced A level course and it is important to select texts which you hope will engage the interest of everyone in the class and stimulate discussion and debate on the issues of race, class and gender. The Introduction stated that A level classes are usually taught by at least two teachers. If they are, then the courses have to be planned and taught collaboratively. This provides a very good opportunity to share ideas and to discuss the progress of individual students. It is also a good method to achieve some professional development for the newer teacher of the pair, especially if he or she is new to teaching A level.

2 Knowledge and understanding

In addition to whatever else has been said and implied by activity instructions, anyone teaching the combined Language–Literature specification will need to be well aware of how enriching of and helpful to the study of literature knowledge about language can be. Some English graduates are well prepared to accept this facet of literary criticism; to others it seems a variety of critical activity that should not claim any specialism or added insight over customary modes. We suggest that, if the combined specification (Language and Literature) is taught by different individuals, then it be done by those with a good understanding of one another's intellectual standpoints. The benefit, of course, is productive in both directions. The current view is that insight into language whets the sharpness of literary critical acumen. Equally, teachers of language usually act in the belief that literary texts and extracts are positively appreciated by language students if they illustrate well some aspect of language use, such as the study of accents in the chapter on A level Language. the part that speech accents play in understanding character in dialogue in a novel (see p. 441).

3.2 Planning, expectations and targets

The teacher will help the students, especially those from backgrounds new to sixth form study, if at the start of the voyage they can see what they have to study, to know and be good at when tested, and what form the testing will take. This might help to set up appropriate expectations about amount of study time demanded and the skills to be developed.

One aspect of planning a one plus one year course is that of deciding when to study which text. Teachers of A level Literature have always had to decide when to study what as well as how, but this is, like so many others, an area where the questions are more obvious than the answers, or where it is easy to duck out of drawing up a list of principles about the order of studying texts by saying that much depends on student inclination, when the local theatre is staging *A Streetcar Named Desire*, and so on.

What a PGCE candidate interviewed recently thought intelligent about the design of her degree course was the way in which texts from very different times (and societies) could be fruitfully compared and critically understood against one another. Her course had not followed a straight historical chronology of authors. When an A level Literature student writes comparatively about *The Scarlet Letter* and *The Handmaid's Tale*, then an interesting juxtaposition of two novels set in the same state and city has been arranged. In terms of general planning, then, there could be much that stands in favour of studying simultaneously texts that are distant chronologically but nevertheless able to inform the student's grasp of each via significant linkages or points of contrast, in style or theme.

3.3 Monitoring and assessment

It is important to provide students with both formative assessment in terms of targets for improvement and summative assessment to inform them of how they are performing in relation to the A level grade criteria. The assessment process must be transparent and it is useful to let students see the grade descriptors and examples of mark schemes provided by QCA and the separate examination boards. As all A levels are driven by the assessment objectives it is crucial that written work is assessed against the relevant objectives with the specified weightings. Teachers assessing work for any of the coursework components will be involved in standardising exercises sent by the examination boards and in moderating assignments with other teachers. Coursework moderation is a valuable chance, not only to establish the accuracy of your assessment skills, but also to share ideas and look at the work of students in classes other than your own.

One of the subtler achievements of the monitoring and assessment process that might also be of direct interest to the students is that of noting the distance they travel, across months, in terms of their increased knowledge and clarity as readers and increased powers as writers. Early scripts from the start of the course could be compared by the teacher with later ones, and where development had occurred this could be pointed out to the student. Even at the age of 17 it is good to know that someone else thinks you show signs of progression and intellectual growth!

Many of the skills required at A level have been practised for GCSE English and students have a body of knowledge stemming from their own reading and life experiences. You need to consider at what level students enter the A level course and what is a reasonable expectation of their final examinations. Many institutions measure this progress from GCSE to A level and term the final outcome the 'value added' performance. There is an inherent notion of progression in the AS and A level courses as students are assessed at AS level at the end of the first three modules and it is expected that there will be identifiable progress by the time they take the examination for the final synoptic module at the end of A2.

3.4 Teaching and class management

See above under 'Organising Activities in Class'

3.3.4 Differentiation

There is usually no 'setting' by ability at A level but there will be considerable differences in the performance of students. A student who enters the course with a low grade at GCSE (usually students have to achieve 4–5 GCSE Grade C and above to enter an A Level course) will need support and encouragement. Writing frames, examples of successful A level essays and tasks that make explicit the assessment criteria are very valuable in raising achievement. High-achieving students will need you to suggest further reading and to structure tasks focusing on independent academic research.

2.5 ICT

The formal assessment of key skills in ICT has signalled their importance at this level of study. There are many opportunities for A Level English students to use ICT and to be assessed as to their competence in it. The coursework components of many English specifications provide an excellent opportunity for drafting and amending work using word processing skills, and desk top publishing programs aid the presentation element of writing for different purposes and audiences. There are endless opportunities for academic research using the Internet. It is usually best to ask students to research one aspect of a topic or a text (for example biographical detail on a particular author for English Literature or newspaper articles on particular topics such as joy riding for English Language) as it is very easy to become overwhelmed with irrelevant information from the World Wide Web.

FURTHER READING

Crystal, D. (1988) *Rediscover Grammar.* London: Longman

Crystal, D. (1995) *The Cambridge Encyclopedia of the English Language.* Cambridge: Cambridge University Press

Dymoke, S. (ed.) (1998) *Critical Reading at post-16.* Sheffield: NATE

Dymoke, S. (1998) *The Handmaid's Tale: a post-16 Study Guide.* Sheffield: NATE

Eagleton, T. (1983) *Literary Theory: An Introduction*. Oxford: Blackwell
Goddard, A. and Keen, J. (1992) *A Level English Language Starter Pack*. Lancaster: Framework Press
Halliday, M. (1994) *An Introduction to Functional Grammar*. London: Arnold
Keith, G. and Shuttleworth, J. (2000) *Living Language and Literature*. London: Hodder
Wardhaugh, R. (1989) *How Conversation Works*. Oxford: Blackwell

APPENDIX 1

A sample of authors from A Level Literature specifications:

Chinua Achebe	Herman Melville
Pat Barker	V S Naipaul
Geoffrey Chaucer	George Orwell
Charles Dickens	Sylvia Plath
T S Eliot	Jean Rhys
E M Forster	William Shakespeare
Elizabeth Gaskell	William Makepeace Thackeray
Thomas Hardy	John Updike
Kazuo Ishiguro	Kurt Vonegut
Ben Jonson	Tennessee Williams
John Keats	William Butler Yeats
D H Lawrence	

APPENDIX 2

Time line	Teacher A	Teacher B
First Half of Term One		
Second Half of Term One		
January – opportunity for AS assessment		
First Half of Term Two		
Second Half of Term Two		
First Half of Term Three		
June – AS examination		
Second Half of Term Three		
Summer Break		
First Half of Term Four		
Second Half of Term Four		
January – opportunity for A2 assessment		
First Half of Term Five		
Second Half of Term Five		
First Half of Term Six		
June – A2 examinations		

REFERENCES

AQA/NEAB (2000) GCE English Literature, AS 5746, A 6746, AQA

AQA/NEAB (2000) GCE English Language, AS 5706, A 6706, AQA

AQA/NEAB (2000) GCE English Language and Literature AS 5729, A 6726, AQA

Davison, J. and Dowson, J. (1998) *Learning to Teach English in the Secondary School: A Companion to School Experience.* London: Routledge

Fleming, M. and Stevens, D. (1998) *English Teaching in the Secondary School.* London: David Fulton

WEBSITES

AQA/NEAB (2000) www.neab/aqa.org.uk

QCA (2000) www.qca.org.uk

chapter 24

TEACHING AS/A2 ENGLISH LANGUAGE

By the end of this chapter you should have begun to understand the extent of knowledge about language required of those who teach English Language at A level and identified issues concerning transition from GCSE to AS/A2 study. You will have gained an understanding of the key requirements of the English Language specifications and experience of devising classroom activities, coursework tasks and plans.

RATIONALE

English Language in its present form, that is as a public examination course that gives insight into key aspects of the 'structural and systematic features of the English language' as well as the 'social functions of language (including varieties)', is a relatively recent arrival on the educational scene. The phrases quoted in the last sentence are from an unpublished paper by George Keith (1995). It was his vision of possible change that lay behind the work of the group that wrote the first JMB syllabus for an English Language A level of the present type in the early 1980s. 'JMB' stands for Joint Matriculation Board – one of the predecessors of the Assessment and Qualifications Alliance (AQA).

English Language studies took a long time in arriving on the educational scene, in England and Wales if not the rest of the UK, as compared with the arrival of Literature studies. This is bound up with a history of the whole subject that lies elsewhere, but, allowing a very brief explanation, what lay behind the lateness of the arrival of the programme as outlined above was a view of the relationship between students in school and the language itself. English teaching in the state schools was conceived in the first place as a planned intervention to correct the language of those whom culture, if not nature, had failed. Rosen (1981), among others, has put it on record that much school English up to the Second World War taught the language as if it were something foreign to the native speakers set to learn it. It took a while, after 1945, for language studies to catch up with the best ways of teaching literature that were being developed and promoted by, most successfully, ex-Cambridge English Literature graduates.

These teachers, working mainly in grammar schools, were teaching the independent and critical reading of serious literary texts. This way of learning to read was argued and argumentative even though subjective, and informed even if ambiguous and out to discover ambiguity. What were needed, it might appear from our own historical vantage-point, were modes of engagement with ordinary language that were equally susceptible to knowledge and equally susceptible to critical discernment. What tended to be on offer instead were heavily guided reading exercises in factual or social prose (an early kind of A level English Language), and grammar studies that (on the English Language GCE Ordinary Level at any rate) were intellectually indistinguishable from train spotting. The complement of a verb might be observed, and duly noted as an instance of itself.

Steadily, however, as participation rates in secondary schooling up to the age of 18 increased, so did the numbers of those doing A level English. Not all were felt, either by their teachers or by themselves, to be best placed in a Literature class. Meanwhile, as it were, the state of understanding about how to study language was being positively transformed by such as Halliday and Crystal. This movement coincided with a third significant force, namely the Language Across the Curriculum movement, based initially in London, and the LATE (London branch of NATE), which promoted, through such figures as Barnes, Burgess, Medway and Rosen, the idea that ordinary language of the kind that the pupils brought to school with them was a subtle instrument for learning, and something that those same pupils could never have developed without intelligence, creativity and cultural alertness. If ordinary everyday language was an interesting phenomenon, then presumably its speakers were perfectly capable of learning about it.

You could argue, then, that the early 1980s were the historically right point at which to launch a new examination syllabus or two (one in the north and one in London) through which students could gain a formal qualification in ways of understanding and studying their own language. Ever since the early 1980s the following have been central to all syllabuses and specifications in English Language at A level:

(a) a system that guides the extent of language study, or series of overarching concepts that articulate the more detailed elements of the language;

(b) the opportunity for students to investigate an aspect of language and language use that interests them, whether as social semiotic or rule-bound system, or something between both of those; and

(c) a concern that students shall not only study language and investigate it, but improve an aspect of their own language use, as reader, writer or editor.

What the teacher needs to know

These things imply, for the teacher of the presently specified courses, that he or she needs:

- a clear understanding of language as a system,
- insight into how best to develop in students the right desire to investigate and the right equipment, intellectually, with which to carry out the investigation, and
- the skill with which to develop an individual's reading, writing and editing powers beyond the limits reached at GCSE.

You also, of course, need to be fully familiar with the specifications of whichever route has been chosen for your students, to have a range of good textbooks in the area of advanced language study, and an abiding interest of your own in language. It may be commonly observed that keen English Language teachers habitually do such things as: tape-record examples of particular varieties of speech when broadcast; photograph signs, advertising hoardings and other kinds of large writing found in the environment; keep a file of cuttings (such as the *Guardian's* Homophone Corner) about aspects of language that are reported frequently; keep up with contemporary slang as much as possible, at least as listener and doubtless as ironic user, and understand something of the linguistic world which the students inhabit. They also keep menus where there is more matter in the words than the food, linguistically rich crisp packets, old advertisements and opinionated letters about accents and dialects from all possible sources.

Some of those about to teach A level English Language for the first time may feel unprepared, compared with starting to teach Literature. English degrees may all include significant electives on one or other aspect of language, but they are not all alike, and it is a common finding on ITT courses that English graduates tend in general to have to catch up with their knowledge of language more than of literature. This feeling, however, of relative unpreparedness to launch confidently into English Language teaching is an echo of what has been experienced across the country by well-seasoned English teachers who decided to add Language to their A level programme. They all set about reading up what they could, attending courses on the subject run by the likes of Keith and Shuttleworth, experimenting with enthusiasm and learning from experience.

The pedagogic point to be drawn from this is that it is perfectly possible to succeed as an English Language teacher by good sense, determination and enthusiasm for the subject. English teachers and lecturers came to discover how they could spread enthusiasm for insights into the language itself, all aspects of its systems for making meaning, whether in speech or in writing. Seeing the language as fascinating was the key to teaching it well. This may seem like a starkly obvious point, but those who fired the teachers in the first place made their sessions pre-echoes and echoes of what should be or was, in many cases already, happening in school and college classrooms. Examples of language of all kinds were available, and interest in aspects of them was generated by showing how keen-eyed but non-technical analysis could reveal much that had previously remained unnoticed. Take one small example. We now all, as English teachers, are prepared, by one means or another, to teach the rules of arranging and punctuating speech in writing – direct speech and dialogue. We know what the rules are and can teach them with confidence. Historically, however, we can watch them coming into being. Some of the early novelists, in English, were less clear, apparently, than we are about the differences between direct and indirect speech, and the representation of them. See how, in Fielding's *Joseph Andrews*, for example, we have the following;

> 'I am convinced you are no stranger to that passion; come Joey,' says she, 'tell me truly who is the happy girl whose eyes have made a conquest of you?' Joseph returned, 'that all women he had ever seen were equally indifferent to him.' 'O then,' said the lady, 'you are indeed a general lover.' (Chapter 5)

It would be an interesting point to show, in a class engaged in an exploration of the whole business of how writers represent speech, that earlier writers than Fielding had tackled with ease the demarcation between their narrative and the actual words used by characters within that narrative. Think of *Paradise Lost*, for example, and the speeches that make up the Great Consult in Hell. Few 19th-century novelists, we feel, would put inside speech marks the sentence in indirect speech, 'that all women he had ever seen were equally indifferent to him.'

From the question of the wording and punctuation of speech, it is an easy but fascinating step to look at how different writers in English have characterised, through such devices as spelling and lexis, how characters are to be understood, heard, tonally, within the play of voices in the tale. This is done, very neatly, by Keith and Shuttleworth (2000) as Activity 8, page 8, quoting from *The Pickwick Papers* by Dickens and Dorothy L. Sayers's *Murder Must Advertise*. They present their evidence under the heading 'Dialect and Accent'. However, their approach could be used to illumine other areas besides.

Activity 1

ACCENT AND CHARACTER

(suggested time: 2 hours)

For the sake of exploring both a phonological question, a sociolinguistic question and one that relates to speech–writing relationships, gather three more examples, from English fiction (at any time) where it is clear that the writer is aiming to catch a particular speech effect through the spelling, word-choice or arrangement of the writing. If you can think of no other point at which to start, then begin with Kingsley Amis's *Jake's Thing*.

Standard addressed: 2.1

If you are engaged in teaching a course, then you have to know the extent of what you will be required to teach and your students to learn. English Language does not have its equivalents to the texts set for study in Literature at the same level. It does have texts, but they are not given from the first day, as it were, and read in detail over months, if need be. However, like Literature, Language has sets of skills that must be developed (and tested) through teaching the content knowledge, and through rehearsal of such skills as investigating, reflecting and editing. Instead of set texts to demarcate the content, there are frameworks; these are commonly employed to classify and elucidate aspects of the phenomenon language. They are given here, below:

From Keith and Shuttleworth *Living Language* (2000)

AS [Advanced Subsidiary] **English Language**

This requires [students] to show knowledge and understanding of:

- The key features of the frameworks for the systematic study of the English language:
  a) phonology (sound and intonation patterns of speech);
  b) lexis (vocabulary);
  c) grammar (of both spoken and written texts);
  d) semantics and pragmatics (the ways meanings are constructed and interpreted in both speech and writing).
- The ways language varies according to whether it is written or spoken and according to the context in which it is produced.
- The ways language varies according to personal and social factors.
- The ways that variations in language can shape and change meanings and forms.

In addition students will need to be able to:

- Write appropriately and accurately for a variety of audiences and purposes and comment on what they have produced.

A-level English Language (in addition to AS requirements)
This requires students to show deeper knowledge and understanding of:

- The frameworks for the systematic study of language.
- The ways in which historical and geographical variation shape and change meanings and forms in language.

You need also, as a student, to be able to:

- Comment on and evaluate the usefulness of your application and exploration of these systematic frameworks in the study of spoken and written texts, including texts from the past.

Activity 2   AUDITING YOUR OWN LANGUAGE KNOWLEDGE
(suggested time: 90 minutes)

Conduct an audit of one aspect of your own level of knowledge about the English language, as it will be required for A level teaching purposes. Use the following list of specialist terms (culled from examination specifications), and ensure that terms not known, or only insecurely guessed at, become well defined and significant in your own mind.

> abstract, accent, adverbials, affix, allophone, analogy, anaphoric reference, antonym, auxiliaries, clause, code, collocation, command, common noun, complex, compound, concrete, connotation, co-ordination, declaratives, deixis, denotation, dialect, discourse, elision, ellipsis, etymology, exclamation, family, finite, form, function, genre, grammar, idiolect, idiom, lexis, metaphor, morpheme, passivisation, pragmatics, pre-modification, post-modification, psycholinguistics, register, semantics, simile, slang, structure, style, synonym, syntax, transitivity, words

Among the best sources of definitions of the terms above are, of course, David Crystal's majestic *Encyclopaedias*, either of *Language* or *The English Language*.

The Assessment Objectives for A level English language (AS and A2) may be obtained from the official examination authority's web-pages (**www.aqa.org.uk/qual**). A reading of the set of them leads the teacher to the conclusion that students have quite a sophisticated task ahead when they begin their two years of study, but that there are some essential skills that are well able to be taught. Students must have some linguistic terminology available to be able to show what they know about language; they must be able to reflect on their own writing, decisions and thinking; they must have some critical ability to comment on the usefulness of approaches taken towards analysing or describing some item of language; they must at a variety of points be able to write well, understanding the things they write about and explaining why (to draw upon Keith and Shuttleworth again) language is used differently in different circumstances; they must analyse and evaluate variations in meanings and forms.

LINKS WITH GCSE AND THE KS3 STRATEGY

Since the start of the A level English Language programme the effects of it have been seen lower down the age range. This is not the place to explore that, but there are now, perhaps, more continuous patterns discernible that link lower school work with sixth form work in language than were once there. The KS3 Strategy's English *Framework* shows how literacy may be developed through a conscious focus on aspects of language at word, sentence and text levels. This degree of explicitness, with pupils coming, for example, to realise how to use connectives more sophisticatedly than they had first thought they could, and conscious of the term 'connectives' and its applicability, points towards similar kinds of overt links between a category and its use at A level.

GCSE English, however, although concerned to do much to develop reading and writing, is relatively unaligned with Language at A level as compared to Literature. Those starting to study English Language may well find the initial encounters technical and demanding. A glance at, for example, the first paper to be examined under Specification B of AQA shows that students have to demonstrate they can discuss, from a variety of provided texts: lexis, grammar, phonology, discourse and pragmatics. More will be said below about the actual processes of assessment, but the point to be made here is that some students may well face initial struggles in getting to grips with a series of powerful explanatory terms that they may have scarcely encountered before. As with much else, there are no royal roads to success when it comes to supporting the strugglers, but a general rule worth following might be to lower anxiety. This might be done by taking an example of an examination paper and just getting the class (or a section of it) to talk about, quite simply, how the different texts are different. Ex-Prime Minister Thatcher's address to a radio interviewer about strong government is utterly unlike, in lexical terms, a preceding conversation about feeding the dog, eating in or going out. Each of those is quite unlike a poem by Byron, and so on. Even an initiate can begin to see that these kinds of distinct text are massively different, and could talk about them, even if, at first, only in their own terms. Speakers could then be nudged by such teacher prompts as, 'Tell me about the kinds of words that Mrs Thatcher uses which could not possibly occur in the domestic conversation', and then point out that the student does after all have worthwhile knowledge about lexis.

What the teacher needs to do

The teacher has, in drawing up plans and schemes of work, not only to keep in mind the content to be covered and the skills that are to be tested, but the nature of the distinct papers, tasks and examinations that occur during the two years of study. If these three are held in balance in the right way, then the teaching stands a good chance of gaining coherence. There is scarcely a textbook written in this area except by a practising teacher, so the novice could do much worse than examine the approaches of the wise and experienced. The following emerge as general truths:

1   Start straight away to introduce some specialist vocabulary, but in a way that begins with the phenomena, not the labels or descriptive terms. Hook the labels on to the phenomenon once it has come to be of interest.
2   The study of English Language epitomises the idea that English is learned recursively. It seems that any starting point may, treated in an enlightened way, enable the students to begin to see how language has sounds, words, grammar and rules for intending and receiving meanings.
3   Studying any aspect of language is likely to involve a systematic and informed examination of something already well rehearsed. For example, all

those who speak English can make the full range of appropriate vowel and consonantal sounds of the language, but not until it is pointed out to most students that 'though' and 'through' start on different sounds (respectively a voiced and unvoiced consonantal blend involving tongue on upper front teeth) are they aware of having made this distinction all their speaking lives.

Doing, then, involves lots of advance planning and preparing materials. In an emergency a new teacher, left with an A level English Language class to foster, could do much worse than buy a set of *Living Language*, and work through the chapters. However, for most student teachers or beginners, the situation is not an emergency, and doing consists in having clear knowledge about what is to be learned, what is to be tested and which approaches to teaching work best. Under this last heading a brief list of how your ideal class would proceed, or what would characterise it, would help your long term planning. It could be that you would like each encounter with your group to be characterised by, among other items:

(a)   increasing security about a technical term learned previously by revisiting it from a new angle (morphology, for example, looked at again under the heading 'grammar');

(b)   plenty of offerings from the students about some phenomenon of language which they've come to notice from having started to study it ('Sir, of all the teachers we see in a week, only you have a tendency to employ the post-vocalic "r");

(c)   group work, pair work and investigatory work – e.g. set pairs or triads to complete an analysis of the transcript of two people talking to one another. As they get more secure and advanced, set them to investigate, through the study of different authors whose words you've presented comparatively (subject to copyright) how 'bound morphemes' and 'inflections' can refer to much the same kind of phenomenon, but that the two different terms come from quite different ways of looking at the language (the first phonological, the second grammatical).

Activity 3 EXTENDING THE PLANNING

(suggested time: 1 hour)

Standards addressed: 2.1, 3.3.2, 3.3.3

Continue the list above by adding two more items (d and e).

Activity 4   INTRODUCING CONCEPT WORDS

(suggested time: 1 hour)

Plan a single session (an hour long) that intends to introduce the students to the following concepts: phonemes, allophones, accents, long and short vowels.

Standards addressed: 2.1, 3.1.1

Available to you (and thus potentially to your class) are copies of the International Phonetic Alphabet, Crystal's *Encyclopedias*, tape recordings of different ages, sexes and social classes of speaker, a tape recorder and microphone, the usual transparencies, pens, etc. In your introduction, you should explain why it is necessary to classify sounds in a rather more exact and systematic way than has been done before.

Assessment processes within the course

Each year of the two-year course contains three elements of assessed work. Depending upon particular examination authority and specification, there will be differences of emphasis over exactly what is assessed when, and how, but common to all examination processes is that students must show a deepening understanding in the second year of their course. A *Teacher's Guide* issued by the Assessment and Qualifications Alliance (AQA) in 2001 sums up very neatly how that 'deepening' is to be understood. They provide (on pp. 9 and 10) a graphic series of models about how the Text (spoken or written) becomes the object of a wider and wider framework of understanding by the student, so that, at first, 'Text' is boxed, as it were by 'Representation, Purpose, Subject Matter and Mode' in the first square, and in the outer square by 'Situation, Writer/Speaker, Reader/Listener'. As the course progresses, more squares (symbolising wider conceptual and social frames) are added, requiring more insight into kinds of variation and causes of variation to which language is subject, and, finally, wider critical perspectives are added that bring yet more light to bear (we hope).

Modern examination board publications provide rich and practical detail about the demands of the assessment elements within the course. You should study such documents under your mentors' guidance; it is not easy to summarise them fairly here, but what is being looked for at each stage of the assessment is, of course, the ability to write confidently about what is under scrutiny. For some papers the candidates (as the students will have become) do not know in advance what they will be reading, only how they are to write about what they meet. For some other papers, however, they do know in advance. For example, in AQA Specification B, for Unit 5 of assessment, in the A2 year, the students are given so-called 'Pre-Release Material', in other words, the texts they are to edit. There are some 20 or more extracts from which they produce a text of their own. In short, the rules about how the extracts – the material released prior to the two and a half hour examination – are to be treated are strict and the task demanding, with no small amount of time required for the proper absorption of the 57 pages requiring to be read, thought about and, once in the examination room, cut, combined and rewritten. The skills are sophisticated, if performed at all well, and yet they achieve, at best, 15% of all the marks for the individual concerned.

Activity 5

DOING THE EXAMINATION TASK
(suggested time: 3½ hours)

Carry out for yourself, in your own time, one of the editorial tasks demanded of the A2 students. Discover from within, as it were, how to re-present and transform (to use the AQA's own terminology) the passages given. You'll need to rehearse subtitling, paraphrasing, annotating, introducing, summarising and glossing. Put the finished product in your English portfolio.

Activity 6

FROM ASSESSMENT TO PLANNING
(suggested time: 1 hour)

Standards addressed: 3.2.1, 3.2.2

Look at pages 152–7 of *Living Language* by Keith and Shuttleworth. Here you will see two essays compared, and, illuminatingly from your point of view as well as that of your students, the comments on each script by examiners. Make brief notes when you have finished on what a teacher or lecturer would, ideally, needed to have taught the writer of Essay 1 to enable him or her to gain a higher grade.

A note on achievement

The following comes from a randomly selected long-past examination script to which the writer was given access by a local teacher. It is headed 'English Language Project' and on NEAB paper, and is thus from an element which no longer survives in the form it once took, and from an examination board that has itself transmuted into the AQA. However, despite the age of this script and the fact that at the introduction to it the teacher has noted the writer as 'a weak candidate', and despite the further judgement that he is unable to exploit fully the data he had gained in his investigation, nevertheless this extract is given in order to prove something positive. I believe that writing of this kind proves that the course in English Language has great strength. Here is one student, by no means a naturally good candidate (and in that sense the test of the value of doing the course at all) able to examine his mother's conversational style in a way that shows he can understand perfectly well which elements of language count. What is being illuminated is not just the writer's grasp of some technical terms (not entirely secure), but an understanding of a phenomenon beyond those terms, namely the way in which a speaker may vary their language according to social context. We all do it, but we don't all do it in the same way; here is a part-picture of someone caught in the act, as it were. The names have, for obvious reasons, been changed.

| 447

Mrs Smith does change her language when talking to different people.

She uses more standard forms when talking to Yvonne in conversation six because she is a new friend and she wants to make a good impression.

Most of the time in conversations one to five, Mrs Smith uses 'yeah' instead of 'yes', but in the final conversation, she uses 'yes' 59% of the time (22 out of 37).

Instead of Mrs Smith saying 'oh God' like she has done in other conversations in number six she uses 'oh Goodness.'

When Mrs Smith turns around the pronoun and the past-participle of the verb 'to be' to form a question such as 'was she?' or 'was he' [sic] she uses the correct form of the verb 'was' and not 'were'. In all the other conversations Mrs Smith has used 'were' for all the pronouns I, he, they, she and you, but in conversation six she says '. . . she was feeling then.' This in my opinion is one of the most interesting line [sic] in the whole of the conversation because it proves that she used the standard form instead of the regional dialect form which means she has changed her language due to the person she is speaking to.

Comment on the above. I have long been of the opinion that at A level some of the weaker grades are awarded because of failure to learn, not to read well or understand well, but to write well. Perhaps reading, understanding and writing are too closely bound up with one another to make it possible to fully separate them, but here is a case, it seems, of a writer who has made some perfectly well evidenced observations, and grasped fairly soundly what a dialect is, and what indices of its use are, but who just fails to see how his sentences could be stronger, and paragraphs more coherent. So –

Activity 7

PLANNING TO HELP THE WRITER

(suggested time: 1 hour)

Standards How do you help this writer to give what is above more writerly force? In any case,
addressed: 1.1, work out from the little given here what his teacher has almost certainly done to
3.1.1, 3.2.1, guide this student to investigate some language in use, and what the writer has had
3.2.2, 3.2.4 to do in order to obtain and report on the data referred to.

Key skills

Any A level course may now expect certain skills to be developed from certain modules. Note how the writer above should gain some credit for 'Application of Number' with his percentages and raw figures juxtaposed. More generally however, anyone engaging in English Language should be able to develop their ICT skills (web searches, word processing, and now, increasingly, the ability to store spoken language on a computer, as sound, and indeed to use some aspect of hardware or software as an object of study, if the programs themselves have intrinsic linguistic interest), their ability to work with others and solve problems as investigator, editor and so on, and, of course, they should be able to improve their own learning and performance.

REFERENCES

Crystal, D. (1987) *The Cambridge Encyclopedia of Language*. Cambridge: Cambridge University Press

Crystal, D. (1995) *The Cambridge Encyclopedia of the English Language*. Cambridge: Cambridge University Press

Keith, G. and Shuttleworh, J. (2000) *Living Language*, 2nd edition. London: Hodder & Stoughton

Rosen, H. (1981) *Neither Bleak House Nor Liberty Hall: English in the Curriculum*. London: University of London Institute of Education.

WEBSITES

Examination boards:
www.aqa.org.uk/qual
www.aqa.org.uk/qual/gceasa/engLaB.html
www.wjec.co.uk
www.ocr.org.uk

RECOMMENDED READING

Crystal, D. (1988) *The English Language*. London: Penguin

Bryson, B. (1990) *Mother Tongue*. London: Hamish Hamilton.

Goddard, A. (1998) *Researching Language: English Project Work at A Level and beyond*. Lancaster: Folens Framework

Fairclough, N. (2001) *Language and Power*, 2nd edition. London: Longman/Pearson

Russell, S. (1993) *Grammar, Structure, Style*. Oxford: Oxford University Press.

Thorne, S. (1997) *Mastering Advanced English Language*. Basingstoke: Palgrave

APPENDIX 1: GRADE DESCRIPTORS

The following grade descriptors for A Level English Language indicate the level of attainment characteristic of grades A, C and E at Advanced GCE. They give a general indication of the required learning outcomes at the specified grades.

The descriptions should be interpreted in relation to the content outlined in the specification; they are not designed to define that content. The grade awarded will depend in practice on the extent to which the student has met the assessment objectives overall. Shortcomings in some aspects of the examination may be balanced by better performances in others.

Grade A

In response to the tasks set, candidates demonstrate a comprehensive theoretical knowledge of the way language works as a multi-layered system, through their analysis and evaluation of a range of material from the past to the present. They select and apply analytical frameworks appropriately and systematically in their own investigation and research, evaluating the usefulness of the approaches taken to the description of spoken and written English. Candidates explore perceptively and critically concepts and viewpoints relating to language in use, supporting coherent, well-argued discussion with relevant examples, using appropriate terminology. Their writing is fluent, well structured, accurate and precise, demonstrating awareness of a wide range of different audiences and purposes.

Grade C

In response to the tasks set, candidates demonstrate secure knowledge and understanding of linguistic ideas and concepts in their use of analytic frameworks to identify and discuss significant features of spoken and written language. They distinguish important elements of language variation in past and present usage, explaining these by reference to context and using examples to support their interpretations. They show awareness of different approaches to language study and different attitudes to language use, informed by their own investigative studies of speech or writing. Their writing in a range of tasks is accurate and clear, showing an ability to use technical language appropriately, and some adaptation to audience and purpose.

Grade E

In response to the tasks set, candidates demonstrate some knowledge and understanding of the way different linguistic frameworks may be used and applied in the study of language. They comment descriptively on some of the ways in which spoken and written English varies according to the context of use, without necessarily distinguishing the impact of different factors. Candidates show an appreciation of topical issues surrounding the use of English which may be informed by some investigation of samples of speech and writing. Their writing conveys basic ideas and is generally accurate if non-technical in expression, showing some awareness of the needs of different audiences and purposes.

(Taken from Appendix A of GCE English Language 2005 Specification B, pp. 44 and 45. She http://www.aqa.org.uk/qual/pdf/AQA-5706-6706-w-sp-05.pdf)

chapter 25

TEACHING AS/A2 ENGLISH LITERATURE

By the end of this chapter you will have reflected on your experiences and perceptions of studying and teaching English Literature at A level and identified issues concerning transition from GCSE to AS/A2 study. You will have gained an understanding of the key requirements of the English Literature specifications and experience of devising classroom activities, coursework tasks and long term plans.

RATIONALE

In assuming the responsibility of teaching A level, English teachers are faced with many challenges. Not all the students will be equally passionate about English, want to study it at university or beyond AS. However, the relationships between A level students and their texts are extremely important ones which teachers want to foster in order that their students can continue to develop as critical readers of texts who enjoy reading, can communicate their ideas fully to others and are able to explore a range of interpretations with confidence and insight.

LINKS WITH THE NATIONAL CURRICULUM

Teaching and learning at AS/A2 level should be informed by students' experiences of English at Key Stages 3 and 4. If you have not done so already it would be a good idea to familiarise yourself with the requirements of GCSE English and English Literature specifications before beginning your reading for this chapter.

On your school or college placement you should:

- Find out which A level Literature specification your school uses
- Read some examples of examination papers
- Ask if you can look at some recently assessed coursework and try to talk to the teacher who marked it
- Observe a number of different A level teachers in action
- Talk to A2 students about their experiences of the first year of the course
- Investigate A level resources in the department, school library and ICT base
- Talk to the teacher responsible for A level Literature. Find out: how the course is planned; how groups are organised; how texts are chosen; how progress is tracked; differences between performance of males and females in the subject
- Broaden your own subject knowledge by reading examination texts you are unfamiliar with
- Take an active role in A level lessons and negotiate to plan and teach a block of lessons.

Activity 1

NATURE OF A LEVEL LITERATURE
(suggested time: 30 minutes)

Standard addressed: 1.7

Begin by reflecting on your own experiences (if any) of receiving A level Literature teaching. How did these compare with Literature study lower down the school? How did your teachers organise the lessons? What kinds of activities did you do? How were you able to express your views about texts? What was expected of you as a learner? Now note down any issues, concerns and questions which you personally may have about teaching at this level. Be honest and try to return to these notes (kept in your English portfolio) once you have completed the rest of this section.

Activity 2

FAMILIARISING YOURSELF WITH KEY PRINCIPLES
(suggested time: 90 minutes)

Standard addressed: 2.1

Read Chapter 11, 'English in the sixth form' in Fleming and Stevens (1998).

Read Chapter 13, 'English at 16 +' in Davison and Dowson (1998).

These chapters will give you an overview of some of the key principles about teaching Literature at A level. However, it is important to be aware that any specific information they provide about syllabuses (now called 'specifications') is now out of date. From September 2000 changes in the assessment structure of all A level courses mean that all students in every subject are to sit AS examinations during the first year of their course. It was not uncommon at the time of change for English teachers to feel that students in Y12 were having to make judgements about texts based on too little experience of reading, interpreting and writing at advanced level, but there is no doubt that the new requirements have been adapted to since they began to take force. One positive compensation for the need to be assessed early is that students have a chance to resit, during their A2 year, a module originally taken at AS level at which they did poorly. The student's growing ability to read and to write well may gain recognition (for A2 award) before the course is over. The idea of intellectual growth not being constant or steady is given formal power in this aspect of the examination arrangements. This can have the consequence that a student may enter his or her last set of exams in confident mood, based on the successful attempt at an upgrade.

Standard addressed: 2.1d

Many of the courses offer examinations in both January and the summer. The results from these courses can then either be 'cashed in' for an AS qualification or used as a building block towards a full A level, which is awarded if students are successful in their A2 examinations at, and coursework completed by, the end of the second year of the course.

Activity 3

FAMILIARISING YOURSELF WITH EXAMINATION REQUIREMENTS
(suggested time: 30 minutes)

Read carefully through the common core requirements, assessment objectives for AS/A2 Literature (obtained on-line from **www.edexcel.org.uk**, **www.aqa.org.uk**, **www.wjec.co.uk or www.ocr.org.uk**), the Further Notes on Assessment Objective (AO) 5i and AO5ii and the Grade Descriptions for A, C and E grade work (Appendices 1 and 2).

Structure of the course

Common to all English Literature examinations are the AS/A2 core requirements.

All candidates complete an AS course (worth 50%) in their first year. This requires them to show knowledge and understanding of:

- a minimum of four texts
- prose
- poetry
- drama
- a play by Shakespeare
- one other text (other than Shakespeare) that was published before 1900.

Those students moving on to A level in their second year (A2) need to show knowledge and understanding of:

- a minimum further four texts
- prose, poetry and drama
- at least one work published before 1770 (pre-Romantic)
- at least one other text written before 1900
- comparisons across texts.

All the core texts studied in both years should be of sufficient substance and quality to merit serious consideration and should originally have been written in English. (Study of work in translation is encouraged in some specifications as an element of wider reading.)

One assessment unit from each year of the course is examined without the texts being available to students during the examination (known as 'closed book'). The A level Literature course (A2) must include synoptic assessment. Coursework options of 30% are available in some specifications. You will find the Assessment Objectives for AS/A2 Literature at **www.edexcel.org.uk**, **www.aqa.org.uk**, **www.wjec.co.uk** or **www.ocr.org.uk**. Further Notes on AO 5i and AO 5ii may be found as Appendix 1 and the Grade Descriptions for Grades A, C and E as Appendix 2 of the present chapter.

Activity 4

FROM GCSE TO GCE
(suggested time: 1 hour)

Standards addressed: 3.1.1, 3.2.4, 3.3.2

What challenges do you think these requirements and assessment objectives present to students who have recently completed their GCSEs? What aspects of A level study will you need to support them with? Make notes by way of answer, and keep these in your English portfolio. Re-read pages 272–3 of Davison and Dowson and pages 123–7 of Fleming and Stevens (both 1998) for practical advice on some of the issues likely to occur.

Activity 5

INVOLVING THE READERS
(suggested time: 90 minutes)

Both Fleming and Stevens and Davison and Dowson stress that it is important for teachers to draw on the good practices for working with texts which have been established at KS3 and 4. Students need to be encouraged early on to participate fully in their A level lessons in order to develop their own personal responses to texts and to share and challenge the interpretations of others. Such activities should include the directed activities related to texts (DARTs) which you will be familiar with from Chapter 13, 'Teaching Reading' and Chapter 14, 'Children's Literature and Narrative Texts' in Section Three (you may want to refer back to the chart of DARTs in that unit to remind yourself).

In the very early stages of a course, novel openings can provide a useful way to open up discussion about texts.

Standards addressed: 2.1, 3.1.1, 3.1.2, 3.3.3

- Select five novel openings (either by the same author or a range of authors whose texts are perhaps thematically linked) and plan a series of DARTs for two lessons of an hour each. The activities should involve some small group work and whole class presentation. The lessons should focus on developing students' skills in A03 and A04.
  (Some suggested authors you could use are: Thomas Hardy, Charles Dickens, Alice Walker, Jane Austen, Raymond Chandler, Edith Wharton.)
- Now consider how you might build on what is achieved in these two lessons. What could this work lead to for the whole class? For individual students?

Activity 6

DESIGNING COURSEWORK ASSIGNMENTS
(suggested time: 90 minutes)

You will see on the second AS/A2 chart the weightings which each examination board has given to different papers. The AQA B Shakespeare coursework paper, for example, emphasises the importance of 'assessing candidates' ability to articulate independent opinions and judgements, informed by different interpretations of literary texts by other readers'.

Standards addressed: 1.1, 2.1,d, 3.1.2, 3.1.3, 3.3.1d

In order to prepare your students for AQA B Paper 3, first select your text (you could choose any Shakespeare play except *Measure for Measure*, as this is assessed elsewhere). Design a selection of coursework assignments for your students to choose from which would cover the appropriate AOs. (Candidates are allowed to submit either one coursework piece of approximately 1,500–2,000 words in length or two pieces of around 750–1,000 words each.)

Activity 7

PLANNING TEACHING OF THE NOVEL
(suggested time: 2 hours)

As a result of the new assessment arrangements many more modular courses are now on offer than previously. Think about the impact of modular courses on A level literature teaching.

- How do you think the knowledge that your brand new Year 12 group are going to sit a modular exam in 15 weeks' time would influence your planning, introduction and teaching of a novel such as *Wuthering Heights* or *The Handmaid's Tale*?
- Choose either of these texts (or another novel) you know well and try to break down the text into sections. Decide which sections of the book you

Standards addressed: 1.1, 2.1,d, 3.1.2, 3.1.3, 3.3.1d

would want to read in class and which students would be required to read independently. How would you ensure the reading has been completed? How much time would you allow for discussion of the whole text? What are the key features of this text which students would need to be familiar with?

- How would your teaching plan differ if the students were to be examined on the novel in nine months' time?

Activity 8   PREPARING FOR THE SYNOPTIC PAPER

(suggested time: 2 hours)

In the A2 part of the course Literature students (along with all students in all other A level subjects) sit a synoptic paper. Synoptic assessment draws on all the assessment objectives and is designed so that students synthesise the skills and knowledge gained during the whole of their course. In A2 Literature they are expected to apply their knowledge and skills to consideration of previously unseen material (in some specifications pre-released material is also included). 'Pre-release' material refers to texts from the examination board distributed, via the centre (school or college) to the candidates, so that all candidates have equal study time prior to the examination on the texts they've read.

Standards addressed: 1.1, 2.1,d, 3.1.2, 3.1.3, 3.3.1d

- For detailed information about synoptic assessment requirements and specific set texts for each paper, consult the examination boards' websites (addresses provided at the end of this chapter).
- How might you need to prepare your students for synoptic assessment?
- How could you adapt your 'Novel openings' activities to use them in the spring term of Year 13 in preparation for synoptic assessment?

Scenarios

1   A talented and conscientious GCSE student seems to be overwhelmed by the pressures of her four new AS courses and is arriving at your Literature lessons exhausted, underprepared and over-anxious. What might you do?

2   A very quiet student who had gained five Cs at GCSE is now in your new AS group. While he is extremely diligent about reading and making notes on other people's ideas, he avoids participation in class discussion and is beginning to be regarded as a bit of a joke by others in the group. What would you do?

CONTINUOUS THREADS

1 Professional values and practice

There is much hope in the discovery that from time to time, but usually under an inspiring teacher, students who were unsure about their capacity to cope in the A level Literature class have in fact discovered in themselves a fascination with what was at first difficult. The Standards for QTS cannot demand inspiration, but any teacher's professionalism may be seen in such attitudes as: their preparedness to think about how to bring students and texts into the most productive alignment; their own preparedness to re-read and rediscover the set texts and read fresh critical commentary about them; their treating encouragingly the first written responses from students and demonstrating in their explanations of texts models of how to think about them. In conjunction with those things come degrees of awareness about context already defined and investigated so far, and rehearsal in assessing well, neither harshly nor softly. Many highly professional teachers at this level are as demanding of their students as they are of themselves.

3.2 Planning, expectations and targets

Careful organisation of structured speaking and listening activities is a very important element of A level teaching. On occasion you will want to build in tutorial time to talk to students individually. There are other notes on this element under the heading 'Organising Activities in Class' in Chapter 23 'English Post-16'.

See also under this planning heading notes for how and when particular texts are taught in the same chapter.

If you have not done so already, read Chapter 26 'Girls and Literature' of Sue Brindley's *Teaching English* (1994). What are the implications of the different agendas an English teacher is faced with for your A level teaching?

When in your secondary placement school, investigate the number of male A level Literature candidates and the centre's results by gender. How do they compare with the GCSE scores and with national averages? What strategies do the staff use when selecting texts, teaching strategies and student groupings?

3.3 Monitoring and assessment

Monitoring and assessing will scarcely, under the post-2000 arrangements, be far from any teacher's mind. Accuracy and fairness of assessment should be accompanied by good feedback and advice. There are teachers who can help their students to improve a coursework essay in progress with swiftly given marginal notes and other prompts about what to leave out, what to insert (by way of ideas) and what to re-word. Some students have been known to gain much from such practical uses of assessment. They go to school with a coursework essay about which they are doubtful, and return home with one which they are confident will help them make the next draft much better. This kind of immediately usable feedback helps to improve the student's writing rather than reading, but other kinds of advice and instruction to the reader about reading again, and what to look for, may be very powerful too. Reading can be monitored and assessed, as when groups or pairs report on what they have found, or have come to think about a critical aspect of a text.

Finally, remind yourself again of the Assessment Objectives. They must inform your planning, be shared with your students and used in your review of what has been achieved.

3.3 Teaching and class management

See 3.2. above, particularly the advice to read the section 'Organising Activities in Class' in Chapter 23.

3.3.4 Differentiation

Although your students will all have successfully passed GCSE, the ability range in any A level group will probably be very wide. How will you differentiate when teaching examination texts and setting assignment tasks? Think about the processes of negotiation which will be needed. Read the section on Differentiation in Scott-Baumann et al.'s book, *Becoming a Secondary Teacher* (1997: 133–8).

2.5 ICT

- Familiarise yourself with the websites listed below and use a search engine to discover other potentially useful sites on specific A level texts.
- How could you use email to encourage students' development of personal response and awareness of different interpretations of texts? Goodwyn (2000) has a number of chapters which could inspire further ideas about using ICT in A level Literature teaching.

FURTHER READING

Critical writing

Bleiman, B. (1999) 'Integrating language and literature at A level', *English and Media Magazine*, 40 (Summer) 19–22

Blocksidge, M. (1999) *Teaching Literature 11–18*. London: Continuum

Eaglestone, R. (1999) *Doing English*. London: Routledge

The English Magazine (The PGCE English team may subscribe to this magazine – ask your tutor about it.)

The English Review

Texts offering practical approaches

Dymoke, S. (ed.) (2000) 'Critical Reading at Post 16' Series (recent titles include *Arcadia*, *The Duchess of Malfi* and *Translations*). Sheffield, NATE/YPS

Hackman, S. and Marshall, B. (1990) *Re-Reading Literature*. London, Hodder & Stoughton

Moon, B. (1992) *Literary Terms: A Practical Glossary*. London: EMC

Royston, M. (1998) *Finding a Voice: Personal Response to AO Level English*. Cheltenham, Stanley Thornes

Ogborn, J. and Webster, L. (2000) *Text, Reader, Critic*. London: EMC

Shiach, D. (1996) *Prose and Poetry: the Reading of the Text*. Cambridge: Cambridge University Press

APPENDIX 1: FURTHER NOTES

AO5i

At AS Level, AO5i requires candidates to show 'understanding of the contexts in which literary texts are written and understood'.

AO5ii

At A2 Level this is expanded as AO5ii, requiring candidates to 'evaluate the significance of cultural, historical and other contextual influences upon literary texts and study'.

The major distinction between AS Level and A2 Level is that in their first year, students will be expected to acknowledge and explore, perhaps from within the texts, the contextual frameworks of literary works. At A2 Level the exploration should be more complex, so that candidates evaluate some of the contextual areas outlined below, and assess the relationship between texts and contexts in terms of ideas and of style.

Candidates should be aware of the significant facts or processes of different kinds which have shaped the writing of literary works and responses to them.

The most important include:

- the context of period or era, including significant social, historical, political and cultural processes
- the context of the work in terms of the writer's biography and/or milieu
- the context of the work in terms of other works, including other works by the same author
- the different contexts for a work established by its reception over time, including the recognition that works have different meanings and effects upon readers in different periods. This could overlap with AO4 in consideration of different critical responses
- the context of a given or specific passage in relation to the whole work from which it is taken: a part-to-whole context
- the literary context, including the question of generic factors and period-specific styles
- the language context, including relevant and significant episodes in the use and development of literary language. This would include matters of style, such as the use of colloquial, dialect, or demotic language.

At AS Level the awareness of context displayed by candidates will be at a simpler level than at A Level, where candidates will be expected to frame considerations of a given text or texts within some of the contextual frames outlined above. Therefore, at A Level candidates should explore contexts as well as texts.

APPENDIX 2: GRADE DESCRIPTIONS

The following grade descriptions indicate the level of attainment characteristic of grades A, C and E at Advanced GCE. They give a general indication of the required learning outcomes at the specified grades.

The descriptions should be interpreted in relation to the content outlined in the specification; they are not designed to define that content. The grade awarded will depend in practice on the extent to which the student has met the assessment objectives overall. Shortcomings in some aspects of the examination may be balanced by better performances in others.

Grade A

Students demonstrate a comprehensive, detailed knowledge and understanding of a wide range of literary texts from the past to the present, and of the critical concepts associated with literary study. Their discussion of texts shows depth, independence and insight in response to the tasks set, and they analyse and evaluate the ways in which form, structure and language shape meanings. Where appropriate, students identify the influence on texts of the cultural and historical contexts in which they were written. They are able to make significant and productive comparisons between texts which enhance and extend their readings, and are sensitive to the scope of their own and others' interpretations of texts. Their material is well organised and presented, making effective use of textual evidence in support of arguments. Written expression is fluent, well-structured, accurate and precise, and shows confident grasp of appropriate terminology.

Grade C

Students demonstrate sound knowledge and understanding of a range of texts from different periods and of different types, and make use of some of the critical concepts relevant to the study of literature. Students comment perceptively on texts in response to the tasks set. They respond to some details in the ways authors use form, structure and language to create meaning, as well as showing some awareness of contextual influences. They relate their own judgements to those of others as appropriate in developing interpretations of texts. They are able to pursue comparisons between texts in order to show how texts can illuminate one another. Their material is clearly organised and presented, and incorporates examples to help sustain a line of argument. Written expression is accurate and clear and shows a sound use of appropriate terminology.

Grade E

Students demonstrate some knowledge and understanding of a range of different tasks and comment on them in response to the tasks set, sometimes supporting their views by reference to the links between meanings and authors' uses of form, structure and language. Students note the possible effects of context and may show some understanding of how other readers interpret the text. They can draw out broad lines of similarities and differences between texts, not necessarily within a wider critical framework. Their written work is generally accurate in conveying statements and opinions, sometimes supported by reference to the texts, and shows the use of some terminology appropriate to the subject.

Taken from 26 UA006108 – Specification – Edexcel AS/A GCE in English Literature – Issue 2 – June 2000. (See http://www.exdexcel.org.uk/VirtualContext/48393/gce_englishlit–iss3.pdf)

REFERENCES

Brindley, S (ed.) (1994) *Teaching English in the Secondary School*. London: Routledge
Davison, J. and Dowson, J. (1998) *Learning to Teach English in the Secondary School: A Companion to School Experience*. London: Routledge

Fleming, M. and Stevens, D. (1998) *English Teaching in the Secondary School*. London: David Fulton

Goodwyn, A. (2000) *English in the Digital Age*. London: Cassell Education

Scott-Baumann, A. and Bloomfield, A. with Roughton, L. (1997) *Becoming a Secondary School Teacher*. London: Hodder & Stoughton.

WEBSITES

Exam boards: www.edexcel.org.uk, www.aqa.org.uk
www.wjec.co.uk, www.ocr.org.uk
www.leicestershire.gov.uk/education/ngfl/literacy/alevel
www.learn.co.uk www.poetrysoc.com
www.shunsley.eril.net http://lion.chadwyck.co.uk/html/about.htm
www.englishonline.co.uk

chapter 26

ASPECTS OF DRAMA: POST-16

By the end of this chapter you will have an overview of two of the most commonly taught courses in Drama and Theatre Studies at A/AS level and a more detailed knowledge of the Edexcel specification. In addition to understanding the specification contents you will also consider teaching methodology and how key skills can be integrated into the subject. The chapter does not directly examine GNVQ Performing Arts as this includes music and dance, but some activities may be relevant to teaching the drama content of this course.

RATIONALE

A level Drama and Theatre Studies is very different to KS3 drama. Post-16 students have chosen to take the subject and the majority will be confident and keen to perform. This is not the case with younger pupils. It is, of course, both possible and desirable to use drama methodology to explore texts through improvisation, etc. as part of the A level course, but much of it is also concerned with performing and devising. This is a natural progression as students have developed their ability to use the art form. There is provision for students to support performance in a technical capacity for assessment at A level, but you will find that most will want to act.

It is important, therefore, to stress that you should seriously consider whether to teach this subject at A level if you do not have any specialist training or experience. It is not uncommon for English specialists to assume that teaching a dramatic text for Theatre Studies is similar to English. There is of course some common ground but you also need a thorough knowledge of how a play will evolve into a performance from the viewpoints of actors, directors, technicians and designers. This is very different from using some classroom drama techniques to investigate characters or fill in the missing parts of the story, although this may be a part of your work. In addition, school students' experience of studying plays will be greatly enriched through knowledge about contemporary practitioners and theatre history and through developing their skills in critically analysing theatre in performance. You do need to know the subject well.

The chapter focuses primarily on the Edexcel specification (**http:// www.edexcel.org.uk/**). This is fast growing in popularity and is, in my opinion, better suited to a mixed ability group of students who might be coming to the course for a variety of reasons. If you are only able to observe the AQA or OCR courses, then adapt the activities to suit the board and specification in question – they are flexible.

The chapter assumes that most English teachers will probably not go on to teach Drama and Theatre Studies at A level. Activities are therefore structured to enable you to familiarise yourself with the specification contents while building in practical approaches for anyone who may be serious about teaching the subject later.

Drama and Theatre Studies at A/AS Level

In the past few years A level courses have undergone a radical restructure. The first year of the new course is known as AS level and can be studied as a course in its own right or as the route to the second, or A2, year. Many of the ideas for teaching and learning in the old syllabuses are relevant to the new courses but it is essential to obtain details about the new specifications from the different exam bodies, in this instance Edexcel, OCR and AQA.

In order to help readers grasp what knowledge and skills are to be taught through the A level drama courses, the following is reproduced from the Edexcel specification;

Knowledge and understanding

In the AS units students will show knowledge and understanding of:

- the use of theatrical forms and genre in relation to the exploration and performance of plays
- how plays relate to the contexts in which they are created and/or performed
- the different ways in which plays are interpreted by different directors, designers, performers and audiences, acknowledging that drama and theatre texts have a range of meanings and that the significance of these is related to the directors', designers' and performers' and audiences' knowledge, experience and ideas
- a minimum of three plays, two of which must be by different playwrights
- the importance of social, cultural and/or historical influences on plays and the relevance of the playwright's, director's, designer's and/or performer's life and his/her other work

- the use of drama and theatre terms and concepts.

In addition the A2 units require students to show knowledge and understanding of:

- the significance of theatrical forms and genre and performance theory in relation to devised work, the performance of a play and the in-depth study of a play
- the ways in which plays have been interpreted and valued by different audiences, directors, designers, performers and critics at different times, acknowledging that the interpretation of plays can depend on an audience's and interpreter's assumptions and stance
- a further three plays different from those studied in the AS units. This will include an in-depth study of a prescribed play examined from the point of view of a director, the research into the production history of a second prescribed play and the undertaking of the role of a performer or designer within the production process of a third play performed to an audience
- how to create an original play using the devising process and how to rehearse and perform it to an audience
- the use and evaluation of higher order drama and theatre terms and concepts.

Skills

Skills in drama and theatre studies refers to the following:

- acting skills
- design skills
- directorial skills (for A2)
- interpretative skills
- creative, devising and improvisation skills
- analytical, evaluative and critical skills
- communication skills
- inter-personal and group working skills.

Generally it is assumed that those in possession of skills are at least in a potential position to teach them, but that those without skills can do little more than outline them. The English graduate therefore, without prior training in drama, might like to examine both the 'Knowledge and understanding' lists above (AS and A2) and the 'Skills' list as a way of auditing what they would need to learn first if they were to try to enter this practical realm. However, there may be some areas in the lists above where the English graduate already feels quite well qualified and able to have something useful to contribute.

Any pair of English and drama teachers might wish to collaborate and co-operate in the interests of the school student cohort that studies both subjects at A level. Students who were studying English Literature as well as Drama and Theatre Studies could be in a position to understand both subjects better at points where they meet, where the knowledge, analytic skills and kinds of explanatory writing in both have much in common. One example of a meeting-point would be where students are required to see how plays relate to the context in which they are performed, in different historical periods. Students of Literature are also required by their own examination specifications to know about texts and contexts; their teachers are likely to supply them with a variety of published interpretations which show how differently the same work may be understood by different critics or different societies. These could surely be made to harmonise with studies in the history of theatre which enable students to see how text and context combine to form that elusive pay-off: meaning. Good texts on drama and theatre (e.g. Cooper and Mackey, 1995) confront the difficulties of the term 'meaning' in a way that a student could benefit from when relating to poems and novels. Such a student might well be guided in their reading by a teacher aware of a good learning opportunity when it arises.

Drama studies will help Literature studies not only by providing further exercises in writing (notes, diaries, observations of performances and critical summaries, etc.), but by helping the student to understand how plays come into being at all, through the skills listed above, of acting, designing, directing and so on. A play is more public than either a poem or a novel. To read the novel or the poem may be to study it, but to read the script of a play is only ever to study, not the play, but part of its plan. These kinds of essential differences relating to reception, to private or public enactments of a work, are not at first obvious to students, but could be made significant.

Through their collaboration we can see that the English and Drama teachers, at AS or A2, may have much to offer their students. This is especially true for those whom they teach in common. If they exchange information and synchronise their approaches, then they can develop in one place skills initially acquired in another and generally improve the necessary thinking about how words, forms and meanings interrelate. They can also guide the reading of certain students (and library provision for them), especially that of the gifted and keen, so that, for example, a single critical text may enlighten some students' understanding of both Brecht and Shakespeare.

Some English teachers will know much about drama through formal study and others through spontaneous interest and an inability to stay out of theatres. Others still will have good practical knowledge through work experience; it is certainly not unknown to recruit on to PGCE English courses students who have previously worked for and with a theatre company. Those wanting to participate in teaching Theatre Studies or collaborate with the drama specialist would have much to learn from such an enthusiastic, broadly exampled and well-theorised account for students as Cooper and Mackey's *Theatre Studies – An Approach for Advanced Level* (1995). Texts of this kind, like the Keith and Shuttleworth (2000) recommended for A level English Language, are invaluable for English student teachers who want to see by example the critical and epistemological basis of a subject which they might like to teach or need to teach.

Activity 1   COMPARING SPECIFICATIONS AT A LEVEL

(suggested time: 40 minutes)

Get hold of the specifications for the Edexcel course and those of one of the two other A level Drama and Theatre Studies courses. Using the course outlines

Standard addressed: 2.1.d contained within each specification make a list of the similarities and differences between them and include this in your portfolio. How does what the specifications contain compare to any preconceptions you may have had about the courses?

One student teacher – Paul Dulley – wrote the following in response:

'Edexcel GCE Drama:

The Edexcel specification "recognises three essential activities in drama":

- the drama process in relation to exploring themes, issues and ideas within the context of the student's own work
- the drama process in relation to exploring themes, issues and ideas within the context of the work of dramatists
- drama products in relation to the performance of the student's own work or the work of others.

60% of the exam is based upon teacher-assessed coursework (paper 1), 40% upon an externally assessed practical examination (paper 2). Paper one is itself divided into two units. Unit one intends pupils to use stimulus material from *different times and/or cultures* in order to explore ideas and issues through drama. Paper two centres upon the "exploration of a complete and substantial play" (chosen by the school) in terms of script, direction, acting and design. For paper two, pupils are required to give a drama performance using "any appropriate material as a stimulus". This can be either a *devised performance, performance support or scripted performance*.'

AQA GCE Drama

The rationale behind the AQA GCE in drama is to offer 'candidates the opportunities to develop their practical skills in drama and to enhance their appreciation and understanding of drama and a range of play texts'.

The actual examination comprises 60% coursework and 40% written examination. For coursework, pupils select two options from the following list, only one of which can be a technical/design skill:

1 *Devised thematic work for performance to an audience*
2 *Acting*
3 *Theatre in Education presentation*
4 *Improvisation*
5 *Dance/drama*
6 *Set*
7 *Costume*
8 *Make-up*
9 *Properties*
10 *Masks*
11 *Puppets*
12 *Lighting*
13 *Sound*
14 *Stage management.*

Each option is assessed through 50% practical work (preparatory work and end-product) and 10% response to the process of development. The written examination consists of a two-hour paper in which pupils must answer any two questions from the following sections: *set plays* (a choice from six) and *response to live productions seen during the course*.

It would seem that the Edexcel GCE places a far greater emphasis upon practical performance than its AQA counterpart. Whereas a pupil on the former course could expect a minimum of 70% of the examination to be based upon her acting performances, the AQA course implicitly stipulates a minimum of 30% in this area. Of course, pupils taking the AQA exam could, through a careful selection of options, choose to have as much as 60% of their mark based upon performance. In this sense, the AQA specification is both broader and more flexible. Not only does it accommodate those pupils with a strong desire to concentrate upon their acting skills, it allows others to study the important technical/design areas of drama. This could, of course, create its own difficulties in terms of delivering the great number of options available to students. The AQA exam, therefore, may require a school able to support cross-curricular study between the English/Drama and Art/Design departments (perhaps even the Science Department for areas such as sound and lighting).

Activity 2

PROGRESSION FROM AS TO A2
(suggested time: 20 minutes)

Standards addressed: 2.1.d, 3.2.3

Looking at both specifications and also at specimen examination papers, consider and make notes on progression through the course between AS and A2. For example, how do the performance-based units change from the first to the second year of the course? Would you have any concerns about any aspect of this?

Activity 3

OBSERVING A LEVEL DRAMA LESSONS: A SCHOOL-BASED TASK
(suggested time in addition to observation time: 1 hour)

Observe some A level lessons being taught, and note how the lessons fitted into the specification in question. Write your observations up briefly for your portfolio under the following headings:

1   Start of lesson
2   Introductory or warm-up activities
3   How lesson content fits into specification
4   Conclusion of lesson.

Activity 4   PLANNING A PATHWAY THROUGH THE TWO YEARS

(suggested time:30 minutes)

Look again at the Edexcel specification in more detail. This one allows teachers a fair amount of freedom to use their own personal areas of expertise in planning the course. Study the exam board's suggestions for pathways, which follow. There is a two-year overall plan for the course.

Pathways

The plays to be studied in Units 1, 2 and 5 are the choice of individual centres but to ensure that there is sufficient breadth and depth across the whole qualification, centres must structure their course in drama and theatre studies using the following pathways as a guide. Each pathway is designed to ensure that centres choose a range of texts and genres to work in. The plays and genres given as suggestions in each pathway are only examples for Units 1 to 5.

Pathway A		
Unit no	**Areas of Study**	**Suggestions**
1	2 plays by different playwrights excluding those prescribed in Unit 6	*Mother Courage* by Bertolt Brecht; *Antigone* by Jean Anouilh
2	Different play by 1 of the 2 playwrights studied in Unit 1	*The Caucasian Chalk Circle* by Bertolt Brecht
3	Contextual study of the play from Unit 2	*The Caucasian Chalk Circle* by Bertolt Brecht and a live performance of any play
4	The creating and performing of a devised production in a different genre from Units 2 and 5	Devising any physical piece
5	Designing or performing role in a production of a different play from that studied in any other unit	A production of *An inspector Calls* by J.B. Priestley
6	An in-depth study of 1 prescribed play and a research study of the performance history of a play written and produced between 1575 and 1720	**Either** *The Beggar's Opera* by John Gay **or** *The Trojan Women* by Euripides **and** *a play written between 1575 and 1720*

From UA006805 – specification. Edexcel AS/A GCE in Drama and Theatre Studies – Issue 3 – September 2002, p. 12.

Pathway B		
Unit no	Areas of Study	Suggestions
1	2 plays by the same playwright excluding those studied in Unit 6	*Fen* and *Vinegar Tom* by Caryl Churchill
2	1 play by a different playwright from that studied in Unit 1 but could be 1 of the playwrights studied in Unit 6	*The Crucible* by Arthur Miller
3	Contextual study of the play from Unit 2 as a performance text and a performance analysis of a production of a play	Production of *The Crucible* by Arthur Miller and a 'live' performance of any play
4	The creating and performing of a devised production in a different genre from Units 2 and 5	Devising a documentary theatre piece
5	Designing or performing a role in a production of a different play from that studied in any other unit	A production of *Art* by Yasmin Reza
6	An in-depth study of 1 prescribed play and a research study of the performance history of a play written and produced between 1575 and 1720	**Either** *The Beggar's Opera* by John Gay **or** *The Trojan Women* by Euripides **and** a *play written and produced between 1575 and 1720*

From UA006805 – specification. Edexcel AS/A GCE in Drama and Theatre Studies – Issue 3 – September 2002, p. 12.

TASK

Copy the pathway grid into your portfolio and fill in any ideas for your own pathway if you were to teach the course. It is important that the students are introduced to a range of theatre forms and practitioners during the course, so your plan needs to reflect this.

Don't worry if you have some gaps. This in itself may be useful in highlighting where you need to develop your own knowledge in order to teach the course. Remember too that many A level teachers share responsibility for teaching a course. It may be that you would feel more confident in teaching certain areas of the specification over others, even if you feel you have some expertise.

Standards addressed:
2.1.d, 3.2.3d

Email your grid and/or any ideas to other modular students and compare notes.

Activity 5   DEVISING AN OUTLINE FOR A WORKSHOP/LESSON
(suggested time: 40 minutes, plus teaching time if relevant)

Using your own pathway grid from the previous activity or any one of those suggested in the Edexcel specification, devise the outline for a workshop/lesson (or part of one) for Unit 1. You may choose to focus on one of the two texts or consider something that would explore a theme for both texts. Use the detailed specification to help you.

Standard addressed: 3.3.3

You could plan a lesson to actually teach, if this is possible on your placement and you think you may wish to teach the subject at A level later. In this case collaborate closely with the class teacher in your planning. You will also need to use the texts that the students are actually studying for their course. If these are different to your own pathway, substitute the ones the students are studying, for this activity.

Include your lesson plan and an evaluation of the lesson in your portfolio.

Activity 6   DEVISING A PIECE OF ORIGINAL THEATRE
(suggested time: 20 minutes)

Unit 4 of the Edexcel course requires students to devise a piece of original theatre for performance to others.

Consider what guidance you might be able to give to students in order to help them to use a stimulus to start a piece of drama, i.e. making a vocal soundtrack for a photograph from a newspaper *or* creating the outline of a character who might own a stimulus object *or* creating abstract still images in response to words such as 'greed' or 'freedom'.

Standard addressed: 3.3.2d

Write down the details of one or two short exercises/activities in your portfolio.

Again, if possible, actually teach some of your ideas and record how successful they were.

Activity 7   DIRECTOR'S NOTE
(suggested time: 30 minutes)

Choose one of the two plays, *The Trojan Women* and *The Beggar's Opera*, outlined in Unit 6 of the Edexcel specification. Students are required to annotate one of the texts as if they were a director mounting a production of the play.

Select an extract of about a page long. Use this to make some director's notes of your own. You will need to consider the following, even if only briefly:

- what the set will be like
- what costumes the actors in the extract might wear
- any sound or lighting effects
- what the actors will do.

Standard addressed:
3.3.2.d

Include your notes in your portfolio.

Activity 8

KEY SKILLS
(suggested time: 20 minutes)

Drama and Theatre Studies provide plentiful opportunities to include and assess key skills activities. Consider an activity you could include in your teaching which would allow you to assess your students. Give one example for each of the following key skills:

1 Communication
2 Improving Own Learning and Performance
3 Working with Others
4 Problem Solving.

Standard addressed:
3.2.3.d

Use any specification for this activity and record your ideas in your portfolio.

Scenarios

1 Both specifications involve students visiting at least one live theatre performance and writing an analysis of it. Imagine that some of your students have seen very little live theatre. What pointers could you give them in order to help them make notes during the performance?
2 In the performance units of both specifications students will need to rely on each other to attend rehearsals and sometimes work without you around. What ideas might you consider to ensure that all students are motivated and committed to such work?

CONTINUOUS THREADS

1 Professional values and practice

There is some scope on the A level course to choose plays to suit your group from within a set list. This may help if you have a large ratio of female students and wish to study theatre and women, for example. However, the emphasis of the courses is still very Eurocentric in its recommendation of types of play and practitioners. This does make it easy to fulfil the requirement to include a European dimension in education, though!

3.1 Planning expectations and targets

There is a natural progression between AS and A2 – the former being more teacher led and the latter offering students more autonomy. The units in the second year often return to the areas of study tackled in the first year, but in more depth, so it is a spiral curriculum. You will need to structure lessons and be prepared to direct in the first year. This will also happen in the second year, but students should be taking more responsibility for shaping the work within your framework.

You will need to be familiar with the GCSE syllabus followed by the students in order to decide which will be the most appropriate specification for A level. Edexcel tends to follow on better from the more practical and coursework GCSEs than AQA.

It is worth bearing in mind that it is probably better to start at KS3 upwards when planning a drama curriculum for the school as a whole. The skills learned in exploratory drama (as outlined in Chapters 19 and 20, 'Teaching Practical Drama' and 'Teaching Dramatic Texts') lower down the school will be developed to allow post-16 students to apply them to investigating an A level text. For these students performance is a natural progression from the skills learned earlier, as it probably was at GCSE. Preparing younger pupils to perform in a production can be exposing and inhibiting for a large number of them and is best kept for those who opt to get involved in the school play. You will gain more meaningful work through directed and structured approaches. A watered-down A level syllabus will not suit KS3 and will exclude all but the already confident.

3.3 Monitoring and assessment

The assessment criteria for A level are contained within each specification. If students study these criteria for both practical and written work, having had them clearly explained, then they should know well what is required of them. Frequently assessed work, with marks explained, implies targets for improvement and enables those targets to be explicated as part of the progression process.

3.4 Teaching and class management

It goes without saying that you will need to have access to at least a basic drama studio in order to teach the course. At a minimum this could be a large classroom cleared of the usual desks, a few stage lanterns on a T-stand and the means to create a blackout. Ideally it will be used only for drama lessons. The studio will need chairs that can be arranged as needed and a few desks stacked in a corner which can be used for writing when required. A large wooden table is a useful piece of furniture as it can be used for a variety of purposes in improvisation; likewise a few rostra. If there is no board to write on you will need access to a flip chart.

Although lessons may seem less formal than at KS3, it is a good idea not to relax your teacher status too much, and to keep a presence nearby when students are working 'alone'. They need time and space to figure things out for themselves but they are more likely to actually be doing this if you are around. Students left to get on with a task unsupervised will often digress or sit around talking about it instead of doing it. As they get to A2 level you may be able to trust them more, but this is something that only you will know at the time. Students' ability to motivate themselves varies enormously from group to group, even within the same school.

3.3.4 Differentiation

Recent changes to the whole structure of post-16 education mean that students may now study a combination of academic and vocational subjects. Traditionally many Theatre Studies students would have taken the course in order to gain entry to a performance-related course in Higher Education or broaden a humanities-based group of A levels. Now you may also have students who wish to build their communication skill for a business course, for example. As a teacher you will need to consider the needs of all such students.

The majority of the students taking the course will have at least four or five GCSEs at Grade C or higher, but their experience of drama may be very diverse. Many will have taken a GCSE in the subject but this is not a prerequisite to the A level course. To some extent differentiation by outcome is expected of practical work: all students have the same tasks to do, but are likely to achieve different qualities of outcome. It may be useful to offer guidelines to writing coursework and provide students with the opportunity to share good written work from their own and previous courses. It is also helpful to direct students' reading to specific pages of books for example, so that research is more productive.

2.5 ICT

In addition to using computers to produce coursework and essays there are now computer packages available for designing stage sets and lighting which are relevant to A Level courses. It is worth developing a website for the Drama Department that includes bookmarks for relevant research at A level. This could also include examples of good essays and course guidelines, as outlined above.

FURTHER READING

Mackey, S. (ed.) (1997) *Practical Theatre – A Post 16 Approach*. Cheltenham: Stanley Thornes

Mackey, S. and Cooper, S. (1995) *Drama and Theatre Studies*. Cheltenham: Stanley Thornes

Neelands, J. and Dobson, W. (2000) *Drama and Theatre Studies at AS/A Level*. London: Hodder & Stoughton

Neelands, J. and Dobson, W. (2000) *Theatre Directions*. London: Hodder & Stoughton

Lamden, G. (2000) *Devising: A Handbook for Drama and Theatre Studies*. London: Hodder & Stoughton

Oddey, A. (1996) *Devising Theatre: A Practical and Theoretical Handbook*. London: Taylor & Francis

THE LEARNING CENTRE
TOWER HAMLETS COLLEGE
ARBOUR SQUARE
LONDON E1 0PS

USEFUL TEXTBOOKS FOR A LEVEL

Artaud, A. (1970) *The Theatre and its Double*. London: Calder

Barton, J. (1984) *Playing Shakespeare*. London: Methuen

Benedetti, J. (1982) *Stanislavski: An Introduction*. London: Methuen

Bentley, E. (ed.) (1968) *The Theory of the Modern Stage*. London: Penguin Books

Boal, A. (1979) *Games for Actors and Non-actors*. London: Routledge

Boal, A. (1979) *Theatre of the Oppressed*. London: Pluto Press

Brook, P. (1968) *The Empty Space*. London: Penguin Books

Brook, P. (1995) *There Are No Secrets*. London: Methuen

Callow, S. (1995) *Being an Actor*, revised edition. London: Penguin Books. First published 1984

Edgar, D. (1999) *How Plays Work*. London: Nick Hern Books

Esslin, M. (1984) *Brecht: A Choice of Evils*. London: Methuen

Hahlo, R. and Reynolds, P. (2000) *Dramatic Events: How to Run a Successful Workshop*. London: Faber and Faber

Holland, P. (1997) *English Shakespeare: Shakespeare on the English Stage in the 1990s*. Cambridge: Cambridge University Press

Johnstone. K. (1979) *Impro*. London: Methuen

Manfull, H. (1999) *Taking Stage: Women Directors on Directing*. London: Methuen

National Theatre. *Platform Papers*. http://www.nt-online.org/?/id=2627

Reid, F. (1982) *Stage Lighting*. London: Focal Press

Reynolds, P. (1993) *Novel Images: Literature in Performance*. London: Routledge

Roose-Evans, J. (1989) *Experimental Theatre*. London: Routledge

Sher, A. (1985) *Year of the King*. London: Chatto and Windus

Stephenson, H. and Langridge, N. (1997) *Rage and Reason: Women Playwrights on Playwriting*. London: Methuen

Willett, J. (trans.) (1984) *Brecht on Theatre*. London: Methuen

REFERENCES

AQA specification for Drama and Theatre Studies 2003/4

Cooper, S. and Mackey, S. (1995) *Theatre Studies – An Approach for Advanced Level*. Cheltenham: Stanley Thornes

Edexcel specification for Drama and Theatre Studies 2003/4

Keith, G. and Shuttleworth, J. (2000) *Living Language*, 2nd edition. London: Hodder & Stoughton

OCR specification for Drama and Theatre Studies 2003/4

INDEX